THE YEAR OF THE THREE KAISERS

Four Generations of Hohenzollerns, 1883. Kaiser William holds his great-grandson Frederick William, while Crown Prince Frederick William and his son, Prince William, look on. Prince William's useless left hand is tucked into his pocket. (Ullstein)

THE YEAR OF THE THREE KAISERS

Bismarck and
the German Succession,
1887–88

J. ALDEN NICHOLS

UNIVERSITY OF ILLINOIS PRESS
Urbana and Chicago

© 1987 by the Board of Trustees of the University of Illinois
Manufactured in the United States of America
C 5 4 3 2 1

This book is printed on acid-free paper.

Library of Congress Cataloging-in-Publication Data

Nichols, J. Alden, 1919–
    The year of the three kaisers.

    Bibliography: p.
    Includes index.
    1. Germany—History—1871-1918.   2. Germany—Kings
and rulers—Succession.   3. Bismark, Otto, Fürst von,
1815–1898.   I. Title.   II. Title: Year of the 3 kaisers.
DD223.9.N53   1987   943.08   86-7028
ISBN 0-252-01307-7 (alk. paper)

To the memory of

SIGMUND NEUMANN
and
GARRETT MATTINGLY

writers, teachers,
scholars, friends,
who deepened
my appreciation
of history

Contents

Preface

IN history there is no substitute for events. Events are more than merely "surface disturbances, crests of foam that the tides of history carry on their strong backs."* Their "brief, rapid, nervous fluctuations" constitute a set of pointer readings that measure the relative strength of basic forces—ecological, demographic, psychological, cultural, social, political, and economic. Sometimes, also, a single event will, like a lightning flash, suddenly illuminate a whole landscape; or a string of events, in cumulative sequence, will form a slow precipitate, clearly revealing the chief ingredients of the basic brew. Above all, events reveal people in action, both individual personalities and groups, and thus infuse life, color, meaning into otherwise impersonal and dead statistics. Like a procession in an antique frieze, events celebrate rituals, attitudes, feelings of moments in the past that once were full of meaning and that for us to contemplate with sympathy adds pathos, height of imagination, depth of insight, and perspective to our present lives. It is this personal relevance that continues to make history—whether written by scholars, journalists, or novelists— compellingly attractive to people of all kinds and in all stations, who have an insatiable hunger for the rich human show, the interplay of personality, belief, and circumstance that only the history of past events can convincingly portray. Learning how past personages dealt with a variety of problems and situations may better prepare people to deal imaginatively, tolerantly, and wisely with present problems.

For the nineteenth century in the West, the best source for events of all kinds is the daily press. Official documents do not describe the tangle of conflicting forces out of which the thread of policy is drawn. Such conflicts, both long-running and ephemeral, the actual ebb and flow of daily incident, can be found in all their fullness only in the press, at a time when there were few other media of communication. In the city of Berlin alone, some twenty-six newspapers—most with more than one edition— competed daily for the attention of fewer than two million citizens. For

* Braudel, preface to 1st ed.

every shade of opinion, for every faction, there was a newspaper, and more than one newspaper editor was also a political party leader. Eugen Richter and his *Freisinnige Zeitung* and Theodor Barth and *Die Nation* on the Left, and Baron Wilhelm von Hammerstein-Schwartow and the *Kreuzzeitung* on the Right—all three editors held seats in the Reichstag. Party organizations were then mostly loose and informal, and the greater part of party leadership consisted in editorial direction of the newspaper. In addition to providing the matrix of events, without which the zigs and zags of policy cannot be fully understood, the party press is thus also the best source for policies, attitudes, opinions, those states of mind that form the parameters of human possibility.*

In Germany under Bismarck the press was also an important part of government. Political initiative came mostly from the top as did instruction in the government press on what attitudes were proper, authorized. Thus, in the *Norddeutsche Allgemeine Zeitung*, the chancellor had his recognized mouthpiece not only in featured articles, but also in the way the newspaper quoted the party press in its "Journal-Revue," constantly explaining, advocating, and defining the viewpoint of the government. For less dignified scrapping with the opposition, various organs of parties friendly to the government were frequently used—the Free Conservative *Post*, the Conservative *Deutsches Tageblatt*, or the National Liberal *Kölnische Zeitung*. On special occasions, or for special effect, items could even be inspired or planted in the opposition press. If necessary, the chancellor would dictate an article himself. More usually, a word or two of instruction or a marginal comment on a newspaper clipping would provide the basis for articles written by the Chancellery or Foreign Office staff, depending on the area of policy. Editors and correspondents of friendly papers, as well as party leaders, also constantly consulted the Foreign Office and Chancellery for information and the latest turns of policy.

To find patterns in the daily chatter of the press, it is necessary to use more than occasional articles. In addition to the indispensable private correspondence, diaries, memoirs, and government reports, this narrative is based on a systematic study of the press, both government and party, day by day, edition by edition. Practical limitations of time imposed a somewhat narrow selection, the *Norddeutsche* and *Deutsches Wochenblatt* for the government, the *Neue Preussische (Kreuz) Zeitung* for the Conservatives, the *Kölnische* and *National Zeitung* for right and left-wing National Liberals, *Germania* for the Catholic Center party, and the *Frankfurter Zeitung* for the *Freisinnige* or democrats. The limitations of this selection were considerably lessened by the habit of German papers of the time of quoting ex-

---

* See Turk.

tensively from each other, so that on most issues the position of other prominent organs, such as the *Post*, the *Konservative Korrespondenz*, the *National Liberale Korrespondenz*, the *Hannoverscher Kourier*, or the South German press could usually be ascertained. Naturally, the point of view of a particular newspaper cannot always be assumed to represent more than the opinion of its editor or correspondent. Public opinion polls had not yet been developed, and even today, when their use is probably excessive, whether they actually represent "public opinion" or whether there really is such a thing are moot questions. Yet attitudes of the rank and file, as expressed crucially in election results, had always to be considered by the party leaders, and most articles reflected this awareness. Admittedly, it was a fault of all the German parties—probably a consequence of inexperience as well as elitist arrogance, somewhat suggestive of the Federal period in American history—not to be sufficiently responsive to such popular attitudes. Regardless of the drawbacks, in the late nineteenth century there is no better source for party and public opinion than the press, and I am more interested in the range and clash of opinion than in the number of people actually represented. This narrative proves that on occasion it was possible for one person, such as Baron von Hammerstein, not only to sway a whole political party with the help of his newspaper, but also to persuade it to defy Bismarck's government. I have not tried to go beyond the political in charting attitudes, although such areas as ideology, religion, nationalism, and psychological sets involving security, authority, and leadership necessarily come under that rubric.

My main intent has been to tell the story of what occurred at an unexpectedly critical time for the nation. The story form is most satisfying because it is more complete; it can—like the life of each individual or nation—accommodate both the obvious and the puzzling, the comic and the tragic, along with the complicated and the contradictory, the inexorable, the unexpected, and the mysterious. My major interest in the telling is not to pass judgment but to try to understand—not to be for or against Bismarck, but to try to explain why it was thus. Perhaps the attempt has made me too indulgent, although I have tried not to shirk the larger issues as I see them, and have tried to put the great man in his place.

My debts are many: to the Library and Research Board of the University of Illinois for providing me with a series of research assistants and runs of German newspapers on microfilm; to the American Council of Learned Societies for summer grants in 1966 and 1975, to finish up work on the Eulenburg papers at Coblenz and to make a tour of various archives in England and Germany; to the late Prince Otto von Bismarck, Princess Ann Mari von Bismarck, and Prince Ferdinand von Bismarck for their kind hospitality and permission to use the family archive at

Friedrichsruh and to their archivists, Kurt Reitsch and Dr. Paul Heinsius, for their kind assistance; to the staffs of the Deutsches Bundesarchiv at Coblenz, the Zentral Staatsarchiv both in Potsdam and in Merseburg, the Haus-, Hof-, und Staatsarchiv in Vienna, the Geheimes Staatsarchiv der Stiftung des preussischen Kulturbesitzes in Berlin/Dahlem, the Geheims Staatsarchiv in Munich, the Hauptstaatsarchiv in Stuttgart, the General-landesarchiv in Karlsruhe and the grandducal family for permission to use the papers of Grand Duke Frederick I of Baden; to Her Majesty the Queen of Great Britain, for her gracious permission to use and to quote from material in the Royal Archive at Windsor; to the Marquess of Salisbury for use of the Salisbury papers; and to Baron Moritz von und zu Franckenstein and Dr. Leonhard Lenk of the Library of the Bavarian Landtag for permission to examine the political correspondence of Georg Arbogast, Baron von und zu Franckenstein. I am grateful to Cambridge University Press for permission to quote extensively from the Norman Rich and M. H. Fisher English edition of *The Holstein Papers*. All other translations are my own unless otherwise indicated in the list of sources. I should also like to acknowledge the work done in my seminar in the summer of 1969 and spring of 1970 on topics included in this narrative by Eleanor Turk, George Libbey, Alfred Bunnett, John Sahayda, and Eugene Gillespie. I am grateful to Ekkehard-Teja Wilke for many kindnesses and for permission to reprint material previously published in his journal, *Studies in Modern European History and Culture*, 1 (1975).

PART 1

The Succession

The capacity of old and new cultures and structures to exist without conflict and even with mutual adaptations is a frequent phenomenon of social change; the old is not necessarily *replaced* by the new, the acceptance of a new product, a new religion, a new mode of decision-making does not necessarily lead to the disappearance of the older form. New forms may only increase the range of alternatives. Both magic and medicine can exist side by side, used alternatively by the same people.

—Joseph R. Gusfield, "Tradition and Modernity:
Misplaced Polarities in the Study of Social Change,"
in Jason L. Finkle and Richard W. Gable, eds.
Political Development and Social Change.

1

The Cartel and the Crown Prince

CRISES, in retrospect, are useful. Facing the unexpected, individuals and factions act without forethought and thereby reveal more of their motives than in more normal times. Forces and tendencies that are ordinarily concealed behind institutionalized facades may thus suddenly be exposed. Germany, in 1887–88, was unexpectedly confronted with a crisis in the imperial succession that, in effect, reversed the whole political field and forced Otto von Bismarck, perennial chancellor and actual ruler of Germany, to recast his policies. By examining this crisis in detail, one may catch a glimpse into the depths of German politics and society on the eve of the fin de siècle. Beside the human elements of a tragic and timeless story, one may recognize the interplay of underlying social and economic forces with attitudes and ideologies, from traditional to liberal, progressive, and revolutionary. In addition, one may note the interaction of bureaucratic authorities with popular political parties, and all of these with the crown. Finally one can examine the role of personalities and obtain a private look at the Bismarck style and system at work, with a possibility of gauging its basic social and political tendencies. From all of this it may be possible to form judgments as to how much was inevitable and how much contrived, and of what the political possibilities and limitations were; to identify the major problems facing the new age to which this was the prologue; and finally to weigh the question of whether, ultimately, it is generally possible for a state to move from a monarchical and authoritarian political system to a more liberal, open, and pluralistic system gradually, peacefully, and without violence, or whether the relative success of the English and North Americans in the eighteenth and nineteenth centuries in so doing resulted only from a run of extraordinary good luck.

The doubt suddenly cast over the imperial succession in Germany in 1887 afflicted a country that was already in the throes of several more basic crises. In the period between 1866 and 1871, Bismarck had created the Second German Reich by forcing Prussia to fight Austria for supremacy in Germany and excluding her from the new arrangements, bringing together first the North German states under Prussian hegemony and then, as a result of the war with France in 1870–71, bringing in also the South Germans down to the Austrian frontier. All this had been a gamble from the first. To be sure, Bismarck had had the advantage, in that simpler age, of believing, with other Victorian statesmen, that he was merely carrying out the will of God; but Germans, located in the middle of Europe, surrounded by historically hostile and predatory neighbors, politically fragmented and powerless for the previous 200 years, and subject to a cultural cacophony out of the West and East and North and South, have always marveled at Bismarck's strength of will—his ability to act decisively and to accept the consequences. If one wants to be critical of both him and the age he typified, one can accuse them both of a certain demonic recklessness.[1]

In creating the new German Empire, Bismarck characteristically used all sides against each other and the middle; that is, he handled an internal Prussian challenge by the Liberal-dominated parliament to the king's authority over the army, in 1862, by gaining victories for that army in the field and using it to create a new German nation—the Liberals' major goal. The new empire was thus created from the top down—by the authoritarian governments of the German kings and princes and the Prussian army. But Bismarck nevertheless resisted the reactionary desires of the conservative Prussian ruling class, the so-called Junker gentry, to take this opportunity to return to royal absolutism, and he not only made political peace with the Liberals in Prussia, but also included universal and direct manhood suffrage for the Reichstag in the new imperial constitution and worked primarily with the great National Liberal party in the early 1870s in laying the legislative foundation for the new nation. The Liberals, after all, not only represented the romantic, emotional desire of citizens of all classes to belong to a united, strong Germany, but also had leadership close to the new industrial and commercial interests whose growing wealth was an important new source of power for the state and could only become more so in the future. Nevertheless, the Liberals' push toward parliamentary government was not satisfied: the essentially authoritarian Prussian government, where the ministers were responsible to the king, not the parliament, was carried over into the structure of the new empire, which was dominated by Prussia, overwhelmingly the largest and most populous state.

The fact of Prussian domination is illustrated by the circumstance that, although there were eventually a number of Reich administrative offices headed by state secretaries, there was never a formal meeting of this group as an imperial cabinet; rather, the chancellor, the only "responsible" Reich official, met regularly with the other members of the Prussian State Ministry, where he held the positions both of minister-president and of foreign minister, since he had constantly to work in the Federal Council (Bundesrat) with representatives of the governments of the other federal states. The chancellor nominally merely presided over the Bundesrat, which was the formal government of the federation, and represented the federated governments before the Reichstag, where other members of the Bundesrat also had a right to appear. But because he represented Prussia, which had the most population, industry, and the dominant army, in actuality he headed the whole government structure. Ultimately the chancellor's position and authority rested on the confidence of the king of Prussia, who had appointed him as Prussian minister, and as hereditary emperor or kaiser of the German Reich had also appointed him as chancellor, and who could, therefore, theoretically also dismiss him when he chose. Since Bismarck had bailed him out of the army crisis in Prussia in 1862, King (later Kaiser) William had become personally and politically committed to his strikingly successful minister, a dependency that increased with his advancing age (he was ninety in 1887). William, who had already been an army captain in the final allied campaign against Napoleon in 1814, always considered himself primarily a soldier, and the army, especially with the new prestige gained through the wars of unification, thus held a position of special prominence in the new empire, independent of the chancellor's direct control. Kaiser William, in his old age, also increasingly objected to any changes in personnel. Bismarck himself was now seventy-two, and Field Marshal Helmuth von Moltke, who had won the victories over Austria and France, remained chief of the general staff at the age of eighty-seven. It was difficult to recommend replacement of old retainers on grounds of incapacity due to age because the kaiser, a gracious, loyal, and gallant old gentleman, if somewhat simple-minded and inflexible, was likely to take such remarks personally. Consequently the whole court was almost as superannuated as he.

Kaiser William had developed an antipathy toward the Liberals as a result of the army crisis of 1862 and had never liked Bismarck's working closely with them. But it was not William's influence that brought an end to the liberal era in the 1870s, but rather the working of the Liberals' own most revered institution, the free market. The economic crash of 1873 was followed by a prolonged period of recurrent slumps and economic adjustment worldwide, the so-called Long Depression, that lasted until 1896. The development of low-cost, long-distance transport, by railroad and steamship, created crisis conditions for European agriculture by inundating European markets with cheap grain from the virgin soil of the

United States, Canada, and Argentina. The drastic decline in grain prices shook the security of the grain-growing Junker gentry in the mid-1870s at the same time that they were becoming increasingly alienated by the Liberals' campaign against the influence of religion, especially the Catholic church, in primary education, the so-called Kulturkampf. Not wishing to push the ruling class—Bismarck himself came from an old Junker family—into permanent opposition, the chancellor began to swing back toward both the Junkers and the Catholics, abandoning free trade in 1879 with the introduction of modest protective tariffs, both for agriculture and industry, and gradually relaxing the Kulturkampf regulations in return for the support of the Catholic Center party for his trade policy.[2]

The more doctrinaire left wing of the National Liberal party was distressed by Bismarck's turn away from the free-trade principle and toward the reactionary Junkers and Catholics. Their distress increased when Bismarck took the opportunity after repeated assassination attempts against Kaiser William in 1878 to force through a repressive law against the political agitation of the revolutionary Marxist Social Democrats, dissolving the Reichstag and fighting a special election campaign on the issue. In the early 1880s, he also launched a new paternalistic program of social insurance for the working classes, which meant intervention of the state in economic affairs, a turn toward collectivism that pleased both the Center-party Catholics and the Junker Conservatives but was anathema to the doctrinaire laissez-faire Liberals, who were also afraid that any increase in the authoritarian state power would prove to be politically repressive. Counting too much on an inevitable victory for liberalism in the rapidly industrializing society and with their eyes on England, where the Liberal Gladstone had returned triumphantly in 1880 to head his second ministry, the left-wingers then seceded from the National Liberal party. In 1884 they united with the democratically oriented Progressives, led by Eugen Richter, an indomitable parliamentary orator with an impressive command of facts and an aggressive black beard. This new party was christened *Deutsch-Freisinnige*—"free thinking" in the general sense of open-minded or progressively liberal.[3]

This German Liberal party tried to raise the banner of modern, progressive liberalism to which all independent and forward-looking citizens might repair in defiance of the rightward tendencies of the Bismarck government. Its timing, however, was unfortunate. As a result of the disruptive power of capitalistic enterprise and the bankruptcies, scandals, and social distress associated with the economic depression, the liberal principle of free initiative and enterprise and the Liberal parties were not doing well now anywhere in Europe. The Austrian Liberals had already had to yield the government to a Conservative in 1879, and in France the liberal

"Opportunists" suffered severe losses in the election of 1885, both to a resurgent Right and the Radical Left. And in England itself, William Gladstone, shying away from Joseph Chamberlain's Radical program, split the Liberal Party over the Irish question in 1886, thus handing the political leadership to the Conservatives. When the German Liberal party was formed, it claimed 105 Reichstag seats. In the election campaign of 1884, Bismarck managed to reduce this to 74 by distracting the electorate by suddenly embracing imperialism and picking up territories overseas. But the remaining German Liberal strength, added to the 99 seats of the Center and the 24 seats of the Social Democrats, plus Danes, Alsatians, and Poles, still produced a majority in the Reichstag (total seats: 397) for forces mostly oppositional to the Bismarck government.

The threat to Bismarck's policies was all the greater since the German Liberal party considered itself the "crown prince's party" and therefore destined to take over the government with his succession, which appeared to be imminent. Crown Prince Frederick William was a tall, ruggedly handsome man with a long red-gold beard and a friendly, winning disposition.[4] He had been in his late teens when Europe broke out in the liberal revolutions of 1848, and a liberal education and marriage to the Princess Royal of England, Victoria, eldest daughter of Queen Victoria, confirmed him in believing that the liberal principles of free thought and inquiry, science, and material progress were the dominant forces of the new age and that Germany should move in that direction. He shared his wife's worship of her father, Albert, the prince consort, who was the model of the enlightened ruler who tries to advance the welfare of his people and who had organized the great English Industrial Exposition of 1852. The crown prince and princess agreed with Prince Albert that it would have been far better for Prussia to have unified Germany through "moral conquests" rather than through the "iron and blood" methods of Bismarck. It was not only Bismarck's devious and brutal methods that the royal couple deplored, but also the fact that by unifying Germany from the top he had helped to maintain the political position of the reactionary Prussian Junkers. Victoria, a handsome, dynamic woman, who was more intelligent and perceptive than her husband, had more political instinct and a much stronger will and therefore tended to dominate him. She considered the Junkers to be culturally backward and boorish. In her later "Account of the Events of 1888" she wrote, "Certainly the members of the Junker gentry have accomplished a great deal in Prussian history, with iron determination, devotion to duty and self-sacrifice they have served the state in the army and as officials. . . . But by and large they are not a cultural force. . . . They want to control their sovereign completely . . . then they will be true to him! . . . They are horrified by everything new and everything foreign, the level of their education is low and their ambition is unbounded!" Disdainfully, the crown princess once told Bismarck that two or three merchant families in Liverpool had more silver plate than the entire Prussian nobility.[5]

Observers are generally agreed that Crown Prince Frederick William's liberalism was more a pious belief than an instinct and was counteracted by very strong personal concerns for uniforms, decorations, ceremonies, and his own royal prerogatives. In the spring of 1885, when the whole nation was showering honors on Bismarck at the time of his seventieth birthday, the crown prince had demonstrated both his royal feelings and his jealousy by a rather illiberal remark: "A minister, what's a minister? Nothing but one of the king's officials. But this man's not a minister, he's a dictator. This means the overthrow of the monarchy." It is a striking fact that, in the crisis of 1862 in Prussia, when King William, at loggerheads with the parliament (Landtag), was talking of abdication, the crown prince and princess reacted to this intention in opposite ways. True to her English liberal heritage, Victoria approved of the abdication; it was just the way a constitutional monarch should act, and it would strengthen the parliamentary forces. But Frederick William was appalled at the prospect and was furious with his father. The king's abdication under pressure of the parliament would amount to a constitutional precedent and would thus diminish Frederick William's own royal prerogatives, and this he clearly did not want.[6]

King William of Prussia had been seventy-four when the war with France was won and he was acclaimed emperor of the new Germany. It was natural that Frederick William—who had commanded an army corps during the war, had become popular even in South Germany, and had supported Bismarck in persuading his father to accept the imperial title— should imagine that he himself would soon take over that title. But his father had lived on and on. As with other heirs to long-lived monarchs, such as Queen Victoria's son, the Prince of Wales, or Crown Prince Rudolf, eldest son of Emperor Francis Joseph of Austria, it was easy to become discouraged, disgruntled, and out of touch with affairs. Also the crown princess's stubbornness and willfulness—like that of her mother and some of her other Hanoverian English ancestors—had over the years alienated most of the more able among their advisors, until by 1887 only Baron Franz von Roggenbach, a former National Liberal prime minister in Baden, was left to confide in. By this time, having had ample time in which to observe Bismarck in action, both the crown prince and princess had decided rather sensibly that for the sake of the dynasty and their own position they would have to keep Bismarck at the head of the government when they came to the throne, at least at the beginning.[7]

In 1885, when Kaiser William had had a rather ominous fainting spell, Frederick William had asked Bismarck if he would be willing to remain in his position after the old man's death. The chancellor had agreed, but under two conditions: that parliamentary government would not be introduced and that there should be no "foreign influence" (England, through the crown princess) on government policy. The crown prince had protested with a wave of his hand that he had "no such idea." Bismarck had suggested that he might retire from the administration of Prussia, confining himself to foreign affairs, and the crown prince had agreed to try a Prussian ministry headed—not by his German Liberal friends—but by the leaders of the more conservative, loyally Bismarckian rump National Liberals, Rudolf von Bennigsen and Johannes Miquel. To her entourage, Crown Princess Victoria had remarked that of course Bismarck must stay on under the new reign. "Why should it not be possible to bring about a general agreement [among] all parties favourable to the monarchy, including the Liberals, to form a front against the Republicans and Socialists?" As for Bismarck's own judgment of Frederick William's liberalism, he declared in September 1886 that he did not take it very seriously: "It was the kind of liberalism that was usual with all heirs to the throne, here as well as in Russia and elsewhere. When the prince later had the authority in his own hands and had to bear the responsibility himself, he would probably think differently."[8]

Nevertheless, as long as the German Liberal party continued to maintain a sizable bloc of votes in the Reichstag so that it could form a majority, say, with the National Liberals and the Catholic Center party, there would be danger that Frederick William and Victoria might be tempted, when they came to the throne, to oust Bismarck and give the German Liberals their head. Such a move would be extremely dangerous, since the German Liberals were strongly middle class, urban-oriented, and sworn foes of the conservative Junker gentry, who still dominated the Prussian army, court, and bureaucracy. Could a Prussian king—especially a weak one like Frederick William—actually challenge the Junkers and try to rule against his own court, bureaucracy, and army? In 1862 the Liberal attempt to bring the army under parliamentary control had failed, and then many of the Junkers themselves had voted Liberal. Since then they had been rallied to the monarchy and to conservatism by Bismarck's victories and the agricultural crisis, and had come largely to dominate the government since the turn to the Right in 1878–79. Being the traditional ruling class, they were the most politically experienced and self-confident. An outright frontal attack on their position would risk serious civil conflict.[9]

Actually, Bismarck had not been comfortable having to rely on the

Conservatives and Center party, and from the very beginning of the Reich he had consistently tried to bring the National Liberals and the Conservatives together, to associate the middle-class industrialists with the agrarian Junker gentry, the new economic power with the old. The secession of the doctrinaire left wing of the National Liberals under his provocations and their fusion with the Progressives to form the German Liberal party in 1884 had given Bismarck a further opportunity to carry out this program. In March 1884 Friedrich von Holstein, senior counselor in the Political Department of the Foreign Office, wrote to Herbert Bismarck, the eldest son and foreign secretary after 1886, that his father's recent speeches had been friendly to the moderate Bennigsen faction of the National Liberals. "He wants to try once more to construct a great moderate middle party, now that [the National Liberal secessionists Max von] Forckenbeck, [Franz von] Stauffenberg and Co. have become *open* enemies." In December 1885 Bennigsen wrote to Dr. Friedrich Hammacher, a National Liberal Reichstag deputy with ties to Ruhr mining interests, that "Bismarck is now apparently, after six years, steering into the right channel, at least he himself as well as his press organs are very sharply and clearly against the Center and the [Conservative] *Kreuzzeitung* reactionaries and not merely against the Progressives." Bennigsen hoped that Bismarck would prepare the ground well in advance, "so as to dissolve [the Reichstag] at the proper moment with an appeal to the healthy national forces."[10]

Undoubtedly the most serious threat to the existence of the new German Reich from the beginning was the attitude of the other European great powers toward this new, strong, dominant state in the strategic center of the continent. France had been too humiliated by her defeat in 1870–71 and was too proud ever really to be reconciled to German preponderance, so it was important to isolate her. Bismarck managed to achieve this in the 1870s by cultivating friendship with England and at the same time uniting the three authoritarian Eastern empires, Russia, Austria-Hungary, and his own Germany, in a League of the Three Emperors, to support monarchical principles against the threat of international revolution as exemplified by the revolt in 1871 of the Paris Commune. This conservative grouping, however, had fallen apart under the impact of rebellious uprisings against the authority of the Ottoman Turks in Bosnia and Bulgaria. Eventually Russia had gone to war with the Ottoman Empire and had forced on them a peace treaty that had created a large autonomous Bulgaria under Ottoman suzerainty but Russian influence and extending from the Black Sea to the Aegean. This was too much, however, for both the English and the Austrians, and British Prime Minister Disraeli sent the British fleet into the Straits. Bismarck then called a conference of the powers at Berlin in 1878, where Russia was made to accept a smaller Bulgaria, without Macedonia, England was awarded Cyprus, and the Austrians received the right to garrison Bosnia-Herzegovina. Although Bismarck maintained that his efforts at the Congress of Berlin had been of service to the Russians, their humiliation there laid the basis for a growing anti-German hostility, so much so that Bismarck felt it necessary to sign a formal defensive alliance with Austria-Hungary in 1879. In spite of this move, however, or even because of it, Russia had indicated a desire to improve her relations with Germany. Eventually, in 1881, Bismarck had maneuvered the other two Eastern powers back into a renewal of the Three Emperors' League, which had then been further renewed in 1884. But the Bulgarians, under Prince Alexander of Battenberg, had not been willing to act obediently as Russian pawns, and Tsar Alexander III, a moody, suspicious man, had grown more and more exasperated with Prince Alexander. Finally, in the fall of 1886, the Tsar had had him kidnaped and then forced Alexander to abdicate. Prince Alexander's brother, Henry, was married to Queen Victoria's youngest and favorite daughter, Beatrice, and English and Austrian sensibilities were strongly affronted by the clumsiness of the Russian treatment of the Bulgarians. Obviously the Three Emperors' League had fallen apart again, and there was danger of a general European war being sparked in the Balkans, which might drag in Germany with who knew what result. The war danger, in the fall of 1886, was probably not really acute, but the atmosphere had grown tense enough that Bismarck could use it for his own domestic political purposes, as a means, say, of rallying the "healthy national forces."[11]

Since the election of an oppositional Reichstag in 1881, the eventual necessity of passing a new army budget had hung over the opposition parties like the sword of Damocles. At the beginning of the Reich, Kaiser William had wanted a permanent army budget with no parliamentary control, whereas the National Liberals had demanded an annual budget, as with other departments and as in England. Bismarck and the National Liberal Bennigsen had then arranged a compromise, with funding for seven years, the so-called *Septennat*. That had been in 1874, and the arrangement had since been renewed once, in 1881. It would have to be voted on again in 1887 at the latest, before it ran out in 1888. A regular election for the Reichstag was also due in 1887, the life of the Reichstag then being three years. The announced program of the new German Liberal party at the time of its formation in 1884 had included a three-year army budget, to conform to the life of the Reichstag. The Center party had also long since committed itself to a shorter period. The issue was thus a kind of time bomb that could be set off at any time. A successful reduction in the budgetary period for the army would amount to a victory of the Reichstag over the government, army, and crown, and thus to a change in the constitutional balance between the people's representatives, on the one hand, and the authoritarian government structure, on the other.

At such a crucial moment in the life of the Reich, with the liberal crown prince and princess about to succeed and a precarious situation abroad, Bismarck was not interested in changing the constitutional balance, at least not so abruptly or so obviously and in defiance of his own leadership. Deciding, apparently, to use the *Septennat* issue to solve some of his domestic problems, he seized the favorable moment and introduced a renewal of the *Septennat* to the Reichstag prematurely, in the fall of 1886. Disdaining to try to make a strong case for his bill and staying away from Berlin at his estate at Friedrichsruh, near Hamburg, until the Reichstag committee had reported the bill negatively, Bismarck then appeared in Berlin. During the second reading of the bill in the Reichstag, Bismarck delivered a frontal assault on the opposition parties. The Reichstag majority, he said, wanted to replace "the royal [*kaiserliche*] army such as we have previously had in Germany, with a parliamentary army."[12] But the majority in the Reichstag, he pointed out, was not a stable one; it was made up of nine or ten different party groupings "united accidentally in negation and in antipathy towards the personalities of the present government; *une haine commune vous unit*; as soon as this ceases, as soon as you have to create something positive, then you will be completely disunited, then you will be no majority at all."[13]

Such blunt speech from the chancellor probably heightened the combativeness of the opposition, which was doubtless his intention. For idealists, the cold truth is always infuriating. Since the problematical nature of the liberalism of the crown prince must have been known to the German Liberal leaders,[14] and since a regular election to the Reichstag was due in 1887, why did German Liberals and the Center party insist on giving Bismarck the opportunity to dissolve the Reichstag and fight an election on the emotional issue of defense of the fatherland? Apparently they were caught in a bind between their ideological principles, on the one hand, and their future political expectations, on the other. In a peroration near the end of the *Septennat* debate, the old Progressive and German Liberal leader Eugen Richter declared, "The future, the not-too-far-distant future belongs to us."[15] Dr. Ludwig Windthorst, leader of the Center party, appears to have hoped to bring the government to a compromise on a budget period of five years in the third reading of the bill. Bismarck, however, foiled such plans by dissolving the Reichstag abruptly after the debate on the second reading.

Immediately after the dissolution of the Reichstag in January 1887, in an atmosphere of tension and excitement, negotiations began under Bismarck's sponsorship among the Conservative, Free Conservative, and National Liberal parties to form an electoral "cartel." The three parties agreed to support each other in the campaign, candidates in the districts to be apportioned generally upon the basis of existing strength. In this apparent fight against parliamentarism and democracy and for the control of the next, presumably liberal, kaiser and king, the Conservatives were compelled necessarily to support the chancellor. To be sure, Bismarck had seemed to be governing in their interest and with their support ever since his break with the National Liberals over the tariff and the antisocialist law in 1878–79 and his introduction of paternalistic state insurance in the early 1880s. There were no National Liberals now in the Prussian Ministry, only Free Conservatives and Conservatives, such as the reactionary and religiously orthodox minister of the interior, Robert von Puttkamer. It is also possible that Bismarck gave the Conservative leaders some private expectation of a truly reactionary policy, including limitation of the suffrage. Even moderate Conservatives, in the excitement of the *Septennat* crisis, were pressing for a coup d'etat and suffrage change, and it appears that privately the chancellor did not discourage such notions. Throughout the 1880s Bismarck had on occasion made disparaging remarks about the Reichstag and spoken of the possibility of changing the suffrage. In 1881 he had remarked to Württemberg Minister-President Baron Hermann von Mittnacht that "possibly the moment might come when the German princes might wonder whether the present parliamentarism is still compatible with the welfare of the Reich. . . . If [he] should sometime have to fear for the monarchy, he would cold-bloodedly put the match to the powder keg."[16] To Moritz Busch, editor of the monthly *Die Grenzboten*, at the end of January 1887, the old man remarked that "our first and greatest necessity is a strong and steadfast army, as that secures . . . our existence. . . . Of course we could defend [this] without the present constitution, and could certainly do so more successfully without a Reichstag like the last one, which was much less an expression of our unity than of our divisions and particularism and which was little else than a hindrance. . . . I could immediately secure the sanction of the emperor to a change in this respect, and that of the federal governments also. But that must wait yet awhile—until we see how these and perhaps the next elections turn out."[17]

Bismarck hardly ever made statements such as these without some immediate effect in mind. In the latter case, he quite clearly threatened the electorate with dire consequences if they did not vote for the cartel. Busch, after all, was a faithful journalistic hack. But a statement to the

Prussian ministers after a disappointment in the 1884 election and a defeat at the hands of the new oppositional majority in the Reichstag may provide a somewhat broader perspective: "He had been able to rule with the Kaiser for four years [1862–66] against majorities in the chamber; the crown prince, however, believes in majorities. One could not get along with this election law. . . . It would be remarkable if now, after governing for twenty-two years, he should end with a budgetless period just as he began."[18] Just before the election of February 1887, the chancellor's oldest son, Herbert, foreign secretary since 1886, wrote to his English Liberal friend, Lord Rosebery, "I do not expect a great change between the different parties; this awkward manhood suffrage will never give a majority to a decent government, because it promotes too much the rise of socialism. However, the 'septennat' is sure to be carried this time by a large majority, even if all the same members should be returned—which is not likely. And that is all we want at present."[19]

From these statements it seems clear that Bismarck had at various times considered a change in the Reich suffrage law, if it was necessary and if the conditions were favorable. In the spring of 1887, however, it is very doubtful that he intended any such thing, especially since the crown prince, who did "believe in majorities," was now very close to the throne. During the campaign, to reassure and publicly assist the National Liberals, the chancellor made a statement in the Prussian Landtag denying any intention of tampering with the suffrage. In fact, any thoughtful political observer who had watched Bismarck's previous career and his continuous balancing between opposed forces should have drawn the inference from his scathing attacks on the left Liberals in the Reichstag that it was the Conservatives who were actually in danger of being taken into camp and that the chancellor was about to move in a liberal direction and to drag the Conservatives along with him. The extreme right wing of the Conservative party, represented by the *Neue Preussische Zeitung*— nicknamed the *Kreuzzeitung* because of the large iron cross it carried between the last two words of its title—did in fact react to Bismarck's maneuvers with deep suspicion. They noted that both Rudolf von Bennigsen, the elderly leader of the National Liberals, who had retired despondently from the Reichstag in 1883, and Johannes Miquel, lord mayor of Frankfurt am Main, who had also retired from the Reichstag in 1884, had not only both hurried to Berlin to participate actively in the negotiations for the cartel, but also had agreed to stand for Reichstag seats once more. To the *Kreuzzeitung* reactionaries, the obvious National Liberal enthusiasm and excitement were ominous signs. In a lead article on January 27 entitled "The Coming Man," they mounted an attack on Bennigsen, now blaming him for the Kulturkampf—the Liberal anticlerical and anti-Catholic campaign of the 1870s.[20]

Obviously the strongly orthodox Protestant right wing of the Junker Conservatives would prefer a political alliance with the Silesian Junkers, South German nobles and peasants, and Rhineland laborers of the religiously oriented Catholic Center party to one with those unreliable middle-class worthies of the National Liberals, with their industrial orientation and leadership, their secular, naturalistic attitude toward religion and education, and their modernizing tendencies. Also, association with the National Liberals displaced the leadership within the Conservative party itself toward the Left: the moderate Conservative Baron Otto von Helldorff-Bedra, a Reichstag leader, and the Free Conservative Wilhelm von Kardorff, long associated with industrial interests, were now in the ascendancy. Furthermore, under Frederick William and Victoria, who had always longed to be progressive, liberal rulers, the center of gravity of the cartel grouping would necessarily move toward the Left. National Liberals would be brought into the Prussian ministry; the anti-Semitic rabble-rouser and Christian Socialist leader Adolf Stoecker would be removed from his position as court chaplain; the strongly orthodox and reactionary Prussian Minister of the Interior Robert von Puttkamer would be replaced; and eventually perhaps Bismarck himself might be succeeded as chancellor by a National Liberal such as Bennigsen or Miquel, while his foreign policy would be continued by his son, Herbert. In 1884 Bismarck remarked to Friedrich von Holstein, his principal lieutenant in the Foreign Office after Herbert, that Bennigsen "possessed far more political acumen than all the Conservatives." Although the rule of the Junker gentry would probably not be fundamentally threatened in Prussia by such a development, it might very well be constrained, modified, or opened up.[21]

In the election campaign of February 1887, the Center and the German Liberals accused Bismarck of planning a coup d'etat and the abolition of universal suffrage, while, of course, the government accused them of deserting the fatherland when it was in danger and made much of the threat, not of Russia, but of the French and their aggressive war minister, General Georges Boulanger. Under the force of the national issue and the scare propaganda of the three parties of the cartel, the essentially conservative elements of the nation began to rally to the government, led by the Prussian Herrenhaus (House of Notables), which voted a declaration of loyalty to the king and assured him of Prussian support for the army. Some German Liberal deputies actually broke with their party and supported the *Septennat* before the electorate. In early February 1887 the pope himself let it be known that he wished all Catholics to vote for the *Septennat*, in spite of the position of the Center party, hoping that this gesture of loyalty would lead to further advantages for Catholics in Prussia. On February 15, thirty-six members of the Catholic Rhineland nobility issued a declaration regretting the opposition of the Center party and especially its alliance with democrats and socialists and announced their intention to found a separate Catholic Conservative party. The Catholic Silesian nobility took similar action. Since the National Liberal was the most national of the parties, with the most variegated social basis outside of the Center party, it was natural that a scare campaign on the issue of national defense should work primarily to its advantage. General participation in the February 1887 Reichstag election jumped from 61.9 percent (1884) to 77.1 percent. Most of this increase went to the National Liberals, whose popular vote (first ballot) rose from 997,033 (1884) to 1,677,979 and whose percentage of the total vote increased from 17 to 22. The percentage rise for the Free Conservatives was from 7 to 10, whereas the Conservative percentage remained steady at 15. With the government laying stress on the moderate "middle parties," the gain in Reichstag seats was disproportionately heavy for the National Liberals, from 51 to 99, with the Free Conservatives going from 28 to 41, and the Conservatives only from 78 to 80. Although the Center party successfully withstood the brunt of the onslaught by government and cartel—and even the Vatican— and actually raised its total vote from 1,282,006 (1884) to 1,516,222, its percentage of the total declined, from 22 to 20. Holding doggedly on to its faithful districts, however, it lost only one Reichstag seat, for a total representation of 98. The Social Democrats also polled more votes (763,128 compared to 549,990 in 1884), but raised their percentage only from 9.5 to 10 and lost heavily in the number of deputies elected, only 11 as against 24 in 1884. The German Liberals, however, experienced disaster, their total vote actually declining, from 1,092,895 (1884) to 1,061,922, and in percentage from 19 to 14, and their Reichstag deputation being reduced from 74 to only 32. Although their share of the popular vote was only 47.3 percent, the three cartel parties now had 220 seats out of 397, a narrow but sufficient majority. Thus, near the end of his career, Chancellor von Bismarck inaugurated the era of popular politics (participation in Reichstag elections never returned to its previous level) and proved himself a better judge of the mood of the electorate than the democrats.[22]

In June 1887 Ludwig Bamberger, a leading member of the National Liberal secession before 1884, confided bitterly to his diary that the fusion of the secession group with the aggressively doctrinaire Eugen Richter's Progressives in 1884 had been a mistake. "More consideration should have been given to the weakness of the German people, who see in Richter their bête noire. If it had remained in being, the Secession would have had good potentialities [*viel Chancen*]. Now National Liberalism has taken over its inheritance. Its spirit, pompous servility, is the expression of the German middle classes, over whom, after the end of the Kulturkampf,

the ancestral rulers, Junkers and priests, will once more become masters."
Surely the German Liberal leaders must have been sufficiently acquainted
with the character of the German middle classes before the election?
Ninety-year-old Kaiser William was charmed with the election results.
Any Conservative, he told some members of the Reichstag, who accepted
a Reichstag seat, he had always considered to be doing him a personal
favor. The election had made him feel twenty years younger.[23]

One liberal historian has written that the cartel victory of 1887 was
"a battle for the maintenance of [Bismarck's] own power position against
the future German kaiser." It is certainly true that the construction of the
cartel and its election victory were aimed at preventing the future kaiser,
Crown Prince Frederick William, from relying for his government and his
policies on his former friends and advisors in the German Liberal party.
But that this was the only purpose of the campaign and represented a
purely personal power drive is a view that would appear to rest on a
one-sided distortion of the facts and to be, in effect, a liberal illusion. In
reality, it seems quite clear that in constructing the cartel and launching
it victoriously on a wave of national enthusiasm, Bismarck was fighting
for the next kaiser; he had actually provided Frederick William and Victoria with a Liberal-Conservative majority with which they could practically and successfully govern. Just as in foreign policy after 1885 he had
gradually moved toward England again, a trend made easier for him by
the fall of the Liberal leader, William Gladstone, in 1886, so now in
domestic politics he had constructed a moderately liberal and effective
power base that would be acceptable to the crown prince but would not
be a fundamental challenge to the traditional Prussian political and social
system. Did not, in fact, a contradictory association of Liberals with
Conservatives very nicely express the crown prince's own political
ambivalence?[24]

At the time when Bismarck constructed the cartel and fought the *Septennat* election in February, he naturally expected that the crown prince and
his English wife, who would soon succeed to the throne, would have a
long reign ahead of them. Clearly the fundamental problem would be one
of transition, especially since he himself could not expect, at the age of
seventy-two, to carry on actively much longer. He was quite aware of his
declining powers. On New Year's Eve 1885, Holstein reports that he was
extraordinarily depressed. "'Another year gone,' he said to [his son] Bill.
'Yes,' Bill replied with a laugh, 'we grow cleverer each year.' 'Oh, no,' said
the old man. 'I used to be cleverer than I am now. I can feel it; I have
far greater difficulty in grasping things, and I have lost my control of
affairs.'" It is probably significant that during the election campaign, in
late January 1887, in the interview with Busch previously referred to, the

chancellor displayed in passing a remarkably objective, detached attitude. The crown prince and princess were both well disposed toward him, he said, and in fact their main worry was that he might prefer to retire from office when they came to the throne. He spoke of the temptations of retirement to his estate at Friedrichsruh. In response to Busch's mention of the necessity of defending his "work" against the crown prince's German Liberal friends, Bismarck reiterated that there was little danger. "People deceive themselves greatly if they imagine there will be any considerable difference under the new king. . . . As to what you say about my work, it looks great, but after all it is of the earth and transient. Besides, what is the meaning of 'great'? Germany is great, but the earth is greater, and how small the earth is in comparison with the solar system, to say nothing of the whole universe. And how long will it last?" The philosopher Hegel had been wrong to claim that life did not exist elsewhere in space. "Certainly there are worlds where things of much greater importance are thought and done."[25] The trend of Bismarck's thought after the cartel victory in the election may be gauged by his statement to the Prussian ministers in the spring of 1887 that it was politically desirable to facilitate the raising of bourgeois to the nobility. "That makes the nobility popular, as is the case in England." A year later, in June 1888, just before Kaiser Frederick's death, Bismarck conceded to the ministers that "he had indeed earlier prepared himself for some National Liberal ministers in the case of a long reign for His Majesty."[26] Through dramatic manipulation and brow-beating of both parties and electorate in the cartel election of 1887, Chancellor von Bismarck had actually created a strong political basis for at least the successful launching, under the crown prince and princess, of what they had awaited so long—a new, fresh, liberal era.

2

Cancer

AT the time of the *Septennat* conflict, Crown Prince Frederick William was developing a persistent hoarseness; on March 16, 1887, a small growth on his left vocal cord was removed by electric needle by Dr. Karl Gerhardt, a throat specialist. The prince's voice thereupon improved, but by March 26 the growth had reappeared. Determined to eradicate it, Dr. Gerhardt burned it with the electric needle in repeated sessions between March 26 and April 7, when he was satisfied that it had been completely eliminated. The crown prince was then encouraged to go to the spa at Ems for rest and recuperation. Dr. Gerhardt was already apprehensive from the persistent character of the tumor, and from its appearance he feared that it might be malignant; he regarded the recuperation period at Ems as a test of this possibility. When the crown prince returned to Potsdam on May 15, the growth had not only returned, but was larger than before. Gerhardt was now convinced that it was cancer, and Dr. Ernst von Bergmann, the foremost surgeon in Germany and director of the Medical School of the University of Berlin, agreed with Gerhardt's diagnosis and advised an immediate operation on the larynx to prevent the spread of the disease and save the crown prince's life. A consultation of a number of distinguished doctors concurred with this recommendation, and, with the consent and cooperation of the crown princess, the operation was set for May 21.[1]

When Bismarck heard of the doctors' plans, however, he insisted that they call in the best non-German specialist they could find, that the crown prince be expressly informed of the nature and seriousness of the operation, and that no such operation take place without the kaiser's and the crown prince's own consent. The doctors had already decided that an outside expert, Dr. Morrell Mackenzie, a Scotsman, who had written a well-known book on laryngeal diseases, should be summoned, and the crown princess requested of her mother, Queen Victoria, that, to avoid comment, she send Dr. Mackenzie over as if on her own initiative. This was an unfortunate move, for it later made it appear that Mackenzie's intervention in the case was an English plot. The queen complied reluctantly. In England, Mackenzie was regarded as something of a charlatan and a money grubber. On May 20 Bismarck called on the crown princess to express his sympathy and urged her not to allow the operation. Both he and especially his wife would prefer in such a situation to put their trust in God rather than in doctors. Dr. von Bergmann had admitted that once he had opened up the larynx, he did not know how much of the left vocal cord or of the larynx itself he might have to remove, and that, in any case, the crown prince would be left voiceless, but the doctor had not conceded that the operation might also cost the crown prince his life. One should not take chances with the life of the heir to the throne.[2]

Dr. Mackenzie arrived on May 20 in Potsdam and immediately examined the royal patient. It did not look like cancer to him, he said, and before the awful risk of a serious operation should be taken, a piece of tissue should be microscopically examined. Only if cancer was definitely present should one operate. Thus the crown princess and her husband found themselves caught in a clash of opinion. Dr. von Bergmann felt emphatically that the possibility of saving the crown prince's life was worth the risk of the operation; others, led now unexpectedly by Dr. Mackenzie, insisted that only God knew whether the disease might be fatal, but that the operation was too serious a threat to the crown prince's life to accept without absolute certainty of the diagnosis—and perhaps not then. In this situation Frederick William and Victoria, seizing the straw of hope that Dr. Mackenzie's position inevitably offered, from that time on gave Mackenzie precedence over the German doctors and listened only to his opinions. The crown prince wrote to his mother, Kaiserin Augusta, that he and his wife found Mackenzie's personality "especially sympathetic." Professor Rudolf Virchow, then the world's greatest authority on cells, examined pieces of tissue removed from the larynx on several occasions but could not say definitely that they were cancerous. He apparently was not very sure what resembled a cancer cell. For their part, the German doctors agreed to let Mackenzie try to cure the crown prince without an operation, insisting only that he sign a statement for the files. They also filed their own dissenting opinion. They presumably saw that it was hopeless to insist on an operation against the will of the imperial couple backed by Bismarck.[3]

As for Dr. Morrell Mackenzie, he evidently was a better psychologist than laryngologist, notwithstanding all of his protestations to the contrary. Sensing that Frederick William and Victoria wanted to be reassured, he reassured them. It is quite likely that Mackenzie had decided from the first that the illness would be fatal, but his own experience convinced him that an operation would also be fatal, and thus pointless. The statistical chances at that time of a complete cure from partial or total extirpation of the larynx were not very high. The whole object, therefore, would be to make the patient as comfortable as possible and to prolong his life with purely palliative measures. In the meantime Dr. Mackenzie was determinedly optimistic. He told Minister of Justice Heinrich Friedberg that he could cure the crown prince in six weeks if he visited his clinic in London "like any other mortal." Unfortunately Mackenzie did not limit his optimism to official circles but released statements in the *Deutsche Revue* and the *British Medical Journal* in July announcing that the disease was definitely not cancer and that "very encouraging progress" was being made. In early August an article in the *Pall Mall Gazette* quoted Mackenzie as saying that the crown prince would make a complete recovery. The day before, Mackenzie had admitted to his young German assistant, Landgraf, that the tumor was growing again. In the meantime, at the end of June, Dr. Mackenzie had submitted a bill for his two visits to Berlin of £2,625 or $13,125, which he claimed was his usual fee, even for "private individuals."[4]

Crown Princess Victoria insisted that Frederick William accompany her to England in June, where he participated in the festivities celebrating the Golden Jubilee of the reign of Queen Victoria. Riding on horseback in the parade to Westminster Abbey behind the queen's carriage among a group of the queen's three sons, five sons-in-law, and nine grandsons, he was a striking figure with his tall, erect bearing, flowing golden beard, white uniform, silver cuirass, and helmet topped by an eagle. He drew the loudest and longest cheers from the crowd, some of whom saw him variously as Charlemagne, Siegfried, Lohengrin, or a new Barbarossa. Dr. Mackenzie's treatment of the illness with the electric needle during the summer was no more successful than Dr. Gerhardt's had been earlier. The growth was clearly increasing, but the imperial couple now refused to listen to the warnings from their German doctors and took refuge in what seems to later observers a kind of symbolic flight from the dread disease: first to the Isle of Wight, whose climate Mackenzie especially recommended, then to Scotland, then to Toblach in the Tyrol, then to Venice, then to Baveno on Lago Maggiore, then finally to a villa on the Italian Riviera, at San Remo. For the winter, Dr. Mackenzie had advised a southern climate, recommending Egypt or Madeira, which the crown prince and princess, however, decided would be too far from Germany. At the request of the crown prince, Queen Victoria knighted Dr. Mackenzie in September.[5]

While the crown prince and princess were engaged in these travels abroad, political leaders at home were adjusting to the new realities.

Already at the end of May, Baron von Roggenbach, former Baden National Liberal prime minister and long-time advisor to the crown prince, had expressed his distrust of Mackenzie in a letter to General Albrecht von Stosch. "Prince William and Herbert Bismarck label him simply a swindler." There was no need for the trip to England. "Meanwhile the enemy in the larynx continues its ravages and as far as I am concerned is leading His Highness [*den hohen Herrn*] toward destruction. The resourceful ones are taking their positions accordingly. They will be proved right in the end." Old Prince Bismarck, who had wept when he heard of the seriousness of the crown prince's condition, talked to Prussian Minister of Agriculture Robert Lucius about it in early June "very seriously, as of a hopelessly ill, doomed man." Bill Bismarck, the chancellor's second son, confessed to Friedrich von Holstein of the Foreign Office that he was mystified that his father should be so upset at the doom hanging over the crown prince. The chancellor had never shown any great regard for him and had been annoyed often enough by his oppositional liberal stance. Yet the psychological insight of Prince William's hypersensitive friend, Philipp Eulenburg, who was impressed by the old man's tears, was surely correct: the chancellor had prepared brilliantly for Frederick William's reign, and now it was not to be. Instead, to have to deal with the grandson, Prince William, would be an entirely different story. Once more Bismarck experienced the truth of the remark about politics that he had written to his wife in the 1860s: "One can be as clever as clever can be, and in the next minute be left like a child in the dark." The seventy-two-year-old chancellor suffered especially severely from neuralgic pains, rheumatism, and insomnia throughout the summer and fall, so that his private physician, Dr. Ernst Schweninger, had to resort to morphine, which he administered in carefully spaced and regulated doses.[6]

As the summer proceeded into fall, and the crown prince's health did not seem to be improving, a pessimistic tone, coupled with harsh criticisms of Dr. Mackenzie, began to appear in the German press. In this situation, German Liberal and independently liberal papers sprang enthusiastically to Mackenzie's and the crown prince's support. Their determined optimism meshed very well with the optimism of the imperial couple, providing it with amplification in the public arena. At the end of October, the crown prince published a letter to the Prussian Grand Masonic Lodge that included the statement, "Full of trust I look to God and hope that, recuperated, in the not too distant future I can return with my family to My Residence in the midst of My beloved Fatherland." A few days later Mackenzie himself admitted to the crown prince that the new developments in his larynx looked "very much like" cancer. On November 9 a general consultation of doctors agreed that the disease was cancer and that not only must an operation at this late stage involve removal of the entire larynx, but also that complete eradication of the disease thereby could not be assured. The crown prince was so informed and stated in writing that he did not wish to have the major operation, but would undergo a tracheotomy if difficulty in breathing made it necessary. On November 11, Crown Princess Victoria wrote her mother, "Yet I cannot and will not give up hope." And again on November 18, "We must leave the future in God's hands and not trouble about it, but fight this illness as well as we can, by remaining cheerful and hopeful. . . . You know how sensitive and apprehensive, how suspicious and despondent Fritz is by nature! All the more wrong and positively dangerous (let alone the cruelty of it) to wish him to think the worst! . . . How long it may please God to leave our darling with us we know not, but this thought, though it embitters every minute of my existence, shall not cast more gloom over him than I can help! . . . I do not know, but I think Prince Bismarck would be on our side." This was the basic sentiment that the imperial couple would hold to, right down to the end, a kind of pretense to each other and to the world that Dr. Mackenzie and the German Liberal press would continue to support and collaborate in. That for the crown princess personally it was not only pretense, but also an integral part of her dynamic, liberal, life-affirming and aesthetic personality is shown in a letter, written in mid-November, that is a rare expression of love and appreciation of her oldest son, Prince William. He had been in San Remo for the consultation and wrote her a warm letter of sympathy upon his return to Berlin, and she replied, thanking him for his thoughtfulness. She had not been fully able then to cope with the stress of the crisis, she admitted, but had now recovered control. "Amongst the flowers, & kind words—& Gifts,—sad thoughts had no time to gain the upper hand—the sun shone on the blue sea,—and it has the power—of being a *cheering* symbol, of Love—& hope—and *these* are one's stay & one's strength. . . . I do *not* look into the future, that is in God's hand—I take out of the *present* —Whatever is *cheering* & *encouraging* (& can find such). We do not lose courage in any way—*die schlechteste Rathgeberin ist die Angst* [the worst counselor is fear]."[7]*

A more political reason for determined optimism was the existence of a group at court, apparently headed by General Emil von Albedyll, chief of His Majesty's military cabinet, or secretariat, who wanted Frederick William to abdicate immediately in favor of Prince William when the old kaiser died. After the doctors' consultation in San Remo, Albedyll had demanded of Herbert Bismarck, foreign secretary and his father's lieuten-

* F. Ponsonby, *Letters of the Empress Frederick*, unfortunately standardized Crown Princess Victoria's highly personal capitalization and punctuation; at the cost of inconsistency I have kept the original form where quoting from the manuscripts.

ant in Berlin, that the public, which was becoming impatient with Mackenzie's pussyfooting medical bulletins, should be told the truth. Herbert cleared the matter with his father, got the kaiser's permission, and arranged publication of a bulletin written by him and amended by Albedyll and Count Udo zu Stolberg-Wernigerode, acting minister of the royal household, on November 12 in the official *Reichsanzeiger* stating that the crown prince's illness had been diagnosed as of "a carcinomatous nature . . . the glands are swollen, and the larynx is inflamed." Another temporizing bulletin from Mackenzie was suppressed. On November 14 Herbert Bismarck wrote to his father that Albedyll had suggested that since the old kaiser was obviously getting weak and could die any day, Prince William must immediately be made deputy or regent. "The crown prince could then . . . accept the title of Kaiser but would not rule. We could not accept a dying Kaiser who was sitting in Italy with a cut-open neck." The crown princess, said Albedyll, was issuing falsely optimistic reports to maintain the idea that her husband was capable of ruling so that she could, in fact, rule herself. In this report the elder Bismarck bracketed the word "deputy" and wrote in the margin, "Sick or healthy, H.I.H. [His Imperial Highness] becomes Kaiser through the death of H.M. [His Majesty]; whether the K. [Kaiser] is 'permanently incapacitated'* is determined according to Art. 56–58 of the Prussian Constitution." These articles stated that if the king of Prussia (who was automatically German kaiser according to the imperial constitution) should become "permanently incapacitated," the next male heir who had reached his majority would become regent, with the approval of both houses of the Prussian Landtag. This heir was, of course, Prince William. In 1858 the mentally ill King Frederick William IV had been persuaded to sign a statement declaring his permanent incapacity, and his brother, the present King William, had been declared regent. In the past, in moments of despondency, Crown Prince Frederick William had expressed the idea that his father had lived so long and the possibility of giving Prussia and Germany a liberal political direction had been so frustrated by him and Bismarck that there was really little hope that he himself could achieve anything positive when he succeeded his father, and that he might as well abdicate in favor of Prince William, whose conservative views would thus perpetuate those of his grandfather. But now that Frederick William's life and succession were under a real threat, neither he nor his wife showed the slightest disposition to give up their chance at the throne.[8]

---

* For the constitutional question of "incapacity," see below, pp. 116–17.

That some of the Prussian army generals should have been hostile to Frederick William and Victoria is not surprising, yet it is unlikely that Albedyll's motivation was consciously political. It is much more likely that he was overly concerned for the smooth running of the government and the chaos that might result if the old kaiser suddenly died while the crown prince was also dying and out of the country. The general wanted an effective commander. To the crown princess the idea that her husband should abdicate in favor of Prince William was "*monstrous*. It was expressed here by Dr. Schmidt,—" she wrote her mother on November 16,

> whether put in his head by Willy or vice versa I do not know,—but Genl. v. Winterfeld [the crown prince's adjutant] seems to agree with it. . . . Do not think I am complaining on interested grounds—I am really *not*!—If Fritz succeeds, he can provide for his daughters—& for his wife!—If he does *not**
> succeed—he can do *nothing* for us!—This is however *not* my motive!
>
> But I think it wd. be such a satisfaction to Fritz to be able to be of use—to his country—nation—army—& to Europe, if only for a limited time! If he felt too ill to discharge business— later on, *he* could then institute a Regency!

On November 21 the crown princess wrote to her mother that Prince Henry, her younger son, had tried to convince her that afternoon of the necessity of his father's abdication. Already in the preceding July, Prince Chlodwig zu Hohenlohe-Schillingsfürst, Statthalter or viceroy of Alsace-Lorraine, had noted in his diary that "there are people who are pushing Prince William forward as successor and apparently agitating for this. The chancellor is for the crown prince." Even Friedrich von Holstein, de facto head of the political section of the Foreign Office, wrote in his diary on November 11, "If the Kaiser dies overnight it seems to me unavoidable that the dying prince shall be made to renounce his claim to the throne, because under present conditions his wife could do all manner of mischief in a few months." The efforts of the German Liberal press to come to the defense of the crown prince only confirmed conservative court circles in these feelings, as again witness Holstein's diary of November 14: "The crown princess and her democratic adherents are spreading barefaced lies about the crown prince's health. The aim is to prevent the crown prince from being made to renounce his claim to the throne on the grounds of incapacity. There will be a really violent conflict between the advocates of abdication and the crown princess's following. The democrats think, quite rightly, that a dying monarch with the crown prince's character, completely dominated by his wife, could do great things in a few months, i.e., he could destroy or severely damage the monarchy."[9]

* No attempt has been made to indicate Crown Princess Victoria's double and triple underlining.

It has been frequently assumed from isolated statements of Bismarck or of Count Herbert that it was a great relief to them that Kaiser Frederick had such a short reign. This view has tied in nicely with the basic assumption that Bismarck was consistently conservative in his later years. The public line taken by the government after Kaiser William II's accession, especially the campaign against the unauthorized publication of Kaiser Frederick's diary, has also been allowed to obscure the facts of the case. It would actually have been easy for Bismarck to have forced Frederick William to renounce his rights to the throne at any time in the period between November 1887 and March 1888, but he did not do it. Such a move would have been risky politically, since it would have provided the left Liberals with a splendid issue upon which to raise a public hue and cry, an issue that, since it involved deep, traditional, and personal emotions of love for and loyalty to the ruling house, could only have an extremely divisive effect on all classes and groups. Holstein's "really violent conflict" would be an unnecessary scandal that had best be avoided. But in addition it is quite clear that even before the Stoecker affair, Bismarck hoped to postpone Prince William's accession until he could better prepare him for it.[10]

The crown princess herself provided the rationale for maintaining her husband's rights to the throne in a conversation with Count Hugo Radolinski, chamberlain and Bismarck's agent at the crown prince's court, as reported carefully by him in a letter of November 21, 1887, to his friend Holstein.

> She herself (she said) set little value on the crown (who really believes that!!) but she would not consent that her husband should be subject to another Kaiser during his lifetime, that is, after his father is dead, of course.
>
> She also thinks that the crown prince can still survive for some years. She added that both the chancellor and Count H[erbert]. B[ismarck]. would certainly prefer to work with a more accommodating master than with the still youthful and consequently impetuous son. This I also leave to your judgment to tell Count H. B. confidentially. The crown princess added that she was convinced that the chancellor would not support the abdication of the crown prince.

Back in June, Holstein had noted in his diary that Herbert Bismarck had just told him that a Hungarian artist who was currently painting Prince William's portrait had remarked astutely, "Nothing pleases him for long." Holstein went on:

> Herbert said this judgement was unfortunately only too correct. The prince had no staying power—he simply wanted to be amused. And all that really interested him in army life was wearing a handsome uniform and marching

through the streets to music. He fancied himself as Frederick the Great, but had neither his gifts nor his knowledge. And Frederick the Great, as a young man, had ceaselessly worked and exercised his intellect, whereas Prince [William] allowed his talents to deteriorate by constantly consorting with Potsdam lieutenants. And as cold as a block of ice. Convinced from the start that people only exist to be used—either for work or amusement—and that even then they only do duty for a given period, after which they may be cast aside. Herbert said the prince was impressed by no one, except, it was to be hoped, the chancellor. If the prince were to ascend the throne now, many blunders would be committed. His views on domestic policy were those of a Potsdam lieutenant and would, if acted upon, easily plunge Germany into a jolly civil war.

Since this was a confidential conversation, and Holstein was close to Herbert, this opinion must be taken seriously, especially since it conforms so well to the generally accepted view of the character of the later William II. It is unlikely that the elder Bismarck's opinion of the prince was substantially different from his son's. In the same passage in his diary, Holstein had also noted that General Leo von Caprivi had remarked that Crown Prince Frederick William "'has never been held in such high esteem as now.' Caprivi is one of many people who regard the crown prince as less dangerous than Prince [William] because the former can be led, but not the latter." On November 22 Bismarck sent a long memorandum to Lord Salisbury, the British prime minister and foreign secretary, arguing that it would be impossible for Prince William to turn German policy in a direction hostile to England when and if he came to the throne because German policy was not formed merely by the kaiser but "proceeds along a route necessarily prescribed by the political situation in Europe." He added a personal note that he had read the memorandum to Prince William, who had approved it, and that he was informing Lord Salisbury of the fact "to make assurance doubly sure." Three days later Lord Salisbury informed Queen Victoria that he had spoken to the German ambassador "on the subject [of a regency] . . . and has received from him the assurance . . . that there was not the slightest ground of apprehending any proceeding of the kind suggested. He dwelt rather upon the great advantage to Germany that would ensue, even if the worst that was feared should turn out to be true as to the Crown Prince's health, if he should live long enough to interpose some interval between the death of the present Emperor and the accession of Prince Wm."[11]

Probably to forestall the intrigues of the Albedyll party, on November 17, Bismarck, in Berlin briefly for an audience with the tsar of Russia, quickly got the old kaiser's signature on an order making Prince William the kaiser's deputy, so that he could sign official documents if his grandfather became suddenly incapacitated, which could be expected almost any day. This act was taken without consulting the crown prince, and the chancellor told the Prussian ministry that it would "infuriate" him, which it did. Prussian Minister of Agriculture Robert Lucius records that in the ministry session on November 19, Bismarck said nothing about the crown prince, but expanded on the fact that other Hohenzollerns, like Prince William, had come to the throne at an early age, including Frederick the Great, who was Prince William's exact age, twenty-eight. "He has obviously ceased to concern himself" with the crown prince, noted Lucius. For the benefit of Berlin court circles, including General von Albedyll, the ministry, the Foreign Office, and perhaps even Count Herbert, who was being encouraged to maintain a close relationship with Prince William, and certainly for the special benefit of the latter, the deputizing order— which could be renewed by the crown prince upon his accession and thus effectively removed any practical, urgent grounds for imposing a regency on him—was to look like a brutal act directed against the crown prince. It might also have the virtue of a shock effect for the imperial couple, remote in their villa in sunny San Remo, of reminding them of the dangers of staying away from Berlin and of the reality of the forces threatening their interests there. Also, by tacitly encouraging the court agitation in favor of raising the position of Prince William, Bismarck could more effectively strengthen his own personal relationship to the crown prince and princess as their one faithful champion and protector and thus tie them all the more closely to himself. Factional extremism within the governing bureaucracy, as also among the political parties, with or without encouragement, allowed him to continue to play the role of mediator and manipulator. On November 29 Bismarck's son-in-law and private secretary, Count Kuno zu Rantzau, wrote Herbert that Franz von Rottenburg, head of the chancellery and the chancellor's chief lieutenant and press officer in domestic affairs, wanted to put through the crown prince's abdication with the help of Acting Minister of the Royal Household Stolberg and Minister of Justice Heinrich Friedberg, an old advisor and friend of the crown prince. He himself, the count wrote, did not believe in the possibility of an abdication and the crown princess would never allow it. "She will win the race with the Kaiser, it is for her simply a question of rank and money, and no other considerations will count."[12]

On November 26 Crown Princess Victoria had written her mother that "Fritz does not dream of resigning his rights, and *no* Law would allow of his being superseded, so on this score—both you, & we ourselves—can set our minds at rest." And, two days later, "Fritz is as well able to *think—read* & *write*—& *transact* business as he ever was." The next day, November 29, she wrote the queen,

As to a certain plot—it has *not* succeeded. They have not been able to tear Fritz out of the Hands of Sir Morell [*sic*], Dr. Krause and Dr. Hovell,—*nor* to drag Fritz to Berlin,—put him under incompetent Doctors, and *force* the operation on him—which wd. either kill him—or reduce him to the *most awful* existence you can imagine.

They *cannot* therefore force—Fritz to resign as they wanted, nor—get rid of me! So far all is right!—but they are still frantic—and *Henry* maintains that *his Papa* is *lost* through the English Doctors & me—& the Germans would have *saved* him with the operation!! The boy is as foolish as he is obstinate & pig headed.

"I have been *so* tormented—" she wrote on December 2,

& had to struggle & *fight*—& pick my way *alone*, as the *2* who resolutely stuck by me—were so *swamped* by the violence fr. Berlin (i.e.—Ct Radolinski—& Ct Seckendorff)—that I did *not* dare—ask them to open their mouths, or they would have been perhaps removed or . . [*sic*] I know not what!—If I had not had Sir Morell [*sic*]—who is wonderfully shrewd & has a *very* good temper & always remains quiet when people lose their heads with excitement—I do not know how I could have stemmed or turned the current wh. was rushing with such fury!—It was *so* wrong of Genl Winterfeld!!—He means well—& does it fr. the best of motives i.e. Patriotism &c . . [*sic*] but he set the *Court*—& the Govt. in the most violent alarm.[13]

On December 2 Bismarck sent a handwritten letter to the crown princess, in response to letters of November 22 from both herself and the crown prince, explaining his action in signing the deputizing order. A model of diplomatic tact, the letter apparently said little, but the crown princess could doubtless read between the lines. Contrary to all other reports from Berlin, the chancellor wrote,

the conviction that the opponents of a precipitous operation in the spring were right is today only rarely disputed, because the success of a forced operation, which was not without immediate danger to [the patient's] life, was always uncertain, even for the six months that have been won since then, or, in case it had been successful, would have been hardly acceptable for the illustrious patient. . . . His Imperial Highness has graciously written me regarding the temporary creating of a deputy [*Stellvertretung*] for His Majesty the Kaiser. . . . I have taken part in the affair only at second hand, could also not create difficulties for His Majesty in fulfilling his justified wish, in case of illness to create work-free days for himself. The question that concerns His Imperial Highness in that connection is only that of prior information; there was no possibility of the latter because of the rapidity with which His Majesty concluded the matter.

The word "temporary" clearly indicated that the order had nothing to do with the succession and would, as Bismarck told the ministry, automatically lapse with the accession of the crown prince, who would naturally become kaiser on the death of his father. In a sixteen-page, dictated letter to the crown prince's chamberlain, Count Radolinski, the chancellor spelled this point out in detail. He also blamed the initiative for the order on the military cabinet (Albedyll) and the royal household (Stolberg). He further made the very sensitive point, as far as the crown prince was concerned, that it was not compatible with the honor of a servant of the crown, just because the kaiser was old and in feeble health, to act on his requests only after prior consultation with and the approval of the heir to the throne! He would, he wrote, if he ever had the honor of serving the crown prince in such a capacity, not be willing to make his carrying out of his duties dependent on the agreement of the heir to the throne (Prince William). He would have a bad conscience, with the present kaiser near the end of his life, if he allowed him to receive the impression that he had let his relationship to him be altered by consideration for the impending succession. He did not doubt that the crown prince would not himself want a chancellor or minister who thought otherwise. Clearly this statement to Radolinski was meant as a sort of pledge of loyalty and faithfulness to the crown prince and princess and of willingness to defend them against Prince William and his backers. In a letter to her mother on December 4, the crown princess called Bismarck's letter "civil & pleasant" and added that Prince Henry was now "nice & amiable." On December 12 Queen Victoria wrote to her daughter that she had heard that Bismarck was "extremely concerned that the life of our beloved Fritz be spared for many, many years."[14]

In late November, because at the dinner for the tsar at the royal palace Bismarck had not been placed near the Russian ruler but at the end of the table with the other princes, he not only had protested in sharply written letters to Superior Court Marshal Count Wilhelm von Perponcher and Acting Minister of the Royal Household Count Udo zu Stolberg-Wernigerode, but also had had complaints run in the *Kölnische Zeitung* that a "court clique" was opposing his foreign policy of good relations with Russia. Having yielded to Albedyll and Stolberg in regard to the deputizing of Prince William, perhaps the chancellor seized this opportunity to belabor the court officials in order to demonstrate his clout and prevent their imagining that their personal influence was on the increase. His public display of ill humor in their direction also lent credibility to his protest to the crown prince and princess that it was Albedyll and Stolberg who had been primarily responsible for the deputizing order.[15]

At the end of December 1887, the crown princess informed her mother that she had learned, to her satisfaction, that the chancellor had taken up a position against any talk of abdication for her husband. In the meantime, on December 9 and 10, the newspapers published a letter of the crown prince to *Geheimrat* Georg Hinzpeter, Prince William's old tutor, declaring, "I do not in any way despair, and hope, even if after a long convalescence [*Schonung*], to be able one day to devote my strength to the Fatherland as of old." There seems to be little evidence that Bismarck shared Holstein's fears of the damage to the monarchy that Victoria and her German Liberal friends might do in a few months if her husband came to the throne in a partially incapacitated condition. Not only was he aware that the crown princess, now more than ever, believed that his own continuance in office would be desirable, but he did not regard the crown princess herself as a political threat. In July he had told Lucius that "the crown princess is no Catherine II, no more than the crown prince is a Peter III.* She is primarily a 'coward'; she wants to be popular, to sparkle in conversation, but she has no real ambition to rule. She has artistic inclinations and will try to be active in that direction. She wants to appear liberal, to embarrass people through paradoxes, but no more."[16]

* Tsarina Catherine the Great of Russia, it will be remembered, succeeded as autocratic ruler in her own right in 1762 upon the deposition and murder of her husband, Peter III.

3

The Waldersee-Stoecker Meeting

IN a private, strictly confidential letter on November 16, Lord Salisbury
summed up the German situation for his ambassador in Berlin, Sir
Edward Malet. "Between us and Prince William's perhaps unchecked
rule there only stand now three lives,—one of ninety-one, one of seventy-
three, and one menaced by a disease 'that does not pardon.' . . . I fear that
Mackenzie has done irreparable damage. . . . I hope that you, my dear Sir
Edward, will be able to persuade Count [Herbert] Bismarck to use his
undoubtedly great influence on Prince William in order to destroy all
prejudices that he may have against our country." Certainly, if the head
of a foreign government was interested in cultivating Prince William's
favor after his father's cancer had been definitely diagnosed, political
leaders inside Germany would not be far behind. The reactionary Junker
Kreuzzeitung group already had the inside track. Prince William was notoriously antiliberal, sincerely and orthodoxly religious, and had developed a
close friendship with the chief assistant to old Field Marshal von Moltke
in the general staff, Quartermaster General Count Alfred von Waldersee,
who was himself a follower of the orthodox, anti-Semitic, Christian
Socialist second court chaplain, Adolf Stoecker.[1]

On November 28 a meeting of dignitaries was called under the auspices
of Prince and Princess William in the quarters of General von Waldersee
in the general staff building to discuss ways and means of collecting funds
to support the work of Pastor Stoecker's Berlin City Mission. About forty
persons attended, mostly political Conservatives and orthodox Protestants, but with a deliberate sprinkling of financiers, industrialists, and
National Liberals so as to downplay the partisan aspect. The group included personalities of high rank and important governmental position,
such as Prussian Minister of the Interior Robert von Puttkamer, Prussian
Minister of Ecclesiastical, Educational, and Medical Affairs Gustav von
Gossler, Chief of His Majesty's Civil Cabinet Baron Karl von Wilmowski,
and Acting Minister of the Royal Household Count Udo zu Stolberg-

Wernigerode. Prince and Princess William and Court Chaplain Stoecker were, of course, also in attendance. Superior Court Chaplain Rudolf Kögel, Chief of His Majesty's Military Cabinet General Emil von Albedyll, and National Liberal party leader Johannes Miquel were invited, but, for one reason or another, did not attend. Representation of the press was narrowly restricted to Pastor Heinrich Engel, editor in chief of the ultra-conservative and orthodox *Reichsbote,* and the Conservative Reichstag and Prussian Landtag deputy, Baron Wilhelm von Hammerstein-Schwartow, chief editor of the *Kreuzzeitung.*[2]

In his opening speech, General von Waldersee pointed out that representatives of all parts of Germany and all religious and political points of view had been invited because the city of Berlin, where the shortage of churches and the need for religious work were so great, was made up of people from all parts of Germany. The City Mission, he said, represented "absolutely no definite political viewpoint, belonged to no political party, but its only norm is loyalty to the king and the cultivation of patriotism." The only effective means of combating the anarchistic, revolutionary tendencies threatening the state, he stressed, was spiritual care, which should be accompanied by material support in poverty and sickness. Only thus could a person by made to be "satisfied with his lot." Following Waldersee, Prince William then gave a short speech, declaring that "as against the revolutionary tendencies of an anarchistic and irreligious party [the Marxist Social Democrats] the most effective protection of throne and altar must be sought in leading the irreligious masses back to Christianity and the church and thus to recognition of legal authority and love for the monarchy. The Christian-socialist idea must therefore be given greater consideration with more emphasis than previously." After these and other speeches, a committee was chosen to organize a drive to raise funds. That evening General Waldersee noted in his diary that the affair "went very well and is, I believe, of far-reaching significance, since Prince William thereby not only took up a firm Christian standpoint, but also advocated it."[3]

Waldersee and his orthodox-Conserative friends, such as Puttkamer and Hammerstein, probably had not intended the Stoecker meeting to be a public demonstration but merely wanted quietly to establish a sort of right-wing beachhead among influential circles and with Prince William in preparation for future developments. And the first reports of the occasion in the party press were rather restrained. The Free-Conservative *Post* and the National Liberal *Kölnische Zeitung* even made a point of explaining that Princess William had raised 45,000 M for the City Mission last year through a bazaar, and that Prince William had originally intended this year to hold a great riding exhibition with the aid of officers of the guards, but that this plan had been given up in deference to the serious condition of the crown prince, and the less public meeting at General Waldersee's had been substituted. The public association of the heir to the throne with the Stoecker-*Kreuzzeitung* right wing of the Conservative party, however, could not go entirely unchallenged. The left-liberal press immediately began to stress the political implications. The very first report of the meeting in the *Börsen-Courier* was headed, "Consolidation of the Clerical-Conservative Elements." The meeting, it said, was attended by "notables from mostly orthodox or clerical-conservative circles." The *Frankfurter Zeitung* agreed. The *Freisinnige Zeitung*, the German Liberal leader Eugen Richter's paper, pointed out that the City Mission was a considerable enterprise, with its own publishing house and a staff of four pastors in addition to Pastor Stoecker, assisted by twenty-seven "so-called City Missionaries" working in the individual parishes. Everyone knew that Stoecker had mixed his City Mission work with political agitation and that "often liberal parish authorities have refused Herr Stoecker the use of churches for sermons in the interest of the Berlin City Mission because of the special orientation of this mission." On December 9 Waldersee noted that "our meeting . . . has been answered by a cry of indignation from all the extreme-progressive papers that are completely under Jewish influence, the same naturally from the Social Democratic papers, but also from *Germania* [the chief organ of the Catholic Center party]. I believe that that these attacks just help the cause. Naturally, however, there are the weak-kneed and indifferent [*Halbe und Laue*] among us who find that the prince has overengaged himself."[4]

Even with the liberal outcry, the incident might not have developed into anything of importance but for Stoecker himself. Adolf Stoecker had risen from a lower-middle-class military family through studying theology and becoming a pastor. He had advanced swiftly in this profession, being called to Berlin to become fourth court chaplain in 1874 at the age of thirty-nine. Here his efforts in behalf of orthodox Protestantism, dominant at court under old Kaiser William, quickly carried over into a political attempt to win back the masses of Berlin from socialism and atheism to Christianity, the church, and the state. This program was to be accomplished through a combination of propaganda and social reform, and in 1878 Stoecker founded his Christian Socialist Workers' party, which called for state aid for the working class. A robust, handsome, naturally combative man with a rich, powerful voice and a flair for popular political oratory, Stoecker possessed a genuinely warm sympathy for the little people and sincerely wanted to bring the church back into contact with the masses. In 1875, partly, no doubt, because of the Kulturkampf law requiring civil marriage, but also because of the lack of churches in the burgeoning city, of 100 Berlin marriages, only 18 to 19 were performed in church, and only 52 out of 100 children were baptized. Stoecker recognized that the new industrial state would have to take responsibility for the welfare of all its citizens and that some sort of socialism was the wave of the future, and he hoped that it would be Christian rather than atheist. Both Bismarck's law against socialist agitation, passed in 1878, and his social insurance program, launched in 1881, however, preempted the program of Stoecker's party, and the working class naturally regarded the court chaplain suspiciously as a representative of the oppressive power structure. Stoecker never did win any significant following among the Berlin workers, and the word "worker" was dropped from the party designation in 1880. Since the chancellor had turned against the Liberals in 1878–79, and the government press began to create an antiliberal atmosphere, Stoecker went along with this tide, his party developing as a petty-bourgeois-oriented, anti-Semitic, and antiliberal movement. In the fall of 1880 the Berlin Movement was formed, to bring Stoecker's Christian Socialists together with the Conservative party and independent anti-Semites under the common aegis of anti-Semitism and opposition to liberalism. In 1881 the Berlin Movement obtained its own newspaper in the *Deutsches Tageblatt* and in the election that year established itself as a developing popular power in the city, with strongholds mostly in the suburbs among the lower middle class. The Conservative vote in that election increased threefold. In the Protestant church organization, the Berlin Movement was especially successful, dominating the Berlin synod by 1889.[5]

Yet from the beginning Stoecker's political activity contained basic anomalies and weaknesses. His great strengths were his personality and his power as a popular speaker. "At that time he was the only great popular personality that the Conservatives possessed." But he, of course, did not lead even the right wing of the Conservative party. Yet he remained tied to it and did not strike out on his own; he did not, for example, try to extend his Christian-Socialist appeal to the large masses of disgruntled artisans, shopkeepers, and peasants outside of Berlin, both in the Prussian and non-Prussian provinces. This failure derived from his personal need to cling to his position at court. Being close to traditional authority and included in the "higher circles" was more important to him than the popular power he was ostensibly trying to arouse. He could not risk becoming an outsider. Thus his movement found itself constantly sacrificed to demands of state and government policy. For example, as a result of the formation of the cartel between the Conservative, Free Conservative, and National Liberal parties for the election of 1887, Stoecker, Professor Adolf Wagner, an economist, and Josef Cremer, editor of the

Deutsches Tageblatt, withdrew under government pressure from their candidacies in Berlin and were replaced by persons acceptable to the National Liberals. On the other hand, although the orthodox Protestant, right-wing leaders and Junker aristocrats von Hammerstein and Hugo von Kleist-Retzow were his close friends and strong supporters, Stoecker's demagogical style as a speaker frequently got him in trouble, involving him in embarrassing libel suits and alienating him from many Conservatives as well as Liberals. Passionately and sincerely devoted to religious values, he was frequently overbold and rash, thereby probably revealing a basic political naiveté. His approach to politics was simplistic, as was his approach to anti-Semitism. Jews at the time were mostly associated with Liberals since the Liberals had been responsible for their recent grant of full citizenship in 1869. Many emancipated Jews were active in the liberal press, and the great liberal newspapers, the *Frankfurter Zeitung, Berliner Tageblatt, National Zeitung*, and the Viennese *Neue Freie Presse*, were Jewish owned and edited. Also Jews had been traditionally involved in money lending and still were, in relatively backward Central Europe. Both Kaiser William and Bismarck had their own Jewish bankers. With the onset of the Long Depression in 1873, accompanied by many bankruptcies and scandals, one could attack capital, high finance, and the new industrial society without running the danger of encouraging revolutionary assaults on property in general, by focusing the hostilities and frustrations of artisans, shopkeepers, white-collar workers, and peasants on the Jews. Stoecker, with his typically mid-century concept of Christianity as a strenuous, heroic combat, found that personalizing modern materialism in the Jew was popular. He thought that offering the masses a scapegoat to vent their rage on was a good way to release tensions that could otherwise endanger authority and order. His critics, on the other hand, thought that he was igniting unhealthy mass feelings that might otherwise have only smoldered. He himself boasted (correctly) that he had "taken the Jewish question out of the realm of literature and introduced it into popular meetings and thereby into political practice." Others took it from there.[6]

Crown Prince Frederick William and his English wife, Victoria, were emancipated and liberal in their religious views, and the prospect of their permanent removal from the succession to the throne must have seemed to the orthodox prelates at the Berlin court like a truly divine dispensation. There had been hints to this effect even before the Waldersee meeting. Speaking at a meeting of Christian Socialists on November 25, Pastor Stoecker had taken as his theme, in keeping with the Advent season, "An Advent for the Workers." Christianity, he said, had the power to make the rich willing to sacrifice and the poor contented. A new time was coming for the workers, and the beginnings had already been made by the social insurance legislation of the German Empire. "We stand," he went on, "under the wing-beats of a new national period." Now united, Germans need no longer be afraid, but *others* were now afraid of them (applause). But serious internal divisions, especially class divisions, remained, and Stoecker went on to attack the Social Democrats for erroneously taking an antinational position. The same day Superior Court Chaplain Rudolf Kögel delivered a sermon in the Berlin cathedral, during the customary service for the Protestant deputies before the opening of the Reichstag, whose text was "Be still and wait upon the Lord." The German Empire and her aged kaiser were undergoing a severe trial in the illness of the crown prince. "A national affliction is also a holy event, where the prophetic word applies: 'The Lord is in his holy temple, let the whole earth be silent before Him.' So humble yourselves under the mighty hand of God, you German people, be still and wait upon the Lord." On November 27 the *Kreuzzeitung* carried a lead article entitled "Advent" that discussed the trials of the church and especially its conflicts with the state. It was now recognized that church and state should be separate, but the article maintained that this should not be a sharp division; rather they must help each other with understanding, since "both orders have indeed *one* final source in God's grace."[7]

In its initial report of the Waldersee meeting, the *Frankfurter Zeitung* had remarked that it was now clear why Stoecker had recently shown so much more confidence and what the significance of his statement to his followers was, that (misquoting him) " 'in political affairs we stand under the wing-beats of a new age.' " Four days after the Waldersee affair Stoecker made the situation worse in addressing another heavily attended meeting of Christian Socialists in the Tonhalle. Anti-Semitism, he said, was not dead. "So far our opponents have always exulted much too soon. At the moment they are only feigning their triumph; in reality they are afraid, and they are trembling (applause)." Jews, he went on, were doubly dangerous since they both aroused the dissatisfaction of the workers by amassing wealth as capitalists and also provided the leadership for the revolution. There had been a lot of comment recently regarding the City Mission, which was purely a work of charity. He had never interfered with affairs of the Jewish faith or Jewish charities. But the Jews had interfered in this Christian work. The *Berliner Tageblatt* had made false and inaccurate statements. Stoecker then went on to deplore the recent rise of a demagogical (!) kind of anti-Semitism that could only hurt the cause of a "rational, calm, successful struggle against Jewry." He carefully distinguished theological, national, and racial anti-Semitism from his own, which was "social-ethical." The theological view saw the problem as purely religious and sought to convert the Jews.

> The national conception protests that a negligible fraction of a foreign nationality spoils our history, destroys our national character, rules our press (applause), and tries to make our policy. The advocates of this view say: Germany belongs to the Germans (applause) and no corner of Germany, no area of intellectual life shall belong to the Jews (lively applause). This point of view is justified; but it is insufficient. It is too one-sided (shout: No! laughter) and runs the danger of developing into racial anti-Semitism, [which] is neither cultured nor Christian. Christianity has overcome the differences of the peoples and races.

His own view was "social-ethical"; the Jews were "morally quite different from us." Stoecker then went on to attack Reichstag deputy Otto Böckel, a racial anti-Semite. Böckel, a person of "intelligence, energy, and good looks," was a student of folklore and librarian at the University of Marburg in Prussian Hesse, who had romanticized and idealized traditional peasant life, now threatened by industrialization. He had tapped anti-Prussian and anti-industrial anger among the peasantry and had built a strong, grassroots, anti-Semitic political party by turning this anger against both Jews and Junkers. He had been elected by a landslide in the largely rural district around Marburg the previous February and sat in the Reichstag as an Independent. It is clear from the news account of Stoecker's speech that the crowd was not quite with the pastor in his fine distinctions. If the emotional appeal of anti-Semitism was merely a convenient means for Pastor Stoecker to promote a traditional ethical, Christian, patriotic, and authoritarian point of view, for his followers the aura of ethical and political righteousness that he supplied was itself merely an adjunct—the expression of frustrated rage was primary, and the Jew a convenient, alien, and vulnerable target.[8]

In the same edition in which its report of Stoecker's speech appeared, the *Kreuzzeitung* replied testily to the attacks of the liberal press. Its irritable tone probably stemmed from editor Baron von Hammerstein's embarrassment over Stoecker's remarks regarding the present fear and apprehension of the Liberals, with their crude and obvious reference to the illness of the crown prince. The meeting at General von Waldersee's, the *Kreuzzeitung* insisted, had been nonpartisan and concerned solely with charity. Nevertheless, the whole liberal press had treated it as an "untoward event." On the contrary, "the action of Prince William, just because it is removed from all party politics, finds general agreement where people do not see things exclusively from the standpoint of the Jewish interest."[9]

The attempt of the *Kreuzzeitung*-Stoecker group to prepare the ground for a "new era" under Prince William, as tentative and essentially harmless as the Waldersee-Stoecker meeting had been in itself, was necessarily aimed by implication at undercutting the position of the liberal crown prince and princess. That Waldersee, a close friend of Prince William, was the prime mover in the affair emphasized the threat, since Waldersee had been conscious for some time that the crown prince and his wife were hostile toward him, because of his conservatism and orthodoxy, as well as his influence on their son. Waldersee's close ties to Chief of the Military Cabinet General von Albedyll and the latter's to General Hugo von Winterfeld, adjutant to the crown prince, also suggest a possibly crucial role for Waldersee in the agitation for a regency. At any rate, the crown princess, at the end of the month, expressed herself to her mother concerning the affair in no uncertain terms. The Stoecker Berlin mission was not at all a harmless institution. Prince William's speech at the Waldersee-Stoecker meeting had

> created great indignation . . . in the Liberal and Bourgeois world at Berlin, and has made William still more unpopular than he already was. . . . The people who for almost 30 years have been nasty to Fritz and especially to me, are the very same who run after William, who have him quite in their pocket and Dona [Prince William's wife, Auguste Victoria] also. . . . Their hope, their wish is that William shall continue the style of Government they are so sadly afraid will be modified if Fritz ever is Emperor. William knows all this! The Court-Clergy at Berlin are most pernicious elements, false, ambitious, narrow-minded and servile, much disliked by the educated and industrial middle class. . . . Much will change if we ever have a chance of putting straight and conciliating.[10]

One may wonder just how "conciliatory" Crown Princess Victoria's "putting straight" would have been if she and her husband had come to the throne under normal conditions. But that she could still be thinking of such possibilities when her husband's days were numbered and the surgeon who was to perform the tracheotomy had been standing by for a month indicates to what an extent it was possible for her to ignore reality when she wished. Her political attitudes were similarly unreal. Like other left-wing or orthodox liberals, she and the crown prince disapproved of Bismarck's powerful and realistic methods. As recently as the preceding September, the crown princess had written her mother that Bismarck "has made Germany great, but neither loved, free, happy, nor has he developed her immense resources for good! Despotism is the essence of his being; it cannot be right or good in the long run!" Yet by the end of November, it was this despotic chancellor in Berlin who was the principal barrier between the liberal imperial couple and the loss of their rights of succession to the throne. To her librarian, the crown princess remarked one day that they were surrounded by spies and traitors. "Why then not get rid of them?" he asked. "Because we cannot; they are imposed on us as overseers. They want to compel the crown prince to abdicate; our own son has put himself on the side of the agitation. His stay here was terrible; he acted like the master; we had already sunk into insignificance; we were not to be considered any more." In regard to the Stoecker meeting, the crown prince remarked, "William does intentionally what he knows is disagreeable to me." He wrote to Minister of Justice Friedberg about the matter and sent Count Radolinski to Berlin. Friedberg and Radolinski both reported that Prince William had not been aware of being exploited by the Conservative right wing. His adjutant Edward von Liebenau wrote the crown prince that the affair was the result of a "well considered intrigue of Stoecker's," and—perhaps inaccurately—that Prince William had been drawn in more by vanity and the high official position of Puttkamer and Waldersee than by political conviction. He recommended that the crown prince wait to write to his son, since at present he was touchy about the matter. But no one else could point out to Prince William that in supporting a partisan viewpoint he had offended royal tact.[11]

On November 28 Prince William had gone straight from the Waldersee meeting to the Foreign Office, where he had told Herbert Bismarck about the meeting in support of Stoecker's City Mission. To critical comments of Count Herbert's the prince had replied, "Nevertheless, Stoecker is something like Luther." He had won many thousands of Berliners away from the Social Democrats and for the kaiser. The contrary was the case, replied Herbert; Stoecker had brought new voters to the polls; the votes of the Social Democrats had continued to increase with each election. In the evening of Thursday, December 1, Prince William departed from Berlin for the royal hunt at Letzlingen, where after dinner he passed around newspaper articles regarding the Waldersee meeting. The prince was upset at the criticism in the liberal press. His pugnacity shocked even the reactionary Minister of the Interior Puttkamer. "When I have the say [*Wenn er einmal dran komme*], I will not allow Jews to operate in the press!" According to the present industrial code, remarked Puttkamer, that could not be prevented. "Then we shall repeal it." Herbert Bismarck returned from the Letzlingen hunt on Saturday evening and took a late train to Friedrichsruh, where he talked to his father on Sunday about foreign affairs and the warlike attitude of the general staff (see p. 000) and presumably also reported the intransigent attitude of Prince William.[12]

Now the affair really began to roll. The Catholic Center party organ *Germania*, sensing discord among the government and cartel forces, began to display keen interest, carefully distinguishing between its religious sensibilities, sympathetic to the orthodox Protestant Right, and its tactical political sense. "Prince William," it wrote on December 6, "wants to favor the Protestant City Mission, which in the light of the desolate religious and church conditions in Berlin is a very meritorious action of the prince's. . . . The supporters of Stoecker, however, are keen to take political advantage [of it]." *Germania* then proceeded to quote the reaction of the *Kreuzzeitung* and key articles in other papers, such as the *Reichsbote* and the *Posener Zeitung*.[13] The *Reichsbote* had pointed out that since liberal science, journalism, and literature had been propagating naturalistic attitudes among the masses, things had been deteriorating. Social Democracy could not be defeated by the egotistical consideration for their own interests that characterized the liberal bourgeoisie. Only Christianity, through a marshaling of free Christian love, could accomplish the task, and such was the Berlin City Mission. Since moral needs were connected to social needs, Stoecker had also agitated for Christian social reform, and it was because this program of social reform threatened the naturalistic liberal Weltanschauung and its principle of laissez faire that the liberals were afraid of the City Mission. "The *Reichsbote*," remarked *Germania*, "thus stamps Prince William's action as political. In addition, there is the *personality of Herr Stoecker*, which finds no sympathy anywhere among the higher circles and really deserves none."* It then quoted the *Posener Zeitung*, which had written, "It is certainly not a trifling matter, when the future German Kaiser declares himself in word and deed in favor of an orientation characterizing the extreme right wing of the Conservative party." Bismarck, it wrote, had never supported or approved of Stoecker. It then quoted the crown prince's well-known denunciation of anti-Semitism as "a disgrace for the German nation" and pointed out opposition to Stoecker within the Protestant church and Stoecker's involvement in unsavory libel suits. The generally authoritative tone of this article suggests that it might well have been written in the Chancellery. *Germania* followed the *Posener Zeitung* article with one from the *Freisinnige Zeitung* claiming that all the liberal parishes in Berlin opposed the City Mission, which was not controlled by the parishes and worked for its own purposes. Directly below this general discussion, *Germania* then placed an item reporting the yearly meeting of the Gustav-Adolf Association (for the propagation of Protestantism) in Potsdam in the Garrison Church, attended by Princess William, at which Court Chaplain Rogge had warned against Catholic advances in Brandenburg. Sectarian rivalry, as well as tactical political considerations, prevented the Catholic Center party from

---

* *Germania* habitually used a maximum of emphasis in its articles. I have used italics for the usual extra separation of the letters in German typographic style.

sympathizing too closely with the orthodox Protestant right-wing Conservatives.[14]

On December 6 Chancellery Chief Franz von Rottenburg wrote to the chancellor's private secretary, Count Kuno zu Rantzau—an old school friend with whom he had an intimate, first-name relationship—that Josef Cremer had complained to him the day before that Stoecker was working against the cartel. Cremer was one of the leaders of the Conservative Berlin Movement and editor of the government-oriented *Deutsches Tageblatt* and was presently receiving 3,000 M yearly from the chancellery for "expenses." "I encouraged Cremer," Rottenburg wrote, "very decidedly, to support the Cartel and attack Stoecker at every opportunity." He had expressed the same sentiments also to Minister of the Interior Puttkamer, who was a personal friend of Stoecker and who agreed with him and promised to speak to Stoecker. "Should the latter," Rottenburg continued, "in any way move publicly against the Cartel, I may presumably consider myself to be empowered to pounce upon him, *even in the* Norddeutsche. [Bismarck's marginal comment: "yes." The *Norddeutsche Allgemeine Zeitung* was the chancellor's recognized journalistic mouthpiece.] Perhaps it would be time to subject Stoecker's social and political endeavors to a thorough criticism and to prove that religion can, indeed, provide a motive for engaging oneself with the social question, but that every attempt to solve it by religion is hopeless [Bismarck's marginal comment: "right"], as has been demonstrated by a hundred years of history." Puttkamer, he wrote, would in any case not use his press (that is, those provincial papers dependent on the Literary Bureau of the Prussian Ministry of the Interior) in this sense. Public attention had been called to Stoecker recently by the Waldersee meeting. "If Prince W. associates himself with such people, we approach a serious time of conflict [Bismarck's marginal comment: "yes!"]." National Liberal circles, wrote Rottenburg, were deeply offended. "The necessity of providing the prince with the support of a sensible official—a man e.g. like [Ludwig] Herrfurth [under state secretary in the Prussian Ministry of the Interior]—appears to me to become more and more urgent. Herbert's enlistment now and again works only momentarily; what is needed is a permanent counter-weight to *Potsdamerei* [that is, the military influence]." In a second letter the same day, Rottenburg pointed out that the situation was especially favorable for giving Prince William a civil advisor, since at any time now he might be called upon to represent the kaiser and could reasonably be expected to be kept informed, which would make the step acceptable to both the kaiser and the crown prince. "If you are able to win H[is]. H[ighness, that is Bismarck]. for the idea, you will have deserved well of the *res publica*." A couple of days later, Minister of Agriculture Lucius noted in his diary that

Bismarck condemned very sharply Prince William's association with Stoecker. "Those who wear long skirts (women, priests, judges) are no good in politics. . . . Stoecker must separate himself both from the prince and from politics. Prince William had the most reactionary impulses and wanted, for example, to prevent Jews working in the press. He would get into the most serious conflicts and must be given a reasonable civilian advisor who could inform and influence him properly." In 1880, in a letter to Puttkamer, Bismarck had attacked Stoecker for stirring up class hatred and the greed and envy of the masses, as did the Social Democrats. Wealthy Jews were loyal to the government, and the liberal, reform Jews active in the press were not wealthy.[15]

The negative diagnosis of the crown prince's illness had suddenly reversed the political prospects of the right-wing *Kreuzzeitung* Conservatives and thus enticed them into bringing about a premature political conflict, not only with the broad spectrum of liberals, including the National Liberals, thereby threatening the cartel, but also with the chancellor, who was naturally concerned at this delicate point, when the lives of both kaiser and crown prince were hedged with growing uncertainty, with keeping the governing political configuration strong and steady. Pastor Stoecker might regularly arouse frenzied enthusiasm among the artisans and shopkeepers of Berlin, but the cultivated and respectable middle classes, who were the staunchest supporters of the new German Reich, found his rabble-rousing style embarrassing and dangerous. Nor in rapidly modernizing Germany in 1887 was a return to orthodox Protestant religion a program with potentially wide appeal. Yet the *Kreuzzeitung*-Stoecker challenge was important and threatening. Because of the old kaiser's piety, the court clergy was solidly orthodox, and, because of Bismarck's political swing to the right in 1878, both court and upper bureaucracy were now heavily Conservative, as symbolized by the orthodox Puttkamer in the strategic ministerial post of the Interior. Prince William was already associated with right-wing orthodox elements in the army in the person of General von Waldersee and might easily carry such religious and political convictions with him onto the throne, where he would command the loyalty and obedience of the whole authoritarian government structure and might through some rash act provoke a fundamental and unbridgeable cultural, political, and constitutional conflict. Chancellor von Bismarck could not allow such a possibility. Ironically, the naive, premature political provocation of the Waldersee-Stoecker meeting had thus increased the importance of his continued support of both the moderately oriented cartel and the desperately ill crown prince.

4

The Stoecker Drive Becomes an Affair

ALTHOUGH public criticism of the Waldersee-Stoecker meeting had begun to take a harder line, as yet it had been confined to the Left. No public protests had been heard from the other cartel parties—the Free Conservative and National Liberal press—nor had the government itself taken any public, official stand. This situation was now to be changed by further action of the Stoecker group. On the evening of December 6, two hundred leaders of Conservative clubs in Berlin, including Stoecker, Landtag Deputy Cremer, and Reichstag Deputy Oscar Hahn, met in a closed meeting and adopted the following resolution:

> Appreciating the significance of the Cartel, especially for the circumstances in the capital city, the meeting resolves: that election alliances among the patriotic [*reichstreuen*] parties as far as the Conservative party of Berlin is concerned can be regarded and executed as valid only when they are brought about with the cooperation of the regular general representation of the Conservative party in Berlin and that those who make political agreements contrary to this resolution thereby separate themselves from this movement.

This action was interpreted by the *Kreuzzeitung* as having "the purpose of putting a stop in the future to the attempt made in the last election to mix the Conservative Berlin Movement with other parties."[1]

On December 7, Chancellor Bismarck's son-in-law and private secretary, Count Rantzau, wrote to Herbert Bismarck that he now had to prepare a memorandum [*Immediatbericht*] for the kaiser requesting that Under State Secretary Herrfurth be designated civil advisor to Prince William. The memorandum, dated the ninth and signed by the chancellor, stated that the prince needed protection against clerical and political influences that would alienate wide circles of the population from him; it also asked that Prince William's residence be moved from Potsdam to Berlin. Herbert, in a letter of the sixth, had called General Waldersee "an incurable chatterbox or twaddle-monger [*Quatschkopf*]," but Rantzau replied that these terms

44

were too mild for the general's recent behavior, which revealed "ox-like stupidity." On December 8, Chancellery Chief Franz von Rottenburg wrote that he did not as yet have a full report on the Conservative meeting of the sixth, but it appeared to him that the Conservatives were assuming too much influence for themselves. He planned eventually to move against Stoecker to indicate to him that he had "not as yet sufficiently recognized the significance of the Cartel." On the tenth, Rottenburg wrote that the following day an article against Stoecker would appear [in the *Norddeutsche*]. "The attack is veiled and hypothetical. Cremer assures me that Stoecker has become more reasonable. I don't believe it and want to draw him out with the article." He was half dead, he added, from writing articles and from twenty conferences that day.[2]

Rottenburg's article, which appeared in the *Norddeutsche Allgemeine Zeitung*, the chancellor's recognized mouthpiece, on December 11, in its forcefulness and pithiness of phrase, literary and historical allusions, and Latin quotations strongly suggested the style of the master himself. The subtly modulated liberal tone—imparted by a few phrases—was probably intended to strike sympathetic resonances with the crown prince and princess, who would certainly eventually read it. The *Kreuzzeitung* was mistaken, the article began: the majority of the Conservative leaders in Berlin were supporters of the cartel. But this error was noteworthy as a "pathological symptom. . . . When a political party confesses to the maxim, *Credo quia absurdum est*,* then even discussion stops. . . .[3] That it would be absurd if the Conservatives allowed the middle parties no room in the Berlin Movement needs no thoroughgoing demonstration. If the local Conservatives, instead of going with the middle parties, adopted an extreme orientation and, for example, amalgamated themselves with the Christian Socialists, they would burden themselves with a dead weight." The Conservatives had won substantially only in the last election when they had been allied with the Free Conservatives and National Liberals and had repudiated "all political and religious fanatics." Germany must stay strongly united to resist the hostility and envy of other nations.

> German history is rich in illustrations of the correctness of Tacitus' diagnosis, that the disputes of the Germans among themselves are their enemies' best weapons . . . we need unanimity above all. *In necessariis unitas, in dubiis libertas, in omnibus caritas.*†

* "I believe because it is absurd." Tertullian's remark regarding the Christian faith.

† Freely: "Unity in essentials, liberty where there is doubt, in all things charity." According to Hugh Percy Jones, *Dictionary of Foreign Phrases and Classical Quotations* (Edinburgh, 1925), 58 n, "A saying generally attributed to St. Augustine, but not to be found in his extant writings."

If one of the parties still contains within itself political elements that are incapable of keeping any peace, that are shortsighted enough as to regard as fundamental the special interest of the political or religious faction to which they belong, then we wish that these enemies of the Cartel still possessed enough patriotic feeling to give up any further political activity.... Where, however, the required patriotic feeling is lacking, the Cartel parties are obligated to assist it with ruthless coercion.

The *Kreuzzeitung* was apparently rather taken aback by the vigor of this assault. It protested that it had always condemned only misuse of the cartel. In rebuttal it quoted an issue of the official Conservative party paper, the *Konservative Korrespondenz*, of the previous October complaining that the National Liberals, with an eye on the succession to the throne, were trying to drag the cartel to the left, toward the right wing of the German Liberals, their old secessionist party colleagues. The right answer to the threats of the *Norddeutsche* was the further statement of the *Konservative Korrespondenz* that the cartel should not be used to "serve *one-sided, middle-party aspirations*," nor should the right wing of the Conservative party "be misused in a frivolous fashion as a general whipping boy." Ought not the *Norddeutsche* to consider, added the *Kreuzzeitung*, that its recent attack "under present conditions bears a strongly anachronistic character?" What good, indeed, were procartel threats if Prince William were soon to become kaiser and king?[4]

The *Norddeutsche* article, however, was the signal for an all-out attack by the cartel and government-oriented press on the *Kreuzzeitung*-Stoecker Conservatives. The "best elements" of the Berlin Movement and the "more reasonable" members of the Conservative party, wrote the National Liberal *Kölnische Zeitung* on December 12, could not approve the action inspired by the Christian Socialists and their allies. The *Norddeutsche* article was "quite splendid," and it quoted it extensively. Stoecker and his friends had no attraction beyond the Conservative party, and the actions they were now taking would soon isolate them even within that party. On the fourteenth the *Norddeutsche* returned to the fray, stating flatly that the *Kreuzzeitung* did not represent the Conservative party, but only "a quite special political and religious group." The *Reichsbote* erred in supposing that the Christian Socialists had brought new life to the Conservative party in Berlin. "It was not the Christian Socialists that were the yeast of the Berlin Movement, but anti-Semitism.... Every tendency that is directed against definite social classes or religious creeds must and will be kept out of the Cartel." Two days before this article, on December 12, Stoecker had addressed a suburban political club and defended himself and the Berlin Movement against the *Norddeutsche*. For the latter to be constantly hindering a movement that had produced eighty-six thousand new voters for the monarchy, he said, was not "practical politics."[5]

General Waldersee confessed to his diary on December 15 that in regard to the Stoecker mission, "the fat is in the fire." People were too much under Jewish influence. "They see in the decline of the crown prince the disappearance of their hopes for a golden time, and they are afraid of Prince William, as are all our enemies: French, Russians, Progressives, and Social Democrats." Minister of the Interior Puttkamer had informed him that the chancellor was angry with them and Prince William, which Waldersee tended to blame on Herbert Bismarck. Puttkamer thought that he might have to resign his ministry. After these two had conferred, Waldersee had gone to see Pastor Stoecker and explain the situation, and Stoecker had offered to resign from the City Mission, which Waldersee, apparently with some relief, thought might bring the affair to an end. He added, however, "I also allowed myself to say a thing or two to Prince William about his friend Herbert Bismarck, and he didn't mind at all."[6]

Although Waldersee and Stoecker might be ready for a tactical retreat, Baron von Hammerstein's *Kreuzzeitung* was of a different mind. On December 16 and 17 it declared that the whole Conservative party shared its viewpoint that the cartel must not be equated with a "mixing of the different parties." Apparently, according to the *Norddeutsche*, a Christian could not be a politician. Since they had already called for the exclusion of anti-Semites from the Berlin Movement, in the future the latter would probably have to look to "Herr von Bleichröder [Bismarck's Jewish banker] and a few *Geheimräthe* [bureaucrats] for its standard-bearers." It reprinted an article of the *Konservative Korrespondenz* that declared that attempts "to force the Christian Socialist party out of the Berlin Cartel" would be unjust and inexpedient. The antiprogressive forces in Berlin were not strong enough to afford this luxury. The *Kreuzzeitung* was right in opposing a "mixing" of the parties under the aegis of the cartel.[7]

In the meantime the more radical Berlin anti-Semites had held a meeting, the evening of the fifteenth, at which they had denounced Stoecker for attacking Reichstag Deputy Böckel and racial anti-Semitism. The principal speaker complained that the anti-Semitic leader Liebermann von Sonnenberg was now fawning on Stoecker because of the latter's "suddenly revealed favor in *very high circles*." The Conservatives had used the anti-Semites for their own purposes; there was only one kind of anti-Semitism, and that was to treat Jews as foreigners. The speaker even went so far as to use the term: "*Cohn*servatism." The meeting ended by passing a resolution approving Böckel's actions in the Reichstag and protesting the attacks by Liebermann and Stoecker on "the best of all anti-Semites." Böckel needed this support from his followers since the same day he had been called to order in the Reichstag for attempting to use a debate on the tariff as an excuse for a diatribe on the Jewish menace. The intervention of the president of the Reichstag, a Conservative, came only after repeated shouts of protest from the floor on the part of the German Liberal leader, Eugen Richter, whom the president finally called to order even more severely than he had Böckel. It was not too surprising, under the circumstances, that the *Kreuzzeitung*, two days later, defended Böckel, declaring that he had not strayed from the subject of debate nearly as far as the German Liberals habitually did. It does seem rather surprising, however, that the *Norddeutsche* made much the same comment. Evidently the chancellor's paper was taking the opportunity to refuse to go too far either toward the Left or away from the Right. In an article the following day it defended itself against the *Reichsbote* by pointing out that it was also being attacked from the Left, which was "the most infallible sign that we are really holding the middle line." Böckel had attacked them as the enemy of Jew baiting but had also praised their articles against abuses in grain speculation (involving a number of Jews). There was no contradiction here: "It would be sad if it were actually possible to fight social and economic excrescences only, as is maintained in some quarters, with the simultaneous dissemination of racial and religious hatred." As for the *Konservative Korrespondenz*, the *Norddeutsche* suggested that it was willing to accept the interpretation of the *Kreuzzeitung* regarding the Berlin Movement because the Prussian Conservative party really had little interest in Berlin. "The Conservative politicians and party leaders know too well what it would mean to make the doctrines of the *Kreuzzeitung* into the sole Conservative watchword in the country as a whole [*im Lande*] for it ever to occur to them to try to do it." In other words, the Conservative organization had better remember that orthodoxy was not that popular, and that as a party of the ruling aristocracy it was vulnerable and thus dependent on the good will of the government for protection, prestige, support in the districts, and especially for jobs, that is, positions at court and in the civil and military bureaucracies.[8]

The applause for Böckel from the Conservatives on the floor of the Reichstag and also in the *Kreuzzeitung* further inflamed liberal suspicions. The *Liberale Korrespondenz* declared that Böckel's speech had been a very timely clarification of "the significance of the new Christian-socialist era that is preparing itself in the German Reich." This accusation, replied the *Konservative Korrespondenz*, was unjustified; it was a well-known fact that Böckel was hostile to the Conservatives, and that they, for their part, despised him as a dangerous demagogue and would certainly try to unseat him in the next election. Furthermore, Free Conservative and Center deputies had also applauded him, mostly because of Richter's unreasonable attacks. August Stein, chief Berlin correspondent of the left-liberal

Frankfurter Zeitung, found these denials unconvincing. The Conservative support for Böckel had been too spontaneous to be without meaning. He was also skeptical of the *Norddeutsche* attacks on Stoecker and the Christian Socialists. "Herr Stoecker has been shoved aside and disavowed as often as necessary and just as often brought forth again as a, to be sure not respected, but nevertheless useful ally. The kick that he has now received by high authority is interesting only because of its source and its timing." The meeting at Waldersee's was the focal point of all the excitement. "The official articles against the Christian Socialists and Herr Stoecker obviously are meant to guard against the attempt to deduce a political future under the aegis of Stoecker from the participation of Prince William at that meeting."[9]

At this juncture the *Norddeutsche* was joined in its anti-Stoecker campaign by the left-leaning National Liberal Berlin paper, the *National Zeitung*. Ever since the election of the preceding year and the formation of the cartel, the *National Zeitung* had been acting as if it considered itself, perhaps not without some justification, to be the chief spokesman for the expected new liberal era under the crown prince.[10] It had also remained in close touch with Dr. Mackenzie, which was a fact of some political significance at this time. Now it declared that the statements of the *Norddeutsche* had been received with great satisfaction by wide circles of the population in Berlin and elsewhere. The anti-Semitism of the Conservatives in Berlin was pushing respectable people into the Progressive party, which was able to use hostility to anti-Semitism as a primary agitational tool. Without anti-Semitism, the cartel parties would do much better. To this the *Kreuzzeitung* responded with scorn and sarcasm. The National Liberal leader Johannes Miquel had been forced by the cartel in February 1887 onto a Berlin district previously represented by the anti-Semite Cremer and had received 300 *fewer* votes. Other figures showed that National Liberal "philo-Semitic" candidates had always run substantially behind the anti-Semitic Conservatives.[11]

On December 22 the *Norddeutsche* came to the assistance of the *National Zeitung* and responded to the *Kreuzzeitung*. One should bear in mind, it wrote, in discussing party movements in Berlin, that Berlin was a metropolis, and that such large cities were very susceptible to democratic tendencies. If Berlin had not developed into as democratically inclined a city as Paris and others, that was because the inhabitants were aware that "Berlin is what it is because the kings of Prussia have made it into what it has become." For this reason, and since the Christian Socialists and anti-Semites were really not political parties, those who were hostile to those movements were driven into the democratic parties. The *Kreuzzeitung* had appealed to election statistics but cited only three cases. Why not

compare the whole election results of 1884 with those of the cartel election
of 1887? In 1884 the Berlin Movement had received 56,028 votes or 28.5
percent of the total, whereas in 1887 the cartel had received 71,756 votes
or 30.8 percent of the total.[12]

What the *Norddeutsche* had omitted to mention in this article was that
the Reichstag election of 1887 was a very special case, held under the
threat of war and with an unprecedented rise in general voter participation. The *Kreuzzeitung*, of course, lost no time in pointing this out, deploring in the process the habit of the *Norddeutsche* of sacrificing the truth to
its political purposes, in this case "to bring the Conservative party into
general confusion—to the benefit of the National Liberals." The failings
of the *Norddeutsche*, it wrote, clearly could not be considered merely intellectual, but were obviously ethical. "Its readers are not *meant* to discover the
truth." Truly the ideological stance of the *Kreuzzeitung* could not basically
reconcile itself with the more purely power-political orientation of the
Norddeutsche, representing the Bismarck regime. But no state can function
without some general power consensus, and a purely ideological stance
fosters partisanship, not agreement. In the previous spring the *Kreuzzeitung* had written: "The political party as such rests on opposition and
can exist only in opposition; in an opposition naturally that does not
exclude *ad hoc* cooperation, but that never may disavow its self-esteem
[*Selbstbewusstsein*] if it is not to end in self-destruction." The preoccupation
of the *Kreuzzeitung* with ideological purity actually assumed the existence
of a strong independent monarchy and administration to provide the
leadership, make the necessary compromises, and accept the responsibility. But by reforming themselves as a national party in 1875, the Prussian Conservatives had seemed to accept an active, responsible role in a
constitutional state, and the *Kreuzzeitung* support for Stoecker and anti-
Semitism implied a bid for a mass following, as the Waldersee meeting
itself also suggested a push toward greater power and influence in the
state. Did they really want power and the responsibility that went with
it (which, as the Prussian ruling class, they already had in considerable
degree) or not? Were the Junkers as a class prepared to rule a rapidly
modernizing empire of Great Power proportions? This appeared to be
doubtful.[13]

At this point a new impulse was given to the Stoecker affair, beginning
with an article in the Viennese liberal *Neue Freie Presse* on December 21,
and bringing the whole incident to a public climax in subsequent articles
in the Berlin Free Conservative and government-oriented *Post*. The *Neue
Freie Presse* article sounded as if it could easily have been inspired in
official quarters in Berlin. "Men who were odious to the father in his
innermost soul now press themselves on the son, misuse his name, pro-

claim that their time has now come and that they have won the powerful arm of the future monarch for their plans." These same people had agitated for a drastic operation on the crown prince and had denied any possibility or error in the cancer diagnosis. "This dangerous illness seemed to promise a new configuration of domestic politics in Germany, and immediately those rushed in who have always exploited the state, the Junkers, for whom the bourgeoisie has always been a thorn in the side, the bigots [*Mucker*], who make Christianity into a cloak for their immeasurable ambition."[14] An article similar to that in the *Neue Freie Presse* had also appeared in the *Berliner Tageblatt*, a liberal and Jewish-owned paper that was close to Dr. Mackenzie. This article stated that there were apparently certain groups "who felt and indeed showed a certain discomfort at every piece of good news regarding the health of the crown prince." Echoes of these feelings had cropped up in the *National Zeitung* (doubtful), the *Kreuzzeitung*, and the *Reichsbote*. These same circles had also planted rumors in the press in November that the crown prince was going to abdicate.

The point of view expressed in these articles was something of a cross between the Bismarck-cartel, nationalist-middle-party concept, as exemplified in the controversy between the *Norddeutsche* and *Kreuzzeitung* regarding the orientation of the Conservative party in Berlin, and the anti-Junker and pro-Mackenzie views of the crown princess—a matter of some interest. The orchestration of this whole journalistic campaign was too careful, too effective to be accidental, and one wonders whether some consultation and even collaboration were involved, say, between Radolinski (representing the crown prince and princess), who was presently in Berlin, and Rottenburg.[15] Also, Dr. Mackenzie had very quickly reverted to his original tendency after his momentary concession of a cancer diagnosis in early November. A constant stream of reports in late November and December in both the German and English press suggested that there were serious doubts that the disease was cancer after all. The symptoms were not typical; even the optimistic mood of the patient practically ensured that it could not be cancer. Undoubtedly acute inflammation of the cartilaginous tissue (perichondritis) was the correct diagnosis, a disease that was also very severe and difficult, but that could be cured. Articles in the *Freisinnige Zeitung*, apparently inspired by Dr. Rudolf Virchow, the famous pathologist (who was also a German Liberal Reichstag deputy), emphasized that there really was no concrete evidence as yet to substantiate the cancer diagnosis.[16]

In the meantime the crown prince was appearing publicly for drives and excursions, and the crown princess even tried to get rid of Dr. Fritz von Bramann, Dr. Bergmann's assistant, who was standing by to do a tracheotomy should it suddenly become necessary. But Bergmann instructed Bramann to stick to his post like a soldier, and, for his own part, Bramann wrote to Bergmann that he could already feel through the skin the spread of the infection from the larynx into the surrounding tissue. In early December the *National Zeitung* published optimistic excerpts from a letter of the crown princess. The left-leaning National Liberal *Magdeburger Zeitung*, citing evidence against cancer, was quite explicit: "To the great good fortune of the Fatherland," it wrote, "there is no indication that the crown prince . . . should be hindered from personally playing a prominent role."[17]

Even when in mid-December a new growth appeared and Dr. Mackenzie hurried over from England, reports were simultaneously released that the site of the older growth was developing scar tissue, which was not at all like cancer, and that the previous swelling of the glands had completely disappeared. To downplay the incident, Dr. Mackenzie soon departed for Algiers to visit another patient, on his way through Marseille declaring to a reporter from *Le Figaro* that the cancer diagnosis had "not in the slightest degree" been confirmed by his recent examination. The condition of the patient was "relatively better" than when he had last seen him, and "hope of complete recovery is permitted." On December 23, two days after the article of the *Neue Freie Presse* quoted above, the *Frankfurter Zeitung* carried a report from Berlin that stated that the present heated conflict in the press over the health of the crown prince could be understood only if one recognized its strongly political background. The following day the National Liberal and governmental *Kölnische Zeitung*, which had previously been taking a very hard line on the crown prince's illness, wrote that the only truly joyful news at this Christmas time was that the crown prince had become at present "the complete master of his disease." On December 29 the crown prince himself wrote to Prince William that if his health continued to improve as it had so far, "I may hope that I shall again be able to work." At the end of the month the grand duke of Baden informed his Landtag that the crown prince (his wife's brother), in expressing thanks for the Landtag's good wishes, had stated that he had the feeling—which was certainly true—that his illness had forged a new bond of attachment between him and his people.[18]

Also on December 23 the Free Conservative and governmental *Post* had published an article under the heading "Political Undercurrents" that began: "The fact that high-church sentiment [*die hochkirchliche Richtung*] declines with the rise of national consciousness suggests the danger that results conversely from a rise in the former orientation." The cultured classes might be thoroughly imbued with nationalistic spirit, but that was not yet true of the great masses of the country. The danger that they might be susceptible to radical and selfish appeals was increased by the necessity for great sacrifices to augment the economic and military strength of the nation. Without special disturbances, however, there was no doubt that feelings of national loyalty would also gradually and increasingly penetrate the bulk of the population. "One of the most drastic disturbances that such a process . . . could suffer would be a reappearance of a strong clerical-Conservative movement in alliance with Stoeckerism [*Stoeckerei*] and Christian-Socialist tendencies. . . . For there is no doubt . . . that precisely among the more highly educated circles of the nation there exists a decided aversion to *Muckerei und Stoeckerei* [bigotry and Stoeckerism— note the use of a similar term in the *Neue Freie Presse* article above, p. 51]." It was the duty of the government to contain this movement. "The assiduity with which *Stoeckerei* seeks to attach itself to the soles of Prince William can have only harmful consequences for him and for his future duties. . . . From whatever side, therefore, one may regard the most recent attempt at exploiting events in the clerical-Conservative, especially Christian-Socialist, party interest, it appears to be pernicious. The sooner and the more thoroughly it is done away with the better."[19]

Where the Free Conservatives were apparently taking the lead, one could expect that the National Liberals would not be far behind. Thus the *Hamburger Korrespondenz*, which was close to the National Liberal leader, Rudolf von Bennigsen, commented that the fact that the *Norddeutsche* had taken so relatively unimportant an incident as the reorganization of the Berlin Conservative party to launch so energetic a campaign clearly showed that they recognized that the Conservative attempt in Berlin was a "symptom of a systematic, deeper movement." The source of this movement lay in "the hopes that the high-church party suppose they can place upon the younger generation of the royal family." In the history of the Hohenzollern dynasty "a high-church orientation [*Hochkirchenthum*] and decline always came together." To cap these statements, on the twenty-fourth Cremer's *Deutsches Tageblatt* stated "from a very good source" that Prince William had never meant to support any political party or to take an antiliberal position and had stated flatly: "I am no anti-Semite."[20]

If any lid remained on the Stoecker affair, the *Post* article certainly blew it off. The phrase *Muckerei und Stoeckerei* was picked up and spread everywhere by the government-oriented press. Even the skeptical and experienced August Stein was impressed. It was noteworthy, he wrote in the *Frankfurter*, that the *Post* had kept quiet for a month and had found the courage to speak out only after the *Norddeutsche* had given the signal. If any government tried to support itself on Stoecker's movement, it would create such an opposition that it would have to yield. It was because of fear of this opposition that the official press had "pressed Herr Stoecker to the wall and are attempting to cleanse certain high-standing persons of their contact with him." The *Post*, continued Stein, was quite right in emphasizing a growing feeling of mistrust. "Therewith is also associated a deep indignation toward anyone who brings upon himself the suspicion that he is irreverently speculating upon a future lying behind the heir to the throne, ill in a foreign land. Herr Stoecker was too rash, he grasped for fruit that were not yet ripe and will feel the evil consequences. His healthy nature, however, guarantees that he will later recover from it."[21]

Whereas the sympathy of the left Liberals could be expected, much more significant was the reaction of the powerful Catholic Center party. Up to this point *Germania* had been reporting on the affair with keen interest, but had taken no position of its own. Now that government papers had mounted an all-out attack, *Germania* rallied, not to the party of religious (although Protestant) orthodoxy—of "positive Christianity"—but rather to the liberal crown prince and the Bismarck regime. The *Post* was correct, it commented, in stressing the deep divisions among Protestants. The orthodox group was a minority and was "persecuted by the majority with a fanatical hatred." That, in allying themselves with Stoecker, the "believing Protestants" should not have considered the liberal antipathy toward him was a great mistake. "The reaction now setting in against Stoecker could easily take on dimensions that could greatly endanger the re-Christianization of society." In other words, the clumsiness and narrowness of view of Baron von Hammerstein, Minister von Puttkamer, and General von Waldersee were endangering the Christian cause in general, Catholic as well as Protestant. One might also add more pragmatically—and the Center party was always pragmatic—that while the crown prince was still alive and Bismarck was still supporting the cartel, it was politically unwise and premature to try to turn the government in a more conservative and religiously orthodox direction.[22]

Baron von Hammerstein had no intention of accepting any criticism of his attitude or that of his right-wing Junker friends toward the monarchy. The National Liberals, now so critical, wrote the *Kreuzzeitung*, "during the summer months in spite of repeated urgent appeals to try to apply a little tact, continually exhorted the Cartel parties in regard to their position toward government bills to consider the presumably imminent change of rulers." The shameless tone of the *Post* and *Hamburger Korrespondenz* would suffice with "all true royalists" to "turn shame . . . into loathing and contempt. . . . The reptiles are leaving their holes, and naturally the *Post* now also appears on the scene, after being silent for a whole month, to spray out its poison in short-sighted trust in the deliberately disseminated report that 'Prince Bismarck has taken occasion to appeal to the influence of an authoritative agency.' Does the *Post* really believe that the standard bearer of the Hohenzollern monarchy, tested through several decades of unswerving loyalty, will lend himself to be the mouthpiece of its shameful attacks against his future king and master?" A sarcastic challenge, this last, to Chancellor Bismarck, as to whether he really wanted to browbeat the monarchy in the person of Prince William—always bearing in mind the tenuous state of health of the crown prince.[23]

The answer was an even more authoritative and official-sounding article on December 27 in the *Post*. The reports regarding Prince William's disassociating himself from the Stoecker party, it stated, were quite believable. The *Post* had exercised restraint at first, exactly for this reason, but when it became clear that the clerical-Conservative party was using Prince William in the same way that the German Liberal party had tried to use his father, it had had to speak out. The prince's association with a particular party would not be in the interests of the monarchy. "Thanks to the royalist sentiment of our people, it is undoubtedly a powerful lever for the endeavors of a political party if it can attach itself to the name of an heir to the throne of Prussia and the Reich." It was especially reprehensible, continued the *Post*, "on the part of a group that likes to talk constantly about royal and monarchical sentiments. . . . Such behavior goes far beyond the saying: 'And let the king be absolute if but our will he execute [*Und der König absolut, wenn er unseren Willen tut*].' It is a piece of the worst hypocrisy to emphasize the necessity of defending the monarchy against anarchism and to justify oneself as a special kind of champion in this struggle and at the same time actually to undermine authority and trust by misusing the royal family as a cover for one's own partisan power drive."[24]

At this point the *Kreuzzeitung* became rather hysterical. The statements of the *Post* were lies and libel, it screamed, and it invoked the *Konservative Korrespondenz* in its support. The latter had declared that the *Post* could not very well write seriously about national unity when it had consistently been attacking the Conservative cause and the "Conservative Era" under Puttkamer, as well as the increase in the grain tariff. The Stoecker-Waldersee meeting had been purely charitable and religious, and this was proved by the fact that the conservative press had not mentioned it until after it was reported in the *Börsen Zeitung* (an ingenuous admission, since such an attempt at secrecy must appear rather to corroborate the conspiratorial aspect). The attacks of the *Post* and *Hamburger Korrespondenz* came only after the articles in the *Norddeutsche*, which had then given the former prominent display and even approving comment in its "Journal-Revue." All this had started the liberal press going again. That these attacks on publicly expressed religious sympathies of the kaiser and Prince William should occur in monarchical Prussia was "an unprecedented scandal." The "kind of 'royalism' that tries to place conditions on its loyalty to the prince is, thank God, not traditional in Prussia." The *Post* had declared that the Christian-Socialist influence should be "done away with": "Who might this authority be who 'does away' with any kind of voluntary act that a royal prince performs publicly with the sanction of his and our king and sovereign?" The manner of procedure of the so-called official press had been damaging the dignity of the state for a long time. It was painful to criticize sources close to the government, but it was to be hoped that those possessing influence over these press circles would remind them that "we in Prussia live under the government of His Majesty the King, and that the first thing we expect from a press working in the service of this government is a proper and respectful attitude toward the members of the royal family."[25]

Germania replied that the *Kreuzzeitung* seemed to be living in a dream world. It might be true that it had itself always handled the Waldersee meeting as a strictly religious affair, but that had hardly been true of the *Reichsbote*, which had definitely put a political stamp on the meeting. Some Conservative publications had picked this up, and others, especially the Stoecker publications, had dealt with the illness of the crown prince in a pessimistic way that had featured Prince William. It was also true that only the left-liberal press had initially launched an attack on the meeting, but there had been a good deal of private discussion and disapproval among moderates, especially in the Reichstag and the Prussian Landtag. This statement of *Germania* was true enough, but it did not touch the real substance of the matter: whether Prince William or Bismarck should dictate what the prince's political stance should be. In this connection the *Kreuzzeitung* hit the nail on the head when it responded to the *Deutsches Tageblatt* and the *Post* that Prince William had never made the remark about not being anti-Semitic that was attributed to him, but that the entire attack on Stoecker had been a probe, a test of strength against the "free expression of a future king of Prussia dedicated to positive Christian activity among his people."[26]

The whole affair inspired the liberal *Frankfurter Zeitung* to attempt a higher level of critical objectivity. In a Christmas editorial it bemoaned the fact that for years the Christmas holidays had been spoiled by war scares, and that this year was the worst ever. Then, in addition, had come the Stoecker affair and the party squabbling over the health of the crown prince. "Recently we have often asked ourselves, does the German people really envisage its future under no other auspices than the views of the person who will one day be called to wear the crown? Has it lost all confidence in its own power to create its own fate, has it lost the most elementary concepts of constitutional government? Does it see its ideal in personal rule, its satisfaction in getting a hearing and currying favor with the ruler? If the rise of the nation is to end in this transformation, then it will not be a blessing, but a curse." This interesting warning would be even more impressive if the *Frankfurter* had not itself been so keenly interested in the health of the crown prince. The chief cause of this evil development the *Frankfurter* saw to be the growth of selfish egoism at the expense of a sense of responsibility to the community as a whole. "Out of such meanness of spirit grow the conflicts of interest, which in serving the rawest materialism dissolve the national community into classes and cliques, and distort the party system, so indispensable and beneficial for political development, into a caricature. In such swampy ground there is no place for the most certain foundation of a state: for compensating justice; caesarism, however, grows there like a vine, it absorbs all the strength and leaves a fatal miasma behind." For the commercially minded (and Jewish-owned) *Frankfurter Zeitung* to write like this was most extraordinary. The same sentiments could be found in almost any issue of the clerical, agrarian, Junker-dominated *Kreuzzeitung*, which, of course, always went on to blame the "raw materialism" on capitalism, industry, and the growth of the "Jewish" money interest. Left and Right might be far apart in German society but they were, nevertheless, as one in their idealistic devotion.[27]

5

Prince William and the Chancellor

WHILE the newspaper war was reaching its height, General von Waldersee and Minister of the Interior Puttkamer were becoming quite apprehensive. Waldersee was shocked that the *Norddeutsche* had "given the signal for more or less insolent attacks, which are partly directed openly against Prince William. The official paper in combat against the heir to the throne!" Puttkamer had given an article concerning the Berlin City Mission to the *Norddeutsche*, and it had been refused! They had advised Prince William to write directly to Bismarck, explaining his views and asking for the chancellor's good will. "I cannot believe," noted Waldersee, "that the chancellor and his son want to break with the prince, but even less that the latter is inclined to give in. In any case, it is an interesting moment." It was indeed, especially since Waldersee was at that time closest to Prince William and, for better or worse, obviously was exerting the most influence on him.[1]

Prince William wrote to Bismarck on December 21. His interest in work among the poor, he wrote, had been distorted by Social Democratic papers, and he had been daily expecting a direct inquiry from the chancellor, considering the intimate relationship between them, which explained his silence until now. He reviewed his plans for the riding competition and the change, because of the crown prince's health, to a direct appeal for the City Mission, and the decision to hold a meeting, which should be as representative as possible of different areas and political groupings. In his remarks to the assembly he had specifically stressed the necessity of keeping the affair nonpolitical. Nevertheless, he was convinced "that a union of these elements for the purpose mentioned is a goal to be striven for and the most effective means of sustained struggle against Social Democracy and anarchism." Efforts were to be made in large cities other than Berlin, so that it was by no means merely a Stoecker affair, and Stoecker would not be given the overall direction. The Berlin Mission was supported by the General Synod of the Prussian church and "the most distinguished

58

and respected people from all the provinces," and it promised the greatest effectiveness in the "moral elevation of the masses." He had been disturbed that this pious work had been undermined by "a clever and well-calculated emphasis on the personality of Stoecker." The effort had been well received until the Social Democratic and German Liberal press had made disgraceful attacks on it. "The great and warm respect and sincere devotion that I feel for Your Serene Highness—I should let myself be hacked limb from limb before I undertook anything that would make difficulties or unpleasantness for you—should, I believe, guarantee that I did not engage myself in this work from any political considerations. In the same manner the great trust and the warm friendship that Your Serene Highness has always extended to me . . . allow me to hope that, after these explanations, Your Serene Highness will extend to me your favor." The most immediate response to the prince's letter was the *Muckerei und Stoeckerei* article in the *Post* two days later. After the second *Post* article of the twenty-eighth, the affair seemed to slacken. Stoecker had in the meantime been removed as head of the City Mission appeal committee, and Herbert Bismarck assured Prince William that neither he nor his father had had anything to do with the *Norddeutsche* article. Waldersee commented on this latter step that obviously Herbert had recognized that he had made a mistake. "He knew very well that it would be all up with the friendship of the prince if the latter caught him in hostile acts." Nevertheless, when Herbert went out to Friedrichsruh on New Year's Eve, he found Prince William waiting for him at the railroad station. The prince assured him that the Stoecker affair was now quite harmless, that attacks had been made in his hearing on Herbert and that he had defended him.[2]

To be a young prince of Prussia at the end of the nineteenth century was undoubtedly to be in a difficult position, caught between the traditions of Frederick the Great and the glorious achievements of old Kaiser William and Bismarck, on the one hand, and the accelerating process of the modernization of society and life, on the other. The future William II would always dramatize, even caricature, in his own personality the contradictions, uncertainties, strengths, and weaknesses of his own "fin-de-siècle" generation, its loss of the simple certainties of previous generations, its curiosity and taste for new experiences, its compulsive activity, its rather callow posturing, and its yearning after new certainties, as yet unfound or untried. The prince also naturally combined in his own nature the characteristics of his parents: the vanity and essential weakness of his father plus the quick intelligence of his mother, as well as the incredible stubbornness and self-will of both his English mother and grandmother. And then there was his birth injury, his useless and wizened left arm, and the distaste that this apparently aroused in his mother, that her first-born child could be less than perfect, which perhaps partly accounted for his rigorous upbringing at the hands of an unimaginative and overdiscipli- nary tutor. He was not his mother's favorite child. It is likely that the strong military tradition of the Hohenzollerns, personified in his grand- father, along with an orthodox religious faith, became for him, the even- tual heir to the throne, both a personal haven and a transfiguring and sustaining, transcendental mission. As early as 1884 the prince had sent his picture to Chancellor Bismarck on the latter's sixty-ninth birthday and had written on it, "Cave: adsum! [Watch out: I am coming!]" This was no doubt meant to be a witticism, but it was not a very graceful one. Years later the old chancellor would show it to Maximilian Harden and quote Mephistopheles' remark to the brash Baccalaureus in Goethe's *Faust*: " 'You do not seem to know how crude you are!'* This youth believes itself to be more terrible than it is." The previous spring, after the over- whelming victory of the cartel election, the crown princess had written to Queen Victoria, "He [Prince William] is probably a playing card in the hands of the chancellor's party . . . but a very dangerous one, because he is young, greenly fanatic, and foolishly believes every single thing that the flatterers and intriguers that he associates with say to him. . . . He does not mean badly and imagines that he is indispensable to Bismarck and the Kaiser. . . . He is not aware of the damage he is doing nor of the way he is being used."[3]

In his outwardly self-assured and possibly compulsive naiveté, Prince William had overlooked the reality of the weakening of the personal au- thority of the Prussian monarchy as it became engulfed in the larger German Empire and had seen only the glory, the magnificent external trappings, the king-emperor as a growing national cult. Thus he took Bismarck's use of the monarchy against the opposition parties in the Reichstag at face value. In a book on Bismarck that quoted one of his speeches twenty-five years previously—"The Prussian monarchy has not fulfilled its mission, it is not yet ripe for forming a purely ornamental decoration on your constitutional structure"—Prince William had written in the margin, "And as far as this youngest one can help it, it will never come to that." Yet the prince was by no means alone in harboring old- fashioned monarchical illusions. The mysterious and magical presence and overwhelming reputation of Bismarck made fundamental and inevit- able changes seem merely a temporary part of his personal phenomenon. It was the function of the great mid-Victorian heroes—Gladstone, Dis- raeli, Lincoln—to carry basic change by means of charismatic personal

* Pt. 2, act 2, sc. 1. Among other statements, Baccalaureus declares that men over thirty are already dead and should be put out of the way and that "the world was not till I created it." Translation by Walter Kaufmann, 37.

dramatization. Thus the extent to which the larger demands of the Foreign Office, Bundesrat, and Reichstag, the growth of an educated public opinion, and a more complicated party life had diminished the power of the Prussian crown tended to be obscured by the continuing Bismarckian political pageant. It is not surprising that Prussian Junker military men around the prince, such as Quartermaster General Waldersee, should tell him that when he came to the throne he should take back some of the power that Bismarck had seized from the king in the 1860s and restore the crown to its old position; but it is rather disconcerting to find an old *Liberal* statesman like the former Baden Prime Minister Franz von Roggenbach advising Prince William the same way: that as ruler he must guard his independence against everyone, especially the chancellor. This meant, of course, that Roggenbach was assuring himself continued access to, and thus presumably influence on, the future emperor, but this petty shortsightedness and instinctive deference for monarchy on the part of a "left Liberal" explains why the English representative at the Saxon court could say that the German Liberal party was "only on the political level of our Tories."[4]

That the Bismarcks should have used Prince William for their own purposes was natural enough. Especially in the 1880s, when the crown prince's Liberal friends had moved over to the political opposition and the kaiser had become too old for ceremonial functions, it was easy to make use of the young prince: for example, to send him to Russia in 1884 and 1886 to strengthen ties with the reactionary Tsar Alexander III. The prince had come away from those trips altogether too pro-Russian for General Waldersee, who set about counteracting that influence. Rather than seeing the precariousness of the Russian domestic situation, the isolation of the tsar, and the harsh contradictions inherent in the painfully modernizing society, the prince had been impressed mostly by the tsar's still awesome personal position, by the romance, extravagance, and pomp of the old autocracy. The Bismarcks also set the prince to work in the Foreign Office, over the crown prince's protests, where he would be close to Herbert Bismarck, who had been foreign secretary since 1886. Herbert could have been a good and useful influence on Prince William, but a hard-driving, hard-working, and equally hard-drinking fin-de-siècle character himself, he apparently overdid it and by being too friendly lost the prince's respect.[5]

The crown prince's illness, suddenly pushing Prince William nearer to the throne, naturally created a very difficult and delicate situation, and the greatest caution and tact were clearly called for. Unfortunately these were qualities he mostly lacked. Less than three weeks after the definitive diagnosis of his father's cancer, on November 29, Prince William sent

Chancellor Bismarck a personal letter enclosing a copy of a proclamation to the princes of the other states of the German Empire, which was to be deposited in all the various ministries and handed over immediately upon his own accession. This would be, he thought, the first succession to the imperial title; almost all of the princes were of his father's generation, and "humanly speaking, one could not blame them if they find it rather trying to come under such a young new sovereign. Therefore the succession by the grace of God must be emphasized to them as an independent fait accompli." He had often discussed the relationship of kaiser to other German princes with his father, who always insisted that it would be his to command and for the princes to obey. But he contended that the princes must not be treated as vassals but more like colleagues. "It will be easy for me, as a nephew with his uncles, to win over these gentlemen with little favors and to tame them with courtesy calls. If I have first reassured them by my actions and manner and got them eating out of my hand, then they will obey me more willingly. For they must obey! But better that it be done out of conviction and trust than by compulsion!"[6]

The chancellor ignored Prince William's proclamation for over a month while the Stoecker affair developed in the press. To Bismarck's request regarding a civil advisor for the prince, old Kaiser William had reacted with misgivings. It might not suffice to protect Prince William from the danger of associating himself with one-sided party activities, he wrote to Kaiserin Augusta, and such a move might also offend the crown prince. The kaiserin agreed, but suggested that if the prince moved to Berlin he could have easier unofficial contact with a possible advisor. On New Year's Eve the crown prince's chamberlain, Count Radolinski, wrote the crown prince that he had spent almost the entire previous day talking confidentially with Bismarck in Friedrichsruh. The chancellor had expressed regret that the influence of the Potsdam garrison had given Prince William false ideas in every conceivable area, which would be dangerous for the future. It was, therefore, of fundamental importance to provide a counterinfluence. Visiting the ministries would not suffice, as it had not in the Foreign Office. The ministers could not devote enough time to him. He would "take a sip here and there in all the branches, learn nothing *thoroughly,* and end by believing falsely that he knew *everything.*" The only way to give him a basic knowledge of the administrative and financial organism was to give him a civil advisor, who would be "older, solid, politically objective, [and] of no definite political coloration," and who could discuss individual subjects with him. But the chancellor doubted that this could be done unless the crown prince himself suggested it to the kaiser. He, Bismarck said disingenuously, would not dare to make such a suggestion to the kaiser himself, but would support it vigorously. Radolinski added that he thought the suggestion a good one and that Minister of Justice Friedberg, the crown prince's old advisor, agreed.

Radolinski proposed Ludwig Herrfurth, under state secretary in the Prussian Ministry of the Interior, for the position. Herrfurth was objective and not on good terms with Puttkamer, his superior, with whose opinions he disagreed. The chancellor had told Radolinski that Puttkamer would be enraged if Herrfurth were to be appointed to such a position. Bismarck had gone on to speak very strongly against Puttkamer, calling him the "soul" of the Stoecker City Mission affair. He deplored the latter and planned to express his opinion on it quite openly to Prince William, who had written him a few weeks before. He also criticized General Waldersee, whose political capacity he rated "less than average." Although the chancellor's opinions were obviously tailored for the crown prince, they were probably also at least partly sincere. An army officer who spent New Year's Day in Friedrichsruh told the Württemberg minister to Berlin, Count Ferdinand von Zeppelin, that Prince Bismarck had been unusually serious. When his wife had urged him to cheer up, since he was surrounded by cheerful faces, he had replied, "Behind them I see faces that are not at all cheerful."[7]

Bismarck replied to Prince William's two letters in an eight-page, handwritten letter on January 6. Really, he wrote, a "historical-political work" was required, but according to the motto that the best is the enemy of the good he would do as well as he could for now. He hoped to be in Berlin soon and would then amplify his writing orally. He was returning the copy of the proposed proclamation with the most respectful and humble advice "to burn it without delay." It would be extremely difficult to prevent premature disclosure of such a document even with only one copy, but if some twenty copies were made and deposited in seven different legations, such a leak would be certain. And such premature disclosure would distress both the kaiser and the crown prince and others, too. Also, even if it was successfully kept secret, the inevitable realization after its release that it had been prepared before the event would make a bad impression. He was happy to see that the prince recognized the importance of *voluntary* cooperation of the federal princes. It was only seventeen years ago that the rallying of the princes to the Reich prevented the victory of parliamentary government, and their assistance would be even more important in the future to protect monarchical institutions. They were "not subjects, but allies of the Kaiser, and if the federal treaty is not observed in their interest, they will also not feel obligated to it and, as they used to do, will seek ties with Russia, Austria, and France as soon as the opportunity offers. . . . The opposition in the parliament would also take on a very different strength if the previous unanimity of the Bundesrat

ceased and Bavaria and Saxony made common cause with Richter and
Windthorst." In regard to the City Mission, the chancellor wrote,
"Against Social and other democrats the national idea, perhaps not in the
countryside but in the cities, is stronger than the Christian. . . . Priests can
do a great deal of damage and help little; the most clerically pious countries are the most revolutionary."

It would not be wise for the prince's name to be so closely attached to
the affairs of the City Mission, especially if expanded as planned, that he
might be affected by its lack of success. He was not trying to sow mistrust,
but experience had shown that a king could not get along without some
mistrust. He wondered how many of the gentlemen would be as interested
in the mission without the sponsorship of the prince, and whether they
might not be more interested in the favor of their future monarch. "*After*
the succession Your Highness will have to use the men and the parties
with caution and with changing relationships according to Your Highness's own judgment, without being able outwardly to devote yourself to
any one of our factions. There are times for liberalism and times for
reaction, also for despotism. . . . I have nothing against Stoecker; for me
he has only one fault as a politician, that he is a priest, and as priest, that
he is engaged in politics." He admired Stoecker's energy and eloquence,
but Stoecker could not build lasting accomplishments. "He stands at the
head of elements . . . upon which a government of the German Reich could
not support itself." He had not written directly to the prince previously
concerning the Stoecker affair because he had not taken it seriously until
he had received the prince's letter. His sense of duty compelled him to
advise the prince "not to lay upon yourself, before you ascend the throne,
the fetters of a connection with any kind of political or religious association." All private associations were "very effective instruments for *attacking*
and *destroying* the existing order, but not for building and maintaining. . . . With us *only* the king at the head of the executive power is able
by means of *legislation* to create and preserve viable reforms. . . . 'Religious
and moral training of the young' is in itself a worthy purpose, but I fear
that behind this front other political and hierarchical goals are being
pursued."[8]

Whether Bismarck's careful amalgam of flattery for the monarchy and
for Prince William personally with admonitions concerning the importance for a king of hard and patient work through established political
institutions impressed the prince is dubious. It certainly impressed Herbert Bismarck, who wrote to Kuno zu Rantzau praising the "powerful
and lofty language of this splendid state paper." The prince would not
fully appreciate it for ten years, he wrote, after he had experienced many
disappointments. "What intellectual effort and wisdom there is in it! 'It

ought to be Prince William's constant bedside reading,' as the English say—his Sibylline Book for all time to come." Certainly the points contained in the chancellor's letter differed hardly at all from the sensational articles in the official and semiofficial press. The chancellor's claim of previous indifference may be interpreted as a suggestion that if the prince had not insisted on maintaining publicly his association with the Stoeckerites it would not have had to be officially noticed. One of the side effects of the letter was its effect on Minister von Puttkamer, who took it to mean a complete repudiation of himself by the chancellor. Under Puttkamer's regime the Prussian Ministry of the Interior had supported both a Conservative and religious point of view, in the districts at election time and in administrative policy. The idea that the king should be above the parties was much closer to the favorite concepts of the Liberals, the crown prince, and the opposition in general.[9]

In spite of the press campaign and the fact that the old kaiser himself had expressed his displeasure over the Stoecker affair to Waldersee, Prince William was apparently still trying to hold his ground. Thus Princess William made an official visit to Stoecker on his birthday. "It appears," wrote Roggenbach to General von Stosch, "that the crown prince was right when he said: Prince William doesn't take advice, he has to break his head." General von Waldersee, however, was betting on the prince. "If the chancellor doesn't give in a little, then I believe a lasting rift is probable between him and Prince William and am inclined to think that Prince Bismarck is bringing this rift about *quite willingly; he has come to a dead end with his politics and would like to find an opportunity to extricate himself under a good pretext*. . . . [sic] So far he has probably hoped to overpower the prince and tie him to his son; I believe, however, that he is making a gross miscalculation." At the end of December, Prince William had remarked to Finance Minister Adolf von Scholz that Prince Bismarck would of course be needed very badly for a few years, but that later his functions would be divided and that the monarch himself must take over more of them, to which Scholz had replied that the chancellor would be needed for a long time yet and that he could never be completely replaced. To his former tutor, Hinzpeter, the prince had been even more emphatic. "For the sake of the chancellor I have, so to speak, for years locked myself out of my parents' house. So I did not deserve such treatment from the chancellor, of all people." And again, "The chancellor cannot go on enjoying the power he wields at present; he simply must realize there's still a Kaiser." And, banging his fist on the table, "He'd better remember that I shall be his master."

Bismarck, however, had a different view. A visitor at Friedrichsruh in early January reported to Roggenbach that "the chancellor holds the loss of the crown prince to be a great misfortune, in spite of his love for Prince William and the prince's devoted love for the chancellor. He is a hothead, can't keep still, is susceptible to flatterers, and can plunge Germany into war without realizing it or wanting it. The value of the reign of the crown prince would be that Prince William would win time to settle down and to learn."[10]

6

General Waldersee and Preventive War

PRINCE William had ended his letter of December 21 to Bismarck with a New Year's wish that the chancellor might continue wisely to lead the country, "whether in peace or in war. In case the latter should occur, may you not forget that here is a ready hand and sword of a man who is well aware that Frederick the Great is his ancestor and that he fought alone three times as many as we now have against us; and who has not worked hard at his ten-years' military training for nothing!" The most ominous aspect of the influence of General von Waldersee upon Prince William, even more serious than his connection with Stoecker, was that he encouraged the prince's natural, neurotic bellicosity. Thus the London *Times* commented on November 9 that "if the Emperor's death . . . had taken place some months ago, when the Crown Prince's illness was still unknown, it would have been regarded here as a pledge of peace, because the Crown Prince's pacific sentiments were well known, whereas the event now appears likely to place virtually on the throne not the Emperor's mild and peacefully disposed son, but William, the most bellicose, impetuous, and impatient of Princes."[1]

General Count Alfred von Waldersee dangerously combined in his personality the simplistic attitudes and loyalties of a soldier—to the army and to his king—with a flair for diplomacy and intrigue. The war with France in 1870, coming in his mid-thirties, had developed and encouraged his talents and his ambition, and he had been noticed favorably by Bismarck, who promoted him from military attaché in Paris to chargé d'affaires. The excitement of the war period, however, had been followed inevitably by ten years of marking time in military ranks before he was again advanced to Quartermaster General, in 1882, a position that amounted to being chief assistant to old Moltke, the aged chief of staff. Even at that time Bismarck would have preferred Leo von Caprivi, a soldier who was more steady, reliable, and intelligent, and with less political ambition; but Caprivi's rugged and touchy independence of spirit could not adapt as easily to Moltke's own stubbornness as did Waldersee's diplomatic tact. Subsequently, in 1886, Bismarck decided that Waldersee must be removed, again in favor of Caprivi, not only because of his tendency to extend his operations beyond his own department, especially into foreign affairs, but also because of his warmongering and the danger that such an attitude constituted when it was combined with his close relationship with Prince William. Now, the developing crisis in the health of the crown prince had suddenly magnified that danger. The possibility loomed that, upon the death of both his father and grandfather, Prince William, at the head of the government structure, with his inexperience, impressionability, and impulsiveness, would provide an opening for Waldersee and other belligerent generals to enlarge the influence of the army beyond the bounds of civilian control and push the German Reich into unnecessary and perhaps fatal military adventures.[2]

As with others who had experienced the heroic 1860s and 1870s when they were relatively young—Foreign Office Counselor Friedrich von Holstein, for example—the growing complexity of affairs in the 1880s, both on the foreign and the domestic fronts, bred in General von Waldersee a certain frustration and a consequent willingness to favor drastic solutions. An able general, quick and decisive, his political naiveté was expressed in a burning hatred of socialists, Catholics, and Jews. The only way to handle these enemies, he thought, was with military force. Thus his concept of statesmanship and the position of the king in the monarchy predated Frederick the Great. Worse was his prescription for solving the continuing threats from France and Russia through preventive war—the sooner the better. Thus a year before, in December 1886, he had noted in his diary, "After a mature weighing of all the odds, I believe that the best thing would be for us to provoke a war with France; to wait until the moment is favorable to our enemies is certainly not right." No doubt this recklessness was fed by the fear of a man in his early fifties that he would himself soon be too old for leadership, and also by the continuing frustration of having to serve under a ninety-year-old king-emperor, a seventy-two-year-old chancellor, and an eighty-seven-year-old chief of staff. Waldersee was thus inclined to feel that Bismarck's efforts to maintain peace were purely selfish, since he had already earned his own laurels and was now merely preventing others from doing the same.[3]

If Crown Prince Frederick William and his wife Victoria had come to the throne normally, in good health, Bismarck would certainly have had his way with Waldersee and ended his political career at the beginning. General von Caprivi was already on the favored list of the imperial couple, and they would have been glad to make the switch. They would certainly have cooperated most eagerly in trying to place Prince William under steadier influences. Waldersee's early successes and the favor of Bismarck, which he characteristically overestimated, had planted in him the wild ambition eventually to succeed Bismarck himself as chancellor. Frederick William and Victoria had stood formidably in the way, but now destiny had quite unexpectedly thrown the cards in his favor, and he found himself competing with Herbert Bismarck, his chief rival for influence on Prince William, soon to be emperor and king. Thus this tacit rivalry gave a sharper quality to their opposition over Prince William's relationship to Stoecker. In opposing Stoecker so strongly at this time, the chancellor was, therefore, not only protecting the prince's future position, his own political cartel, and carrying out the wishes of the crown prince and princess in San Remo, but also simultaneously supporting his eldest son as the bearer of his own name, tradition, and authority in contest with Waldersee, Stoecker's friend and supporter, for control over Prince William. It was thus his own concept of the German Reich—a construction attempting stability, equilibrium, and balance—that Bismarck was protecting from Waldersee, from unnecessarily rash and provocative moves in domestic politics, and, in foreign affairs, from an unnecessary preventive war.[4]

There was no doubt about the major source of the war threat. Tsar Alexander III of Russia, personally piqued over the recalcitrant behavior of the Bulgarians and especially their electing a new prince with Austrian connections, had allowed his generals to mass troops along the Austrian frontier, in Galicia. This had been going on for weeks. A slight improvement had come with a courtesy visit of the tsar to Berlin in November. Apparently using the carrot and stick method on the suspicious and rather fearful tsar, Bismarck had it announced in the *Norddeutsche* that he was coming to Berlin for the tsar's visit only "at the Kaiser's command," and a week before the tsar's arrival he had directed the Reichsbank not to accept transactions in Russian securities. When Paul Shuvalov, the Russian ambassador, protested this action to the chancellor after his arrival in Berlin, Bismarck had told him that it was only the first of a series of such measures if Russia did not change her present policy. He had also used a report of Waldersee's on Russian troop movements to berate Shuvalov. The Russians, he had said, had forced him to ally with Austria, then with Italy; next they would force him to ally with Turkey, and finally to sic the Chinese on them. Shuvalov, Waldersee noted, had departed "like a whipped dog." In October, Herbert had written to Rantzau that the tsar's limited understanding gave him such a thick skin that "it takes a moral bludgeoning for him to feel it." At his personal audience with Tsar Alexander in November, Bismarck had then been all cordiality and deferential courtesy. The difficulties between their countries had been due to misunderstandings and plots; reports that he was supporting the Bulgarians against Russia had clearly been forged, and he subsequently released a series of sensational reports concerning the "forged documents" in the *Kölnische Zeitung*. Shuvalov was given the Order of the Black Eagle, the highest Prussian decoration, by the kaiser. All this had produced momentary talk of détente, but the Russian troop movements had continued. By Christmas, therefore, the government press, probably with the intention of encouraging the Austrians to step up their military preparations and at the same time warn them that if they provoked a war with Russia it would be at their own risk, was taking a very ominous tone. The *Post* declared that the "dawn" of a Russo-Austrian conflict over Bulgaria could already be detected.[5]

General Waldersee's approach to the situation was very logical in its simplicity. Germany could not afford to allow Russia to annihilate Austria (here he was in agreement with Bismarck), but to wait and maintain neutrality, as the chancellor was proposing, until *after* a Russian attack would be to run precisely this risk of annihilation or, conversely, a quick Austrian submission that would then leave Germany to face Russia alone. It was therefore urgent, in the face of what appeared to be Russian preparations for a full-scale war in the spring, to concert military plans with the Austrians and take the offensive at their own, not the Russians', convenience. At the end of November Waldersee drew up a memorandum on Russian armaments for Moltke to present to the chancellor and the kaiser. Through the military attaché in Vienna he was also trying to promote his more belligerent policies with the Austrians. Bismarck's response was contained in a directive to the Foreign Office from Count Rantzau, on December 7, asking them to advise Vienna not to pay attention to the statements of General Waldersee, that Moltke in his recent memorandum had recommended that Germany and Austria mount an offensive as soon as possible to forestall the inevitable Russian attack, but that "His Highness could not agree for political reasons, no matter how correct the military judgment might be." A week later the chancellor wrote the ambassador in Vienna, Prince Reuss, "As long as I am minister I shall not agree to a prophylactic attack on Russia." In his diplomatic judgment Bismarck, in fact, felt that any war would be the worst of all possible results; that certainty of German intervention if Russia threatened Austria militarily would in itself limit the scale of any possible Russian attack; that the timorousness and natural caution of Tsar Alexander meant, no matter what the military preparations, that the latter were probably intended only as diplomatic pressure to produce a favorable result for Russia in the Bulgarian question; and that war would therefore not break out. Belligerency in the press—to the distress of the *Frankfurter Zeitung*, which seemed to think that if people would only stop talking about war the danger of it would go away—would warn both the Austrians and the Russians and might help prevent actual belligerency. In maintaining the fine line between encouraging the Austrians to take a strong stand and provoking them to irresponsible and dangerous actions, the chancellor found that General Waldersee was working at cross-purposes with him. To make the situation even more complicated, it seemed that Friedrich von Holstein and others in the Foreign Office agreed with Waldersee. To some extent this hostility to Russia was a natural result of a growing sense of national pride and a feeling of rivalry with the great Eastern empire that affected all classes, all parties, and the general public. Even Herbert Bismarck leaned more toward supporting German Austria unconditionally against Russia than did Bismarck himself.[6]

Here, too, the illness of Crown Prince Frederick William came to Waldersee's aid. He could now thrust Prince William forward in this foreign policy area to counteract the age and weakness of the kaiser and the apparent timidity of the chancellor. In November he had written the military attaché in St. Petersburg, Yorck von Wartenburg, that "we must not leave out of consideration that His Majesty the Kaiser is unfortunately very feeble and a small shock can suffice to bring about the end, that we therefore can be faced suddenly with a completely different situation, since according to human reckoning the crown prince will not ascend the throne, we shall then have a twenty-eight-year-old, energetic, ambitious, and fearless kaiser, who certainly has no desire to wait until it suits our enemies to start the war." At about that time Waldersee had advised Prince William to ask the kaiser to allow him to be present at all audiences, so that he would be fully familiar with the various governmental functions and could take over if necessary that much more easily. This move would scarcely have been acceptable to the crown prince or to the Bismarcks, and it was not done. The old kaiser, however, had recently, after showing lively interest in a report, fallen promptly asleep while Moltke was reading it, although it had not lasted more than ten minutes. This fact gave Waldersee his opportunity. On December 17 the kaiser received Chief of Staff General von Moltke, Minister of War General Paul Bronsart von Schellendorf, Chief of the Military Cabinet General von Albedyll, Quartermaster General von Waldersee, and for the first time in that connection and company, Prince William. The kaiser protested to the assembled generals that it was very hard even to think of war with Russia, but in the end he approved military staff talks with the Austrians. It was apparently this association of Prince William and the kaiser with the "war party," even more than the Stoecker affair, that provoked Bismarck the most. The peak of the Stoecker attacks—which were aimed at least as much at Waldersee as at Stoecker—came immediately after this meeting, and Bismarck once more began to agitate for replacing Waldersee. As the *Frankfurter Zeitung* wrote a month later, those who wanted to guard against overconfidence regarding the achievements of the second half of the nineteenth century might consider that "worried patriots believe that the future of our Reich depends basically on the question whether a fanatical cleric and an equally pious as well as warlike general have already laid their hands upon one of the next heirs to the throne," and that simultaneously people were waiting with a feeling of helplessness to see whether the tsar of Russia would decide for peace or war.[7]

Bismarck's strongest weapon in trying to counteract all of these personal influences was public opinion. Thus in the speech from the throne at the end of November (read by Reich Secretary of State for the Interior Heinrich von Boetticher to a sparsely attended opening session of the Reichstag in the Berlin *Schloss* [castle]), the statement had been made, to the general applause and satisfaction of the deputies, that "the foreign policy of His Majesty the Kaiser is endeavoring with success to strengthen the peace of Europe, which it is its duty to maintain, through the cultivation of friendly relations with all Powers, through treaties and through alliances, which have the purpose to avoid the danger of war and to oppose unjustified attacks. The German Reich has no aggressive tendencies and no needs that could be satisfied through victorious wars. The un-Christian inclination to attack neighboring peoples is alien to the German character." The day after the military conference with the kaiser, Herbert Bismarck instructed the press through the Foreign Office press officer not to mention the words "council of war" and not to discuss the content of Moltke's report. The *Frankfurter Zeitung* carried a telegram obviously based on false Foreign Office information that stated that the report of the audience given by the kaiser the previous day to Prince William, Generals Moltke and Waldersee, and the minister of war had given the appearance of "an important military conference," and that this had "caused a panic in Vienna. Here," it went on, "nothing is known of any such conference. The individuals named appear to have been received, not together, but one after the other."

Genuinely disturbed by the military conference, the elder Bismarck reacted privately as strongly as possible. In a memorandum to Albedyll he noted that according to Albedyll it had been agreed at the meeting that Germany would provide at least a few army corps to assist the Austrians in the East "under all circumstances and in any case." That would presumably include cases where the *casus foederis* of their alliance treaty did not apply: i.e., in the case of an Austrian attack on Russia. Such cooperation with Austrian aggressive acts would be contrary to Germany's secret treaties (i.e., the so-called Reinsurance Treaty with Russia, signed in June 1887, which provided for neutrality if either country were attacked by a third power). Such positive decisions went beyond Bismarck's concept of the purpose of the talks with the Austrians. Since the Austrians had requested the talks, they could not be avoided, but no positive engagements or any initiative should be advanced by the German side, and in any case the Foreign Office could not recognize the talks officially, because then it would have to accept responsibility for what the generals said, and this would mean putting an unacceptable restriction from the military side upon overall diplomatic policy. It was not in Germany's political interest to in any way encourage the Austrians to start a war with Russia. In an accompanying memorandum the chancellor requested the Foreign Office (that is, Herbert) to report to the kaiser in the above sense and to emphasize that he himself could not accept the responsibility of carrying on the government under any other circumstances and that he had to guard himself from "the direction of political affairs devolving to a certain extent upon the general staff, and the military men from urging war at all costs in Vienna."[8]

When Herbert Bismarck approached Generals Albedyll and Moltke with his father's criticisms, they both claimed that there had been a misunderstanding. Albedyll had used careless language, he said. He was by no means a warmonger, but agreed absolutely with the chancellor's policy. The other generals had accompanied Moltke in his audience with the kaiser to try to temper [!] his belligerency. He regretted that the meeting had been called a "council of war." Moltke insisted that all arrangements had been considered only on the assumption that the *casus foederis* would be in operation with Austria, and determination of that contingency was the business solely of the chancellor. He would not reply to any of the Austrian staff proposals, but would refer them to the chancellor first. Herbert reported that he thought there was no danger from Moltke, who seemed quite reasonable. Albedyll, he wrote, was "an unbelievably superficial, egoistic customer, who is now not only unfit but also dangerous for his position. Nothing but a manufacturer of commissions for protégés." It was a delight to deal with Moltke directly. "In comparison with Waldersee, it is like a rubber-tired [trap] on asphalt to a peasant's cart with no springs on a swampy corduroy road." The elder Bismarck sent a new instruction anyway, for both the kaiser and Moltke, pointing out that it was in the Austrian interest to extend the terms of the alliance with Germany if possible. "The present purpose of His Majesty's policy is to keep the peace, and our system of secret treaties sets a premium upon peaceful behavior in that we support Austria if Russia breaks the peace and according to the Russian treaty remain neutral if Austria breaks the peace. We can and may, therefore, promise the Austrians nothing, no disposition of troops, no mobilization, if they are the aggressors." He could not maintain his responsibility for the conduct of foreign affairs as Reich chancellor if Moltke were to be authorized by the kaiser to promise troop dispositions without his approval. He requested that the kaiser be asked to authorize the Foreign Office to inform Moltke personally about the secret Russian treaty. Privately Rantzau wrote that Bismarck had said to tell Herbert that he could eventually let the military know that "if they continued to make trouble [*Knüppel zwischen die Beine zu schieben*]" for the chancellor, "he would stay away from Berlin completely and dump the whole kit and caboodle in their lap [*den ganzen Bettel vor die Füsse werfen*]." Kaiser William assured Herbert that his own views corresponded exactly with his father's: he had no intention of approving a war of aggression against Russia. Christmas day Herbert walked with his father through the snow-filled woods in Friedrichsruh and noted in his diary, "Future politics, Pr[ince] W[illiam]. & Russia-Austria. In spite of her weakness, we depend on the latter."[9]

Although the chancellor's personal support for what little future remained to the crown prince, and his efforts to contain Stoecker, Albedyll, Stolberg, Puttkamer, and Waldersee and maintain peace might have been appreciated by Crown Princess Victoria, she was nevertheless still complaining, in a letter to her mother in early January, about Bismarck's methods. "These 'middle ages' fashions of treating Politics I cannot admire and in the 19th Century it is hardly the thing to take a leaf out of the Book—of the *Medici*." Bismarck was a great man who had done great things, but he could not give Germany what she most wanted, "*Peace* amongst its classes, races, religions & Parties,—good & *friendly* relations with its neighbours, *Liberty*,—& the respect of *right* instead of *force*, the protection of the weak against the oppression of the strong." Bismarck's methods had been corrupting, and his followers were fifty times worse than he himself. It was probably natural for royalty, even in the late nineteenth century, to feel that all the ministers and statesmen who came and went while they remained in their high positions, although necessary and therefore to be tolerated, were rather a nuisance nevertheless and that they themselves knew better—one does get such an impression from reading at length in the correspondence of the crown princess of Prussia with her mother, Queen Victoria. Certainly the warm, liberal sentiments of the crown princess were admirable—even though it is clear that the ideal political image in her mind was more English than German. And it was true that Otto von Bismarck, like many politicians then and now, had more faith in the efficacy of power, pressure, and maneuver than of vague, idealistic generosity and good will. But the crown princess appears not to have considered whether actual conditions at the time and forces both inside and outside Germany were conducive to relaxation, conciliation, and consensus. Her confidence in the inevitability of the advance of liberalism, like that of her friends in the German Liberal party, was still undaunted. It is unfortunate that she did not in the end have more time on the throne. Perhaps she and her husband would actually have been able to soften and liberalize the general tone of politics, to a degree, but one suspects nevertheless that, as Germany and the rest of Europe passed from the 1880s to the 1890s, she would also have continued basically to be frustrated and disappointed, with or without the tutelage of the "Iron Chancellor."[10]

7

The Cartel and the Grain Tariff

IF Bismarck's strongest resource against power plays on the part of the military and the clerical Conservatives was in public opinion and the Reichstag, he was especially fortunate in this period of double doubt and anxiety—over war and over the succession—that he had just created a strong majority in the Reichstag election of the previous year to back his personal policy: the cartel, established among the National Liberal, Free Conservative, and Conservative parties. Even for the Conservative party, to maintain the existing majority, a political constellation already established, would be more reasonable than to speculate on other, chancy possibilities. For Bismarck, the cartel in this uncertain period was thus a kind of insurance. And yet, with the final diagnosis of the crown prince's cancer, the original orientation and thrust of the cartel idea, its specific coloration, and the balance of the elements within it, had been suddenly and irrevocably destroyed. "What sad events and stupendous changes we are in for," wrote the National Liberal leader, Johannes Miquel, to his friend and colleague Rudolf von Bennigsen, "through the illness of the crown prince! Above all, that means holding together all the national forces." He expressed the hope that Bennigsen—the more "doctrinaire liberal" of the two and not so close to the Conservatives—would take over the leadership of the coming Reichstag session and steer the budget and the planned extension of the legal term of the Reichstag through the legislative process quickly. Most National Liberals would vote against the increase in the grain tariff, he expected, but they must allow full freedom to their deputies on the issue. "One must try all the more to avoid speaking too harshly in the debate and offending the agrarians [Landwirte]."[1]

Unable to counteract the virulence of the liberal-conservative conflict of ideologies and interests except through general appeals to nationalism and patriotism, which tended to work only in a crisis but not for a positive, peacetime consensus, the Bismarck regime had responded to the onset of the Long Depression in the 1870s by appealing to both groups through a double-barreled tariff policy. But, under the impact of grain imports from the New World, German agriculture was in much greater need of assistance than was its rapidly developing industry. Higher German tariffs on grain, however, might encourage retaliation against German manufactures. In special session at the end of November, representatives of chambers of commerce passed a resolution denying the need for an increase in the grain tariff. Urban-oriented politicians, whether National Liberal, German Liberal, or Social Democratic, had small sympathy with the agricultural point of view and tended to assume that if German agricultural producers could not compete in the world grain market, they should shift to something else. They also were especially sensitive to charges that the tariff was a tax on the daily bread of the working poor. Liberal critics assumed from the fact that the bulk of wheat and rye was grown on large Junker estates that the peasants, most of whom had to do wage work, were thus, as consumers, actually hurt by the grain tariff. In rebuttal to this charge that the tariff assisted only the large estate owner, the *Norddeutsche* pointed out that the small holder had to buy many items for cash—oil for light, coffee, salt, spices, beer, wine, and most of his clothes— as well as make mortgage payments and pay taxes that did not decrease with falling prices. He commonly sold most of the butter and cheese and pork he produced and lived very frugally, eating very little meat. He usually raised wheat for sale as a cash crop and did not himself eat white bread. Certainly the grain tariff program did have a wide appeal in the country districts, as the eventual support for the increase in the rate from some twenty National Liberals from South Germany, an area of mostly small peasant holdings, would seem to indicate. One petition to the chancellor from the Peasants' League called for complete exclusion of "unnecessary" foreign grain and meat and pointed out that it was dangerous for a nation to become dependent on foreign countries for its food. An increase in the tariff on grain had been promised to the agrarians by Prussian Minister of Agriculture Lucius the preceding spring. The present rate had not been successful in maintaining price levels, and the government probably also wanted to mollify the agrarian Junker Conservatives for its sponsorship of the rise of the National Liberals to a position of dominance in the cartel and the new Reichstag.[2]

The Reichstag was opened on November 24, and a government bill to double the existing tariff (3 M per double *Zentner*) on wheat and rye was introduced. The increase would bring the rate to about 66 percent of value and would probably mean an increase in the price of bread. Long before the Reichstag met, however, the party press had been preparing their several constituencies for the issue. In early October, for example, the Free Conservative *Post* had urged moderation on the agrarians, reminding them that the present era of protectionist policy was relatively recent and depended on the good will of the industrialists. It would not be wise to endanger this policy and weaken the cartel. Evidently the *Post* was afraid that in the coming liberal era under the crown prince—whose cancer diagnosis had not at that time been authoritatively announced— any liberal, free-trade reaction against higher tariffs and bread prices would be reinforced by the liberal tendencies of the administration and would result in a sharp swing to free trade, to the ultimate disadvantage of the agrarian Junkers. These fears were immediately confirmed by a German Liberal victory in a Reichstag by-election in the Silesian district of Sagan-Sprottau on October 8. The district, which had been National Liberal secessionist, or German Liberal, since 1881, had gone for the cartel the previous February, 8,513 to 7,943. But now the German Liberal candidate Forckenbeck—*Oberbürgermeister* of Berlin and an old friend of the crown prince—had won by a margin of 7,656 to 5,119. It was immediately apparent that whereas the German Liberals had actually received 287 fewer votes than in February, the cartel parties had attracted 3,394 fewer. As the *Frankfurter Zeitung* pointed out, this was clearly the result of a smaller overall participation in the voting.[3]

The *Post*, blaming the negative result in Sagan-Sprottau on the proagrarian liquor tax passed the previous spring, was now convinced that if the cartel was to continue, it must swing away from the agrarian Right and refuse to raise the tariff. It called to mind the sequence of elections after 1878, when a dissolution and special election that year on a scare issue (an assassination attempt against the kaiser) had been followed in 1881 by a swing to the Left, a trend that had lasted until the recent cartel election (again on a scare issue) the previous February. In 1881, continued the *Post*, the political swing had not influenced the new protective tariff policy, but now it would very likely be different. The *Frankfurter Zeitung* recognized the validity of the *Post*'s concern for what might happen to the policy of protective tariffs when the liberal crown prince came to the throne, and urged its liberal readers also to prepare themselves for opportunities that might then arise—"We think in this connection of the first elections to be carried out uninfluenced by the pressure of the whole government apparatus."[4]

The reaction of the Conservative agrarians to these developments was, of course, diametrically opposed. The cartel, declared the *Reichsbote* and the *Kreuzzeitung*, had been designed from the first to split the Conservatives and to lead the clerical right wing to a kind of suicide. As for the tariff, the government-proposed rate of 6 M was not nearly enough—it should be at least 8 M. The cartel parties in Sagan-Sprottau would have done better to put up their own candidates instead of uniting upon one.

If the National Liberal party was so concerned with industrial interests, let it confine itself to the industrial districts and leave the rural districts to the Conservatives. The Conservative party, wrote the official *Konservative Korrespondenz*, had no intention of supporting ulterior liberal motives under the flag of the cartel. To this the *Post* replied that a Conservative candidate would have done even worse in Sagan-Sprottau, that the voters knew quite well that Forckenbeck was a dedicated free-trader. The defeat in Sagan-Sprottau demanded, not dissolution of the cartel, but even greater efforts at cooperation.[5]

The *Frankfurter Zeitung* agreed that from the beginning certain National Liberal leaders had had a great moderate majority in mind, one very much directed toward the impending succession and that would include the German Liberals. In this debate most interesting was the noncommital stance of the chancellor's *Norddeutsche Allgemeine Zeitung*. Mostly it advocated a middle line, supporting the cartel, disparaging any future hopes for the German Liberals, and, for example, deprecating an attack by the left-Liberal *Berliner Volksblatt* on the reckless high living of the agrarian Junkers as the source of their distress, but nevertheless quoting the article in question at length. In early October, in fact, Minister of Agriculture Lucius had been informed by Chief of the Chancellery Rottenburg that Bismarck was "taken aback by the greed of the agrarians." He recognized the necessity of introducing the tariff increase, but would not "hold it against the National Liberals if they voted against it." An appeal to economic interests would not work as a program for bringing industrialists and Junkers together if attitudes toward such matters were allowed to become doctrinaire, and the chancellor's newspaper appealed for a more rational approach. "Political convictions," it wrote, "appeal mostly to the feelings of the heart. Some formulate their program by heading it with concepts that electrify the masses, such as Liberty, Equality, Fraternity; others support themselves upon the authority principle as incorporated in monarchy.... But ... in economic questions reason alone decides. The latter are matters of practical utility ... their actual determination rests upon a function of the intellect; it is, as it were, a matter of calculation."[6]

To the National Liberals, however, rationality extended beyond merely economic affairs. The very basis of the cartel, wrote the official *National Liberale Korrespondenz*, was the rational appreciation that "as over against the power of the negative and destructive elements in Germany the positive forces must necessarily hold together because they are individually too weak." The reactionary clerical wing of the Conservatives, which did not represent the whole party, naturally would prefer to work with the Catholic Center party and was attacking the cartel out of sheer "blindness and frivolity." On the contrary, replied the *Kreuzzeitung*, the National Liberal tendency was to use the cartel purely for their own benefit. To this, Catholic *Germania* could only agree. Just as, from the Left, the German Liberals were constantly attacking and deriding the cartel as an agent of reaction and the National Liberals for turning reactionary and betraying their liberal principles, so also from the Right the Center-party press was constantly attacking the cartel as a Liberal plot and clucking their tongues at the Conservatives for betraying their Christian and monarchical principles. The difference between the National and the German Liberals, declared *Germania*, was not one of principle, but merely of tactics. "After the National Liberals have become a strong party through the Conservatives and when in the coming 'New Era,' they amount to something, then they will drop the mask and again be openly what they are, liberals." Recently they had been trying to attract liberal Catholics, over the head of the Center party, but this would not work; the Liberals did not understand religion and were themselves a philosophical cult, like the Masons.[7]

At the end of October, in a major article set off by larger type on the front page, the *Norddeutsche Allgemeine Zeitung* pointed out that the left Liberals and the Center had consistently attacked the cartel as being "unnatural" since they were the ones that would suffer most from its success. The alliance of the National Liberal, Free Conservative, and Conservative parties in the cartel, however, did not mean that they had to give up their individuality as parties, but only that they agreed to put the *national* point of view ahead of partisan attitudes. One of the great defects of the German Liberal party was that it was devoted to the cause of "true" parliamentarism. But parliamentary government required a stable majority, and this was especially hard to accomplish in Germany because of "our partisan exuberance [*Parteiüppigkeit*]." Recently, in his weekly *Die Nation*, Dr. Theodor Barth, a German Liberal leader, had admitted that the present cartel was the only lasting association of that kind that was possible. Although the Catholic Center, German Liberals, and Social Democrats had worked together in elections, their widely divergent philosophies—Catholic Christianity, secular individualism, and revolutionary, atheistic Marxism—rendered any lasting association or working legislative majority of those parties impossible. Barth was hoping that the basic differences between Conservatives and National Liberals would eventually cause the cartel to fail, but he was overlooking the fact that the differences were not so crucial as the points of agreement. And it was precisely the hopes of the Center and German Liberals for its early demise that would assist the cartel leaders in emphasizing the unifying tendencies.[8]

Undoubtedly what the *Norddeutsche* and the Bismarck government were getting at was the idea that the material interests and political and social position of the traditional agrarian Junker gentry and of the newer industrial and commercial elites could be supported and the authority of the state and public order protected only by cooperation of the interests with each other and the government. They also believed that the power factor of political and social supremacy would in the end outweigh any particular ideological or economic differences and encourage mutual give and take and a spirit of sacrifice. But, since it was the bureaucratic government itself that had sponsored the cartel and was still taking the responsibility for actual political decisions, the inevitable jockeying of the factions for advantage and overbidding for purposes of bargaining could take place in public and be carried to extremes of intransigence that could only weaken the cartel association and encourage its enemies. Thus it was possible for the conservative *Kreuzzeitung* to claim that the agricultural classes constituted "the wide, strong foundation of the Prussian state," and that, if agriculture were to receive no assistance, then "the foundations of the monarchy, of morals, of religion, the welfare and finally even the existence of the state" were in question. The state, in other words, could not continue as it was without the support of the Junker class. To this the National Liberals turned a disdainful and deaf ear. The agrarian agitation, wrote the official *National Liberale Korrespondenz*, did not involve the whole Conservative party but only the *Kreuzzeitung* and "a narrow circle of politicians of harshly agrarian character." It was, wrote the National Liberal *Hamburger Nachrichten*, "completely impossible in our time, in a country with universal suffrage, to maintain artificially through legislation and through the sacrifice of the remaining classes of the population the property and social position of a single class that lacks the material means to support them." The Junkers were obsolete and should admit it.[9]

At the beginning of November the *Norddeutsche Allgemeine Zeitung* took the discussion a degree further. The origin of the cartel had been the recognition by the three parties that partisan viewpoints should be subordinated to patriotism and defense of the nation as a whole. The realization of this necessity, among both party leaders and the electorate, and the willingness to work and sacrifice for it amounted to "a significant advance, and one will not go too far in asserting that the parliamentary elements and the masses of voters that stand for this principle represent the politically mature part of the nation." Particularism had always been the main German weakness—"Our future well-being can be perceived only in a union of all parties loyal to the state." In his search for stability and consensus, the chancellor appeared to be calling for a single party led by the bureaucracy.[10]

Germania accused the *Norddeutsche* of attempting to cover over very real differences between liberalism and conservatism with a thick fog. The

National Liberals, after all, wanted to subordinate the church to the state, and their policy toward education was "nothing more than the propaganda of Indifferentism or unbelief." In economic affairs they had indeed given up extreme free trade out of expediency, but one would find out how little they cared for agriculture if any measures were suggested for its support beyond merely raising the tariff. They represented the most extreme individualism and capitalism in industrial affairs and had no interest in "organizing a strong, independent body of *handicraftsmen* [*sic*] as a counterweight against the leveling operations of the factory." They opposed the Conservatives in their tax policy and even more in their basic attitude toward the constitution and delimiting the rights of the crown and the parliaments. Above all, they wanted a share of the power. The Conservatives, however, were just as determined, and so this "mixed society" would not work; but over against it the Catholics themselves were "holding always ready a solid, united, and strong Center party, which presents a fixed point around which later the conservative elements of the nation can rally."[11]

It would no doubt have been interesting to observe, in the normal course of events, how Chancellor Bismarck would have instructed both Liberals and Conservatives further in "political maturity" under the new reign of the crown prince, but the announcement of the definitive diagnosis of the crown prince's cancer on November 12 put an end to all such possibilities. Suddenly the certain vista of an imminently approaching liberal era faded into doubt and ambiguity. With a conservative, orthodox instead of liberal kaiser in the offing, the swollen roster of National Liberal deputies in the Reichstag could easily become a mockery rather than a promise, and the results of the by-election in Sagan-Sprottau could indeed become prophetic. The change in future prospects on the throne did not lessen the bickering among the parties of the cartel—it probably increased it—but now the rivalry was carried on with different motives: new confidence (as expressed in the Stoecker affair) instead of apprehension on the side of the *Kreuzzeitung* Conservatives, and disillusionment and frustration on the side of the National Liberals, who now found themselves caught inextricably in a false position. Ever since their brilliant electoral victory of the preceding February, they had been bending over backward to soothe and please the agrarian Conservatives, keeping their special liberal plans and aspirations more or less to themselves, as *Germania* said, waiting for the right future moment in which to launch the new liberal era with sufficient éclat to fortify and establish permanently their dominant position with the electorate. And now there was to be no liberal future, and the German Liberals were enthusiastically exploiting this opportunity to tar them with the brush of "Reaction," and undoubtedly would make the most of this advantage in the next elections. The National Liberals thus now possessed additional, urgent reasons for emphasizing their liberalism and, in spite of Miquel's appeal for tact, detaching themselves from the agrarian cause.[12]

As early as the general budget debate in the Reichstag, at the end of November, the National Liberal leader, von Bennigsen, explained that he was personally against the rise in the grain tariff, especially because of the agitational issue that it gave the German Liberals. Bennigsen admitted that his feelings about the tariff were similar to theirs, but he closed his speech by carefully emphasizing the differences between them. Prophecies by the German Liberal press that the National Liberals, who had divided evenly over the tariff increase of 1885, would now bow to government pressure and produce a majority for the bill were subsequently not borne out. In the committee on the tariff bill the National Liberal and the Center representatives attacked the rate increase at least as strongly as the German Liberals and Social Democrats. The Conservatives thus found themselves outvoted, but they stubbornly would not compromise, letting the bill be voted down by the committee and holding out for "all or nothing." There was some indication that the Conservatives were expecting special support and pressure from the government, perhaps even an appearance and speech in the Reichstag by Bismarck himself. Apparently the *Kreuzzeitung* was hoping that, since both National Liberal and Center parties had agrarian as well as urban wings and therefore were divided on the tariff issue, by taking a strong stand the agrarians could split these parties and, in effect, create an overall Conservative majority on the basis of the agricultural interest that would pass the government bill. Such an alignment would also provide an appropriate basis for the New Era under Prince William. The Stoecker-Waldersee meeting had taken place a few days after the opening of the Reichstag session.[13]

If the government had wished to make an issue of the tariff increase, it undoubtedly could have forced the 6 M rate through, but the rather unseemly overconfidence and naive arrogance of the *Kreuzzeitung* wing of the Conservative party, as evidenced also by the Stoecker affair, fitted neither the requirements of the very delicate political situation nor the chancellor's point of view. The day before the opening of the second reading of the tariff bill in the Reichstag it was announced that a slight indisposition had required the chancellor to limit his attention to only the "most important questions," of which the tariff did not appear to be one. Rottenburg's "dead weight" article against Stoecker's Christian Socialists had appeared the previous day. Government restraint in the tariff question, however, presented the Center leader Dr. Windthorst with a first-class opportunity, which he seized with the greatest dexterity. Although the Center press was capable, along with the *Kreuzzeitung*, of advocating from time to time clarity and clear demarcation along ideological lines in party politics, the heterogeneous economic and social composition of the Center party itself did not recommend a realignment according to economic interests. To keep his party together—and also to demonstrate to both the Conservatives and the government that the Center party still existed and could be useful—Windthorst managed to persuade the free-traders in the Center party to agree to a compromise tariff rate of 5 M. He advanced this compromise in the second reading of the bill; it was quietly accepted by the agrarians (probably with government encourage-ment); and the amended bill passed by a small margin. In the crucial vote on December 13, sixty-nine National Liberals voted against the bill and only twenty-two, mostly South German agrarians, for. The *Kreuz-zeitung* admitted that Windthorst had achieved a major victory for his party—"never has a party leader maneuvered his party more elegantly under fire"—but blamed it on the weakness of the Free Conservatives, especially the *Post*, in questioning the higher tariff rate in the first place. The German Liberals were as shocked by the Center party tactic as they were pleased by the National Liberal vote. The Center party would have difficulty maintaining its stance as a Catholic "people's party" now that it had voted for an increase in the price of bread, declared the *Vossische Zeitung*. The *National Liberale Korrespondenz* recognized that the Center party had refused to split along aristocratic-democratic lines but saw it moving toward the Conservatives, and Catholic *Germania* seemed rather smugly satisfied that the clash of economic interests that the secular, nationalist, rational appeal of the cartel had not been able to master had in the end, as far as the Center party was concerned, been effectively reconciled by religion.[14]

8
==

Legislative Term and
Antisocialist Law

THE significance of the momentary Catholic-Conservative majority for the tariff bill was substantially lessened by the fact that on other pressing issues no agreement was possible between Conservatives and the Center party; namely, over the extension of the length of the Reichstag session and the renewal of the law against socialist agitation. Well before the opening of the Reichstag, the leadership of the cartel parties had agreed to introduce a bill extending the term of the Reichstag from three years to five. This was a perfect compromise issue for the cartel, since the National Liberals were basically convinced that lengthening the term of a deputy to five years would greatly increase his effectiveness and independence and thus ultimately strengthen the influence and esprit de corps of the Reichstag as a whole, whereas the Conservatives were mostly intent upon reducing the frequency of elections, the accountability of the deputies to the passing moods of the electorate, and the opportunities for agitation of the mass parties of the Center and the Left. The cartel majority thought in terms of the effectiveness of government, whereas the opposition parties were more interested in the closeness of the deputies to the voters. The left-Liberal by-election victory in Sagan-Sprottau, where the lack of an overriding national issue had caused a drop in voter participation and thus a reversion to oppositional politics, had also provoked other suggestions in cartel circles, such as compulsory voting and a plurality election system like the one in Saxony, instead of the absolute majority system prevailing. For the purpose of trying to buttress the national consensus block of the cartel, these other measures would no doubt be more effective than merely lengthening the legislative term, but the latter was less controversial and more easily put through.[1]

The German Liberals, of course, homed in on the extension of the Reichstag term as a betrayal of the National Liberal campaign promise that they would not tamper with the constitution and as only the beginning of a planned campaign of political reaction. In a speech in late October to his constituents in Ober-Hilbersheim, the German Liberal leader, Ludwig Bamberger, had denounced the proposed lengthening of the Reichstag term as only a preliminary exercise, "as when a pianist seats himself at the grand piano and first lets his fingers glide over the keys in a few runs and chords in order to satisfy himself that his hand is sure and the instrument well tuned. If this trial succeeds, then he has the assurance that he can do what he likes with the instrument, and only then does the big piece begin." Bamberger, an old 1848 revolutionary like Miquel, had become a successful financier and an ally of Bismarck's in the liberal nationalist era of nation-building. He had helped found the Reichsbank and put Germany on the gold standard. The cartel press was now citing his own speeches from the 1870s in favor of the longer Reichstag term; it was interesting to read them, he said, and see how much more faith he had had then in "certain individuals" and in the German people. He still thought that a five-year term for a legislature was better for "a genuinely constitutional and parliamentary state, but not in a situation in which the whole constitutional and parliamentary system has already sunk to a mere sham and where even this sham is threatened . . . with being gradually destroyed." In other countries the power of the crown to dissolve the parliament was counterbalanced by the power of the parliament to dissolve the ministry. "With us all power is on one side; the parliament is sent home, and the ministers remain." The result was that every dissolution involved a serious conflict and a threat of coup d'etat, so that the voters were successfully cowed. When the ministry could thus choose the moment for dissolution, it would be "the height of stupidity" to give them their favorable majority for five instead of for only three years. If this blast of Bamberger's had come after the mid-November diagnostic sentence on the crown prince, it might have had more real political justification. But, coming before that crucial event, its effect is vitiated by our suspicion that the vituperative tone and pointed personal references to Bismarck's dictatorship represented a bid for royal support. Curiously, not even the liberal *Frankfurter Zeitung* was impressed. The government had been just as powerful in relation to the Reichstag in the late 1860s and early 1870s, it pointed out, when Bamberger, with his oratorical eloquence, had been one of Bismarck's chief supporters.[2]

In reply to the accusation of the German Liberals, the *Konservative Korrespondenz* denied categorically that the Conservatives had any thought of attacking universal suffrage. The *National Liberale Korrespondenz* issued a statement maintaining that a lessening of the frequency of elections was necessary if "our whole public life is not to degenerate more and more into demagogic electoral agitation." Less frequent elections would try the public's patience less and would thus actually tend to protect the system of universal and equal suffrage. The government's *Norddeutsche Allgemeine Zeitung* in the meantime buttressed the cartel position by pointing out that "reaction" meant going back to a previous condition, but that the characteristic of the present age was the *new* activity of the state in "reconciling social conflicts as much as possible," and that the old-fashioned liberalism of the German Liberals was against this kind of social intervention. It was precisely the failure of Manchester liberalism to accept the consequences of its law of competition that was responsible for the startling rise of the Social Democrats.[3]

The basic question, however, was not whether the state would exert more influence over the life of the nation—of that there was little doubt, no matter how much the German Liberals disapproved of the trend. The question was, what kind of state would it be? Even with the certain prospect of a long reign for the crown prince, the chances of an easy transition from the controlled manipulations of the Bismarck dictatorship to a freer, more open, spontaneous, and responsible system had been problematical, but now? What really did the government and the parties intend? An indication much clearer than the cartel sponsorship of an extension of the life of the Reichstag should have been given by the government bill to extend the law against socialist agitation; but this did not, in fact, prove to be the case. The government had held back its antisocialist bill until after the Christmas recess, ostensibly to prevent the Social Democrats from beginning an agitation against it; instead, during the Christmas holidays the press was occupied with the full fury of the anti-Stoecker campaign. Nevertheless, rumors of the major outlines of the bill gradually crept into the press, contributing, along with the increase in the grain tariff and the Stoecker affair, to the growing conflict between the Liberal and Conservative wings of the cartel. Apparently the new antisocialist bill was to call for an extension of the law for five years instead of two or three and for banishment upon conviction for socialist agitation, not just from towns and cities, as before, but from the whole Reich. These provisions went completely against the inclinations of the National Liberal leadership. In the light of the major defeat delivered to the Social Democrats in February and considering that the previous banishment provision had not been effective, but had actually served in many cases merely to transfer the agitation along with the agitator into areas where it had not formerly existed, the National Liberals were much more inclined to soften the law and perhaps to end its exceptional character by substituting for it more strict general provisions in the existing laws dealing with speech and assembly. This tendency was, of course, especially strong within the left wing of the party, as evidenced in the *National Zeitung*, and included attacks on Minister of the Interior Puttkamer, chief representative of the recently prevailing Conservative domination in Prussia.[4]

What, in fact, did Bismarck intend by allowing Puttkamer to bring forward a more severe antisocialist law at this time? He must have been aware that the National Liberals would not support it. The harsher provisions were Puttkamer's idea, but Bismarck certainly did nothing to discourage him, having replied to his letter proposing the more stringent provisions that avowed revolutionaries like the Social Democrats did not deserve any protection from the state, and that expulsion from the country was the logical result of their hostility. There was no objection to the bill in the Prussian State Ministry, although some of the ministers had misgivings, and in the Bundesrat, Saxony proposed amendments even more strict, which were accepted by Prussia and the other states. The Bavarian minister of the interior thought the new banishment provision would be "very effective," but the Bavarian ministry as a whole thought it was at least doubtful that the Reichstag would accept it. Although the Württemberg government supported the new bill, it too was skeptical concerning its political chances. In other matters the chancellor had shown the greatest sensitivity to National Liberal sensibilities, but in regard to the crucial antisocialist bill they were apparently not even consulted. Bavarian Minister to Berlin Count Hugo zu Lerchenfeld-Koefering reported that, as far as he knew, Bismarck had not changed his personal opinion that the law was of no political value; he had regularly worked to renew it only because old Kaiser William urgently desired it. If there was really going to be a new liberal era under the crown prince, Puttkamer, the symbol of the conservative era, would eventually have to go. Was Bismarck trusting in his own prestige to force the harsher bill on the National Liberals? Was he overbidding to gain some kind of compromise? Had old age and ill health merely made him inattentive and careless? Or was he cold-bloodedly planning from the beginning to let Puttkamer compromise himself and break his neck on this clearly provocative bill? It would not be the first time that he had publicly sacrificed a cabinet colleague to a change in policy in Prussia; in 1881 he had forced the resignation of Puttkamer's predecessor Botho zu Eulenburg, by publicly disavowing him in the Landtag. Ever since spring the press had been prophesying Puttkamer's replacement by Miquel. If he were forced out in a public fight over a "reactionary" measure such as this bill, it would provide a very satisfying but cheap Liberal victory.[5]

For the orthodox conservative *Kreuzzeitung* there was no question that the more drastic antisocialist law was necessary and even crucial. Banishing the chief Social Democratic agitators completely from the Reich and depriving them of citizenship would largely destroy the party in the Reichstag. The opponents of the law were correct, it wrote in a lead article on December 7, that the present law had not prevented the growth of the Social Democrats, but one did not do away with laws merely because crime was increasing. Without the present law, Social Democratic successes would have been much greater. In the 1870s they were beginning to make astonishing conquests in the countryside, but the exceptional law had stopped this development. If the law were allowed to lapse altogether, the country would immediately be flooded with propaganda and the Social Democratic party would increase its strength by leaps and bounds. Even the Center party was beginning to realize that outright repeal would be irresponsible and that if the law were to be dismantled, it would have to be done gradually.[6] In this article, published only a few days before the *Norddeutsche* attack on Stoecker, the *Kreuzzeitung* tried to associate Bismarck closely with the antisocialist law and a general, all-out fight against social revolution, and thus, by implication, also with Puttkamer and the clerical-Conservative, Stoeckerite campaign. The article thus began by denying the common assessment that Bismarck's foreign policy had been more successful than his domestic policy. It was the Liberals who had insisted on going too far in the Kulturkampf. "Where is there more security and order, where is there a more careful, more effective administration, a fairer administration of justice than in Germany?" The *National Zeitung* had advocated a return from exceptional laws to "a normal condition." "We cannot regard as a 'normal condition' that revolutionaries should enjoy the same freedom as peaceful and loyal citizens." With enemies such as the Social Democrats there could be no compromise.[7]

The growth of the Social Democratic party in Germany certainly did pose a difficult problem. Although the February cartel election, with its artificially inspired war scare, had reduced its Reichstag seats by half (see above, p. 16), it had nevertheless, in the face of this all-out attack, actually increased its total vote. *Germania*, representing another mass party, pointed out nervously that the Social Democrats had not been prepared for that election, but that they were now preparing for the next one, and that the liquor tax, the higher tariff on grain, the generally high level of taxation, the longer Reichstag term, and perhaps a more severe antisocialist law would give them a strong basis for agitation. In early October the Social Democrats had held a party congress in St. Gall in Switzerland, and their revolutionary rhetoric had caused a stir in the bourgeois press. The German Socialist leaders had also sent a telegram to the governor of Illinois, urging leniency for the convicted anarchists in the affair of the Haymarket bombing. In the Reichstag budget debate the Social Democratic leader August Bebel had declared that German statesmen, intent on raising the tariff on grain, were acting as if the "state were an insurance society at the cost of the poor. . . . Yes, when I see how you are operating in every area, then I must say: you are in fact working for the overthrow of the present order of state and society in such a way that almost nothing remains for us to do."[8]

Nor were the threats of disorder and revolution confined to Germany. In America there were the Haymarket bombing in Chicago, constant reports of anarchist activity, and the open publication by Tammany Hall in New York of a scale of financial contributions to the party necessary to ensure Democratic nomination to various state and local offices. In France the Daniel Wilson scandal had just broken, wherein it was discovered that the son-in-law of President Jules Grévy was selling high decorations out of the Elysée Palace. The *Frankfurter Zeitung* might protest that the French system was only a travesty of parliamentary government and by no means the real thing, but it was hard to refute the Conservative argument that France was clearly ruled by the changing majorities of the Chamber, and that if parliamentary government meant the rule of the majority, then the obvious muddle and scandal of the French situation were inherent in the system. "What a bottomless abyss of dirt and immorality is here revealed!" wrote the *Kreuzzeitung*. "How much, in fact, does a nation lack that has no prince by the Grace of God in whose person the idea of the state is concentrated, in whom the nation sees itself as one, whom it can love and cheer with enthusiasm!" And even in liberal England, the city of London in the fall of 1887 was being terrorized by riots of the unemployed in Trafalgar Square and elsewhere, and the Liberal party was trying to capitalize on these disturbances and the continuing violence and disorder in Ireland by supporting the cause of the rioters and rebels and accusing the Salisbury government of police brutality. Queen Victoria herself protested to aristocratic Liberal leaders that William Gladstone was directly inciting "resistance against all authority." Even liberal Germans were shocked by these excesses, and the *Norddeutsche* was able with some satisfaction to quote at length an article by the London correspondent of the left-liberal *Berliner Tageblatt*, complaining in regard to the English situation, "Of what use is the very best constitution, written or unwritten; of what use are the most beautiful speeches of Gladstone to the ordinary peaceful citizen, if he may not dare to walk on the street without running the danger of being murdered by a mob?"[9]

Although the Center party was quite concerned with the challenge of the mass appeal of the Social Democrats, and although the possibility of a basic turn to a Conservative-clerical block, as advocated by the *Kreuzzeitung* and suggested in the Reichstag majority for the tariff bill, might seem attractive, nevertheless the Center party was not ready to support any strengthening of the antisocialist law. First, the Center had had its own bitter experience with exceptional laws in the Kulturkampf—the only precedent for banishing German citizens from the Reich was the 1874 law against the Jesuits. Second, as already indicated by the attitude of *Germania* in the Stoecker affair, the party leadership was more interested in the attitude of the government than it was in that of the Conservative party or of the *Kreuzzeitung*. Third, the Center party believed profoundly, with the left Liberals, that the only way to bring the working class out of its alienation was through positive reforms and positive recognition of its needs and rights. In its opinion, however, it was the fight that the modern world had waged against religion and the church that had developed the basis for socialism. It was liberalism that had first developed naturalistic philosophy and the revolutionary myth and that had seduced state and society into devoting themselves to purely materialistic purposes. Thus the Center agreed with the anticlerical left Liberals that the working class should be conciliated, but put the emphasis more on social than on political reform. It agreed fundamentally with the *Kreuzzeitung* Conservatives that the best solution was to return the church to a larger role in school and society, but it disagreed on the necessity of retaining harsh disciplinary measures in the meantime, such as the antisocialist law. The latter should be repealed completely, but from a practical point of view it would be better to do this gradually.[10]

If, after the November sentence of the doctors on the crown prince, it had been so important for the National Liberals to disassociate themselves from "agrarian reaction" that they had voted against the tariff bill by more than three to one, certainly it was even more important now for them not to get caught in the trap of the more drastic provisions of this antisocialist bill. The National Liberal *Kölnische Zeitung*, which was close to the government, in a thoughtful, two-part article rehearsing the history of the law against socialist agitation, pointed out that the German people were especially susceptible to "theoretical views of situations" and were thus easily persuaded that socialism was as respectable a Weltanschauung as any other. Consequently the great virtue of the antisocialist law had been to point out to the masses that socialism was not compatible with the "existence of the state and common morality," and to thus force a milder, reformist tone on the Social Democratic party. Nevertheless, the paper also refrained from approving the severer measures contained in the new bill. The official *National Liberale Korrespondenz* stated simply and diplomatically that passage of the bill would be "difficult." The left-leaning *National Zeitung* went further and declared that National Liberal party approval of the stronger measures was "out of the question." To this negative Liberal stance the *Kreuzzeitung* responded that if the government had found from experience that it needed stronger measures against the socialists, then it was the duty of the "parties of order" to give it what it asked. It then quoted the *Konservative Korrespondenz* in saying that it assumed that the left-Liberal habit of automatically attacking every legislative measure designed to "safeguard order and authority" had ceased to dominate the National Liberals, but if not, then the basis for political cooperation with them would have been "strongly shaken."[11]

This Conservative statement provoked an even stronger and clearer declaration from the *National Zeitung*. The antisocialist law—since the Center party was negatively disposed toward it—would simply be renewed "in a fashion to be determined between the National Liberals and the government." The Conservative party would have to agree to it. As for Conservative threats, the National Liberals had allied with the Conservatives a year ago in the cartel in order to defend the Reich. On the basis of that alliance it had been possible to develop a wider agreement concerning domestic affairs, "and we desired it." But such cooperation was possible only if due consideration was given to the "moderate liberal viewpoint." Neither the Conservatives nor the government, however, had responded adequately so far. If things continued this way, then there was no point in Conservatives threatening to leave the cartel, because the National Liberals would not be interested in it any longer either, and they questioned whether the planned lengthening of the term for the Prussian House of Deputies was now desirable.[12] This clash between *Kreuzzeitung* and *National Zeitung* clearly demonstrated the lack of general consensus within the "state-supporting" parties of the cartel, a lack deriving not only from differing economic interests but also from basic disagreement on the relationship between the citizenry and the state power. And, as in the clash over the tariff, so also with the antisocialist law the polarizing tendencies within the cartel were markedly increased by the political reversal of field caused by the cancer of the crown prince—resulting in new confidence among the *Kreuzzeitung* orthodox Conservatives, and confusion and loss of confidence among the National Liberals.

9

The Stoeckerites Breathe Defiance

THE chancellor was not ready to give up the cartel, and, regardless of his original intentions, his present annoyance over the Stoecker affair and the dangerous warmongering of General von Waldersee tended to strengthen the Liberal position in the antisocialist law dispute. The important thing was to prevent the Conservative party from coming under the control of its right wing and destroying the cartel. Thus in early January the governmental *Norddeutsche Allgemeine Zeitung* began to attack the *Konservative Korrespondenz* for supporting Stoecker and the *Kreuzzeitung*. The official Conservative paper did not understand the true defense of conservatism, it wrote. To this the *Konservative Korrespondenz* responded hotly that it understood political tactics perfectly well, but that in regard to the fundamental principles of upholding "the standard of positive Christianity and the Hohenzollern Dynasty" there could be no compromise. The *Kölnische Zeitung* contributed an article ostensibly from a correspondent in South Germany, which pointed out that the value of the new Reich was more appreciated in the South than in Prussia, but for that reason the South Germans would not care to see national politics come under the sway of "a narrow-minded [Prussian] clique." In the National Liberal *Magdeburger Zeitung* an article appeared suggesting that the stand of the *Konservative Korrespondenz* could be explained by the fact that the Conservative party leader most responsible for its direction, the leader of the Conservative Reichstag delegation, Baron Otto von Helldorff-Bedra, unlike his counterpart in the Prussian House of Deputies, Wilhelm von Rauchhaupt, was coming more and more under the influence of Pastor Stoecker and his friends. Soon after the reconvening of the Reichstag after the Christmas recess, it continued, the Conservative Reichstag deputies would have to consider what might be done concerning the line their official paper was taking.[1]

The *Magdeburger Zeitung* ran simultaneously an article that claimed that the attempt of the Stoecker-Waldersee meeting to encourage contributions from wealthy bourgeois to the City Mission had failed completely, that the appeal had not even been drawn up, and that many of those who had attended were trying, because of the press campaign, to disassociate themselves from the mission as much as possible. Prince William would have nothing more to do with it. The *Reichsbote* replied that this statement was completely false, and that Prince William was much too high-minded and courageous to back down before a press campaign. One suspects, however, that there was probably considerable truth in the *Magdeburger* report. On January 3, in a large hall in Berlin, the Christian Socialist party celebrated its tenth anniversary, an event described by the *Kreuzzeitung* as a "victory celebration." Court Chaplain Stoecker's chair at the middle of the head table was decorated with laurel, as was a bust of the kaiser in the center of the stage. At the start of the meeting two magnesium flares were lighted on either side of the bust while the members sang the national hymn (to the tune of "God Save the King" and "America"), "Heil Dir im Sieger-kranz [Hail to Thee with Victory's Laurels]." The editor in chief of the *Kreuzzeitung*, Baron Wilhelm von Hammerstein-Schwartow, was also seated in a place of honor at the head table, along with Pastor Engel, editor of the *Reichsbote*. In his speech Stoecker recognized with gratitude the strong defense against their enemies that the conservative press had recently been providing. He hoped that National Liberals and Free Conservatives would eventually also cooperate with them. "We are not so extreme as they say; we are moderate towards them. We are merely extremely loyal to our king; we are extremely convinced that only a living, practical Christianity can help our people."[2]

At this meeting an address of loyalty to Prince William expressing gratitude for his support of the Berlin City Mission was circulated and signed by those present. At about the same time another address to Prince William from the lower Rhine signed by large numbers of working-class people was reported in the press. It thanked Prince and Princess William for their efforts in behalf of the City Mission. A few days later the press revealed that the Berlin court and cathedral chaplains had sent Prince and Princess William a New Year's greeting that included the passage: "If in the last few weeks of the old year You have experienced that sincere participation in the work of the Kingdom of God may also not occur without opposition, then may the word of the Lord be your guide: 'Whosoever acknowledges Me before men, him will I also acknowledge before My Heavenly Father.'" This message brought a rather noncommittal response from Prince William that made specific reference to his father as well as his grandfather. Eduard von Liebenau, the prince's adjutant, released the statement to the *Kölnische Zeitung* and wrote the crown prince that he hoped it would calm the atmosphere.[3]

When Pastor Stoecker's monthly *Kirchliche Monatschrift* appeared in mid-

January, it contained very vigorous language against the critics of the City Mission, denouncing all of the hostile press as "Jewish papers" and accusing them—including the governmental *Post* and *Norddeutsche*—of "an inexhaustible hatred, a boundless impudence toward the sometime heir to the throne . . . such as one has not heretofore been accustomed to in Prussia." At a meeting of the Conservative association of the Hallesches Tor on January 11 Stoecker reviewed the events of the past year, praising the diplomatic skill of the chancellor and the cartel electoral victory but regretting that the middle parties had not proved to be more reliable. The government social insurance program was excellent, but it should be extended to cover restrictions on hours and conditions of work and unemployment insurance. If one established such measures, there would be no need for an exceptional law against the socialists. In the meantime, however, the present law should be renewed, but in contrast to the position of the *Kreuzzeitung*—Stoecker, after all, fancied himself as a leader of the masses—without any stiffening of its terms. As for the attacks against himself, he certainly was no *Mucker* [bigot]—a man "who sits in the corner and has nothing to do with the world. . . . We are fighters, have practical ideas, and we oppose the enemies of the Fatherland and of the church. . . . Above all, we are also positive Christians. With the half belief such as the *Post* advocates no one will accomplish anything. . . . Most disturbing, however, is the fact that this half-official press dares to assail a Prussian prince. . . . When Social Democrats and democrats undermine the throne, that is understandable; but that one should dare in official papers to deride the future German Kaiser and make him out to be a man who does not know what he wants, that is terrible." This "downright brutal frankness" of Stoecker's provoked the *Frankfurter Zeitung* to admire his courage for openly defying Bismarck's press campaign.[4]

Of greater actual political significance than these defiant gestures of the Stoeckerites were two provocative suggestions of Hammerstein's *Kreuzzeitung*: first, that the campaign against Stoecker had been based on the mistaken assumption that the famous articles in the *Norddeutsche* in December had been officially inspired, whereas they had actually been a purely "private" affair. On January 15 the *Kreuzzeitung* denounced the *Norddeutsche* for deliberately starting the press campaign against Stoecker and the City Mission, encouraging the liberal and "Semitic" press by quoting their articles in its "Journal-Revue" and allowing them to wrap their anti-Stoecker campaign in "the princely mantle of Bismarck." The *Norddeutsche*'s "official drapery," it wrote, was "pure humbug, . . . the Reich Chancellor has taken occasion to give Prince William full assurance that he exerted no influence upon the attitude of the press toward the meeting of November 28." This statement was, of course, true enough, but Bismarck's assurance was false: he had approved Rottenburg's article in advance (see above, p. 42). Hammerstein was trying to turn a private, diplomatic falsehood into a public scandal, to turn the chancellor's weapons back on himself. The second suggestion of the *Kreuzzeitung* was that it was the Liberals that were destroying the cartel and that they were actually opposing the government in their attacks on the Right. The more severe antisocialist bill was a government bill, approved by the whole government, not merely Puttkamer. The National Liberals, however, were apparently not prepared to support the bill, and since the *National Zeitung* had also questioned the usefulness of the extension of the legislative term, there was now really no cartel program left at all.[5]

Along with this pointed criticism of the National Liberals and the attempt to identify its own extreme Conservative viewpoint with that of the government, on January 6 the *Kreuzzeitung* had also gone on the political offensive and, in a lead article, "The Founding of a Christian-socialist Union," had suggested a general association of "believing Christians," both Protestant and Catholic, around a basic program of social reform. The National Liberals, it stated, when they attacked the "high-Tory Hammerstein-Stoecker right wing," were really attacking the conservative *idea*, with the purpose of luring Conservatives into "the great National Liberal mish-mash swamp." National Liberal papers were quick to respond to Social Democratic attacks on plutocracy or the "aristocracy of money," but remained silent when landed property or the agrarian aristocracy came under fire. Besides, the "freedom" program of the Liberals was antediluvian, whereas the great question of the future was the social question. If a true social revolution occurred, it would make the overturnings of 1789 and 1793 in France look like child's play. "Salvation can come only from Christianity and monarchy." Frederick the Great had said once that he wanted to become a true "king of the beggars," and Bismarck had quoted this statement approvingly in the Prussian Landtag in 1865. Bishop Jacques Benigne Bossuet, a hundred [*sic*] years ago, had already warned that the rich must help the poor and ameliorate social conflicts, and the Catholic Bishop Baron von Ketteler had written his famous book *Christianity and the Labor Question* earlier in the nineteenth century, upon which had been founded a Catholic social movement. The efforts of the Protestant ministers Rudolf Todt and Stoecker had come later, but had also been very beneficial. The *Kreuzzeitung* did not advocate a complete amalgamation of these independent movements, but rather *"a union of respected leaders of all parties [sic]* who do not stand for sterile negation, which should have as its goal to work together in the spirit of the Imperial Message of November 17, 1881."[6]*

---

* The speech from the throne to the Reichstag of November 17, 1881, announced a new program of state assistance for the working class.

The comment of the *Norddeutsche* on this *Kreuzzeitung* proposal was that the cartel was also dedicated to a program other than "sterile negation," but that there was no question that the *Kreuzzeitung* Conservatives would rather be politically allied with the Center party than with the National Liberals and Free Conservatives. It doubted, however, that the Center would be interested, especially since they could not hope to gain more than a couple of votes in the Reichstag from such a maneuver. In other words, the chancellor's newspaper was pointing out that the bulk of the Conservative party would not take up a new alignment unless the government approved of it and sponsored it, and, furthermore, a formal Conservative-clerical alliance might very well split the Center party into its aristocratic-agrarian and democratic constituent parts. In the event the *Norddeutsche* was proved to be quite right. A Center-party Berlin newsletter almost a week later retorted that Hammerstein was hardly the one to make such a proposal for unity among Conservatives and the Catholic Center party since he had been involved in the origin of the cartel, which had fought the Center party in the last election. If he was now dissatisfied with the old cartel and wanted to start a new Christian-socialist one, that was hardly surprising, but it did not awaken their sympathy for him. His Conservative Protestant group was neither strong nor independent enough to contribute on an equal basis with the Center party to such an enterprise. "The whole Conservative party organism depends on the good will of the government. If one fine day it should withdraw its hand from the Conservatives, then a remnant would remain large enough, as the old joke has it, to drive away in a cab." If the *Kreuzzeitung* thought that *Stoeckerei und Muckerei* appealed to the Catholics as a program to attract a future following, it added, then it understood neither their feelings nor their taste.[7]

In the meantime, the desire of Prince and Princess William on the one hand and the National Liberal and Free Conservative leaders on the other to somehow soften the Stoecker conflict and extricate the prince from his exposed position without dealing him an obvious defeat led to suggestions in the *Post* and in the *Hannoverscher Kourier* that if Stoecker had the grace to retire from the leadership of the City Mission, then the political aura would be dispelled from it and the purely religious and charitable purposes would remain. This would then draw considerable financial support, which had, after all, been the ostensible purpose of the campaign from the beginning. Even the *Reichsbote* acknowledged that since the organization of the missionary activity was to be expanded, a new, full-time person would be needed for this position, and Stoecker himself declared, in the Hallesches Tor meeting on the eleventh, that the work of the City Mission took up too much of his time. On January 14 Prince William replied to Chancellor Bismarck's letter of the sixth, protesting that he had always tried to remain free from any particular political attachment or association, but that he did not regard his support of the City Mission as in any way political. Having given the chancellor's arguments the most serious consideration, nevertheless he could not in conscience withdraw his support from such an important enterprise, of whose value he was sincerely convinced, a sentiment that was also supported by countless letters and addresses of support that he had received from all parts of the monarchy, especially from Catholics and the lower classes. He would, however, request Stoecker to withdraw from his position as official director of the mission. "Before such a demonstration every suspicion, I believe, of my intentions and my position must cease—if not, then woe to them when I shall give the orders!" The prince evidently was daring to challenge the authority of the all-powerful chancellor and warn him that he would soon be his master. That after growing up in the shadow of the brilliant political manipulations and the personal domination of this extraordinary minister of his grandfather's, Prince William, now aged twenty-nine, should imagine that politics at the end of the nineteenth century was a matter of a king's "giving orders" shows quite clearly what the chancellor was up against.[8]

Prince William had also not yielded completely in the area of foreign affairs and preventive war against Russia. To a great extent his stubborn adherence to a warlike stance was the result of the example of people around him, among whom General Waldersee was only the most significant and influential. Thus Waldersee noted in early January that he was afraid the chancellor was making an enemy of Austria, and that he himself desired "an open and solid reliance upon Austria.... I am not the only one who has the impression that the chancellor is no longer what he was. It becomes ever clearer to me that his son is not the man that we shall need for later." On January 11 Friedrich von Holstein, de facto head of the political section of the Foreign Office, noted that a few days before, Prince William had said, "I have ceased to understand the chancellor's policy; he will yet succeed in estranging us from Austria." And the day before, "The chancellor, for purely selfish reasons, doesn't want another war, although he and my grandfather between them have a moral value of 250,000 men so long as they live. I shall have to pay the interest on this delay later on. I shall have to bear the brunt of the crisis, though I shall be young and weak"—a most interesting comment, indicating that Prince William's belligerency did not come so much from self-assurance as from fear and lack of confidence. On January 9, at a dinner given by Count Lerchenfeld, the Bavarian minister to Berlin, Prince William was still talking very belligerently in regard to Russia, which apparently provoked Herbert Bismarck to snub him openly. By the end of the month the prince and Count Herbert seemed once more to be on friendly and intimate terms, but when Herbert showed the prince a long memorandum from his father to Prince Reuss in Vienna concerning the dangers of preventive war, the prince was still capable of replying—in words reminiscent of Waldersee—"That is very nice, but your father must nevertheless not forget that sometimes the best defense is to attack."[9]

Waldersee's mention of others who agreed with him on the chancellor's deterioration probably referred to Holstein. In the same passage quoting Prince William, Holstein wrote that he agreed with the prince, and that Bismarck's policy reminded him of that of Frederick the Great during the Bavarian War of Succession—"It lacks drive. And he makes it only too clear that he would like to push others forward while sitting still himself. That is why people have lost their trust in him and in Germany." And then, practically in Waldersee's own words, "If I seem to be talking lightly about war, it is because I regard it as inevitable. The only question is whether it will break out at a moment favorable to us or to our enemies." When Count zu Solms-Sonnenwalde, ambassador at Rome, wrote to Holstein in early January, "I know that neither H.M. the Kaiser, you, Count Bismarck, or our officers, would be displeased if war were to break out, but that His Highness [Bismarck] is strongly opposed to it," he was exaggerating only slightly. With August Eulenburg, court master of ceremonies and faithful conduit of court gossip for the *Norddeutsche*, Holstein agreed that "the continuing anxiety is worse than war." Against these reckless sentiments of the younger generation old Prince Bismarck had only the same weapons: public opinion and his own prestige. To two Italian general staff officers he declared forthrightly, "It is my settled conviction and firm intention that we shall have peace for three or four more years. However, we have a military party intent on waging war quite soon. Prince [William] belongs to this party. The only question is whether he will find a minister to carry out this program once he is Kaiser." The officers were impressed by the way Prince Bismarck's hands shook as he spoke. In the National Liberal *National Zeitung* and the Conservative *Deutsches Tageblatt* the chancellor had articles published attacking "the military and war party." "That means the field marshal [Moltke] and me, but also Prince William," noted Waldersee. "I am in a position to prove that these articles come from Bismarck."[10]

Emil Pindter, the pious editor in chief of the *Norddeutsche Allgemeine Zeitung* (he opened each new month in his diary with the words: "Guard and bless me and mine, dear God, also in this month; lead us on every path and graciously watch over us"), had learned on January 10 from Chief of the Chancellery Rottenburg, with whom he regularly consulted, that Chancellor Bismarck had no special message regarding the *Norddeutsche*: "*Ergo content*," he noted. But on the sixteenth, the day after the *Kreuzzeitung's* bold revelation of Bismarck's denial to Prince William of any connection with the anti-Stoecker articles, Rottenburg, freshly returned with Count Herbert from Friedrichsruh, came "flying" to Pindter to prevent the *Norddeutsche* from answering the *Kreuzzeitung* in too strong a manner. "For it is true," Pindter wrote. "Bismarck did write that. 'Obviously,'" Rottenburg had remarked, "'he has forgotten his instructions.'" The Stoeckerites were stirring up Prince William through flattery and were filling him with mistrust of "his grandfather's Richelieu." Perhaps the chancellor could still influence the prince through the weight of his personality, but he was not due to return from Friedrichsruh to Berlin for a while yet, and in the meantime Herbert, Rottenburg, and Holstein had agreed that it would be best to let the matter rest for a bit. "Bismarck," added Pindter, "obviously does not have either the mental or physical endurance for a fight against this Fronde." The ambitions of the Stoeckerites went far beyond the City Mission. "Poor Reich! What kind of times must you live through, and the crown prince hopeless, as Rottenburg also confirms. A gloomy future."[11]

As all these maneuvers and machinations amply prove, it was never necessary in Germany for Bismarck artificially to provoke or manufacture conflict; there was always more than enough to allow him continually to occupy a middle, mediating position. He did prefer, however, to *anticipate* conflicts before they became serious, to nip movements in the bud by depicting them as full-grown plants and thereby arousing against them counterforces inimical to their growth. This was what he had done in both the Stoecker case and that of the "war party." If the crown prince and princess had been able to enter upon a long reign, clearly the tirelessly self-generating bogey of the *Kreuzzeitung* would have helped Bismarck and his heirs and associates immeasurably in keeping them in line. At the other end of the spectrum, the democratically oriented German Liberals and the Social Democrats could always be counted upon to provide the necessary threat from the Left for use in controlling the Conservatives. In the current situation the *Kreuzzeitung* warned the government that if it strayed too far from the Right, it would inevitably strengthen the allure (especially in the event of a quick accession to the throne of the crown prince) of the German Liberals, whereas the *Post* was just as insistent in warning the *Kreuzzeitung* that if it succeeded in leading the Conservative party away from the cartel and the moderate middle toward obvious reaction, this could only cause a public swing to the Left and strengthen the German Liberals in the next election. More specifically, if Bismarck went too far at this point in repudiating Puttkamer, it would amount to a Liberal victory, and he would likely lose the antisocialist law altogether. But if he rallied to Puttkamer and the more severe measures of the government-sponsored bill, he would accept defeat from Prince William and

Stoecker and put himself fatally in the hands of the *Kreuzzeitung*. After the middle of January, the chancellor's return to Berlin was expected, the Conservatives confidently asserting that he would speak in the debate on the antisocialist law, and the Liberals asserting just as confidently that he would not.[12]

Puttkamer had written to Bismarck, explaining and defending his position in regard to the Stoecker affair, and he had received an uncompromisingly severe reply. He was sure, he told Waldersee, that the chancellor was trying to force him out of office, and he was determined to go rather than withdraw his signature from the City Mission appeal. Waldersee noted that he himself, Puttkamer, and Albedyll were agreed that the chancellor was jealous of anyone who wanted to alienate Prince William from his son Herbert. He was seeing ghosts, added Waldersee disingenuously (cf. above, p. 47). It was a "great moment" for Prince William. "If he yields to the chancellor, it will be difficult for him ever to free himself from him." On January 16 Count Herbert informed his father that Radolinski had heard from a number of sources that Puttkamer was advising Prince William "not to allow himself to be dominated by a powerful minister, but that he should rule alone, since he [has] the stuff for it!" Herbert observed that if Puttkamer did not publicly disassociate himself from Stoecker, that might push the task of handling the affair in the party debates in the parliaments onto Bismarck himself. "Puttkamer likes being a minister; I would vote for holding on to him for a while, but with the stipulation that he separate himself from the City Mission. If one forces him out now, he will depart as a 'martyr for Prince William' with the expectation of being re-employed in the top position [Bismarck's marginal comment: "Let him"] after the accession of our hot-headed grandson. To create this platform for him would mean exposing our country to great dangers." On the following day Count Rantzau reported to Herbert from Friedrichsruh that his father did not believe that Puttkamer was consciously double-dealing, but that he was ambitious, irresponsible, and tactless. On January 17 the Conservative party leader in the Prussian Landtag, Wilhelm von Rauchhaupt, was summoned to Friedrichsruh, and on the twentieth the Conservative Reichstag leader, Otto von Helldorff-Bedra. At about the same time old Kaiser William also admonished Prince William about the Stoecker affair and blamed it all on the pious Countess Waldersee.[13]*

---

* Mary Esther Lee Waldersee, the daughter of a wealthy American, was very religious. Her first husband had been the prince of Augustenburg, heir to the duchies of Schleswig-Holstein. She apparently played the role of confidante and sympathetic mother figure for Prince William and introduced him to his eventual wife, Auguste Victoria, an Augustenburg princess.

Meanwhile, the National Liberal party organ, the *National Liberale Korrespondenz*, declared on January 8 that the cartel had been formed to support a national policy and that the continued cooperation of the three parties could be maintained only on this basis. The union had not been formed to conduct "reactionary politics," and the National Liberals would not allow themselves to be enticed away from their moderately liberal position and into becoming merely a Conservative cohort. If the Conservatives wished to strengthen their relationship to the moderate Liberals they would therefore have to refrain from "completely unjustified and impossible expectations and demands." It was not the whole Conservative party that was causing the trouble, but only its extreme right wing, which possessed more influence in the party than it deserved because of its "confidence and assertiveness." A few days later the *National Liberale Korrespondenz* adopted the point of view of the *National Zeitung* and remarked that so far there had been no conference among the cartel leaders in regard to introducing a bill lengthening the term of the Prussian House of Deputies, and it questioned whether now such a measure was "expedient." There was no compelling reason to lengthen the Prussian Landtag term merely because the term of the Reichstag was to be extended, and the Reichstag bill had not been passed yet. Also, Landtag elections did not involve nearly so much agitation as elections to the Reichstag.[14]

On January 13, the day before the opening of the Prussian Landtag, the *National Zeitung* published an article calling for an end to Conservative predominance in Prussia. Since 1879, it wrote, when the Conservatives had taken over the presidency of the House of Deputies from the National Liberals, their numbers had continued to increase so that now the two Conservative parties together were only some twenty votes short of an absolute majority in the House, a position that they had not enjoyed since a brief period in the 1850s. During this time, however, they had done nothing of any significance. The few notable legislative achievements had come on government initiative, and the real program of the Conservatives—increasing the influence and independence of the Protestant church in the state and in the schools—had failed only because of government resistance. Thus in the early 1880s Stoecker and the Center-party leader Dr. Windthorst had led an attack on teachers of natural science in Prussian universities that had the enthusiastic support of a large majority of the House and had forced Minister of Ecclesiastical, Educational, and Medical Affairs von Gossler to come to the defense of academic freedom. In the Reichstag, however, the Conservatives were weaker than the National Liberals, and for the sake of their own non-Prussian members also had to maintain a less one-sided and parochial stance there. Important reforms in the areas of administration, education, and taxation were needed in Prussia, and the record of the past three legislative sessions indicated that not only would a continuation of such Conservative strength accomplish nothing progressive, but that it would be downright dangerous. The *National Zeitung* hoped, therefore, that in the present session, the last before the Landtag election in the fall, the moderate Liberals would demonstrate to the voters, especially in the eastern provinces, the necessity of creating a different division of political power. The same day the *Post* observed that the outbreak of "boundless rage" recently in the clerical-Conservative press indicated a guilty conscience. Their accusations of attacks on Prince William were intended to obscure the fact that they themselves had introduced the political element into the City Mission affair. As for Stoecker's circulating an address of loyalty to Prince William, such an act went against the *Post*'s monarchical feelings since "the reverse of the medal cannot be avoided." The response of the *Konservative Korrespondenz* that "a Hohenzollern prince does what seems good to him, by his own free decision" and that the *Post* was trying to destroy the image of the prince's "unusually clear, sharp intellect and great firmness of character" before the public seemed rather overdone.[15]

On January 14 both houses of the Prussian Landtag assembled in the White Hall of the old Berlin castle, where Vice-President of the State Ministry von Puttkamer read the king's speech before the draped throne, followed by the usual three cheers for the king, led by the president of the Herrenhaus, the duke of Ratibor. There was nothing in the speech from the throne, observed the *Kreuzzeitung*, that would support the prophecy of the *National Zeitung* of the "end of the Conservative era." With the political leaders now once more in Berlin, the National Liberal leadership (Bennigsen, Miquel, Heinrich von Marquardsen, Hammacher, and Robert von Benda), along with the Free Conservative leaders, under pressure from Bismarck via Rottenburg, signed the City Mission appeal, thus freeing it from a one-sided political aspect. In Friedrichsruh the chancellor read Helldorff his letter to Puttkamer, and the Conservative leader agreed to work to downplay the Stoecker affair. This, Rottenburg wrote to Rantzau, must have required "a decided glance from H.H.'s eyes. Five days ago Helldorff had quite a different attitude." An attempt was apparently also made to get the crown prince and princess to join the City Mission drive, but they would have none of it. Among their private papers there is an undated, unsigned draft in pencil that states: "Every attempt to deprive Stoecker of his activity is to the good. Since we, however, cannot judge the lay of the land, we remain, true to our principle, aloof from all such enterprises. We cannot beforehand grant express permission in this matter."[16]

At the end of January the City Mission appeal (having in the meantime been slightly amended by a committee made up of Waldersee and Puttkamer as well as Court Chaplains Kögel and Stoecker and President

Ottomar Hermes of the Evangelical Superior Church Council and then redrafted by the National Liberal leader, Johannes Miquel) was published in the press, Stoecker's name having been removed from among the signers. When the Conservative deputy von Minnigerode tried to provoke a debate on the City Mission affair in the Prussian House of Deputies, he was promptly put down not only by the German Liberal Alexander Meyer but also by the Free Conservative leader, Octavio von Zedlitz-Neukirch, who merely remarked that such references (that is, to the royal family) were not proper in the House. At the end of December the *Frankfurter Zeitung* had made the sarcastic suggestion that Stoeckerites and government papers could easily make peace if "Herr Stoecker declares that he has never seen Prince William and confirms this with a sworn statement; then the *Post* can declare itself satisfied and formally withdraw the accusation that any attempt has been made to secure the prince for '*Stoeckerei und Muckerei*.' The *Reichsbote* and *Kreuzzeitung* then in turn take back their verbal insults against the *Post*, the *Kreuzzeitung* especially confesses that its 'last shaft, that the *Post* henceforth bears on its brow the brand of felony and common slander and has incurred the general contempt of all true royalists' was not so badly meant." Things had not actually gone quite that far, but a certain similarity in the line of development was nevertheless recognizable. Court Chaplain Stoecker, however, was not the sort to drop modestly out of sight. In the Reichstag, during the debate on extending the legislative term, he seized the occasion to thank the National Liberals ironically for overcoming their scruples and joining in the support of the City Mission. It did not need their patronage, he said, but he was grateful for it. The unofficial wit of both Reichstag and Prussian House of Deputies, German Liberal Alexander Meyer, remarked subsequently in the House that the Stoecker affair reminded him of the story of the soldier who called to his captain, "*Herr Hauptmann*, I have taken a prisoner, but the nasty fellow won't let go of me! (much laughter)."[17]

10

The Chancellor Appeals to the Nation

ON January 28 Chancellor von Bismarck finally arrived in Berlin. Minister of the Interior Puttkamer, who had stated that day in the Reichstag in response to a jibe of the German Liberal leader, Eugen Richter, that he was proud to serve the Reich chancellor and hoped that the latter would continue to head the government for a long time to come, hastened to report to the elder Bismarck, still convinced that he would be summarily dismissed. To Puttkamer's surprise, the chancellor brushed off his signature on the City Mission appeal as a matter of no importance. The Reichstag debate on the antisocialist law had begun the day before, but the chancellor did not intend to speak in that debate; Puttkamer was to be left to bear that burden alone (see below, pp. 124, 127). He did plan to speak in the debate on the new defense bill. General von Waldersee, when he heard of Bismarck's change of attitude toward Puttkamer, was amazed and overjoyed. "Prince William," he wrote, "has achieved a great success in this matter, which is due solely to his steadfastness. An event of great significance." Waldersee also noted with satisfaction that at a meeting of Free Conservatives and National Liberals, where Princess William's chamberlain had explained the City Mission situation, there had been much criticism of the duplicity of the two Bismarcks. "While they declared to Prince William in the most definite way that they had nothing to do with the articles of the *Norddeutsche* and the *Post* and had done nothing to oppose the prince's purposes in the whole affair, several of the men present said that they had proof that the chancellor has incited other papers, such as, for example, the *Hamburger Korrespondenz*, against the prince. These revelations are very sad, but cannot be denied." Waldersee was convinced that such a manner of acting had cost the chancellor support in every party.[1]

It is likely that the men of the moderate parties did indeed go out of their way to convince Prince William's confidant Waldersee that they were all for the prince. At the same time one remains skeptical that they really cared about the Bismarcks' cavalier double-dealing. As basically hostile to the Stoeckerites as they were, they could only be grateful for the opportunity to place most of the blame for the anti-Stoecker campaign on the old chancellor and his son. In a sense the Bismarcks, because of the old man's prestige and actual political clout, were just as much above the parties as the monarchy. Foreign Office Counselor Holstein agreed with Waldersee that the chancellor had made a mistake in the method he used to instruct Prince William. Holstein thought that Bismarck should have approached the prince privately and not in the public press. But since Count Herbert had at the very beginning of the Stoecker affair privately admonished Prince William, and it had done no good, there was every reason for giving the naive and opinionated prince, before he succeeded to the throne, a strong taste of what kind of trouble unthinking and headstrong behavior could get him into. The tendency of both government officials such as Holstein and party men, however, to treat the young prince's personal inclinations—in the style of the *Konservative Korrespondenz*—as an overriding political factor indicates how strong the traditional, monarchical, authoritarian habit of mind still was, even among experienced public men and after twenty-five years of the Bismarck system. Whether the Bismarcks could continue for long to control this factor would depend ultimately on their political credibility; and the elder Bismarck was seventy-three years old and in precarious health.[2]

Although the *Septennat* defense bill had been introduced and fought through only a year before, nevertheless the government had introduced a new defense bill in mid-December. The new bill did not touch the peacetime strength of the army, which had been set in the *Septennat*, but substantially raised the number of troops available in wartime by lengthening the term of service in the reserve from twelve to nineteen years and reintroducing a second Landwehr (National Guard), which had been abolished in the 1860s. *Germania* and some of the liberal papers greeted the bill with hostility and complaints about the militarization of life. Bismarck had claimed, wrote Catholic *Germania*, that his policy of the 1860s (construction of a "little" Germany under Prussia) would bring peace and security, but the opposite had been the case. The new Germany had been forced into constantly increasing armaments, and its security was more tenuous than ever. Similar articles complaining of ever-increasing defense burdens and constant terrorizing of the public appeared in the *Frankfurter Zeitung* and even the *National Zeitung*. The radical *Berliner Volkszeitung* denounced the "Moloch of Militarism."[3]

It soon became apparent, however, that for many reasons Center and German Liberal deputies in the Reichstag were not inclined to oppose the government's new army reform. For one thing, since the reorganization would come into full effect only in wartime, it would not require any great

immediate expenditure of funds. Second, in a time of genuine international tension, with Russian troops continuing to mass on the Austrian
frontier, it would not do to deny the nation any reasonable increase in
its defenses, especially considering the reaction of the public to the defense
issue the preceding February. For these reasons only the Social Democrats
opposed the bill in the first reading, and it was approved unanimously in
committee. Even the left-liberal *Frankfurter Zeitung* had to admit at the end
of January that the bill would easily pass. It hoped that in exchange the
nation might receive some tranquillity. It was the duty of the government
to see that this occurred. The *Times* of London wrote admiringly, however,
that Germany was making "a splendid—almost sublime—effort for the
maintenance of peace."[4]

On January 31 the *Kölnische Zeitung* announced that Chancellor Bismarck would speak in the Reichstag on the second reading of the defense
bill, and on February 1 the *Frankfurter Zeitung* confirmed this with a report
that the chancellor would speak on the general diplomatic situation. On
Friday, February 3, the Austro-German Dual Alliance treaty was simultaneously published in Vienna and Berlin, causing a small sensation. In
the meantime, Bismarck had called leaders of the Conservative party, the
National Liberals, and the Center individually to the Chancellery for
consultation. In political circles speculation began to grow over the likely
contents of the chancellor's speech on Monday, February 6, and the impression spread that it might announce a decision as to peace or war.
When that day dawned, the atmosphere of Berlin had become electric
with expectation. The Leipzigerstrasse, site of the old Reichstag building,
was closed off. Seats in the galleries of the Reichstag, noted Baroness
Hildegard von Spitzemberg, were selling for as much as 500 M. Hours
before the Reichstag session began, the building was surrounded by a
dense crowd, eager to catch a glimpse of Bismarck. A dozen policemen,
on foot and on horseback, kept order with difficulty. Inside, the vestibule
was packed with people and the galleries were overflowing in a crush such
as the oldest members could not recall. The court and diplomatic loges
were filled with ambassadors, court officials, and royal princes, including
Prince William. At the long Bundesrat table on the dais to the right of
the president only the chancellor's seat at the end was empty. On the
floor, where for the last two weeks debates had been carried on without
enough deputies present for a quorum, the seats were only about two-
thirds occupied. "A new indication . . . ," wrote the *Frankfurter Zeitung*'s
'N' correspondent, "that no one is more indifferent and obtuse politically
than German representatives."[5]

Shortly after 1:00 P.M. Reich Chancellor Prince von Bismarck rode up
to the Reichstag building in a coupé drawn by two horses. The crowd
broke into shouts and cheers that could be clearly heard inside, where the

president of the Reichstag was waiting for the chancellor's arrival to begin the session. Both Minister of Agriculture Lucius and the *Magdeburger Zeitung* reporter agreed that the tense and expectant atmosphere in the House was like that at the beginning of the Franco-Prussian War. At length the little door behind the rostrum opened, and the towering figure of Prince Bismarck was there, as usual wearing his gray cuirassier's uniform with the yellow collar and carrying a red dispatch case. The House rose, he acknowledged the gesture with a wave of his hand, bowed to the president, and sat down. *Germania* described him as looking tired, the *Magdeburger Zeitung* as "powerful and energetic, otherwise rather pale, but not like a man in his seventies upon whose shoulders rest heavy cares." After the president had opened the session, he recognized the chancellor, and the old man rose and delivered a speech that lasted almost two hours. His normally high, weak voice seemed weaker than usual and could be heard only with difficulty in the galleries. He spoke with his hands clasped behind his back, emphasizing important points by bending forward at the waist. Frequently he refreshed himself with glasses of wine and seltzer water, which Count Herbert, standing behind him, especially mixed for him. After about an hour he had to sit, and remained seated while he continued to speak for about a quarter of an hour, when he stood again and remained standing until the end. The House listened with strained attention in a hushed, absolute silence.[6]

Only at the beginning of the speech did Bismarck refer to the army bill. He hoped, he said, that the Reichstag would pass it with a large majority. He then proceeded to survey the history of Germany's foreign relations for the past fifty years in a very judiciously mixed combination of emphasis on peace and on Germany's military strength and new national unity and determination, along with a rather remarkable clarity of perspective and calm sense of humor. Germany, he said, would never begin a war; there had been many occasions when war tension was greater than now and war had not actually occurred; it was better not to try to second-guess Divine Providence; and the Bulgarian question was not important enough to be allowed to break the previously good relations with Russia. If any other nation began a war, however, it would feel all the force of the *furor teutonicus*. He also suggested obliquely that if the Russians tried to settle the Bulgarian question diplomatically, they would be supported by Germany. Wilhelm von Kardorff, leader of the Free Conservative party, wrote to his wife that the speech was probably the most outstanding of all Bismarck's performances. The speech, noted Baroness Spitzemberg in her diary, impressed her as "splendid; moving in its earnestness, its manly dignity, the calm self-confidence such as is possessed only by the truly strong; it appears to me as a legacy of the great man to his people, an appeal to them to guard the greatness that he has created." The *Börsen Zeitung* commented in a similar vein: "He has shown us that we are operating conscientiously, honorably, but that above all we must build on our own strength."[7]

After the concluding peroration, containing the well-known words, "We Germans fear God and nothing else in the World!" the House broke into an uproar of applause and cheers. The statement, of course, was far from true; it was an exhortation on the part of the chancellor to his countrymen *not* to be afraid; and doubtless it was the reality and depth of the fear that made Germans seize upon the phrase with such enthusiasm. After the old man had sat down, and the president had continued the debate, the leader of the Center party, Baron Georg Arbogast von und zu Franckenstein, immediately rose and moved that the Reichstag adopt the defense bill in its second reading en bloc and without further debate. In an atmosphere of great enthusiasm and excitement, punctuated by cheering and applause, the leaders of the Conservative, Free Conservative, National Liberal, and even the German Liberal parties gave their affirmative support. The president asked for objections—there were none, and the bill was passed unanimously. The whole extraordinary proceeding had taken fifteen minutes. The silence of the Alsatians and the Social Democrats, who were fundamentally opposed to any such bill, was caused either by their complete absence from the hall or by the intimidation of those deputies who may have been present by the general atmosphere of enthusiasm and expectation. When Heinrich Rickert, the German Liberal leader, rallied to passage of the bill en bloc, Prince Bismarck was seen to nod his head in satisfaction and to mouth the word, "Bravo!" After the president announced unanimous passage of the bill, Bismarck again rose and thanked the deputies not only for the demonstration of their confidence in the government, but also for the support they had thereby given to the further guaranty of peace.[8]

When Bismarck emerged from the Reichstag building, he found that because of the shortness of the session his carriage had not yet arrived, and, in the face of the huge, cheering crowd in the street, he decided to walk the short distance back to the Chancellery in the Wilhelmstrasse. Five mounted policemen went ahead to clear a passage, and the excited, cheering crowd followed all the way to the Chancellery door, many trying to touch the great man, Court Herbert fending them off as best he could with his back and his elbows. At the Chancellery followed more cheers and singing. Probably no statesman, wrote the *Kölnische Zeitung*, had ever been so greatly acclaimed. The whole event was a splendid production, a national celebration of confidence and good feeling. All the major newspapers carried the full text of the speech; the *Norddeutsche* issued it also in a special, extra edition; and 235 officials of the telegraph office worked night and day at 222 separate machines to send the speech out in 1,218 separate telegrams to 326 different places inside and outside Germany. The whole press, with the exception of the far Left, greeted the speech with enthusiasm and praise. "No German," wrote the *Kölnische Zeitung*, "has ever recognized as the Reich Chancellor did yesterday the value of the spirit that lives in the people." The left-liberal *Weser Zeitung* wrote that "never yet has the nation been shown by a great man its own likeness in such proud lines and luminous colors, and it would be strange if these words did not kindle in the hearts of the listeners an urge to resemble the picture." Perhaps Baroness Spitzemberg best summed up the general feeling when she noted in her diary that the moment when Franckenstein arose to first move en bloc approval of the defense bill was "overpoweringly beautiful and moving. . . . It was a beautiful, proud day for us." Minister of Agriculture Lucius was able to detect larger political implications. "In these difficult times," he wrote, "the feeling of solidarity, of trust, the knowledge that the political guidance of the country is in the firm hands of the chancellor, this is an immeasurable advantage. The life of the crown prince and the preservation of peace, those are the two driving concerns, and one appears as uncertain as the other."

The very uncertainty of the situation in both foreign and domestic policy, the danger of war, the contradictions and intrigues among parties and cliques, all these factors had been brilliantly exploited by the chancellor, as impresario, in order to accomplish several things at once: to appeal once more to the tsar in a reasonable and convincing way; to calm the general international atmosphere and yet warn Russia against provoking a war; to impress Prince William with the dangers of warmongering and with the nobility, sanity, and popularity of a peaceful policy; and to nail that policy so firmly to the masthead of the Reich in a public fashion that no one, whether prince, Foreign Office, or general staff, could haul it down. Also, by stepping into the breach in a dramatic, public way, the chancellor reassured the nation and emphasized a united, national (cartel) policy, once more bolstering his own political position, reaffirming his unique standing in the hearts and minds of the Germans, and displaying and further strengthening his political prestige and power.[9]

In subsequent days reactions to Bismarck's February 6 speech continued. Tsar Alexander sent him a big barrel of caviar. A jeweler in the Friedrichsstrasse advertised a small commemorative medal in silver and gold with the bust of the chancellor on one side and the "We Germans fear God" quotation and the date on the other. In Chicago a meeting of Germans sang a special set of words to the tune of "Die Wacht am Rhein," with the chorus, "Furor teutonicus, teutonicus! [repeat]." The city of Cologne planned to send the chancellor, an honorary citizen, a silver platter with the "We Germans fear God" quotation engraved on it. To the members of the Prussian State Ministry, Bismarck confessed that he had noticed the effects of his age in speaking, that connections between ideas did not occur to him as quickly as before, but the ministers assured him that the audience had certainly not had that impression.[10]

One of the more notable results of the speech was a toast that Prince William delivered on February 8 at a banquet for the members of the Brandenburg Provincial Landtag given by the governor [*Oberpräsident*] of the province. He was well aware, he said, that the general public, especially abroad, considered him to be eager for war—"God preserve me from such criminal frivolity; I reject such accusations with indignation!" Then he closed with a special adaptation of the words spoken to the Reichstag on the sixth by "our great chancellor"—"We Brandenburgers fear God and nothing else in this world!" Afterwards the prince sent a major with a copy of the toast to Pindter for the *Norddeutsche*; Pindter wrote in his diary, "Bravo! So he too does not want to be a warmonger! Very good." A couple of days later the *Frankfurter Zeitung* noted that the prince's toast was being purposely circulated as widely as possible in the official press in order to deny the existence of a war party in Berlin. The prince, reported Austrian Ambassador Count Imre Széchényi to Vienna, was trying by his remarks to remove the bad impression left by the Stoecker meeting and the tension that had resulted in his relations with the chancellor. Even General Waldersee confessed to his diary that he had advised Princess William to give vent to her annoyance with the Bismarcks less in public, since it was necessary for the prince to continue to work with them.[11]

Reaction to the Bismarck speech, however, was not uniformly favorable. Later in the same afternoon it was delivered, Pindter met Foreign Office Counselor Holstein in the Tiergarten and found him upset by the peaceful tone of the chancellor's speech. It only showed, he said, that one should never develop an opinion of one's own. "The gentlemen do seem to have been agitating strongly on their own hook," noted Pindter. Four days later Pindter wrote that Holstein, and Dr. Rudolf Lindau (the Foreign Office press officer), as well as Count Herbert Bismarck himself, all seemed to disapprove of any calming of the international situation. As far as they were concerned, Bismarck's speech had been merely a comedy, which he did not himself believe. His own comprehension, commented Pindter, did not extend to that degree of hypocrisy. Furthermore, it was not clear to him why the Foreign Office should seem to be concerned mostly with whether the stock market went up or down.[12]

On February 7 August Stein reported in his column in the *Frankfurter Zeitung* that in the Reichstag immediately after the chancellor's speech he kept hearing people in the foyer asking each other, "But what did he really say? Are we going to have war or not?" thus demonstrating to what degree they had missed the main point of the speech: that Germans must learn to live with uncertainty and be confident in their own strength. During the early part of the speech, Stein observed, he had seen much head-shaking when Bismarck had made light of the international crisis. Public opinion in Europe generally was so overheated that a calm appraisal of the situation appeared unbelievable and false. The *Frankfurter Zeitung* itself was pleased with the speech; it had wanted peaceful assurance from the government, and Bismarck had given it. *Germania*, although applauding the patriotic behavior in the Reichstag of the Center party leader, Franckenstein, and generally treating the Bismarck speech with approval and reverence, nevertheless showed distinct misgivings. The Reichstag had passed unanimously and with not the slightest protest a bill that imposed heavy new financial and personal burdens, especially on "hus-bands and fathers of families." In later issues it dealt rather gingerly with the speech itself, clearly demonstrating distress over its pro-Russian tone. The chancellor, for example, had said that at the time of the Treaty of Berlin in 1878 everybody had expected that Russian influence would be preponderant in Bulgaria, but, protested *Germania*, there was "*nothing at all* [sic] about this in the peace treaty!" The sovereignty over Bulgaria was left to the Sultan in Constantinople, and therefore other nations (namely, Catholic Austria) had as much right to influence in Bulgaria as Russia! On the far Left the Social Democratic leader, August Bebel, had already declared in the debate on the antisocialist law in the Reichstag a week before the chancellor's speech that Bismarck's attitude in the Bul-garian question made one wonder "whether he is a German or a Russian minister." On February 17 the left-liberal *Berliner Volkszeitung* carried an article headed "On Future Occasions" that declared that Liberals, instead of joining unthinkingly in "great moments of German history" and "a general hurrah," would do well to consider soberly the heavy burdens being increasingly laid on the necks of the people. German foreign policy had no call to encourage the megalomania of the tsar.[13]

11

Tracheotomy

A few days after the chancellor's speech in the Reichstag, one of the two great uncertainties facing the German people suddenly increased in intensity. A rapid swelling in the larynx of the crown prince had made it progressively difficult for him to breathe, and on February 9 Dr. Bramann performed a tracheotomy, administering chloroform (Dr. Mackenzie apparently was against this, but had himself no experience in surgery), very swiftly and expertly making a small incision in the trachea just above the collarbone, and inserting a silver tube through which the crown prince could now again breathe freely. Mackenzie and the crown princess had delayed the operation until the last minute, and Dr. von Bergmann had not had time to travel to San Remo to perform the operation himself. He now arrived, however, to oversee the process of healing and recuperation.[1]

At the end of December 1887, Queen Victoria had written in her journal of "the great improvement in dear Fritz's condition!" and two days later Lord Salisbury wrote to the queen congratulating her "on the encouraging news which has been received from the Crown Prince. His recovery will give universal joy in this country as well as in Germany." Two weeks later the queen sent a coded telegram to Sir Edward Malet in Berlin asking what was the real state of health of the old emperor and declaring, "Think there is little doubt C[rown] Prince's trouble in throat is not malignant and life not imperilled; but the throat will remain troublesome and, whatever happens, he could not return in the winter to Berlin. Most important that the C. Prince should be kept informed of what is going on, for he is perfectly well and able to transact any business." To this Sir Edward immediately replied that he had asked Herbert Bismarck the same day if the crown prince was kept informed, and Herbert had assured him that a special courier was sent every ten days to San Remo with summaries of reports and events. "Sir Edward Malet's conviction is," he continued, "that his Imperial Highness may trust implicitly in the present crisis to

Prince Bismarck, and that his Imperial Highness's rights and interests will be jealously guarded by him." None of the favorable reports on the crown prince impressed the hardheaded Dr. von Bergmann, however. At the end of December he predicted a turn for the worse in February.[2]

The speech from the throne opening the Prussian Landtag on January 14, it was noted, was more positive in tone as to the possible recovery of the crown prince than the speech opening the Reichstag had been in November. Dr. Mackenzie was still saying that it was not cancer, and he assured the crown prince's chamberlain, Count Radolinski, that the illness could go on for three or four years. In his reply to the New Year's greeting of the Protestant pastors of Berlin, the crown prince expressed the "hope, that with God's help through continued improvement my health will strengthen and establish itself." Only at the end of January did a special consultation of Mackenzie and the other doctors in San Remo give some hint of a more serious turn to the disease. The bulletin from the assembled doctors stated cryptically that breathing was normal and that there was no need for an operation. Only on February 1 did a report appear that the crown prince was suffering from coughing and neuralgic pains of the head. Actually, he had indicated in his diary already on January 19 that he was feeling generally unwell. As late as February 3, however, Dr. Mackenzie was still issuing positive bulletins.[3]

The report of the tracheotomy caused a sensation in Berlin. Members of the Reichstag crowded around the bulletin board with the latest telegrams, and the crown prince's health became the sole topic of conversation. In court circles the operation was regarded as the beginning of the end, which was now expected in four to six weeks. "An extremely tragic fate," wrote Lucius, "without parallel in history. This handsome knightly figure! The next to the throne for almost thirty years, field commander in three victorious campaigns, brave, mild, nobly human, and this end! . . . With this certainty attention is naturally strongly attracted to Prince William, who is highly gifted, full of temperament, but who also fills even his most enthusiastic admirers with some anxiety. . . . All observers are always emphasizing his lack of maturity—especially striking at the age of twenty-nine." Shortly after the report of the tracheotomy had reached Berlin, Prince William had approached Bismarck with the question whether he would serve him when he came to the throne as he had served his grandfather. Yes, said Bismarck, if the prince did not plan to make war and was ready to profit from his own considerable experience. The prince seized his hand and shook it warmly.[4]

Although the tracheotomy was followed by reports that the incision was healing nicely, it was clear that the crown prince's general health was declining. Headaches and sleeplessness became more common, and the discharge now expectorated through the tube was more copious and stained as if with blood. To counteract the effect of these reports, Dr. Mackenzie prepared a report of his own on February 12, which he had the crown prince authorize to be published in the official *Reichsanzeiger.* On February 16, possibly because he (or the crown princess) feared that Berlin court circles might hold up the report and prevent its publication, Mackenzie also released it to the *Berliner Tageblatt.* This report, published in the *Reichsanzeiger* on February 16, reviewed the history of the case since November, emphasizing the lack of any conclusive, factual evidence of the presence of cancer, especially the negative results of the microscopic analyses of Dr. Virchow. Mackenzie's conclusion was that the only certainty was the existence of a "chronic, deeply seated inflammation of the larynx combined with perichondritis." Mackenzie also issued reports to the press that the bloody discharge was caused by irritation from the German-made tube, which did not fit correctly. Reports also surfaced in London papers claiming that in his nervousness, Dr. Bramann had not exactly located the trachea and had got the incision off center. The ill-fitting German tube had been successfully replaced by an English tube. Actually, the right-angled English tube provided by Mackenzie had proved uncomfortable to the patient, and the curved German tube had had to be put back in place. The discharge obviously came from the cancerous larynx itself.[5]

Naturally the dogged optimism of Mackenzie was picked up and supported by the left-liberal press, which sensed that it was thereby supporting the crown prince and princess. On February 16 the *Norddeutsche* reprinted a report from the *Freisinnige Zeitung* stating that the already feverish excitement of the Berliners over the condition of the crown prince had been increased by new reports of plans for a deputizing or regency law, "by means of which the crown prince is to be eventually either temporarily or permanently excluded from the government." Although these reports stemmed from a "respectable source," the *Freisinnige Zeitung* did not believe them, but if such intentions actually existed, then the reports of Virchow and Mackenzie would take on special significance. The *Norddeutsche* commented that the author of this article had been identified as the German Liberal Reichstag leader, Eugen Richter himself, and went on, "What can he intend with such completely unfounded remarks?" This, wrote *Germania*, was "a very legitimate question." The National Liberal *Hannoverscher Kourier* suggested that Richter was trying to *create* "feverish excitement" with unfounded rumors. Doubtless, in calling attention to the *Freisinnige Zeitung* article, the *Norddeutsche* was pointing out to the more rabid Conservatives, especially at court, what a marvelous public issue they would present to the left Liberals if they again tried to force a regency on the royal couple against their will. That such intentions were once more flourishing among right-wing Conservatives may easily be surmised.[6]

On February 19 the *Frankfurter Zeitung* tried to put the regency rumors to rest with a sensible, carefully reasoned lead article, possibly inspired by the government, that pointed out that, according to the Prussian constitution, the heir to the throne automatically became king upon the death of the present king, whether he was capable of ruling or not. The constitution stated that if the king was "permanently incapacitated," the next male heir who had reached his majority would become regent, with the approval of both houses of the Landtag. But whether "incapacity" existed could not, of course, be decided by anyone other than the king himself. That is, the king could give up his right to rule voluntarily, but could not be deprived of it. He could appoint a representative or deputy, however, at his pleasure. If the crown prince as king, for example, had to remain outside the country, he could appoint Prince William as his deputy. Since the king of Prussia was automatically also German emperor, these rules also applied to the Reich. Three days later the semiofficial *Berliner Politische Nachrichten* commented that such discussions were unecessary since nothing of the sort was contemplated. On the same day Chancellor von Bismarck told the Prussian Ministry that there was no need for a regency law. There was no vacuum—"The crown slips through the keyhole of the sick room. Meanwhile the ministry continues to conduct affairs until the further determination of the sovereign." Bismarck, noted Lucius, was "especially calm and definite in everything he said, and obviously prepared in his decisions for all eventualities."[7]

A week later, on February 27, the *Kölnische Zeitung* also carried an authoritative article, repeating the statements in the *Frankfurter* and emphasizing that the stipulations of the Prussian constitution on the succession and the incapacity of the king were so clear and the application of these regulations to the Reich so obvious that no special regency law was in any way required. Two days later the left-liberal Berlin *Vossische Zeitung* carried the discussion a stage further by pointing out that the difficulties did not lie in the legal stipulations for a regency but in the actual conditions under which it might be carried out. The questions of under what circumstances the king was to be declared "permanently incapacitated" and who was to be the final authority in making this decision were matters of "outstanding importance." In an article on March 1, the *Frankfurter Zeitung* declared flatly that absence from the country and inability to speak, even if declared incurable, would not constitute permanent incapacity. It had determined, however, from a "reliable source" that the old kaiser had already signed an order that Prince William should represent him if he were to be temporarily incapacitated. Since this report was subsequently reprinted in the *Norddeutsche* without contradiction, the press generally accepted it as true.[8]

Given the obvious weakness of the crown prince and the appearance of the colored discharge, two schools of thought developed in Berlin as to likely future developments. The pessimists, including not only such enthusiastic right-wing Conservative supporters of Prince William as General von Waldersee, but also such moderates as the Reichstag Conservative leader, von Helldorff-Bedra, many National Liberals, and even a left Liberal like Roggenbach, assumed that the discharge was coming at least partially from the lungs, and that therefore the crown prince's life would soon be over. This development, they believed, was to be preferred, since a short reign for the crown prince would create great confusion and uncertainty. (It was because Dr. Mackenzie had prevented the drastic operation the previous year, which they assumed would have decided the life-or-death issue at once, that this group so resented him.) The optimists, on the other hand, believed that the lungs were not affected, and that the crown prince would soon recover his strength and would live for some years. To try to bring more certainty into the situation, the doctors called in a lung specialist, Dr. Adolf Kussmaul from Strassburg, who examined the crown prince on February 26 and 27 and pronounced the lungs as yet unaffected. In the meantime, however, Dr. von Bergmann and Dr. Bramann had prepared a microscopic display from the discharge and declared cancer cells were present in it, an opinion with which Dr. Kussmaul agreed. Dr. Mackenzie, however, insisted that a pathological specialist be called in to examine the preparation, and, since Professor Virchow had gone on an archeological expedition to the Near East, Professor Waldeyer of Berlin was chosen. In his report Waldeyer agreed on the evidence of cancer, but the report was suppressed, which was regarded by the public as ominous in itself.[9]

By the end of February it was clear that the crown prince's general health was superficially improving again, and Bergmann urged that he immediately be brought back to Berlin. It was generally agreed that it would be neither politically advisable nor proper for the crown prince to die abroad and that he personally would not want to, but it was difficult to convince the crown princess. On February 22, at a meeting of the State Ministry in the Chancellery, Bismarck complained that it was practically impossible to get through to the crown prince directly, and that the crown princess kept him isolated. The animosity between the German and English doctors had grown to unbelievable proportions. The kaiser, however, would not command his son to return, and the chancellor was afraid that if the crown prince was ordered to do so, "the Anglophiles and the democrats will raise a cry that it is murder." The crown princess was willing to consider moving her husband in April to Wiesbaden, where the climate was milder than in Berlin, and then back to Potsdam in May, but Dr. von Bergmann warned that if the present favorable conditions were not taken advantage of, it would then be too late to bring the crown prince back to Berlin at all. The main difficulty was the steadfast refusal of the crown princess to accept the idea of cancer and her husband's imminent death. "Although the crown princess," Radolinski wrote to Holstein, "has heard from all sides that cancer has been diagnosed, . . . she nevertheless obstinately maintains that it is all nonsense, that he will recover, and that . . . Mackenzie will prolong his life by all sorts of devices, etc. She is very optimistic and gay." Radolinski stressed to the crown princess the impossibility of the crown prince's actually ruling from abroad, and this seemed to make an impression. Rumors surfaced in the press that the crown prince and princess were considering returning to Berlin at the end of March.[10]

12

An Advisor for Prince William

SINCE Prince William was the nearest male heir, the question of his father's "permanent incapacity," especially in the event of the sudden death of his grandfather, was a matter of personal concern and responsibility. During February he became progressively more wrought up over the situation, spending a good deal of time with General Waldersee and confiding in him. He wanted to go to San Remo, but his mother told him to stay away. Very likely, there was pressure from the ultraconservative *Kreuzzeitung* side upon the prince to prepare himself to declare a regency, on his own responsibility if necessary. On February 23 Waldersee expressed to his diary his concern over the situation that would be created if the old kaiser were suddenly to die. "The worst confusion would be unavoidable. The crown prince can certainly not rule, but under pressure from his passionate wife can probably do damage enough. And precisely because she knows that her rule will be of short duration, she will try to avenge herself on her adversaries and ensure her future. It is questionable to what extent Prince William allows this to happen." On the twenty-seventh he also noted "how much influence Prince William is winning and [how he] is actually feared by most people; he can definitely not be so immature as many like to imagine." After dining with Holstein—with whom, he noted with satisfaction, he was once more "on the good old footing; he is really working in my interest, as I discover from many sources"—Waldersee wrote on March 3 that it was astonishing how opinion concerning Prince William had changed recently. "He is supposed to have become more serious, more mature, and I don't know what all." This was all nonsense, added Waldersee; people merely knew that he could soon be kaiser and wanted to place themselves in a good position. Prince William had not changed a bit, but had learned a few things in recent months.[1]

On February 22 Chancellor Bismarck told the Prussian Ministry that he sympathized with the prince's desire to go to San Remo. It was unnatural that he should be the only one of the children not near to his father at this critical time. On the one hand, his staying away was regarded by the public as hardheartedness, but on the other, if he went to San Remo he would be accused of going to find out how much longer his father had to live. A few days later the kaiser designated Prince William to attend the funeral of young Prince Ludwig of Baden, and the prince requested Bismarck to intercede with his grandfather to let him proceed from Karlsruhe to San Remo. The old kaiser reluctantly agreed but stipulated that Prince William should come right home again and not go off on a pleasure trip to Rome. He arrived in San Remo on March 2 and stayed until the fifth. Although Radolinski wrote to Holstein that "while here he was very nice in every respect," the crown princess—who had vainly telegraphed Prince William not to come—was sure that he was acting in San Remo as if he were already king.[2]

Meanwhile on Prince William's birthday, January 27, Kaiser William had finally yielded, in spite of the inevitable extra expense, and had raised his grandson to the rank of major general, which would mean that the prince would have to move away from the Potsdam garrison and to Berlin, where he would be closer to responsible government and army leaders. "The previous, rather confined life of the prince in Potsdam," wrote Ambassador Széchényi to Count Gustav Kálnoky von Köröspatak in Vienna, "and his intimate association with the officers of his regiment, whereby his undeniable predilection for roisterous Junkerism was ever more encouraged, have not exerted a favorable influence on him and have lost him the sympathies of many people." The prince had been so fond of his hussar uniform that the old kaiser joked that they would have to chloroform him to get it off. Herbert Bismarck wrote to his brother Bill, "Now the prince moves into the [Berlin] *Schloss*; I am happy that he is finally out of Potsdam, but [in English] a precious time has been irretrievably lost!"

National Liberals, including Miquel and Bennigsen, made attempts to develop ties with Prince William to offset the number of Conservatives among his associates. The government also finally appointed a civil advisor for him—two, in fact. The crown prince had accepted Bismarck's suggestion and had made the request of his father. Although Minister of Justice Friedberg praised Under State Secretary of the Interior Herrfurth as "extremely knowledgeable, moderate, disinclined to any extremism, judging and handling everything objectively," the crown prince remained hostile to him because he had been brought into the Ministry of the Interior by Puttkamer. Also, Prince William himself, who had met the bearded Herrfurth at a dinner, declared that he reminded him of Rübezahl (a wood demon of the Riesengebirge) and was too old and boring. The prince wanted a companion who would hunt, converse, and play cards with him. The chancellor told the Prussian Ministry that he thought it would be wise to go along with the prince's preference as much as possible. The prince had a candidate of his own, a counselor to the governor in Magdeburg named von Brandenstein, whom he had met at a hunting party. Minister of the Interior Puttkamer observed that the man was very competent but rather inclined toward frivolity and carousing. Bismarck thought that did not matter as long as he was capable. For serious instruction, the prince would also be given as advisor the seventy-two-year-old professor of law at the University of Berlin, Dr. Rudolf Gneist, who had previously instructed the crown prince and would thus be acceptable to him. Herbert Bismarck had written his father that Prince William would not be sufficiently impressed by a younger man, and Bismarck had decided that the advisor should be a lawyer so he could "make clear to him the powers [*Machtbefugniss*] of a Kaiser and king." To the ministers he explained, "The prince has as yet very little understanding of and respect for the law." Gneist would give the prince two lectures a week, and Brandenstein, who would also attend, would then go through the material of the lectures with the prince and supplement and explain them—"a very good plan," said the chancellor.[3]

Professor Gneist was a National Liberal, and the *Kölnische Zeitung* disgusted the *Kreuzzeitung* by reporting proudly that Gneist "enters a position of trust similar to that at one time occupied by the present minister of justice [Friedberg] with the crown prince." The appointment, added the *Kölnische*, was at the direct suggestion of Prince Bismarck. The appointment of a Liberal as advisor to the prince, commented the *Frankfurter Zeitung*, "has the same significance as the signatures of the National Liberal leaders under the Stoecker appeal." The *Kreuzzeitung*, however, growled that "we do not believe that it is 'good' politics for the *National Liberals* [*sic*] to advertise their man in this way."[4]

Inhibited from attacking the crown prince outright because of their deference to the monarchy, the Conservatives tended to take out their apprehension and frustration on Dr. Mackenzie. In late February a dispute broke out between the *Vossische Zeitung* and the *Berliner Tageblatt* over which was the official newspaper for Mackenzie, and the Conservative and government press found this disgusting. On the twenty-fourth the *Kreuzzeitung* printed a lengthy article from the party *Konservative Korrespondenz* pointing out that respectable German newspapers had reported on the illness of the crown prince with great restraint out of regard for the prince's feelings, since he could easily read the reports himself. But other papers, especially the Jewish press, had printed all the information and rumors they could dig up, exploiting the sympathies and interest of the general public and swinging from optimism to pessimism in the most sensational and irresponsible way. Dr. Mackenzie had not given his information to all the papers, but only to the two (the Jewish-owned *Vossische* and *Tageblatt*) that paid the most for their articles. The German people were indignant over this creature who had inserted himself between them and the sickroom of the crown prince. An Italian paper had complained that whereas Mackenzie had always been very friendly and cooperative, Dr. von Bergmann, when its reporter had approached him, had thrown him out. Commented the conservative paper: "We thank God for the *German* doctor, who . . . thus restores the disgraced nobility of his profession." At the end of February, apparently under pressure from Berlin, the crown prince forbade his doctors to give out any more information to the press. Whether this order would improve the situation was doubtful. On March 6 the *Reichsanzeiger* published a statement signed by all doctors in attendance in San Remo—including Bergmann and Mackenzie—that denied any basic disagreement among them, stated that the specific situation of the crown prince had not changed, that there was no immediate danger, and that appealed to the press to refrain from discussing the handling of the case, overall responsibility for which remained in the hands of Dr. Mackenzie.[5]

13

Puttkamer on the Defensive: The Antisocialist Law Debate

NATURALLY the new crisis in the health of the crown prince placed further stress upon the relations of the parties of the cartel. These relations were already strained enough, as was clearly evidenced in the debate in the Reichstag over the government bill to extend and strengthen the antisocialist law, which began at the end of January (see above, p. 105; for previous reaction to the bill, pp. 87–92). As early as January 8 the *Hamburger Nachrichten* had announced the basic position of the National Liberal party. In contrast to the assertions of the right-wing conservative *Kreuzzeitung* that the cartel was conservatively oriented, the *Hamburger* declared that it was the duty of the National Liberals to maintain their independent identity as a liberal party, especially in the light of attacks by the German Liberals. Therefore, continued the *Hamburger*, the National Liberals should unite behind a proposal to renew the antisocialist law for the usual period, with no change, with the understanding that during this period a plan would be worked out to make the law unnecessary. This would be a reasonable compromise. It was generally realized that the secret agitation under the law was dangerous, and that the measures already used or proposed to contain it were useless. The Center party's *Germania* called this suggestion "practical" and "quite correct." Probably the National Liberal party was trying to show both government and crown prince that it could rise to the occasion and save the situation in a reasonable, responsible way. The *Kreuzzeitung*, however, was not impressed. The necessity to prove their liberalism, it wrote sarcastically, was understandably causing the National Liberals "anxiety . . . such as genuine 'reactionaries' can hardly imagine. This continual limping toward both sides must actually be a quite tiring way to walk." But in the special political situation, National Liberal concerns were likely to receive more sympathy in the Chancellery than those of the right-wing orthodox *Kreuzzeitung* and the Stoeckerites. At the end of December Chancellery Chief Franz von Rottenburg had written Herbert Bismarck that the new expatriation provision was quite unworkable and, in any case, undesirable; and that Social Democrats would be more dangerous in the United States than at home in Germany under the eyes of the police. The important thing was to "handle the dissenting National Liberals with indulgence" in the debate.[1]

On January 16 the text of the antisocialist bill and the government's explanatory argument for it were published. The statement admitted that although the law had prevented revolutionary outbreaks and the spread of socialism to the countryside, growth of the movement had not been prevented. Nor had the revolutionary orientation of the party been changed. At least ten thousand copies of the Zürich *Sozialdemokrat* were currently being secretly circulated among German workers, plus several thousand copies of a couple of anarchist papers. Persons who were concentrating professionally on overthrowing the state should not be allowed to continue to belong to the state. Agitators who were judged by a court to be liable to expatriation would then be subject to actual expulsion and deprivation of citizenship by the individual state to which they belonged; this action would then be respected by all the other states in the empire. The fact that the expatriation provisions had not been taken out of the bill, in spite of all the negative comment, was something of a shock to the *Frankfurter Zeitung*. The main purpose of the bill, it noted, had not been mentioned: to banish all Social Democratic members of the Reichstag from Germany.[2]

The day after the publication of the bill, the National Liberal leader, Rudolf von Bennigsen, informed Rottenburg that it had no chance of passage in its present form. Even some of the Conservatives would vote against it. Both he and Johannes Miquel assured Rottenburg that a renewal of the present law was all that could be expected. Bennigsen asked Rottenburg in some excitement if it was true that the old kaiser was putting special importance on the new, harsher provisions of the bill, which, with other comments by Conservatives, led Rottenburg, as he wrote to Bismarck's son-in-law Kuno Rantzau, to suspect that Stoecker and the Conservative right wing were planning an all-out attack on the National Liberals and the cartel over the issue. But Count Rantzau replied that Stoecker himself, according to press reports, had spoken publicly against the expatriation clause. Rottenburg had also written that he assumed that the chancellor could not speak against the bill and would not speak against the National Liberals, and if he wanted the timing of the debate speeded up so that it would be over before he came to Berlin, to let him know. Rantzau replied that His Highness would not speak on the antisocialist law in any event, so it did not matter whether he was in Berlin or not. He had said that if he was really to expect any success from the law, expatriation would not be enough. The only effective measure would be to place socialists under the ban and take away all their legal rights and protection. But the situation "was not ripe" for that; perhaps if the law was repealed outright, it would be. So he was uncertain as to whether it might be better to have no antisocialist law at all, but rather to take extreme measures instead. Expatriation was a "half measure." Thus the chancellor covered up his actual retreat with belligerent and threatening language.[3]

With the publication of the bill the discussion in the press intensified. The left-wing National Liberal *National Zeitung* stated flatly that the Social Democrats would have to be allowed to operate publicly like any other party. One should remember, growled the *Kreuzzeitung* in response, how things had been ten years ago, when Social Democrats could indeed "operate like any other party. . . . an unbelievably wild agitation raged through the entire Reich . . . because . . . the naïve part of the population said to themselves, if something like that was permitted it probably wasn't so bad." These were irreconcilable revolutionaries; they would not be conciliated by social reform; and if the movement could not be suppressed entirely, at least it could be contained. On the contrary, wrote the left-liberal *Frankfurter Zeitung*, history had shown that "the use of police power against ideas" had never worked.[4] In reply, the *Kreuzzeitung* conceded that the socialist movement, international in scope as it was, might not be completely or permanently suppressed. But if the Reichstag could summon nerve enough to deprive the Socialist party of its leadership by strengthening the present law, it would be possible to contain the movement for a long time. The history of the success of the Counter-Reformation in Austria and South Germany and of the crusade against the Albigensians in medieval France proved that it was indeed possible to suppress ideas. In the United States a law was currently being prepared that would provide for deporting notorious anarchists, and there seemed to be very little opposition to it. But of course anything the Americans did was all right with the liberal press since they were republicans, whereas the same sort of measure in Germany was "reactionary." To this the *Frankfurter* replied that the *Kreuzzeitung* had overlooked the fact that the American law was to apply only to foreigners, whereas the German Reich was recommending such a measure against its own citizens.[5]

At this point the *Kreuzzeitung* brought heavier guns into the exchange. The oppositional attitude of the National Liberals toward the government's antisocialist bill was merely a further indication of their "drift to the left," of their hankering to work toward the formation, with the German Liberals, of a "great Liberal party," doubtless cooperating in the next Prussian Landtag election in the fall against the Conservatives, especially in the eastern provinces. The *Kreuzzeitung* did not suppose that the National Liberals wanted to break up the cartel; it would be useful to maintain it. Rather, it suspected them of wanting to create "a second purely 'Liberal' majority" next to the cartel.[6] The current party strength in the House of Deputies of the Prussian Landtag was as follows:

Conservatives	132
Center	98
National Liberals	72
Free Conservatives	62
German Liberals	40
Poles	15
"wild"	14
	433

Since the two Conservative parties together lacked only twenty-three votes of a majority, it would be difficult to explain this professed concern of the *Kreuzzeitung* over a "Liberal majority" if one did not consider the possible effect on the next Landtag election of a swing in the support of the *government* toward the Liberals, possibly under the aegis of a new Liberal minister of the interior in the place of Puttkamer after the accession of the crown prince.

The Prussian agrarian Junker gentry had always been dependent on the crown, largely because of their relative poverty but also because of the essentially military character of the Prussian state. The entrenched position of Junkers in the military and civil bureaucracy and the restricting effect of the Prussian three-class voting system tended to perpetuate this dependence. The notorious three-class system was an arrangement of indirect elections, inserted in the constitution in the postrevolutionary era, in 1850, whereby equal numbers of electors with the duty to meet together and choose the deputy for the district were elected by three classes based on a division of the tax list. Taxpayers were arranged according to the amount of taxes paid. Those at the top, whose payments constituted a third of the total taxes, made up the first class; those whose payments amounted to the second third made up the second class; and the rest the third. The members of the upper two classes of this Landtag electorate, the taxpayers responsible for two-thirds of the taxes, were a small group (about 15 percent of the population), especially in the country districts, and together they usually elected the deputy through their two-thirds majority among the district electors, to the complete exclusion of the votes of the representatives of the huge third class. As a small group they were easily influenced by the Landrat, the local magistrate, who was on the state payroll, under government discipline, and serving at government pleasure. Thus, although Conservative strength in the House of

Deputies, as a result of the pre-Bismarck liberal era, had fallen by 1862 to the extreme low of only 11 members, Bismarck's successful confrontation with the Liberals during the *Konfliktzeit* caused Conservative strength to rise by 1870 to 116. Then, as Bismarck, engaged in constructing his new Reich, moved back toward the Liberals, the Landtag Conservatives came into conflict with the government, with a resulting drop in strength in the House of Deputies in 1873 to only 32. The subsequent turn of the Bismarck government toward protective tariffs and away from the Kulturkampf had meant a swing back toward the Conservatives, and under the Puttkamer regime the Conservative party had risen to its present point.[7]

With the cartel in disarray over the antisocialist law and the government, as evidenced in the *Norddeutsche Allgemeine Zeitung*, taking up a remarkably noncommittal or quiescent position, the Social Democrats themselves seized the initiative and mounted an effective offensive of their own. A week before the opening of the Reichstag debate on the antisocialist bill, the Social Democrats distributed among the members an impressive summary of court and police actions taken against individuals under the provisions of the present law. Then on the opening day of the debate the Social Democratic leader and deputy from Berlin, Paul Singer, led off with a long, detailed exposé of the activities of agents provocateurs on behalf of the Prussian political police among Social Democrats and anarchist exiles in Switzerland, obviously prepared with the assistance of Swiss police authorities. Put on the defensive in this manner, since the police came under his department (and conscious of a lack of all-out support in the Chancellery), Minister of the Interior Puttkamer was clearly embarrassed and had difficulty in responding in an effective, convincing way. It was apparent that the government would be willing to accept a compromise. In fact, the only speaker who supported the sharper measures of the government bill was Baron von Helldorff-Bedra, the Reichstag leader of the Conservative party. The National Liberals chose as their speaker neither Bennigsen nor Miquel, but the second-string South German Marquardsen, who spoke only in favor of extending the present law. Many liberal employers, he said, had told him that it had basically improved the situation and that they feared a return to the conditions of 1878.[8]

The course of the Reichstag debate naturally distressed the right-wing conservative *Kreuzzeitung*, which saw it as not a matter of factual criticism of the bill, but rather a concerted attack on the "Puttkamer System." With their expectations on the crown prince, the National Liberals were willing to cater even to the Social Democrats in their attempt not to appear reactionary. Since the Center party, however, was also against the government bill, there was nothing the Conservatives could do; they would have to accept the National Liberal formula. The *Kreuzzeitung* pointed out bitterly that it was liberals who had started the revolutionary process, and "liberalism must regard socialism as its pupil." The *National Zeitung*, it went on, which had been most prominent in leading the National Liberal party to the left in recent months, was really delighted with the Social Democratic attack on Puttkamer. Actually, the effectiveness of the Socialist attack on Puttkamer and his ineffective defense had indeed done him considerable damage.[9]

In the Reichstag commission the new, harsher measures in the bill were rejected, and a large majority voted merely to renew the present law for two years. The lack of a strong defense of the bill by the government astonished the *Frankfurter Zeitung*. Only last year the Reichstag had been dissolved merely over the difference between a three-year and a seven-year term for the army budget. "This benevolent tone toward the Reichstag," wrote August Stein, "is new and unusual." In the second reading of the bill on February 13 the proposed changes in the law were rejected against the votes of the Conservatives, and the old law was renewed for two years with a vote of 164 to 80, 11 Center party members voting for the extension, and 40 against. On February 17 the bill passed the third reading with the same majority. It was approved by the Bundesrat on March 1.[10]

In an article published a few days before the beginning of the debate on the antisocialist law, the *National Liberale Korrespondenz* had complained that the government could have avoided a likely defeat for the bill if it had consulted the "authoritative factors" in the Reichstag. The *National Zeitung* had then announced that the National Liberal party would decide what should be done with the bill, and, in the event, the National Liberals had indeed led the cartel majority to successful passage of their own compromise two-year extension of the existing law. The two-year term was chosen so as to give the present Reichstag a further opportunity to deal with the antisocialist law before its term expired. In order to achieve this success the National Liberal Reichstag leadership had had to enforce the strictest discipline, threatening any deputies who did not vote as instructed with expulsion from the party. They had thus been able to dominate the situation in the Reichstag and direct the whole cartel majority. In demonstrating their political power, however, they had also taken on the responsibility for what happened next, as both the government *Norddeutsche Allgemeine Zeitung* and the Free Conservative *Post* reminded them. Since the government in introducing its stronger bill had declared the present law inadequate and ineffective, the two-year extension of this law without change was bound to dissatisfy everybody. Nor was it easy to decide how to replace it, since strengthening the civil code against various kinds of political agitation or threats to law and order would limit the rights of free expression and assembly of all the other parties as well as the Social Democrats. In reality the two-year extension was merely a delaying tactic, because the National Liberals had no idea what to do. The electorate would not be impressed.[11]

The implications of this quandary were boldly confronted by the *National Zeitung* in articles on February 21 and 23 that declared that the social "peace" achieved by the present law was false in that it had created an underground defiance of the government that was seriously undermining general respect for law and authority. If one wanted to return to the basis of the common law and give up special laws against the socialists, this would necessarily mean granting the Social Democrats the same rights to act and agitate publicly as other parties. It would be healthier to have the agitation out in the open where it could be watched and controlled. More normal circumstances would also improve the positive impact of the government's social insurance legislation upon the working class. Repressive measures under the present law had tended likewise to repress any workers' efforts to organize for purely practical and material purposes. Repeal of the exceptional legislation would again make it possible to distinguish between revolutionary sentiments and revolutionary acts, only the latter being punishable under the criminal code. Doubtless a general Reich law regulating organizations and assembly would have to be passed. The *National Zeitung* also thought that since monarchy and religion were already sufficiently protected by laws in force, as were public and state officials, private property also needed to be protected. How typical of the "Manchesterish" *National Zeitung*, commented the *Norddeutsche*, that it should regard throne and altar as sufficiently protected, but not property! The *Preussische Jahrbücher*, on the other hand, was shocked that Germany's "whole political life should be placed under laws strict enough to contain a movement like the Social Democratic! . . . Our restraining legislation is truly severe enough." The National Liberal call for a return to the common law simply meant repeal of the antisocialist legislation. The *Kreuzzeitung* agreed: the "threads" that the *National Zeitung* was spinning would not suffice to restrain the socialists. Furthermore, a new provision it recommended against "inciting the masses" appeared to be directed more against the anti-Semites than against the Social Democrats. It would gladly free Singer in order to contain Stoecker![12]

14

The Cartel Unites on
the Legislative Term Issue

IN enforcing a compromise solution to the imbroglio over the anti-socialist law and in signing the City Mission appeal (see above, p. 103), the National Liberal leaders had moved to reassert the claims of the cartel program and the power of their own position at the head of "the most favored party in the Reich" (to use the *Kreuzzeitung*'s phrase) against the now rather unreliable Conservatives. They had also, however, it now became apparent, made the Conservatives the positive concession of continued support for the extension of the length of the legislative session, both in the Reichstag and in the Prussian House of Deputies. Although the Reichstag bill had been discussed extensively in the press it was not brought up for debate until February 1. In this first reading of the bill, Rudolf von Bennigsen lent the prestige of his personal leadership to the debate. In reply to an accusation of the Center leader, Windthorst, he declared that it would be irresponsible to tamper with universal, equal, secret, direct suffrage. "We [the National Liberals] do not want a jot or tittle of the existing fundamentals to be changed. (Bravo! on the left)." He pointed out that a three-year legislative term existed elsewhere only in Scandinavia; that Holland and Belgium had four years; Spain, Italy, and Hungary five years; Austria six; and England seven. The government power of dissolution, so stressed by the German Liberals, was not so easy to carry out; one could not always count on the success of the preceding year. With a longer term the Reichstag would be more effective and would therefore acquire more authority. It was true that Germany did not have parliamentary government. And he must admit that he did not think such an arrangement would suit Germany; he wondered, in fact, if it was not already obsolete in England. Germany had "a monarchy that is still so strong and effective (lively applause right and left) that it is hardly likely to reduce the monarchical principle [*Fürstenthum*] to the point of playing the role of merely putting the dot on the i, as in other constitutions." For the people really to participate in power, the Reichstag must take its place alongside the monarchy, the army, the church, and the bureaucracy, and it could do this better if it "were not torn apart through the miserable personal battles of the party leaders, through being split into factions in such a way that finally neither a majority nor an agreement is possible. (lively applause right and left)."[1]

On the other side of the issue, the German Liberal leader, Ludwig Bamberger, declared that the National Liberals were "past[ing] liberal labels on reactionary measures. . . . They are not stopping the reaction, but are being dragged ever further along in its train (very true! on the left). . . . The basic idea of our Conservatives, however, is to do away with the constitution (contradiction on the right). Ask in England, or in Italy, or in Belgium, Gentlemen, countries that you are always holding up to us as horrible examples because of the misfortune of their parliamentary constitutions, ask anybody if he would exchange his situation for ours, and you will see what a contemptuous [*verachtende*] reply you will receive. (great disturbance on the right and among the National Liberals)." The German Liberal and old Progressive leader, Eugen Richter, explained that the times had changed since 1867, when there was some hope of a new liberal Germany. Now, rather than the chancellor being responsible to the Reichstag, the Reichstag was practically responsible to the chancellor. The new National Liberal strength had been accomplished with the assistance of the government. Back in the early 1880s National and German Liberals together were strong enough to hold off the reaction, but then the National Liberals had moved to the right and had supported the Conservatives instead of the left Liberals in the run-off elections of 1884 and 1887 and thereby helped the Conservatives achieve a position where they could form a majority with the Center party and put through "certain reactionary plans." The conservative press was full of suggestions for changing the suffrage and perhaps even replacing territorial with corporate representation. The National Liberals were "optimistic upwards [toward state authority] and pessimistic downwards."[2]

The cartel party press naturally heaped praise on the Bennigsen speech. Even the ultraconservative *Kreuzzeitung* called it "generally splendid." The government *Norddeutsche Allgemeine Zeitung* called the speech "convincing." The National Liberal *Kölnische Zeitung* pointed out that the "reactionary" drift of the National Liberals claimed by Bamberger hardly squared with the fact that it was the National Liberals who were at that very time most responsible for beating back the attempt to strengthen the antisocialist law. The *Konservative Korrespondenz* observed that the German Liberals were trying unsuccessfully to discredit the National Liberals with the electorate. The *National Liberale Korrespondenz* pointed out that Germany had achieved a position of power such as it had never possessed in its whole history, and that political, economic, and social conditions were "more favorable and more gratifying than those of any other country." The *Hannoverscher Kourier* asked who in Germany would want to exchange the government of Bismarck for one of Richter, Rickert, and Bamberger? No doubt the question and the warning were aimed at San Remo as well as at the *Kreuzzeitung*.[3]

Strong in their Reichstag majority, the cartel parties refused to send the bill on the legislative period to commission, putting it through its second and third readings on February 7 and 9, during which the Free Conservative leader, von Kardorff, reminded the parties that since it had just won a great election victory, the cartel had no reason to be dissatisfied with universal suffrage. "Every party today," he went on, "that mounts an assault on universal, direct suffrage cuts its own throat." The Center party leader, Ludwig Windthorst, declared that a longer period between Reichstag elections would mean merely that the agitation would be that much more intense, not less. "In the next [elections] it will be war to the knife." The bill was passed overwhelmingly and accepted by the Bundesrat on the twenty-third.[4]

In the meantime a similar bill had been introduced into the Prussian Landtag, where, because of the much greater strength of the Conservatives and the upcoming election in the fall, the tone of the party conflict was even more strident. To embarrass the National Liberals, the German Liberals had introduced an amendment to the Reichstag bill calling for provisions of per diem expenses for members of the Reichstag, and now in the Landtag they submitted an amendment providing for the introduction of the secret ballot for Landtag elections. Since a vote for these measures, which were also favored by the National Liberals, would destroy the alignment of the latter with the Conservatives, they had to vote them down. The electorate, declared the National Liberal *National Zeitung* confidently, would not be misled by this opportunistic tactic of the German Liberals. Baron Hugo Sholto Douglas declared in the House that the government's right of dissolution did not necessarily represent merely the power of the government, but also that of the people. "What success [a dissolution] has when government and people are united we saw most strikingly last year." To speak of constant conflict between the crown and the parliament, stated the Free Conservative leader, von Zedlitz-Neukirch, showed "a complete ignorance of the foundations of the Prussian constitution," which rested on "the trust of the crown in the people and of the people in the crown."

The aristocratic Center party leader from Westphalia, Baron Burghard von Schorlemer-Alst, saw it differently: "When the participation of the people [in government] is . . . more limited—as it is with us—then the constitutional rights of the people and the voters should not be tampered with." An enlightened absolute monarchy would be preferable, he declared, to the "pseudo-constitutionalism" that was developing, in which "no one knows and can tell who is finally responsible." The National Liberals, said Windthorst, to the amusement of the House, were mere "pseudo-Conservatives." In a lead article on February 15, the *Frankfurter Zeitung* wrote that the National Liberal party had sunk to the position of "lackey of the reaction." The cartel parties, suggested Catholic *Germania* sarcastically, were extending the legislative period merely to demonstrate that they could accomplish something together. "They want thereby to take precautions that the fragile Cartel does not fall apart *before* the 'New Era.'" The bill was passed in the third reading in the House on February 13 by a large majority. According to the provisions for amendment of the Prussian constitution, it would have to be voted again after a lapse of at least three weeks.[5]

During the Reichstag debate the *Kreuzzeitung* had once more suggested that for the extension of the length of the life of the legislature to become fully effective, the present system of majority elections should be changed to a plurality system, as in Saxony. The plurality system, by eliminating the run-off elections, would prevent the parties from making purely tactical and "unnatural" alliances, which so benefited the opposition parties. In the election of 1887, for example, the German Liberals had received only eight or nine seats on the first ballot. It was true, commented the left-liberal *Frankfurter Zeitung* on this proposal, that under the plurality system, since neither the Center nor the Social Democrats would be willing to refrain from putting up their own candidates, the Conservative parties would win the plurality in a number of districts presently German Liberal. Stoecker, for example, would win in Berlin, a result that in itself was sufficient explanation for the *Kreuzzeitung*'s view. During the debate Stoecker himself had denied any opposition to universal suffrage as such, but had suggested raising the minimum voting age from twenty-five to thirty. To a meeting of his Christian-Socialist followers in Mundt's Salon on the Köpernickerstrasse on February 10 he had repeated his denial concerning universal suffrage, but had pointed out that if voting were organized corporately instead of territorially, then people would be voting according to their profession instead of by where they happened to live or how much money they had, and so "like could elect like to represent them, not, as the situation is now, the workers the big capitalist [laughter] or the pensioned lieutenant."[6]

To Catholic *Germania* the purpose of the government in encouraging the extension of the legislative period was to further reduce the populace to "trusting submission." They did not want parliamentary government, they stressed, any more than the government did, but there should be "understandings" between the government and the people. The parliamentary deputies "should not be the *guardians* of the people, but their *proxies*, they should be the *expression* of the people's wishes and desires." The cartel majority was obsequious toward the government and arrogant toward the electorate. The voters, however, would not be pleased to have themselves declared immature in this fashion, and they would chastise the cartel parties at the next election. The cartel deputies were forgetting that they were deputies, not "government officials." They were making the parliaments even more oligarchical in a time when the masses, the "fourth estate," were necessarily making their historic bid for recognition and power. The cartel policy of "increasing the people's burdens, reducing their rights, and avoiding or refusing necessary religious and social improvements, this is driving the *masses* of the people gradually to Social Democracy and in the end to violent *revolution*."[7]

Ten days previously *Germania* had pointed out disparagingly how proud "middle-party" leaders had been the preceding spring of their new "national majority," and how soon it had become apparent that for a number of purposes, from the liquor tax to the tariff, other majorities, especially the Conservative-Center combination, had become necessary. "Because of the *different kinds* of questions that concern our parliaments and which, according to the *nature* of the individual parties, bring them together, in different ways, without *artificial* combinations, such a situation is not at all striking. Furthermore, each of the factors that at present has some prospect of positive success *desires* the possibility of *various* majority combinations." Since many Liberals were still too devoted to free enterprise, the government wanted to be able to use the support of Conservatives and Center for its economic and social reforms; the Center needed the possibility of an alignment with the left Liberals to defeat any attacks on political liberties and to prevent the imposition of too heavy burdens on the people; the Conservatives wanted to be able to construct a majority against the Center party as well as with them; and the National Liberals felt the same way about the Conservatives and the left Liberals.[8]

Although the eloquence of the Center party's *Germania* on the dangers of inflexible paternalistic government appears convincing and in some ways prophetic, such emotional, idealistic, and partisan denunciations did tend to cover up a basic issue. In emphasizing the necessity of frequent elections because of the importance of constantly gauging the sentiment of the masses, the Center party, German Liberal, and Social Democratic leaders were in the first instance disingenuous since none of them was himself a peasant or worker nor by any means backward in instructing the masses on how to think as well as vote. In the second place they were taking the same line as Stoecker: that is, if purity of representation was the paramount concern, in search of a more exact image of political or ideological opinion one would logically have to go ultimately to some scheme of proportional representation; for a more exact reproduction of economic or social interest, one would ultimately have to adopt a system of corporate representation. In either case the stress on pure representation as the primary function of the legislature suggested a merely advisory function—one cannot get responsibility or initiative or much political power out of heterogeneity. The interest of both the right-wing, orthodox Protestant *Kreuzzeitung* and the Catholic, Center party *Germania* in a multiparty, fragmented situation in the parliaments stemmed from their conception of politics as a means of protecting or advancing their own special ideological and social interests. (The Social Democrats looked forward to the day when their party would simply capture the government and impose the "dictatorship of the proletariat.") But pressure-group politics is not the politics of power or responsibility; it assumes that the power and the responsibility and the initiative lie elsewhere. The conflict over the length of the parliamentary term was to some degree merely a matter of ins and outs. Those parties in power wanted a longer term; those out of power wanted more frequent elections. But it was not only that. The opposition parties necessarily fought against any further consolidation of power in Berlin, even within the parliaments in which their own representatives sat, because they were thereby protecting their interests and their identity against the threatening encroachments of the modern state. The only political group in the German Reich at the time that was interested in encouraging a unifying consensus within the existing system focused in a parliament intent on developing its political and governing power was the relatively small group of heterogeneous leaders and followers in the much harassed and much maligned "middle parties."[9]

From the above point of view the speech of the elderly Rudolf Gneist (*Ordinarius* Professor of Law at the University of Berlin since 1858 and National Liberal deputy in the Prussian Landtag since 1859) in the renewed debate on the bill extending the legal term of the House of Deputies, on March 6, was especially interesting. A certain amount of time, Gneist pointed out, was necessary before a parliament acquired an esprit de corps. The deputy had first to achieve an understanding with the most extreme on his side, then an understanding with the opposition, "because the majority and the minority must mutually understand each other if their decisions are to be significant." Then came understanding with the other house and also with the government, without which decisions of the legislature would not be carried out. Not only understanding, but a certain cooperative habit had to be established in order to make a parliament effective. Constant working together in the House, in the committees, in the party delegations, "at the green and the white tables," was necessary to produce a capacity for action. Only thereby could a "will of the whole" be created. In this respect the first chamber, with its permanent appointed or hereditary personnel, had the advantage. In the "historically famous case" of the lengthening of the term of the English parliament from three to seven years at the beginning of the reign of the House of Hanover (by Sir Robert Walpole in 1716), the purpose of the Whig party had been not only to lessen the "more violent and lasting heats and animosities among the subjects of this realm," but also to increase the power and strengthen the position of the House of Commons against the House of Lords. This aim, said Gneist, "was in fact achieved. With the seven-year period the lower house very soon established its complete equality with the upper house, . . . soon its superiority, and gradually its so-called omnipotence, and . . . the system of parliamentary government began." Among all the trenchant reforms of the last half century, all parties in Great Britain had agreed on retaining the seven-year period. Within the German states, the three-year period in Prussia and Electoral Hesse was the shortest, whereas Bavaria, Württemberg, Hesse-Darmstadt, and Brunswick had a six-year term, Nassau had seven, Baden had an eight-year term, and the Kingdom of Saxony, a nine-year term. Prussia's great size and diversity were arguments for continuing the short term, but with regard to Reichstag elections, as well as local elections, the five-year term in conformity with the Reichstag would be the most practical. The government had itself considered that a longer life for the legislature would be a step toward parliamentary government and had wanted to ask for a two-year budget in return, but financial complications caused by relations between the Prussian and Reich budgets made the one-year budget easier to manage, and the five-year legislative term would also hinder any recourse to a two-year budget period. Foreign countries might indeed wonder why a measure that promised to raise the significance and influence of the parliaments as well as their esprit de corps should be received with such an outburst of partisan spirit, such a typical *querelle allemande*. Perhaps they might guess that one purpose of this contention was to demonstrate to the government how far removed the parliaments were from the solidarity that could produce responsible party government. After a few years, the longer period between elections would seem just as natural as the five-year census, since by then the natural logic of the step would have won out over party election propaganda.[10]

In responding to Gneist's speech in the House of Deputies, the German Liberal wit Alexander Meyer remarked that Dr. Gneist's championing of parliamentarism astonished him. "If he had had the pleasure . . . of hearing the lectures of Professor Gneist on constitutional law at the local university (laughter), he would have learned that parliamentary government according to the English model would be an absolute misfortune for a country and that one should therefore never try to introduce the English parliamentary system here." And it was true; Gneist had indeed in all his books pointed out at great length and in detail how different the historical development had been in the two countries and how little, therefore, the English model applied to Germany. Had he changed his mind in his old age? Or had his recent appointment as special advisor to Prince William made him change his tune? Was his speech in fact aimed at San Remo? August Stein thought so. In his piece for the *Frankfurter Zeitung* he wrote that Gneist had proved that he could make a case for anything. He was presenting his credentials to the government for his new position. The *Kölnische Zeitung*, on the other hand, called the Gneist speech "constitutionally the most significant that has been given on the question."[11] Both judgments were probably correct.

15

The Government Assists the Cartel

WHILE in Reichstag and Landtag the cartel leadership strove to keep up at least an appearance of prestige and effectiveness, the government also gave it the assistance of its considerable authority. On the very day that Chancellor von Bismarck returned from Friedrichsruh to Berlin the *Berliner Börsen Zeitung* carried a possibly inspired article proclaiming, "The spirit of the times strives for the deepening of the world of perception, the ennoblement, the perfection of humanity, but without opposing itself to the real circumstances of existence. It strives for the raising of morals, the generalizing of the feeling for justice, wishes to teach toleration and true charity, and thereby protect the particular nature of the German character [*Deutschtum*]." True justice, which recognized no distinctions, and a law above all corruption were to be recognized as the highest factors in the development of the life of the individual. This spirit of the time had found its stimulus in the genius of both Kaiser William and Chancellor Bismarck, especially in their recognition of the duty of the state toward the welfare of its citizens and in their goal of achieving the reconciliation of opposing viewpoints through peaceful competition. This spirit of the times was neither reactionary nor libertarian (*freisinnig*) and was subject to no party. Naturally this article was reprinted without comment on page one of the chancellor's *Norddeutsche Allgemeine Zeitung.*[1]

Two days before Bismarck's dramatic appearance in the Reichstag, the *Norddeutsche* carried also on its front page an article reporting on a lecture by Prof. Dr. Alfred Schoene of the University of Königsberg on "The Development of Our National Consciousness." Germany, the writer stated, was not inclined to chauvinism, but was much more likely to find pleasure in identifying its own faults and weaknesses. Fortunately the educated younger generation was not so susceptible to this tendency. Prussian and German patriotism had developed from the same root and had grown together in the recent period of national greatness. The teachings of the Königsberg philosopher Immanuel Kant had made possible the development of a strong Prussian administration incorporating "unbending rectitude and self-denying devotion to duty," and the ideas of Herder, another Prussian, had awakened understanding for the specifically national, especially in literature. But even scholarship, especially in law and history, could not flourish without the national spirit. This spirit was developing now in the most healthy way. Germans were no longer paying so much attention to things foreign, foreign given names were being abandoned for good German ones, and the language was being "cleansed" of "superfluous" foreign phrases. It was a happy symptom of the growing patriotic devotion, remarked the writer, when not only professional politicians but also German scholars, in contrast to an earlier time, expressed their patriotism publicly, and when all leading personalities among the people recognized a higher calling than their own professions in selfless devotion to the fatherland.[2]

Chancellor Bismarck's choice of the issue of national defense and the tenseness of the European diplomatic situation as the basis for his February 6 speech and his achievement of a dramatic demonstration of national patriotism and unity in the Reichstag on that occasion had also naturally served to buttress mainly the "national" parties of the cartel. On February 21, the anniversary of the cartel election to the Reichstag, the *Norddeutsche* carried a front-page article that in spite of the recent acrimony of the antisocialist law debate, hailed the cartel Reichstag majority as one "that in harmonious cooperation with the Federated Governments wants to provide for the welfare of our people, the protection of our ethical and material values, the continuing reform of our political, social, and economic conditions . . . that places the *national* above the party interest." Comparing the present majority with the "energetic cooperation of the moderate liberal and conservative parties" that had given the Reich its basic framework in the first ten years of its existence, the writer blamed the breakup of this previous block on the willfulness of the free-trading Liberals, who had split the National Liberal party and, joining with the Progressives, had brought on a victory in 1881 for "democratic and particularistic elements" and an unfortunate interval of oppositional majorities. Unfortunate, because this majority included elements "opposed in principle either to the modern state itself or to the new German Reich" and was "united solely on the point of fundamental political opposition"—an "unhealthy . . . situation." The cartel had ended this era and that had been possible only because a year ago the two Conservative parties and the National Liberal party had buried their differences. The achievements of the present Reichstag as opposed to the former Richter-

Windthorst-Bebel majority clearly showed "which way those elements must go in the future that wish to further national interests and not cripple themselves through party conflict."[3]

The government did not confine itself to admonitions and exhortations. In the Prussian Landtag it introduced bills to raise the salaries of Protestant pastors and Catholic priests—presumably to disarm the clerical hierarchies—and also to use the available surplus of state money to contribute to the support of local schools on the basis of a stipulated sum per teacher, in return for which the local communities were to cease collecting school fees of any kind (*Schulgeld*), thereby finally carrying out in practice the principle of free education for all guaranteed in the Prussian constitution of 1850. Although the orthodox, right-wing conservative *Kreuzzeitung* acknowledged recognition of the importance of the "church movement" in the bill raising clerical salaries, it complained that the 744,000 M provided was not nearly enough—it should be 1,900,000 M—and that nothing was being done to buttress the Protestant church as an independent institution. Baron Hammerstein and Kleist-Retzow had introduced a motion in the House of Deputies the previous year asking for a set yearly money grant to be given to the church to administer as it wished, but the government had not responded to this bid for greater church independence, and when Hammerstein and Stoecker tried to amend the present bill in this sense, they found themselves again opposed in the House, not only by the government, but also by National Liberal and Free Conservative speakers. In particular, the Free Conservative leader von Zedlitz-Neukirch accused the high-church party of wanting to strengthen their domination in the church and suppress other factions by increasing the power of the central organizations, which he linked to an attempt to mix church affairs with "one-sided party politics." Prussia's interests in the Reich did not permit the encouragement of such tendencies. A mild protest of Wilhelm von Rauchhaupt, the Conservative Landtag leader, that it was questionable for the government to reject the amendments of a party that was allied with it, brought forth a blast from the *Berliner Politische Nachrichten*, which had connections with Finance Minister von Scholz, that on the contrary it was extremely questionable for the leader of a party that supposedly supported the government and "whose members have been elected under this basic assumption" to publicly denounce the government. Such action would "saw off the branch upon which the Conservative party sits." The Conservatives, commented the Center party's *Germania*, after a long time were again being reminded "that they are sitting in parliament by grace of the government and therefore have no right at all to independent action, certainly not before the elections. . . . It is a hard row that the Conservatives have to hoe, but they don't deserve any better."[4]

What had aroused the government's ire in this instance, of course, was that the leader of the Conservative party had championed the right-wing orthodox clerical cause of Hammerstein, Stoecker, and the *Kreuzzeitung* against both the government and the cartel. The National Liberals might get away with throwing their weight around in the Reichstag, where their superior numbers dominated the cartel—as in the case of their treatment of Puttkamer and the antisocialist law—but in the Prussian Landtag the Conservatives, with their 132 votes, enjoyed the superior position. They also rested on the relative security of the three-class, indirect election system, which, as long as the propertied leaders in the two upper classes of the districts were in agreement, was bound to produce safely conservative and antipopular results. With a conservative and orthodox-clerical orientation evident in the young prince about to ascend the Prussian throne, it was understandable that the Landtag Conservatives should imagine that they had the whip hand, not only over the National Liberals but over the government too, especially since the expectation of a young conservative kaiser in the offing should discourage any public swing of the government against the Conservatives in the election. This conflict between cartel and government on one side and the *Kreuzzeitung* on the other was a struggle for control over the Conservative party rank and file, and von Rauchhaupt's attitude indicated that the *Kreuzzeitung* had at least an immediate chance of winning.[5]

A similar conflict between government and Conservatives also gradually emerged over the school-aid bill (*Gesetz betreffend die Erleichterung der Volksschullasten*). It soon appeared that the government grant would not in all districts cover all the income lost through abolition of school fees, so that many local communities would have to make up the difference by raising general community taxes, a prospect that did not please the big taxpayers. Also in some of the larger cities special schools had been developed by the wealthier districts with higher fees and an enriched curriculum to give their children special preparation for the gymnasium. If all the fees were abolished, these schools would be open to poorer children whose parents had not previously been able to pay the fees, and it was quite clear that the wealthy parents did not want their children to be threatened with association with children from a lower social and cultural level. Certainly these considerations would affect as many of the leading National Liberals as Conservatives, but the principle of free education was so fundamental a tenet of the liberal point of view and the cartel was being so seriously attacked from the Right, that they—perhaps also aware of the scrutiny of San Remo—for the time being loyally adhered to the government bill. An opportunity thus presented itself for the Conservatives and the Center party to take over the issue and come together politically on the basis of it. The National Liberal leader and Berlin Landtag deputy Arthur von Hobrecht declared in the initial debate that the virtue of the bill was precisely that it would redistribute the tax burden onto the people more able to pay, and he called for an administrative reform (*Land-gemeindeordnung*) of the rural communities in the eastern (conservative) provinces. Rauchhaupt, in whose own country district relatively high school fees were collected, spoke against the bill, as did the aristocratic Center party leader Dr. Baron von Schorlemer-Alst, an association that Catholic *Germania* found "significant."[6]

The *Kreuzzeitung* naturally seconded Rauchhaupt's criticisms. It would be better to allow the localities more latitude in determining how to spend the funds allotted to them than to create new burdens on the taxpayers, many of whom no longer had children in school, by prohibiting school fees. The primary responsibility for providing schooling was not with the state or community, but with the parents. Hobrecht's rallying to free schools, his mention of administrative reform in a "more liberal" direc-tion, and especially the approving comment in the left-liberal press were further proof to the *Kreuzzeitung* of the drift of the National Liberals to the left. In the committee on the bill a Conservative representative maintained that school fees were a popular custom. As for the Catholic Center party, it did not want any strengthening of state as opposed to church influence in the schools. An amendment presented by Rauchhaupt providing that school fees could continue to be collected to the extent that they were not covered by the government payments was passed in the committee by a Conservative-Center majority. If allowed to stand, commented the *Frankfurter Zeitung*, this action of the committee would accentuate the already existing tendency toward separate and lower-level schools for the poor (*Armenschulen*). The *Kreuzzeitung*, however, declared that out of a total state expenditure for education in 1883–84 of 3.37 M per capita, the cost for the primary schools constituted the greater part—2.25 M— and that the working man had never begrudged paying his 35 pfennigs per month per child because he told himself, "In return my child is learn-ing something."[7]

To a degree the difference between the parties over the school-aid bill rested on a basic ideological divergence. The conservative *Kreuzzeitung* insisted that it was a good thing for parents to be personally involved in paying for their child's education, that they paid school fees much more cheerfully than general taxes, and that completely free schooling would thus relieve the parents of their personal responsibility for educating their children. It quoted a letter from Westphalia to "a deputy close to us" that stated that for parents to have to pay through the general tax rate for "strange children" as well as their own was "a dangerous advance of communism." On the other side, the left-liberal *Vossische Zeitung* pointed out that the city of Berlin had long since dispensed with school fees, which did not mean that its school costs were lower than those where school fees were still collected. Should Berlin and other cities that collected very low or no fees be penalized for adhering to the letter of the constitution? Free primary education was a natural right for the children and at least a partial reimbursement to the lower classes for the indirect state and imperial taxes on consumption. This tendency toward social amelioration was the most important aspect of the abolition of school fees and would also contribute toward strengthening loyalty to the nation. This article was carried in the *Norddeutsche*'s "Journal-Revue," and in another issue the *Norddeutsche* itself pointed out that none of the petitions to allow retention of school fees had come from fee-paying parents. Also, in recent years the number of cases where localities had had to resort to legal force to collect school fees had amounted to 6⅔ percent; in the first three months of 1887 it had risen to almost 8 percent; and in Silesia almost 13 percent. Late in February the Landtag commission on the school-aid bill held its final session, and in spite of the protests of Finance Minister von Scholz, who, with ministerial authorization, threatened government opposition to the commission's bill, the same Conservative-Center majority approved an amended version that raised the total amount of the state grant and allowed districts to continue to collect school fees if these were not completely covered by the grant.[8]

16

New Attacks on Waldersee,
the *Kreuzzeitung*, and Stoecker

AT the same time that the parties were engaged in these new maneuvers, the government press was renewing its attacks on Waldersee and
Stoecker. On February 14 the *Deutsches Tageblatt* published an article entitled "The War Party before and after Prince Bismarck's Speech" that
called for national loyalty in domestic as well as foreign affairs, accused
the "war party" of intriguing against the chancellor's foreign policy, denounced high army officers for interfering in politics, and suggested that
scare articles in the *Kreuzzeitung* and the *Kölnische Zeitung* on the danger
from Russian troop movements, as well as these other actions, had all
stemmed from one individual, a "*spiritus rector*." "Hardly is the City Mission conflict over with," General Waldersee wrote in his diary, "than a
new one threatens. . . . Doubtless I am meant above all, then probably the
general staff as a whole, in any case also the minister of war and the field
marshal. The affair would be laughable, if I were not convinced that the
attack comes from the Wilhelmstrasse. Besides, it is doubtless also directed to the address of Prince William. I am eager to see what will come
of it; the field marshal shakes his head doubtfully."

That such an attack should be made on Waldersee and the *Kreuzzeitung*
was not surprising in the circumstances. But the National Liberal *Kölnische Zeitung* was generally regarded as one of the most faithful of the
government papers. Its Berlin editor, however, *Justizrat* Dr. Franz Fischer,
was very close to the senior Foreign Office functionary Friedrich von
Holstein. The suggestion of a single *spiritus rector*, intriguing and attention-
getting in itself, was a bit of journalistic fiction that would serve to swat
at least two flies with a single blow. As Waldersee put it ten days later,
"In any case the instigator is the chancellor and not his son; the latter
used the *Kölnische Zeitung* without his father's knowledge to agitate against
Russia, as he generally departs from his father's policy in small nuances;
therefore the article in question also attacked the *Kölnische*." It is, however,
also quite possible that Foreign Minister Herbert Bismarck had, in fact,

found it convenient to blame Holstein for the fact that the Foreign Office and government press had taken a stronger anti-Russian and pro-Austrian stance than the chancellor (then in Friedrichsruh) had intended. And perhaps Holstein's friendliness to Waldersee had been noticed. Prince William, indignant over the article, assumed it had been written by a Russian agent, and Bismarck agreed. Chancellery Chief Rottenburg even told the *Norddeutsche*'s Emil Pindter that Bismarck was not only not responsible for the article, but would very much like to know who wrote it. All these attempts at camouflage, however, did not persuade Waldersee. The article, he was quite sure, was the work of "the House of Bismarck and their mamelukes." He had also discovered that he himself was distrusted by the Liberals, who were afraid that Prince William would keep him as his advisor, "and then we will make war together."[1]

The only Berlin newspaper to take the "war party" article of the *Deutsches Tageblatt* seriously was the right-wing conservative *Kreuzzeitung*, which scented blood and reacted accordingly. The article, it wrote, was "the most monstrous ever perpetrated by a *German* paper in this difficult, sad time." It was most shameful to suggest that high military officers—including, it hinted, the revered Field Marshal Moltke—were not maintaining the proper relationship between the military and civilian spheres. The chancellor and the army knew each other and their relationship to each other; it had been best demonstrated by the handclasp with which the aged Moltke had greeted Bismarck in the Reichstag after his great speech of February 6. The *Kölnische Zeitung* responded, for its part, with wounded dignity. Even foreign newspapers, in all their recklessness, it pointed out, had never suggested the existence of an actual "war party" in Germany. Bismarck had said in his speech that Germany would not break the peace, and they had seen no contradiction in any of the German press. The concern over Russian troop movements had been shared, not only by other newspapers, but also by "the highest political officials."[2]

What disturbed the *Kreuzzeitung* most about the "war party" article was the suggestion that out of patriotism all Germans should rally to a "national" policy also in domestic affairs. It was true enough, it observed, that in only twenty-five years Prince Bismarck had succeeded in establishing a German unity of feeling such as had never existed before in their long history. But what did that have to do with domestic policy? Unity toward the outside world was a simple matter of defense against attack on German soil, but in domestic affairs, where this common defense was not in question, conformity of opinions *must* cease, "because the sources and roots from which every individual life flows and grows are *infinitely diverse.*" Naturally every individual and party must concern itself with the welfare of the nation, but an artificial unity would not be in the national interest. In a most extraordinary statement for a right-wing journal it went on: "The inner development of a people is not effected through a monotonous nodding of heads, but through the *clash* of opinions." Such a clash, "within certain limits," was indispensable for the development of national consciousness, but required an "immovable ruler" standing above the parties "who is independent of fluctuations and imposes peace when the situation demands it." The approach of the *Deutsches Tageblatt*, said the *Kreuzzeitung*, blurred all useful distinctions. "Why this continual pressure toward the middle-party 'indifference point,' where all independent life ceases?" Thus the orthodox Protestant Junker Baron von Hammerstein demonstrated that partisanship within European nations did not arise only with the middle class—to say nothing of the proletariat!—but was historically rooted in the aristocracy. Doubtless his rallying to divine-right monarchy was based on his confidence in his own party's ability to control the future king.

It was probably true that in appealing to Reichstag, parties, and press in trying to build a national, popular political consensus around himself as a national hero and symbol, Chancellor von Bismarck was actually setting up national public opinion, national welfare, and a feeling of national identity as an authority superior to the throne and also to any party, including the right-wing Junker clique represented by the *Kreuzzeitung*. But the *Kreuzzeitung*'s concept of limiting popular national feeling to the sphere of external policy was a curious one. If the right-wing Junkers really wanted to continue to rule such a rapidly modernizing state as Germany, they would have to find a way to popularize both their ideals and their interests. The possibility, however, that groups and parties other than the *Kreuzzeitung*, as well as the mass of voters, might also regard the middle of the road, the way of compromise, as a "point of indifference," remained a serious threat to the middle parties. What generally accepted principles, besides patriotism and pride in Germany's new power, did the Bismarck regime stand for? Was a national consensus chimerical?[3]

Only a few days before the "war party" article, reports appeared in the Berlin press that the *Deutsches Tageblatt*, which had previously been close to Landtag deputy Cremer and the Conservative "Citizens' Clubs," had been bought up by a consortium headed by local National Liberal leaders, Reichstag Deputy Dr. Hammacher and City Councillor Kyllmann. Actually it appears that the reorganization of the *Deutsches Tageblatt* also involved a number of Conservatives, such as Counts Arnim Muskau and Otto Karl von Manteuffel and Baron Julius von Mirbach-Sorquitten, and Free Conservatives, such as Baron Douglas and the industrialist Carl Stumm. Saxon Conservatives apparently also were involved. Thus all three cartel parties were represented. In any case, the purpose was to make sure that the paper adhered to a "national," that is, a cartel or Bismarckian, policy. Both Herbert Bismarck and his father appear to have sponsored and pushed the reorganization. The underlying intention clearly was to try to prevent the Conservative party from falling into the hands of the *Kreuzzeitung* orthodox reactionaries. The reorganization of the ownership of the *Deutsches Tageblatt* thus represented a rallying by the Bismarcks of support among the Conservative and cartel leadership in defense of the carefully constructed alliance of agrarian and industrial interests, of moderately progressive Junkers and respectable Liberals represented by the cartel. In addition to this move, on March 6 the chancellor's *Norddeutsche Allgemeine Zeitung* announced the founding of a new weekly, the *Deutsches Wochenblatt*, to serve the "union of the three national parties." The paper would begin publication on April 1 (coincidentally Bismarck's birthday) and would be edited by Dr. Otto Arendt, a thirty-four-year-old Free Conservative Landtag deputy of Jewish origin who was a bimetallist and a friend of the Free Conservative Reichstag leader, Wilhelm von Kardorff. "Numerous parliamentarians from the National Liberal, Free Conservative, and German Conservative parties, as well as a number of prominent representatives of the learned professions (*Wissenschaft*) are named as collaborators," added the *Norddeutsche*. No doubt the choice of a strong agrarian as editor of the new cartel-oriented weekly was intended to spike the *Kreuzzeitung*'s guns. Since there was little doubt that Prince William would soon be kaiser and king, these journalistic maneuvers against his orthodox Conservative friends also carried an inevitable aura of potential agitation by the Bismarcks and their loyal followers against the throne itself.[4]

Since the reorganization of the *Deutsches Tageblatt* was a cartel move, the anticartel parties—German Liberal, Center, and *Kreuzzeitung*—all agreed in stressing the allegedly National Liberal character of the enterprise. It would be difficult to derive any benefit for the National Liberal party from the paper, wrote Catholic *Germania*, since there was no following for National Liberalism in Berlin, and the *Deutsches Tageblatt* had always been a strictly government paper. The orthodox Protestant *Reichsbote* complained that although the *Deutsches Tageblatt* had been founded with the financial support of Conservative party members, it had never been "seriously conservative." Rather, in trying to compete with the left-liberal *Berliner Tageblatt* and in hewing too closely to the government line, it had been not conservative enough for the Conservatives and not liberal enough for the Liberals. The National Liberals, it observed, apparently thought that by buying a paper connected with the Conservative Citizens' Clubs and the

Conservative Berlin Movement they would be able to keep the readership and move them over into the National Liberal party. Berliners, however, would not let their souls be bought in this fashion.[5]

The *Kreuzzeitung* declared that they did not mind if the right wing of the National Liberals in Berlin developed a journalistic outlet of their own to compete with the left-oriented *National Zeitung*. What they objected to was that the National Liberals should "gather together a reading public under *their colors* that according to its whole manner of thinking belongs to *us*." The new *Deutsches Tageblatt* ownership intended to destroy the conservative character of the paper, but keep the readership. "Clear lines" must be drawn between the party viewpoints. The conservative press, both in Berlin and in the provinces, "do not desire that under the name of 'national' mishmash politics should be carried on."[6]

In response to this challenge, the *Deutsches Tageblatt* declared that the *Kreuzzeitung* had long since lost any understanding of truly middle-class (*bürgerlichen*) interest, whereas they had striven, from the beginning, "with great success to prepare a place for Conservatism in the houses of middle-class people [*des Bürgerstandes*]." Meanwhile the *Kreuzzeitung* printed a statement from the *Konservative Korrepondenz* that denounced the *Deutsches Tageblatt* for sowing discord in the Conservative party.[7] The *Deutsches Tageblatt*, wrote the *Kreuzzeitung*, was no longer a Conservative paper. In response, the *Deutsches Tageblatt* cited some remarks of the *Norddeutsche Allgemeine Zeitung*. Aha! replied the *Kreuzzeitung*, the *Norddeutsche* also was not a Conservative paper and *could* not be. This was no reproach: "Its tasks are quite different from the defense of the Conservative party." On February 24 General von Waldersee noted in his diary that "quite obviously the chancellor is conducting a sharp battle against the *Kreuzzeitung*; undoubtedly he decided on it after the City Mission affair. He wants to move closer to the National Liberals and boost the *Deutsches Tageblatt*. That newspaper, however, has had bad luck with its article on the 'war party,' which has damaged it with all respectable people."[8]

On February 17, three days after the publication of the "war party" article by the *Deutsches Tageblatt*, the chancellor's *Norddeutsche* carried a report from the left-liberal *Berliner Tageblatt* that in the sixth Berlin Reichstag district, where a by-election was coming up, the Stoeckerites were spreading "inflammatory and defamatory writings of the lowest kind." The passages quoted by the *Berliner Tageblatt* from one of the pamphlets, went on the *Norddeutsche* primly, could not be reproduced because of the press law. On February 20 the *Norddeutsche* repeated its earlier remarks concerning the likelihood of the scurrilous pamphlet's having been distributed by Stoecker and that it could not quote from it because of the press law and because of "literary scruples." The *Kreuzzeitung,* of course, was quite scornful. The very same people who were still openly disapproving of Stoecker frequently gave him "a silent handclasp." The only difference between National Liberal and Conservative anti-Semitism was that the National Liberals did not admit it publicly. This private anti-Semitism was also widespread among both the German Liberals and Social Democrats.[9]

In reply to the *Norddeutsche*'s "literary scruples," the *Kreuzzeitung* on February 23 reprinted the Stoecker pamphlet on its front page. It was entitled "Workers! Friends! Comrades!" and tried to distinguish the true interest of the workers, which could best be met by social reform, from that of the international revolutionaries, who were interested in the workers merely as cannon fodder in their attack on society. The pamphlet, explained the *Kreuzzeitung,* had been written in reply to a Social Democratic one that ended, "Long live the international revolutionary proletariat!" attempting to stir up the workers against the government. Under these circumstances any objective observer would see that the Stoecker pamphlet did not deserve the criticism the *Norddeutsche* had given it. In reply, the *Norddeutsche* declared that it was against all harassment, whether of an individual or a class. "We can only hope that in the next Landtag elections the Conservatives do not have to reap the harvest from the seed that the *Kreuzzeitung* is so tirelessly sowing."[10]

The fact that the chancellor's *Norddeutsche* was taking part in the attacks on Stoecker, wrote August Stein in the *Frankfurter,* showed apprehension that he might be "the man of the imminent future. . . . Many who, in expectation of the future as they had understood it for some years, used to love now and then confidentially to press one's hand have completely lost their memory." It was thus no accident that Stoecker was becoming more active and prominent than he had been recently.[11] Meanwhile Pastor Stoecker had addressed a capacity crowd of his Christian Socialist followers in the Tonhalle on the subject of "Social Reform and the Social Monarchy." The object of social reform must be to give a large part of the population a more just position in society and to create for labor a more favorable relation between profits and wages to prevent concentration of wealth in a few hands and the consequent impoverishment of large groups of people. The social monarchy stood above the classes. "Our Prussian kings have been an unbroken chain of fathers of the people. . . . The social kingship, however, cannot exist without Christianity, nor monarchy without religion." After Stoecker, Professor Adolf Wagner spoke, emphasizing the disparity between technological advance and the law, which had lagged behind. "In order to bridge the omnipresent antagonism between capital and labor, the principle of free competition must be broken, the handworker and the peasant must be protected and supported by the state, and workable labor legislation must be passed."[12]

In a front-page article on March 2, the *Kreuzzeitung* proclaimed that the present anti-Stoecker agitation was "the exclusive work of the Jews and a few so-called Christian newspapers that have 'from destitution' become subordinates to them." Fear of Stoecker on the part of the Jews, such as was evidenced in the attacks of August Stein in the *Frankfurter Zeitung*, was understandable, but it was unjust and untrue to accuse Stoecker of intrigue and of trimming his sails to the wind; he had always been open and public in his actions and had resolutely gone his own way. Stoecker had not changed; he had not become more active—it was his enemies that had done that, "because they see God knows what 'coming.' That merely expresses their own guilty conscience and no more. The scourge that they fear they have deserved; but whether they will get to feel it so soon is not in the power of mortal man."[13]

This reference of the *Kreuzzeitung* to the "scourge" was, as the left-liberal *Frankfurter* put it, of such "staggering frankness" that it attracted attention. This promised chastisement would involve not only the Jews but all liberals, wrote Stein on March 6. "The connection is clear: the scourge is coming when fate robs the German people of the life upon which great hopes for the future have been placed." Their anxiety over Stoecker, wrote Stein, was not merely in apprehension of specific anti-Semitic measures that might be passed under his influence. Rather, not only the Jews but all liberals feared that the present reaction in the church, schools, administration, and in economic and political legislation might be strengthened and given a permanence "that it would not have if fate did not rudely intervene in the regular course of events." A government under the influence of Stoecker would mean the "rule of the Junkers and the parsons."[14]

On March 2, the day of the *Kreuzzeitung*'s "scourge" article, Pastor Stoecker had addressed a large gathering in the Berlin City Mission on the text: "Providence and God's Governing of the World." Human suffering and misfortune came from God's punishment for sin, declared the pastor. Four thoughts helped in facing sorrow: that everything comes from God, and that what God sends is good; that every Christian is tested by suffering: "'Through the cross to the crown!'"; that Christ himself suffered and was crucified for us; and that this life is only a short preparation for eternity. "If we ask in this moment, what God can intend with the great testing with which he has afflicted our imperial and royal family, one thing must be certain to all of us if we are Christians: the ways of the Lord are just, even if we do not understand them. . . . Here is strife and sorrow! Beyond, eternity awaits us, where all mysteries are solved! (lively applause].” It was more than doubtful that all of Pastor Stoecker’s expectations were of the next world.[15]

At the end of February, Emil Pindter, editor in chief of the *Norddeutsche Allgemeine Zeitung*, noticed that the *Kreuzzeitung* was giving an unusually strong play to attacks in the Russian press on the chancellor’s foreign policy. “Is the military party trying to force Bismarck into a blind alley?” he wrote in his diary. “*Rottenburg*, who thinks my guess about the blind alley is perhaps not without . . . [*sic*].” At the end of February Bismarck asked Field Marshal von Moltke if he was sure that General von Waldersee was the “right man for the job.” “Definitely yes,” responded Moltke. Early in March General Wilhelm von Heuduck told Prince Chlodwig Hohenlohe, the Statthalter in Strassburg, that a powerful party in Berlin was trying to remove Waldersee from his post at the general staff. One of Pindter’s confidential military informants also confirmed the rumor that Waldersee would be going soon. Waldersee himself noted on March 6 that the attacks on him in the press were becoming more and more open. The *Deutsches Tageblatt* had reported that he was leaving

> because of differences with a very highly placed personality, who is not the chief of the general staff. Naturally it is clear that Prince Bismarck is meant. This article was probably not written by the prince himself; it does express his point of view, however, of which I do not doubt for a moment. It is scandalous, however, or better, sad that such procedures are possible. If I am uncomfortable for the chancellor, he can say so to the Kaiser; but to operate against me in such a manner is [. . .] [*sic*] and shows that we are going backwards. I am eager to see what position [Chief of the kaiser’s military cabinet General von] Albedyll will take; in his heart he is really on my side; whether, however, he will now oppose the chancellor only the future can tell.[16]

17

##

Protestant Clericals Court
the Center Party

S INCE the Conservative party was not strong enough in either Prussia or Germany to govern alone under the coming reign of Prince William, the *Kreuzzeitung* and Stoecker continued to woo the Catholic Center party. Their principal advantage was the basic ideological agreement shared by both sides: orthodox Christianity, whether Protestant or Catholic. Thus in mid-January Catholic *Germania* had quoted at length and with approval an article on the antisocialist law by the Stoecker-oriented orthodox Protestant *Reichsbote* that pointed out that Social Democracy could not be legislated away because it expressed the widespread acceptance of philosophical naturalism and its application to political and social affairs. *Germania* had agreed that it was not material security that mattered the most, but hunger for "the higher values."[1]

Both parties also possessed a special interest in the social groups hardest hit by industrialization: the peasants and the artisans. In defending Stoecker, also in mid-January, the *Kreuzzeitung* had attacked the basic tenets of economic liberalism: Mercier de la Rivière's "Let things alone and let them go, the world runs by itself," and Thomas Malthus's statement: "A man who is born into a world already possessed, if he cannot get subsistence from his parents on whom he has a just demand, and if the society do not want his labour, has no claim of *right* to the smallest portion of food, and, in fact, has no business to be where he is. At nature's mighty feast there is no vacant cover for him. She tells him to be gone, and will quickly execute her own orders." These liberal theories, wrote the clerical *Kreuzzeitung*, fitted the atheistic state very well and had ended by conjuring up Social Democracy. The liberals had given up the authority of God and the king for that of man and had proclaimed their "inalienable rights." The socialists had gone to this school, and the liberals were therefore the more guilty. The masses were beginning to lose interest in constitutional conflicts. "It is very likely that in twenty-five years we shall have only two parties: a Christian socialist and a social-revolutionary."

The *Kreuzzeitung* had proposed a grand alliance of groups with Christian and conservative interests under the banner of social reform (see above, pp. 96ff.), but the "Augustinian brothers" of the Center party press had read the government *Norddeutsche* and said to themselves, "Nothing at all will come from this Christian-social union since the chancellor is not protecting it," and had turned a disdainful shoulder. But there were other, more reasonable people among the conservative Catholics, such as Baron von Schorlemer-Alst, who had united both Protestants and Catholics behind him in his Westphalian district.[2]

Although the Center party's *Germania* labeled the orthodox Protestant *Kreuzzeitung*'s program "a beautiful dream" and observed caustically that Baron Hammerstein was merely trying to get out of his "political isolation," nevertheless, as the *Kreuzzeitung* had pointed out, the pervasiveness and strength of the liberal point of view naturally brought believing Catholics and Protestants together in self-defense. On January 22 the *Kreuzzeitung* denounced a new Protestant catechism prepared by Dr. R. Schramm of Bremen, which answered the question, "Why do we call ourselves evangelical Christians?" with "We call ourselves Christians because Christ is our greatest prophet and common master." This was the same as Islam, noted the *Kreuzzeitung*. The only correct answer was "because Jesus Christ, truly God, born of the Father in eternity, and also truly man, born of the Virgin Mary, is our Lord." Schramm's catechism denied the divinity of Jesus (he was the best and most perfect man that had ever lived) and defined God as "the world spirit, reason in all things . . . the spirit of the universe." Actually, wrote the *Kreuzzeitung*, there was no Christianity left in this catechism. "There is no sin, no salvation, no miracle, no Providence, no prayer, there is no personal God, no Creation, no angels, no devil, no Son of God—Jesus is an ordinary man—no Resurrection, no Ascension of Jesus Christ, no Redemption through His blood, no Holy Ghost, no Church, no forgiveness of sins, . . . no Heaven, no Hell, no Judgment, no eternal life." Later the *Kreuzzeitung* reported that as a result of a petition against the use of Schramm's catechism for the instruction of school children in Bremen, the Bremen Senate had directed that the phrase that described prayers to Jesus as "idolatry" must be deleted, but that the book otherwise could be used.[3]

In February, on the unanimous recommendation of the theological faculty, Minister of Ecclesiastical, Educational, and Medical Affairs von Gossler decided to call Professor Adolf Harnack from Marburg to the August Neander chair at the University of Berlin, news that created a wave of concern among both orthodox Protestants and Catholics. Harnack was known to be of the school of Albrecht Ritschl, liberal professor of theology at the University of Tübingen. Catholic *Germania* quoted with approval the statement of Stoecker's *Deutsche Evangelische Kirchenzeitung* that "Ritschl Christianity . . . destroys the trust . . . in the fundamental teachings of the Christian faith . . . the divinity of Christ is denied." Stoecker's paper was confident that the true faith would finally defeat this liberal heresy, but *Germania* thought that "the present condition of Protestantism" did not justify such optimism. A week previously *Germania* had also attacked Professor Ritschl for making a political speech the preceding summer at an official celebration at Tübingen. He had found the basis for the political association of the Center party, German Liberals, and Social Democrats in their attitudes toward natural law. The speech had been answered by Professor Georg von Hertling of Munich, a member of the Center party, and *Germania* reported his arguments at some length. On March 7 the Center party leader Ludwig Windthorst also complained about the Ritschl speech in the Prussian House of Deputies. Ritschl had officiated at the Tübingen ceremony in his capacity as rector, and it was not tactful for him, in the presence of the minister of education, to make controversial statements to which his audience was in no position to reply. On the same day the Evangelical Superior Church Council, under the influence of Superior Court Chaplain Kögel, formally objected to the Harnack appointment. There already was a Ritschl follower on the Berlin theological faculty, and another such appointment would move the whole faculty to the left.[4]

In mid-February Stoecker found another issue which happily combined morality, patriotism, and anti-Semitism: a committee had asked permission to erect a monument to the poet Heinrich Heine in his hometown of Düsseldorf. Heine, wrote the *Kreuzzeitung*, might be a great lyricist, but his wit had mostly been turned against his own people and specifically against the Hohenzollern family. On February 24 Pastor Stoecker spoke in the Tonhalle on "Heinrich Heine and His Monument in Düsseldorf" before a capacity crowd of two thousand that included a number of students and some members of the Salvation Army in uniform. Stoecker said that to want to "put up a monument to the abysmally malicious writing of Heine, the most un-German of Germans in our time of national and religious struggles, that is a slap in the face of the new united Germany (lively applause)." Behind the reformed Jews pushing Heine was a whole host of enemies of the church—Christ-haters, lusters after the flesh, licentious people. One might make allowances for Heine, but one should not give him a monument. A resolution requesting the minister of the interior (Puttkamer) and the local authorities to prohibit erection of a monument to Heine in Düsseldorf was passed with only seven opposing votes.[5]

Stoecker's speech was denounced by the left-wing National Liberal *National Zeitung* and defended by the *Kreuzzeitung*. Catholic *Germania* had not paid much attention to the Heine affair until the attacks on Stoecker's speech, when it rallied to Stoecker's side. The content of Stoecker's criticism, it wrote, was completely justified. Heine had "ridiculed Germany in the most shameless way; everything that was German, princes, nobility, burghers, scholars, the German fatherland, the Hohenzollern family, he slandered in such a way that he cannot be quoted at all." In spite of this agitation and considering that the money for the Heine monument had already been provided by Empress Elizabeth of Austria, the Düsseldorf city council authorized erection of the monument by a margin of one vote. The German people would take note of the name of this wretched person, wrote the *Kreuzzeitung*. Later, when a petition against the monument was presented to the Prussian State Ministry by "the most distinguished residents of Düsseldorf," Minister of the Interior Puttkamer reported that according to administrative regulations he had no authority to interfere in the decisions of the city council. On the advice of Minister of Ecclesiastical Affairs von Gossler, who suggested that the eventual monument might turn out to be only a "Lorelei fountain" with a bas-relief, the ministry then decided to let the matter drift and avoid taking any position on it. The monument, by Ernst Gustav Herter, completed in 1897 in white Tyrolean marble, was indeed a fountain, with a buxom figure of the Lorelei uncomfortably seated on a nine-foot column, a bas-relief of Heine's head on one side, and three Graces gamboling about the base. The city fathers of Düsseldorf did not like it and refused it, as did Frankfurt am Main, Hamburg, Berlin, and Mainz. Eventually it was successfully erected in The Bronx.[6]

Along with this general doctrinal and moral agreement, the Conservative party and the Center party had also found themselves representing a common point of view in regard to the Prussian school-aid bill (see above, pp. 141ff.) and had been able to impose their views on the commission. At the end of January the two parties also acted together in introducing a motion in the Reichstag to require certificates of competence in handicrafts, hailed by the Center spokesman as a protection against shoddy workmanship, an assistance to education, and a new foundation for the flourishing of the guilds. At the beginning of March the two parties even managed to pass the bill by one vote, in its second reading, apparently because of the failure of some of the Liberal troops to appear. The association of National Liberals, German Liberals, and Social Democrats in opposition to this bill was duly noted by both *Germania* and the *Kreuzzeitung*. The latter wrote that although the "good Aryans" among those parties might sympathize with the handicraft workers and appreciate the power of their votes, they did not possess the courage or the strength to oppose the "Jewish influence," which "in the interest of easier exploitation" was hostile to any craft associations. It amounted to a fight of the big capitalists against the small capitalists. If the government, stated the *Kreuzzeitung*, did not support the strengthening of the guilds, handicrafts would be hopelessly lost.[7]

In spite of their similar ideological outlook and even their occasional practical cooperation, the Conservative and Center parties continued to be separated by their respective attitudes toward the government and state. Thus they had fought on opposite sides over the antisocialist law and the lengthening of the legislative period in Reichstag and Landtag. Whereas, on the one hand, the conservative *Kreuzzeitung* warned the Center that the church could never survive in modern society without the support of state authority, Catholic *Germania* took its stand on a preexisting natural law and accused the Conservatives of regarding all law as founded in the historical state—"Not principles, not what ought to be, but utility and what is possible decide with us; that has been adopted as the rule officially by the 'Conservatives,' and by the middle parties." Anti-Prussian, Catholic particularism, of course, inevitably colored this judgment. The *Kreuzzeitung* expressed this difference in attitude by continually trying to separate the Center party press—run, they insisted, by the "Augustinian brothers"—from the aristocratic party leadership, represented by Baron von Schorlemer-Alst. The Catholic press might protest that the Augustinian Society was "a completely innocent thing, which vegetates more than it agitates" and which served mostly very practical purposes, such as the preparation of stenographic reports of meetings and the sending out of greetings and addresses for ceremonial occasions. The *Kreuzzeitung* insisted that it might well have had a modest beginning, but that it had now grown to the point where it competed in authority over the Catholic population with the Center party and the church hierarchy, declaring, "Le peuple c'est moi." Because the pope and the hierarchy were now cooperating with the government, the *Kreuzzeitung* pointed out, the "Augustinian" press was showing hostility to the hierarchy and was in general taking a much more democratic stand than the Center party leadership. The *Kreuzzeitung* naturally tried to encourage this divisive tendency. As far as it was concerned, now that the Kulturkampf had been overcome, the Center party must become conservative. Unlike the Social Democrats or German Liberals, the Center party was a *positive* party; it should make its peace with the state and government. One had only to look at France and Belgium to see what could happen to the church without the support of the state.[8]

That such divisions and conflicts existed within the Catholic Center party was undoubtedly true, but that the party would follow the *Kreuzzeitung*'s advice and split into its constituent parts was not likely. Especially not when an election for the House of Deputies of the Prussian Landtag was slated for the fall. Furthermore, with the coming reign of the liberal crown prince now in question and Liberals and government on one side and the Conservatives on the other engaged in a struggle for control over Prince William, the Center party certainly had nothing to gain politically by taking a stand prematurely on one side or the other— especially since the new situation had already created a certain amount of rivalry between the two factions in bidding for the Center party's favor and support. For the sake of its own unity and morale, the Landtag elections, and to take full advantage of the new political configuration, the Center had to raise the level of its own demands. Although a modest motion introduced into the House of Deputies by the conservative Center leader Prince Franz Ludwig von Arenberg to grant the recently restored Catholic religious orders full corporate rights was quickly accepted in principle by the government, the Center was far from mollified. It objected to continued government support for the antipapal Old Catholics.* It was known that Bismarck personally felt that support for them should cease, wrote *Germania*. Surely he could enforce his will in this as in other things. "We expect Prince Bismarck finally to take drastic measures! Our patience is at an end." With the help of Rauchhaupt and half of the Conservatives and with the support of the German Liberals, the Prussian government budget item to support Old Catholic university training was at length successfully cut. In the debate on the budget for the Ministry of Ecclesiastical, Educational, and Medical Affairs in the Landtag at the beginning of March, the Center leader Dr. Ludwig Windthorst demanded the restoration of a separate Catholic section in the ministry, the appointment of a substantial number of Catholics to it, the repeal of the imperial ban on the Jesuit order, and the relinquishment by the government of all funds sequestered during the Kulturkampf. In response, it was noted that Minister von Gossler was very mild and accommodating toward the Center, whereas he treated criticisms from Rickert and the German Liberals with considerable harshness.[9]

The pièce de résistance, however, in the new forward program of the Center party was a motion introduced by Windthorst into the Prussian House of Deputies on February 27 calling for a bill to guarantee control by the church hierarchy over religious instruction in the schools. The first clause of this motion declared that "in the office of primary teacher [*Volksschullehrer*] only such persons should be appointed against whom the church authorities have made no objection in a clerical-religious sense. If such objections are raised later, the teacher may not be allowed further

* The Old Catholics had split from the church over the proclamation of papal infallibility by the Vatican Council in 1870.

to impart religious instruction." Actual plans of religious instruction and textbooks must also be approved by the church. Windthorst's motion raised a great hue and cry. The basic difficulty was the same that had produced the fight over religious instruction in the schools during the Kulturkampf in the 1870s. According to the constitution of 1850, "Religious instruction in the elementary schools shall be superintended by the religious organizations concerned," but the same article also provided that teachers should be appointed by the state, and the fact was that most of the Prussian primary schools were still held in one room with one teacher, and in every school the teacher responsible for religious instruction had other teaching duties as well. In the 1850s, the *Frankfurter Zeitung* pointed out, the state had practically let the churches run the schools; then during the Kulturkampf the state had tried to control everything in the schools, including religious instruction. Now a sort of compromise had been reached, where the church authorities were informally consulted, but Windthorst's demands for legal guaranties of church influence must end in furthering the only logical, clean solution for schools in modern society: a separation of religious instruction from the schools altogether and permission for the churches to operate their own schools if they wished. But even the Liberal parties were not yet willing to demand that religion be taken out of the schools. Consequently, from the Liberal point of view Windthorst's motion appeared to involve, as the (Bennigsen) *Hannoverscher Kourier* put it, "the surrender of the whole primary school system to the church."[10]

The main reason for Windthorst's school motion, declared the Free Conservative and governmental *Post*, was that his position in the Center party was so uncertain that only heroic measures could strengthen it. He was trying to arouse his followers by a new conflict between church and state and bolster his own authority in the process. The party press—except for the Center party—was generally in agreement with the *Post*, including even the *Kreuzzeitung*. It was, in fact, extremely difficult for the orthodox Protestants around Stoecker and Baron von Hammerstein to handle this Center party move. Basically, of course, they were just as intent as the Catholics on strengthening and extending the authority and impact of religion, and they sympathized with the Catholic desire to protect religious instruction in the schools from interference by the state. On January 24, Baron von Schorlemer-Alst had complained in the House of Deputies concerning the inroads of modernism among teachers, to vocal approval from the Right as well as the Center, and considerable sympathy did exist for the Center school motion on the Conservative side. As the *Post*, however, pointed out, support of the Windthorst school motion by the Conservatives would not be very popular at the polls, and then there was government disfavor to consider. Under the circumstances, therefore, the *Kreuzzeitung* and *Reichsbote* stifled their religious feelings and deprecated the Center bill, much to the disgust of *Germania*, which accused them of pusillanimity, of "opportunism and governmentalism." Peaceful, organic cooperation between state and church would be threatened by a new conflict over authority, agreed the *Konservative Korrespondenz* and the *Reichsbote*; in fact, the latter went so far as to accuse the Center of endangering the cause of religious instruction in the schools with its rash actions, which was the exact criticism that the Center's *Germania* had previously thrown at Stoecker![11]

18

Greiffenberg-Kammin and
the National Liberals

IN the midst of these party bickerings another Reichstag by-election in the Pomeranian district of Greiffenberg-Kammin, near Stettin, threw oil on the fires of party conflict. The district, consisting of large estates and scattered villages, had been strongly Conservative since 1867, and the preceding year it had voted, as usual, overwhelmingly on the first ballot for the Conservative *Landrat* Ernst von Köller, a relative of the president of the House of Deputies, by 8,276 to only 1,471 votes for his German Liberal opponent. Since then Köller had accepted a post as chief of police in Frankfurt am Main and had chosen another relative, a retired army major, von Köller zu Hoff, to succeed him. The Conservatives in the district, however, had not all been agreeable to this family succession, with the result that in the initial balloting of February 21 two Conservative candidates had split the vote: 3,732 votes for Köller-Hoff, 1,161 for the other Conservative, von Neumann, and 3,492 votes for the German Liberal Kohli, a city recorder from Stettin. This result was disconcerting, and the *Kreuzzeitung* took the local Conservatives strongly to task and appealed for unity in the runoff in defense of Conservative ideals. Whereas, however, in the first election the total number of voters was only 8,637 (out of some 15,000 eligible), with the added interest caused by the Conservative disarray, in the runoff election on March 1 the total grew to almost 11,000, over 1,000 more than in the great cartel election of the preceding year, and the victor was—wonder of wonders—the German Liberal Kohli, by 5,597 to 5,375 votes. That an agricultural Junker district in pious Pomerania could suddenly produce a victory for a left Liberal was as much of a political shock, wrote the *Frankfurter Zeitung* gleefully, as if the "Woods of Dunsinane" were on the move.*[1]

The blame for the Conservative defeat was immediately placed by the

---

* It was, of course, in Shakespeare's *Macbeth*, Birnam Wood that moved to Dunsinane Castle.

Free Conservative *Post* on the "noticeably stronger emergence of the extreme clerical and political Right since the fall, as it has expressed itself namely in the *Kreuzzeitung*." The left-wing National Liberal *National Zeitung* took an even sharper tone: the election was "a severe warning . . . both to the government and to the . . . Conservatives." The German people had not voted on February 21, 1887, for "an era of domination by 'Junkers and parsons.'" The *Weser Zeitung* pointed out that this was the third district lost by the Conservatives since the last election, and that at least half of the electorate had had its eyes opened to the fact that "agrarian politics is merely a system of privilege for the large estate owner (*Rittergutsbesitzer*) at the expense of the cities, the rural lower middle class, and the rural wage worker." The jubilant German Liberal press denounced the National Liberals for having assisted in creating, in the cartel, the basis for the greater arrogance of the Right. In the Landtag the German Liberal leader Heinrich Rickert told the National Liberals, "I am convinced that . . . you will achieve something that you did not wish to achieve. . . . You have worked for us . . . (lively applause on the left.)"[2]

The *Kreuzzeitung* admitted that the Conservative defeat in the Pomeranian district was a serious affair. Against the evidence, it complained that it was becoming more and more difficult to get the peasant to the polls. He was convinced that the "half measures" in favor of agriculture, such as the recent raising of the tariff, did no good at all, and the liquor tax had imposed a new burden on him. The left Liberals had been most effective in passing the word among the working men, "Vote for Kohli, then schnapps will be cheaper again." The invocation by the *National Zeitung* of the "cultivated people" who hated Stoecker and the Junkers and parsons could hardly be applied to rural Greiffenberg-Kammin, where the cultivated people *were* the Junkers and parsons. Nothing substantial had been done in favor of agriculture, and thus the Conservative party had nothing to offer to the people.[3]

Both the *Konservative Korrespondenz* and *Kreuzzeitung* also accused the National Liberals of treachery. Several National Liberal papers had interpreted the failure of the Conservatives to win a clear majority on the first ballot in Greiffenberg-Kammin as the result of the growth of "clerical reaction." Naturally the National Liberals and Free Conservatives in the district would then have either stayed home or voted for Kohli in the runoff. The Center party's *Germania* also did not miss the opportunity to point out that in the Reichstag election of 1881 in Greiffenberg-Kammin there were 3,777 National Liberal votes; these had now "disappeared without a trace"—that is, they had now swung to the left. The Conservative arguments were relatively weak. If it was true that the peasants and agricultural wage workers were dissatisfied with a tariff increase on grain of only 67 percent rather than 167 percent, why did they vote for a German Liberal, whose party was notoriously in favor of no tariff at all? It appeared much more likely that the local voters, of whatever social or ideological grouping, were rebelling against the arrogance of the local Junker notables, against being taken for granted. *Germania*'s contention that the voters rebelled because the Conservative party, in cooperating with Free Conservatives and National Liberals in the cartel, had betrayed the true social and religious ideals of Conservatism was just as unconvincing as the argument of the *Kreuzzeitung*.[4]

The analysis of the government *Norddeutsche*, that the by-election had no larger political or ideological significance at all, but was entirely a local affair having to do with a lack of personal following for Köller-Hoff, might be largely true, yet a disquieting implication remained for the moderate parties as well as the Conservatives. In strongly religious, authoritarian, and conservative areas, such as Pomerania, if a revolt, for whatever reason, did break out against the local authorities (whose political, social, and economic domination was real enough and could probably ordinarily control the political process), it would be natural for such a revolt to swing to the opposite left-Liberal or even Social Democratic extreme, not to stop in the moderate middle. For this reason, the National Liberal leader Bennigsen's *Hannoverscher Kourier* agreed for once with the *Kreuzzeitung*, declaring that it did not believe that the German public really feared "an era of domination by Junkers and parsons," and that it was foolish to encourage artificially such an apprehension, which could only work in favor of the German Liberals. Neither the liquor tax nor the higher tariff, it said, had been passed to "raise the income of the big landowners." Rather, these measures had been recognized by all the parties of the cartel as necessary for providing more revenue for the federal government and alleviating the genuine distress of agriculture.[5]

What, actually, except national loyalty and patriotism, did the National Liberals have to offer as a positive program? How could they continue, without war scares, to attract the mass of voters and maintain the leading position in the Reichstag so brilliantly achieved for them the preceding year? Even in more normal circumstances, if they could have envisaged a long reign for a new liberal king-emperor who, with the government, would have sponsored a new liberal era of reform legislation, even then they would have been faced with the practical problem of organizing and buttressing their new strength at the local precinct level. In April 1887 one of the local party workers in National Liberal Deputy Hammacher's Ruhr district had written that miners and factory workers must be brought onto the local party committee and means be found to spread the ideas of the National Liberal party among the masses. Now, with the future of the crown prince extremely dubious, such a necessity was even more pressing and more difficult. The National Liberals had, indeed, made some noteworthy gestures in the direction of social welfare. They had introduced a bill into the Reichstag to set federal standards for housing; in the previous session they had joined the Conservatives and Center is supporting Reich legislation controlling the labor of women and children; in this session they now supported a Center-German Liberal bill prohibiting work on Sundays, which passed almost unanimously. The problem in this area was to get the Federated Governments to accept such bills in the Bundesrat, which they had so far shown no disposition to do. Meanwhile the *National Liberale Korrespondenz* tried to make the most of the party's positive attitude toward labor legislation, and Bennigsen's *Hannoverscher Kourier* claimed that German labor had never been exploited as it had been in other countries (Frederick the Great had even called himself "king of the beggars") and that the social insurance legislation already achieved under William I was in this tradition. The left-liberal *Frankfurter Zeitung*, however, remained skeptical concerning the degree of enthusiasm of the big-industrialist-dominated National Liberals for labor legislation. It pointed out that the National Liberal Reichstag deputy most outspoken in his support for labor legislation was Wilhelm Oechelhäuser, but that the Continental-Gesellschaft of Dessau, of which he was managing director, had expended only 1.56 percent of its profits for the welfare of its workers, which was much less than some other companies.[6]

In late February 1888 the National Liberal *Jenaische Zeitung* carried an article calling for a thorough shake-up of the party organization in Berlin. The old leadership under Kyllmann had been too conservative and too inactive; they should be expelled from the party and a stronger, younger organization constructed. In early March a similar article appeared in the *Kölnische Zeitung*, calling for rejuvenation of the party organization in Cologne. "It does not suffice for a committee to come together a few weeks before an election, to go through the lists and with much difficulty search out a candidate, . . . without bringing itself into harmony with the great mass of the voters, who after all give the final decision." It was much easier for the Center party, whose Catholic "troops" were always mobilized and ready to march to the ballot box at the command of a few leaders. Windthorst's school motion had given them a new standard to rally to in the Prussian Landtag elections in the fall, and the citizenry must be alerted to this threat. Such statements at least demonstrated an awareness among the National Liberal leadership of the necessity of learning how to construct a mass party. Whether they could successfully accomplish such a goal, however, remained to be seen.[7]

19

Death of Kaiser William

AT the height of the controversy over the Greiffenberg-Kammin election the attention of the press was suddenly diverted by the news that old Kaiser William was gravely ill. He had caught one of his frequent colds, which had brought on another attack of his bladder trouble; the morphine given him to ease the pain had reduced his appetite, and the resultant weakness in the almost ninety-one-year-old monarch had quickly become critical. Although the kaiser's illness had begun on March 5, the public became aware of the seriousness of its development only gradually, so that on the seventh there was the usual crowd in front of the palace at noon, hoping to see the kaiser come to the corner window, as was his custom, to watch the changing of the guard. Since the illness of the crown prince these crowds had been growing in size, especially on Sundays, as though the public wanted to show its sympathy with the misfortunes of the royal family. Three Sundays before, on February 19, the crowd in front of the palace had been estimated at between four and five thousand. They had had a special treat that day. While they watched the window, the curtain parted, and three small blond heads appeared— Prince William's oldest children. A servant then removed the curtain and the old kaiser appeared, standing behind his great-grandsons in their white suits, resting his hand on the head of the youngest. Presently they were joined by the kaiserin in her wheelchair and by Princess William, holding her youngest in her arms. At the sight of this family tableau the crowd let out a great roar of cheering and then sang the slow, solemn strains of "Heil Dir im Siegerkranz."[1]

On March 6 Bismarck telegraphed the crown prince and urged him to return to Berlin immediately. A subsequent telegram to Prince William from his brother, Prince Henry, in San Remo, however, stated that his father would go first not to Berlin, but to Wiesbaden, where the air was less raw; the ministry could carry on until further instructions. Reports that the crown prince was going to Wiesbaden appeared in the press.

Bismarck then telegraphed Radolinski at noon on the seventh that if the crown prince did not return at once to Berlin, he personally would not answer for the consequences. To the State Ministry on the eighth the chancellor complained that having the crown prince in Wiesbaden would be no better than his being in San Remo. The presence of the ruler would be necessary for the transition and for fulfilling the constitutional stipulations. The State Ministry could carry on constitutionally by itself only if there were no king or regent available (Article 57). Only the king, for example, could order the swearing of the troops. The public would not understand the king's choosing Wiesbaden over Berlin and would easily interpret it as indicating a "permanent incapacity"—i.e., reason for a regency. The ministry agreed to a collective telegram requesting that if the crown prince was at all able to travel he should come directly to Berlin "in the interest of the state and of the dynasty." Bismarck also told the ministers that the crown prince had decided to take the name of Frederick and was thinking of taking the number IV in the line of the old Holy Roman emperors. Bismarck had told him that there was no connection whatever between the new empire and the old Holy Roman Empire, and that if he wanted to be called Frederick he should take the numeral from the Prussian kings and be Frederick III. In the meantime the crown prince had received a telegram from his mother-in-law, Queen Victoria, imploring him for the sake of his health not to go to Berlin. The queen also telegraphed Sir Edward Malet to remonstrate with Bismarck against urging the crown prince to leave San Remo. The embarrassed ambassador approached the chancellor somewhat gingerly after he had addressed the Reichstag on the ninth and was calmly told—falsely—that Bismarck had not urged the crown prince to come to Berlin. However, for the queen's benefit Bismarck added that there were "the gravest reasons of state" for the crown prince to return and that if he stayed in San Remo it would be necessary for him to name a regent.[2]

Early on the morning of the seventh Prince William, back from his visit to San Remo, arrived in Berlin and learned of his grandfather's serious condition. In the evening he sent for Waldersee and talked at length with him in the flag room of the *Schloss*. "He was very excited and moved," wrote Waldersee in his diary. "All kinds of things are now going through his head!" Thursday morning, March 8, the official *Reichsgesetzblatt* carried the text of the kaiser's cabinet order of November 17 authorizing Prince William to sign papers for him if the condition of his health required it. Various members of the royal family now began to gather in the palace, including the kaiser's daughter, the grand duchess of Baden, and her husband. The court theater canceled its evening performance. Out of respect for the kaiser's condition, the Prussian House of Deputies adjourned. Prince Bismarck, Field Marshal Moltke, and Prince William were now spending much time in the palace. In its evening edition the *Norddeutsche* carried a eulogy of the dying monarch, clearly meant to indicate his approaching end, in which it called him "a shining example of the duties of his high office." The danger now threatening him must bring all Germans even closer together, "in calm and devotion, but also in courage and self-confidence."[3]

By Thursday evening, the eighth, dense crowds surrounded the palace, standing silent and conversing in whispers. Around six o'clock one newspaper prematurely announced the kaiser's death, which caused a short-lived sensation. The paper was confiscated by the police. Later it began to rain hard, but the crowd stayed on under a forest of black umbrellas. Special services were being held in the churches. Late in the evening the dying kaiser surprised the doctors by coming out of his coma, speaking to the grand duchess of Baden, and taking some nourishment. Early in the morning he slipped back into a coma, and the court officials sent a carriage at half-past three to wake the elderly Bismarck and bring him once more to the palace, where he remained until after five, and then, returning to the chancellor's palace, found that he could not sleep. At 8:32 in the morning of March 9, in the presence of his wife, the grand duchess of Baden, and Prince William, the old man finally died. Special sessions of the Prussian House of Deputies, the Bundesrat, and the Reichstag were set for 11:00, 11:30, and 11:45 A.M., so that ministers and deputies who were members of more than one could attend. The morning editions of the *Frankfurter Zeitung* reported that the crown prince would leave San Remo by special train the next day, one report saying for Wiesbaden, another Berlin.[4]

When the Prussian House of Deputies met, President von Köller recognized Vice-President of the State Ministry von Puttkamer, and the deputies rose. Puttkamer, in a voice shaken with emotion, announced the death of Kaiser William, but quite unaccountably then failed to mention the succession of the new kaiser, Frederick. Von Köller, in expressing the general sorrow of the deputies and closing the session, also omitted any mention of their new kaiser and king. One could hardly suppose that such an omission was inadvertent, since continuity in a hereditary monarchy is the very essence of the institution. To add to the certainty that there was, indeed, no mistake, Puttkamer specifically declared that "the sorrow of our exalted ruling family is our sorrow, and that, the deeper the general pain is over the departure of the unforgettable king, the tighter and more indestructable will prove to be the tie that, in good days and bad, binds Prussia's ruling house with Prussia's people." Likewise von Köller ended his short statement with the call, "God save the royal family! God save the fatherland!"[5]

The Puttkamer-Köller omission is all the more suggestive when one finds that the acting governor of the Berlin army garrison, in announcing the death of Kaiser William to his assembled troops, also did not mention the succession of Kaiser Frederick, but merely added, "Further orders are to be awaited." When the members of the House of Deputies realized that there had been no mention of the new king, there was consternation and heated discussion, which was not alleviated by the explanation of some Conservative deputies that official word of the new kaiser's succession had not yet been received from San Remo. Succession from father to son was automatic; it did not need a proclamation. As Landtag deputies arrived at the Reichstag, reports of what had happened in the House started agitation there, and some of the Reichstag party leaders approached the president and received assurances that he would be more tactful.

At 11:45 the Reichstag deputies filed in and took their places in the chamber. "Each sat in his place, no walking around, no whispering, deathly silence, sorrow on all faces. . . . The time lengthened. Over half an hour, mute and silent, the representatives of the German people waited. It seemed so simple and so natural, and yet the impression was extraordinarily moving." A servant carried in the chancellor's yellow leather armchair and set it at his place at the end of the Bundesrat table. Eventually Herbert Bismarck appeared through the little door in back of the podium and beckoned to the Reichstag president, Wilhelm von Wedell-Piesdorf, who followed him back through the door to the room where the Bundesrat was sitting. A few minutes later von Wedell-Piesdorf reappeared and was soon followed by Bismarck and the members of the Bundesrat, who took their places. "The House rose, the members of the Social Democratic delegation this time making no exception. The president's bell did not sound, no routine introduction was spoken, only a brief, 'The Herr Reich Chancellor will speak.'" With a fine sense of appropriateness, Prince Bismarck spoke simply and plainly: "It is my sad duty to report to you officially what you actually already know, that this morning at half-past eight His Majesty Kaiser William passed away to his fathers. As a result of this event the Prussian crown and, according to Article Eleven of the Reich constitution, the imperial title have passed to His Majesty Frederick III, King of Prussia."

Thus simply were the doubts and fears allayed and the decorum of form and tradition preserved. Kaiser Frederick, announced the chancellor, would leave San Remo tomorrow and arrive in Berlin in due time. The chancellor then related that the day before the kaiser's death he had handed him the order for the closing of the Reichstag session to sign and had suggested that he merely initial it. The old man, however, had insisted upon writing his full name. The signature, which was his last, was now neither valid nor necessary, since the Reichstag would not want to adjourn until the new kaiser had arrived, but it remained a historic document. He did not need to tell the Reichstag of his personal feelings, which were shared by every German. Two things had comforted the kaiser in his last hours: the worldwide concern expressed over his son's illness, which had shown that the dynasty had won the trust of all nations; and the demonstration of national unity in defense of the fatherland in the Reichstag in February. "Gentlemen! The heroic gallantry, the high, national sense of honor, and above all the loyal, industrious fulfillment of duty in service to the fatherland and the love for the fatherland that were embodied in our departed sovereign, may they be an indestructible heritage for our nation, . . . " At this point the old man, who had been struggling to control his emotions and his voice, lost control of both. Tears ran down his cheeks, which he wiped away with his hand, and the assembled members of the Reichstag, standing in awed silence, savoring the historic quality of the moment, clearly heard the Iron Chancellor sob. Loyal, industrious service, simplicity, humility, responsibility: these were the virtues of the grandfather. They were conspicuously not the virtues of the grandson, Prince William, the real heir. Surely the experienced party leaders standing there must have realized that the old man wept, not only for his departed sovereign, but also for the future of the German Reich, with which he had so closely identified himself. The chancellor continued: "—which the departed kaiser has left behind for us. I hope to God that by all of us who take part in the affairs of our fatherland, in war and in peace, in heroism, in sacrifice, in diligence, in devotion to duty, this heritage shall be loyally preserved." "One saw," Miquel later wrote, "many serious men with tears on their cheeks. We all maintained our silence. And so we departed, with the awareness that a serious time could now be beginning."

After the president had closed the session, Bismarck came down from the dais and shook hands and talked for a while with Field Marshal von Moltke. He also handed around the document with the kaiser's last signature. Many newspapers carried a facsimile of the signature the next day, beside one of the normal signature of the old man. Later Friday the minister of war issued an order to the officers and officials of the ministry announcing the death of Kaiser William and continuing, "We can express this gratitude in no better way than by serving His Majesty King Frederick III of Prussia, who has now been called to rule, with the same devotion with which we served his deceased father." When a special session of the Prussian House of Deputies was called to receive the official announcement from the State Ministry of the accession of Kaiser Frederick and his expected arrival in Berlin, President von Köller used the same stylistic formulation. The State Ministry statement had rather awkwardly referred, contrary to fact, to the "official communication delivered orally to the House of Deputies today of the decease of His Majesty Kaiser and King William and the succession to the throne of His Majesty King Frederick III." *Germania* reported in its second Sunday edition that Puttkamer had neglected to announce Kaiser Frederick's succession to the throne in the House because the telegram reporting the kaiser's choice of official title had not yet been received, and that the Reichstag session had been delayed for the same reason. It may never be known whether this interpretation of Puttkamer's and Köller's silence is true or not. It does appear, however, that these two had made no special efforts to remedy the situation and that they had rather too easily adopted the very unusual and provocative course that they took. In the circumstances the left Liberals no doubt were willing to believe the worst.[6]

Evening editions of the March 9 papers were edged in black, and several carried large crosses centered above leading articles announcing the death of the kaiser. Every detail of the last hours was reported, frequently more than once: what prayers had been read, what the old kaiser had eaten and drunk, what he had said at this or that time. Given a great deal of prominence was his reply to a remark that he must be tired and must rest: "I have no time to be tired." The *Norddeutsche* published a telegram from Kaiser Frederick thanking Bismarck and the State Ministry for their loyalty and service to his father and requesting their continued support of his new government. It was announced that the new kaiser would leave San Remo by special train Saturday morning, the tenth, and travel over the Brenner through Munich to Charlottenburg, just west of Berlin, where he, the kaiserin, and the doctors would take up residence in the palace there. His daughters would live in the old Berlin *Schloss*. Of Kaiser William, among many eulogies, the *National Zeitung* wrote, "What made him more revered than his age or his fame was his selflessness. . . . Consciously for the few, unconsciously for all, in him was embodied the monarchial idea. . . . The more vaguely the mystical aura surrounding monarchy threatens to evaporate in the democratic movement and feelings of the peoples, the more glorious and majestic the figure of Kaiser William towered over us. . . . We, the living, however, know that with him the nineteenth century has gone to rest, and a new age begins to dawn."[7]

PART II

The Ninety-Nine Days

We are a people of the middle, of the world-bourgeoisie; there is a fittingness in our geographical position and in our *mores*. . . . A people settled in the bourgeois world-middle must needs be the *täuschende* (deceptive), protean folk: a race that practises sly and ironic reserve toward both sides, that moves between extremes, easily, with noncommittal benevolence; with the morality, no, the piety of that elusive 'betweenness' of theirs, their faith in knowledge and insight, in cosmopolitan culture.

Fruitful dilemma of the middle, thou art freedom and reserve in one!

—Thomas Mann, "Goethe and Tolstoy"

20

The New Reign

AT 11:04 Sunday night, March 11, the special train carrying the new German kaiser arrived at the Berlin Westend station, nearest to Charlottenburg. Long beforehand crowds had begun to gather, undeterred by the onset of a heavy snowstorm about eight o'clock, driven by an icy wind, so that one could scarcely see. Several thousand people had gathered around the station, and more lined both sides of the road all the way to the Charlottenburg palace. The train, due at 10:37, had been delayed by the storm. The *Kreuzzeitung* reported that one frequently heard people in the crowd remark, "We are not leaving here even if it takes until early morning and we can see the imperial carriage only in the distance"; and "Our Fritz deserves that we should get our feet cold and wet for him." To protect the ailing kaiser from the raw weather, a sort of pavilion had been erected between the train tracks and the street. This tent or pavilion was hung with black on the outside and red on the inside, and was elaborately decorated with rugs, laurel, palms, flowers, silver candelabras, and gilded chairs emblazoned with the imperial eagle. Shortly after ten, Crown Prince William, the crown princess, Prince Henry, and Princess Charlotte and her husband, the hereditary prince of Saxe-Meiningen, arrived, and when the train finally came in, they entered the imperial coach to greet their parents. A formal welcome had been strictly forbidden, but local officials appear to have been present regardless. At length Kaiser Frederick emerged, dressed in a long gray military coat with fur collar and forage cap, and walked quickly through the tent to a closed carriage, which then set off for the Charlottenburg palace, preceded and followed by mounted detachments of the *Gardes du Corps*. The faithful crowd, baring their heads in the driving snow, raised lusty cheers.[1]

The kaiser's train of three coaches, two salon cars, one sleeping car, and three baggage cars had departed from San Remo the morning of the tenth, had been visited by the king and prime minister of Italy at San Pier d'Arena, and had crossed into Germany in the early morning of the

eleventh. Since the scheduled arrival in Berlin would be so late, and
Kaiser Frederick wanted to meet the ministry as soon as possible, he
ordered them by telegram to meet him in Leipzig. Although Bismarck
was experiencing physical disabilities, mostly in his legs, as a result of the
strain of the last few days, he felt that it was important to make the
additional effort of the trip to Leipzig, since, as he told M. Jules Herbette,
the French ambassador, he was afraid that in his absence some of the
ministers (probably Puttkamer) might not get along with the kaiser. As
extra support, he took his personal physician, Dr. Schweninger, and Herbert along with him. In Leipzig Bismarck was the first to enter the imperial car, and through the uncurtained windows observers could see that
Kaiser Frederick immediately hurried forward to meet him, embracing
him and kissing him three times on both cheeks. After a brief conference
with the ministers, during which the kaiser agreed to all their suggested
dispositions, they returned by separate train to Berlin, while Bismarck
and Herbert continued on in the kaiser's train. It was agreed that there
should be no changes in the ministry, Bismarck declaring himself against
it; and in general the Bismarcks found the kaiser "extremely reasonable
and sensible." Although still lively in his movements, he was thin in the
face and his complexion ashen. He did not speak, but used a pad and
pencil to write down his wishes and replies. All the ministers found it
difficult to accustom themselves to the gurgling, whistling sound of the
kaiser's breathing through the tube in his neck. "That the *novum regnum*,"
Herbert wrote to his brother Bill, "can last more than 3-4 months seems
out of the question, perhaps even less."[2]

This fundamental problem of Kaiser Frederick's health placed a very
large question mark over the new regime. The succession, wrote Ambassador Széchényi to Vienna, was best described by the tragic cry, "The
emperor is dead! Long live the dying emperor!" He had already heard
people say openly that it was unfortunate that Kaiser William had not
outlived his son, since "only confusion and obstruction can be expected
from the ephemeral rule of the present kaiser." Kaiserin Victoria herself
wrote to her mother the queen,

> I think people in general consider us a mere passing shadow, soon to be
> replaced by reality in the shape of William. I may be wrong, but it seems to
> me as if the party that opposed and ill-treated us so long hardly think it
> worth while to change their attitude except very slightly—as they count on
> a different future! . . . Yes, we are our own masters now, but shall we not have
> to leave all the work undone which we have so long and so carefully been
> preparing? Will there be any chance of doing the right thing, any time to
> carry out useful measures, needful reforms? . . . All the more we shall strive
> to do what is wisest and safest and best! Prudence and caution are necessary

now where fresh and vigorous regeneration of many an obsolete and used up thing would have been desirable! . . . Prince Bismarck has been civil and nice and I think feels quite at his ease.

The day after Kaiser William's death Bismarck had asked Dr. von Bergmann how much longer Kaiser Frederick had to live. He would not survive the summer, replied the doctor. Thus there was little reason for engaging in any new departures. Meanwhile perhaps such an interim before the succession of Crown Prince William could be used to try to gain further control over him. Before his actual meeting with Kaiser Frederick, Bismarck's greatest fear was that he would have to forcefully and ruthlessly block inappropriate proposals of a dying man. The reasonable and cautious recognition of their difficult position by the royal couple therefore relieved him greatly. All observers bear out the kaiserin's judgment that the chancellor was very pleased and satisfied with his relations with the kaiser. It was only looking at him that he found distressing—not his physical appearance, but the "dumb anxiety in his eyes when he wanted to say something and couldn't." A week later Kaiserin Victoria wrote to her mother that Bismarck was "not a bit shaky—I never saw him looking stronger—as hale—as a bell—rosy in the face & . . . [*sic*] He is only troubled with a varicose vein on one Leg. He seems *bien disposé*, and we do all we can to keep him so.—"[3]

The relations between kaiser and chancellor, however, by no means took care of all the factors at work. In his report to Vienna of March 10 Ambassador Széchényi had remarked that a regime made provisional by the precarious health of its leader would have difficulty competing with the definite expectations embodied in the presence of the heir to the throne. It would help to minimize intrigue if the crown prince were deputized to represent his father in official affairs. Some sort of deputy was definitely needed. Although Kaiser Frederick applied himself diligently to the stacks of official papers, the doctors would not allow him to risk getting overtired; and especially before and after his father's funeral, there were courtesy calls of royal and princely personages and representatives that he could not very well avoid, as well as the ongoing, routine conferences with the chancellor, the ministers, and the cabinet chiefs. In Prussian affairs everything had to be signed by the king. He had signed a hundred papers on the train from Leipzig to Berlin, but Kaiser William's illness and death had produced a stack of over five hundred. "Of course the change is immense, from the life of an invalid to one of business and excitement," wrote Kaiserin Victoria to her mother the queen, "far beyond what he is at present fit for."[4]

The main obstacle preventing the quick reappointment of Crown Prince William as the kaiser's deputy was the lack of trust between son and parents. The day of the old kaiser's death, in reply to a telegram from the crown prince announcing the event, Kaiser Frederick had written, "In deep sorrow over the death of my father, at which you not I were privileged to be present, in ascending the throne I express the firm confidence that in loyalty and obedience you will be an example to all." This consciously formal and solemn statement from father to son on a solemn occasion could have been taken as in fact complimentary, but the crown prince read it as hostile and threatening. He showed it to Waldersee, who noted in his diary that in "coldness" it "surpassed all bounds." Waldersee also recorded his suggestion to the prince that "the opinion of all of us, that it would be a misfortune if Kaiser William died before the crown prince, was quite erroneous; the new imperial couple would perpetrate so many absurdities that they would prepare the ground in the best way for him, the new crown prince." He advised the prince, therefore, to remain as inconspicuous as possible, and later he praised him for his caution and discretion. Ambassador Széchényi, however, reported that the society and court circles hostile to Kaiserin Victoria were able to gain support from deprecatory and critical statements of the crown prince. The "Bonn manners" of Crown Prince William, wrote Széchényi (Prince William had attended the university at Bonn), were too much in evidence, "and the authoritative and hasty manner in which the prince deals with serious questions, as well as his incautious and intolerant proceeding in religious matters produce much head-shaking, and there are therefore not many left, even in military circles, who anticipate the no-longer-distant accession to the throne of Crown Prince William completely without alarm."[5]

Negotiations had apparently been proceeding indirectly for some time between the chancellor and the crown princess, later kaiserin, over who was to be appointed deputy: she had resisted the appointment of her son and attempted to have herself placed in the position, remarking that if her mother could rule over a world power so well for so long, she could certainly be entrusted to sign a few papers. There appeared to be nothing in the law that would have prevented the appointment of a woman as representative for the kaiser and king, but it was, of course, not very sensible politically, especially considering the hostility toward the kaiserin among the right wing. Outwardly Bismarck maintained a strictly correct posture in the matter, refusing to suggest a deputizing order until the kaiser had ordered him to do so. Privately, of course, he was as outspoken as usual and was naturally backed up by Crown Prince William and his brother, Prince Henry, who declared that "Hohenzollern Prussia and the German Reich must not allow themselves to be led by a woman."

The kaiserin's position in the matter being basically weak, the chancellor merely allowed the various pressures to build against her, including the advice of her brother, the Prince of Wales, when he was in Berlin for the old kaiser's funeral. Eventually she gave in, and on March 21 Kaiser Frederick sent word to Bismarck that he would like to be relieved of as much work as possible through the deputizing of the crown prince. Bismarck then presented for his approval an imperial order that, since it was not a question of either complete or temporary incapacity, was basically different from the order of Kaiser William of the previous November, and also provided face-saving phrases to protect the kaiser's dignity. The order was headed "Concerning the participation of His Imperial and Royal Highness the Crown Prince in state business" and declared that the purpose was to make the crown prince acquainted with state affairs. He was to have the right to sign such papers as the kaiser presented to him, thus making the prince, as Széchényi reported, a sort of secretary. Certainly, wrote the *Frankfurter Zeitung*, to relieve the kaiser of routine signatures was not to limit his power. Why should it be necessary for the king of Prussia to sign every second lieutenant's commission and the letter of appointment for every *Landrat*? This sort of thing should be left to the respective ministers. A point of view that certainly appears sensible, yet in a relatively closed, hierarchical society such as nineteenth-century Germany still was, appointments and promotions to official positions, civil and military, were especially important. The more conservative newspapers, such as the *Kreuzzeitung* or the *Norddeutsche*, regularly carried lists of royal appointments in the leading column on the front page, and people with social or political aspirations perused them avidly, to see whose nephew had finally got his commission or how such and such a family was doing. As head of the administrative hierarchy—where the real power lay—the king could not easily or safely delegate his ultimate authority and responsibility.

The mere signing of the representation order by Kaiser Frederick did not immediately change the situation. The kaiser, Waldersee complained, was reluctant to hand over anything to his son William, so that he remained overworked as before. At the end of the month, therefore, Bismarck procured a second order from the kaiser announcing his intention of defining more precisely what matters were to be handled by the crown prince. In a meeting of the State Ministry, to which both cabinet chiefs were invited, the latter both declared that His Majesty was not likely to want to give up signing many commissions and appointments or imperial decrees that were to be published. The ministers then offered categories of papers in their respective departments that could be sent to the crown prince for signature, and it was decided to present a unified list of these to the kaiser for his approval or amendment. Thus the chancellor by formally spelling out the lines of responsibility sought to reassure the various parties and to minimize occasions for backbiting, criticism, and intrigue.[6]

While the deputy issue was still being negotiated, Berlin and Germany had taken official leave of old Kaiser William in a grand funeral procession. The city voted to spend 600,000 M on decorations, and the funeral route was elaborately draped and ornamented, including lines of flaring gas torches on tall tripods on both sides of Unter den Linden from the cathedral to the Brandenburg Gate. Immediately after the kaiser's death people had poured into the streets, well dressed, wearing mourning. In dense, silent rows the crowd converged upon the royal palace, demonstrating their wish to share in the family's sorrow. Late in the night of Sunday, March 11, the old kaiser's body was transferred, through a double line of soldiers holding torches, to the Berlin cathedral, where it lay in state until the funeral ceremony Friday, the sixteenth. The snow that had begun on Sunday continued to fall for two days, and although the viewing hours were lengthened to begin at 8 A.M. and extend to 10 P.M., thousands nevertheless were left frustrated when the cathedral closed at night, having stood in the packed streets most of the day and evening without being able to gain entrance. Clearly a new phenomenon was developing: the life and death of the king and emperor were no longer the concern merely of a limited group, a closed hierarchy. He had been transformed into the popular symbol of the new nation; and old customs, institutions, and dispositions, adequate to a small, provincial, agrarian kingdom, were no longer suited to the new, larger, urban, mass empire. The Berlin cathedral was too small for the tremendous crowds that wanted to enter it. The office of the court marshal was not prepared to handle the floods of requests from groups of all kinds, many of them from outside Berlin and some from abroad, for special permission to view the body and to take part in the funeral. There was also no coordination among the court authorities, the city police, and the army—a difficulty compounded by the transition from the administration of Kaiser William's court marshal, Count Perponcher, to Kaiser Frederick's court marshal, Count Radolinski. The noble army officers, headed by the crown prince, also felt it to be their right and duty to lead their various units to view the old kaiser as an act of instructive patriotic piety, especially for the young recruits. Consequently the general public were being continually held back from the cathedral while military units were given special access.

The rather humorous climax of this frustrating procedure was reached during the evening of March 14, when members of the Bundesrat and Reichstag, by arrangement with the court marshal, attempted to enter the cathedral but were given no recognition or consideration by the police—evidently because they were not in uniform—and were prevented from entering and even pushed back rather unceremoniously to allow some military unit to go in. The liberal press raised a storm over this incident, in spite of the temporarily dominant atmosphere of restraint and piety, and the chancellor promised an investigation. It turned out that the marshal had failed to inform the police. On the other hand, the court marshal's office continued to take the unrealistic position that everyone who wished should be allowed to view the body, but at the same time it disdained giving any special consideration to the popular press. The crowds of Berliners were also strongly reinforced by thousands of people from outside who streamed into the city in an unprecedented way. The *Norddeutsche* estimated that a total of four hundred thousand outsiders came into the city during the week. Outside as well as inside the cathedral the crowd was packed so tightly that people could not move their arms, and it was difficult to breathe. Among the thousands of strangers were also an international collection of professional pickpockets. Many of the police were injured in the crush, and one mounted policeman and his horse were overturned by the crowd. By the end of the week, stated the *Norddeutsche*, the police were quite exhausted.[7]

It was commonly felt that the old kaiser's death marked the end of an era. He had been seventeen years old and already an army captain when Prussia helped defeat Napoleon in 1814, had gone into exile during the revolutions of 1848, had presided over the unifying of most of Germany and its rise to a position of dominant power. He had come to symbolize that historical achievement and that position. With him now gone, everything seemed put in question. In an editorial that sounded as if it had been dictated by Bismarck himself, the *Frankfurter Zeitung* assured its readers that Germany's position and peaceful policy need not suffer any significant change with the kaiser's death. The new Germany was a nation, and therefore a peaceful empire, dedicated to the welfare of its citizens and to allowing other nations the same concern.[8] Later generations might find it odd that there should be any question of the ninety-year-old kaiser's death actually affecting the policy or position of Germany. But at the time it was a common tendency to perceive the nation's power as residing entirely in the person of its monarch, perhaps a matter of symbolic imagery. Even London papers suggested that Russia might seize the occasion to make a bold move. Some French papers assumed that the end of the creator of the new German empire must herald the end of the empire as well, and they quoted the *Bayrisches Vaterland* of the Bavarian eccentric Dr. Sigl, which stated that the difficulties of the Prussian royal house, with one king dead and another dying, "appear to be bringing about a great change in German politics. We believe that the time is at hand, when certain German federal states will win back their former independence."

The *Kölnische Zeitung*, the day following the kaiser's death, carried a sensational article quoting a parliamentary leader quoting Field Marshal Moltke to the effect that foreign enemies should beware of attacking Germany in this difficult time because everyone would be united. The *Konservative Korrespondenz* the same day declared that there could be no danger of external attack since Germans were as devotedly united around the throne as before, and Bismarck and Moltke, "who embody the trust of the German people and the fear of the foreigners [*des Auslandes*]," still stood next to the throne. Not surprisingly, such emotional feelings of insecurity and apprehension came to a head in the *Kreuzzeitung*, which wrote, "With his incomparable prestige the kaiser protected the tender plant that no one around it wanted to allow to grow up into a strong tree, nor does yet today." And then, in an open expression of what for this disciplined, orderly society must have been the key to the complex, "Our father has left us, we have become orphans."[9]

In the funeral procession on Friday, March 16, Kaiser William's casket, covered by a cloth of imperial purple embroidered in gold, was mounted on a carriage drawn by eight horses draped in black. A canopy of yellow silk embroidered with a border of black imperial eagles was carried over it by twelve major generals walking on either side. After the funeral car came the kaiser's horse, empty boots reversed in the stirrups. Next came the imperial flag, followed by the crown prince walking alone in the uniform of a general, with military coat. This position Kaiser Frederick had reserved for himself, but he had been prevented by the doctors from making the effort in the raw weather. Crown Prince William held himself very erect, walking very solemnly and seriously, looking neither to right nor to left. To the public, aware that his father was dying too and that the whole burden of the Reich would shortly descend upon his shoulders, he made a poignantly appealing figure. After the crown prince came a motley and rather ragged crowd of more than a hundred German and foreign princes and rulers, with the kings of Saxony, Belgium, and Rumania at the front, and including Crown Prince Rudolf of Austria-Hungary, Tsarevich Nicholas of Russia, and the Prince of Wales. This group was followed by diplomatic representatives, members of the parliaments, representatives of the universities, and other dignitaries. The whole procession was headed by eight squadrons of cavalry, a body of infantry, twelve guns, three regimental bands, and court officials, followed by the ministers carrying the imperial crown, sword, scepter, and orb. Bismarck and Moltke had been excused from taking part in the procession, so that the kaiser's scepter was carried, rather ironically, by Puttkamer.

The funeral route down Unter den Linden through the Brandenburg Gate and the Tiergarten to the mausoleum in Charlottenburg was strewn with yellow gravel and evergreen twigs, and five-hundred thousand people lined the way within the city, where standing room was limited to officially recognized guilds and corporations, displaying their individual flags. At the Brandenburg Gate there was a brief flurry of fisticuffs as two different groups tried to occupy the same place, but it was quieted just in time for the procession to pass. All the way through the Tiergarten, crowds three hundred feet deep continued to line the route, in spite of a foot of snow. A number of intrepid souls climbed the trees, stubbornly maintaining themselves there during the long wait, immobilized, exposed to the icy wind. In Charlottenburg the procession passed close by the palace, where at a second-story window stood Kaiser Frederick at attention, in a general's dress uniform, with the ribbon of the Order of the Black Eagle, remaining there until a cannon volley signaled that the final ceremony in the mausoleum had ended. The press, almost without exception of party, devoted itself to eulogies of the departed monarch; even the German Liberal *Freisinnige Zeitung* wrote that the old kaiser's funeral was a final victory parade—"a victory march into immortality!"[10]

It was, in cruel contrast, ineluctable mortality that shadowed the new regime of Frederick and Victoria. Once having decided to brazen it out, to put on a confident face and defy the dread disease—a stance that was not only natural to Victoria's stubborn Hanoverian English heritage but also fundamentally necessary to Frederick's sensitive, weak nature—they were obliged to act positively, at least to some degree, and therefore engage in an increasingly grotesque charade. Thus it was natural that Dr. Mackenzie should now release new reports to the newspapers questioning the cancer diagnosis.

On the train from Leipzig to Berlin, Kaiser Frederick had handed to Bismarck copies of two proclamations, carefully written out in his own hand, one "To the Reich Chancellor and President of the State Ministry," and the other "To My People." Somewhat taken aback, Bismarck had asked for time to study the documents, but as he later told the ministry, having done so, he had found them to be "beautifully written" and quite unobjectionable. In his audience with Kaiser Frederick in Charlottenburg on the twelfth he had recommended that they be published immediately and substantially without change. These proclamations had been drawn up in a series of meetings in the summer of 1885, when Kaiser William was in ill health and appeared not to have long to live, by a small group of the then crown prince's closest advisors: Baron von Roggenbach, General von Stosch, and Minister of Justice Friedberg. Heinrich Geffcken, a former professor of public law and government at the new University of Strassburg and a rabid Bismarck-hater, who had known the crown prince in their student days at Bonn, had added himself to the group, acting as secretary. Letters to the kings of Bavaria, Württemberg, and Saxony were also drawn up, to reassure them that Frederick William did not intend to infringe their constitutional rights. All these documents had received the crown prince's approval after "two contentious days with Roggenbach and the grand duke of Baden." The purpose of this labor was primarily to prevent the crown prince from fatally alienating both Bismarck and the princes in the first days of his reign, and the proclamations now, in a very different situation than was then envisaged, did serve this purpose. But their tone of setting a positive, confident program for the future, in light of Frederick's illness, produced a most peculiar, eerie effect. Pindter put it bluntly in his diary: the documents, he wrote, were "beautifully styled, but contain mere words. Who will carry [them] out?"[11]

It was also difficult for Frederick and Victoria, with their sudden accession to power, not to make gestures expressing their own independent point of view. Indeed, the tentative nature of their situation and the oppressive consciousness of time running out may well have increased their urge to make some kind of personal mark. Even before they had left San Remo, Kaiser Frederick had telegraphed to the State Ministry an order proclaiming that no set period of public mourning for his father was to be prescribed, but that each German was to be left free to express his sorrow in his own way. This liberal-minded order produced a measure of dismay and resentment in Berlin. Some of the ministers wanted to hold up its publication and remonstrate. In the first place, this and other orders from San Remo had not been based on recommendations of the ministers and could therefore not be legally countersigned; secondly, it would cause a great deal of confusion. Bismarck, however, maintained that it would not do to oppose the first independent acts of the new ruler, that the matter was not all that important. The kaiser had taken the responsibility upon himself and would have to accept any painful repercussions. The order naturally offended the conservatives around the court and caused a flurry of consultations, especially among the representatives of the federal princes, whose rights of sovereignty over the acts of their own subjects appeared to be infringed by the kaiser's reference to "every German," but who did not want in their own dispositions to ignore Prussian regulations and also did not want to appear to be lacking in respect. In the end they decreed the traditional six weeks' period of public mourning, so that Waldersee noted scornfully, "Most of the German princes have proclaimed public mourning; the king of Prussia leaves it to each person to do what he wants!" As a gesture of mourning Kaiser Frederick also took the opportunity to do away with epaulets on army uniforms. Bismarck and the minister of war appearing in military coats with bare shoulder straps, wrote Lucius, was an "unusual sight."[12]

Orders, uniforms, and decorations had always been very important to Frederick III. His concept of monarchy was rather naive and romantic. Ambassador Széchényi reported that the main reason the kaiser had dropped the "William" from his name was because he was so commonly known as "our Fritz," but Frederick's insistence down to the last minute on the numeral "IV" indicates rather that he wanted very much to put himself in the romantic line of the medieval Hohenstaufen Holy Roman emperors, descendants of the similarly red-bearded Frederick I, that figure who in popular myth slept in a cave under the Kyffhäuser mountain, waiting to be awakened, when he would once more, in a new incarnation, lead Germany to glory. In the first days of his reign Kaiser Frederick pasted into volume thirty-seven of his diary (a sort of catchall) a sentimental poem, "To the New Kaiser," that began,

> Kaiser Frederick Barbarossa,
> Our Great and noble Kaiser,
> Once again has he arisen,
> From the depths of the Kyffhäuser . . .

Upon Frederick's accession he presented his wife with the most distinguished Prussian Order of the Black Eagle, copying his father's gesture upon his own accession. Also, after he had dismissed the ministers in Leipzig, and with Bismarck's agreement, he called Minister of Justice Friedberg, his advisor for twenty-six years, back into the salon car and, to his surprise, hung his own Black Eagle ribbon and cross on him. Since this special recognition of Friedberg gave him preferment over Ministers von Puttkamer, Maybach, and Lucius, who surpassed him in length of service, Albert von Maybach, who was due for recognition anyway, subsequently was also given the Black Eagle. Puttkamer, whom no one expected the new kaiser to decorate, had to bear the oversight as best he could; Lucius realized the personal reasons for Friedberg's recognition and was not affronted. Conservative court circles, however, were scandalized by the decoration of Friedberg, a commoner, and equally so when the Black Eagle was later presented by the kaiser to Dr. Eduard Simson, presiding judge of the Supreme Imperial Court, who had been president of the Frankfurt Assembly in 1848 and the first president of the Reichstag. This recognition of a prominent National Liberal had been previously planned under Kaiser William, but that made small difference to the Conservatives. Not only were both men commoners, who, since the Black Eagle order was limited to nobility, thus had to be ennobled, but they were also both of Jewish origin. Maybach too was merely a middle-class Catholic. Waldersee saw the Friedberg decoration as in itself the announcement of a liberal program. Friedberg was claimed by the Liberals, and the kaiser's gesture, he wrote, "reveals the attempt to make himself popular among the liberals and the Jews." Aristocratic Berlin society had never liked Kaiserin Victoria—a feeling that was heartily reciprocated— and they now, under the uncertain circumstances, allowed themselves to be provoked into unrestrained criticism and hostility. The *Kreuzzeitung* Conservatives, it was reported, were privately calling Kaiser Frederick "Cohn I, king of the Jews." One well-informed person, reported Ambassador Széchényi, expressed wonder that Conservative hostility had not gotten into the press, which appeared to have "more tact and feeling of decency . . . than the upper ten thousand." Another Reich official remarked that it was fortunate for the monarchy that such attitudes were not shared by the middle classes. "The monarchy would be in a bad way if one were to judge . . . by the conduct of court society."[13]

The party press, had, indeed, been maintaining a most exemplary reticence, a sort of political truce in deference to the old kaiser, at least until the funeral. But it was not unanimous; on both Right and Left the urge to guide and admonish the new regime was not entirely resisted. In its welcome to Kaiser Frederick of March 13 the *Kreuzzeitung* declared that the whole world recognized that the German Reich as it stood was a guarantor and defender of the peace. "To want peace, therefore," it went on, "means to take things as they are, no more, no less." Rather inadvertently the *Kölnische Zeitung* had made the same point quite baldly already on the tenth. In the sensational article previously referred to (see above, p. 180), the reporter quoted "trustworthy circles" to the effect that "Prince Bismarck could not have grown up in monarchical sentiment and could not have helped found and construct the German Reich if in the hour of need he did not declare his solidarity with every individual Prussian minister. Let it be noted, with every individual. He would not lend his name to an overturning even of Prussian relationships." This obvious declaration of support for Puttkamer could not be overlooked by other party papers, and the *National Zeitung* remarked sharply that nothing could more severely injure monarchical sentiment than that kind of declaration of solidarity, which would "hinder [the new ruler] in the choice of his advisors." The statement that the *Kölnische Zeitung* had picked up had probably originated with bureaucrats who felt threatened rather than from the chancellor himself. That this was likely the case was indicated when the *Kölnische* explained lamely in an article on the twelfth that the previous article contained a printer's error: a "not" had crept in that did not belong there. Thus the statement should read that Bismarck would not have strong monarchical sentiment, etc., if in the present difficult time he declared solidarity with every individual, etc. So that now, instead of a defense of Puttkamer, it became an attack on him.[14]

The *Freisinnige Zeitung*, Eugen Richter's paper, went further. The German people knew, it wrote as early as the tenth, that the very core of the new kaiser's being was formed by "a humane impulse and universal understanding of different political, social, and religious tendencies, only from whose conflict and adjustment the True, Right, and Good can work its way out." Kaiser Frederick, it wrote, would examine the situation to see "whether, in favor of one-sided party domination, forces have not been repressed and embittered whose cooperation in the long run and in time of danger no state can do without; . . . whether that has not suffered and been deeply wronged upon which in the last resort nevertheless the power of the state alone rests: the freedom, the self-confidence, and the strength of character of the citizens." This attack on the tendencies of Bismarckian rule was followed a few days later in the same paper by the declaration that "we are approaching an eventful time. The people too are summoned to a concern with the shaping of their destiny. Elections for the Prussian House of Deputies are expected in the fall. . . . An immediate dissolution of the Reichstag is not out of the realm of possibility. . . . Therefore, party comrades, build liberal associations, where they do not already exist, all over the country!"[15]

Kaiser Frederick's proclamations, which appeared in the morning papers of March 13, naturally called forth some political comment from the party press, but such comments were unusually mild and unanimous in their general approval. In the first place, the proclamations were long-windedly banal. All the stops were pulled out, but the chords struck and phrases expressed were carefully ordinary. There were gratitude for the achievements of Kaiser William, gratitude to Bismarck, and an appeal for his help in implementing the kaiser's program. There was assurance that Germany must continue to be the support for peace in Europe. There was gratitude to the people for their age-old loyalty to the royal house. To be sure, the proclamation to the chancellor declared that in order that "the constitutions and the laws of the Reich and of Prussia . . . may strengthen themselves in the respect and customs of the people," it was important to avoid as much as possible "shocks . . . caused by continual changes in state institutions and laws." This could be taken to be a criticism of Bismarckian rule by conflict and crisis, but it was, on the face of it, also a very conservative statement, and the following phrase even more so: "The demands posed by the tasks of the Reich government must leave undisturbed the firm foundations upon which the Prussian state has so far rested." This impression was strengthened by the statement that the best supports of national welfare were the army and navy, which must be maintained at their present level of effectiveness. The "firm foundations" of Prussia, declared the *Konservative Korrespondenz*, were "fear of God, devo-

tion to duty, and strong authoritarian rule." The interpretation of the
relation of Prussia to the Reich and the kaiser to the people in Kaiser
Frederick's proclamations was equally cautious and conservative, and
drew Bismarck's special commendation in remarks to the ministry. The
fact was that Frederick's former liberal advisors were really conservative
in their concepts and attitudes, their liberalism being limited—as was
equally true of many members of the left-wing German Liberal party—to
an emphasis on political respectability and proper form: strict legality,
fairness, and accountability. They fondly imagined that the mass of the
people would always be willing to follow (their own) enlightened, intelligent leadership if given a fair chance. Their dislike for paternalistic authority was limited to policies and groups they disagreed with, so that Bismarck's constant accusations of "republicanism" were mostly unfair. They
undoubtedly did have tendencies in that direction, but they were mostly
unconscious and unadmitted. Hence the enthusiasm of even such an uncompromising liberal doctrinaire as Eugen Richter for a possible new era
of freedom led by Kaiser Frederick.[16]

The conservative statements in the kaiser's proclamations were emphasized by the Conservative party press and pointed to as evidence that
Kaiser Frederick intended no basic changes in government policy or personnel. The most the liberal papers could do was to emphasize the rather
strong statement on religious toleration, "a holy principle in My house
for centuries. . . . Every individual [in the various religious communities]
is equally close to My heart." *Germania* naturally applied it mostly to the
Catholics, and the *Frankfurter Zeitung* and the *National Zeitung* considered
it a declaration against anti-Semitism and Stoecker. But, on the other
side, the *Reichsbote* explained that religious toleration need not hamper
anti-Semitism, which was not directed against the Jewish *religion*. All in
all, declared the German Liberal *Weser Zeitung*, the proclamations had a
liberal tone. "New hope enters into all hearts once more. The lovely faith
takes on new strength, that even in advocating free politics one does not
need to be opposed to the monarch, whose exalted position is above all
parties."[17] But the *Kreuzzeitung* pointed out that the proclamations had
properly emphasized the "three strong roots" of the great tree "under
whose shadow we Prussians and Germans can live well and safely . . .
Christianity, monarchy, the army."[18]

The governmental *Post* noted that neither proclamation carried a countersignature, which was proper in Prussia. Kaiser William's proclamation
upon his accession in 1861 had also not been countersigned. The signature
of a minister might be constitutionally necessary for legislation, but that
did not mean that "the personality of the monarch ceases, even in its
relations to the people, to be active and free." The *Kölnische Zeitung*

thought the proclamations supported the cartel. They were the product of years of ripe consideration and experience, it pointed out, and mixed tolerance for innovation with insistence on the "enduring fundamentals.... Behind the sheltering [*sturmsicheren*] walls of this philosophy of moderation [*Weltanschauung der Mitte*] the German people may regard the future with tranquility." The kaiser had tactfully indicated in his proclamations that he intended to retain the great statesman who had accomplished so much, "but he fosters also the proud and calm confidence that, when there is no statesman standing above the average of the mass of humanity to raise the nation above itself by volcanic politics, . . . the German nation will become the forger of its own happiness and will have that destiny that it deserves according to its political maturity and culture." The following day, March 14, the *Kölnische Zeitung* modified its previous position on ministerial personnel to state now that changes "even insofar as only personalities are concerned are presently not to be expected and are also not foreseen for a later time."[19]

21

===

Political Relationships
and Maneuvers

THAT even a dying German kaiser remained a considerable political
factor was indicated by a subtle but decided shift in the public position of the parties. The fact that in spite of Kaiser Frederick's physical
condition and negative prognosis, he had actually lived long enough and
had been allowed to succeed to the throne forced the *Kreuzzeitung* group
of Conservatives to restructure their assumptions. Suddenly, from stri-
dently advocating independent leadership for the Conservatives toward a
new Christian-Socialist era, the *Kreuzzeitung* now began to stress solidarity
and continuity with past traditions and the policies of the revered Kaiser
William. All at once its tone began to coincide with that of the rest of the
cartel and government press. It even proclaimed that "political conflict is
not an end in itself and parties have higher goals than the [previously
sacred (see above, pp. 145–46)] interest of their factional existence."
Together with the *Berliner Politische Nachrichten*, it chided the left-liberal
papers for stressing the new sense of freedom and liberation under Kaiser
Frederick, which constituted a libel against Kaiser William, whose reign
certainly had not been oppressive. In an editorial on March 15 entitled
"The Imperial Legacy" the *Kreuzzeitung* declared that the three pillars of
the tradition of Kaiser William were the same as those that Luther had
said supported true fear of God: "'fear, love, and trust!' A *state* [*sic*] that
is not *feared* is despised!" Kaiser William had made the new Germany
strong enough to be feared, "which in foreign policy is the same as to be
respected. From this respect sprang the love of the people. Every true love even
in the family and school springs from fear—respect—so also in Germany."
It was Germany's new strength that made her capable of alliances
(*bündnissfähig*), and this capacity created for her a predominant position
in Europe. And from this position of power came the trust of all the
nations, trust in her peaceful disposition.[1]

On the other side, the *National Zeitung*—asserting its political leadership with new confidence and apparently determined to derive some Liberal advantage from the new reign, while it lasted—began a forceful new attack against Minister of the Interior Puttkamer. The shocking failure of law and order in Berlin during the days of Kaiser William's lying in state clearly resulted from lack of coordination among court, police, and military agencies, and the only official with sufficient authority to intervene and organize the situation was the Prussian minister of the interior. "The superior and responsible chief of police is Herr von Puttkamer. In the last few days he has shown a strange uncertainty." He had first neglected to announce the succession of Kaiser Frederick in the Prussian House of Deputies; he had then neglected to take adequate measures to ensure order in Berlin.[2]

In an issue of March 18 the *National Zeitung* carried its campaign against Puttkamer onto the higher ground of general policy. All Germans, it stated confidently, were united on fundamentals, but day-to-day government could best be carried out by the cooperation of "the moderate Liberals and the moderate Conservatives." How things might have been if, years before, the development of the Liberal party had taken a different turn, could now be passed over. Only the moderate Liberals and Conservatives were sufficiently agreed regarding political goals to provide the necessary security and continuity. In contrast to the Progressive demand for a parliamentary government, they were united in maintaining the constitutional monarchy, the existing arrangements concerning the army, and Reich finances. They were agreed in regard to social policy, both being willing to at least maintain the present tariff system. And they were both for "constitutional development of the Reich while respecting its federal character." To be sure, the two parties differed on the issue of the rights of the individual versus the state, on the organization of the school system, and on the "consequences of the constitutional state [*Rechtsstaates*]," but these differences could be adjusted. Other parties were incapable of leadership. The German Liberal program, "if realized, would bring about an upheaval that, outside of their narrow party camp, would nowhere find approval." The Center could cooperate from time to time with this or that party, but "a lasting connection with it for positive achievement is not possible for any other party, not even for the extreme Right." Undoubtedly political dissatisfaction, as indicated by recent by-election victories for the German Liberals, who were in this respect a sort of barometer of dissatisfaction, had grown since last year. It was the agitation of the extreme Right in the tariff question and in the area of religion that was responsible. The paper maintained that "the sole guaranty" of the perpetuation of a Liberal-Conservative majority lay in "a *composition of the government* by which the lack of prospects of all political and clerical reactionaries, of all extreme economic and political tendencies is assured. Which does not in the slightest mean that a 'parliamentary regime' is desired."[3]

The "exclusion of all extreme tendencies" from the government meant the ousting of Puttkamer. That a publicly acknowledged connection between a parliamentary majority and the selection of government ministers did not necessarily mean "parliamentary government" was a distinction that the Center's *Germania* at once repudiated. The demand of the *National Zeitung*, it proclaimed in the heading of an article on March 20, was for "A parliamentary government on the basis of the cartel!" This demand, wrote *Germania*, was the long-term purpose of the whole cartel campaign. Although the cartel did not represent a majority of the electorate, the government was not only supposed to follow its policy but "to ensure its majority!" The extreme Right was to be given "a fist in the eye, in that it conforms or disappears, and the cartel thus has a majority, not through its own strength, but through the *government*, a *party government*! And that over against the quite different proclamation of our Kaiser and King Frederick!" Stressing in the course of this article that it agreed with the kaiser's proclamations and supported his right to choose his own ministers, *Germania* seems to have been announcing the possible readiness of the Center itself to become a "government party."[4]

The *National Zeitung*'s ascription of "strange uncertainty" to Puttkamer was a shrewd guess. Not only had he been passed over when two of his ministerial colleagues had received the highest decoration, but his general attitudes could not be expected to coincide with those of the new ruler. In the early days of the new reign he had submitted the draft of a proclamation announcing Kaiser Frederick's accession only to have Minister of Justice Friedberg criticize it as too pious in tone and not in accord with the simple style of Kaiser Frederick, who hated any trace of sanctimoniousness. Puttkamer gave in to the judgment of his colleagues, and, according to Lucius, several "Christian phrases" were deleted. Realizing generally that he was no longer in step, under different circumstances Puttkamer might very well have resigned, but as it was, with the kaiser's death expected in a few months, he was undoubtedly encouraged by the right-wing Conservatives to stick it out until Crown Prince William came to the throne. His friend General Waldersee, for example, admitted to his diary that if Kaiser Frederick were in good health he himself would be leaving Berlin immediately, but he doubted now that the kaiser would find the time to concern himself with him. "If he does, it is all right with me; anyone who is overthrown now will soon rise again." It would be another matter if Bismarck took advantage of this opportunity to get rid of him. But Bismarck too would surely realize that "the new rule cannot last long." Taking no chances, Waldersee spoke to Chief of Staff General von Moltke, who assured him, warmly shaking his hand—"which he rarely does"—that Waldersee must remain with him "under all circumstances." Waldersee also spoke to the crown prince, emphasizing the danger of Bismarck's interfering in army affairs. "The prince, however," he wrote, "thank God, understands this completely." The prince promised to warn Herbert Bismarck that the newspaper attacks on Waldersee must cease. "I do believe," remarked the prince, "that the good Herbert places some value on the preservation of my friendship." The prince was also indignant over the decoration of Friedberg and Maybach and said that "Puttkamer must not leave or anything, but wait quietly; it could last only a few months." Later Waldersee reported hearing from a high source [Albedyll?] that the newspapers had been ordered to stop attacking him, which he ascribed to the effects of the crown prince's talk with Herbert.[5]

Surrounded by all these competing interests and personalities, and beset by the implacable disease, Frederick and Victoria could not very well take any strong initiatives or mount any bold new program. However, there is also evidence that they, in fact, had very little program—Victoria's protestations to her mother to the contrary—or initiatives to offer. They had very few of their old advisors left, Victoria having long since alienated them all with her willfulness, and when it came to making up their court they seem to have had no lists of names prepared. Radolinski replaced the elderly Perponcher as superior court marshal, and Götz von Seckendorff, Victoria's favorite, became superior court master of ceremonies, but, although Frederick originally intended to make a clean sweep of his father's military entourage—always an important factor at the Berlin court—he had no list of names to propose, with the result that Chief of the Military Cabinet General von Albedyll eventually succeeded in persuading him to retain all of his father's military suite, including Waldersee. During his long wait for the succession, Frederick—who never had much political instinct—had lost touch with the ongoing course of political affairs. If one takes the average age of his and Victoria's principal advisors: Roggenbach (63), Stosch (70), Friedberg (75)—Radolinski (47) was admittedly a representative of Bismarck—along with those German Liberals, Bamberger (65) and Forckenbeck (67), whom Victoria later mentioned as favored ministerial candidates, plus possibly General Walter von Loë (60) and Caprivi (57), and compares it with the average age of Bismarck's ministers: Puttkamer (60), Maybach (66), Lucius (53), Scholz (55), Bötticher (55), Gossler (50), and Bronsart (56)—even including Friedberg and omitting Herbert (38)—the chancellor's group turns out to be six years younger, 59 to 65. The kaiser's favored group would have been at the formative age of twenty in 1843, in the *Vormärz*, before the revolutions of 1848, while the chancellor's group would not have reached that age until 1849, the year of reaction. Liberal idealism had been out of style ever since. It is probable that not all of the vacuousness and lack of direction of the Charlottenburg court resulted from the kaiser's cancer.[6]

The general uncertainty and the mutual antagonisms of the various political and personal factors in the Berlin situation presented Bismarck, the old, experienced political hand, with an unusual opportunity to practice his manipulative skill, and thus increase his power momentarily. "He remains," wrote Lucius, "the past master in all transactions—thus the care with which he is now operating as over against the kaiser, the crown prince, and the kaiserin is unsurpassable." Bismarck was careful from the beginning to give the new rulers all due respect and deference. As he confidentially reminded the Prussian ministers, it would not do to in any way publicly downgrade the monarchy. Domestic relations with the other non-Prussian German royal and princely states would be immeasurably more difficult if the importance of the Prussian royal house were not maintained, as would diplomatic relations with imperial Austria and Russia. As long as these states remained in the hands of the traditional power structures it was an advantage (a kind of leverage that Republican France, for example, did not now possess) to retain such a structure in Prussia, and for this the amenities had to be scrupulously observed. From the first day, therefore, to the very last, the chancellor conscientiously consulted the kaiser, regardless of his conditon, on all important questions, traveling regularly—and publicly—out to Charlottenburg for official audiences. The chancellor's *Norddeutsche Allgemeine Zeitung* hailed Kaiser Frederick immediately upon his accession as a true Hohenzollern, who in returning to Berlin had responded to duty with no hesitation. "Already as crown prince the darling and pride of the Nation, His Majesty has become so even more, since he has struggled manfully with and heroically withstood the insidious disease!" All elements of the nation loyally rallied around him, in whom "the national idea of the empire [*des Kaisertums*] is so nobly embodied." With the royal couple, and especially Victoria, Bismarck exercised his courtly flattery and charm. The kaiserin's own statement is noteworthy: "The Reich chancellor during the whole period was especially nice and pleasant, came often to Fritz, and was considerate and easy in manner! So that the audiences didn't tire Fritz!"

Clearly Bismarck was deliberately accommodating in small matters of decorations, uniforms, and court appointments—of special importance to Kaiser Frederick—so as to win the kaiser's trust and be able to impose his will more readily in important questions of policy. Count Radolinski also continued to work hard at mediating and eliminating conflict between the imperial couple and the chancellor. The only change the chancellor made in Kaiser Frederick's proclamations, according to a later press report, was to change the word describing his own relationship to Kaiser William from "collaborator" to "servant," which did not fail to please the son. He arranged with dispatch for the constitutional provision for the king's swearing to observe the Prussian constitution before both houses of the Landtag to be satisfied by written messages—since the king could not speak—to both Landtag and Reichstag, drawing up the Reichstag message himself and appearing personally in both parliaments to read the messages, wearing dress uniform, sword, gloves, all his Prussian decorations, and holding his helmet in his hand. Grumbling privately against the idea of a royal amnesty—he told the ministers that "it was a singular kind of grace that let loose a band of criminals over the country"—Bismarck nevertheless agreed to accept it, but not for traitors and Social Democrats. The Bavarian minister to Berlin, Count Lerchenfeld, was amazed at the chancellor's uncharacteristic patience and tolerance with the new rulers.[7]

Bismarck behaved toward Kaiserin Victoria, he later told Minister of Agriculture Lucius, "like an infatuated graybeard." At the very beginning he had confided frankly to the French ambassador that the new reign would be "a feminine interregnum of a few months." The day before Kaiser William's death he had told the Prussian ministers that Victoria "did not have the ambition to be a ruler; she was predominantly egoistic and self-indulgent. Widowhood as kaiserin would suit her best. During the short reign she could be bountifully provided for." This matter of arranging for the future financial security, after Kaiser Frederick's death, of Kaiserin Victoria and her daughters, which had also been an important factor in avoiding a regency, remained Bismarck's trump card in dealing with her. Meanwhile he could use the Conservative solidarity of the ministry and the hostility of the court and aristocracy to the new rulers in maintaining his moderating influence with them. It was especially easy to use the ministry since Frederick and Victoria tended to want to deal with it as a single, collegial, mutually responsible, policy-making body, like the English cabinet, rather than deal separately with the individual ministers. Bismarck had decided at the beginning that under the circumstances it would be unwise to make any significant changes in policy or personnel, and for the most part he or others managed to prevent any. Since the crown prince would soon rule, it would have been reasonable to consult him on major decisions, but he was allied with his mother's enemies, and collaboration of any kind with his parents was impossible. Bismarck could mediate there too and could use his difficulties with the kaiser and kaiserin—real or imaginary—in handling the court Conservatives and ministers, as well as the crown prince. Especially with the latter, who had now been given authority to sign some official papers, he was also careful regularly to consult, and doubtless he was able to use the situation educationally, to try to point out to the politically naive prince the distinction between individual personalities and wishes and the public dignity and political functions of the crown.[8]

On March 22 Chancellor Bismarck informed the Prussian ministers that Kaiser Frederick wanted to meet with them the following day in a crown council, which was now to be called *Kronrat* in good German, by order of the kaiser, instead of the traditional Prussian *conseil*. The ministers were to swear their new oaths of loyalty, and matters of general policy were to be discussed. He had suggested an agenda to the kaiser, which he now proposed for approval. First there would be a discussion of the Reichstag resolution proposing a monument to Kaiser William; then a survey of foreign policy by himself; then an item suggested by the kaiser: "Whether the political activity of Court and Cathedral Chaplain Stoecker could be regarded as compatible with his position as court and cathedral chaplain." He was not, Bismarck explained, himself opposed to Stoecker's political activity, and he recognized that any alteration in his manner of agitation would probably reduce his success, nor did he regard political activity as necessarily incompatible in general with clerical positions; but it was compromising for a court official. Kaiser Frederick was very much interested in the matter and had thought he could transfer Stoecker at will. A court chaplain, however, could be removed only through a proper disciplinary inquiry. Kaiser William had begun such a process, but it had resulted merely in a censure by the Superior Evangelical Church Council. Perhaps this process could be opened up again. He requested Minister of Ecclesiastical Affairs Gossler to report on the matter at the crown council the next day, which Gossler, with rather bad grace, agreed to do. Minister of the Interior Puttkamer asked whether the crown prince should also be invited to the crown council. Bismarck replied that he had considered that, but since His Majesty had not included the crown prince in his invitation and he was therefore not certain whether the presence of the crown prince would be in accord with His Majesty's intentions, he believed that he himself should not take any initiative in the matter.[9]

Since at the crown council in the Charlottenburg palace on March 23 Crown Prince William and his brother, Prince Henry, were present, one must assume either that the kaiser had thought of this himself or that Puttkamer had exerted his own initiative through his connections at court. After the ministers had kissed hands and sworn allegiance, the kaiser handed Bismarck a note stating that he wanted to build his own monument to his father. A bit nonplussed, Bismarck avoided discussion by handing the matter to Gossler to arrange the details. Then the chancellor launched into a brilliant, full-scale elucidation of Germany's foreign policy. After the new nation had achieved through successful wars the position of power necessary to it, Bismarck's chief object had been to prevent the formation of coalitions against it, such as had been formed among Austria, France, and Russia against Prussia during the Seven Years' War. Now possessing the "right" frontiers, Germany had no interest in wars of conquest and could not easily conduct them with a mass army based on universal service. Even a successful war against Russia would produce no gains for Germany. He had explained to the Austrian emperor in 1879 that if Russia pushed into Bulgaria and even Constantinople, it would thereby expose and weaken its European position, militarily speaking. Austria ought not to act against Russia until English cannons boomed in the Bosporus, as in the Crimean War. Nor could Germany lend support to an Austrian attack on Russia, but should refrain from any action, at least initially. It could not allow Austria to be destroyed, however. It could also not allow England to be defeated by France, but must maintain it, too, in its European position. One could not count on Italy's military assistance, because "one cannot rely on a country where the parliament has a voice in whether the troops should march or not"; but the Italian alliance was nevertheless valuable.

The princes, noted Lucius, followed this recital with rapt attention, but passively, whereas Kaiser Frederick involved himself personally, frequently nodding his head in agreement. The exposé was slightly slanted for Frederick's benefit, and Bismarck repeatedly stated that he could carry on only a German, not a foreign-oriented (English) policy. Later Bismarck was to cite as an example of Frederick's political naiveté and basically pro-English disposition that he had inquired whether the English had been informed of Germany's secret treaty with Russia. A major article in the *National Zeitung*, published on the same day and entitled "The German Change of Rulers and the Bulgarian Question," explained the Russian connection in greater detail. It had been a fundamental axiom of Prussian policy since Frederick the Great "to live in peace with Russia as long as possible." Russian persecution of Germans in the Baltic area was regrettable, but one could not interfere with the internal affairs of another state, and the same situation existed in Hungary and Bohemia. Also, Germany would never be tempted to parry Russian commercial blows with diplomatic weapons. "Every German statesman must regard it as his task to conciliate Russia as far as Germany's honor and interests allow." Since the time of Peter the Great, German power had kept pace with Russian, in spite of the conquests of the tsars, "which often absorb more strength than they produce." Germany must not take sides with either Russia or Austria in the Balkans.[10]

After the chancellor had finished his foreign affairs recital, Finance Minister Scholz reported, to the kaiser's great interest, that it would be necessary to mint ten to twelve million new gold pieces and as many silver; these would, of course, bear the likeness of the new ruler, which Frederick subsequently gave much attention to choosing. Then Gossler gave a dry, heavily documented report on the Stoecker case, which was in the hands of the Superior Evangelical Church Council. Stoecker had stated that he was willing to retire on a pension of 3,000 M, and the Finance Ministry had agreed to pay it. Bismarck then suggested that Gossler be instructed to bring the disciplinary inquiry into motion again and to report further. For the benefit of the princes he praised Stoecker's talent and energy—"He has a mouth like a sword!"—and maintained that his work in rallying the masses to the monarch in Berlin had been politically useful and for that reason he should not be too harshly treated, although such activity was not appropriate to a court chaplain. Stoecker also stood politically further to the Right than he, in the camp of the *Kreuzzeitung*, which had been fighting Bismarck for ten years. The princes seemed to go along with Bismarck's light tone, smiling politely, but Kaiser Frederick was not amused, took the matter very seriously, and was obviously holding back feelings of strong hostility toward Stoecker. But he nodded his head finally in agreement with the suggested procedure. At the end the kaiser shook everybody's hand, somewhat curtly with Puttkamer.[11]

Crown Prince William had evidently taken the Stoecker discussion more to heart than he demonstrated at the time. From Charlottenburg he went directly to General Waldersee and told him about the chancellor's action against Stoecker and his attack on the *Kreuzzeitung*. He apparently was not sure whether the initiative had been Bismarck's or his father's, with Bismarck going along to ingratiate himself. "Presumably," noted Waldersee, "they will also try to bring about Puttkamer's downfall as well. The prince was very indignant and felt quite correctly that the blow is aimed at him too. The chancellor is not acting wisely if he offends the crown prince." But he had heard, he wrote, that the kaiserin was beginning to create problems for the chancellor. With obvious satisfaction he continued, "I expected this from the beginning, she can't stand him and keeps making difficulties for him." The following day he added that he had learned that the move against Stoecker did not stem from the chancellor but was the work of the kaiserin. What the general could not imagine was that Victoria and Bismarck could be in perfect agreement and cooperation in this matter. No doubt it was Bismarck himself who encouraged such illusions.[12]

Aside from the struggle over deputizing the crown prince, the first real clash between the new rulers and the government came over the bill, approved by both Reichstag and Bundesrat, to extend the length of the

Reichstag session from three to five years. When Civil Cabinet Chief Wilmowski presented it to Kaiser Frederick, he refused to sign it, citing all the usual German Liberal arguments: that it would reduce the rights of the voters, etc. He also refused to sign the antisocialist law renewal. Bismarck went at once to the kaiserin. He took a forceful line: both bills had been passed by large majorities in Reichstag and Bundesrat. Once both legislative houses had passed a bill, the kaiser, as president of the Federation, had no choice but to sign it; the Reich constitution did not give him a veto, as in Prussia. Furthermore, to oppose the (cartel) majority of the Reichstag and the expressed wish of the other federal states in the Bundesrat would contradict the policy of the present government, and it would have to resign. And then the final threat: such a move would "prejudice the future of the crown prince"—a not too subtle reminder that her and Frederick's continuation on the throne depended almost solely on his, the chancellor's, continued favor and support. Whether purposely or not, the old man evidently let his determination and anger flash in his manner; later Victoria wrote that she had "seen his claws." She gave in immediately. There must be a misunderstanding, she said; if the kaiser constitutionally had to sign, why then he must. At that Bismarck recovered his composure—"and withdrew his claws like a tiger that changes its mind and decides not to attack its prey." The kaiserin excused herself for a minute, and when the chancellor later went in for his audience with the kaiser, the latter handed him the two bills, with his signature on them still wet.[13]

When on March 21 Bismarck arrived for an audience with Kaiserin Victoria, he found with her three ladies: Frau von Helmholtz, Frau Schrader, wife of a Reichstag member of the German Liberal party and former railroad director, and Frau von Stockmar, widow of Ernst von Stockmar, former secretary to the kaiserin and son of the advisor to both Albert, Prince Consort in England, and King Leopold of Belgium. These women obviously formed the political connection with the oppositional German Liberal party, a connection whose efficacy in producing Kaiser Frederick's refusal to sign the two bills was shocking to an observer such as General Waldersee, who noted that he had not believed "that progressive influences would make themselves felt so quickly and so thoroughly." After the kaiser's proclamations had forced the German Liberals to give up their expectations of a complete change of government, they had nevertheless been actively agitating for specific changes in policy, such as dropping the cartel-sponsored antisocialist and legislative period laws. Their initial tactic in this regard was rather foolish. The Berlin correspondent of the German Liberal *Breslauer Zeitung* advanced the theory, which was immediately taken up by other German Liberal papers, that since the preamble to all legislation in Prussia and the Reich—"We William, by the Grace of God King of Prussia and German Kaiser, do proclaim and establish as follows:"—had been duly debated and voted in the respective parliaments word by word, all bills that had already been passed but not yet signed by Kaiser William must now be reintroduced, debated, and passed all over again in order to change "William" to "Frederick." Thus by instructing the Prussian representatives to the Bundesrat not to approve the antisocialist law extension and the bill extending the length of the Reichstag session in their new "We Frederick" form, the new kaiser could veto them at the last minute in spite of the Reichstag majority.

Even the *National Zeitung* was shaken by this argument and advocated that the parliaments immediately pass bills authorizing the name change in blanket fashion. As the *Norddeutsche* pointed out, however, the wording of the preamble to bills might be the result of legislative acts, but the *name* used in the preamble was hardly under the control of the parliaments, but was the natural result of the fact of the old kaiser's death and his son's succession. Subsequently the party leaders in the Reichstag and Prussian Landtag tacitly adopted this view, and the matter was never mentioned in debate. After Kaiser Frederick signed the two imperial bills, the issue ceased to be discussed even in the liberal press. Even liberal people, noted Waldersee, felt "that the Progressive party, to which also these [Jewish] circles mostly belong, are operating in an unbelievably stupid way. The crown prince will have an easy time taking care of them later." [14]

The left-liberal press also continued to instruct and encourage the new rulers in other ways. It carried a series of rumors of the removal from Berlin of Stoecker and Waldersee to positions in the provinces. The *Freisinnige Zeitung* announced that the real reason for Minister of Justice Friedberg's receiving the Order of the Black Eagle was that he had fought against the attempt to impose a regency. Friedberg publicly denied that a regency had ever been discussed in the Prussian Ministry. The liberal *Börsen-Courier* announced on March 21 the retirement of Minister von Puttkamer and gave as the reason that he had been the one who, before the death of Kaiser William, had advocated in the ministry—not in official sessions—that the succession to the throne be changed, but he had been strongly opposed, not only by Friedberg, but also by Bismarck. He could not expect to remain in office under the king whom he had worked against. The *Frankfurter Zeitung* added skeptically that if Puttkamer fell, it would not be as a sacrifice to the Liberals, but because Bismarck had long been dissatisfied with him, as the antisocialist law debate had shown, and would use this favorable opportunity to get rid of him. The *Frankfurter* then quoted the Italian *Diritto* to the effect that under the new ruler the repressive tactics of the German government might be lifted. Germany would then reach a higher peak of greatness and power. "Everyone sees what fortunate effects it would have if the new kaiser is allowed to introduce a truly constitutional regime." Kaiser Frederick had always had such ideas. He had written in his diary in 1870 that he prayed God the new German empire might "put itself at the head of civilization, developing and bringing to bear all the noble ideas of the modern world, so that from Germany the world would be humanized, morals uplifted, and people turned away from the frivolous French influence."[15]

On March 22 the *Frankfurter* viciously attacked the cartel, and especially the National Liberals. Whereas, it claimed, in November both Conservative and National Liberal newspapers had joined in the attack on *Muckerei und Stoeckerei*, things had suddenly changed with the crown prince's tracheotomy, which indicated that his days were numbered and that he might not succeed to the throne. This change found its "sharpest expression" in the signatures that prominent National Liberals placed under the Stoecker City Mission appeal. But the actual succession of Frederick and Victoria put an end to these illusions. Suddenly *Muckerei und Stoeckerei* fell silent—waiting confidently for the future. But among the National Liberals reigned bewilderment and perplexity.[16] To this the *Kölnische Zeitung* replied with some credibility that the bitterness of the left Liberals was caused by their realization of their weakness and isolation, a condition that had its origin in the wrong turning many of the leaders of their party had taken when, in the early 1880s, they had split off from the National Liberal party and had joined with Richter's Progressives. It was natural that they should consistently use the National Liberals as a scapegoat for their own frustration. "What can in reality not be forgiven the National Liberals is the circumstance that they were not so obliging as to disappear from the scene in shame and remorse after Herr Bamberger had denied them their liberalism ex cathedra." Bamberger and others had actually maintained that Bismarck was more liberal than Bennigsen. The suggestion in a Berlin-inspired article in the Vienna *Neue Freie Presse* (probably written by Bamberger) that it would be interesting to see how Bismarck now adapted himself to a progressive-minded monarch after having served for so long a conservative-minded one was inaccurate and unfair to both rulers.

Kaiser William, wrote the *Kölnische*, had been liberal in his generation and had been responsible for providing a liberal education and liberal advisors for his son. To see a conflict of generations was to libel both and Bismarck as well. The previous day the *Kölnische* had pointed out that at the head of a great state the personal options of a ruler were limited. Kaiser Frederick placed primary importance on stability even to the extent of not changing ministerial personnel (Puttkamer) who otherwise might not be especially compatible with his preferences. He certainly would not let himself be dictated to by the German Liberals. The attacks on Puttkamer, wrote the *Hamburger Nachrichten*, were likely to entrench him further in his position. The *Hannoverscher Kourier* pointed out with irony that the parliamentary-oriented German Liberals were now urging personal, absolutistic rule on Kaiser Frederick to the extent of urging him to veto laws that had been duly passed by majorities of the parliaments. On the other hand, it was surprising to find the absolutistic (see above, p. 103) *Konservative Korrespondenz* emphasizing, against the attacks of the German Liberals, that the Bismarck government was supported in both Reichstag and Landtag by parliamentary majorities.[17]

Insisting on continuity, government and cartel papers, led by the *Norddeutsche*, attacked the German Liberals for a record of negativism. The German Liberals, the *Norddeutsche* pointed out, frequently cooperated with the unpatriotic Social Democrats and the particularistic Center. They might have true national feeling, as in the case of supporting the recent military bill, but unlike the parties of the cartel, they placed the "party catechism" first. In their press, the cartel parties rallied around the chancellor, the *Kölnische Zeitung* quoting articles from English and Russian papers pointing out the indispensability of Bismarck. "The political party," wrote the Russian *Grashdanin*, "that stands behind Prince Bismarck is all Germany. Bismarck is no minister; Bismarck is Bismarck, that is, an historic political personality, without whom the Germany of today is quite inconceivable. To say to him: 'Step aside into the shadows, we have a replacement for you'—no one can do that, for there is no substitute for him and there is no shadow into which he can walk." Appreciation and support of the cartel parties for the chancellor appeared to be reciprocated. After the Reichstag session in which Bismarck delivered the kaiser's message, he had a long conference with von Bennigsen in the Reichstag building. He was also openly friendly to National Liberal leaders in the parliaments, congratulating them on the high decoration of Dr. Simson. At the end of March Bismarck informed Bennigsen that he was about to be given the Order of the Red Eagle, first class—which Lucius called "an unheard-of innovation," that a mere third-class counselor who was not an Excellency should receive such a high decoration. Bennigsen replied to Bismarck's note with thanks for his thoughtfulness and good wishes for his birthday, and continued: "The more serious the times are in which we live and which Germany will confront in the future, the more strongly the wish forces itself upon me as on every German patriot that this day will for many more years find you at the head of those political affairs that to Germany's benefit you have through every danger successfully conducted for so long. In old veneration I remain Your Serene Highness's sincerely devoted R.v. Bennigsen."[18]

The rallying of the cartel parties around the chancellor persuaded August Stein, in a thoughtful column in the *Frankfurter* on March 27, that Professor Theodor Mommsen, the famous historian of ancient Rome, had been quite right with his reference to Bismarck's *Hausmeiertum*—literally "mayoralty of the palace"—that position at the medieval French Merovingian court that eventually enabled the Carolingians to replace the old dynasty with their own. Such a position, wrote Stein, could be dangerous if it were not for Bismarck's own feudal loyalty. Every successor to Kaiser William would find him a power to deal with, but "presumably quite willingly." Changes, therefore, in the system would come slowly and administratively rather than legislatively. Perhaps there was some justification for the hope that at least the conditions of battle might now be fairer and "that many of the means with which the opposition has previously been suppressed will no longer be practical in the future." The opposition parties, he thought, were now more confident than the cartel, among which parties there was uncertainty and confusion. The Conservatives, for all their silence, were the most uncertain of all. "Prince Bismarck, their protection and their hope, is on much better terms with his new imperial sovereign than many previously imagined."

The Conservatives were also not especially pleased that Bismarck had managed to integrate the crown prince into the functioning of the new government. The chancellor was notorious for his ability to change his policies to suit the occasion, and the Conservatives, thought Stein, were worried that he might adjust too well to the new kaiser. For example, they had already privately written off Puttkamer. It was an open secret where the attacks on Stoecker and Waldersee had originated, and it was by no means likely that the chancellor had forgotten the attempt of the *Kreuzzeitung* clique to use the crown prince in an orthodox, anti-Semitic way. "It is not at all unthinkable that under the changed circumstances he can endeavor to prepare a future that will, to be sure, not satisfy real Liberalism, but that will please the Conservatives even less." The following day Stein wrote that one of Bismarck's characteristics was merely to deny policies he had previously fought for when they no longer worked. "He then simply leaves the unfortunate department head in the lurch. One thinks of the Kulturkampf and the fate of Herr Falk [the minister of ecclesiastical and educational affairs]! It can eventually happen the same way to Puttkamer." Stein's sources were probably similar or identical to those of Austrian Ambassador Széchényi, who wrote to Foreign Minister Count Kálnoky on the twenty-ninth that Puttkamer had ignored the hints that the kaiser had given him and had persisted in holding on to his ministerial post, hoping to outlast the new regime. According to a "high official," although the chancellor wanted to avoid changes, nevertheless he was disenchanted with Puttkamer, especially since the debate on the antisocialist law, and therefore an expressly stated wish of the kaiser in regard to Puttkamer would not meet any serious opposition from Bismarck.[19]

If, on the one hand, the German-Liberal opposition could be more objective than the cartel parties, and, on the other hand, they could and did continue to advocate rather impractical and idealistic goals, both characteristics stemmed from their noninvolvement in actual power. It was precisely, then, because they were on the outside of the power structure that they could rally so wholeheartedly to the liberal principles with which they knew the new kaiser sympathized, and with so little thought for the practical results. In so doing—in at best providing Kaiser Frederick with personal support and liberal alternatives—they were choosing sentiment over the reality of power and, more than they probably realized, deliberately choosing a role as pressure group rather than political party. No doubt they had little choice. And yet the Center party, also in opposition, showed more practical flexibility. While it continued to maintain an intransigent position against the government in the Prussian parliament, its Berlin organ, *Germania*, took a very positive attitude toward Kaiser Frederick. But its two-part leading article, "A New Advance in Labor Legislation," published on March 27, claiming to see in Kaiser Frederick's accession to the throne new hope for further support for social welfare laws, seemed to be aimed in other directions as well. The imperial message in 1881, *Germania* pointed out, had not only based the duty of the state to assist the unfortunate on the "moral foundations of a Christian society [*christlichen Volkslebens*]," but had advocated the organization of society "in the form of corporative bodies supported and encouraged by the state." But in the course of the development of social legislation this latter purpose had been dropped, and Bismarck had concentrated only on state social insurance laws. The whole program had lost its impetus, and the recent attempts of the Reichstag to pass labor protection bills had been completely stymied by the government. They hoped that under Kaiser Frederick a positive program of labor legislation might once more get under way. Emphases on corporative organizations and state support for the upholding of the Christian foundations of society, however, were more likely to appeal, not to Kaiser Frederick, with his already old-fashioned liberal-individualistic orientation, but rather to Crown Prince William and his Christian-socialistic Conservative friends. With another—imminent—change of kaisers, there might possibly be another

change of party constellation, and at least some of the Center party leadership were ready.[20]

Party and political constellations depended in Germany on government
initiative, and that government was responsible to the king and kaiser.
The political future, then, depended upon who managed to control Crown
Prince William, if anyone could. "The Bismarcks," wrote Holstein on
March 27,

> both father and son, stand in wholesome dread of [Crown Prince William].
> The chancellor is fond of telling his intimates that he feels sure of the crown
> prince. I do not believe that and I rather doubt whether the chancellor
> believes it himself. The chancellor's military opponents tell the crown prince
> that Frederick II would never have become Frederick the Great under the
> political tutelage of a minister like Bismarck. In addition they keep telling
> the prince that the Bismarcks, father and son, are not over-scrupulous about
> the truth, and try to take him in.
>
> The conflict will arise over the war question. Bismarck wants to put off
> making war while he remains at the helm. The generals, regardless of their
> views on other matters—Waldersee, Bronsart, Verdy, Loë, Caprivi—think
> time is running *against* us, that 1889 will be a particularly unfavorable year,
> and that we ought not to allow certain military preparations along our fron-
> tier or the Galician frontier. . . . I hope for many reasons that Bismarck
> remains at the helm for a few more years, but on the other hand I feel:
> "Cobbler, stick to your last!" An intelligent general is surely better able to
> judge of the *military* necessity for defense than a civilian in uniform.

That a senior official in the political department of Bismarck's own
Foreign Office could be so willing to hand the initiative for war or peace
over to the military technicians—and should regard the chancellor, in
effect, as himself merely a technician—reveals one perspective on the
disadvantages of government by bureaucracy. The general public no
doubt desired peace, but the political parties, supposedly closer than anyone else to public opinion, were not in the habit of taking political initiatives, especially in foreign affairs, and they in fact usually vied with each
other in belligerent patriotism, especially against Russia. Also, although
the *Kreuzzeitung* Conservatives were being relatively discreet in the press,
in the Prussian Landtag they lined up again with the Center party to vote
down a small additional subsidy for the Old Catholics, against the National Liberals, Free Conservatives, and the government. Among both
parties and bureaucrats, the uncertainties of the time did not produce
flexibility, tolerance, a disposition to reconcile viewpoints, or a broadening
of perspective. There appeared to be little capacity for creative, imagina-
tive leadership, for envisioning, let alone carrying out, an overall, consistent, stable, national policy. Rather, there seems to have been a clinging

to previously held convictions, a greater dogmatism, a seeking for assurance in narrow partisanship or technical expertise. No wonder individuals like Bennigsen hoped that the elderly chancellor could remain in control for at least the immediate future.[21]

With so much political significance riding on the state of Kaiser Frederick's health, it was probably inevitable that the medical facts themselves should continue to be the subject of a public conflict. Less than a week after the succession, the *Kölnische Zeitung* published a serious, straightforward survey of the kaiser's physical condition. Although very positive in its praise for his courage—"He is a martyr in the fullest sense of the word"—and conceding that in the current pause, characteristic of the disease, his general health was impressively good, the article nevertheless made no attempt to conceal or soften the fact that the "local affliction" had made "great progress" and that there was now no hope of a cure. This article was immediately denounced by the German Liberal *Freisinnige Zeitung* as concealing "sordid political purposes"; it was a disgrace for the Rhineland that such a newspaper could maintain itself there. Court circles, it claimed, were very indignant over the article, which they regarded as an attempt for political purposes to intimidate the kaiser and shake his morale.

On the other side, Mackenzie released reports in the *Berliner Tageblatt* that hinted at "new developments" that were not typical of cancer and that gave hope for a "satisfactory development" of the illness that would refute "the pessimistic prophecies from a certain side." In turn, the kaiserin's natural reliance on and preference for Mackenzie as opposed to the other doctors was interpreted as being entirely because he was English, and all kinds of scandalous rumors were circulated around the court as to the incompetence of Mackenzie and the other English doctor, Mark Hovell. Bismarck told Prince Hohenlohe humorously that if everything people reported was true and not exaggerated, "one ought to send a public prosecutor to protect the kaiser." Conservative circles spread rumors that Mackenzie was really a Hungarian or Polish Jew, whose grandfather came from Posen. His real name was Moritz Markovicz. "It is astonishing," noted Pindter, "what sorts of phenomena have been produced, even highly treasonous placards on the Brandenburg Gate and the like. And yet it is finally simple and explicable . . . : an operation in May last year could have been immediately fatal and of no help in the long run, the Mackenzie methods guaranteed at least a certain length of time and eventually the throne—therefore the anger against Mackenzie." Lest this medical conflict go too far, the kaiserin apparently sent Dr. Hermann Krause, an assistant to Mackenzie, to offer Pindter regular reports on the kaiser's health for the *Norddeutsche*, which Pindter accepted, a fact that horrified Holstein and others. "Krause had made such an offer to all the newspapers, he wanted to plant cuckoo's eggs. . . . What is all the fuss! If the *N.A.Z.* wanted to print notices from Dr. Rinaldo-Rinaldini the ardor could not be greater.* If something a bit more favorable should actually be presented, that would be a cuckoo's egg!! Vis-à-vis the kaiser. Wretched bunch, they are themselves conjuring up a social revolution." On the other hand, the left-liberal press went so far in their enthusiasm over the state of the kaiser's health as to claim that he did not need a deputy, which the *National Zeitung* compared to the obtuse officiousness of Shakespeare's Malvolio.[22]

In the meantime the Berlin public, on a Sunday, had begun, in spite of the continued inclement weather, to stream out to Charlottenburg, to stand patiently in front of the palace, waiting for Kaiser Frederick to come to the window—and not in vain; he would appear occasionally, dressed in his general's uniform, waving benevolently at the crowd. On March 28 the weather took a turn for the better, and Kaiser Frederick was allowed to take a walk in the palace park. On the following day he and the kaiserin drove from Charlottenburg to Westend and back, cheered by the public along the way. On the thirtieth he went for another walk in the palace grounds, then later drove with the kaiserin for the first time to central Berlin and visited his mother, the Dowager Kaiserin Augusta, in the palace. The imperial couple drove in an open carriage drawn by four horses, followed by four other carriages carrying the three unmarried princesses, Victoria, Sophie, and Margaret, the married daughter Charlotte and her husband, the hereditary prince of Saxe-Meiningen, and their suite, including Dr. Mackenzie. On the return drive the kaiser, dressed in uniform and military coat with fur collar and wearing a helmet, was cheered endlessly by thousands of Berliners massed on both sides of the street all the way through the Brandenburg Gate and into the Tiergarten. The progress of the carriages was slowed to a walk by the press of the crowd, and the kaiser's carriage was filled with bouquets of flowers. For the Berlin public he had come home at last.[23]

---

* *Rinaldo Rinaldini, Robber Captain* was a popular early romantic novel by Christian August Vulpius.

22

The Battenberg Crisis

ON March 31, when Chancellor von Bismarck arrived in Charlottenburg for an audience, the kaiser handed him a note saying that he wished to give Prince Alexander von Battenberg a Prussian army command and decorate him with the order *Pour le Mérite*. Prince Alexander was arriving in Berlin within the next few days to become engaged to his daughter Victoria. "What do you say to that?" Replied the chancellor, "Impossible!" Forcefully he explained that since Tsar Alexander III of Russia notoriously had an obsessive hatred for Prince Alexander, and since Bismarck's own opposition to the marriage on this ground was well known to the Russians, it would be impossible for him now to change his attitude toward the marriage without its being taken by the Russians as a shift in policy, so that if the marriage plans were persisted in Bismarck must resign. Kaiser Frederick, apparently convinced, nodded and scribbled, "What to do?" "Telegraph him not to come," replied the chancellor. The kaiser wrote out such a telegram and gave it to Radolinski, at which point Kaiserin Victoria, who had evidently been lurking in the corridor to see how the interview went, burst in and made a stormy scene. He had given his solemn promise; he was ruining his daughter's happiness and breaking her heart merely for reasons of state. The kaiser wrote on his pad, "I cannot plunge this country into a war with Russia on account of her marriage." The kaiserin became even more violent. Radolinski, alarmed, protested, "But Your Majesty, I implore you to think of the kaiser's health!" She paid no attention. The kaiser wept in agitation and frustration, tore his hair, and gasped for breath, but did not yield. He eventually rose, pushed his wife out the door, and closed it. He then asked Bismarck to present him with his arguments in writing.[1]

Prince Alexander von Battenberg and his brother Henry were sons of a morganatic marriage between a lady-in-waiting at the Russian court and Prince Alexander of Hesse, who had given them their names and royal status. The younger Alexander had been made prince of Bulgaria by Tsar Alexander of Russia, but had become more Bulgarian than Russian and had drawn upon himself the hostility of the tsar, who eventually forced him out of his position as ruler and out of the country. In the meantime his brother Henry had married Queen Victoria's favorite and youngest daughter, Beatrice; and her older sister, now Kaiserin Victoria, then crown princess of Prussia and Germany, had singled out the handsome, bearded "Sandro" as a fine match for her own daughter Victoria, who had a crush on him. The emphatic opposition of Bismarck, old Kaiser William, her son William, and in the beginning her husband as well had merely hardened her determination. "I love a fight," she had written Prince Alexander in October 1885 in the course of a twenty-eight-page letter from Venice. Immediately after Frederick III's accession to the German throne, Kaiserin Victoria had written Prince Alexander, reviving the idea of the marriage and promising a definite decision in the near future. Alexander, painfully aware of the opposition among the Berlin royal family, especially of Crown Prince William, soon himself to be kaiser, replied to the kaiserin in a diplomatically worded letter that plainly indicated his loss of interest. But Kaiserin Victoria was blind to anyone's feelings in the matter but her own. It is probable that it was now she, not the youngest Victoria, who was in love with the prince. Since Prince Alexander had in the meantime acquired a passion for an actress in Darmstadt, he then asked his brother in England to explain to Queen Victoria that the marriage would be impossible due to the opposition of both Bismarck and the crown prince, and urged him to get the queen to try to persuade her daughter to be reasonable. This the queen did, writing on March 21 to the kaiserin, "Above all, do not even consider such a step without William's consent. You must consider him since he is crown prince." But this too was ignored. Even more than Kaiserin Victoria's trying to be named deputy for her husband or influencing him to grant amnesty to Social Democrats or to refuse to sign bills, this Battenberg incident indicates how right Bismarck was in his judgment of her character: that she had no real interest in power or a consistent political program, but was primarily devoted to the satisfaction of her own immediate, personal desires (see above, pp. 31, 193; below, p. 237).[2]

Bismarck had already heard of the renewal of the marriage project when he met with the kaiser on the thirty-first. General von Winterfeld, the kaiser's adjutant, had shown him the telegram inviting Prince Alexander to Charlottenburg, and in directing Albedyll to arrange for Prince Alexander to be appointed commander of the *Gardes du Corps* Kaiser Frederick had stipulated that the chancellor should be informed first. Immediately Bismarck informed the other opponents of the marriage, Crown Prince William and the grand duke of Baden, who happened to be in

Berlin. The latter warned the kaiser, just before the audience with Bismarck, not to provoke the chancellor's resignation, to which the kaiser repeatedly indicated he agreed. The grand duke also commissioned his Berlin Bundesrat representative, Adolf Marschall von Bieberstein, to remonstrate with the grand duke of Hesse. After the chancellor's audience with the kaiser, Kaiserin Victoria wrote another wild letter to Prince Alexander, suggesting elopement, a secret marriage, and a position in the Austro-Hungarian army if he could not serve in the German. Count Radolinski wrote Holstein that the kaiserin was determined to make the kaiser accept Bismarck's resignation. "All she wants is to force through this marriage, and she is indifferent to everything else." On April 4 Kaiserin Victoria instructed Radolinski to make arrangements for the celebration of the engagement of her daughter to Prince Alexander on her birthday, the twelfth. Radolinski reported this at once to the crown prince, who informed the grand duke of Baden and then called on Bismarck, who dictated a letter for him to Prince Alexander that stated flatly, "I shall regard everyone who works for this marriage not only as an enemy of My House, but also of My country, and will deal with him accordingly!"[3]

On April 3 Bismarck wrote a thirty-page exposé of his objections to any connection of the German royal family with the prince of Battenberg. Not only did Tsar Alexander of Russia hate him, but the prince's popularity with the Bulgarians made him a continuing source of suspicion. The German policy since 1871 of preventing hostile European coalitions had its focal point in Russia, thus the attempt to maintain the confidence and trust of the tsar. Even if a war conducted simultaneously with France and Russia were to be victorious, it would remain "one of the greatest calamities that could befall the German people." Italy could not be counted on, and Austria was weak, so that Germany would be left to rely chiefly on her own strength. Whether they would have to face such a two-front war was a decision that lay "solely with Emperor Alexander." France would not bring about a war without Russian support, but if assured of such support, certainly would. There had been general fear of war six months ago, but now, through correct diplomacy, they had succeeded in restoring a measure of trust with the tsar sufficient to promise a prospect of continued peace. It would be a disaster for all Europe if a mistake in German handling of the tsar destroyed all previous diplomatic success. The previous reserve toward Prince Alexander was an important part of German diplomatic policy. The chancellor personally would not care to take the responsibility for the possible effects on the tsar of a change in this policy. Indifference on the part of the dynasty to the effect of its actions on "the peace and welfare of the country and its subjects . . . is, however, not in the tradition of the Prussian monarchy." It would be impossible to provide an acceptable or even believable motive for such a break in German relations with Russia to public opinion, the parliaments, or to history. Quite aside from his own personal honor, such a drastic change in policy, if he remained in office, would destroy the trust in his steadiness of purpose built up among the European cabinets and German public opinion over his long years of service. He would have lost his political usefulness. That Bismarck in this memorandum overstressed the trust of the tsar in himself and his policy and exaggerated the European importance of the prince of Battenberg is probable, but he was surely correct in assuming that a reversal of his attitude toward Prince Alexander would have some kind of negative effect on relations with both the tsar and the Russian public.[4]

Bismarck's memorandum for the kaiser was sent off on Wednesday morning, the fourth. Later in the day he sent after it a postscript to the effect that a reception of the prince at court would be regarded as a political demonstration against Russia by the public. They would assume that such a turn in policy toward Russia could have been brought about only by English influence at court, which would be blamed on Kaiserin Victoria. Ill feeling between Germany and Russia would be advantageous to English policy. Such hostility among the public would be difficult to handle. On the same day Bismarck sent off telegrams reporting his reaction to the Battenberg crisis to Ambassadors Hans Lothar von Schweinitz in St. Petersburg and Prince Reuss in Vienna, asking if they and the governments to which they were accredited shared his view that special recognition of the prince of Battenberg by the kaiser would amount to an anti-Russian demonstration. In these telegrams he stated that he suspected that the prince's proposed visit to Berlin had been "inspired by the queen of England." Whether he actually believed this is doubtful, but it was a possibility that he could use advantageously in two directions, and he did. On the fifth he telegraphed Count Paul Hatzfeldt in London that the "Battenberg marriage project with our princess is again being more actively promoted from the English side and personally through Her Majesty Queen Victoria." Hatzfeldt was instructed to inform Lord Salisbury that if the marriage went through, Germany would have to reorient her policy "necessarily and permanently" more toward Russia in compensation. Bismarck also asked the English ambassador, Sir Edward Malet, to use his influence with Kaiserin Victoria against the marriage, and Herbert told Sir Edward that Queen Victoria could prevent the marriage if she wished and that encouraging it was "an unfriendly act."[5]

Against the kaiserin, Bismarck discreetly used his strongest weapon. Radolinski warned her that if she persisted the chancellor would raise the question of her husband's fitness to rule. Apparently also on the fourth,

Bismarck began an orchestrated press campaign. In 1884, when the chancellor had been told that Crown Princess Victoria was determined to bring about her daughter's marriage with Prince Alexander regardless of opposition and might do it secretly and thus present him and the old kaiser with a fait accompli, he had replied that he would then be obligated in view of Germany's relations with Russia "to cause 'a scandal.' He would hand in his resignation and keep it in force until he received guaranties which would prove to the Powers concerned that he had no part in the intrigue."[6]

In the morning edition of the *Kölnische Zeitung* on Thursday, April 5, a short notice appeared under an April 4 Vienna dateline that stated, "In usually well informed circles a rumor circulated this noon that Prince Bismarck is about to hand in his resignation. The motive given is reasons of health, but it is probable that a secret conflict exists." In the first evening edition of the same paper on the same day a Berlin article reported that the chancellor's intended resignation had been brought about, not by any differences over foreign policy, but by a disagreement in matters of "a family nature." There was still hope, the *Kölnische* continued, that the difficulties might be settled by compromise and that Kaiser Frederick might repeat the "Never!" that his dead father had written on a resignation statement of Bismarck's in 1876. "Arrangements that had been made at the cost of the tried and tested Reich chancellor could never be fully approved of by the German people." In a second article on page 2 with extra leading between the lines to give it special prominence it was reported that "diplomatic circles" were greatly excited by the report of Bismarck's intention to resign because of a renewal of the proposed marriage between Princess Victoria and Prince Alexander of Battenberg. A "reliable source" reported that the prince was to come to Berlin in the near future to carry on his courtship, and that Queen Victoria of England was herself expected to visit Berlin on her return from Florence "in order to act as matchmaker for the brother-in-law of her favorite daughter." Such a marriage could not be regarded in the same light as any other princely alliance. "As long as the Bulgarian question is not settled, Prince Alexander will carry on his forehead ... the mark of the Bulgarian crown." Germany's policy toward Bulgaria must be completely disinterested. Only this disinterest gave Germany the possibility of maintaining the trust of both regimes—Russia and Austria—most opposed to each other in the Bulgarian question. "This trust would naturally be destroyed with a single blow ... if the most hated personal enemy of the tsar became the son-in-law of the German Kaiser." So much was clear to "any German who loves his fatherland." This authoritative article was obviously official and seemed to bear the stamp of the chancellor himself. Simultaneously with the release of these articles both Pindter of the *Norddeutsche Allgemeine Zeitung* and Schweinburg of the *Berliner Politische Nachrichten* received strict orders not to discuss the matter in their papers.[7]

While these *Kölnische Zeitung* articles were causing a sensation among both the populace and the political leadership in Berlin, the chancellor went to Charlottenburg for an audience with Kaiser Frederick, who wrote that he approved Bismarck's memorandum, but requested him to talk with the kaiserin and expressed concern that the affair might damage the monarchical principle. Bismarck then suggested that the kaiserin might make a tour of the areas in Prussia currently suffering from severe spring flooding. The kaiser would see how Her Majesty would be acclaimed by the people. Afterward Bismarck had an audience with the kaiserin. This interview apparently began on a stern note—according to the chancellor's habitual modus operandi—but upon the kaiserin's statement that the marriage could be postponed, Bismarck then turned all sympathetic, protested that he personally had nothing against the marriage, and that after her husband's reign it could certainly be carried out. He then offered the kaiserin, for the assurance of the future of all four of her daughters, a sum of 9,000,000 M from the crown property left by Kaiser William: 2,000,000 M for each daughter and one million for herself. Holstein (who probably heard the details from Radolinski), boasting in his diary that he undoubtedly had the most "rounded view of the affair" since everyone confided in him, was disgusted. The kaiserin, he wrote, had "got round the chancellor completely." With the nine million marks the elderly Bismarck had made the marriage possible, probably because he was

> afraid of dismissal. Similarly, his apparently furious opposition to the marriage springs from his fear of the crown prince. It is the same double game he plays in foreign policy, between the Russians on the one hand and their enemies on the other. It is a measure of Bismarck's immense prestige that such behavior did not render his position impossible long age. Does H[is]. H[ighness]. imagine, then, that Prince William will never hear of this later on? . . . I do not think the chancellor will strengthen his position with the future William II by his present double game. Surely the prince must be aware of it—Waldersee sees to that.

Holstein apparently did not ask himself why, then, Bismarck had been able to build such immense prestige with such policies or whether, in either domestic or foreign policy, there was a sound, viable alternative to a policy of balance, or whether Bismarck's concern with Prince William might go beyond merely winning his favor. Pindter heard of the financial deal with the kaiserin on the seventh, writing in his diary, "The old business, clink, clink." On the following day the chancellor arranged the legal details of the nine-million-mark transfer with the rather astonished

Minister of Justice Friedberg and Acting Minister of the Royal Household von Stolberg.[8]

According to Radolinski via Holstein, during Bismarck's audience with Kaiserin Victoria on the fifth she assured him that he "could curse her up hill and down dale and lay all the blame on her afterwards." Later the same day Victoria telegraphed her mother in Florence, "Please be in no anxiety. Crisis of chancellor is an invention: we have never been on better terms and the understanding is perfect. Your visit 'must on no account be given up." Later she wrote the queen,

> I do not wonder that you should have been startled and alarmed as many people were, by the *senseless*, ridiculous and violent storm in the press, about Vicky and Sandro! If you knew *why* all this row was made, you would see more clearly that the reason was a futile one! *Our* relations with the chancellor never have been more cordial or agreeable; and you well know that Fritz is too calm and prudent and experienced to jeopardize peace or the interests of Germany in any way. . . . Pray pay no attention to the newspapers—there is no "*Kanzler* Crisis"—All this row is made for a *purpose*, & is really very silly.[9]

One could assume that the reason the press conflict was allowed not only to continue but to become even more extreme was to make sure of impressing the tsar. It is even possible to explain by that motive, because of the English connection, the attacks on the kaiserin personally that actually developed and that she herself, according to Radolinski, approved so cheerfully. But Queen Victoria certainly knew about Bismarck's apprehensions concerning the effect of the Battenberg marriage on Russia; it was in all the papers. And yet the kaiserin wrote, "*If* you knew . . . " Also, why should Kaiserin Victoria willingly approve scurrilous press attacks on herself that she thought were futile? Why the emphasis on "*our* relations" with the chancellor? Was it only the money that made her understanding with Bismarck so "perfect"?

The only hypothesis that clarifies these perplexities and throws light on the larger issues of the Battenberg crisis is to assume that the press outcry was aimed, in large part, at the edification and instruction of Crown Prince William and at helping to immobilize his *Kreuzzeitung* and Stoeckerite friends. Bismarck's banker Gerson Bleichröder, told Pindter that the chancellor had remarked that what bothered him the most in the Battenberg affair was that in contrast to his simple, open, confident relationship with Kaiser William, this development had occurred without his knowledge and in spite of his known sentiments; he did not know what to expect next from Charlottenburg and did not feel comfortable in the relationship. "The situation must be kept clear for William II." On April 1 Herbert had noted in his diary, "Long conference re: Charlottenburg difficulties, *Battenbergerei*, 'take it coolly,' but Papa wants to provide for the future." In other words, the crown was acting irresponsibly, and an incident that, as Queen Victoria indignantly protested, could have been and indeed was settled quietly between king, queen, and responsible minister was therefore seized upon by the chancellor—especially since William was already excited about it—not only, as Holstein surmised correctly at the beginning, "to use this opportunity of winning back the position of trust he formerly enjoyed with the crown prince, before the Stoecker affair," but also to bring the crown prince and his right-wing Conservative friends back into a progovernment position. Deputy Schrader wrote Bamberger on April 5 that as far as he knew, there was no conflict, that Bismarck was merely trying to get attention. He added that recently he had heard that Puttkamer and friends also wanted to remove Bismarck and were thinking of Stolberg as a replacement. It is possible that Bismarck was also trying to provoke the reactionaries into attacking the crown so strongly that even the formidable naiveté of the crown prince would not be proof against such a demonstration of the selfish shallowness of the much-vaunted monarchical loyalty of the right wing and also of the vulnerability of the crown itself to pressures from parties and public opinion. Such an attempt to educate Crown Prince William and compromise the reactionary Junkers could easily have charmed and intrigued Kaiserin Victoria—Bismarck was letting her into his secret operations—and account rather better than merely the promised money for Bismarck's later statement to the journalist Maximilian Harden that she was "enchanted" with him at the end of this interview. Yet, knowing William, she was quite sure the whole comedy would, in the end, prove to be "futile."[10]

23

Party Reaction

THE surmise that public exploitation of the Battenberg crisis by Bismarck served largely political purposes explains why the press campaign was begun in a prominent National Liberal paper, an orientation that was accentuated by Bismarck's interview with Rudolf von Bennigsen on April 9. He had written the National Liberal leader on the sixth—with the papers now full of rumors of his resignation—that he had money for victims of flood conditions in Hanover, asking him either to visit him to discuss its disposition or write him. It is very doubtful that the more than two-hour discussion with the chancellor that followed on the ninth was limited to assistance to flood victims. And immediately after the visit the newspapers announced that in both Berlin and Leipzig petitions were being circulated by National Liberals for signature among cartel circles appealing to the kaiser not to allow Bismarck to resign but to find a way "to save Germany from such an irreparable loss." The grand duke of Baden—probably with the chancellor's approval, and perhaps at his urging—had summoned Baron von Roggenbach to Berlin to assist him in influencing the kaiserin. Rumors circulated in the press that Bismarck would be succeeded as chancellor by either Bennigsen or Roggenbach, noted liberal figures whose candidacy had enough credibility to fill Junker Conservatives with a cold apprehension. On April 11 a public meeting was called in Breslau by the chairmen of the local Conservative, National Liberal, and Free Conservative organizations: namely, a retired lieutenant-colonel, a lawyer, and a count, to approve and sign a petition to the kaiser. The petition (headed by the traditional ceremonial salutation: "Most Serene, Most Mighty Kaiser and King! Most Gracious Kaiser, King, and Lord!") recalled that more than ten years earlier the country had also been shocked by the report of Bismarck's possible resignation. That time Kaiser William put all fears to rest with one word: "Never!" It then continued, "Your Majesty! In deep respect and unswerving loyalty [*Untertanentreue*] we beseech Your Majesty, considering the anxiety weigh-

214

ing heavily upon the country, likewise to speak a word of comfort [*erlösendes Wort*] to your people." According to *Germania*, the meeting was attended largely by government officials of all ranks, and the informal cheer for Bismarck at the end was louder than the formal cheer for Kaiser Frederick at the beginning.[1]

The attempt to rally the public through the press against the crown would normally have outraged the Conservatives, and privately they were indeed disturbed by the chancellor's "methods." It was clear to the initiated, noted General Waldersee, that whether the *Kölnische Zeitung* articles were datelined Vienna or wherever, they had been written in the Wilhelmstrasse. "A chancellor who carries on a war in the press against his own sovereign! If Kaiser Frederick were a man, he would get rid of the chancellor today and rule himself; but he won't do it, he will yield, and the monarchy thereby takes a great step backward." Even if the Kaiser did dismiss the chancellor and the latter were quickly brought back upon the accession of the crown prince, he would return with an acquisition of moral superiority over the monarchy, and, added Waldersee, "In my view everything [his own career?] depends on making the future kaiser gradually independent of the chancellor." Yet, when the crown prince had come to him on the thirty-first, Waldersee, the advocate of a preventive war against Russia, had apparently accepted the crown prince's statement that the Battenberg marriage project was an English intrigue to alienate Russia from Germany, merely adding piously in his diary, "Sad that our kaiserin allows herself to carry on an anti-German policy. Everything is working out just as we feared it would." He thereby demonstrated how the hatred of Kaiserin Victoria—and fear of her "liberal" orientation—among the far Right made it relatively easy to take them into camp through a campaign against her. Even after the press campaign had aroused in General Waldersee the above misgivings concerning the authority of the crown, he refrained from warning the crown prince—contrary to Holstein's assumptions and in spite of his awareness of the Bismarcks' hostility to himself—and actually earnestly advised the prince to get closer to the National Liberals, who were afraid that as kaiser he would support himself solely on the *Kreuzzeitung* party, and that "in the present world situation the only possible government was one supported by the cartel parties, that all men of patriotic feeling must stick together."[2]

Waldersee's sudden concern for the cartel was probably also brought about by Kaiser Frederick's request to Chief of the Military Cabinet General von Albedyll to remove Waldersee from his present position and appoint him to command an army corps away from Berlin, where his opportunities to maintain his influence with the crown prince would be at a minimum. This action was apparently launched on the fourth, and this simultaneous timing with the Battenberg crisis creates a suspicion that it was Bismarck himself who had suggested such a move to the kaiser in his audience on the thirty-first, perhaps as a kind of consolation prize for the kaiser's self-abnegating support against his wife in the Battenberg affair and under cover of that crisis. At any rate, the main question in Waldersee's mind, as he confessed to his diary, was "After how many weeks or months will [the kaiser's] suffering have come to an end?" The disagreement among the doctors was very great, and Waldersee would be justified in assuming that, if he were sent away from Berlin, even six months of Kaiser Frederick's continued rule could suffice to attenuate the general's influence with the flighty and impressionable crown prince to the point where it could not be restored. Waldersee also wrote that in such a period, without Bismarck, a Liberal ministry could do all kinds of damage; dissolution of the Reichstag under such auspices would especially be "a deeply damaging misfortune for the existence of the Reich that never could be made good." If Waldersee had had to rely on the chancellor alone, he would surely have fallen at this time; but Albedyll appealed to Waldersee's superior at the general staff, the aged Field Marshal von Moltke, who gave him a strong, uncompromising statement concerning Waldersee's irreplaceability and threatened his own resignation if he were removed, a challenge that neither the kaiser nor Bismarck cared to pick up. So the general survived.[3]

Throughout the Battenberg crisis both Bismarck and Herbert consulted constantly with Crown Prince William, thus drawing him into the agitation and committing him to it. "At the moment," wrote Holstein, "it strikes one with unaccustomed strangeness to see how full of attention the two Bismarcks are for the crown prince. And to think how inconsiderately they treated the noble old Kaiser. But his grandson, I feel sure, will pay off many an old score. The chancellor is striving desperately to make people think he is the object of the crown prince's deepest respect. We shall see how long that will last." At the outset certainly the crown prince struck as enthusiastic and devoted a note as one might wish—even more. Bismarck's birthday came on April 1, and Crown Prince William, dressed in his new general's uniform and bearing a big bouquet, had invited himself to the celebration. At the dinner that evening, undoubtedly responding spontaneously to the quality of the moment, the crown prince toasted the chancellor by comparing the Reich to an army corps "that has lost its commanding officer on the battlefield and whose first officer is badly wounded! In this critical moment forty-six million true German hearts turn in anxiety and hope to the flag and to its bearer, from whom all is expected. But the bearer of this flag is our illustrious prince, our great chancellor, he goes before us, we follow him! To his health!" Besides indicating that Crown Prince William had as naively romantic a concept of battle as of politics, this toast also showed a few other things quite clearly to those who read it. "Well," wrote Pindter, "and isn't Frederick then also the commanding officer? The dynastic instinct is becoming lost, and it is not nice for the son to emphasize his father's severe illness that way. *Les Dieux s'en vont* [the gods are departing]." The *Frankfurter Zeitung* remarked acidly that the speaker's imperial father did not in fact lie severely wounded, but had received the enthusiastic ovations of the Berlin public in the streets of the capital hardly an hour before and held the reins of the government in his hands "to the joy and satisfaction of the German people." Kaiser Frederick himself sent his son William a note deploring his clear suggestion that his father was unfit to rule and continued, "You have probably not considered how lacking in loyalty it sounds to describe the minister, at the expense of the monarch, as the only active force in the government, and also how unsuitable it is for you especially to speak about it." The chancellor evidently helped the crown prince to doctor his words, and the "authorized version" of the toast, full of loyal praise for the kaiser, was then printed in the *Norddeutsche* and other government-oriented papers. Interestingly, however, the real version had been initially revealed by the *Post*, also a government-related paper.[4]

That Bismarck's press campaign against the Battenberg marriage was a scandalous assault on the prerogatives of the crown might be uncomfortably felt by Conservative Berlin society, but publicly it was the left-liberal press that picked up and trumpeted the theme. The marriage, commented the *Berliner Tageblatt*, could not possibly be the real reason for the resignation rumors. If the queen of England could accept a Battenberg as her son-in-law, the German kaiser certainly could do as much. Bismarck's resignation would "precisely at the present moment be advantageous." To suggest that the kaiser could not dismiss a minister, wrote the *Freisinnige Zeitung*, was to limit his freedom of decision. The *Frankfurter Zeitung* agreed: "It is putting the rights of the crown in question if the 'Never' that originated in Kaiser William's free decision is made into a rule." The *Vossische Zeitung* found it completely unbelievable that the position of the German Reich could be endangered by a royal marriage. The exaggerated concern for the feelings of the tsar, wrote the *Frankfurter Zeitung*'s August Stein, contrasted "in an almost painful way" with the famous statement, "We Germans fear God and nobody else." In an editorial on April 9 the *Frankfurter* declared that the sequence of official reports in the *Kölnische Zeitung* had been planned "to alarm public opinion and by this means to bring pressure on the crown [*höchster Stelle*].... Whoever remembers the last twenty years of German politics could not have been surprised; one knows the tune, one also knows the Herr composer." At least part of the cartel formed a sort of "chancellor party" that was preaching the doctrine that if there was a basic dispute between chancellor and kaiser, for the good of Germany the kaiser must yield. The National Liberal petition campaign was directed at forcing the will of party assemblies on the kaiser. "That in imperial Germany, in monarchical Prussia—what a triumph for the most fanatical radicalism!... A leading minister and statesman that the monarch will not dismiss, whom parliamentary majorities *cannot* remove" amounted to "ministerial absolutism." If Kaiser Frederick were in good health the ministry would be changed "from top to bottom." On the thirteenth the *Frankfurter* wrote that "with a shadow monarchy on one side and a majordomo [*Hausmeiertum*] on the other ... nothing would be lacking in order to reproduce the situation under the *Merovingians* [*sic,* see above, p. 201] than that the *chancellorship* should be made *hereditary.*" This was a nasty dig at the position of Herbert Bismarck in the government.[5]

Naturally the cartel press seized this opportunity to point out the glaring contradiction between the new-found concern of the left Liberals for the rights of the monarchy and their oft declared democratic, parliamentary principles. "It is heartening," wrote the *Kölnische Zeitung* sarcastically, "to see with what victorious strength the *monarchical principle* is momentarily developing in Germany." Those who were trying to protect the nation and the dynasty from the possible resignation of the chancellor, however, were more devoted to both dynasty and nation. The German Liberals' new-found monarchism was merely a mask that they had momentarily put on for purely tactical reasons out of their hatred for Bismarck.[6]

The *Kölnische Zeitung* also made it quite clear that it was Kaiserin Victoria who was pushing for the Battenberg marriage, backed by her mother, the English queen, who was due to visit Berlin on April 12, Princess Victoria's birthday. For highly placed women in such affairs of the heart momentarily to lose sight of politics and the interests of the dynasty was not only understandable, but "noble and truly womanly." For this reason it was fortunate that such decisions did not lie with the kaiserin, but according to "our Prussian institutions" had to be made by the kaiser and "his responsible advisor." In response to the *National Zeitung,* which, evidently on the strength of information from sources close to Charlottenburg, was vainly protesting that there was no chancellor crisis, that the marriage plans had been postponed, that there was therefore no longer any conflict between the chancellor and the imperial couple, and no thought of the chancellor's resignation, the *Kölnische* simply stated disdainfully that the left-wing National Liberal paper was "completely uninformed."[7]

When Moritz Busch, editor of *Die Grenzboten* and a publicist who had long worked off and on for Bismarck, read the initial articles about the Battenberg crisis in the *Kölnische Zeitung* on the sixth, he sent Bismarck a note offering his services and received a summons to the Chancellery the following day. He found the chancellor complaining of nervous excitement and insomnia; he had to take morphine to get only a little sleep. He blamed the Battenberg marriage plans on Queen Victoria. "The old queen is fond of matchmaking, like all old women. . . . But obviously her main objects are political—a permanent estrangement between ourselves and Russia." The kaiser, said the chancellor, was glad that he had come to his assistance in resisting his wife over the marriage, since "she is too much for him in argument." The marriage had only been postponed. "It is true that in Charlottenburg they are most anxious to retain me—she also. They wrap me up in cotton wool and velvet." Bismarck suggested that Busch write an article for the *Grenzboten*, "showing how England has at all times sought and still seeks to influence us for her own ends, and often against our interest." He could survey English policy of the last two centuries and how it had set the continental European powers against each other. "Remember the press laws," cautioned Bismarck. "Be very cautious, diplomatic, and not too venomous; and always emphasize the fact that it is foreign influences that are working against me; not the emperor, but the reigning lady and her mother." The following day Busch was recalled to the Chancellery, where he found Prince Bismarck reclining on a chaise longue and reading the *Kölnische Zeitung*. "The main point," he said, "is that the emperor is on my side." Bismarck had scathing things to say regarding the kaiser's Liberal friends: "These Byzantine hypocrites, these democrats who wag their tails and crawl more abjectly than the most extravagant absolutist." In 1885 Holstein had written that "the crown princess is a coward in the face of public opinion." Although the chancellor was exploiting the crisis for political reasons and in agreement with Kaiserin Victoria herself, the public agitation also provided insurance against the unpredictability of the kaiserin.[8]

The partly false appearance of a full-blown, basic conflict between the chancellor and the left-Liberal, pro-English influence at court that the left-liberal press was unwittingly assisting Bismarck in projecting, did not fail to rally the Conservatives to the chancellor's support. Reacting to statements in the left-liberal press, the *Konservative Korrespondenz* denounced as completely frivolous any thought of experimenting with how far in the present dangerous situation the German ship of state might manage to proceed without "the best pilot available to us." The Conservatives, however, agreed with the left Liberals that the real issues went much deeper than merely the Battenberg affair. "It appears to be much more the case, that the Reich chancellor has received the impression . . . that his advice does not enjoy the same esteem from the crown as in the time of the late kaiser." The *Kreuzzeitung* printed this statement of the conservative paper without comment, and generally maintained an air of discretion and restraint. But in the face of the all-out attacks on the kaiserin and "English influence" from the *Kölnische Zeitung* and other cartel or government-oriented papers, this restraint in itself spoke forcefully for the chancellor and against the crown. They, too, declared an editorial on the eighth, had thoughts about the "chancellor crisis," but saw no reason for expressing them. For one thing, the crisis by this time might not be so severe as it had seemed for a few days (as usual, the court connections of the *Kreuzzeitung* were very good), and also the number of persons actually informed of what was going on was bound to be very small (again, a correct appraisal: Holstein wrote that he doubted that even Herbert was aware of the substance of Bismarck's interview with the Kaiserin). Nevertheless, to the *Kreuzzeitung* it was also quite clear that such a crisis could not have been caused by merely a trivial disagreement between Bismarck and the crown. Two days later the *Kreuzzeitung* became quite aroused by what it thought was "a happy springtime rustling through the leaves of the German Liberal press [*Blätterwald*]." It especially denounced the Berlin correspondent of the German Liberal *Breslauer Zeitung* for "kneeling at the feet of Herr von Bennigsen." The German Liberals were clearly willing, like the French Radicals who groveled before the tsar, to take any pose and make any alliances if it would bring them to power. With their parliamentary orientation, if they were to take over the government they would have to have the support of a Reichstag majority, and this could be produced for them only with the assistance of both the National Liberals and the Center. The *Kreuzzeitung* was sure, however, that the Center party would never support such a liberal regime.[9]

In a later issue, on April 20, the *Kreuzzeitung* further assisted the chancellor's purposes by distinguishing between two different phases of the chancellor crisis: the acute phase, which had been surmounted when the impending visit of Prince Alexander had been canceled; and the latent phase, which would continue until "the planned decoration of the Prince of Battenberg and his coming here have been definitely given up." A conclusive settlement of the Bulgarian question would have the same effect by doubtless removing the suspicions of the tsar in regard to the marriage. Since such a Bulgarian settlement was not likely soon, the *Kreuzzeitung* thus in effect warned of a continuing threat hanging over the chancellor. In the same issue they also deplored plans in "national circles" in Leipzig to circulate a declaration of loyalty to Bismarck. Although they were "completely on his side" in the current dispute, they regarded such an act as "completely improper." Jewish journalists on both sides, the *Kreuzzeitung* complained in an article on the eleventh, were exceeding the bounds of decency and falsifying the facts, which was an example of a general lack of morality in the press.[10]

Although the rallying of the conservative *Kreuzzeitung* to Bismarck and against the crown was discreet and hedged about with solemn protestations of undiminished monarchical loyalty, Pastor Engel's conservative and orthodox *Reichsbote* was more open. The German Liberals, it wrote, were thinking in terms of English parliamentarism; they assumed that because the monarchy ought not to be significant in the life of the state, in Germany as in England it therefore did not matter whom royal princes and princesses married. The Prussian monarchy, however, "belongs to the state, as the state to the monarchy; concern for the state [*Staatsbewusstsein*] is its soul, just as royalism is the soul of the people." The German Liberals, in their pettiness accusing the chancellor of being afraid of the tsar, could never reach Bismarck's high level of responsibility, that of guarding the peace of Germany and of Europe. Such language coincided absolutely and most surprisingly—coming from the Stoeckerite, right-wing conservative paper—with that of the government-inspired articles of the *Kölnische Zeitung*. As against a possible political threat from the liberal Left, the *Reichsbote* clearly did not have much sensitivity for the personal rights of the royal family. In a later article it declared that the German people wanted to be ruled by a king, but not by women. The Prussian people could envisage their king only as an actual ruler and military leader. "Just as the little son of the crown prince recently thought that Kaiser William must have taken his sword with him up to heaven, so in the thoughts of the . . . Prussian people the king is unthinkable without the sword." Presumably to bring into the open the even more drastic things the Conservatives were saying in private and to lift their mask of royalist respectability, a journalistic agent of the Berlin political police was sent, probably on the chancellor's secret instructions, to plant an article in the Saxon conservative *Dresdener Nachrichten*, the most widely read paper in Conservative circles in the area. The article appeared on April 10 and was picked up by some provincial conservative Prussian papers as well. The article attacked Kaiserin Victoria in the most vulgar way, under the title: "No Petticoat Politics [*Frauenzimmerpolitik*]! And No English Politics in Germany!" The left-liberal press also assisted Bismarck in documenting the monarchical disloyalty of the Right. The *Frankfurter Zeitung* pointed out that "certain circles" had been agitating against the then crown princess and now kaiserin for months "with vicious zeal" because of her "alleged religious and political liberalism." This agitation had had some success in a shameful way among "the so-called cultivated." And if one demanded sources and evidence, one received for an answer, "After all, she is not German." The *Freisinnige Zeitung* included "High Conservative Nihilists" in its denunciations.[11]

The rallying of the right-wing Conservatives through the Battenberg crisis takes on even more political significance when one considers the tense relations among the cartel parties just before it broke. On April 6—the same day that the startling reports of the *Kölnische Zeitung* regarding the chancellor's intention to resign were being commented on and widely disseminated in the press—the Free Conservative *Post* had carried a very hard-hitting attack on the *Kreuzzeitung* clerical Conservatives. The German Liberals, the *Post* pointed out, were taking a very moderate and sensible line in preparation for the fall Prussian Landtag elections. They were not speaking any more of a complete change in the political system, but rather were basing their appeal to the electorate on the necessity of blocking further reactionary tendencies. The parties of the cartel must remember "that the prospects of the German Liberal party basically depend upon whether they succeed in winning the great bulk of those elements that do not . . . belong to a definite party persuasion, and that therefore everything must be carefully avoided that could drive those elements over to the German Liberals. The government and the Conservatives would be doing the work of the latter if they did not make clear beyond any doubt that high-church reactionary tendencies have no place either in the government or in the national majorities of both legislative houses." The article was, of course, reprinted the following day in the *Norddeutsche Allgemeine Zeitung*'s "Journal-Revue."[12]

This blast of the *Post* was probably called forth by the cooperation of the Conservatives with the Catholic Center party in emasculating the government's school-aid bill in committee (see above, p. 143). On March 30 the *National Zeitung* had complained that the Conservative members of the committee had arranged their agreement with the Center without making any attempt to arrive at an understanding with the Free Conservatives and the National Liberals. The Center was basically hostile to the bill because it strengthened the public schools and therefore made their own goal of replacing the state schools with church schools more difficult to achieve. That the German Conservatives should play into the hands of the Center in this way could be explained only by the Conservatives' "well-known, irresistible inclination to cooperate with clericalism." To this article the *Kreuzzeitung* replied disdainfully that it was well known that the *National Zeitung* had been trying for some time to develop a "moderate" party constellation, but that attacking the Conservatives over the school-aid bill would not work. The voters would care much more about having to pay higher taxes in the districts if the government provisions went through. The *Kreuzzeitung* advised dropping the bill altogether, since the disagreement over it was so basic, and using the money for flood relief. The latter suggestion was picked up and seconded by the *National Liberale Korrespondenz*, but the *National Zeitung* stuck to its guns. Giving up the bill, it wrote, would be "most regrettable" and would be "exclusively the fault of the German Conservatives."[13]

Significantly, not only did the government *Norddeutsche* reprint the articles of the *National Zeitung* and the *Post* in its "Journal-Revue," but on April 4 it also reprinted on page 1 an article by the German Liberal Eugen Richter in his *Freisinnige Zeitung* that called for a stop to government influence and interference in elections. Referring to the mention in Kaiser Frederick's proclamation of "the trustful cooperation of all classes of the population," Richter wrote, "Elections should not be a test of power for the current direction of government policy, but should make it possible for the people to play an independent role in the formulation of state affairs." After quoting this article at length, the *Norddeutsche* merely added the rather weak statement that one must wait to discover to what extent these views were shared by the whole German Liberal party and by the rest of the party press before commenting on them. On April 15 the *Norddeutsche* even went to the extreme of quoting the radical *Berliner Volkszeitung* to the effect that the provision for the abolition of school fees in the government's school-aid bill and the payment of money grants to the local communities did not add up to a net increase in tax burdens, as the people were quite aware. The appearance of these articles in the *Norddeutsche* seemed to indicate that the Bismarck government had by no means given up on the school-aid bill. Furthermore, it was placing the Conservative party in a two-way crunch by threatening them, on the one hand, with a left-Liberal government to replace Bismarck as a result of the Battenberg crisis and, on the other hand, with an implied threat, in case they continued their noncooperation with the middle parties, of a withdrawal of government support in the election for the Prussian Landtag in the fall.[14]

In response to the criticism of the *Post*, the *Kreuzzeitung* complained that the *Post* had appealed for unity among the "national parties," yet in the same breath it had loudly attacked the "clerical Conservatives." These repeated attempts to shake off a faction of the Conservative party would not work. Left Liberals were determined in any case to apply the term "reaction" to the whole cartel, not just the right-wing Conservatives. This reply of the *Kreuzzeitung* was published on April 6. Its response in a serious way in the following days to the possibility of a Liberal ministry's following the chancellor as a result of the Battenberg crisis and its implicit and explicit support of Bismarck and of the "national" point of view thus marked a weakening in its previous attitude of defiant independence toward the cartel and the government.[15]

A strong, politically independent position for the *Kreuzzeitung*-Waldersee-Puttkamer-Stoecker group, even if they succeeded in carrying the rest of the German Conservative party with them, could ultimately be guaranteed only by the support of the Catholic Center party. Thus the *Kreuzzeitung's* call in January (see above, p. 96) for a new "Christian-socialist union," to include Catholics as well as Protestants, and its recent confident assertion that the Center party would never support a German Liberal regime. The situation must indeed have been a difficult one for the Center party. *Germania* simply refused to take the first reports of the chancellor crisis in the *Kölnische Zeitung* seriously and gleefully quoted the *National Zeitung's* quip that perhaps the *Kölnische* articles originated in another "printer's error." No doubt Bismarck had often thought of retirement; but in the present situation he would "not want to introduce a change." There were no special threats to present programs in domestic policy, but in foreign affairs the situation was so complicated and delicate and so much hung on Germany's position that "the slightest mistake can bring about unforeseen explosions, the slightest suggestion could decrease Germany's influence in foreign affairs and thereby set the ball rolling. Such a suggestion would clearly be created if Prince Bismarck were to resign over a matter of foreign policy."[16]

Suspicious of the *Kölnische Zeitung* and other cartel papers from the beginning, however, *Germania* was quick to detect the focus of the attack on the kaiserin. "It is clear against whom these attacks are directed. One does not so much mean England as the English royal family and especially one of its members who lives among us." Yet, as late as April 8, a Sunday, *Germania*, in reporting the opinion of the *Konservative Korrespondenz* that the crisis must have deeper roots in domestic policy, reserved its own opinion "until further statements are available." By its next issue on Tuesday the tenth (neither *Germania* nor the *Kreuzzeitung*, of course, worked on Sunday), it had made up its mind—or had received definite orders from the Center party leader Windthorst. To experienced observers, the possibility of Bismarck's actually resigning in the current situation might indeed appear to be nil, but that would not prevent changes in the ministry—and possible opportunities for Center party leaders—if indeed the crisis originated in domestic policy. *Germania* consequently now changed its tune and accused the cartel papers of trying to rewrite Bismarck's ringing declaration of German self-confidence in his February speech to, "We Germans fear God *and the nerves of the tsar.*" It was clear, it declared, that the cartel press *"has raised a false alarm to play the chancellor off against the kaiser [sic]* and control the latter's political decisions." If the cartel parties, either with or without the help of Bismarck, were actually trying to browbeat the monarchy, as the German Liberal press—which could be expected to have good connections with Charlottenburg—was strongly maintaining, then the Center party, if only to protect its own independent political position, was more or less forced to help the German Liberals in providing the kaiser with an alternative to both the cartel and if necessary Bismarck as well. The Center party deputy Baron Schorlemer-Alst later assured minister of Agriculture Lucius that because of the close friendship of Kaiserin Victoria with Frau Schrader, wife of one of the German Liberal leaders, the German Liberals were confident of being called to form a government if Bismarck fell. "Richter had strutted around like a stork in the lettuce patch!"

Even if they had not seriously believed they had such chances, the necessity of publicly maintaining such a claim would have forced the German Liberals to rally to the defense of the crown under the cartel onslaught. The kaiser's physical condition, the basic hostility to Frederick and Victoria of Prince William and the far Right, and the imperial couple's fear of a regency, however, had rendered Bismarck immune from this kind of challenge from the beginning. In fact, under these conditions—where sustaining the precarious position of the imperial couple apparently rested upon Bismarck alone—the shrill insistence of the German Liberal press that the chancellor could easily be dispensed with might well have appeared to the kaiser and kaiserin to be not only dangerously frivolous but disloyal. On the other hand, by going along, at least tacitly, with Bismarck's press campaign, Kaiserin Victoria was unwittingly or carelessly placing her true Liberal supporters in a false position. On Wednesday April 11 the *Konservative Korrespondenz* reported that before and during the session of the Prussian Landtag that day Dr. Ludwig Windthorst and Eugen Richter had conferred together in a corner of the foyer for more than an hour. "What topic was dealt with in this council of war one can hardly fail to guess." In noting this report, the governmental *Deutsches Tageblatt* remarked sardonically that Richter was probably inquiring about becoming a "Krongardist mit Welfenhosen [royal guard in Guelf pants]," a reference to Windthorst's former position as prime minister of the (Guelf or Welf) Kingdom of Hanover before it was annexed by Prussia after the Seven Weeks' War with Austria and its German Confederation allies in 1866.[17]

Germania was especially upset by a report in official Viennese papers evidently stemming from Berlin, that Bismarck "is determined to *make an example* of this case, and will not let this opportunity slip to permanently insure a completely free hand." To attempt such a thing, declared *Germania*, would amount to "ministerial absolutism." With the reports of petitions being adopted in public meetings and signed by the public imploring Kaiser Frederick to find a way to keep Bismarck, *Germania* flew into a rage of denunciation, branding such efforts "German Boulangism"—a timely reference, since the ambitious General Boulanger was currently beginning his successful series of campaigns in French by-elections as a sort of running plebiscite in his own support and against the French republican regime. *Germania* was convinced, however, that "the inviolability of legal dispositions [*Rechtsordnungen*] and above all of the monarchical principle mean more to the *immense* [*sic*] majority of the Germans than a hundred Bismarcks!" Such campaigns would in fact be embarrassing for the chancellor; he would not accept such petitions from the German Boulangists. The cartel operators had better watch out lest they provoke a movement of counterpetitions in support of the kaiser that would overwhelm them. The *Kreuzzeitung, Germania* observed, had proclaimed the right of the kaiser to dismiss anybody, but had not defended him against the attacks of the cartel press. The whole Battenberg crisis, it declared, was merely a mask for a putsch against the crown by the servile cartel "majordomoists [*Hausmeieraner*]," who were thereby doing the work of the Social Democrats. Just as partisan and ethnocentric hatred of Kaiserin Victoria made the right-wing *Kreuzzeitung* and Stoeckerite Conservatives susceptible to the Bismarck Battenberg campaign, so also *Germania*'s and the Center party's suspicious oppositional and particularistic stance toward both government and cartel made it easy for them to be drawn into Bismarck's artificial chancellor crisis and compromise themselves in it. The *Kreuzzeitung* was thus proved wrong; the Center party was indeed prepared to support a possible new left-Liberal government; and Bismarck had thus successfully, at least for the moment, driven a wedge between the Protestant clericals and the Catholics.[18]

24

Foreign and Public Reaction

THE reaction abroad to Bismarck's Battenberg initiatives was mixed. Lord Salisbury had advised Sir Edward Malet that the chancellor's communication to him should go directly to Queen Victoria personally, since it concerned her private family, and not through the government, and he further telegraphed Sir Edward on April 8 in a coolly negative tone: "I am very sorry not to be able to comply with Prince Bismarck's wishes, but he is asking me to assist him in thwarting the wishes of his Emperor and my Queen in order to gratify the malignant feelings of the Russian Emperor. This would certainly be inconsistent with my duty &, if German cooperation can only be had at this price, we must do without it." Nevertheless, Salisbury, being not only a responsible minister but also a careful politician, simultaneously warned the queen in Florence not to go to Berlin. "I have received several private telegrams from Sir E. Malet," he telegraphed the queen in code,

> showing that Prince Bismarck is in one of his raging moods about the proposed marriage. . . . He has a vast corrupt influence over the press and can give enormous circulation to rumors. I would humbly advise Your Majesty to avoid any action which could operate with the controversy which is going on. The newspapers say that Your Majesty is going to Potsdam or Berlin. I would humbly submit that this visit at this time would expose You to great misconstruction and possibly to some disrespectful demonstration. German Chancellor is reported by his son to be in a state of intense exasperation, drinking stimulants all day and narcotics by night.[1]

Upon receipt of Sir Edward Malet's letter, the queen directed her private secretary to inform Sir Edward that the queen had nothing to do with the proposed Battenberg marriage, that she had instead strongly advised against it. This information Sir Edward passed on to Herbert Bismarck, who appeared pleased and surprised and promised to see to it that the press discontinue its attacks on England and Queen Victoria.

The queen was disturbed that her ambassador in Berlin had been so easily stampeded by the Bismarcks that he had sent "what almost amounted to a message! to the Queen. It was too outrageous." Political considerations did not prevail over the queen's strong family feeling and human instincts. She informed Lord Salisbury that she would not give up "going to see my poor sick son-in-law." Disgusted by the intrigues in Berlin, she instructed her secretary to "write to Lord Salisbury about the outrageous conduct of Pce. Wm., and of the terrible *cercle vicieux* which surrounds the unfortunate Emperor and Empress and which makes Bismarck's conduct really disloyal, wicked and really unwise in the extreme! . . . How Bismarck and still more William *can* play such a double game it is impossible for us honest, straightforward English to understand. Thank God! we *are* English!"[2]

In spite of both Lord Salisbury's and the queen's protestations, the English essentially cooperated with Bismarck in the affair by taking the crisis seriously and continuing family and discreet diplomatic pressure in Charlottenburg against the marriage. Articles in the *Times* and the *Standard*, the newspaper closest to Lord Salisbury, were so in favor of the Bismarckian position that the *Kölnische Zeitung* quoted them prominently at length. The response from Russia, on the other hand, which in a sense was the hinge of the whole press campaign, was disappointing. The pan-Slav press, rejoicing to find their chief enemy, Bismarck, in apparent trouble, proclaimed loudly that Russia had no interest at all in what happened to the prince of Battenberg, and that his marriage to a Prussian princess would put him under German control and make it less likely that he would return to Bulgaria. Even Foreign Minister Giers took a politely noncommittal stance and told the German ambassador that the proposed marriage would of course not shake the confidence of the tsar and the Russian government in Germany's friendly policy toward Russia. The chancellor found this reply unsatisfactory and responded tartly that that was not what Giers had telegraphed his own ambassador in Berlin and would the ambassador please clarify whether the Russian foreign minister was concealing his real opinions. He had assumed from Giers's and Ambassador Shuvalov's earlier attitudes that they would give him strong support in opposing the Battenberg marriage, but the lack of such support was making it difficult for him to oppose the kaiserin in her determination to bring it about. He could not be "more Russian than the Russian government."[3]

Austrian Ambassador Széchényi had written Foreign Minister Kálnoky that it was "incomprehensible" that the kaiserin, "precisely at a moment when everything here hangs by a hair, putting the monarchy completely aside and responding only to the feelings of the woman and mother, solely through an affair of the heart, in which she herself has so unwisely constantly prompted and encouraged her daughter, could bring things to a break with the Reich chancellor," and that it had to be recognized that Bismarck's objections were, from his point of view, "in many respects justified." Nevertheless, like his St. Petersburg counterpart, the Austrian foreign minister also responded skeptically and cautiously. He was not quite sure why Bismarck had asked for his opinion, he told the German ambassador, apparently suspecting some ulterior motive. He simply did not believe that in the current situation, at home and abroad, the chancellor would actually resign. Of course, it was understandable that Bismarck would prefer to see the marriage plans given up, "if only on account of the crown prince."[4]

In contrast to the skepticism of the professional diplomats, the initial public reaction to the news of the chancellor's possible resignation apparently left little to be desired. The first *Kölnische Zeitung* report, wrote Széchényi, reacted on the public "like a bomb." Everyone—except part of the German Liberal press, quoted above—reacted in unbelief and dismay. "One fancies oneself back in the era of Louis XIV," wrote the liberal *Frankfurter Zeitung*, "when one hears that sort of thing, but more thorough examination forces the conclusion that we really are not yet at all removed from that era, that purely personal moods . . . unfortunately still play a more significant role in politics than the will and interests of the peoples." Although the left-wing National Liberal *National Zeitung* supported Charlottenburg by continuing to insist that there was no crisis, it nevertheless took an increasingly strong position in favor of Bismarck and against the marriage. "There are dynasties," it wrote, "whose members may marry whom they wish because in their countries the crown does not direct affairs. With us the monarch is the highest leader of the state; from that follows that the family alliances of the dynasty can never be politically meaningless." "The excitement is tremendous," noted Baroness Spitzemberg, who so often convincingly mirrored the feelings of the cultivated, politically alert German public, "and I hold it to be simply impossible that such a monstrous frivolity will occur, in spite of the obstinacy of the kaiserin, the weakness of the kaiser, and the wailing of an infatuated girl, who is not at all respectable, has in the interim taken every guard officer, and coquetted in the most common way with every man who has come down the pike." It was, she wrote, "revolting and shameful to discover so little princely feeling, so little understanding for her duty and her position in the kaiserin; she is pushing this love intrigue of her man-crazy, ill-bred daughter as if she were a chamber maid, not a woman of quality." The duke of Ratibor, president of the Prussian Herrenhaus, wrote to his brother Prince Hohenlohe that being willing to sacrifice "the man whom the whole world envies us" for such a marriage amounted to treason.[5]

The non-Prussian federal princes and governments also backed the chancellor. The kaiser's sister, the grand duchess of Baden, wrote to Kaiser Frederick and remonstrated with him for not respecting their father's wishes in regard to the Battenberg marriage. Frederick replied testily that their father had had limited information on the matter, and that he had to consider his children's welfare. King Albert of Saxony appealed to Kaiser Frederick "to spare us this irreparable loss." Kaiser Frederick replied that it would be best to allow the present storm to go calmly by. "We, Victoria and I, are in the very best harmony with the chancellor, and there is also no ground for assuming that this will be disturbed." On April 9 the grand duke of Hesse wrote the kaiser renouncing the marriage in the name of Prince Alexander. The liberal Bavarian *Münchener Neuste Nachrichten* announced that "a resignation of Prince Bismarck would be a misfortune for our people, for Europe. When eventually inexorable fate cuts the thread of life of the great man, Germany and the world will have to see how things go without him. As long as he lives, however, may he dedicate his strength to the fatherland!" The court paper of the Kingdom of Württemberg and the National Liberal *Schwäbischer Merkur* supported the chancellor's position. Along with the unexpectedly good news that Queen Victoria was against the marriage, the Bismarcks also soon discovered from the English family connections and also from Darmstadt that Prince Alexander, having fallen in love with a local actress, was actually no longer really interested in marrying Princess Victoria.[6]

25

Partial Resolution of the Crisis

IT was in the nature of Bismarck's campaign that it could not be kept up for long. He had achieved the effect he wanted; the *Kreuzzeitung-Reichsbote*-Stoecker party had once more been rallied to the cartel, and the Center had been separated from the clerical Protestants in the *Kreuzzeitung*-Stoecker group. Also, regardless of Bismarck's private arrangements and understandings with Kaiserin Victoria, the intensity of the public outcry had effectively underscored his own opposition to the Battenberg connection and made the latter impossible. As Bismarck later told Roggenbach, he could not rely on "a woman's word." General von Stosch agreed. He thought that the attacks on the kaiserin in the press had not been sharp enough. She was undermining monarchical power and had told him often herself that "she was to be led only by fear." Bismarck was very likely also aware that the shock and resentment at the cartel assault on the crown were beginning to gather negative force; *Germania*'s threat to organize a countermovement of petitions in support of the kaiser was serious enough to want to avoid. At the same time, Kaiser Frederick's health began to deteriorate again. Consequently on April 10 Bismarck arranged a well-publicized conference with the kaiserin in Berlin, at the former crown prince's palace, where they talked together for two hours. In this conversation, according to Holstein, Bismarck advised the kaiserin against buying a palace in Berlin for her daughter and Prince Alexander to live in with the money she was to be given from the crown holdings, "because you never know whether Their Highnesses will like it here afterwards," a hint at the hostility of the crown prince. Holstein also stated that Bismarck and Kaiserin Victoria agreed "that the appearance of a quarrel must still be kept up. So the press battle still goes merrily on."[1]

The meeting with the kaiserin on the tenth was followed by an audience with the kaiser on the eleventh, who inquired of Bismarck in writing, "if he regarded the crisis as ended?" When Bismarck replied that he did,

Kaiser Frederick then handed him a previously prepared statement that read, "You will have realized from your interview with the kaiserin yesterday that the fullest consideration has been given to all the points raised in your memorandum. I therefore regard the matter as settled." Confidentially the chancellor informed the Prussian ministers of this exchange in a meeting on the twelfth and pointed out that although he now regarded the affair as ended, he could not publicize it because it would appear to be a "shout of triumph." He had, he said, sent word to Breslau and Leipzig to call off the petition movement, "which was embarrassing to him." Although doubtless well meant, such a movement was just as out of place as the sharp polemics against the kaiserin. Bismarck gave a darkly colored account of his conversation with the kaiserin: he had been severe with her and had told her that the marriage would not bring honor to the royal family, and that Battenberg was not disinterested; if, under different circumstances, perhaps after a change of rulers, the couple wanted to marry and live in Darmstadt, that was another matter. The kaiserin had given in. The same day, the twelfth, Kaiserin Victoria sent Bismarck a note marked "secret" that read, "I hear, most esteemed Prince, that you are afraid that I wish now to influence the Kaiser in the matter in question. You know quite well my recent words; and I can assure you, that I shall hold strictly to what we recently discussed. No step at all will now be taken,—and *you* alone know what I modestly expect from the future." "What a farce!" Holstein wrote of the whole affair. "Each bent on tricking the other, but the poor Kaiser is tricked the worst."[2]

Holstein was partly wrong about the press. Already by April 11 the government-inspired papers began to tone down their position and to suggest that an acceptable modus vivendi had been reached—not, of course, a final or definitive agreement that would put an end to a conflict that was politically too useful. The *Post* gently deprecated the petition movement on April 11, and the issue the same day of the new nationally oriented *Deutsches Wochenblatt* reported a story that when old Kaiser William had gone against Bismarck's advice, and the latter had offered his resignation, the kaiser had merely ordered him to remain. The personal relationship with the new kaiser was doubtless different, but in the objective situation nothing had changed. How simple! Bismarck resigns, makes his point, and then the kaiser merely orders him to continue, and he does, having relieved himself of the responsibility. A possible scenario, which might even have satisfied the tsar in the present case, but probably not one that Bismarck would prefer. It seems more likely that the suggestion was meant for consumption in Charlottenburg, as well as to soothe the monarchical feelings of not only Prince William and the far Right, but also the ministers and upper bureaucracy.[3]

The first issue of the weekly *Deutsches Wochenblatt* appeared on Wednesday, March 28. Viewpoints were to be expressed in the new journal that were widespread among the public but were not being completely expressed by any of the existing political parties. Its task would be to fight against lack of national pride and efforts directed against the national idea, and to try to strengthen *Deutschtum* both at home and abroad. It would defend the monarchy and the constitution and oppose both particularism and unjustified centralization. Historical development had sanctioned federalism as the proper form of government for Germany, and the German kind of constitutionalism recognized the right of the parliament to legislate jointly with the crown. Although the journal would be conservative in the sense of defending the present constitution against every revolutionary party, "in economic affairs social reform is the best means of defense of the existing social order against threatening social revolution." It would advocate peaceful relations with the church, but also recognized the necessity for the supremacy of state authority in a state divided between two faiths. The main goal would be "union of all those elements of the nation that today are divided by party conflict . . . but nevertheless agree on fundamentals." It thus recognized a special duty to defend the cartel. Conciliation among the parties required calm, factual discussion: "The daily press serves the party, and will never do justice to opposed points of view." A weekly with a distinguished body of contributors could contribute much toward clarification and conciliation.[4]

In its second issue, April 4, the *Deutsches Wochenblatt* pointed out that Germany had been especially fortunate in that those figures who had been so instrumental in creating the new Reich had been able to continue to protect it for half a generation. Kaiser William had died in the knowledge that Germany had become one nation. Only areas of economic or religious interest now provided sources of conflict. National confidence, however, provided a firm basis for accommodation. As in foreign policy, so in domestic, "no fearful yielding, but also no unprofitable challenges. Moderation in goals and endeavors, but ruthless energy when the highest values of the nation, national unity, monarchy, and constitution, cultural progress and economic reform are endangered from any direction."[5]

Although the *Deutsches Wochenblatt* specifically recognized the rights of the crown in an April 11 article entitled "Bismarck," on the Battenberg affair, nevertheless it proclaimed its gratitude "to fate for every day that Kaiser William's paladins continue in office. Theirs is now the difficult task of preparing the way for the transition from Kaiser William's time to the new era. The more time they allow to the newly developing generation the better for the fatherland." Bismarck had raised himself to too high a position to be able to enjoy the perquisites of old age: "His life belongs to his people." Like Kaiser William, "he must die in office."

People who spoke of "majordomoism" were judging him by ordinary political standards, which did not apply. He had devoted himself to serving the monarchy from the beginning. On April 18 the paper wrote that "it was at least inept to try to influence the imperial decision through petitions and meetings." They deplored the publicity given to the crisis. The *Deutsches Wochenblatt*, while seeming—like the meetings in Leipzig and Breslau—to demand Kaiser William's "Never!," thus also calmly stole the *Kreuzzeitung*'s critical thunder and inferentially denounced the press of the Conservative Right as well as that of the National Liberals for the recent Battenberg excesses.[6]

On the morning of April 12 poor Pindter, who had been kept waiting for authentic information and instructions on the crisis for a week—humiliating and frustrating for the editor of the recognized government paper—finally received an article for the *Norddeutsche Allgemeine Zeitung*, "written," he noted, "as it should be, simply making the majordomo legend ridiculous." Since the original draft of this article has been found among Chancellery Chief Rottenburg's papers, it is worth examining to throw a bit more light on Bismarck's press methods. The original text of the article, probably written by Rottenburg, began very formally, "We have until now not commented upon the question of the chancellor crisis because it appeared to us futile to add another to the countless conjectures that have shot up in the press in recent weeks." Almost all of this text was crossed out by Bismarck and a new version written in his own hand that while following the same basic interpretation as that in the *Deutsches Wochenblatt*, was at once more forceful and more provocative, turning the defense of the chancellor's party into an attack focused on the German Liberals, thus fanning the partisan flames, no doubt for the benefit of the *Kreuzzeitung*, Stoecker, Waldersee, and Crown Prince William. "The progressive press is connecting with the alleged intention of the Reich chancellor to resign an attempt to accuse Prince Bismarck of lack of courage toward foreign nations and insubordination toward the kaiser ... [I]f avoidance of unnecessary wars by taking precautions to avoid international quarrels were able to produce the suspicion of cowardice, then all statesmanship would consist merely in threatening with strong armies and energetic laying about with the sword. But for that neither political experience nor skill are required."

The question at issue also had nothing to do with insubordination toward the kaiser. The suspicion of "majordomoism ... shows the intellectual poverty of the party from which it emanates. A fantasy image of that sort can arise only in the heads of politicians who, with all the erudition of their cryptorepublican and classically educated talents, have as much conception of the existing residue in Prussia of Germanic fidelity to the king and of the mutual relations of the king with his servants that proceed from it as the blind man does of color." Such suspicions made as little impression upon the reigning kaiser as they had on his father. Both had appointed the chancellor to advise them "according to his knowledge and conscience [*Wissen und Gewissen*]" and never doubted that he would "carry out this service with as much regard for the interests of the dynasty as for those of the country." The monarch could not long retain trust in the advice of his minister without the presence in the latter of "a measure of loyalty to his convictions and *honesty* [*sic*]." Recognizing that the origin of this article was "hardly to be sought in the editorial office of the *Norddeutsche Allgemeine Zeitung*," the *Kreuzzeitung* remarked that its "calm and serious tone" contrasted favorably with the tactlessness and coarseness of other official and semiofficial papers on the subject. It regretted that the *Norddeutsche* had not set the correct tone much earlier in the affair, so that less damage would have been done to the monarchical principle. Detecting in the article "the style of the master," the *Frankfurter Zeitung* pointed out that on the basis of the argument in this article the present campaign in national and official newspapers was proved to be "not only antimonarchical, but downright revolutionary."[7]

The clamoring of the public meetings of the cartel parties for Kaiser Frederick to repeat his father's "Never!" and the proclamation by the *Deutsches Wochenblatt* and other government-oriented papers that Bismarck must be kept in office for life had less application objectively to the few remaining weeks of the life of the reigning kaiser than they did to his successor, Crown Prince William. The same can be said for the passages in Bismarck's *Norddeutsche* article on true statesmanship, diplomacy, and the necessary relation of sovereign to minister. No doubt the more experienced and responsible party leaders, especially in the middle parties, were aware of this factor, and a good part of the enthusiastic support for the chancellor in the National Liberal and Free Conservative press can probably be ascribed to approval of this attempt of Bismarck's to educate the crown prince on the limitations on the personal prerogatives of the crown. Doubtless a substantial part of that two-hour conference with the old, experienced National Liberal leader Bennigsen had been devoted to a frank explanation by Bismarck of how he envisaged exploiting the Battenberg affair in order to contain the potential dangers, both personal and political, of the next reign. On April 14 the Free Conservative *Post*, in welcoming the end of the "chancellor crisis," warned that all "danger for the future" could not be regarded as removed. It hoped that the recent incident would have a "preventive effect," but it would nevertheless be wise "to keep one's eyes open and powder dry." It is an indication of how blind and hysterical the cartel attack on the kaiserin had made the left

Liberals that the *Frankfurter Zeitung* completely missed the true thrust of
this warning and interpreted it as meaning that the *Post* was foolishly
convinced of a left-Liberal plot against the chancellor. The *Kreuzzeitung*,
on the other hand, immediately scented danger. "It would actually be
interesting," it wrote, "to discover *against whom*, when the case arises, the
Post intends to shoot with its dry powder." Ten years later, after Bismarck's
death, Kaiser William II wrote to his mother that during his father's
short reign he had not supported the dismissal "of the then allmighty
[*sic*] chancellor" because

> The death of Grandpapa had so fatally upset and even unnerved the country,
> that it was quite out of its mind; and in a state of hysterics. In this state it
> looked at Bismarck, *not* at *us* [*sic*] as the sole transmitter and *keeper* of the old
> tradition—it was wholly wrong and was his own crafty doing—but it was a
> fact! Had Papa and I with him sent Bismarck home, then such a storm
> would have broken lose [*sic*] against him and you, that we would have simply
> been powerless to stay it. . . . For the moment Bismarck was the Master of
> the situation and the Empire! And the house of Hohenzollern was nowhere!
> Had we only even tried to touch him, the whole of the German Princes—I
> was secretly informed of this—would have arisen like one man and would
> have made us take back the chancellor, to whom we and especially later I
> would have been delivered over bound hand and foot! The situation was
> simply impossible. I from that moment perfectly understood the terrible
> task, you then did not foresee, which Heaven had shaped for me; the task of
> rescuing the Crown from the overwhelming shadow of its minister.

That Crown Prince William consistently envisaged the said "task" in the
spring of 1888 is quite doubtful. His recognition of the nation's psychological rallying around Bismarck in the crisis of the dynasty had already
been probably quite sincerely expressed in his famous toast of April 1.
But one wonders if all the press articles, the quite unprecedentedly rough
language used, the sight of respectable Prussian officials, Conservative
Junkers—even army officers!—rallying publicly in favor of the chancellor
and against the crown, if perhaps these experiences did not, indeed, have
some effect, and may even actually have succeeded in shaking Crown
Prince William's naively personal, storybook concept of the relations of
king to ministers, to parties, to people. After his accession, William II
displayed a veritable fixation on the cartel.[8]

On the evening of April 11, the day before the publication of Bismarck's
article in the *Norddeutsche*, a small party was held in the Reich Chancellery
to celebrate the birthday of Princess Johanna von Bismarck, the chancellor's wife. The chancellor was in a good mood, and when one of the
company in a toast to the princess referred to the "old familiar group,"
he poked his old friend Baroness Spitzemberg, whom he had placed on

his right, in the ribs and protested softly, "Familiar we are, yes, but old, no Higachen [for Hildegard], that we won't allow!" The baroness took advantage of sitting next to him to quiz him "brazenly" on the Battenberg affair. He believed it was now over, said Bismarck. One could not estimate, however, such a seriously ill person. The old kaiser had also been dominated by his wife, but he had admitted it frankly and often asked Bismarck for help. The present kaiser was too proud for that but was unbelievably dependent, "like a dog." The most painful thing was the necessity to remain polite and not to interfere. The kaiserin, the "middle Vicky," was the main problem in the Battenberg case; she was in love with Battenberg and wanted to have him around her, as her mother—whom the English called "the selfish old beast"—had his brothers. The kaiserin was a "wild woman": "When [Bismarck] looks at her picture he often shudders at the untamed sensuality in her eyes." Old Kaiserin Augusta had also caused him a lot of trouble, "'but she remained always a woman of quality and full of a sense of duty, which is completely lacking in the new one. That kind is dying out.' 'Who?' I asked. 'The monarchs, they are no longer being born.'" And then, apparently in response to the shocked look on the face of the sensitive and intelligent baroness, "'I hope for it from our young master, his difficult youth has helped him, but already Prince Henry is no longer good for much [*ist nichts rechtes mehr*]. His present painful situation he bears easily, with callousness.'" Bismarck, noted the baroness, did not look tired, but talked brightly and without strain. He lay on the chaise longue smoking and reading the papers until nine o'clock.[9]

In spite of Bismarck's disclaimer in favor of Crown Prince William, he it was who had clearly inherited his mother's willfulness and lack of a sense of duty along with his father's weakness. The pressing problem concerning monarchs and monarchy was at the moment focused inexorably on his personality. One might object to Bismarck's formulation by recalling that historically very few monarchs had ever had a sense of duty, but ever since the enlightened despots of the eighteenth century, exemplified most notably by Crown Prince William's ancestor Frederick the Great, the increasing usurpation and magnification of power by the central monarchical governments had been justified by claims of greater rationality, efficiency, justice, and order. Romantic nationalism had strengthened the obligation of monarchs to embody the ideals and serve the welfare of their people, and the twin challenges of the French Revolution and the Industrial Revolution had imparted a new earnestness and self-discipline to monarchs such as Queen Victoria and Prince Albert and Kaiser William and Kaiserin Augusta, along with their people. But now, at the beginning of the fin de siècle, with the great heroic conquests of new wealth and glory already accomplished and with new, perplexing social and cultural challenges of insidious complexity to face in a strange new atmosphere of combined overconfidence and self-doubt, the younger generation of princes—one thinks of Crown Prince Rudolf of Austria, Tsarevich Nicholas of Russia, and even the Prince of Wales—did seem to deserve Bismarck's deprecating judgment. Pindter was right: the gods were indeed departing—the old beliefs, the old loyalties, the old simplicities. The exchange with Baroness Spitzemberg is interesting from the standpoint of revealing the train of the chancellor's thought. Intellectually he would seem to have already written off, if not the institution of monarchy, at least the possibility of any real reliance upon the personality of the future monarch.

A further sidelight was cast on Bismarck's preoccupation with the position of the crown when he talked with Carl Schurz, the old "forty-eighter" revolutionary and American statesman, at the end of April. Schurz, on a second visit to his homeland since he had left it in his youth, was given a very friendly reception by official circles in Berlin, presumably partly for the sake of German-American relations, but also perhaps to prevent his old liberal friends, now mostly in the oppositional German Liberal party, from extracting any political advantage from the visit. He was given an official banquet and a three-hour-long private interview with the chancellor. After his own fall from power, Bismarck told the German Liberal parliamentary wit Alexander Meyer that in this conversation with Schurz he had inquired especially about the powers of the U.S. president. As Schurz described them—probably with reference to what Abraham Lincoln had been able to make of them during the Civil War—Bismarck had interrupted him with the exclamation, "That is a monarchy with a limited term! Or rather, almost a modern monarchy with a limited term; and it has very much in its favor." The king of Prussia and German kaiser did not rule for a limited term but for life, and that could prove catastrophic for Germany unless the old chancellor succeeded in basically influencing or controlling young William at the beginning.[10]

Kaiser Frederick had been correct in worrying about the negative impact of Bismarck's press campaign upon the monarchical principle. The dramatic public revelation of the irresponsibility of the crown must have tarnished its luster to some degree, which was likely what the chancellor intended. As in the case of his war scare the previous year, Bismarck had taken a real threat and by magnifying it and dramatizing it publicly had shocked and disciplined the various political elements into a more useful, manageable, and less threatening configuration. The potential threat, this time from the crown backed by the Left and Center, had been used to strengthen the cartel, which once more had been associated with patriotism and national security, and the *Kreuzzeitung* and even General von Waldersee had thereby been brought back to support it. Crown Prince William had been once more bound intimately to the Bismarcks, had been shown dramatically how disastrous royal irresponsibility could be, and had himself been drawn into the attack on the royal prerogative—a point that may well have rankled later on and led him to reconstruct his memory of his own role. Also, by identifying himself with the national interest and security, even against the crown, Bismarck had made it that much more difficult for young William subsequently to separate himself from him. There were limits, however, that even Bismarck was careful not to overstep. Kaiserin Victoria did visit the flooded areas in East Prussia and was enthusiastically acclaimed. The chancellor felt it necessary to dissociate himself from the mass meetings and petitions even in confidential discussion with his own ministers. He also was careful to let the most vulgar attacks on the kaiserin appear in the party press, keeping the semiofficial government papers above the battle. But the whole display was too familiar by now for many to be unaware of who was behind it all. It is likely, therefore, that everyone concerned emerged from the crisis with the consciousness that whether for better or for worse, he had been used.[11]

26

Medical Crisis in Charlottenburg

THE turn for the worse in Kaiser Frederick's condition that had contributed to the early dampening of the Battenberg crisis now
developed in a most ominous way. The cancerous tissue had spread noticeably into the glands in the neck and now began also to extend from inside
the larynx downward into the trachea, enveloping the inside end of the
tracheotomy tube and creating difficulty in breathing. The kaiser spent
an especially bad night April 11, and on the afternoon of the twelfth had
such a fit of choking that Dr. Mackenzie sent for Dr. von Bergmann, who,
finding the royal patient blue in the face and struggling for breath, solved
the difficulty by poking his finger into the opening in the throat and
pushing aside the threatening tissue. The kaiser's breathing was immediately eased, but Bergmann's forceful handling had been painful, and
Frederick was shocked by his roughness, an attitude that Dr. Mackenzie
apparently encouraged. In the book that he published after the kaiser's
death, *The Fatal Illness of Frederick the Noble* (London, 1888), Mackenzie
even suggested that Bergmann had been drunk, had missed the opening
in trying to reinsert the tube, and had thus created a wound that had
become abscessed, causing a fever and immediate decline in the kaiser's
condition and ultimately hastening his death. This book, which was an
ill-advised extension of the newspaper and propaganda conflict among
the doctors during Frederick's reign, was so scandalous and obviously
unethical and unfair to his medical colleagues that Dr. Mackenzie was
censured for it by the British Medical Association and the Royal College
of Surgeons, had to resign from the Royal College of Physicians, and
suffered a catastrophic decline in his career. The crisis in the German
ruling structure caused by Frederick's cancer, aside from procuring Mackenzie a title, extra money, and some decorations, thus eventually proved
professionally fatal to him as well.[1]

A longer tube helped the kaiser's breathing, but the continued discharge
from the larynx had created an inflammation in the bronchial tubes and

a sharp fever, accompanied by an increasing general weakness. The critical point came on April 15, when Kaiser Frederick's temperature rose to 103° (39.4° Celsius), with a pulse rate of 104 and rapid breathing. Understandably the doctors assumed that the inflammation had now spread to the lungs and, therefore, that further rapid deterioration was to be expected. Dr. von Bergmann reported that the kaiser had only two or three more days to live. When Bismarck met with the Prussian ministers on the sixteenth he told them, "The end is coming!" The kaiser would probably not live more than twenty-four hours. Both Bismarck and Crown Prince William had been summoned to the palace that morning, and the rest of the royal family were alerted.[2]

Kaiser Frederick's condition, however, did not worsen as expected. Instead the fever lessened somewhat, then fluctuated until another crisis on the eighteenth, when it rose to 104°. This crisis, however, was accompanied by an especially copious discharge of pus, after which the patient felt relieved and breathed easier. Over the next week the fever gradually lessened, and rather more slowly the kaiser began to regain some of his strength. Apparently the lungs, remarkably enough, were not yet affected. The doctors probably further slowed his recovery by insisting that he remain in bed and abstain from working as much as possible.[3]

The news of the crisis in Kaiser Frederick's condition did not take long to get around the city. "Again," confided Baroness Spitzemberg to her diary, "that eerie, ominous unrest prevailed that precedes great events that one knows are coming; everywhere groups of people stood together whispering, for the news had spread quickly that the kaiser had a bronchial infection, that is, the beginning of the end had come." By train, horsecar, private carriage, and on foot Berliners began to stream out through the Tiergarten to Charlottenburg, to stand respectfully in front of the palace, behind the fence, waiting for news, reading bulletins tacked up on the trees, noticing who went in and out, and occasionally getting a few words of information on the kaiser's condition from the doctors as they passed through. Several "elegant ladies" were observed handing in baskets of flowers at the palace gate. During the first few days the kaiser would occasionally manage to show himself at the window, to the roaring acclaim of the crowd, and when Chancellor von Bismarck drove up in an open carriage, which he did almost every day, he too was greeted by the crowd with lusty cheers. Some of the twenty-six newspapers then publishing in Berlin took advantage of the public interest to bring out frequent "extras," which contained mostly stale news and rumors. Sunday, April 22, was an especially pleasant spring day, and thousands went out to Charlottenburg. Baroness Spitzemberg drove out herself with some friends. "I wanted very much," she wrote, "just once to see the scene where such a drama is being enacted, although one experiences almost a feeling of shame at intruding oneself, like the gaping crowd, in order to share the last struggle of a poor, tormented man. . . . The palace lay there still and desolate . . . ,only the imperial standard flapped lustily in the spring wind, and shadows flitted past the great windows—I felt so sad [*das Herz tat mir so weh*] that I was glad to return home."[4]

One might have thought that the new crisis in Kaiser Frederick's condition would produce at least a momentary muting of conflict among the parties and their respective newspapers, but the opposite occurred. The *Kölnische Zeitung* emphasized that in the crisis of April 12 it was the German doctors who had had to be called in to rescue the kaiser from the inadequacy of the English doctors and Mackenzie's right-angled tube. The English doctors responded by accusing Bergmann of causing an abscess by his brutal handling. Further revelations of callous indifference on the part of Dr. Hovell were made by the *Kölnische Zeitung* on the evidence of one of the kaiser's male nurses, who was then fired by Dr. Mackenzie, which produced more agitation. Dr. von Bergmann eventually publicly withdrew from the case, remaining available only in case of emergency. The newspaper uproar was largely the result of the campaign of the kaiserin, carried on recklessly by Dr. Mackenzie, to put as optimistic a face as possible on her husband's condition. Her intention basically in so doing was to encourage the patient, who was simply unable to face the horrible truth. He apparently needed his wife's constant cheerfulness to assure him that everything would be all right—like a calm and confident mother comforting and cajoling a child. It is revealing that in the later stages of this crisis, when Frederick had become physically quite weak, Bavarian Minister to Berlin Count Lerchenfeld reported that whereas his entourage had previously been certain, when the kaiser was feeling reasonably well, that he was fully aware of the hopelessness of his position, now he seemed less aware of it. The relentless cheerfulness of the kaiserin appeared bizarre, unfeeling, and brutal to members of the court, whose resentment also affected wider circles. Then there was the regency threat, and the desirability of staving it off with optimistic reports. Dr. Mackenzie had by now collected a veritable palace press corps of some twelve or fourteen correspondents, mostly of foreign and left-liberal papers, who met with him at Charlottenburg every day. Although, at a dinner for German Liberal party leaders at Bamberger's on April 7, the doctor assured the guests that the kaiser's disease was indeed cancer, optimistic and clearly untrue press reports continued to come out of Charlottenburg.

This attempt to deceive the press affronted the feelings of reporters who were not committed to the defense of the imperial couple on every issue, as the left Liberals were, and who were trying to be responsibly objective. With such a smoke screen emanating from the Charlottenburg palace, it was more or less natural for the more hardheaded cartel papers like the *Kölnische Zeitung* (probably with an eye to Crown Prince William) to rely more heavily than necessary on the opinions of the German doctors, especially Dr. von Bergmann. The professional pride and scientific integrity of these doctors were also affronted by Mackenzie's distortions. Their basic conviction, arrived at in May of the previous year and adhered to ever since, that a surgical removal of the larynx was the one hope of saving the patient's life in the long run, made them regard Dr. Mackenzie as practically a murderer for having prevented such a radical operation. On the other side of this medical dispute, *Germania* pointed out that a patient of Dr. von Bergmann whose larynx had been "successfully" removed in November had died after eight days, another had died after fourteen days, and another had recently died after three weeks. Although the German doctors tried to remain discreet, the anti-Mackenzie press forced them into the fight against their will.

In addition to these medical factions, there was the anti-kaiserin party around Crown Prince William and the *Kreuzzeitung*, who were convinced that Kaiser Frederick was not fit to rule and that Kaiserin Victoria was actually ruling and trying to realize as many as possible of the political purposes of her left-Liberal friends. Out of respect for the monarchical principle, the *Kreuzzeitung* tended to be more restrained and dignified in its hostility to Dr. Mackenzie, and it is possible that some of the anti-Mackenzie partisanship of respectable National Liberal papers like the *Kölnische Zeitung* represented an attempt to continue the anti-kaiserin campaign of the Battenberg affair with the purpose of keeping the *Kreuzzeitung* Conservatives close to the cartel and away from possible alliance with the Center party. If Bismarck himself was giving the directions for this possible campaign, it was done very discreetly, since Pindter of the *Norddeutsche Allgemeine Zeitung* does not appear to have experienced any pressure to discontinue his connection with Dr. Mackenzie's assistant, Dr. Krause, and the *Norddeutsche* came to the defense of the kaiser and kaiserin in a number of instances, such as denouncing as false the report given prominent display by the *Kreuzzeitung* and other conservative papers that Kaiser Frederick had handed a note to one of the court chaplains saying, "Do not pray for my recovery; pray for my release [*Erlösung*—an ambiguous word meaning both "salvation" and "release"]."[5]

There was also a deeper, more general, cultural dimension to this partisan conflict around Mackenzie and the kaiserin. Berlin society hated Kaiserin Victoria because she despised them as basically unprogressive. In a lead article at the end of March the radical *Berliner Volkszeitung* had placed the kaiserin on a cultural pedestal. She admittedly was not, it declared, a present-day "German woman"—who knew nothing of culture and toadied to the pastors. The life of such a "German woman," it wrote, was "a bleak round between thoughtless bigotry and thoughtless luxury. ... No serious thinker doubts that the cultural battles of the future, which will free mankind from all oppression and compulsion, can never be won without the women in the front rank." Count Lerchenfeld reported to Munich that this sort of eulogizing was typical of the treatment of the kaiserin by the left-liberal press. The kaiserin, however, in her politically delicate position, apparently was more embarrassed and annoyed than pleased with such partisanship.[6]

A writer in the liberal Vienna *Neue Freie Presse*, on April 19, combined idealization of Frederick III with a sense of loss:

> All around the world stands armed and staring, the freedom of the peoples has become a fable...; brutal and selfish, hateful and intolerant, egoism shrieks through the streets, popular culture [*Halbbildung*] presses toward the tribune and the pulpit.... This is the so-called Realism of our time. When he mounted the throne of the most powerful empire, Kaiser Frederick wanted to restrain it; to oppose it with the idealism of a clear world view dedicated to the highest human goals.... But he is an ill kaiser, ... a martyr of that great idealistic viewpoint, which has more and more succumbed to the weight of the military spirit, which arms the peoples against each other and places their welfare upon the point of the bayonet. It is more than a human tragedy, more than a tragedy of kings [*Herrscher-Tragödie*]; with it is bound up the deep trouble of a whole epoch. In front of the chamber in which Kaiser Frederick lies on his sickbed lean the old trees of the Charlottenburg Palace park; on their branches the first buds of spring are opening.... Will spring also come then for the German people? Or shall it have seen the glorious figure of Kaiser Frederick again in its midst only to become aware of what a people possesses in such a ruler, what it can lose in him? Much was given by fate to this nation, it has become great and powerful; but he who wanted to make it happy and free lies sick and silent.

Whereas the *Volkszeitung* writer hailed the inevitable future victory of freedom, the writer in Vienna appeared mournfully to relish the foretaste of liberalism's inevitable defeat. The willingness of these radical social critics to identify the fate of their country and their culture with individual rulers is notable in both instances.[7]

Crown Prince William had just returned from participating in the exercises of the first regiment of the Royal Guards, of which he was now brigadier general, on Tempelhof field on the morning of April 16, when he was informed of the crisis in his father's condition, and he immediately galloped his horse out to Charlottenburg, leaving word for General von Waldersee to meet him there. Later they walked and talked together in the palace garden. Waldersee complained that influences at court were privately working against him, which the crown prince blamed on his mother, who was trying to alienate all his friends from him. The crown prince confided to Waldersee that his father might have only a few hours to live. Waldersee had been quite right, it had been better that his father had had a short reign before he himself came to the throne. He intended to make a clean sweep of the more important court officials. This, to Waldersee's regret, included his friend General von Albedyll. "The crown prince," wrote Waldersee in his diary, "said many flattering things to me, and I saw that I have a reliable friend in him." The crown prince also mentioned that he had already taken certain steps in preparation for his father's death. One of these was an order to the major commanding the palace guard: "The moment you hear the news of the kaiser's death, man the entire palace and let no one go out, without exception."[8]

During the following days Waldersee and the crown prince thoroughly discussed reorganization of the army commands under the new reign. Waldersee recommended encouraging many of the older generals to retire. It was agreed that General Wilhelm von Hahnke would be appointed chief of the military cabinet to replace Albedyll. (Albedyll had wanted General von Winterfeld to succeed him, but the crown prince would not hear of it.) Waldersee agreed that it would be best to have a cabinet chief who had had no connection with the present regime. He sounded Hahnke out and found him "very reasonable." Hahnke agreed with Waldersee that they must try to persuade the new kaiser, as Waldersee was now calling him, to postpone administrative and personnel changes during the first few weeks of the reign so that they could be prepared carefully and thoroughly. Hahnke, wrote Waldersee, was "completely honest" and devoted to the crown prince. The crown prince assured Waldersee that he was aware of how much Waldersee had suffered politically on his behalf and that he would show his gratitude.[9]

The sudden and severe crisis in the kaiser's health made Kaiserin Victoria's stubbornly continued effort to maintain a positive and optimistic front extremely difficult. Aside from Mackenzie, Hovell, Krause, Pindter, and the left-liberal press, there was almost no one in court and government who sympathized with or supported her attempts at deception. Members of the immediate royal family resented the fact that they could not see the kaiser without her presence, and that most often she prevented them from seeing him at all. Frederick's sister, the grand duchess of Baden, for example, was consistently kept away from him because she was only too likely to talk to him at length about setting his soul right with God, which he did not appreciate. Resentment of the kaiserin and criticism and backbiting came to a rather dangerous head. In this situation it was significant that Bismarck understood, sympathized, and stood by her, making an ostentatious point of continuing his regular visits and audiences and sending flowers every day. He decided that it would be possible quietly to extend the deputizing functions of the crown prince without bothering the kaiser with another formal order. To several people Kaiserin Victoria was quoted as saying at this time, "The chancellor is really our best friend."[10]

27

Queen Victoria Arrives

WHILE Kaiser Frederick's condition was still critical, Queen Victoria of England arrived in Berlin. She had traveled from Florence north over the Alps, meeting with Emperor Francis Joseph of Austria-Hungary at Innsbruck. As early as April 15 the *National Zeitung* had written that the report that the queen was against the Battenberg marriage must be regarded as authentic. Two days later the semiofficial *Berliner Politische Nachrichten* denied reports that special security measures were to be taken during the queen's visit. "Her Majesty never supported the marriage project with the Battenberg prince. But even if Queen Victoria had taken a different position, the fears expressed ... would be unfounded. The Berlin population is too morally cultivated [*geartet und zu gesittet*] to greet the mother of the German empress other than with respect." At about the same time the elder Bismarck told British Ambassador Sir Edward Malet that the German government welcomed the queen's visit, even if the Kaiser should die in the meantime. It would be desirable if she could be accompanied by a minister. "The thereby announced intention to give the presence of the queen a political character," wrote Marschall von Bieberstein to the grand duke of Baden, "appears to me to derive from the wish to emphasize our political freedom of action in regard to Russia after the events of the last two weeks." This was true especially since the recent appointment of the well-known Pan-Slavist Evgenii Vasilyevich Bogdanovich to an influential position in St. Petersburg had made a very painful impression.[1]

In further preparation for the visit, Bismarck had also instructed Count Hatzfeldt, the ambassador in London, to ask Lord Salisbury to urge the queen to be careful in talking with Crown Prince William, presumably in regard to her feelings about his treatment of his mother. Lord Salisbury wrote to Queen Victoria in Florence that

It appears that his head is turned by his position.... Evidently, ... they are afraid that if any thorny subject came up in conversation, the prince might

247

say something that would not reflect credit on him, and that if he acted so as to draw any reproof from Your Majesty, he might take it ill, and a feeling would rankle in his mind which might hinder the good relations between the two nations. Lord Salisbury strongly discouraged the idea that he could be made the channel for any representations on such a subject. But it is nevertheless true—most unhappily—that all Prince William's impulses, however blameable or unreasonable, will henceforth be political causes of enormous potency; and the two nations are so necessary to each other that everything that is said to him must be very carefully weighed.[2]

On April 23, the day before the queen's arrival, the *Kölnische Zeitung* recalled that she had last visited Berlin with her consort, Prince Albert, in 1858, for her daughter's wedding, when Berlin had 600,000 inhabitants. It had now grown to 1,400,000, but the queen would not be able to see any of the new sights since she was concerned only with comforting with her presence a severely ill kaiser whose condition the whole world was watching with rapt attention and growing sympathy. The same day, the *Norddeutsche Allgemeine Zeitung* announced that Lord John Manners, the duke of Rutland, and his wife had arrived a few days previously to attend the queen during her visit. On April 24 the *Norddeutsche* carried a special message of welcome to the queen in a prominent place on page 1. She would be received, it wrote, by the whole population of Germany and especially by the inhabitants of Berlin "with that respect and sympathy . . . which is to such a high degree appropriate to the long-term ruler of a friendly state and the mother of their own kaiserin. All German hearts will recognize with gratitude as a sign of the deep sympathy of Her Majesty the Queen of England for the fate of our ruling house that Queen Victoria comes to the sickbed of our dearly beloved kaiser and thereby personally shares in our heavy trouble and great concern. May it be granted to her to bring comfort and hope."[3]

The queen's arrival has been best described by herself:

After I had tidied myself up a bit, dear Vicky came and asked me to go and see dear Fritz. He was lying in bed, his dear face unaltered; and he raised up both his hands with pleasure at seeing me and gave me a nosegay. . . . Afterwards saw Sir M. Mackenzie with Vicky. He seemed to think Fritz was better. Before luncheon . . . went again for a short while to dear Fritz, and afterwards Vicky sat talking with me for some time in my room. She is very sad, and cried a good deal, poor dear. Besides her cruel anxiety about dear Fritz, she has so many worries and unpleasantnesses. The whole dreadful bother about poor young Vicky had been purposely got up, and they had never had a quarrel with Prince Bismarck.

Previously, in a two-hour audience with Bismarck on the nineteenth, the kaiserin had still been planning on the Battenberg marriage, and

Bismarck had apparently gone along with her fantasies and had said that it was all right with him if the prince promised never to return to Bulgaria and if it occurred without his knowledge. He would then hand in his resignation, but the kaiser would not have to accept it. Bismarck also told the kaiserin that the Prussian minister in Darmstadt reported that Prince Alexander was no longer in love with Princess Victoria, but the kaiserin refused to believe it. Later she wrote happily to the prince suggesting a visit to Homburg Castle (near Wiesbaden) in May, where the marriage could be secretly performed. In her talks with her daughter at Charlottenburg Queen Victoria apparently came down hard on these flights of fancy. It was all well and good for her to remember her own country so fondly and to be sympathetic to its policies, but her position required her to respect German interests and German wishes. The marriage was against those interests and must simply be given up. Even her own English mother thus put down the kaiserin's romantic idealism and personal feelings in favor of rational discipline, duty, and cold *Staatsraison*. It is also likely, judging by the course of the queen's later interview with Bismarck, that in these talks the younger Victoria enlightened her mother concerning the chancellor's political motivation in creating the chancellor crisis.[4]

By the time the chancellor was ushered in to his audience with the queen at noon on April 25 both parties were clearly prepared to treat the other with special consideration. In emphasizing foreign policy in his approach to the queen, Bismarck may have been trying to appeal to her experienced statesmanship as a way of minimizing her family sympathies, as well as attempting to extract a maximum amount of diplomatic advantage for Germany from the visit. The approach seems to have worked. The queen described the interview as a "most interesting conversation" and wrote that she "was agreeably surprised" to find the chancellor "so amiable and gentle." She expressed her satisfaction that

> there was no idea of a regency, as I knew it would upset dear Fritz dreadfully, and he assured me there would be none. Even if he thought it necessary, which he did not, he would not have the heart to propose it. I appealed to Prince Bismarck to stand by poor Vicky, and he assured me he would, that hers was a hard fate. I spoke of William's inexperience and his not having travelled at all. Prince Bismarck replied that [William] knew nothing at all about civil affairs, that he could however say "should he be thrown into the water, he would be able to swim," for that he was certainly clever.

The audience lasted about three-quarters of an hour, and the queen told the chancellor she quite understood and supported his position in the Battenberg affair. She also promised to try to reconcile the crown prince with his mother and apparently had some success in that, at least momentarily.[5]

Although Queen Victoria's visit was strictly private, she did drive into Berlin to visit old Kaiserin Augusta and the crown prince and princess. Large crowds along the Charlottenburger Chaussee and Unter den Linden cheered with enthusiasm. That evening, when the queen remarked to Bismarck at the banquet table how pleased she was with her public reception, the chancellor responded that it was quite spontaneous "and that ... the Germans liked the English and preferred them to any other foreign nation." In her journal the queen described how her daughter really felt about her situation. "Vicky took me back to my room and talked some time very sadly about the future, breaking down completely. Her despair at what she seems to look on as the certain end is terrible. I saw Sir M. Mackenzie, and he said he thought the fever, which was less, though always increasing at night, would never leave dear Fritz, and that he would not live above a few weeks, possibly two months, but hardly three!!" One almost suspects the queen of having enjoyed her daughter's grief—it was, after all, many years since her own incomparable husband had died. She left Germany on the twenty-sixth. "Dear Vicky came into the railway carriage, and I kissed her again and again. She struggled hard not to give way, but finally broke down, and it was terrible to see her standing there in tears, while the train moved slowly off, and to think of all she was suffering and might have to go through. My poor poor child, what would I not do to help her in her hard lot!"[6]

The following day the *Norddeutsche*, in its lead article, referred to the appropriately respectful and sympathetic reception the queen had received in Berlin. "Her visit in a serious time will remain in the grateful memory ... of all good Germans [*Deutschgesinnten*] as a demonstration of beneficent personal sympathy. We regard it as only natural that this visit ... can have only the most favorable effects on the political relations between Germany and England." In a report to Prince Reuss in Vienna on the twenty-eighth, Bismarck wrote of the "very satisfying impression" he had received from his audience with the queen. She had exhibited an unconditional sympathy for the peaceful policy of the three central powers. "It was especially gratifying to me that during my audience the queen refrained from any attempt to interfere with our domestic policies." He had attempted to calm her apprehensions concerning the future policy of the crown prince and assure her that he did not want war, and was too intelligent to entertain preconceived ideas in any direction in European politics, or to follow any interests save the larger interests of Germany. Reuss showed the letter to Austrian Foreign Minister Count Kálnoky, who was favorably impressed and said so to the English ambassador, who reported it to London.[7]

Sir Edward Malet reported from Berlin that the "general feeling with regard to the result of the visit is that it has done great and, it is hoped, lasting good." The chancellor had spoken openly of his great satisfaction with his conversation with the queen and "has said that if the action of England should correspond with the sound sense and practical character of the views held by Her Majesty, the danger of a European war would be minimised. . . . Altogether I may say that on this side there is an evident desire, not to say anxiety, to come round to the point at which we were when the 'Chancellor Crisis' arose and caused our confidence to waver." Sir Edward thought that the queen had been much pleased with the whole visit. In returning the queen's memorandum on her conversation with Bismarck, Lord Salisbury remarked that Bismarck's attitude was gratifying but "leaves in as much mystery as ever Prince Bismarck's extraordinary language with respect to your Majesty's supposed action, and the supposed intentions of the emperor and empress about the marriage. However, it is evident that the prince, as your Majesty saw him, was in his habitual frame of mind; and that the two memorable conversations with Sir E. Malet must have been held under circumstances of mental excitement and depression which passed rapidly away. This anxious incident has ended as well as it possibly could have ended."[8]

Austrian Ambassador Count Széchényi reported with satisfaction to Vienna that the public reception of Queen Victoria had been much warmer than its response to Tsar Alexander III the previous fall. The "inner political meaning" of the visit, he wrote, was expressed in Bismarck's statement that "the less England leaves the world in doubt as to her determination to oppose disturbers of the peace, the more will the preservation of peace be assured." He had been told that the queen had had a very beneficial effect on her daughter and that she had treated Crown Prince William with special consideration and affection, as contrasted to her treatment of him during her jubilee celebration the previous summer, from which he had returned with bitter feelings toward his grandmother.

In the evening of the day of the queen's departure a dinner was given at the Russian embassy in honor of Grand Duke Vladimir, and the following day Herbert Bismarck wrote out a report of his impressions there. Ambassador Shuvalov had immediately remarked to him that he hoped that they would not sign a treaty with England, and that the queen's visit made him nervous. Such a development would ruin his career. Herbert had replied that it was well known that the English did not make binding treaties, and especially not the queen unaccompanied by her foreign secretary. He hoped that the ambassador would remain in Berlin the rest of his life, unless of course he was recalled to head the Foreign Office, a remark that, Herbert reported, had pleased Shuvalov very much. Later at table the grand duke had made deprecating remarks about the French to Herbert and had assured him that his brother the tsar did indeed hate Prince Alexander of Battenberg. Taking him aside into another room, he had explained confidentially that Foreign Minister Giers' apparent diffidence during the recent crisis had been caused by his knowledge that Tsar Alexander was insurmountably suspicious of Bismarck. "He recognizes his genius, but he is always afraid of being tricked by him." Herbert thanked him for his frankness, protested that Germany's policy had always been straightforward and honest toward Russia ever since the Congress of Berlin, added that his father had always been able to reassure the tsar in personal conversations, and regretted that he visited Berlin so seldom. The difficulty, responded the grand duke, was Germany's treaty of 1879 with Austria. It was true that they had been informed of the terms, but the fact rankled. The fault, said Herbert, had been Russia's illoyal behavior after the Congress of Berlin in 1878. (To this Bismarck added a marginal comment on Herbert's report that ever since that time they had had to be prepared for surprising moves in St. Petersburg and could not therefore give up other connections.) Germany, said Herbert, had always regarded Bulgaria as Russia's domain, and at the straits not only could Russia count on their benevolent neutrality, but he doubted that the Austrians really cared about it. Herbert tried to emphasize dynastic solidarity in the face of continental revolutionary movements, and the grand duke assured him that he had complete confidence in the chancellor and would do what he could to influence his brother in that direction. As a result of Queen Victoria's strong family concerns and Bismarck's dexterity, the Battenberg affair had in the end not changed the balance of the international situation one way or the other.[9]

A week before the queen's visit, on the nineteenth, the issue of *Die Grenzboten* with Busch's article attacking "Foreign Influences in the Reich" had appeared (see above, p. 219). The Battenberg crisis, it had stated, hinged on the question of whether the personality of Prince Alexander or of Prince Bismarck was to weigh more heavily in ruling circles, and it had denounced the interference of Queen Victoria in German affairs. The attitude toward England and the queen, however, having in the meantime changed radically in the government press, a clearly inspired article in the *Berliner Börsen Zeitung*, on April 29, now declared that the chancellor was indignant over the *Grenzboten*'s "notorious" article, which slandered the kaiserin, and that he "has given expression to his condemnation in very strong terms. In this connection exceptional importance is to be attached to the sympathetic article in the *Norddeutsche Allgemeine Zeitung* [see above] on the queen of England's visit." The *Börsen Zeitung*, noted Busch, was in the service of Bismarck's banker, Bleichröder. "Well informed? Possibly, indeed probably. A disclaimer? Why not! Quite in order! Tempora mutantur [times have changed]? But I shall never change toward him, nor he doubtless toward me." Busch's use of the word "doubtless" was a brave assertion, which did not prevent him when next in Friedrichsruh from asking anxiously if the chancellor had really disapproved of his article. "Nonsense!" replied the chancellor, smiling. "The article was really quite first rate."[10]

28

The Honors List

IT was probably characteristic of the Bismarck regime that while newspapers of the loyal Bismarck parties were continuing heavy attacks on the kaiserin and Dr. Mackenzie, Bismarck himself was showing special consideration for the wishes of both kaiser and kaiserin. Not only did he allow a general amnesty—the liberal *Frankfurter Zeitung* regretted the exclusion of Social Democrats, but said that "everyone" would approve the exclusion of "light women" and vagabonds— but he also proved remarkably tolerant in handling the kaiser's long list of decorations and honors. Although honors had been distributed under Kaiser William at the beginning of the year, as was customary, the ministers again sought out new names in their respective departments for Kaiser Frederick's approval and, since he wanted it to be done right away, with less careful consideration than usual. Nevertheless, reported Count Lerchenfeld, people could hardly object to any one case, since they were all persons whose social station and income were appropriate to their new rank. Of some twenty persons to be added to the list to be ennobled, Puttkamer reported to the ministry, most were owners of large estates "from all the provinces." Evidently there was some grumbling in the ministry against the unnecessarily large number of people to be ennobled, and Bismarck wrote Puttkamer, "I hold it in general to be one of our political goals to ease the transition into the nobility and thereby to hinder the reawakening of the animosity toward the nobility, which dominated the situation about twenty years ago to a much greater degree than is today the case. It is in the interest of the nobility itself to assimilate those elements [*Existenzen*] whose standard of living [*Wohlhabenheit*] is more or less permanently established. I should therefore have desired an even greater number of ennoblements than those at hand."

Among those ennobled at the kaiser's special request were all four brothers of the Stumm iron and steel family. Friedrich Alfred von Krupp was also offered a title but rejected it decidedly as being bad for his

254

business, which amused and impressed the chancellor, who suggested to the Prussian ministers that in order to counteract the hatred between nobility and middle class, the kaiser should ennoble the whole population. Professor Gneist was ennobled, and the loyal Chief of the Chancellery Franz von Rottenburg achieved the highest possible rank for his position, *Wirklicher Geheimer Oberregierungsrat* (Actual Privy Superior Administrative Counsellor), which was equivalent to ministerial rank and carried with it the title Excellency. Superior Court Marshal Count Radolinski became Prince Radolin, and, at Bismarck's suggestion, the loyal Free Conservative Minister of Agriculture Robert Lucius was made Baron von Ballhausen, thus eliminating the last commoner from the Prussian ministry. Kaiser Frederick also wanted to make Bismarck himself a duke and Herbert a prince, but the old man begged off in both cases, remarking to the ministers, "Sure, and if I had two million thaler, I should have myself made pope."[1]*

Foreign Office Counsellor Holstein suggested to his friend Radolin that Herbert Bismarck might be made a Prussian minister, which was promptly done, as the *National Zeitung* commented, as an indication of the Kaiser's special consideration for Bismarck, who had refused other honors. Herbert was surprised and moved by the kaiser's benevolence toward him but apprehensive concerning the effect. The action, he wrote to his brother, Bill, was "pointless, and will anger a lot of people, who already envy me unreasonably. I can't do anything about that!" His misgivings were quite justified, *Germania* immediately pointing out that he would be the youngest minister Prussia had ever had, and that two close relatives had never before served together in the ministry. In response, the chancellor's *Norddeutsche Allgemeine Zeitung* claimed that an eighteenth-century ancestor of the Bismarcks had been a minister at thirty-two (Herbert was thirty-eight), and others had also served at correspondingly young ages. The day after Herbert's appointment General von Waldersee came to see Holstein and remarked "with obvious satisfaction" that General von Caprivi had been passed over in Herbert's advancement (Caprivi was older and had been a state secretary—Admiralty—for a longer time). Holstein wrote a note to Herbert suggesting that something be done for Caprivi, and Herbert wrote to Rottenburg, asking that the matter be brought to his father's attention. The result was that fourteen lieutenant generals were advanced to full general's rank, Waldersee becoming general of cavalry and Caprivi general of infantry; and the chancellor made an especially laudatory mention of Caprivi in a meeting of the Prussian ministry. Waldersee considered his a good advancement for his age of fifty-six.

---

* A Thaler was equivalent to 3 M or 71.4 cents.

Herbert, probably the busiest man in town, soon found ministerial meetings a waste of his valuable time and resolved mostly to stay away. Holstein had written in his diary that when he had previously discussed such an appointment for Herbert with Minister of Ecclesiastical, Medical, and Educational Affairs von Gossler, the latter had protested, saying, "At the moment, whenever the big bowwow is not actually attending a session, we can at least grouse to our hearts' content. But that will have to stop if his son is listening." Holstein, however, thought the appointment was necessary "on objective grounds." Apparently he was afraid that Bismarck might otherwise lose control of the ministers. He wished, he wrote, that he knew "how we could manage to keep Caprivi and Rado[lin]. in Berlin as Bismarck's allies in the struggles of the coming regime. But I have not enough power and H.H. not enough tact; Herbert is intimidated by the crown prince."[2]

It was natural that the honors list should include mostly representatives of the ruling political groups, Bismarck's loyal agrarian Conservative lieutenant von Mirbach-Sorquitten, for example, being made a count. In return, the kaiser and kaiserin felt that they should be allowed some special designations of their own, that is, of their former liberal friends. They made a special case for the German Liberal Lord Mayor of Berlin Max von Forckenbeck, finally on the grounds—since he was a prominent leader of the opposition—of his assistance to flood victims, and Bismarck accepted this and put it through the ministry. Then, after the main list had been announced, the kaiserin had Radolin sound out the chancellor on an additional list, including three prominent German Liberals— Rudolf Virchow, the pathologist; Georg von Bunsen, member of the Prussian Landtag and Reichstag; and Karl Schrader, the railroad magnate. According to Radolin and Holstein, Bismarck made no objections to the list, saying that since he had put Forckenbeck through, no doubt he could do the same for these. "What disquiets me is the crown prince's lust for war. I shall have no hand in that." Radolin subsequently drew up a formal order to present to the Prussian ministry, but when the ministry met on May 13, Bismarck read them the draft of a very stern and uncompromising statement rejecting any recognition for Bunsen and Schrader, who had performed no public service other than to oppose the present government. He could not act in the matter, he said, except with the support of the ministry, and the agreement of the ministry was formally incorporated in the statement. Virchow was a famous scientist and could be decorated for his assistance in dealing with the diagnosis of the kaiser's illness. In a letter to Radolin the chancellor delivered a fine essay on constitutional government. "As long as His Majesty does not dismiss the ministry, upholding its dignity is also in the interests of the crown. The results of a royal preferment [*Gunstbezeugung*] of the opponents of the government would make themselves felt practically, in the first instance, at the approaching elections, just as the recognition granted to Herr von Forckenbeck is already now being actively exploited in his election district. If, however, progressive, according to my view, cryptorepublican, elections are to be encouraged, such encouragement cannot be the task of the *present* State Ministry, appointed by Kaiser William."

Thus a resignation threat was implied, and the incident became a potential crisis. Bismarck also suggested to Radolin that since Virchow already had the order of the Red Eagle third class, giving him the second class would be better than the proposed order of the crown. Kaiser Frederick subsequently added the star to the Red Eagle second class, but when Radolin protested that that would be out of line, the kaiser hit his chest with his fist, which Radolin interpreted as "Sic volo, sic jubeo [my wish is my command]" and without further ado handed the matter to Chief of the Civil Cabinet Wilmowski, who made out the appropriate order and gave it to Minister of Ecclesiastical, Medical, and Educational Affairs Gossler. Rottenburg wrote to Kuno Rantzau in Varzin that Gossler was ready to countersign it if the chancellor had no objection, in which case an open telegram to him with the word "agreed" would suffice. The chancellor so indicated on the margin. Both Forckenbeck and Virchow, noted General Waldersee, had voted against the *Septennat* bill the preceding year and under Kaiser William, had no longer received invitations to court.[3]

When Minister of Justice Friedberg told Lucius the kaiserin's side of the story—that Bismarck had originally made no objection to decorating Bunsen and Schrader—Lucius supposed that the chancellor had reacted too quickly and later changed his mind. But generally when dealing with Bismarck, when one finds a handful of very frank and forthright but contradictory statements of the chancellor, rather than take the easy way out and assume, as his contemporaries were more and more inclined to do, that the old man was merely showing his age and becoming forgetful, one can usually find the thread of a consistent—if devious—policy by taking a long look in perspective at the total picture. Bismarck was capable of using even his own physical decline to possible political advantage. Taking the long view, one must agree with Holstein, who, writing on May 15, stated that "a strange chapter of human history could now be written by any one taking as his theme the powerlessness of the dying Kaiser and his wife." It was good, he thought, that Kaiser Frederick had not been able to "realize his liberal fantasies." But, as a royalist, he himself was shocked at how completely powerless the kaiser had become. In government circles the unpopularity of the kaiserin was being taken as an excuse for ignoring and turning away from the kaiser and toward the crown prince. Holstein then gave the story of Bismarck's behavior in the ministry as an example of how the royal couple were being used. "Their Majesties are actually the object of a wanton sport." The ministers were hostile because of "all the anxiety they have felt at times." Herbert, Holstein wrote, was one of the worst. Bismarck was undoubtedly using the kaiserin's request regarding Bunsen and Schrader as a means of fanning the hostility of the ministers toward her and of encouraging their fears that their own positions were being undercut by left-Liberal influence at court. But his motivations in so doing, as we shall see, were much more serious than Holstein imagined. The unfortunate imperial couple were, indeed, being used, and even brutally, but in the cause of rationality, moderation, and control, a cause that was ultimately their own.[4]

29

The Kaiserin's Secret Advisor

WITHIN a week of the May 13 ministerial session the *Frankfurter Zeitung* reported that there had recently been danger of a new crisis: the kaiser had wanted to decorate two public figures, but the ministry had objected in writing, and the decorations had had to be canceled. It had become quite clear that the left-liberal press had recently developed even closer connections at court than previously; they were beginning to be better informed even than the Junker-oriented *Kreuzzeitung*. Shortly after the Battenberg affair, the old Liberal politician and advisor to Frederick and Victoria, Baron von Roggenbach, had stopped in to see the German Liberal leader Bamberger and had mentioned that it was true that on the day the newspaper campaign began in the *Kölnische Zeitung* the kaiser and kaiserin had already accepted the chancellor's point of view. Bamberger responded to Roggenbach that the court suffered from insufficient connections with the press, which prevented their defending themselves against misrepresentations. A week later a neighbor, Baroness von Stockmar, who was also an intimate friend of Kaiserin Victoria, called on Bamberger and informed him that the kaiserin would like to develop the idea of press connections. The *National Zeitung* had been recommended to her. No, said Bamberger, the *National Zeitung* was pure Bismarckian. The kaiserin, said the baroness, was afraid of German Liberal papers. Bamberger nevertheless recommended the *Weser Zeitung, Münchener Allgemeine Zeitung, Breslauer Zeitung,* and *Liberale Korrespondenz*. It was too good of Dr. Bamberger, the kaiserin wrote to the baroness, chivalrously to take up the defense of "an unjustly attacked woman. . . . Since I now have the *honor* to belong with *body* and *soul* to those who would lift, ennoble the nation, bring it forward—see it mature, but above all *peaceful, happy, free,* worthy of itself, I thereby also come into the line of fire and am a small part of those things that *must* be *destroyed*, and must be held up to my *sons* as a *frightening example*—*lest* in the end they should run the danger of being *infected,* as Kaiser Frederick is." She had to suffer such attacks because she would not go along with "Stoecker and company." The sad thing was that people were thereby led to believe that they possessed "such a wretched mother of the country. If my friends want to try to instruct the people otherwise and better, that can naturally only please me."[1]

Ludwig Bamberger was an excellent choice to advise the kaiserin in matters of publicity and to serve as a conduit to the left-liberal press. After his youthful involvement in the 1848 Revolution, he had resigned himself to a career in the international financial world, where he had had substantial success. In the liberal period of the late 1860s and early 1870s he had become prominent in the National Liberal party in Germany and, in cooperation with the Bismarck government, had led the moves to found the Reichsbank and adopt the gold standard. When, after the onset of the Long Depression, Bismarck had moved to the Right politically and had given up free trade for a program of tariff protection, Bamberger had joined the secession of the National Liberal left wing and its eventual fusion with the Progressives to form the German Liberal party. This new political group had been founded as a strong hindrance to Bismarck's state-oriented social policies and also to establish a foundation for a more liberal future. The chancellor, however, had not been greatly hindered, and the liberal future appeared now to be remote. Bamberger was a gifted orator, probably the most fluent and dramatic speaker in the Reichstag, and he was equally effective with his pen, writing thoughtful political analyses regularly for the German Liberal weekly, *Die Nation*. From the letters that Frau von Stockmar showed him, Bamberger could see that the kaiserin's heart was still set on the Battenberg marriage. She and Kaiser Frederick, she wrote, had sources of information of their own in Russia and knew that it was no longer diplomatically dangerous. The "laughable exaggerations as well as the *exploitation* of a simple family affair—not of serious political consideration—occurred *only* with *evil* intent. It was to benefit the chancellor and William, but to *injure* me, Prince Alexander, and my dear child." She advised the baroness not to call on Bamberger and to tell him not to visit her. "One cannot know, whether *you* or *he* are not being watched; it could only cause trouble."[2]

Bamberger was moved by the kaiserin's words, and he wrote Baroness von Stockmar that he had engraved them permanently on his memory. They made the unutterable misfortune that faced them all even more keenly felt: "what we all see eluding us; what splendid things would have been accomplished under such auspices." It did not help to sigh over the unavoidable, but defending the integrity of such a highly placed personality was another matter and not at all futile. "Tell her that the small fragment of society that gloats over this distorted picture prepared and spread by the *Camorra* [clique] is extremely small in relation to the great mass of the people. The latter do not believe a word of all this devilry, but rather, in their natural instinct, surmise the good, beautiful truth. Among the truly cultivated there are very many who feel a deep shame for what we are experiencing and see in it a sign of the severe decline in the ranks of the upper ten thousand." All his acquaintances felt this way. But the truth would prevail. The first great step was the journey from San Remo. "What might have been attempted if one had stayed away!" And they had failed to prevent Queen Victoria from coming. "That one did not allow oneself to be intimidated, that one showed oneself open and trusting had a wonderful effect, changed the situation with one blow." It was not possible to do anything in the larger questions. For "the great fight of light against darkness . . . years of healthy work" would be necessary, and "the most splendid forces" would not be excessive. But one could nevertheless issue carefully chosen statements at propitious moments that would work positively on well-intentioned minds and would provide continuing sources of inspiration.[3]

In a further communication to Bamberger of twenty-four pages on May 16 the kaiserin wrote that the ministers were supposed to be the servants of the kaiser, but in fact they were his enemies and "*strongly oppose every single thing* that he wishes and orders in the sense of his conceptions and of his decrees.—The Kaiser is ill—therefore out of caution he is compelled to alter nothing in regard to the personnel and machinery of the government, which were arranged in the preceding reign! Ill as he is, the Kaiser cannot think of reforms, crises, and changes that cannot be put through smoothly and peacefully—otherwise *only* occasion for confusion, conflict, and fighting, which would lead to sad results. . . . There *is* a *strong* party that *wants* to introduce a regency." This had begun already in San Remo, and the people so concerned were precisely those who had seen their ideal in the government of Kaiser William "and knew *certainly* and counted on it, that the *present Crown Prince* William *also* thinks so." If the old Kaiser or the grandson had been the ones who were ill, there would have been no such talk. "If he had been healthy, the present Kaiser's regime would have been *endured* as an unavoidable evil—the present ill Kaiser will be endured *as long as* he does not hinder the machinery of the ministry through any kind of initiative. Crown Prince William is regarded as the real Kaiser, Kaiser Frederick only as a shadow. *If* these *ministers* had any *reverence, respect,* or sense of propriety, they would at least not expect the Kaiser to make concessions to them that are *against* his views. I cannot fault the Reich chancellor, he is *not so petty,* he is more accommodating [*coulanter*]."

The chancellor, wrote the kaiserin, had found the decorating of Forckenbeck "quite justified, promised it, and put it *through* against the heavy opposition of the ministry, who saw a defeat in it. Puttkamer wanted to go—but he *didn't*! Crown Prince William went to Puttkamer and then to the chancellor, made a scene with the latter and reproached him over the Forckenbeck decoration and afterwards said—the chancellor is getting foolish, for he is giving in to the wishes of the Kaiserin, which is *unheard of*." She had asked for the decoration of Bunsen and Schrader because of their long friendship and service to her—"The Reich chancellor was quite affable, quite agreeable, made no objection. . . . [*sic*] But the ministry made a *terrible row*—namely *Maybach*, Scholz, and Boetticher, and the chancellor could not put it through; they threatened to *resign* immediately." The kaiser had been very disgusted.

> The chancellor is *becoming older* and is becoming *tired* and is terribly tyrannised by the harsh people around him. When, which may God grant, the Kaiser is better, so that one does not have to worry *at all* about the effects of a crisis upon his health, the following must occur: on the next occasion the proposals from the ministry for decorations will be *rejected* by the Kaiser. If it asks for a reason, it will be stated that the royal proposals were previously rejected—or—one will make one's own proposals once more—and if the ministry *again* threatens resignation, one will *calmly accept* it. But this could cause difficulties, and one *must* consider *carefully* what one would do in such a case.

The kaiser did not have a single political friend or supporter near him. Chief of the Civil Cabinet Wilmowski was "quite the *opposite, really bad*." He was "so old and blind, that he *must* be replaced"; but by whom? Someone who would not "immediately be overwhelmed with Bismarck's hatred, but who would support the Kaiser, help him, above all keep him au courant and keep in *touch* with our friends." The German princes had been given the idea that things that the ministry disapproved of and that were said to threaten the tranquillity of the Reich came, not from the kaiser, but from her. Since this showed them that the kaiser no longer had any will of his own, at the next such crisis the princes were all as a body to demand a regency. "Crown Prince William is said to have *strongly* favored this idea and to have pushed it after he was *provoked* into it." She did not share the fear that if the kaiser turned down a proposal for a regency the troops would refuse their allegiance and give it only to the future kaiser. "What would come of it if Bismarck *also* went, if one dismissed the ministry? I do *not really* believe it, but it would perhaps be possible if he is himself tired and believes the Kaiser is better?—again a 'chancellor crisis,' again a *threat* from the German princes to *force a regency* in such a case!? . . . The chancellor behaves *well* toward [the kaiser] and also toward me. . . . The Kaiser cannot rely on his military entourage—with few exceptions they are already serving their future master."[4]

These messages of the kaiserin to the German Liberal leader Bamberger present some interesting problems. Her idea that the monarch should not be required by his ministers to do anything against his own inclinations and her seeming willingness to create a political crisis over medals and decorations are interesting from a liberal, constitutional viewpoint. Her willingness to lump all of the cartel parties and factions into one reactionary group hostile to herself, although certainly the German Liberal view, was also characteristic of her own tendency not to recognize nuances or complications in politics, an inclination that in this case would have been reinforced by the cartel unity in attacking her in the recent Battenberg affair. On the other hand, she never revealed this connection with Bamberger to anyone, not even her mother; Bamberger's papers are the only source. In spite of her spontaneous, naive, emotional approach and tone, she was also capable of discretion and even of duplicity, a point that is borne out by her description of the Battenberg agitation as being for the benefit only of Crown Prince William and the chancellor, without mentioning her own complicity in and approval of the campaign. Her constant stress on her own isolation and helplessness, while to a large extent doubtless sincere, nevertheless appears to be a conscious appeal to Bamberger's (and his party's) sympathies, as is to a degree also her emphasis on the liberal tenor of her husband's and her own plans for the future of Germany.

There is reason enough to assume that the kaiserin truly wanted to counteract the attacks on Mackenzie and herself in the cartel press. What makes one suspicious of her motives, however, is that Bismarck was also trying at this time to magnify the threat from the Left and its influence at court—even privately to his ministerial colleagues, as in his exploitation of the Bunsen-Schrader incident. The kaiserin, in taking the trouble to write these statements to be shown to Bamberger, was raising German Liberal confidence in their influence and importance and was thus supporting the chancellor's more or less secret political machinations. Was she doing so consciously? Had she perhaps mentioned Roggenbach's communication from Bamberger to the chancellor and asked him (on the basis of their cooperation in the Battenberg affair and in light of the kaiser's anxiety over the damage done thereby to the dignity of the crown and in her own defense) if he would have any objections, or would such a publicity link between the German Liberals and the court perhaps help him in his struggle to control Crown Prince William and the *Kreuzzeitung*-Stoecker clique? And had he jumped at it as something that by making the threat of German Liberal influence on the crown more real, could only indeed assist both of them? It is a fascinating possibility, whose truth or falsity can most likely never be known. The kaiserin's care to defend

Bismarck to Bamberger and separate him from the ministry and "the party," while holding out the tempting bait of the possibility of his retirement, adds a certain credibility to such a hypothesis. It is not very likely that Bismarck would have seriously suggested his early retirement during Kaiser Frederick's reign—it would not, for one thing, have squared with his personal stance toward Their Majesties as their loyal and heroic defender. The kaiserin's optimistic treatment of her husband's health and future prospects is also not in line with the attitude revealed to her mother—although it is likely that she was capable of considerable vacillation and self-deception in this regard. Especially as Kaiser Frederick's health began again to improve, it would have been easy for her to believe some of her own optimism. Yet, shortly after the queen's visit, she had secretly packed off a box of private papers, including two volumes of Frederick's diary, to her mother for safekeeping in England. "All the Emperor William's *most secret* & *intimate* papers," she wrote to the queen, "are being sorted & looked through at the '*Hausministerium*' by utter strangers & handled by all these officials!!! To *me*—that seems strangely indelicate & a want of respect & '*pietät*'—such measures ought to be guarded against."

The extent of the kaiserin's optimism as expressed to Bamberger is therefore suspect, although she also wrote her mother on May 9, "People are most kind & civil to me whenever & wherever I appear—*touchingly* so,—but in *official*—Government & *society circles*,—and a certain military Court party,— the *backbiting*— & sneering—the calumniating & intriguing goes *on*.* ...A few months of health—or comparative health would enable Fritz to put an *end* to this." And later, on May 19, also to her mother, "What I said about William is in no way exaggerated. I do not tell you one third of what passes, so that you, who are at a distance, should not fancy that I complain. He is in a 'ring,' a *côterie*, whose main endeavor is as it were to paralyse Fritz in every way. William is not conscious of this! This state of things must be borne until Fritz perhaps gets strong enough to put a stop to it himself." A further piece of negative substantiating evidence: the Prussian political police apparently did have the court under careful and efficient surveillance; they must have known that Baroness von Stockmar, along with Frau Schrader and Frau Helmholtz (see above, p. 197), was one of the kaiserin's most intimate friends and also that she was a neighbor of Bamberger. Yet no suspicion was ever placed on Bamberger, whereas Schrader—a much less prominent member of the German Liberal party (Count Lerchenfeld called him one of the "most superficial")—was mentioned more than once and quite falsely as the likely secret advisor to the Kaiserin. (See below, pp. 316, 323).[5]

---

* No attempt has been made to represent the kaiserin's double and triple underlining.

Bamberger found the picture of Bismarck as "the poor man with good intentions who is tyrannized by 'the harsh persons around him'" "droll" and "for us others so familiar. . . . I have never seen him in all his Tartufferies carry humor so far. For the same purpose he is also using the terrible German princes and the coup-d'état–making troops!" Bamberger guessed that Bismarck had, ever since San Remo, used the threat of a regency and his rejection of it as proof of his own special loyalty and friendship. Baroness von Stockmar urged Bamberger to write a reply to the kaiserin, and he found himself up against the difficult question: "To what extent should one open her eyes regarding Bismarck? It really doesn't help." In his "Discussion of the Confidential Memorandum of May 15" Bamberger agreed that at the moment there was "only *one* all-powerful enemy: that is the disease." There could therefore be no question of significant changes in the carrying on of state affairs. Especially since any resistance would bring on resignation of the ministry, "and the resulting confusion could not now be overcome." It was therefore necessary "to bear the unavoidable with patience." If the disease were conquered, deficiencies could be better made up then than now. If the disease were not conquered, then all reforms now instituted would be transitory, and the inevitable reaction more severe. But there was no need for the kaiser to feel obligated to accept things now that he did not approve of. "He is not forcing any positive acts and can demand that he not be forced into any." Under heavy pressure, he could handle things in a dilatory manner, even invoking the intervention of the doctors if necessary. Bamberger had already suggested this procedure in regard to the extension of the legislative period of the Prussian Landtag, and he was informed on May 21 that the kaiser was indeed postponing signing the bill. There were no other important measures that would require such handling, Bamberger wrote, "and the chancellor is too clever to put himself in the wrong." Bamberger did not think it worth the trouble to make a stand on refusing decorations or insisting on decorating those persons mentioned, even though they were his own party friends. One could certainly refuse to reward outright enemies of the kaiser such as Stoecker or his associates, but opportunities for that were unlikely to arise. "The chancellor is hardly inclined to encourage the ambitious and power-thirsty clericals [*Pfaffentum*] and build up rivals to himself among them." One important thing could still be done, and that was for the kaiser to make a statement in favor of "free voting and against the intervention of officials." This could be done just before the next elections, say in September, and in a special message that would not require the countersignature of a minister. Kaiser William had already done that sort of thing. It could be done earlier, at a good opportunity, if not so formally. "Such an occasion can be contrived."

As long as the kaiser retained possession of his mental faculties, wrote Bamberger, there was no question of imposing a regency by force. "All threats of this sort are mere bluff, conjured up in order to intimidate. Minister Friedberg will certainly regard it in the same way." Nor was there a remote chance of intervention of the army. "We have no officers and soldiers who would allow themselves to be used for such things." As for the German princes, "there is only one person to whom they now listen. If the chancellor instigated them to attempt something of the sort, they would all consider it, several would obey, but most of them? It is doubtful." Since the chancellor did not want a regency, there was no danger. As to Bismarck's claims not to be in control of the situation, of suffering under pressure from his associates, of being tired and thinking of resigning, it was not easy to speak when complete frankness was desired and yet delicate considerations existed. It would, he wrote, be "presumptuous and offensive" for him not to believe the chancellor's reports of actual occurrences. "Only this much can be said here: there is hardly one among politically experienced people in Germany who believes that one of the present ministers would allow himself to resist strongly anything that the chancellor seriously wants and holds to be necessary for the public welfare. One is also not inclined to believe that these ministers would easily decide to give up their portfolios." If any one of them resigned in opposition to both chancellor and kaiser, the nation would not give it a second thought, even if a man like Puttkamer "came to such an unlikely decision." The whole National Liberal party had expected and wanted Puttkamer's resignation. "Only the Ultras would mourn him." But he would not resign, and for such technicians (*Fachministern*) as Scholz, Maybach, or even Boetticher it was unthinkable. One could also not avoid recalling that "it is one of the chancellor's customary tacks to prefer to put the responsibility for a *Non possum* [a refusal] on a third party rather than himself." Bismarck had frequently used old Kaiser William in this way. During the last ten years he had also frequently complained of being tired. But if Bismarck claimed that Puttkamer or Boetticher was opposing him it would be better to let it pass rather than to irritate him through skepticism. "He commands the situation, and according to his disposition and the whole constellation he has no interest in driving things to extremes, but rather to hold them to a gentle pace in which he will live and let live, if one adapts oneself to him in the main and does not take up a distrustful stance toward him. To his temporizing one must oppose one's own in the best possible manner." There was no chance of a change of ministry that ousted Bismarck, and as long as he remained, one of the other ministers could fall only if Bismarck wanted to be rid of him.

The question of a trusted advisor close to the kaiser, continued Bamberger, was another matter. He defended the experienced Wilmowski as "on the whole an honest, well-meaning, humane man. His age and the realization how difficult it might be to force something or other through might make him appear to be succumbing to attacks of too much anxiety." Finding the kaiser an assistant who would possess the requisite sentiments, independence, and the favor of the chancellor would not be easy. Perhaps Dr. von Bojanowski, currently president of the Patent Office and long general consul in London, might do. He had the reputation of a humane man with enlightened and independent judgment who had felt at home in England. He had worked for a time in the Foreign Office and had won the chancellor's approval. In general, Bamberger's statements were surprisingly mild and responsible. The extent to which he assumed— and counted on—complete control by Bismarck of even the army and the federal states is noteworthy. One senses a certain oppositional dogmatism and naiveté of the outsider.[6]

In reply to Bamberger's message, the kaiserin responded on May 21 that Bojanowski would be good if he was not neurotic, and she listed other possible names for appointments. Certainly a statement could be made regarding elections. The question was *"How much* will one be able to salvage and attempt" during the kaiser's reign, which could last "a long time." She came back to the matter of the German princes forcing a regency. During the Battenberg affair Crown Prince William, the king of Saxony, the grand duke of Hesse, and perhaps even the grand duke of Baden had spoken that way. "An unpolitical private affair out of hatred, revenge, arrogance, etc., was made into a cause célèbre in order to destroy me." Prince Bismarck had told her that since Prince Alexander was no longer in Bulgaria, the marriage did not matter to him, but that he was compelled to speak otherwise in order to please the crown prince, "and the whole party—Kaiserin Augusta and above all the grand duchess of Baden [Frederick's sister] cooperated with them!!!!" If she could only settle this affair once and for all she would gladly sacrifice herself. In reply to this note, Bamberger urgently warned against publicly pushing the Battenberg marriage; in the recent crisis most of those who had sympathized with the kaiserin had done so in the belief that she was wrongly accused of pushing the marriage. If the affair were to be taken up again, things would be worse than before. To Frau von Stockmar he remarked that it would justify Bismarck's remark to Roggenbach about his skepticism regarding a woman's word. Bamberger advised patience. The threats of the German princes were simply nonsense. It is notable that the kaiserin did not respond to Bamberger's questioning of Bismarck's veracity, and again insisted on separating him—correctly to a degree—from the rabid regency party. She knew, doubtless, as Bamberger did not care to know, how much the chancellor was truly disturbed by the threat to the Reich of the influence of the Waldersee-Stoecker-*Kreuzzeitung* group on the crown prince.[7]

30

Bismarck, the Crown Prince, and Russia

ALTHOUGH Bismarck may well have been less than truthful with Radolin when he indicated to him that he had no objections to decorating Bunsen and Schrader (he may have immediately recognized his opportunity, and there is no doubt that he despised the German Liberals in general) that is no reason for assuming that he was not quite serious about the rest of his remarks: that what really worried him was not the kaiserin's interest in decorations but the crown prince's "lust for war." Radolin, after all, was an intelligent, trusted lieutenant, for whom he had just approved a princely title. The crown prince's views and actions were a continuing worry. On April 19, for example, Bismarck had been informed of the crown prince's plans, on his father's death, to put the whole Charlottenburg palace under siege. The next day, he had given the prince a serious lecture on the legal possibilities and limits of placing private citizens under detention. Nor were the prince's new advisors pleased with their charge. Professor Gneist complained to French Ambassador Herbette that he was supposed to completely reeducate Crown Prince William in three sessions per week. Like other princes, he said, the crown prince believed that "he knows everything without having learned anything. . . . For them life is easy, and they don't like to trouble themselves." At the end of March Herbert Bismarck had noted in his diary, "Long talk with [the Prince's other advisor] Brandenstein, who is rather upset."[1]

That the chancellor should be primarily concerned with matters of war and peace was in line with his general political and personal orientation and, as far as the crown prince was concerned, there was still cause for alarm. In late April Foreign Minister Count Kálnoky of Austria-Hungary had remarked to the German Ambassador Prince Reuss that perhaps it would have been better, after all, if war had broken out with Russia in the preceding fall when the Russians, upset over Austrian support for the new regime in Bulgaria, had begun massing troops on the Austrian frontier and things were so tense. Reuss had reported this remark to Berlin, and Bismarck had immediately sent a dispatch refuting such a viewpoint with his usual arguments: that nothing was to be gained by war, that public opinion was against a war of aggression, etc. The chancellor then sent Reuss's dispatch and his own reply to the crown prince. When he later went to talk with him, however, he found Crown Prince William apparently stubbornly determined on war. Disturbed, Bismarck then wrote out sixteen closely written pages of argument opposing war with Russia, which he again sent to the prince. Significantly, Crown Prince William then called General Waldersee and conferred at length with him before sending the chancellor a written reply reiterating his own position. When Foreign Office Counselor Friedrich von Holstein went to Bismarck on May 10 to thank him for a recent decoration and asked after his health, the prince complained of sleeplessness "because the crown prince's wishes were going round and round in my head. That young man wants to pursue a policy which would cause me to resign after our first three months together." That same day, talking of Crown Prince William's policy over lunch with Herbert, the chancellor exclaimed, "Alas, my poor grandchildren." Holstein noted in his diary that he had told Bleichröder, Bismarck's banker, that the chancellor was talking of resigning and had asked him to go see Bismarck and ask him, "Your Highness, when a pair of horses stampede, is it better for the coachman to be hurled from his box or to remain in his seat where he can still control them a little?" Bleichröder later reported that Bismarck had spoken of the crown prince with great restraint—"a sign he is afraid of the young man," noted Holstein—and had made no objection to Bleichröder's metaphor of the runaway horses. "Prince Bismarck," the banker commented, "wants to avoid war if at all possible, but if it is unavoidable he will go along and not resign."[2]

On Sunday, May 13, the chancellor suddenly summoned a meeting of the Prussian ministry, where he launched into a long exposé—nearly two hours—on foreign policy, delivered in a grave, belligerent tone. Things were such that they would not try so hard to avoid war with France as formerly. They would neither provoke nor attack that country, but if there were another Schnaebelé* affair or similar incident, war could occur. It was certain, if Germany should be involved in war with Russia, that France would attack, whereas it was not at all certain that Russia would take part in a Franco-German conflict. It would presumably be better to dispose of France first, before a two-front war developed. It had not been possible to make war with the old kaiser, nor with the peaceable, severely

---

* Guillaume Schnaebelé was a French frontier official who was arbitrarily arrested on April 20, 1887, by the German police. He was subsequently released with an apology.

ill present ruler, but when the bellicose young master came to the throne things would be different. It was merely an objective historical (*naturgeschichtliche*) observation on his part that the crown prince could easily decide for war and if one did not, as previously, anxiously and studiously avoid it, it would occur. A month before, Bismarck had advanced a project for introducing strict passports for travel between Alsace-Lorraine and France, to which the Statthalter (viceroy) Hohenlohe had strongly objected as an unnecessary provocation. Now, to the ministry the chancellor declared that he would not accept Hohenlohe's refusal in the matter, but would counter with a threat of his own resignation. If Hohenlohe resigned, then he should be succeeded by a "stiff-necked military man [*mit steifem Kreuz*]—such as Caprivi."

It was at this meeting that Bismarck brought up the matter of the decoration of Bunsen, Virchow, and Schrader. After reading his draft of protest to Their Majesties, he remarked that such arguments meant nothing to the kaiserin, but ran off her like water off a duck's back; it made little difference whether they explained the decision or not; all that she paid attention to was the "yes" or "no." "It was a pure fiction that [the kaiser] was ruling," wrote Lucius, describing the meeting. "Government was made possible by himself [Bismarck] and the two cabinet chiefs. His Majesty was now not capable of governing. . . . [Bismarck] was in a very serious mood and not inclined to joking [*causerie*] as usual." The session, he wrote, opened up very serious perspectives for both foreign and domestic affairs: "war and a serious domestic crisis." Bismarck had announced that he was going off to his estate in Varzin in Hither Pomerania in the next few days. "He is at the point of allowing things to take their course [*biegen oder brechen lassen*]. Her Majesty's willfulness is heading recklessly and apparently consciously toward serious conflict. The situation can very quickly become critical," continued Lucius, but "Bismarck will nevertheless presumably master it." In this last remark one senses a mild critical skepticism toward the chancellor's dramatics. Holstein reacted the same way: "My general impression," he noted in his diary, "is that Prince Bismarck, despite his spirited speech, which was no doubt aimed at H.I.H. [the crown prince], is not likely to force matters to a crisis." Holstein's own opinion was that this was the best year for a war; Caprivi had told him, "*Time is running against us* [*sic*]."[3]

Two days later, on May 15, General Waldersee dined with the crown prince, who greeted him with the news that his letter to the chancellor had had an excellent effect. According to Waldersee's diary, Bismarck had told Prince William that "he had decided that war was no longer to be avoided, which he also held to be necessary for our internal development. Accordingly they would now attempt to provoke the French in order to induce them to attack. The chancellor thinks he is sure of the Russians for a while. Naturally one must first wait for the death of Kaiser Frederick, which does seem to be dragging itself out. I am convinced," continued Waldersee, "that the chancellor came to this decision through knowledge of the character of the crown prince; he sees that the latter is a determined man without fear and not inclined to depart from an opinion that he believes to be right. Whether his decision is final I can't say as yet; it can also be that he wants to make himself agreeable to the prince in order to get more control over him. We shall see."

In executing his dramatic turnabout, Bismarck was taking the same tack that he had in the crisis over the army bill the preceding year (see above, p. 15): if a real danger of conflict with Russia existed, stir up the French, where there was little danger. It was of course true that provoking the French might contribute to the success of the ongoing electoral campaign of the fire-eating French General and former Minister of War Boulanger, but Herbert later wrote to his brother-in-law Count Rantzau, with his father in Varzin, that the best thing they could do would be to bring Boulanger to power, who "will *have* to do stupid things and will be unable to leave us in peace." That the elder Bismarck was inclined to be this rash is doubtful. It is true, however, that a campaign was launched in the government newspapers against both Russia and France. In addition to continuing the campaign against Russian securities, formal advances were made to the Austrians to take joint action to raise the tariff on Russian grain, hints of which were of course released to the press. Bleichröder was annoyed by the press attacks on France and Russia, which, he told *Norddeutsche* editor Pindter, were "solely to create relief for the crown prince." At the end of May, however, Ambassador Schweinitz was received by Tsar Alexander in St. Petersburg and assured of his complete trust in the peaceful policy of Chancellor von Bismarck, with which he quite agreed, after which the anti-Russian press campaign and the tariff plans were suddenly called off.[4]

Prince zu Hohenlohe was not the only one who was distressed over the severe passport measures being introduced into Alsace-Lorraine. Both kaiser and kaiserin strongly disapproved. The grand duke of Baden was much concerned, but eventually advised Hohenlohe to give in, as did Friedberg, Holstein, and the duke of Ratibor. The National Liberal leader Miquel, in nearby Frankfurt, was also quite upset. The Prussians, he told Hohenlohe, had no talent for assimilating conquered territories. Bismarck regarded Alsace-Lorraine merely as a territorial buffer for military purposes; "whether people also lived there was a matter of complete indifference to him." The *Frankfurter Zeitung* deplored the fact that national animosities were obstructing business and the free flow of peoples across frontiers. It was inclined to see the press campaign as serving Junker agrarian interests. Threatening a rise in the grain tariff while actually doing nothing about it, it pointed out, ironically had brought about an extra surge of Russian grain imports into Germany. The left-liberal paper doubted that the attempt to seal off connections between Alsace-Lorraine and France would work in the long run; instead of reducing hostility against Germany in the conquered territories, it would probably increase it.[5]

Bismarck's sudden acceptance of the position of the "war party"—but with the notable switch from Russia to France—appears to have worked. Confronted with the likelihood of war, the crown prince became more aware of sober military facts; he told Herbert that he was upset with Austrian ineffectiveness. They were so stupid, sloppy, and clerical that it was impossible for Germany to keep them [in English] "on a tolerable level." If the war was to break out in the West, then it became important to keep the Russians neutral. The crown prince was planning a summer Baltic cruise on the royal yacht *Hohenzollern*, and he suggested to Herbert that he might meet the tsar in Copenhagen (home of the wife of Alexander III). The elder Bismarck replied to Herbert from Varzin through Count Rantzau that he entirely approved of the crown prince's meeting with the tsar, which would be very useful. It would not be proper, however, for the prince to suggest a rendezvous with a reigning monarch; rather, he should request permission to visit the tsar in Peterhof, on his own territory. Herbert then wrote to Rantzau that he had the impression that the crown prince was thinking of making the trip after he became kaiser, "which he expects with certainty in probably four to six weeks."[6]

31

The Government Disciplines
the Conservatives

WHEN Chancellor von Bismarck informed the Prussian ministers on
May 31 that he was going to his estate in Varzin for a few weeks,
depending on His Majesty's health, his primary reasons were, first, to
avoid the wedding of Prince Henry, and, second, to avoid the vote in the
Prussian Landtag on the school-aid bill. (There was probably also a more
important third event that he wanted to avoid; see Chapter 33.) Prince
Henry's wedding to Princess Irene, daughter of the grand duke of Hesse-
Darmstadt, took place in the chapel in the Charlottenburg palace on May
24. The kaiser himself had enlarged the guest list and increased the formal-
ity and pomp of the occasion, and he appeared briefly in the chapel,
unassisted, for the crucial part of the ceremony, in his general's dress
uniform, but looking very weak and pale and fanning himself continuously
to make breathing easier. The improvement in his condition had again
been accompanied by an offensive in the left-liberal papers denouncing
negative reports and attitudes and questioning the diagnosis of cancer.
On May 19 the kaiser had driven to the Tiergarten in Berlin with his wife
and daughters and was greeted, as he wrote in his diary, with "unbelievable" enthusiasm by the crowds. The kaiserin told Lucius von Ballhausen
and his wife that there was no question of cancer. She thought a change
of scene would be good; first to the New Palace in Potsdam—or "Friedrichskron," as the royal pair had renamed it. Later the kaiserin thought
they would go to Homburg, near Wiesbaden, or to the palace of
Wilhelmshöhe, near Kassel, where there was shade from the mountains
after three in the afternoon. Herbert Bismarck had an audience with
Kaiser Frederick on May 18 for the first time in four weeks and found
him in a very good mood, quite emaciated, but bright-eyed and fresh. He
was able to follow Herbert's foreign-policy account quite well and showed
fleeting amusement, but when Herbert asked if he wanted to retain some
of the more important reports for study, he waved them away with a sad
smile. He seemed, Herbert wrote to his brother-in-law Kuno Rantzau, as

if he was beyond all mortal ambition and concern, in general appearing like a consumptive in his last month.[1]

Bismarck's desire to avoid the final vote on the school-aid bill (see above, pp. 141–43) sprang from the critical situation into which inept party leadership and apparent government laxity had maneuvered the Conservative party. The crucial discussion of what attitude the government should take toward the attempts of the parties to amend the government bill, as reported out of the Landtag commission, took place in the Prussian ministry on April 12, just as the Battenberg crisis was being brought to a sort of truce and the same day that Kaiser Frederick suffered his severe breathing crisis. In this session the ministry decided, on the recommendation of Finance Minister Scholz and Minister of Ecclesiastical, Educational, and Medical Affairs von Gossler, that the commission's attempt to raise the total amount of the government grant to the primary schools must be rejected out of hand, but that whereas the government would stand by the original form of its bill, attempts to amend it so as to allow continuation of school fees would not be declared unacceptable. There is no indication in the minutes of the meeting that the question of whether or not the bill required an amendment to the constitution—as voted in the affirmative by the commission—was even discussed. It is certainly true that the chancellor was preoccupied with the Battenberg affair, and also that there were indications that a possible compromise proposal from the National Liberals would restore cartel cooperation on the measure and replace the Conservative-Center-party lineup that had emerged in the vote of the commission. Ultimately it was the ineptitude of the National Liberal leaders stemming from their own ulterior motives in the matter of the continuation of school fees, that caused a politically explosive situation to develop in the handling of the bill in the House of Deputies.[2]

In simple terms, the National Liberals in the House of Deputies, under the leadership of Arthur von Hobrecht, a deputy representing a Berlin district, proposed as a compromise that school fees might continue to be collected by primary schools with an enriched curriculum—such as existed in the wealthier areas of the larger cities, where the National Liberal party was strong—and that as a concession to the Conservatives, other communities where the government grant would not completely cover the existing income from fees might continue to collect fees for a transitional period of ten years only. Thus they supported the principle of free schooling at least for the poor, but for the (Conservative) country districts only at a future time. The National Liberals also adhered to the government position that an amendment to the constitution was not necessary to permit such government assistance. What the National Liberal leaders were apparently too myopic to see was not only the discrimination in their compromise amendment in favor of the large cities over the country districts, but also that the constitutional issue was symbolically important for both Conservatives and Center. The constitution provided that school costs must be borne by the local communities, but that the state might assist communities that could prove financial inability. Conservatives and Catholics, intent on preserving the independence of the schools from the state as a means of upholding both local authority and church influence, insisted that any general aid by the state to local communities for the support of the schools was prohibited by this constitutional provision, whereas the government and the Liberals (supporting state secular authority in the schools in preference to that of the church) pointed out that the ability of the state to assist anyone it wanted could not practically be limited, and that it had already reached its financial arm into the local schools in establishing, for instance, the teacher pension system.

The National Liberal leaders, conscious of the support of the government, were clearly overconfident. Protests by the right-wing Conservative *Kreuzzeitung* that the proposed National Liberal compromise was inadequate, unfair, and typically inconsistent were ignored. Hobrecht then went into the House of Deputies session expecting cartel solidarity in the second reading of the bill, only to be deserted by the Conservatives at the last minute, who rallied as a united body to the commission version, allowing continuation of school fees wherever the grant was inadequate to cover them and amending the constitution to allow state assistance to the local school districts in this one instance, as an exception.[3]

Since the National Liberal amendment undercut the government bill almost as much as the Conservative-Center commission version, the position of the government in trying to defend the original bill but also uphold a cartel compromise was very difficult, and it is not surprising that Minister of Education Gossler should have given a weak, ineffective response. There apparently was no strong initiative taken in the matter by the chancellor—whether intentionally or not—and in the absence of such a forthright political initiative Gossler evidently did not feel justified in developing one of his own or was not capable of it. The *National Zeitung* and other National Liberal papers suggested strongly that their compromise could very well have succeeded if only the government had wielded its authority over the Conservatives. Yet the decisive factor in the end was the attitude of the Conservatives under the leadership of Wilhelm von Rauchhaupt, a backcountry Junker: they allowed themselves to be stampeded by the orthodox Protestant reactionary Baron von Hammerstein into a defiant demonstration of their independence of the moderate middle parties and repudiation of the arrogant leadership of the National

Liberals. In his newspaper, the *Kreuzzeitung*, after the third reading of the bill, Hammerstein pointed out smugly—and shortsightedly—that since the Conservatives were fortunate enough to be able to form a majority in the House of Deputies with two different party constellations, no one should blame them if they wanted to make use of that possibility when their Conservative principles and their electoral interests were in question. It was also, he wrote, time to demonstrate to the National Liberals and Free Conservatives that the Conservatives did not have always to follow their lead. The indignation shown in the debate by the National Liberal Hobrecht and the Free Conservative leader Zedlitz-Neukirch, he added, demonstrated how accustomed these other parties had become to Conservative subservience. In the third reading of the bill, on April 21, von Rauchhaupt evidently gave the other two cartel leaders the impression that he would accept their compromise amendments, but then he and his party once more voted with the Center for the commission's version. Defying the cartel leadership of the middle parties—judging by the noisy behavior of the rank-and-file Conservatives during the debate—was heady stuff for the Conservative Junkers, and those who retained misgivings could be persuaded to go along by appeals to unity. But this rebellion was bound to be expensive. In the first place, it was based on very shaky constitutional grounds that could not very well be accepted by the government. Also, to defy the middle parties was to repudiate the cartel, and to reject the cartel was to defy the government and the chancellor. At such a critical political juncture, with the new reign of the heir to the throne at hand, such a defiance was premature at best, and in any case extremely reckless.[4]

Attacks on Rauchhaupt's treachery appeared the day after the third reading of the bill in all the chief middle-party papers. He could not be trusted in the future, wrote the *Kölnische Zeitung*. His behavior had dug the grave for his continuing influence in the Conservative party. The school-aid bill would have to be repaired in the Herrenhaus, declared the Free Conservative *Post*. The time had come seriously to see to it that the clerical-extreme-Conservative tree did not grow any larger. It was clear, wrote the *National Zeitung*, that the *Kreuzzeitung* was now leading the Conservative party, and the voters in the fall election should "see to the necessary weakening of this party." A "lasting healthy relationship" between the moderate parties and the Conservatives could not exist, stated the *National Liberale Korrespondenz*, if the Conservatives were always veering toward the Center party in important matters. Rauchhaupt had chosen a time for cooperating with the Center leader Windthorst when the Center (in the Battenberg affair) had been attacking the chancellor almost more violently than the German Liberals. On the other side, the Center party's

Germania maintained that such conflict among the parties of the cartel was only natural since the cartel itself was *un*natural. For Prince Bismarck to intervene to discipline the Conservatives simply for voting according to their convictions and political interests would be immoral and unconstitutional. It did not believe that the Herrenhaus would reject the version passed by the House of Deputies since that would endanger the bill as a whole. According to *Germania*, for the Conservatives, church and school policy was a matter of life or death.[5]

In an article on April 26, the National Liberal *National Zeitung* suggested that in rebelling in such cavalier fashion against the cartel, von Rauchhaupt (under the instigation of von Hammerstein) was challenging the chancellor over control of the future government of the crown prince. Rauchhaupt's defiance of the cartel, however, also had ramifications that were greater than he and Hammerstein probably realized. Defiance of government policy and government direction by the strongest political party in the popularly elected part of the Prussian Landtag suggested a bid for parliamentary power independent of the government bureaucracy and over it. Such a challenge—as unwitting as it probably was—could not be calmly accepted if the Prussian government was to retain its traditional authority over the parliament; nor was this critical period, with a change of personalities on the throne in the offing, a good time for constitutional innovation. The Conservative leaders probably did expect that the government would withdraw its bill, but promising the local communities a substantial grant of state money and then going back on that promise would be humiliating and just as much a defeat for the government as accepting a bad bill. Also, the Conservative-Center position on the constitution as embodied in the amended bill could not be accepted by the government.

If the Conservative leaders had been capable of thinking things through politically, they would have realized that the government could not afford to let them get away with their little rebellion, and that the resources of any Prussian government in handling the parliament were many. Nor could Bismarck allow Crown Prince William, at this delicate juncture, to witness a successful challenge to his personal power. Hammerstein and Rauchhaupt, relying on their orthodox Christian ideological association with the crown prince, were challenging the chancellor's authority, and Bismarck immediately reacted. At a time, wrote the *Kölnische Zeitung* on April 27, when the government of the Reich was under attack from all directions internally and externally, "one does not understand how leading Conservative parliamentarians can willfully manufacture pretexts for sowing dissension among the parties faithful to the Reich." It hoped that at least in the country at large (a sly reference to the fall elections) followers and friends of the Reich chancellor would stand together against his enemies. The following day Chancellery Chief Rottenburg told Emil Pindter, editor of the chancellor's *Norddeutsche Allgemeine Zeitung*, that there was to be a press campaign "against Rauchhaupt's arrogance in the House of Deputies." "Are they now also becoming alarmed about the Junkers?" Pindter asked his diary. "Hopefully it is not too late."[6]

According to the Prussian constitution, the process of amendment— now part of the House of Deputies' version of the school-aid bill—required a second vote in the same chamber not less than twenty-one days after initial passage before the bill could be presented to the other house, where the same process was required. In a meeting of the Prussian State Ministry on April 29 Minister von Gossler informed his colleagues that the commission of the Herrenhaus wanted to begin its discussion of the bill before the House of Deputies voted on the bill for the second time. He also reported that there was a chance of procuring changes in the bill as passed by the House of Deputies that would conform more closely to the government's point of view. He declared that he was personally inclined toward the Hobrecht amendment, which had been defeated in the House of Deputies by the Conservative-Center coalition. Minister of Finance Scholz stated that he was quite in agreement with Gossler, and Minister-President Bismarck remarked that quite aside from the technical provisions of the paragraph in question, he held it to be politically correct in any case to oppose the inclination of the Conservatives to go along with the Center. The whole ministry agreed that Gossler might represent this point of view to the Herrenhaus commission.[7]

On the same day as the ministerial session, the chancellor's *Norddeutsche Allgemeine Zeitung* quoted the warnings of the National Liberal *Kölnische Zeitung* with approval and added an article from the governmental *Berliner Politische Nachrichten* stating that the recent occurrences in the House of Deputies presented the government with the question whether it wanted to support itself in the Prussian Landtag on a majority led by the Center party leader Windthorst and suggesting that the government would have to answer such a question in the negative. In the *Norddeutsche*'s "Journal-Revue" in the same issue, an article in the Free Conservative and governmental *Post* was quoted extensively, stating that effective cooperation of the cartel parties in the Reichstag would be immeasurably hindered by lack of unity and harmony in Prussia. In addition, the *Norddeutsche* quoted the official Conservative organ, the *Konservative Korrespondenz*, as pointing out how the Center party's *Germania* was trying to encourage and exploit the cleavage between the Conservatives and the other parties of the cartel and that this effort would not succeed. It also quoted the *National Liberale Korrespondenz*, which pointed out that Windthorst had not brought up his own school bill for debate yet in the House of Deputies, although there had been ample opportunity. Apparently he was trying to avoid any occasion for discord between his Center party and the Conservatives that might push them back toward the middle parties. On the other hand, *Germania* declared that the suggestion of the *Post* that the strength of the cartel ought to be the main guideline for the parliamentary activity of deputies in the three parties was "immoral and unconstitutional." Each deputy should speak and vote according to the facts of the case and his own conscience.[8]

The *Konservative Korrespondenz* might join the *Post* and the *Norddeutsche* in trying to play down the threat to the cartel, but Baron Hammerstein's right-wing conservative *Kreuzzeitung* would have none of it. The position of the Conservative party in the school-aid bill debate had not been a matter of factional maneuvers, it declared with indignation, but rather of fundamental principles and beliefs. Collaboration with the Center party did not at all mean, as the *Berliner Politische Nachrichten* claimed, that the government was in danger of being dependent on Windthorst, since it was the Conservative party itself, not the Center, that was the largest, dominant party in the House of Deputies, and, added the *Kreuzzeitung* pointedly, this was "a situation that surely cannot be displeasing to a conservative government"—a mild suggestion that perhaps the Bismarck government was not truly conservative. Furthermore, it went on, the government had passed its social insurance laws, tariff laws, and the recent clerical legislation ending the Kulturkampf with the Center and against the votes of the National Liberals. Whether consciously or unconsciously, the *Kreuzzeitung* was here overlooking the difference in general political impact between a Conservative-Center alliance on relatively unemotional economic or social issues, such as the tariff or social insurance, and an alliance on ideological grounds, such as they saw in school aid.[9]

Two days before, Pastor Stoecker had addressed a Christian socialist meeting on "The Prussian Monarchy" in the course of which he had eulogized Kaiser William as one of the greatest and most venerable monarchs of all time. Strong in war, yet sensitive to social problems, he had revived and strengthened the idea of the Prussian monarchy after it had been weakened by revolution. Not only the moderate liberals, but even the radical liberals, as a consequence, had ceased to talk of their ideal of parliamentary supremacy. Only the Social Democrats remained openly antimonarchical. Actually the workers loved the kaiser as much as any other group. Unlike in Switzerland and France, in Germany a monarchy respecting the rights and freedoms of the people had developed historically as the only right form of government. The constitutional position of the kings in Prussia had actually not changed that much over the centuries; the kings had always maintained close connections with the people and their opinions, and today the king remained "absolute master of the army and as before chooses the ministers according to his own judgment." The whole executive administration remained in the hands of the monarch, and all legislation required his consent. It was senseless to talk of democracy: "Who could possibly fill the gap if we did not have our royal family?" Doubtless Stoecker was speaking for the benefit of the crown prince as well as to his immediate audience; his formulation thus provided a significant gloss on the *Kreuzzeitung*'s reference to a "conservative government." This emphasis on Prussia's authoritarian traditions appeared to suggest that the future king-emperor should try to dispense with the powerful chancellor and rule by himself. It also seemed to invite the crown prince to adopt a narrow, reactionary approach to the governing process. Such a suggestion was dangerous, since Crown Prince William was already too much inclined in that direction.[10]

Like the *Kreuzzeitung*, but for diametrically opposite reasons, the *National Zeitung* was also not inclined to play down the defection of the Conservatives over the school-aid bill. Its ideal of liberal-responsible government was now fading along with the vitality of the stricken ruler in Charlottenburg. Rauchhaupt's action, declared the National Liberal paper, merely exposed in an especially crass way a condition that was constantly threatening German parliamentary life and had been the rule before the election of 1887: "the lack of a consistent line of domestic policy guaranteed by the government that would make possible mutual trust among the parties called upon to support the government." On that day (April 28), for example, a Reichstag by-election was taking place in the Westphalian district of Altena-Iserlohn. It would probably go to a runoff, and naturally the Center party would support the oppositional German Liberal against the National Liberal and Conservative (cartel) candidate. And yet the chief issues being exploited by the German Liberal candidate were the liquor tax and the boost in the grain tariff, both of which had been backed by the Center. Caught between simple, idealistic party slogans on the one hand and such complicated and contradictory maneuvers on the other, the ordinary voter could be excused a certain cynicism. Rauchhaupt's recent action was a further manifestation of the attempt of the orthodox Protestant right-wing Conservatives to try to dominate the future regime under the crown prince. Rauchhaupt personally did not belong to the high-church party; he was interested merely in power— perhaps a ministry in the Bismarck administration. But the coming to power in Prussia of the clerical far Right would have a strong negative impact in south Germany and elsewhere among precisely those elements that from the beginning had been the strongest supporters of the Reich.[11]

The by-election in Altena-Iserlohn went approximately as the *National Zeitung* expected. Although the National Liberals won a plurality on the first ballot (8,719), the German Liberal vote was so close (8,442) that the votes of the Center (1,812) and Social Democrats (2,376) were sufficient to deny them an absolute majority. As in other recent by-elections for the Reichstag, voter participation dropped substantially from the high of the previous year—some 4,000 fewer votes in this case. Since a runoff vote would be necessary, and it was a foregone conclusion that the Center and Social Democratic vote would be added to that of the German Liberals, an eventual defeat of the National Liberals—not only in spite of their strength in the district but indeed because of it—was quite certain. Under these circumstances it was understandable and objectively interesting that the *National Zeitung* took the occasion to mount an attack on the absolute-majority election system as a whole, which encouraged the extremes, sacrificed the middle, and in general favored a negative, special-interest approach to party politics that was downright frivolous. The Center represented the most reactionary tendencies in German life, and for Social Democrats and German Liberals to claim they were fighting reaction by cooperating with it was a misuse of the language. "A deputy who is elected by German Liberal, ultramontane, and Social Democratic votes . . . is there merely to prevent the presence of someone else; but that is not the purpose of elections." Such an election system crippled the effectiveness of the parliament. With a plurality system, however, suggested the *National Zeitung*, parties with nothing in common would find it difficult to unite even for one election. Neither the Social Democrats nor the Center could give up their existence as a separate party. To copy the French and allow all candidates to run in the second balloting with the decision by plurality would be better than the present system of a runoff between the two strongest candidates. This attack on the runoff system brought unusual approbation from the conservative *Kreuzzeitung*, and this agreement between the National Liberal and Conservative papers led the left-liberal *Frankfurter Zeitung* to speculate that perhaps the cartel parties were planning to bring in another constitutional amendment to that effect in the fall. The *Kreuzzeitung*, however, was not disturbed by Center support of the German Liberals in Altena-Iserlohn. They were demonstrating German Liberal dependence on their votes and also their independence, which might, for example, one day make it possible for the Center to vote for a Conservative.[12]

It was, no doubt, the conservative *Kreuzzeitung*'s habitual self-confident myopia that led it to approve a plurality election system, expecting that the tendency would be to divide for and against authority or for and against revolution, which would support its own ideological stance. The

National Zeitung, on the other hand, expected more realistically that a plurality system would encourage the middle—that "mishmash" ideological "swamp" that the *Kreuzzeitung* unreservedly detested. This point was clearly recognized by the *Frankfurter's* Berlin correspondent, August Stein, who disapproved of the plurality system precisely because it would deny minority groups the chance to demonstrate their strength and would discourage the formation of new party groupings. It would thus lead to a "stagnation" of party relationships and might therefore very well appeal to the parties of the cartel. This academic discussion of election systems might be very interesting, but, as the *Frankfurter* pointed out, it did not help the National Liberal party members in the district itself who had to try to take the runoff seriously and increase their vote as much as possible. The Center party's *Germania* made no bones about its position in the matter. It was merely a question, it declared, of helping to elect a deputy who would be "least dangerous" or "most useful" to the Center, and it urged the party faithful to go to the ballot box and vote "as one man" for the German Liberal candidate. The National Liberals were the "enemies of our church," and any Catholic who voted for them was "without character" and "*betrays* his church!" The German Liberals, unlike the cartel parties, were not in a position to build a majority potentially dangerous to the Center. Although in the runoff in Altena-Iserlohn the National Liberals increased their vote to 10,621, they were easily submerged by the added Center and Social Democratic support for the German Liberal candidate, who received a total of 13,412 votes.[13]

In regard to the school-aid bill, the *Kreuzzeitung,* in an article May 1, declared that the cartel and government attempt to make it into a matter not only of national, but even of international, politics was "absolute foolish sophistry." The *Post* ought to come right out and declare that unlike the National Liberals, who could vote with the German Liberals and Center whenever they wanted, the Conservatives were not to be permitted to align with the Center party. The *Kreuzzeitung* did not doubt that the middle parties were trying to establish the indispensability of the National Liberals, but it was less sure that the government was really convinced by these efforts. It had, after all, itself been making conciliatory gestures recently toward the Center.[14]

As if to underline the *Kreuzzeitung's* apprehensions, an article appeared at this point in the weekly *Die Gegenwart* advocating the formation of a great "constitutional party" that would accept and defend the constitution as it was and submerge all doctrinal quibbles in a national program of progress and social reform. Even if the chancellor, it stated, had wanted to base his policy on a Conservative majority in Germany, he would have had to accept the fact that it was presently impossible. But his continued encouragement of the middle parties in recent years and his resistance to the extreme, reactionary economic and religious efforts of the Conservatives indicated that he did not in fact want such a majority. But the middle parties constituted only a third of the parliaments, and a larger configuration was therefore called for that would base itself firmly on Kaiser Frederick's program and resist all attacks from Right, Left, and Center. It would thus not include the *Kreuzzeitung* anti-Semitic reactionaries, who now seemed to be dominant in the Conservative party, nor the Eugen Richter group of fanatical Liberals; nor, of course, would it include the Social Democrats nor the Center "in its present composition." The article denounced the extreme Conservatives as not truly conservative, because they did not really accept the constitution. The loss of the bulk of the Conservatives would be made up from the more moderate German Liberals.

In reprinting this article, the Free Conservative and governmental *Post* identified its author as probably a left-wing National Liberal or a right-wing German Liberal. The called-for shift of the middle parties to the Left, the *Post* thought, was too dangerous. The National Liberal leader Bennigsen's *Hannoverscher Kourier* also expressed skepticism; the idea was attractive, but if the right-wing German Liberals wanted to rejoin the National Liberal party, there was danger they would try again to dominate it. If the moderate German Liberals wanted to expel Eugen Richter and form an independent party, that was something else again. Catholic *Germania* detected more sympathy in these middle-party papers toward the German Liberals than toward the extreme Conservatives, whom all joined in denouncing. The *Konservative Korrespondenz*—controlled by the Reichstag Conservative party leadership under Baron Otto von Helldorff-Bedra—reacted nervously to the "constitutional party" article and warned the National Liberals that this was no time for political experiments, a remark that applied equally to the *Kreuzzeitung*'s and Rauchhaupt's dalliance with the Center party. At a time, it continued, when the German Liberals were engaged in "their last desperate battle" (in support of Kaiser Frederick) they must be opposed by a united patriotic front. German Liberal papers appeared to be taken by surprise by the *Gegenwart* article and to regard it as untimely. Since Kaiser Frederick was clearly in the last few weeks of his life, such a proposal of a leftward political shift was indeed a bogey that served cartel and government purposes by inflating the threat from the Left, thereby providing further means for trying to hold the bulk of the Conservative party in the cartel and away from a basic alliance with the Catholic Center. For these reasons one suspects that the *Gegenwart* article originated, not in the study of a well-meaning liberal, but in Franz von Rottenburg's Chancellery.[15]

In a similar vein, on May 1 the semiofficial *Norddeutsche Allgemeine Zeitung* carried a lead article pointing out that with so many celebrations, it was odd that the democrats had made no move to celebrate the fortieth anniversary of "the crazy year" of 1848. This was probably because everything had turned out differently from their expectations then. Much of what was hoped for had actually been accomplished not as a result of popular impulse, but rather from the joint political efforts of princes, statesmen, and legal representatives. The democrats, however, the chancellor's paper warned, were the same now as then, when, copying the French and believing that nothing could withstand their principles, they had tried to force a revolution upon a people "who throughout showed no inclination for it."[16]

On May 4 the commission of the Herrenhaus met to discuss the school-aid bill, with Minister von Gossler attending. As Gossler reported to a meeting of the Prussian State Ministry on the sixth, the commission rejected the idea that the bill required an amendment to the constitution, but rather than endanger passage of the bill in the House of Deputies, the commission voted oddly to recommend that the Herrenhaus accept the amendment provision while passing a resolution declaring it unnecessary. If the government wanted to accentuate the disagreement between the two houses, said Gossler, and, as suggested by Minister of Finance von Scholz and Minister of Public Works von Maybach, close the Landtag session as soon as the Herrenhaus had voted on the bill, it would be better for the Herrenhaus to stand up for its convictions and vote down the constitutional amendment clause, which he thought could be arranged. Minister-President Bismarck agreed that the Herrenhaus would better defend its independent constitutional position if it rejected the clause outright, rather than merely passing a disapproving resolution. It was not necessary, he thought, to decide yet on when to terminate the session.[17]

Government moves at this point in relation to the Conservative party were not only negative. In the press and through informal, personal connections with party leaders it supported an attempt by schnapps-producing farmers and estate owners to form a monopolistic producers' cooperative, a "Spirits Bank," to control and allocate production and maintain an adequate price level. Articles in the *Norddeutsche* in early May took an optimistic view of the chances of organizing the producers. The *Konservative Korrespondenz* reminded the owners of distilleries that time was running out before the deadline that had been set for joining the organization, pointed out the importance of potato and schnapps production for the sandy soil of the north, and urged producers to join to save agriculture from destruction and to strengthen the financial resources of the Reich. Those who were not joining the Spirits Bank, wrote the Free Conservative Reichstag leader Wilhelm von Kardorff in a statement printed in the *Kreuzzeitung*, were irresponsible. The duke of Ratibor, president of the Herrenhaus, wrote to Rottenburg that he would hold a meeting on the Spirits Bank in the Herrenhaus building on May 16, hoping that the largest possible number of persons who might be interested would then be available; this, Rottenburg wrote to Kuno Rantzau, Bismarck's secretary, on the sixteenth, included the Silesian magnates—a group of large estate owners (the most prominent of whom was Count Guido Henckel von Donnersmarck) who were also industrialists. Rottenburg wrote that he had drawn up a list of important points to be made. Two days ago he had explained to the House of Deputies Conservative leader von Rauchhaupt that the peasants had to have an organization that would protect them against the merchants and that the thrust of the Spirits Bank would be chiefly against the middle men and would therefore actually result in cheaper prices in the long run, and Rauchhaupt had declared himself convinced and said that he would give up his opposition. But now he had presented Rottenburg with a memorandum reaffirming his former opposition, which Rottenburg was enclosing. He thought that Rauchhaupt was backed in this position by Baron von Hammerstein of the *Kreuzzeitung*. "I hope," Rottenburg wrote Rantzau, "H.H. will simply throw the letter in the wastebasket and have the sender attacked in the press. . . . As soon as the Silesians have come to a decision, Rauchhaupt, in my opinion, must be advanced against in the *Politische Nachrichten*, *Post* (I have already spoken with Zedlitz), etc. The fellow is impeding business to such an extent that a slaughter is necessary. I suspect—and that also speaks for radical handling—that Rauchhaupt and Hammerstein are making politics for the future [*Zukunftspolitik treiben*]. They are 'betting on the crown prince,' with Stoecker sitting in the prompter's box."[18]

In mid-May an appeal was distributed in favor of the Spirits Bank signed by such notables—and staunch Bismarckians—as the duke of Ratibor, Count Henckel von Donnersmarck, and Count von Mirbach-Sorquitten. One communication from the organizing committee threatened noncooperators with punitive or discriminatory action after the organization was successfully launched. Similar threats were suggested in articles in the *Berliner Politische Nachrichten* and the *Norddeutsche*. Even the *Kreuzzeitung* was drawn through its sensitivity to agrarian causes to defend the right of agrarians to form cartels if they wished. Liberals did not seem so affronted by cartels in industry. Existing letters of Prince Radolin to Chancellery Chief Rottenburg indicate the superior court marshal's efforts in promoting the Spirits Bank. This fact, in connection with an announcement in the *Norddeutsche* that the Royal Court Commission for the Estates of the Royal Family had joined the Spirits Bank, suggests that this Bismarckian move to hold on to the Junkers by means of their economic interests was understood and approved of in Charlotten-burg. All of these efforts nevertheless proved inadequate to raise the number of participating distillers above 76 percent of total production, which was considered insufficient. If organizing distillers on a private basis could not be accomplished through the considerable efforts and agitation just experienced, wrote the *Börsen-Courier*, then it would always be impossible. A government, wrote the *Frankfurter Zeitung*, that had for-mally proclaimed its desire to assist the weak and the helpless should not be supporting a group of producers to the disadvantage of the consumers. Aside from the failure of the Spirits Bank project, it is nevertheless likely that during May the agitation helped the government to control the Con-servative party and challenge the leadership of Rauchhaupt and Ham-merstein. The Conservative Junkers would accept the whip more easily if accompanied by *Zuckerbrot*.[19]

The hardening of the attitude of the Prussian State Ministry toward the House of Deputies in the affair of the school-aid bill could not be known to the general public or the party press, and since the report of the Herrenhaus commission was not necessarily binding on the full house, and the second vote of the deputies had to be taken before the bill could be brought to the floor of the Herrenhaus, it made some sense for the Conservatives to stand their ground in the House of Deputies and hold to their earlier position in the second vote until they could at least discern how strong the government position was. It would only cause confusion for the Conservatives to change their vote at this point, advised the Center party's *Germania*, anxiously trying to gauge the pressure mounting against the Conservatives to bring them back into the cartel fold. The National Liberal *National Zeitung* was disturbed by the failure of the Herrenhaus commission to mention "advanced" primary schools [*Volksschule*]. "With all the consideration that one is inclined to give to the poorer classes," wrote the left-wing National Liberal paper, "such consideration would nevertheless be carried too far if... one wished to compel the classes living in better circumstances... to allow their children to learn *less* in the obligatory *Volksschulen* than they could in the advanced schools, solely on the grounds that they would then be sitting with the children from the poorer classes." In spite of warning articles in the *Berliner Politische Nach-richten* recommending that the Herrenhaus reject the constitutional amend-ment provision outright, neither *Germania*, the *National Zeitung*, nor the *Kreuzzeitung* took this warning seriously because, as the *Kreuzzeitung* itself warned, that would surely defeat the bill as a whole, and no one believed that the government would be willing to go so far.[20]

Meanwhile pressure mounted. The Free Conservative *Post* declared that if the bill failed to pass in this session, it probably never could because the same forces would be against it. Such an outcome, however, would be a victory for the Center party leader Windthorst in his opposition to the government school system. It would also amount to a setback for the cartel and would prepare the way for a successful campaign of the opposition parties in the fall Landtag election. On the other side, a Center party correspondence sheet declared that if the Conservatives failed to stick to their position (and their alliance with the Center), "then they are politically dead and can have themselves buried." *Germania* wrote that the middle parties were demanding "the *humiliation* of the Conservatives." The right-wing conservative *Kreuzzeitung*, however, did not intend to be humiliated. The idea of the *Post* that it was the function of the Conservative parties to protect and defend the National Liberals, it wrote, was "especially senseless right now." Who cared about Liberals with Crown Prince William so close to the throne? On May 14 Rauchhaupt announced in the House of Deputies that for now the Conservative party would stand by its position in the third reading of the school-aid bill, but its further action would depend on the action of the Herrenhaus. The bill was then passed again by the Conservative-Center majority in the House of Deputies in its previous form.[21]

The debate on the floor of the Herrenhaus was set to begin on May 16, with Bismarck now in Varzin, and the day before, Minister of the Interior and Vice President of the State Ministry Puttkamer called the ministers together to decide on what position the government should take. Minister von Gossler reported that he had just come from a session of the Herrenhaus commission on the bill, and for fear of a possibly negative effect on the elections, an overwhelming majority of the commission had voted to approve the constitutional change clause as passed twice now by the House of Deputies. The Conservatives were afraid that the electorate would blame them for the failure of the bill and that this, added to the tax on schnapps, would mean a loss of some of their seats in the East. Although, said Gossler, he would regard such a result as just retribution for the tactics of the Conservatives in the House of Deputies, nevertheless an increase in oppositional strength would be disadvantageous also to the government. He thought that the government should maintain the principle of no necessary change in the constitution, but that the clause in the contrary sense should not be declared unacceptable. If the Herrenhaus rejected the constitutional change clause, then the Landtag should be closed, since the vote in the House of Deputies had been by roll call, and they would not be able to change their position. He thought that the Herrenhaus would accept the clause if the government declared it not unacceptable. That kind of action, declared Finance Minister Scholz, would not avoid a defeat for the government and a triumph for the Center party leader Windthorst. He would regard it as an advantage if the members of the Conservative party were made to feel their guilt, if those who had led them into a position of hostility toward the government were not reelected, and if the party were taught by the consequences of their policy to be more of a support for the government in the future. The government must declare, as in the House of Deputies, that the bill did not require a constitutional change, above all for the sake of similar measures in the future, and that the constitutional clause was unacceptable.

Puttkamer sided with Gossler. His trip to the East to inspect the flooded areas had persuaded him that the bill must be adopted. The agricultural population there would regard government aid for the schools as a kind of compensation for the liquor tax. As wrong-headed as the leadership of the Conservatives might be, the government could not refuse to support them against the German Liberals. He agreed that the House of Deputies was unlikely to reverse its roll-call decision and accept the bill without the constitutional clause. But if the Herrenhaus rejected the clause and the government closed the Landtag, the bill must be brought in again in the fall. Reich Secretary of the Interior and Vice Chancellor Boetticher and Minister of War General Bronsart von Schellendorf, however, agreed with Finance Minister von Scholz that the constitutional clause should not be accepted by the government at the same time that they declared it to be unnecessary. A vote was taken, and the unacceptability of the constitutional change clause was affirmed by five to two—Gossler and Puttkamer. It was, however, decided to ask for the opinion of the minister-president in Varzin immediately by telegraph. It was agreed to work privately for an appropriate vote and definitely to reintroduce the bill in the next session. It would be naive and foolish to suppose that this ministerial solidarity behind Scholz and against Puttkamer and Gossler and the Conservative leadership in the House of Deputies was fortuitous. Bismarck might be in Varzin, but both Scholz and Chancellery Chief Rottenburg had doubtless received quite explicit instructions before his departure. It is interesting that Minister of War General Bronsart von Schellendorf here took a position directly hostile to General von Waldersee's friend Baron von Hammerstein. No doubt for him the principle of government authority overrode questions of mere party or ideological or even army loyalty.[22]

The following day the ministry met again in the Herrenhaus, and Puttkamer read a telegram from Bismarck in Varzin declaring his agreement with the vote of the ministry the day before but suggesting for discussion the possibility of letting members of the Herrenhaus themselves lead the attack on the constitutional change clause. If the government simply declared the clause unacceptable, it could be justifiably criticized for not having done this in the House of Deputies. Puttkamer stated that he regarded this suggestion as a directive not to declare the constitutional change clause unacceptable. Boetticher thought that speakers representing the majority of the Herrenhaus would speak out in the desired sense. But the government should emphatically state that it did not recognize the necessity for a constitutional change and that the acceptance of the clause would prejudice the situation in an unfortunate way. The ministry as a whole agreed with Boetticher's statement and that before the beginning of that day's session individual members of the Herrenhaus should be confidentially advised of the ministry's position.[23]

In the same session of the ministry Gossler again brought up the Stoecker question. He had a report from the minister of justice advising that since the earlier action against Stoecker under Kaiser William had resulted in a reprimand from the Evangelical Superior Church Council, the disciplinary procedure against him could not be considered as continuing nor his offer to resign as still in force. Stoecker, however, had clearly not heeded the warning to cease his political agitation, and the present kaiser held that such activities were not compatible with Stoecker's functions as a court and cathedral chaplain. It would therefore be possible for His Majesty simply to issue a cabinet order that Stoecker desist from his political activity, as Kaiser William had already done. It would be the duty of the minister of ecclesiastical affairs to report to the kaiser in this sense and to submit the draft of the appropriate order. Gossler said that he agreed with this point of view and from his own research into the case believed that a new disciplinary process against Stoecker with the aim of removing him from office could be successfully instituted. The ministry agreed with the views of both ministers and decided, "after a thorough discussion," that it would be most appropriate for the previous order of Kaiser William to be attached to the new one with authorization for the Superior Church Council to take prompt disciplinary steps if the provisions of both orders were not strictly adhered to.[24]

Unaware of these moves in the Prussian ministry, Stoecker and the *Kreuzzeitung* were both riding high on the "wave of the future." In its Ascension Day issue on May 9 the *Kreuzzeitung* had written that the celebration of Christ's rising to heaven to take His place at the right hand of His Father was a reminder that the Kingdom of God was all-inclusive and eternal, and that ultimately therefore there were only two parties: "the party of the Lord and the party of His opponents." And Stoecker, speaking on May 15 to a Conservative meeting on the topic "The Significance of the Church for Conservatism," declared that the greatest evil of German party life was the failure of all the Christian parties to have the same love for religion and the church as the Conservatives. "Only Christianity can bind all the German tribes, all the parties, all the ranks and vocations permanently together, can soften all antagonism." They must try to eliminate the differences among Christians so that they could better oppose the Jews.[25]

It was no doubt the threat of such extreme ideological tendencies and personalities gaining political power that led the left-liberal but independent *Frankfurter Zeitung*, in a remarkable editorial on May 16, the day that the debate on the school-aid bill opened in the Prussian Herrenhaus, to practically beg the government to exert its authoritarian power to force the Conservatives back into the cartel. It was in the government's interest to do this; there were signs that it was already working in this direction; and undoubtedly it would be successful. The Conservatives probably could strengthen the position of their party in the Prussian House of Deputies if their alliance with the Center was carried over into the fall elections. But the stronger their position in the Deputies, the less consideration they would show toward the National Liberals, and they would "show their power toward the government in a quite different way than has hitherto been the case. Our Conservatives know nothing of the selflessness and modesty that the National Liberals are so good at. . . . In theory they condemn parliamentary government, but in practice they are its most stubborn champions, in that they want the government to accommodate itself to the will of their majority. They cannot do that inside the cartel . . . [where] various forces hold themselves in balance, whereby it becomes possible for the government to lead and rule along the diagonal." Thus the democratic *Frankfurter*, which habitually denounced the "reactionary" Bismarck regime, here admitted that it usually governed "along the diagonal." Also, its obvious fear of potential Conservative-clerical power demonstrated its tacit realization of the entrenched position in the state of Junkers, church, and monarchy. It was also clearly hostile to parliamentarism if it was reactionary. How easy it would have been for a "liberal" monarch and government to rally these people to the support of continued authoritarian rule in "liberal" interests! It is also clear that the *Frankfurter* expected support for liberal interests from the Bismarck regime because such interests were modern and progressive in terms of developing new sources of state power, as the clerical-Conservative interests were not.[26]

In the debate in the Herrenhaus on May 16 Finance Minister von Scholz delivered a strong attack on the constitutional change clause. The government had issued warnings, but the House of Deputies had paid no attention. It would be dangerous to limit the power of the government to aid the schools through a constitutional amendment. For example, the government had originally wanted to place its money grant on the basis of 600 M for a first-rank teacher, not 400 M, as eventually stated in the bill. It would like, however, to raise the grant to 600 M when possible, but if the constitutional change clause were now passed such an increase would require another amendment to the constitution! If the bill failed to pass in this session, the government would definitely reintroduce it in the next. In seizing the initiative in the debate, as in the ministry, in an anti-Conservative sense Scholz was continuing the role of disciplinarian of the Conservatives that he had played before (see above, p. 140). The appeal to the dignity of the Herrenhaus as an independent part of the legislative process did not fail to arouse general enthusiasm, and although several Conservative party leaders urged accommodation with the House of Deputies, others, following Scholz, gave ringing declarations that heeding their own consciences in the matter of the constitutional change clause was more important than concern over possible embarrassment of the other house. The result was an overwhelming rejection of the clause—96 to 25. By taking a strong, uncompromising stand and encouraging the Herrenhaus to do the same, the ministry had, as the *National Zeitung* immediately observed, led the House of Deputies and especially the Conservative party into a blind alley from which there were only two equally painful exits: to publicly knuckle under, reverse their position, and change their vote, or to take the responsibility before the electorate for depriving them of the money offered in the government grant. The voters would certainly not care about the niceties of the constitutional question. The whole thing, wrote August Stein in the *Frankfurter*, had been done very slickly, the ministry had indicated that it would not accept the constitutional change clause and had promised more money. It was a complete rout, which the House of Deputies had not expected. It was very unlikely, he thought, that the deputies would reverse themselves, since "the humiliation for the Conservatives would be very shameful."[27]

On May 17, the day following the Herrenhaus debate, Vice President of the State Ministry Puttkamer again called the Prussian ministry together. They must decide, he pointed out, now that the Herrenhaus had rejected the deputies' version of the school-aid bill, whether the Landtag should be immediately closed or not. He had found that no one in the House of Deputies expected the session to be closed, and from a number of sides he was informed that it was possible that the deputies might accept the bill as passed by the Herrenhaus. In the previous voting in the House of Deputies many Conservatives had not voted; others had gone along with the leadership for party reasons or in order to put the bill through, but would presumably be willing now to vote for the Herrenhaus version for the same reasons. All the other ministers present spoke decidedly for further debate and voting on the bill in the House of Deputies. Passage of the bill by both houses was not only desirable in itself but could also be "regarded as a significant parliamentary victory for the government." The ministers decided that the opinion of the minister-president should be obtained by telegraph, and Bismarck presumably agreed, since the debate took place.[28]

For Baron von Hammerstein's *Kreuzzeitung* the action of the Herrenhaus was "almost inexplicable." It could have happened only under the impact of Scholz's onslaught. Was this, it asked, perhaps part of a deliberate attempt of the government to establish sole dominion over the schools through a casual, step-by-step process? Also, the fact that Scholz led the attack, not Gossler or Puttkamer, demonstrated that it was a political move against the Conservative party in the House of Deputies. But, the *Kreuzzeitung* proclaimed, the House of Deputies would not yield. About ten days before the debate on the bill in the Herrenhaus, the *Kreuzzeitung* had observed that the cartel was all right for special crises such as had existed at the time of its formation in the winter of 1887, but that it was not "suited to prosaic, everyday use." This statement had been challenged by the party's official paper, the *Konservative Korrespondenz*, and a dispute between the two conservative organs had ensued over whether the cartel, created for a Reichstag election, should be enforced in the Landtag, suggesting a dispute between the leadership of the two parliaments.[29]

On Saturday, May 19, Hammerstein's *Kreuzzeitung* in a lead article commemorating Pentecost uncompromisingly laid out the ideological basis for the paper's stubborn stand on the school-aid bill. The Spirit of God and the spirit of the times (*Zeitgeist*, or the worldly spirit) were in constant conflict, it wrote, but eventually the former would conquer. It was the Spirit of God that filled not only every individual, but also social life and "all the dispositions of the state." The conflict between the two spirits thus existed in every individual soul, as well as in social and political life. It was the church that carried the eternal Spirit of God, and for this reason the *Zeitgeist* especially opposed it. People did not want a church that was presumptuous enough to attempt to overcome the world. It would be much more convenient for the secular spirit to have a church that expressed worldly attitudes; and modern theology, attempting "to reconcile faith and knowledge," was trying to permeate the church with the worldly spirit. Attempts to bring the church under the domination of the state were aimed at hindering the free spiritual expression of the church, and well-intentioned attempts to democratize the church were likewise serving the secular spirit. The worldly spirit was now very strong, but there were signs that the Spirit of God was growing in strength among the youth, from whom the future leadership must come. In spite of all the conflicts, the present time was thus a blessed time and the Pentecostal Spirit still effectual.

In the same issue the *Kreuzzeitung* reported that the Association of Freethinkers intended to present a petition to the Reichstag opposing the religious form of the oath of loyalty now required of members of that body and asking for repeal of the clause in the present criminal code providing punishment for blasphemy. Four days later the *Kreuzzeitung* reported various ways that the liberal press had treated the Pentecost theme—in general, "honoring the creation instead of the Creator." The National Liberal *National Zeitung* had written regarding the "unity and brotherhood of humanity"; the left-liberal *Berliner Tageblatt* had run an article on the "education of neglected children"; the German Liberal Charlottenburg *Neue Zeit* had criticized the church for preaching love but actually sowing race and class hatred; the *Kleines Journal* had associated the Holy Spirit with putting on extra trains in the spring for people in Berlin to go out to the countryside; the *Berliner Börsen Zeitung* had written that the crowds of Berliners hurrying to the railroad stations to get out into the country, the new-leaved trees, the birds, all were expressions of the Holy Spirit; the radical *Berliner Volkszeitung* had called for criticism of the biblical myths and liberation of the moral sense of the people from its religious component. A new age and a new spirit might very well be in the offing; there appeared, however, to be little agreement with the *Kreuzzeitung* as to their true character.[30]

Pentecost seemed to provide the *Frankfurter Zeitung* with, if not the spirit of prophecy, at least a closer feeling for reality. It found the present period darker and more anxious than for many years. "Error and confusion [*Irrungen und Wirrungen*] wherever we look, no certainty of goals, no clarity of outlook . . . hope and fear contend with each other." The kaiser's illness had prevented him from developing the free initiative from which so much had been hoped. It was blindness or self-delusion if one still thought in terms of a new era for Germany. "In Germany and in Prussia today the Reich Chancellor Prince Bismarck rules more absolutely than ever before, and the governmental program of Kaiser Frederick has become a historical document." The *Frankfurter* nevertheless maintained hope for the future: "No prince can bring freedom to a nation that lacks the impulse for freedom, but neither can the most brilliant ruler permanently withstand the will of a people that perseveres in striving for freedom."[31]

The pressure now mounting on the House of Deputies in regard to the school-aid bill brought to a head the question of who was to control the German Conservative party. Was it to continue to follow Bismarck, or was it to follow Baron von Hammerstein and the *Kreuzzeitung* and, dedicating itself to the service of the crown prince, defy the chancellor while Kaiser Frederick still lived by offering the future William II an alternative? More generally, was it as a party to continue to support the bureaucratic, authoritarian Prussian state, or should it declare its political as well as ideological independence and attempt to coerce the government in a parliamentary or semiparliamentary sense? It is a measure of the ideological inflexibility and stubbornness of Hammerstein, first, that he should have got Rauchhaupt and the party into such a situation and, second, that he should have persisted in his error. Since the Herrenhaus debate, the *Kreuzzeitung* observed on May 20, a campaign had been mounted against the Conservatives throughout the whole middle-party and official press. Yet considerations of friendship and party loyalty made it necessary for the *Kreuzzeitung* itself to publish a series of articles by von Kleist-Retzow, a member of the Herrenhaus, explaining why the bill did not necessitate a constitutional amendment and why the Conservative party should, in any case, follow the lead indicated by the government and the Herrenhaus. Kleist was the most venerable and respected of the clerical right wing, having been one of the founders of the *Kreuzzeitung* in 1848. The Conservatives, wrote Kleist, must be careful; "if they do not operate correctly, they can through this vote be pressed hard against the wall." It would be well to avoid such a possibility in advance. It would be irresponsible to kill the bill at this point. "The Conservative party . . . may not permanently entrench itself in an untenable position." Persistence in holding such a position might bring about a fatal split in the party. Every organized activity demanded concessions and accommodations, and since Conservatives supported the independent authority of the crown, they must yield when royal government and upper house were united against them.[32]

On May 24 Baron von Hammerstein replied to the arguments of von Kleist-Retzow in the *Kreuzzeitung* with a signed leading article. The time was past for discreet anonymity; this was an open bid for leadership. Kleist, he wrote, was wrong about the attitude of the members of the Conservative delegation in the House of Deputies toward the constitutional clause. It had been thoroughly discussed and no pressure had been put on individuals, who had therefore voted their personal convictions. No new substantive arguments had since been raised; why should Conservative deputies give in to the clever tactics of Minister von Scholz? The government had also not been as united in its stand as Kleist had suggested. Minister von Gossler had on several occasions indicated his willingness to accept the constitutional clause. The fact was that the government had taken a hostile stand only after Conservative–National Liberal cooperation broke down and the Conservatives "had temporarily allied themselves so firmly with the Center that they could not retreat without a severe moral defeat. . . . Apparently it is a question of the first step *of a great political campaign to eliminate the danger of a clerical-Conservative alliance.*" Von Kleist had evidently recognized this situation but was afraid of a defeat for the Conservatives in the elections. "I," wrote Hammerstein defiantly, "do not share these anxieties." It would be better, he wrote, to be "numerically weakened than morally broken."[33]

The major assumption behind Baron Hammerstein's defiance was that with the new kaiser and king there would also be a new government. Only a government other than Bismarck's would be likely in the fall to bring in a new bill acceptable to a clerical-Conservative majority. To a later observer his defiance of Bismarck is amazing. Apparently Hammerstein's thinking was rigorously simplistic: like General Waldersee, he assumed that everything must bow to the will of a new, dynamic young king. And he was justifiably sure of Crown Prince William's orthodox Protestant orientation. Yet the political situation was quite complex. The chancellor had prestige, habit, and a powerful machine of patronage and propaganda in being. Furthermore, not all members of the Conservative party were as orthodoxly oriented as Hammerstein, Waldersee, Puttkamer, and Stoecker. A clerical-Conservative majority emphasizing ideology and orthodoxy would challenge not only the chancellor, but all liberal and even moderate opinion. An article printed in the *Hamburger Korrespondenz* suggested that if the Conservative party changed its vote in the House of Deputies and followed the lead of the government and Herrenhaus, then the sins that had been committed against the cartel in the last few weeks would be forgiven the party as a whole and charged only against the account of "von Rauchhaupt, Hammerstein and friends." Here was an out for the rank-and-file Conservative deputy. Also the raucousness with which the German Liberal and Center party press demanded that the Conservatives stick to their convictions made it easier for the government and cartel press to rally the Conservatives back to support of the government and against the opposition, especially with the continuing supposed threat from the left-Liberal coterie around the kaiserin and the kaiser. Even the orthodox Protestant *Reichsbote* advised the party to give in and change its vote, much to the disgust and fury of the Center's *Germania*. A Conservative deputy, declared the Catholic paper, who, having gone on record as favoring the constitutional clause in the bill, now changed his vote and rejected it "would be *stigmatized* for all of public and private life." The "ruling and leading classes," it wrote, should take care lest they present the public with further bad examples. "It is a matter of not calling down the justice of *God* because of such a subjection of conscience and conviction to party and power interests!" Social Democrats, it added in a later issue, should take note. "This society is ripe for *destruction!*"[34]

There was no question of the primary targets of the government and middle-party press campaign. Rauchhaupt and Hammerstein were singled out by name, and a day or so before the opening of the new debate on the school-aid bill in the House of Deputies, the *Norddeutsche* ran a quotation from the *Zeitung für Hinterpommern* suggesting that Hammerstein's Landtag district of Stolp, considering the necessity of the cartel for national policy, might very well elect someone else to represent them. This personal attack, however, gave Hammerstein the opportunity to compel the *Norddeutsche* to print a reply, citing his objections not to the original cartel of February 1887, but to what had become of it since. It represented a hindrance to the Conservative party, preventing introduction of legislation dealing with their special interests—the welfare of the working classes, agriculture, and handicrafts—since nothing could be brought forward that might be opposed by the other two parties. The rise in the grain tariff had been put through by the Conservatives in alliance with the Center, not the middle parties. He was pledged to his constituents to uphold the interests of handicrafts and agriculture. "I believe I am acting according to their wishes when I oppose a political movement that aims at barring the Conservative party from free activity and its own initiative in these areas."[35]

The debate on the bill in the House of Deputies began on Friday, May 25, and in its lead editorial that morning the *Frankfurter Zeitung* forecast a government victory. Finance Minister Scholz might have been the leading government figure in the Herrenhaus action, but "the Conservatives observed with that governmental instinct that distinguishes them that someone stronger than Herr Scholz had come upon them, that a person other than the finance minister was speaking." Why this stronger person had not intervened in the affair at an earlier stage was a mystery. "It is not improbable that the leading statesman wanted also to make the Conservatives the object of a 'test of strength,' to 'make an example.'" A Conservative-Center alliance would threaten all the efforts of the chancellor over a period of years to build "a great middle party.... He will probably also have ascertained that in that quarter that is authoritative for the future configuration of politics [the crown prince] no inclination is at hand, through favoring or tolerating an alliance that outwardly carries the stamp of reaction, to drive wide strata of the middle class, which through lengthy efforts have been won for the government, once again into the ranks of the opposition." Most of the Conservatives would submit; Bismarck would celebrate another triumph. "He will come another step closer to his goal, the construction of a middle party to serve the government. He has gradually driven liberal desires out of the National Liberals, now it is a matter of driving from the Conservatives the last remnant of the inclination to go with the Center and at the same time the last impulse toward independence. Herr von Rauchhaupt has brought the beast so happily into his sights that the shot cannot possibly miss."[36]

The evening and morning before the debate in the House of Deputies, the Conservative Landtag delegation held caucuses that were attended by the leader of the Reichstag Conservatives, von Helldorff-Bedra, who had made a special trip to Berlin for the purpose, and whom the *Frankfurter Zeitung* called "the real head of the party." A majority of the Conservative deputies voted to support the Herrenhaus version of the bill. In the session of the House of Deputies on May 25 von Rauchhaupt declared that the Conservative party had always been ready to sacrifice its own interests for the good of the whole. Some of the party would stand by their previous position, while others would vote for the Herrenhaus version of the bill so as to avoid conflict with the other house and with the government. The Center leader Windthorst stated that when a serious constitutional question was at issue it was "not permissible" to change one's opinion for purely tactical reasons within a couple of weeks. He could not understand how the piously religious von Kleist could recommend handing the schools completely over to the state. There were no factual reasons for Finance Minister Scholz seizing the initiative instead of Ministers Gossler or Friedberg, or for the way that Scholz had acted—"merely an exchange of letters between Varzin and Berlin." In the House of Deputies on the twenty-fifth the constitutional clause was voted down, 179 to 148, a small group of Conservatives, including Rauchhaupt and Hammerstein, still voting with the Center. In the final vote on the whole bill, which was 194 to 121, only Hammerstein and two others among the Conservatives voted against it. According to the *Frankfurter*'s Stein, Helldorff had still been working on Conservative members in the lobby before the session, and the party in general resented the pressure that was being applied by the government. That day Chancellery Chief Franz von Rottenburg wrote to Kuno Rantzau in Varzin that he had been in the House of Deputies session twice. "Since Rauchhaupt knuckled under [*unter das Caudinsche Joch gekrochen ist*], I have for the present put aside the article against him. He can be attacked at the time of the elections, and it is probably better to save the powder until then." Two days later he commented, "I am really sorry about the school law affair. We shall feel the results only too keenly [*am eigenen Fleische spüren*]." For its part, Catholic *Germania* printed a list of names of those Conservative deputies who had absented themselves or changed their vote.[37]

32

An Opening toward the Center

AS well as sparking Crown Prince William's enthusiasm for Russian friendship by agitating for a war with France, it is possible that Bismarck also managed to turn him away from Stoecker, Hammerstein, and the *Kreuzzeitung* by dramatizing, in the school-aid bill affair, the necessity of defending the national unity of the cartel against the machinations of the Center party at such a time of crisis. Certainly the crown prince later proved hostile toward the Center. Yet, in the long run, the innately conservative and orthodox religious orientation of the crown prince remained, reinforced by his close personal ties with individuals such as General von Waldersee. The right wing of the Conservative party were the prince's natural allies, and as in the case of the warlike tendencies of the prince, Bismarck might prove more effective in controlling both the ultra-Conservatives and the future kaiser by ostensibly going along with them rather than trying to maintain a potentially dangerous, uncompromisingly hostile stance against them. If it were to become necessary in the future to mount a struggle to control the crown, it would be safer and more effective to do so from the Right, rather than the Left, since the Right represented leading elements of the power structure.

It would not have been like Bismarck to have overlooked any eventuality, and the fact was that he had already at the time of the Conservative slaughter taken the initial step toward the possibility of governing with a Conservative-Center party alignment. Since the late 1870s he had, of course, been moving toward an end to the Kulturkampf and an accommodation with the Catholic church, but had managed to carry out the gradual relaxing and repeal of the specific Kulturkampf legislation through negotiations with the pope, not with the opposition Center party. He had, in fact, as in the case of the *Septennat* of 1887, used his influence with the pope to try to drive a wedge between the conservative wing of the Center, led by the Bavarian aristocrat Baron Georg Arbogast von und zu Franckenstein, titular head of the Reichstag Center delegation and former vice-president of the Reichstag, and the more particularistic and democratically oriented elements of the party under the leadership of Ludwig Windthorst, with his Hanoverian ties. During the winter of 1886–87 Bismarck had negotiated directly with Franckenstein in regard to possible support for the *Septennat* bill, and although for the sake of party unity Franckenstein had ultimately followed Windthorst's lead, nevertheless the relations between the chancellor and the Bavarian conservative Catholic remained cordial. Franckenstein, of an old noble family, held the position of grand chancellor of the Bavarian order of Saint George, an order of knighthood originating in the Crusades and the center of influential social and economic circles in Munich. He was also president of the upper house of the Bavarian Landtag. Yet he was not a member of the Bavarian government, nor were conservative Catholics influential in that government, a situation that probably harked back to the days of royal absolutism.[1]

Like other German states, Catholic Bavaria was run by a bureaucracy—in this case liberal and even Protestant—from which the ministers were chosen in a self-perpetuating fashion. There were actually several Protestants in the ministry. Under the remote and increasingly eccentric King Ludwig II, the ministry had had things much its own way. When, in 1886, Ludwig had been deposed, there was for a while some concern because of the Catholic piety of the late king's uncle, Prince Regent Luitpold, but the latter was under the influence of his adjutant, General Ignaz, Baron Freyschlag von Freyenstein, who was made chief of the regent's privy chancellery in 1886, and who had a German national, military orientation and was therefore hostile to ultramontane and Center-party influences. The liberal-bureaucratic government had thus gone on much as before. Since the war against Prussia in alliance with Austria had excited the general populace in 1866 and resulted in the formation of an oppositional "Patriot party," allied with and now indistinguishable from the Center party, that party, representing the Catholic masses, had held a majority in the Chamber of Deputies of the Landtag. With assistance from Berlin during the Kulturkampf, the bureaucratic government had successfully governed against it and in spite of it. But with increasing political awareness on the part of the populace and with the turn in Berlin away from the Kulturkampf and toward conciliation with the Catholics, it became progressively more difficult for the Bavarian ministry, under the leadership of Baron Johann von Lutz,* to maintain its position.[2]

---

* Lutz was a Catholic, the son of a schoolteacher, who had entered the Ministry of Justice in 1860, was named cabinet secretary and ennobled in 1866, was made minister of justice in 1867, minister of the interior in 1869, chairman of the council of ministers in 1880, and a baron in 1883.[3]

The narrow elitism and self-satisfaction of the leading liberal bourgeois and aristocratic classes in Bavaria were revealed in a remark of the *Münchener Allgemeine Zeitung* (one of those liberal papers recommended by Bamberger to the kaiserin) during the press controversy over the majority election system, when it had called universal suffrage "a false step that can no longer be reversed." Rather than broaden this leadership cadre by taking Catholic leaders into the government, the Lutz administration preferred to buy the party off with concessions (such as calling the neo-Thomist Professor Baron von Hertling from Bonn to the University of Munich in 1882) and to soften the Center party leadership with favors and appointments. The result of this practice had been, however, by 1888, the discrediting of the older leaders and the emergence in the Center party of new, more intransigent, "fiery" leaders. As the growing political awareness among the masses and greater alienation from the government of the Center leadership gradually undermined the position of Lutz and the liberals, they also automatically enhanced the political prospects of the Catholic aristocrats in the "court party." This group included such people as the minister to Berlin, Count Hugo zu Lerchenfeld-Koefering and the under secretary in the German Foreign Office, Count Maximilian von Berchem.

There were few ties between the tight aristocratic circle of the court party and the raw, uncultivated and bigoted democratic elements of the Center party. Here Baron Franckenstein, with his Center connections, had both an advantage and an opportunity; a Catholic ministry under his leadership could possibly use religion as the basic cement for constructing a broad consensus in Bavarian politics such as had not previously existed, perhaps making some social and economic gestures to appease the masses and at the same time restraining the party's more extreme ideological and social tendencies with the reins of responsible statesmanship. Such an enhancement of the position of the conservative Catholics in Bavaria would give them more weight in the Center party as a whole and render it more cooperative with the Reich government in Berlin through the necessary continuous coordination of policies between Bavaria and Prussia in the Bundesrat. A rapprochement of this sort between the Center, with much of its electoral strength in Bavaria, and Bismarck would also give the chancellor a non-Prussian force to use to help control the extreme Protestant clericals in the Conservative party. Bismarck had fought the Center party in the early 1870s because it had represented anti-Prussian, particularistic forces. But German nationalist sentiment was stronger now and those dangers less important. Basically the Catholic church stood for authority and deference to the existing social order. Ideologically it was as antipathetic to both liberals and socialists as the Conservatives were. The Center party, as widely based as the church, was a genuine mass party, whereas the Conservatives mainly represented the Prussian ruling class. The kind of arrogant narrowness and Prussian provincialism of outlook illustrated by the blunders of Hammerstein and Rauchhaupt in the school-aid bill affair could perhaps be offset by the more relaxed, cosmopolitan, and pragmatic view of the South German Catholics.[4]

Exerting influence from Berlin of the kind suggested on Center party and Bavarian politics naturally required the utmost discretion and sensitivity to the chancellor's intentions. The Prussian minister to Bavaria, however, Count Georg von Werthern, had been posted there in 1867 and, now seventy-two, was wholly devoted to the earlier, liberal-oriented, Kulturkampf line. His secretary of legation happened to be an intimate friend of Crown Prince William, Count Philipp zu Eulenburg-Hertefeld, whose Protestant, North German view of Bavarian politics agreed with Werthern's. In early June 1888, Eulenburg wrote to Herbert Bismarck, an old school friend, that "Berchem is close to the [Bavarian] party that wants a Catholic ministry loyal to the Reich, this monstrosity of tight rope walkers that always topple toward the Roman side." By 1886 the elder Bismarck had decided that he must replace Werthern, who had ceased to be useful to him in the changed situation, but he had postponed the move because of the crisis in Bavarian politics caused by the removal of King Ludwig II. Now, in February 1888, Werthern was somewhat unceremoniously hustled into retirement, and the position was given to Bismarck's son-in-law, Count Kuno zu Rantzau, who as private secretary was by now quite familiar with the workings of the old man's mind. The appointment was evidently arranged with the active cooperation of both Berchem and Lerchenfeld, Holstein reporting to Eulenburg that Berchem was taking credit for it.

The Catholic party in Munich naturally read Rantzau's replacement of Werthern as an indication of a possible turn by Bismarck away from the liberals and toward the Center. Eulenburg and Holstein saw it the same way and set out to oppose it. In addition to his ideological orientation, Eulenburg also wanted to become Prussian minister himself in Munich— a comfortable spot for his artistic and other tastes—and had no compunction about enlisting the crown prince in his support. The crown prince told Herbert in April 1888 to get another post for Rantzau, that Philipp Eulenburg must become minister in Munich. It is an interesting and striking measure of the importance the Bismarcks placed on Rantzau's Munich mission that they, at this critical time, completely ignored and resisted this request of the crown prince. The most important and influential element of the Catholic court party were the royal Bavarian princes, and it is interesting to find Herbert writing his brother-in-law on June 10 that, now that he had his formal reception by the prince regent behind him, "you can now devote yourself to the princes." To the Protestant Foreign Minister Christoph Kraft, Baron von Crailsheim, Rantzau delivered a message from the chancellor that—contrary to appearances—"things had remained the same and would remain the same." which Crailsheim reported with satisfaction to Lerchenfeld in Berlin, remarking that it "should be of interest" to him.[5]

A significant aspect of this move of Bismarck's toward a possible alignment with the Center was the fact that it was a move toward a mass party. In a modern constitutional, electoral system if it was the personality on the throne that was the main problem, if it was the authority of the crown that was to be opposed or controlled—as already momentarily in the Battenberg affair—a counterauthority of sufficient ultimate power could be found only in the people. This is not to say that Bismarck was considering revolution or even a truly popular movement—whatever that might be. It was more a matter of ultimate legitimation and organization of public opinion. The traditional aristocratic, secular leadership in Bavaria would tend to offset the clerical fanaticism and international entanglements of Roman Christianity. On the Protestant side Bismarck had been trying to do the same thing for some time by appealing to the economic interests of the Prussian Junker gentry with his protective tariff—an issue that also attracted the peasantry. Given the strength of the liberal tendency in Protestantism, it would not be possible for the Junkers to attract a mass following on the basis of orthodox Protestant Christianity. The economic appeal to the peasants, handicraftsmen, and shopkeepers was undoubtedly the more practical, as even Hammerstein and Stoecker at least partly recognized. If it came to an impasse with the future kaiser and it became necessary to develop the Conservative Junker elite as a political power independent of the crown and exerting power over it (under the leadership and tutelage of the chancellor, not against him), they would have to develop a wider political base than they had so far. Also, a less fanatically ideological, more pragmatically economic and social basis for a Center-Conservative lineup might make it possible to extend such a government block to include the moderate Liberals.

In late March Bismarck sent a message through Chancellery Chief Rottenburg to an old friend and loyal follower whose estate was in Prussian Saxony, asking if the peasants' leagues in that province had proved politically useful. Material interests were tangible, had limits, could be rationally compromised and adjusted, and would not challenge an overall national consensus; ideological loyalties recognized no limits, demanded total irrational devotion, and could not be compromised with honor. For the practical politician to attempt to move politics onto the material, economic level was to try to move it from the irrational to the rational and from the impossible to the possible.[6]

33

The Fall of Puttkamer

WHEN Bismarck left Berlin for Varzin on May 15, he had likely
planned a third event to take place in his absence, along with the
wedding of Prince Henry and the disciplining of the Conservatives over
the school-aid bill. In her reflections on the year 1888, Kaiserin Victoria
wrote that "it came to Fritz's ears that in his heart the Reich Chancellor
wanted to remove Puttkamer, but would never take the initiative in it
because of collegial, family [Bismarck's wife Johanna was a Puttkamer],
and party considerations! . . . Fritz had only been waiting for an opportunity to rid himself and his government of a minister whose orientation
and principles appeared to him to be so pernicious." When he heard that
Bismarck was willing to sacrifice Puttkamer, Kaiser Frederick's eyes, she
wrote, "lit up with satisfaction." A week after her husband's death, the
kaiserin told approximately the same story to Prince Chlodwig Hohenlohe
during an audience at Friedrichskron. The fall of Puttkamer had been
brought about by the kaiser, the kaiserin said, not by her. "Bismarck
wanted himself to get rid of Puttkamer and had transferred the odium
of the dismissal to the kaiser, as he indeed always understood how to
unload the odium of what he did onto other people." On May 22 Kaiserin
Victoria wrote to her mother that her husband was eating a bit better and
was feeling stronger and less depressed "and is able to think of all sorts
of things & . . . [*sic*]." The following day Pindter noted in his diary that
Dr. Mackenzie had told a reporter that in a few days great things would
happen, that Puttkamer and von Richthofen, the president of the Prussian
police, would fall. In her written account the kaiserin stated that Prince
Radolin was the only one who was in on the Puttkamer affair, that Radolin
"in a truly moving way" had done his utmost "to support his dying
Kaiser and to bring his will to bear, always concerned in the process to
smooth the way and maintain a good relationship with the Reich
chancellor."[1]

With the chancellor's personal barometer set on "storm," other factors naturally cooperated in bringing it about. As he had done with the ministry (see above, pp. 256–58, 271), before he left Berlin he had told his banker Bleichröder—a notorious gossip—that he was concerned not about a possible turn for the worse in the kaiser's health in his absence, but rather "that the kaiserin might carry out some sort of coup that would be difficult to put right." And when he did not sleep well on the night of the twenty-fourth, he told Rantzau that it was because he was worrying about the possible acts of the kaiserin. Rantzau speculated that it was a report that Dr. von Bergmann had said that the present condition of Kaiser Frederick could continue indefinitely that had upset the prince. Bismarck had complained that one could manage if necessary for six to eight weeks with a kaiser who was unable to rule, but not for any manner of months. "He . . . would not be able to endure it," wrote Rantzau, "eternally on the qui vive, to stand up against impossible feminine demands along with a kaiser without a will of his own. One could naturally not mention it publicly, but he would look to his health and resign." The sleepless night might very well have been provoked by the concern that Bismarck's contradictory, complicated double-dealing could not successfully be prolonged indefinitely, that after a certain time he would be sure to be exposed. The fact that he was not letting even his family in on his arrangements with the royal couple meant that he was also using them, especially encouraging, with his complaints of the kaiserin, Herbert's natural irritability. Thus, after Prince Henry's wedding on the twenty-fourth, Herbert insensitively complained to the Prince of Wales—Kaiserin Victoria's brother—that a king who could not discuss really could not rule. The affronted prince wrote to his mother indignantly that if it had not been for English-German relations he would have thrown the fellow out.[2]

The heightened sense of crisis, of a threat from the Left, which the chancellor had been deliberately promoting, along with the expectation of the imminent succession of the crown prince, produced in Puttkamer himself—as in the group closest to him politically, the *Kreuzzeitung* Conservatives—exaggerated expressions of his own authoritarian tendencies. Early in May the German Liberal delegation in the Prussian House of Deputies had introduced a motion, in line with their general agitation against government influence on elections, asking the government to instruct its local officials to abide more strictly by the law in drawing the boundaries of electoral precincts. This was an especially touchy subject for Puttkamer since the House seat of his own brother, Puttkamer-Plauth, was at that moment in the hands of the election commission, which was about to recommend its invalidation because of gerrymandering of district boundaries as well as bribery of electors. Under the circumstances it would have been more sensible merely to have ignored the motion.

Puttkamer, however, entered energetically into the fray, declaring the resolution to be an attempt by the House of Deputies to get control over the administration and thus infringe upon the rights of the crown. Making such an issue of the matter, as the *National Zeitung* pointed out, guaranteed that "all constitutionally minded citizens" would rally against him, and in fact the National Liberals voted along with the Center and German Liberals to pass the motion, Puttkamer being supported only by the Conservatives. Defending Puttkamer, the *Kreuzzeitung* stated that it was necessary to oppose even the first tentative attempts at parliamentary government. The *National Zeitung* thought that the Conservatives, in their noisy support of Puttkamer in the debate, were acting as if they wanted to give up the cartel and try for a majority of their own in the upcoming elections. In the debate the two party groups, Conservatives on one side and German Liberals on the other—the dedicated supporters of the crown prince and Kaiser Frederick respectively—had been too excited to remain in their seats. "Crowded closely together," wrote the *Kölnische Zeitung*, "they stood on the two wings of the house and set up a terrific racket, so that it was a good thing that the calmer elements of the National Liberals and the Center remained in their seats and thereby kept the two warrior bands apart."[3]

Ambassador Széchényi, in a report to Count Kálnoky on May 5, put the air of excitement and crisis in a more general context.

> Since the death of Kaiser William, I no longer know my Berlin and its inhabitants. A piece of water flowing quietly and peacefully in its stone-lined channel has become a wild woods' brook that breaks through all gates. ... The people of the previous administration to whom no attention is paid any more by the present one give their ill humor regarding everything that occurs all the freer rein since they know that their time has gone by, while the place hunters who believe they can rely on Kaiser William II place no restrictions on their criticism because they hope thereby to make for themselves a little impression for the perhaps quite near future. In between lies the great mass of the unambitious but careful who prefer to avoid all unpleasantnesses, but they too are grumbling, on the one hand because the others are doing it, on the other hand because, given the undoubted shortness of the present reign, they are in a position to give themselves this pleasure— and it is one for them—without experiencing any further consequences.

Even the Foreign Office, he noted, seemed preoccupied with domestic affairs to the extent of not reacting to the mention of General Boulanger. Herbert Bismarck had seemed not to be aware of a report from Russia that had been in the papers for two days.[4]

The report of the election commission asking for the invalidation of two seats in the House of Deputies, including that of Puttkamer-Plauth, came up for debate in the House on the last day of the session, May 26, right after the vote on the school-aid bill. Heinrich Rickert and Eugen Richter, leaders of the German Liberal party, apparently "contriving" an "occasion" in line with Bamberger's suggestion to the kaiserin, mounted an outspoken, emotional attack on the progovernment influence of the local *Landräthe* on elections and the unequal handling by the government of governmental and opposition newspapers. German Liberal papers had been indicted for reprinting the article of the *Dresdener Nachrichten* entitled "No Petticoat Politics!" whereas cartel papers had printed with impunity slanders against the kaiserin that were just as bad. Rickert declared that electoral influence was no service to the crown but only to the ministers. The bureaucracy was acting "as if state institutions were their private property." The German Liberal Alexander Meyer reminded the House that in 1858 Kaiser William, then regent, had issued an order to the local officials to refrain from exerting any influence on the elections, and it had given new life and spirit to the country. A new order of that kind was now needed. Meyer was telling only part of the story. Kaiser William had later regretted that order when the parliament opposed his army reforms, and in 1882, when a German Liberal-Center-Social Democratic oppositional majority existed in the Reichstag, he had issued a new order declaring it to be the duty of officials "to represent the policy of my government [in] the elections." In effect, the German Liberals wanted Kaiser Frederick to reverse this order of 1882 and thereby inaugurate a new era in Prussian politics, where voting was open and influence relatively easy. Eugen Richter homed in on the underhanded influencing of the press by the Bismarck regime in the Battenberg affair. Official documents and details that were known only to the imperial family and the chancellor had been published.

> If the hundredth part of the abuse had been thrown at Prince Bismarck that in those weeks was hurled against Kaiserin Victoria (very true! on the left; stick to the subject! on the right) That is on the subject! You don't like it!—then the prisons would be filled with hundreds of people. . . . If the elections are merely a test of how far the . . . power of the ministers . . . extends over the free will of the people, then the popular assembly is itself only a creation . . . of the government. . . . Rather than allow such a pseudo-constitutionalism to develop . . . we should rather return to the absolutist system (quite right! on the left).

Free elections, said Richter, would guard the rights of the crown because the crown would never rule against the people's will.[5]

One wonders which left Liberal it was who shouted his approval of a call for a return to absolutism. The extreme virulence of feeling displayed by Right and Left in the debate cannot all be attributed to differences in social and economic status: agrarian Junker gentry against middle-class money men. The emotional heat was engendered more by the clash of the diametrically opposite ideals held by the two warring bands—embodied in the persons of Crown Prince William on the one hand and of Kaiser Frederick on the other. No doubt economic and social self-interest provided the fuel, but it was idealism that made it take fire: on the Right, devotion to Tradition, Discipline, Authority, emanating from the Divine Mind and represented on earth by church and king; on the Left, devotion to Individual Freedom, rooted in confidence in the powers of the human mind. Both groups were uncompromisingly dedicated and sincere. The one thing they both agreed on was that the middle parties and the Bismarck regime they supported were immoral, because they did not hew consistently to an ideological line. Both sides deplored Bismarck's use of deception, trickery, and coercion because they were convinced of the inevitable victory of their own ideal. But their devotion, their mutual strength, and the intensity of the hostility between them refuted that basic assumption.

Stein in the *Frankfurter Zeitung* applauded Eugen Richter's bold attack, which had caught the cartel off guard and expressed openly what many people had been thinking for a long time and had thus cleared the air. Herbert Bismarck was shocked that the president of the House of Deputies had allowed Richter to mention members of the royal family in debate and also that none of the ministers had tried to reply—apparently because it was at the end of the session and unexpected. "To have let Richter have the last word that way is a scandal and detrimental, 500 of the best articles in all the papers won't help against it." The *Norddeutsche* commented that Richter had merely taken advantage of parliamentary immunity to say on the floor of the House of Deputies what he could not print in his paper. The National Liberal *Hannoverscher Kourier* suggested that the German Liberal attack meant they were trying to replace Bismarck, which in the present critical situation amounted to putting their own party interests above those of the nation. People in many countries, including Germany, did not want parliamentary government, were tired of party bickering, and longed for the "return to a solid, secure, and orderly state of affairs." The governmental *Berliner Politische Nachrichten* suggested ominously that in depicting the kaiser as helpless in the hands of the ministry Richter was probably advocating a regency. The *Reichsbote* quoted Richter's own previous words that "whoever carries the imperial standard into electoral conflicts . . . does not contribute to the cherishing of the monarchy [*Kaisertums*] among the German people." Count Lerchenfeld reported to Munich that Richter's speech was clearly an electoral campaign speech, claiming that the German Liberals were the party that truly supported the kaiser, and that this approach would not be without effect. The *Freisinnige Zeitung* stated that when Kaiser Frederick read the stenographic text of the House of Deputies session containing Richter's speech, he wrote on a slip of paper, "The right word at the right time." This was immediately denied by the *Berliner Politische Nachrichten*, but nevertheless carries the ring of authenticity. The kaiserin wrote to Bamberger that the kaiser had "nodded and smiled" when he read the speech, and Crown Prince William wrote that his mother had exclaimed enthusiastically over the speech, "At last there is someone who defends [me]!" Marschall von Bieberstein reported to Karlsruhe that usually informed circles were describing Richter's speech as "a task ordered from Charlottenburg."[6]

In spite of the provocation of the Richter speech, a majority of the House of Deputies voted to invalidate the seats of the two deputies, since the evidence of improper influence was too glaring. This action was so late in coming, however, that the deputies had been able to complete their full term—a situation that the various newspapers agreed was by no means unusual for either Landtag or Reichstag: it took a whole session to get the committee to act, another for it to make its report, and a third for the full House to act on it; by then that particular House had run its course. On May 26, the day of Richter's speech, Minister of the Interior Puttkamer presented the bill extending the life of the Landtag from three years to five to the kaiser for his signature. The bill had been passed by both houses for the first time in February and again in early May, and Puttkamer had conscientiously been holding it back because Kaiser Frederick, following Bamberger's advice, had indicated that he did not want to sign it right away. Now, when it was presented to him, the kaiser refused to sign. Puttkamer withdrew without comment, handed the matter over to Minister of Justice Friedberg, and asked him to use his influence. The following day Friedberg spent over an hour explaining to the kaiser why he should sign the bill. Kaiser Frederick wrote on a piece of paper, "That will be a bitter disappointment for the German Liberals!" Friedberg emphasized that the kaiser could not support his government on the minority German Liberals nor go against the majority cartel parties and especially the middle parties that supported his government in a matter of some importance to them. The middle parties, wrote the kaiser in response—accepting the German Liberal line—were "in the hands of the Conservatives." Finally, however, he gave in and wrote, "Speak with my wife!" He then signed the bill. The same day, however, he wrote a letter to Puttkamer informing him that he had signed the legislative period bill but that such an extension of the life of the legislature meant that officials must exert even more effort to make sure that the electoral process was completely free of influence of any kind.[7]

These events took place over the weekend, and on Monday and Tuesday quite accurate and detailed reports of the kaiser's objections to the bill and his signing under pressure appeared in the *Freisinnige Zeitung* and *Münchener Allgemeine Zeitung.* The latter also reported that Kaiser Frederick had accompanied his signature with a letter to the minister of the interior concerning the greater necessity for protecting freedom of voting. Marschall wrote the Baden government that this report concerning a letter from the kaiser to Puttkamer was believed because it had appeared in German Liberal papers. Bamberger noted that it had acted like "a spark in a powder keg."[8]

In the meantime, Princess Johanna von Bismarck had become very ill with bronchitis, and the doctors requested the chancellor to return to Berlin. The princess began to recover almost before Bismarck returned, but there was now no way for him to avoid involvement in the gathering Puttkamer crisis. He had returned to Berlin on May 27, and on Monday the twenty-ninth he had an audience with the kaiser. When the latter indicated that he had signed the legislative period bill, but against his inclinations, the chancellor told him that was unfortunate. The left-liberal press was claiming that he had no will of his own; here was an opportunity to show them that, as an equal part of the legislative process, he had rights too. If he felt strongly against the law he could still refrain from publishing it, since no law could go into effect until it was published in the official *Reichsgesetzblatt.* This concept apparently appealed to the kaiser, and he so directed in a note. Bismarck denied that there had been any official influence on elections. The kaiser's letter to Puttkamer, however, had "done good." According to Minister of Agriculture Lucius, Bismarck then went directly to the adjutants' room in the palace and told the whole story, "as merry as an ensign, joking, and drinking cognac." Minister Friedberg was naturally quite flabbergasted. He had asked himself, he told Lucius, "whether it was *he* who was becoming senile or someone else!" He was not sure whether Bismarck's action had been a deep plot, perhaps to give the kaiser the opportunity to change at least some members of the ministry by creating a general crisis, or merely a sudden whim.[9]

The Prussian ministry met three days later, and the chancellor, having encouraged the kaiser to be politically irresponsible and having related the details where they would be sure to be immediately and widely broadcast—especially among Conservative Junker circles—was apparently somewhat embarrassed at having to defend his unorthodox behavior before his very serious colleagues. He had advised the kaiser, he said, for once to carry out his own wishes against ministry and legislature. To this Ministers Friedberg and Scholz objected emphatically that such a procedure would damage the standing of the government and the parties supporting it, and in fact already had. Further delay and confusion would only increase the damage and would eventually be a bad influence on the fall Landtag elections. If the ministers acquiesced in the kaiser's arbitrary act it would look as if they were only holding onto their posts and had no principles. Also, the chancellor had acted in a Prussian matter without consulting his ministerial colleagues; it looked, said Scholz sharply, as if he wanted to get rid of them.

According to Lucius, in response Bismarck then digressed and talked of all sorts of apparently unrelated subjects—at least as far as the bureaucratic ministers were concerned, who were narrowly fixed on the business at hand, on maintaining the façade of authority, respectability, and power, and on keeping the governmental machinery running smoothly. The chancellor complained about Eugen Richter's agitational activity. He criticized Puttkamer (which might have been noted if the other ministers had not been so excited and preoccupied with the present issue) for having delayed so long in presenting the bill for signature (he must have known the reason). He, Puttkamer, would discipline one of his own counselors who acted so. The kaiserin had indicated that her chief opponents were Stoecker and Waldersee (Puttkamer's right-wing friends). None of these hints made any difference; the other ministers were basically affronted that proper procedure had been arbitrarily violated, and they lined up solidly against their old chief. The necessity of confronting Kaiser Frederick with collegial ministerial solidarity had led to a much greater frequency of ministerial sessions under his reign and had thus raised the importance of the ministry and the individual ministers. The other ministers—none of them with anything approaching Bismarck's political backing—appear to have taken this development seriously. Well, said Bismarck, after all, publication of the law had no time limit and could be carried out at any time (the kaiser would not live long). "Formally correct," wrote Lucius, "but still against all usage and custom!"

In the end Bismarck gave in to the other ministers, and it was decided that the law should be published soon. Lucius thought that Bismarck was using the ministers to make a tough stand so as to ingratiate himself with the kaiser and kaiserin. There was more to it than that. Encouraging Kaiser Frederick to do what the opposition German Liberals wanted not only cast an ironic light on their parliamentary principles by associating them with an arbitrary act of the crown, but it also created a bogey of sub-rosa German Liberal influence over the crown with which further to excite the *Kreuzzeitung* Conservatives and thus keep them in line and to provide a basic explanation for the eventual removal of Puttkamer. There was also another factor. To one of his colleagues Bismarck complained that the other ministers did not understand his politics. There was only one person who did understand, and that was His Imperial Highness the crown prince. With his naive concepts of the royal prerogative, Crown Prince William was naturally concerned that his father's ineptitude and illness would damage the powers and prestige of the monarchy before his own succession. The laws lengthening the legislative period of both Reichstag and Prussian Landtag had been one of the few major legislative measures upon which the cartel parties had been able to agree in both parliaments and effectively marshal their majority. Encouraging the kaiser to oppose the cartel and the Landtag precisely where they were strongest was probably not a matter of accident or whim with Bismarck. He had a point concerning the royal prerogative that he wanted to dramatize for the crown prince, and the choice of this issue at this time heightened the drama.[10]

Baroness von Stockmar reported to Ludwig Bamberger that Minister Friedberg had used the regency threat in his talk with the kaiser. She showed him a notebook that Friedberg had prepared on the subject, drawing material from the Ministry of Justice files related to the imposition of a regency on the mentally ill King Frederick William IV in 1858. Bamberger wrote the kaiserin that there was no connection with the present situation, since there was nothing wrong with Kaiser Frederick's mind. And yet the phrase "permanent incapacity" in the constitution certainly did leave room for dispute. A pamphlet attacking the German Liberals and English concepts of parliamentarism and advocating a strong monarchy was distributed in Berlin on May 29, unhindered by the police. Bamberger thought it was intended to prepare the ground for a regency but believed it would actually provoke a counterreaction of loyalty and indignation. Bamberger pointed out that the kaiser's signature on the legislative period bill had disposed of his veto. The delay in publication was therefore meaningless. He noted that Kaiserin Victoria refused to give up her faith in Bismarck. They had discovered, the kaiserin had written, that the *Kölnische Zeitung* articles on the Battenberg marriage had been written by Chancellery Chief Rottenburg, behind the chancellor's back. "Sancta Simplicitas!" wrote Bamberger in his diary. For the kaiserin he wrote, melodramatically and with doctrinaire exaggeration, to Baroness von Stockmar, "That the article in the *Kölnische Zeitung* was by Rottenburg is very likely, but that it was written and dispatched without higher orders I can simply *not* believe. In all these regions no one allows himself an original thought or stroke of the pen. One stroke strikes the thousand connections. The rest is silence." The dismissal of Puttkamer, he thought, would be "very desirable," and he urged that he be replaced by a bureaucrat, not a National Liberal.[11]

The Reich chancellor's interpretation of Kaiser Frederick's withholding publication of the legislative period law, as explained to the ministry, duly appeared in the governmental *Berliner Politische Nachrichten*: the law had not yet been published, and if it were indefinitely held up, though they would regret it on the basis of the bill itself, which they supported, they would welcome such a demonstration of royal authority. The parliamentary principles of the German Liberals would reduce the king to "merely the weathervane on the church steeple. Its only function is to show the direction of the wind. It would be good if these gentlemen were shown for once that . . . according to our constitutional law the king has a very decisive influence in determining the direction of the wind." In his report to the Baden government, Marschall von Bieberstein wrote that if the ministry went along with this interpretation he was afraid that "the result among the public will be regarded much more as a triumph of the German Liberal party than as a blow against the 'parliamentary system.'"[12]

The point of view of the *Berliner Politische Nachrichten* found little credence or even serious attention among the party press. The *Kreuzzeitung* declared confidently that no one would dare to question their support for the power of the crown against parliamentary tendencies, but the legislative period law had been supported and passed by the cartel majority with the agreement of the ministry; it had been bitterly opposed, and if the law "does not receive the royal sanction, political consequences automatically flow from it; no disguise can alter that fact." The German Liberal party would be considerably strengthened. The left-liberal papers naturally agreed wholeheartedly with the right-wing conservative *Kreuzzeitung*. If Kaiser Frederick declared himself against the legislative period law, wrote the *Vossische Zeitung*, "then it will be known among the people that one can be a true royalist [*durchaus königlich gesinnt*] and still be in the opposition against the government in office."[13]

Significantly, the strongest attack on the government-inspired *Berliner Politische Nachrichten*'s interpretation came from another government-oriented paper, the *Kölnische Zeitung*, which was most likely replaying its role in the Battenberg crisis, except that in that affair the official government press had kept silent, whereas now it was defending the crown's arbitrary act. There was no doubt, reported the *Kölnische* on June 2, that for the second time since the accession of Frederick III a crisis existed in Prussia. If the legislative period law were not to be published, the result would have to be the retirement of the entire ministry. The probably government-inspired article took a surprisingly parliamentary view: "If His Majesty is of a different opinion from that of the majority of the parliament and the whole ministry, . . . then clarification of our situation requires that His Majesty try it out with new advisors and discover the opinion of the country concerning these new men through new elections. As little as we hold the so-called parliamentary system to be salutary, we are, on the other hand, decidely of the opinion that in important questions there must be agreement between the crown and the ministry."[14]

If it was true, the *Kölnische* wrote on June 4, that Kaiser Frederick had directed that the legislative period law should not be published, "that fact would have a very unpleasant significance for the national and state-supporting parties." For months the German Liberals had been trying to create the impression that the kaiser was at heart not inclined toward the government or the parties friendly to the government. A clear statement should be made destroying this legend, or, if there was truth in it, the constitutional conclusions should be drawn. The claim of the *Berliner Politische Nachrichten* that the kaiser's holding up publication of the legislative period law would be a lesson for the German Liberals was "too ingenious." The *Kölnische* agreed with Marschall von Bierberstein that such "fine dialectic" would have no chance of impressing the voting public. The country wanted an assurance of unity among its ruling groups. "What is of use to us is not proof that we live in a monarchy, but proof that in this monarchy the continuity of the governing principles has not been interrupted by the succession to the throne and that behind government policy the authority stands firm and solid of all those men to whom each German looks up with love and reverence." What was needed was not "the tightrope-walking sophistry of official underlings," but clarity, decisiveness, and courageous openness. This was certainly not the *Kölnische*'s normal style, nor was even Rottenburg usually this incisive. Who on the government side other than Bismarck himself would dare describe his own arguments so accurately as "tightrope-walking sophistry"? One senses here the genuine fervor of an experienced statesman fighting to protect his statecraft—not from this present artificially contrived threat, but from possible similar threats in the next reign. The language also expressed vividly the frustration of the government parties and served as a rallying cry for the cartel. In a later edition the same day the *Kölnische* wrote that the position of the chancellor in the crisis was not clear. It was therefore uncertain whether the matter was of basic importance or something that could be smoothed over. If—as the *Freisinnige Zeitung* was proclaiming—the legislative period law could be published only in conjunction with a new royal edict regarding freedom of elections, the fact that Bismarck had energetically defended Kaiser William's disciplinary edict of 1882 and could not now very well reverse himself would doubtless prevent his remaining as first minister in the government.[15]

In a letter to his friend General von Stosch on June 2, Baron von Roggenbach agreed that things would not last long enough for a serious crisis to develop. The kaiser, he wrote, would surely not live through the month. Politically he had already become absolutely powerless "and just as insignificant and submissive from sickness as his predecessor from age." Consequently the chancellor, the ministers, and the cabinet chiefs had become used to ordering things in their own way. Two persons, he went on, were keenly sensitive to this decline in the position of the monarchy: the kaiserin and the crown prince. In line with this observation, it is not too surprising to find evidence at this time of a certain softening in the relationship of mother and son. Crown Prince William seems to have been restraining himself quite admirably. Probably his father's imminent end made it easier for him. But it is also clear that various people, not only the chancellor and Herbert, but also Roggenbach and even General von Waldersee, were advising him to hold himself back in a dignified, responsible way. As a special gesture, on May 29 the crown prince led his own brigade of the guards into the Charlottenburg park and past the palace, where his father, dressed in his general's uniform with helmet, reviewed them from the seat of a carriage. Kaiser Frederick seems to have been pleased to have had the opportunity to review his troops for the first—and last—time since his accession, yet one wonders if the obvious visual contrast of the ill father in the carriage and the healthy young son on horseback did not produce a strong, tacit undercurrent of contradictory feelings in them both. Kaiser William II later wrote that this had been one of the most important moments in his father's life—no doubt he meant his own.[16]

How the crown prince really felt about the overall situation is revealed in a letter he wrote to his uncle, the grand duke of Baden, the same day. The lull since the Battenberg crisis, he wrote, was only superficial; a quiet undermining process had continued.

> De facto Mama decides everything. Since she, however, has no political sense, but rather strong personal sympathies and antipathies, there are continuous small clashes, frictions, naggings which have really got on the nerves of the ministry as well as the chancellor. Laws are suggested, rejected, then signed, but the execution is accompanied by a handwritten letter offensive to the ministers; then the publication is again postponed. Suddenly orders without countersignatures are sent for publication to third parties that have nothing to do with them, and decorations are given to those who ought not to receive them.

The person directing it all was Deputy Schrader, whose wife was in constant contact with the kaiserin. The wishes of the German Liberals were transmitted to her in this manner, and Eugen Richter had then repaid her with his defense of her in the Prussian Landtag. The crown prince had spoken with the chancellor today, who had declared that he could not continue to oppose this machine in the long run. "His nerves are completely shot, he can no longer sleep since the constant worry over unpleasant surprises combined with the anxiety over his severely ill wife allows him no rest." If the kaiser continued in this manner, he would resign to preserve his health. Crown Prince William wrote that he, therefore, feared a second and much worse crisis. The following day General von Waldersee noted in his diary that "the kaiserin is now ruling the country. . . . The chancellor is just about fed up with the situation [*Sache*]. But also in the Royal Household, in the Court Marshal's office, in the Royal Stables, etc., there is discontent as a result of the thoughtless, mostly aimless interference of the kaiserin." Needless to say, as Ambassador Széchényi had pointed out, if Kaiser Frederick had been in good health, these various court functionaries would have managed quite well to put up with the kaiserin's eccentricities.[17]

On June 1 the royal court moved from Charlottenburg to Potsdam. The kaiser's health had improved enough in the meantime for him to drive with his wife in an open carriage through the Tiergarten, to the great joy of the crowds, to walk in the palace garden or ride around it in a pony cart, and to sit outdoors under a specially constructed tent. The *Frankfurter Zeitung* reported much less discharge, peaceful sleep, and a good appetite. Professor Virchow had examined him and pronounced the lymph nodes "quite healthy," which was a good sign, throwing doubt on the possibility of cancer. The trip to Potsdam was made by water, on board the new, white-painted, eighty-foot steam yacht, *Alexandra*, through the Spree Canal to Lake Havel. The expedition was under the overall command of Crown Prince William, dressed in naval uniform. Azaleas, rhododendrons, and chestnut trees were in bloom, and although the weather was stormy, crowds had assembled early along the banks. The kaiser came down to the ship in his pony cart, dressed in his general's uniform with helmet and overcoat. As he walked over the gangplank the purple royal standard was raised on the mainmast, the imperial standard being carried on the stern. As the ship left the pier thousands broke through the police lines and rushed down to the water's edge, cheering as the kaiser appeared, waving, at the cabin window. Among the crowd were deputations representing various organizations, such as guilds and the Charlottenburg Rowing Club. The railroad bridge of the Ringbahn was decorated with flowers, and at the Charlotten-Brücke in Spandau, in addition to flowers there were flags and pennants, and both approaches to the bridge were lined with young school girls "in holiday dresses with flowers in their hair and hands." Houses along the bank were decorated with flags, and every window was occupied. Factories had been closed, and the workers made up much of the crowd along the banks, along with schoolchildren and fishermen. All the boats in the various harbors were decorated. From the pier at Potsdam the royal party drove in a closed carriage through more crowds past the palace of Sans Souci to the palace of Friedrichskron. The occasion of the trip was taken advantage of to arrange a conciliatory conference on shipboard between the kaiserin and the crown prince. Both agreed that people were sowing discord between them, but each blamed the other's entourage. The kaiserin appears to have been unable to avoid a hectoring tone. In reporting the coming move to Potsdam to Kuno Rantzau in Varzin on May 23, Herbert Bismarck had complained that such a move would be "very inconvenient; God damn this whole abominable Potsdam!" Rantzau agreed; every audience in Potsdam would require a trip of at least three hours. "Heaven knows that monarchs should not get sick or not meddle in affairs."[18]

It is significant that both Count Lerchenfeld and Baron Marschall reported during these days of late May and early June that in spite of complaints, Chancellor Bismarck was in good health and seemed generally to be in good humor as well. He might talk of retirement to the crown prince, but to Minister of Agriculture Lucius von Ballhausen he took a quite different and much more convincing line. Under the present circumstances, he told him on June 4, the ministers must all hang together and not allow even one individual to be peeled off. The kaiserin wanted "to make a sacrifice for her progressive friends because in certain things she is non compos mentis." In such circumstances one could not simply resign and let things deteriorate. "He would hold fast to his chair and not go, even if they wanted to throw him out. He would not go even if they sent him his dismissal, since he would not have countersigned it. If he had allowed himself to be persuaded to go so easily, he would never have accomplished anything, not even the Austrian war. He had had many hard struggles with the last kaiser, one must not go so easily." The legislative period law had been proposed by the Landtag and, although accepted by the government, had not been regarded by it as necessary. Anyway, it could be published at any convenient time. "In the meantime His Majesty was probably already shocked at the significance his refusal had taken on. Things would not last beyond August at the most. Bergmann had forecast that if he lived through May an improvement would take place at that time, which would, however, soon result in new suffering, which would be very painful." Bismarck then complained that the cartel parties were fighting among each other and that they had no appeal for the government. Lucius noted that Bismarck had never favored a longer life for the parliaments, believing that it would strengthen them, whereas the other ministers had all favored it as providing "greater stability and continuity for the government." Bismarck's exhortation to

Lucius in favor of ministerial solidarity should be regarded with skepticism (see below, p. 322), but the determination to stick it out, the harder attitude toward the cartel, and the casting about for more effective party constellations ring true. Bismarck was already living through the problems of the next reign.[19]

When Pindter visited Rottenburg on June 5, the Chancellery chief told him he had a long article for him regarding the crisis. The ministers were going along with the kaiser because they regarded the time as too serious for a crisis—"and ultimately they are right," wrote Pindter. The article in question appeared in the evening edition of the *Norddeutsche Allgemeine Zeitung* the same day. Having promoted an artificial conflict between crown and parliamentary majority, between the governmental *Berliner Politische Nachrichten* and the governmental *Kölnische Zeitung*, the chancellor now took the opportunity, in his semiofficial paper, to deliver a lecture (for the crown prince) on the proper relationship of monarch, ministers, and parliament. The legislative period law, the article began, had been ready for publication for a month, but had not been published; that was the fact. All further speculations lacked firm evidence. It was not known, for example, whether Kaiser Frederick was postponing publication of the law only until he had satisfied himself on the point of governmental influence on elections or whether he had fundamental objections to the law as such. But it was certain that the "parliamentary fiction, according to which there is no question of the opinions and personality of the monarch, does not conform to our constitutional institutions." Since the constitution stipulated, in Article 62 that the agreement of the king along with that of the two houses of the legislature was necessary for legislation, it was important for a minister who was dealing with one of the houses to be sure of the king's approval. The article then quoted Bismarck's speech to the Reichstag in defense of Kaiser William's disciplinary edict of 1882.

Before the granting of the constitution, Bismarck had declared, the king had possessed all the legislative power; the constitution had then given up two-thirds of it to the two chambers, and this had been accepted by the people. Ministers were not mentioned in the constitution and were practical stopgaps. But after the king had appointed his ministers and delegated his share of the legislative power to them, it was not so easy for him to get rid of them or to control them. "A minister is irremoveable if he has a strong majority in one of the chambers or indeed in both chambers or in the Reichstag and satisfies this majority with rights and concessions that he wins from the king," Bismarck had said. That the legislative power of the crown should again be clearly delineated, the article continued, was a good thing. "The proposition that a difference of opinion between the crown and the ministry can find its resolution only in the separation of both from each other finds no support in either our written law or in our tradition." It was a matter of forty years' experience that the ministry frequently could not get the king's agreement for its decisions. "If the cabinet wanted as a consequence to resign every time, our usage of ministers would have almost equalled that of the French. Every minister will be ready to resign when he believes that the position required of him will damage the communal life [*Gemeinwesen*] of the fatherland. Such a danger does not exist in the case in question." The ministers had to consider the effect that a change of ministry would have on public confidence inside the country and in the attitude toward Germany of foreign powers. With sarcasm the article stated that it had been a great advance that the progressive party had come so clearly to recognize the rights of the crown, which they had earlier so heatedly opposed.[20]

In case the crown prince and others did not immediately grasp the hidden implications of the "loyal" *Norddeutsche* article, the *Kölnische Zeitung* spelled them out. Although the *Norddeutsche* article was undeniably adroit, it stated, nevertheless its reasoning remained too fine. For the king to, in effect, cancel a law that had been approved by his own ministry and by both houses of the legislature through the majority parties that supported his government, a law that the opposition parties had attacked most sharply, was clearly to act in favor of the opposition, and no "devious dialectic" could conceal that political fact. Also, it was the opposition press that had revealed the kaiser's hostility to the law and his letter to Puttkamer regarding freedom of elections. It was not merely a question of Puttkamer, who could have been removed "at any politically neutral time" without benefit to the opposition, but rather of the policy orientation of the whole ministry. If the question was not of fundamental importance, nevertheless it was an amendment to the constitution and required serious handling. No doubt all these considerations had been weighed in "responsible circles," and if it had been decided nevertheless that the action of the king should not be greeted with a general resignation of the ministry, such a decision could have been prompted only by "a manifestation of deep and genuine love for the king." One was concerned—unlike the German Liberals "in all their wretchedness"—with sparing His Majesty the work and excitement that a sudden change of ministry would necessarily entail.[21]

In the legislative period affair, the chancellor had encouraged Kaiser Frederick to act out to the letter Crown Prince William's own naive notions of the royal prerogative. Thus—because words and rational argument did not make much impact on the flighty and dramatically inclined crown prince—he had demonstrated (with the assistance of Rottenburg and the *Kölnische Zeitung*) just how much uproar could be caused by the king's ignoring legislature, parties, and public opinion. Also, as in the Battenberg case, that in the face of a highly personal act of the king, even the avowedly monarchist and Christian reactionaries of the *Kreuzzeitung* and *Reichsbote* could not be counted on to be unstintingly loyal, but would react just as much in accord with their particular political interests as any other party. In this demonstration Bismarck was exploiting the political naiveté both of Kaiser Frederick and the German Liberals. He was clearly motivated not as much by his "love for the king" as by a burning concern for the future stability and security of the state—the German nation that he himself had created.

Since receiving Kaiser Frederick's letter admonishing him about governmental influence on elections, Minister of the Interior von Puttkamer had been preparing what he called a "quite conclusive" report denying any such influence and defending his administration. He was inclined, he told Minister of Agriculture Lucius on June 6, to give up the game, in spite of the chancellor's urging him to remain. Everything, in any case, depended on His Majesty's reaction to his report, which he had prepared three days before, but which had not yet been laid before His Majesty, so that "it must have been held up somewhere." In his most recent audience, the kaiser had been quite apathetic and negative toward him so that he had not been able to accomplish anything. Lucius agreed that Puttkamer was being deliberately treated badly and that he could respond only with his resignation. Puttkamer, however, wanted also to ask Minister of Justice Friedberg for his advice. The day before, the kaiserin had declared flatly to Bismarck that under all circumstances Puttkamer must go, which Bismarck had now confirmed to Puttkamer. The crisis would end, therefore, wrote Lucius, at least with Puttkamer's resignation. "Therefore Her Majesty will have realized a further point of her program."[22]

Puttkamer was not the only one who realized the potentialities of the kaiser's possible reaction to his report. On June 1 the German Liberal leader Ludwig Bamberger had written the kaiserin suggesting that "if H.M. replied to Herr v. Puttkamer in a dissatisfied, ungracious way, he would *have* to go, and none of the other ministers, in particular the chancellor, could complain of the kaiser's replying as he pleases to a letter he has received from a minister." It would not be possible to bring Puttkamer back once he was removed. For Puttkamer to maintain his innocence in face of his past boasting about his influence on elections and in face of the case of his own brother would be impermissible arrogance toward the kaiser. Baroness von Stockmar delivered Bamberger's letter to the kaiserin in Potsdam on the next day, June 2, and reported that the kaiserin had read it with great attention and nodded her head "very approvingly" over the passage regarding Puttkamer. The kaiserin, however, was completely taken up by a twenty-page letter she had just received from Prince Alexander of Battenberg. Although the letter was full of warm protestations, it clearly meant to suggest strongly that the marriage scheme was quite hopeless and to imply discreetly that the prince might be let off the hook. But the kaiserin refused to understand the message. She wanted Bamberger to go talk to the prince and encourage him to stand fast, and she wrote of reopening the question with Bismarck. To bring up the Battenberg affair all over again and especially at this ticklish point appeared to Bamberger to be too frightful to contemplate, and although the baroness warned him that anyone who spoke against Battenberg was likely to incur Her Majesty's disfavor, he determined to risk it and dashed off an impassioned plea to the kaiserin not to hand her enemies this devastating weapon when things were going so well. There were already signs, he thought, that a new "crisis" was being prepared; the article of June 2 in the *Kölnische Zeitung* (see above, pp. 314–15) Bamberger regarded as the "first signal shot" in such a campaign.[23]

On June 7 Herbert Bismarck wrote in his diary, "Radolin comes because of Puttkamer crisis, whom H.M. wants to get rid of. I therefore to [Wilhelm, Count von] Hohenthal [the ministerial representative of the Kingdom of Saxony] at noon. Ate alone with parents and Marie. Evening again with Radolin, Puttkamer with Papa, received ungracious letter, handing in resignation." The visit to Count Hohenthal was doubtless to inform the chief non-Prussian states of the Bundesrat of the impending dismissal of Puttkamer and to explain that it was of no political significance. The kaiser's second letter to Puttkamer read as follows: "After I have read your memorandum, I must insist that I disapprove of such excesses of electoral influence such as have become known in the case of Puttkamer-Plauth, and I regret that you have not taken occasion earlier to clear my government of any suspicion of connivance with such abuses. Nevertheless I will allow the law regarding the lengthening of the legislative period now to be published because the Reich chancellor and the other members of the State Ministry wish it. Frederick R."

The expert phrasing of this letter, which made it clear beyond a shadow of a doubt that the kaiser was expressing his lack of confidence in Puttkamer, was very likely composed by Radolin. The fact that he had come to see Herbert Bismarck in the morning, probably before the letter was sent out, raises the suspicion that they may have collaborated on it. To Puttkamer himself the elder Bismarck was all sympathy and indignation, while agreeing that it was now impossible for him not to resign. He had, said the chancellor, in his recent audience with the kaiser, advised that at least the minister's dismissal might be postponed so that it would not look like a German Liberal victory, and he had thought that the kaiser had agreed. In a meeting of the ministry on the eighth Bismarck suggested that Schrader had written the kaiser's letter to Puttkamer and added that the kaiser's signature was "especially graceful." He declared, however, that it was the patriotic duty of the other ministers not to resign at such a critical time, but to remain at their posts to prevent further damage. To his wife (Puttkamer's cousin) and especially to Bleichröder, Bismarck displayed anger and vexation, threatening to resign. Kaiser Frederick naturally immediately granted Puttkamer's request for dismissal, but with a very gracious letter and bestowal of the Grand Cross of the Hohenzollern house order. Ostentatiously Bismarck visited Puttkamer on the ninth and gave a farewell dinner for him on the twelfth at which the whole ministry was present. As the ministers arrived, the chancellor, displaying his fine sense for nuances, asked Minister of Public Works von Maybach, the senior member of the ministry, to make the toast to Puttkamer. He himself would give the toast to the kaiser and king. Consequently, observed Lucius, Maybach's toast was rather lame, whereas Puttkamer's toast to Bismarck was carefully prepared and effective, being mostly a paean of loyalty and recognition that all that he had become and achieved he owed to the chancellor's patronage. Such demonstrations, as Pindter observed, were not likely to raise Bismarck's estimation of human nature. After the banquet, Lucius left the Chancellery with Friedberg, who told him that the relationship of the kaiserin to Bismarck was very close and that she regarded him as her best friend.[24]

The end to the Puttkamer crisis came so suddenly and was known at first to so few that it took a while for the news to become known in political circles, so that the party press continued for a few days to carry on as if the "crisis" was still in force. On the one hand, the German Liberal and Center party press proclaimed that the legislative period law could not be published without simultaneous publication of Kaiser Frederick's first letter to Puttkamer, and that a royal decree on freedom of elections would be issued before the Prussian Landtag election in the fall. Even the *Kreuzzeitung* assumed that such a decree would indeed be forthcoming. They seemed confident, however, that the content of the decree would not satisfy the left Liberals and they insisted that Puttkamer would be able to persuade the kaiser that there had been no "improper" influence on elections and that the ministry would stand solidly together. For once—again rallying to the cartel—they applauded the position of the National Liberal *Kölnische Zeitung*. The *Konservative Korrespondenz* stated that one used to joke about a Richter ministry and what it would do, but no longer. To weaken Kaiser William's decree of 1882 on the duty of local officials in elections would be for the crown to give up undoubted rights, which would endanger its position. On the other hand, the German Lib-

eral leader Heinrich Rickert declared at a party meeting that a new spirit
had arisen in the country, which the present Reichstag no longer represented. "The people should be permitted to think freely, to believe freely,
and to act freely." In the meantime, in lieu of a new Reichstag, he seemed
ready even to strike a pragmatic political alliance with Bismarck. "We
must come to the point when one can go in and say to the Reich chancellor, 'Your Highness, there are times when one must govern liberally. The
present is such a time, rule liberally!' (long-lasting, stormy applause)."[25]

The sudden publication of the legislative period law in the *Reichsanzeiger*
in the evening of June 7 caught everybody by surprise and was followed
by much relief among the cartel press and taunts directed at the German
Liberals because no decree on freedom of elections accompanied it. The
German Liberals, wrote the *Kreuzzeitung*, had duly sacrificed their liberal,
constitutional principles, but had received no reward. It is, in fact, striking
that Kaiser Frederick's holding up the publication of the law and then
letting it be published showed practically no consideration for the political
position of his German Liberal friends, whom it put in a very awkward
spot. Since the legislative period law had now been published, after the
kaiser had received Puttkamer's report, the *Kreuzzeitung* thought that the
"Puttkamer crisis" was over.[26]

In its confidence that Puttkamer would emerge triumphant the *Kreuzzeitung* was practically alone. Both the *Vossische Zeitung* and the *Frankfurter*
reminded their readers that friction had developed between the minister
of the interior and the chancellor, especially after the Stoecker meeting at
General von Waldersee's and that it could not be assumed that Bismarck
would regret Puttkamer's political demise. On June 6 August Stein wrote
from Berlin to the *Frankfurter* that Puttkamer's position was generally
regarded as shaken. Nor did the publication of the legislative period law
change Stein's assessment; the government press had merely been unusually successful in confusing public opinion; all the fuss over publication
or nonpublication had been contrived to cover up the retirement of
Puttkamer and obscure the connection with the principle of freedom of
voting. "The severely ill kaiser, so fundamentally limited in his freedom
of action, will put at least one thing through, that the minister whose
political character is least sympathetic to him will be replaced by someone else."[27]

Nor would it have been like the government to have left the public
totally without any warning of things to come. Behind the dramatic fire-
works of the exchange between the *Kölnische* and the *Norddeutsche Allgemeine
Zeitung*—in which both, in effect, stressed or assumed complete ministerial
solidarity—contrary indications quietly surfaced in other governmental
outlets. The Free Conservative *Post*, for example, belittled the idea of a

crisis, pointing out that the German Liberals, in concentrating on Puttkamer, were attacking the government at its weakest point and that it would strengthen the government to replace Puttkamer with a "stronger and more firmly rooted" minister of the interior. The governmental and conservative *Deutsches Tageblatt* reported flatly that the crisis involved only reconstruction of the ministry, and that Puttkamer was determined to resign. Finally the *Berliner Tageblatt* (a left-liberal, not a government, paper, but very likely used in this instance for precisely that reason) reported on the sixth that in his audience with the kaiser on the preceding day the chancellor had reached a compromise whereby Puttkamer's retirement was conceded in principle, but that he was to remain temporarily in office, and the precise timing of his departure was to be determined by the chancellor. This report thus confirmed the story that Bismarck himself told Puttkamer and others—which made the sudden dismissal a completely arbitrary and irresponsible royal act—and was significantly referred to as substantiating evidence by Baron Marschall in his report to Karlsruhe.[28]

In the same issue in which it printed the text of the legislative period law, and before the news of Puttkamer's fall had hit the newsstands, the *Norddeutsche* replied to the criticism of the *Kölnische Zeitung*—reprinting its article at length in the process—in an urbane article that appeared to seek to establish a precedent for the next reign and simultaneously to set the stage for the cartel campaign in the fall Landtag elections. The *Kölnische* had complained that the reasoning of the *Norddeutsche* was too fine to be convincing, but it had not been their purpose to convince anyone, rather merely to inform those "whose view is directed beyond the dust of momentary conflicts." They agreed completely that the way that intimate happenings at court were immediately reported in German Liberal papers was "offensive and dangerous" for the ministry, and that it would be tempting for the ministry to resign. But such a move in a difficult time would be irresponsible. Resignation of the ministry would produce a vacuum in the state that the opposition was incapable of filling.[29]

The exchange between the *Norddeutsche* and the *Kölnische Zeitung*, commented Catholic *Germania*, appeared almost as a deliberately created game of badminton between Berlin and Cologne. The left-liberal *Frankfurter* thought, with some justice, that the *Norddeutsche* article was an ultimatum delivered to the crown. In this connection, an article published at about the same time in the *Schlesischer Zeitung* and quoted at length in the *Norddeutsche* seemed to fill out the argument in favor of the ministry and the ministers in a positive way (for the benefit of the crown prince, not Kaiser Frederick, and perhaps for the ministers themselves). It was, it wrote, "the principle of authority" that had brought Prussia from its small beginnings to its present position of power. Officials represented the authority of the king. Even the parliaments had so far been mindful of this, and—unlike in France—there had been no general tendency toward personal hounding of ministers from office. The parliaments had the right of petition and of interpellation; they in effect controlled the whole system of finances; and they could criticize operations of the government at will. But nevertheless the ministers were independent enough that they were not regarded as "ephemeral figures, who have to deal only with the parliaments and leave the administration of their departments . . . to routine professionals [*geschulte Routiniers*], people whom no one knows and who are responsible to no one." It was the orthodox Protestant, politically reactionary, Stoeckerite *Reichsbote*, so strongly supportive of the crown prince, that summed up the lesson in a statement prophetic of the next reign. "The kaiser could hardly have taken such a step [as the dismissal of Puttkamer] without some advisor or other. It has never been good, however, as history demonstrates, when a ruler has bypassed the advice of his legitimate publicly responsible advisor and has followed the advice of secret advisors. God forbid that such a thing might gain ground with us in Prussia!"[30]

The news of the resignation of Puttkamer provoked the German Liberals into proud claims of responsibility for the deed, thus helping Bismarck maintain his camouflage. Before the event there had been some skepticism. August Stein, in the *Frankfurter*, had pointed out that replacing Puttkamer was really more important to the middle parties than to the opposition, especially if a National Liberal should succeed him. In a Bismarck ministry it did not matter who was minister of the interior. Government influence on elections was not a matter merely of a decree; it was the result of a whole entrenched system. Deputy Rickert, in the speech to his German Liberal followers previously quoted, had referred to even more basic obstacles: "One must see to it that the fawning [*Piepmeierei*] and cringing [*Katzenbuckelei*] stop, for as long as they dominate, no kaiser and king can help. . . . Also the bad social deference must cease; the middle class must not hanker after association with officials and military men." In his article after Puttkamer's resignation, Stein also cautioned that even though the direct influence on elections of local officials might conceivably not be authorized under a new minister, nevertheless, long-ingrained habits of behavior were not likely to change that much. As long as opposition to recognized authority was considered to be a stigma that created social and professional disadvantages, removal of whatever official influence on elections existed would accomplish relatively little. If Stein and Rickert were correct—and one's general impression is that they were—that subservience to authority was deeply ingrained in German society, then the determined blindness of the opposition parties to Kaiser Frederick's precarious health and their public and private encouragement of Frederick and Victoria to oppose the Bismarck regime on this or that measure amounted to an exploitation of the unfortunate couple that was just as ruthless as Bismarck's, although undoubtedly idealistic and well meaning.

The same shortsighted partisan fervor provoked Stein, in the same article and against his better judgment, to proclaim that Puttkamer had fallen as a direct result of the action of the opposition parties. Other left-liberal papers agreed. The editorialist of the *Frankfurter Zeitung* saw a decisive defeat for Bismarck and limitation of his power. Catholic *Germania* declared that the "first *break* in the system of *compulsion* [*Drucks*]" had occurred. On the other side, the reactionary conservative *Kreuzzeitung* wrote that it was an incontrovertible fact that the chancellor had been surprised by Puttkamer's dismissal and published a poem saying that like so many earlier Puttkamers, the minister too had fallen fighting for "kaiser and Reich," which implied that Kaiser Frederick was not the true kaiser.[31]

National Liberals and Free Conservatives found themselves in a quandary. The long-wished-for fall of the ultra-Conservative orthodox minister and the further weakening of the *Kreuzzeitung* wing of the Conservative party that it symbolized, under the special circumstances that made it appear as an opposition victory, could not be rejoiced over quite as freely or enthusiastically as might otherwise have been the case. In actual fact, however, the oppositional victory was illusory. The fall of Puttkamer might indeed, under other circumstances, once have heralded a new liberal era (the reaction of the German Liberals indicates how difficult it would have been for them to resist it), but now it amounted to only a measure of insurance that the actual new era about to break might not be hopelessly reactionary. The inability of the middle parties to derive much benefit from the event demonstrated the changed position of the cartel and of the National Liberals within the cartel on the eve of the accession of William II. The special political juxtaposition of monarch and parties that would have promoted Liberal leadership and a freer, more liberal atmosphere and that for so long had seemed inevitable had already gone by.[32]

When General von Waldersee first heard the news of Puttkamer's fall, he asked his diary, "Has Bismarck sacrificed him?" But by the next day the combination of Bismarck's confidential reports blaming the kaiserin and the outburst of rejoicing in the German Liberal press had begun to mitigate his suspicions. "It is solely the work of the kaiserin," he wrote. "On the 5th she told the chancellor she wanted under all circumstances to dismiss Puttkamer, and added, 'I can't get at Waldersee, since Moltke, Albedyll, and he hang together like a pack of rats [*Rattenkönig*]!'" A day later, June 10, he noted that "Puttkamer is convinced that his fall occurred without Bismarck's being involved; that is certainly correct, but nevertheless I maintain that the chancellor let the affair happen, although he could have prevented it. He is above all a man of affairs [*Geschäftsmann*]." Later, however, he added that he had learned that "the otherwise so clever Puttkamer has let himself be fundamentally deceived by Bismarck." When the kaiserin had insisted on dismissing Puttkamer, the chancellor had given in to save his own position. Puttkamer had quite forgotten his conflict with the chancellor over the Stoecker meeting. "He also did not consider that it could not possibly be acceptable for the chancellor to work with a minister who stood close to the future kaiser." Puttkamer had also reacted unnecessarily hastily; he could have stalled for time; he knew that the kaiser had only a short time left. Only five day's delay would have sufficed.[33]

Whatever the final judgment of Crown Prince William concerning the resignation of Puttkamer may have been, his immediate reaction reflected the chancellor's story. What he had previously feared, he wrote the grand duke of Baden on June 10, had been borne out only too well. "Mama and she alone, in league with the German Liberals, overthrew Puttkamer, according to all the corroborating testimony in the palace that much is completely clear." It was possible that other ministers would follow. They "no longer feel secure, and the ground shakes under their feet." The style and the form of his father's second letter to Puttkamer so differed from the kaiser's usual style that the source was easy to surmise. The crown prince was right about the mood of the ministers; they took the ungracious tone of the kaiser's second letter as a personal affront and danger to themselves. The chancellor, of course, encouraged this feeling, reading them the text of the letter and contrasting the gracious tone of the third letter with the previous one and saying that he himself would have sent back the decoration. "He then," wrote Lucius, "elaborated on the bad handling that Puttkamer had received, as if that could yet happen to others too."[34]

Rumors of further resignations—Finance Minister Scholz, Minister of Justice Friedberg—did crop up in the press, probably at the chancellor's instigation, Scholz perhaps as a reprimand for daring to speak up against the chancellor in the ministry and to remind him that he too was expendable, and Friedberg to suggest to the public and the Conservatives a possible culprit for the quick dismissal of Puttkamer. Naturally these reports were immediately and emphatically denied in the chancellor's *Norddeutsche Allgemeine Zeitung*. For a successor to Puttkamer, both Lucius and Friedberg urged the nomination of the National Liberal leader Johannes Miquel. Bismarck, however, was not interested. He preferred the energetic, diplomatic, strongly Christian, conservative, and ruggedly independent governor of the province of Posen, Count Robert von Zedlitz-Trützschler, who even August Stein conceded had risen in the Prussian administration solely through his "outstanding ability." Clearly Bismarck wanted a minister in this key position who would be basically sympathetic to the new Kaiser William II in his religious and political views and yet who would be of sufficiently strong character to act responsibly and oppose any arbitrary whims. The succession of Zedlitz would also reassure the right-wing Junker Conservatives. Initially this suggestion aroused opposition from Kaiserin Victoria, who protested that that would mean a continuation of *Stoeckerei*, that Zedlitz was just as pietistic as Puttkamer and had married a daughter to a Kleist-Retzow. Since, however, the choice was soon formally authorized by the kaiser, Bismarck must have been successful in pointing out the advantage of the ministry's including a strong, judicious character within the orthodox Protestant camp who could help control them. The resignation of Count Stolberg, acting minister of the royal household, was also rumored, but eventually denied. The report of the imminent resignation of Chief of the Civil Cabinet Wilmowski, however, was officially confirmed but was generally regarded as nonpolitical because of his advanced age (seventy-one) and poor eyesight.[35]

The kaiserin's own reaction to the dismissal of Puttkamer was not surprising. "Fritz has after much difficulty and some diplomacy got rid of Puttkamer," she wrote her mother, "which I consider a great step! He will be able to carry all sorts of things if he can break through the wall of opposition already so cleverly organized at San Remo, and in which William is so deeply involved. He would be different to us, I am sure, when these people and influences have gone, that use him for their purposes against us! . . . If I could think we had a year before us! How much could be done, but that is so uncertain!!" The "clique" were enraged, but the people constantly showed their support, and so the former were frustrated in their attempts to hurt her. "And what if they do succeed? If Fritz goes I do not the least care what becomes of me. I do not want these people's love and I scorn their hatred. Fritz and I shall be more than avenged some day by the course events will take when these people come into power." A few days later, Kaiserin Victoria informed her mother that she was sending another box of papers through the English embassy, to be put with the others. Sir Edward Malet thought the box contained jewels. Almost a year later, the kaiserin rather thoughtlessly allowed Bamberger, through Baroness von Stockmar, to read her account of the year 1888, where he found indignantly that she had "falsely" given the credit for the fall of Puttkamer only to Bismarck and Prince Radolin and had not even mentioned his own "role."[36]

Of all the interpretations of Puttkamer's fall, the judgment of Kaiserin Victoria, that Bismarck had wanted him out and had accomplished the ouster in such a way as to put the blame on Kaiser Frederick, remains the most credible. Once more the old chancellor had manipulated individual personalities, parties, and public opinion in a brilliant display of improvisation that had served a number of political purposes: first, it removed a man whose conservative ideological rigidity was not only no longer useful, but had become dangerous, whose naive loyalty to the crown prince threatened any kind of responsible, constitutional government as well as Bismarck personally. Second, it concealed Bismarck's own initiative in this move so as not further to disturb his relations with the crown prince and the *Kreuzzeitung* party. Third, it clearly pinned responsibility on the kaiser and by inference the kaiserin and the oppositional German Liberal party in order to demonstrate dramatically to the crown prince once more, as in the Battenberg affair, how much furor could be caused by arbitrary acts of the crown. But also, fourth, by conjuring up this bogey of a Liberal threat—a "camarilla"—again as in the Battenberg affair, it helped to hold the *Kreuzzeitung* Conservatives in a cooperative position within the cartel majority. Incidentally, fifth, in the process it demonstrated once more to the crown prince how easy it was for these rabid monarchists to desert the king and oppose his personal initiative when it was directed against them. Finally, sixth, there was probably a degree of genuine pleasure in giving Kaiser Frederick this satisfaction before he died. The irregularity of holding up publication of a law legally passed and signed, since it was associated with Kaiser Frederick, would not cause any permanent damage. Certainly, in achieving these purposes, Bismarck, the complete politician, had displayed as usual small regard for customary forms and the personal feelings of individuals.

All these accomplishments, however, had been achieved at a price. During these last days of the reign of Kaiser Frederick, Bismarck's concept of the importance of the position of the monarchy in Prussia-Germany is revealed, more significantly than in the carefully shaded articles in the press, by the drastic nature of his acts. To gain control over the crown prince's belligerence and hostility to Russia and to undermine the influence of Waldersee, he had mounted strong actions against France and had himself actually spoken (privately) of the possibility of war—thus contradicting his own basically peaceful policy. To try to prevent the right-wing *Kreuzzeitung* Conservatives from taking the whole Conservative party into a political position hostile to the cartel, he had publicly humiliated that party over the school-aid bill—thus exacerbating the hostility of the Stoeckerites and *Kreuzzeitung* clique toward himself and very likely storing up resentment within the party as a whole. To remove the danger of the presence within his own government of a representative of the *Kreuzzeitung*-Stoecker faction who had already shown himself to be unreliable as far as the crown prince was concerned, he had engineered the dismissal of Puttkamer by Kaiser Frederick and made it look as if it had been done against his own wishes—thus suggesting that he himself was no longer capable of controlling the political situation in Germany. No doubt the crown prince was sufficiently aroused emotionally over the apparent irresponsibility of his father's and mother's behavior so that he would try, at least initially, to act responsibly himself when he came to the throne. Marschall von Bieberstein reported on June 14 that two days before, the crown prince, in a talk with the chancellor, had agreed to the nomination of Zedlitz and had promised, when he became kaiser, not to try to bring back Puttkamer. This, wrote Marschall, showed a firm grasp of the domestic political situation, where it would be the task of the young monarch to mediate the conflicts among the (ruling) parties, not to sharpen them. Regarding the same talk, Bismarck told the Prussian ministers that the crown prince had been "very careful and reasonable." He had said that he wanted to rule in the sense of his grandfather, to respect the rights of the sovereigns and of the legislature, not to support himself on the political extremes, but on the parties of the cartel. "The orthodox Conservatives would never have a majority and at the most could lead through the extreme wing of the party, which was half-crazy and too narrowminded."[37]

This statement of Crown Prince William represented a considerable achievement for the elderly Bismarck. Through his own special blend of persuasion, pressure, manipulation, maneuver, double-dealing, stage management, and outright intimidation he had brought the crown prince to a point, just before his accession, where he realized the importance for the crown itself and for the continued strength and stability of Prussia-Germany for him as kaiser to represent the whole nation, to stand above the political battles and to support, not only Bismarck himself personally, but also the middle-of-the-road, compromise, moderate bloc of respectable parties Bismarck had brought together to support his regime in the cartel. This achievement of the old man, as admirable as it was, had, however, been costly. Might not the crown prince also have carried away with him from the events of these weeks the false image of a Bismarck who was too old and in too ill health to stand any marked political strain and who had already lost his ability to control people and events? Once more, as in the Stoecker and Battenberg affairs, Bismarck had drawn heavily on his own accumulated prestige and credibility. At the end of May, Count Lerchenfeld had already reported that from what he heard, Bismarck had lost the "lust for battle" that he had shown as recently as the Battenberg affair, and a day later Count Zeppelin had written to Stuttgart that the chancellor was showing an "apathetic" attitude toward domestic affairs. Lerchenfeld wrote the same day that Conservative party leaders could not understand the "compliant" behavior of the chancellor toward the kaiser and kaiserin. After Puttkamer's dismissal, he reported that it had been the result of "influences at court that the Reich chancellor can no longer control" and that "probably for the first time during his administration the chancellor has adopted an equivocating [*lavirende*] position toward oppositional influences at court." The ministers, wrote Lerchenfeld, were disturbed by the fact that "in the otherwise so orderly Prussian governmental organism [*Staatswesen*] underground influences have achieved a strength against which the chancellor himself is struggling in vain, and also by the feeling that as a consequence the position of this man is no longer the same."[38]

One does not mean to suggest that the chancellor made mistakes in his operations at this time or that his acts were not necessary in the context— he probably remains the best judge of that. Yet the historian must at least pose the question and not automatically assume a sort of political infallibility for Bismarck. Had he perhaps, as Holstein suggested, grown too vain and arrogant with his many successes to bother to develop more reasonable, conciliatory methods? Was it only a personality trait—fatal for Germany—that made him prefer deviousness and forceful manipulation to the honest, straightforward, open, and consistent handling so longed for by Kaiserin Victoria and the *National Zeitung* (see above, pp. 74, 281)? Or did the complexities and contradictions of the German situation demand a leader with his special tendencies and talents? Could he not have openly shown his cards to the ministers, and party leaders, public opinion, and the crown prince and appealed for reasonableness, compromise, unity, as he had more or less done in foreign affairs in his speech to the Reichstag in February?

The answer is indicated by the way that the good effects of the February speech had quickly been dissipated, especially with the crown prince, in a system where responsible decisions had always been made by a few people at the top behind closed doors and where the parties and the public were not used to taking the initiative or accepting responsibility, *and did not want it.* The very severe limits within which the German parties and public were willing to tolerate public pressure on the crown—on respected traditional authority—were clearly shown by the Battenberg affair. Just as Bamberger preferred a bureaucrat as minister of the interior to a leader of the rival National Liberal party, so all the parties, in making the most of their right to agitate, criticize, and make extreme demands, preferred that ultimate responsibility continue to be borne by the authoritarian, bureaucratic government. The cartel was a loose association of mutually hostile and suspicious groups incapable of supporting the government, in fact constantly in need of being supported by the government. This was not because German politicians were incorrigibly craven, selfish, shortsighted, and stupid (although their various newspapers might give that impression), nor because, under the cynical handling of Bismarck, they had lost their idealism and succumbed to the politics of special interests (*Interessenpolitik*), but rather because the vision of ultimate political truth to which each of the parties remained intensely devoted ran the gamut—even within the cartel—from the secular liberalism of the *National Zeitung* to the orthodox Christian piety of the *Kreuzzeitung*. To assume that the political parties could have stood the strain of continual basic compromise of their principles is to assume a political sophistication and a national consensus in domestic affairs that at the time did not exist. Yet a degree of consensus is essential for the effective functioning of any state, so that if it does not naturally and organically exist, then it must be artificially constructed, mediated, or forcefully imposed from the top. Neither the *Kreuzzeitung* nor the Conservative party nor Crown Prince William could have publicly accepted the deliberate jettison of Puttkamer.

Lack of basic political consensus, at the end of the nineteenth century, was not exclusively a German problem. In the French republic traditional preoccupation with local, regional, and diverse economic interests and continuing basic ideological hostilities had created such weakness and instability in the parliamentary government that the actual rule was, in effect, being handed over to the bureaucracy (see above, p. 326). With no effective government authority separate from and above the parties—as German critics, from the *Kreuzzeitung* to the *Frankfurter*, constantly pointed out—French party conflicts made governmental instability the norm. Currently the French republic was just entering a period of large-scale crises and scandals, from Boulanger (1889) to Panama (1892) to Dreyfus (1894–1906). The French, being used to public conflict since 1789, with their historical experiences of serious political fragmentation, civil war, and prolonged periods of conquest and occupation by foreign armies several centuries before, and with their two-hundred-year tradition of strong central government, could doubtless stand more scandal and disruption and may even have found them to be a convenient diversionary tactic in avoiding drastic social change. But for the Germans, with the loose federal structure of their new nation—less than twenty years old—their strong regional and religious divisions, their long history of fragmentation and weakness, and their central, exposed position in Europe; with their conquest and domination by Napoleon as recent as the adolescence of Kaiser William; and with the last war among the German states themselves a scant generation ago, the preservation of order and public decorum was of primary importance and a responsibility that none of the political parties, not even the Conservative, was eager to take on and that only the Social Democrats were willing to challenge. French national pride and cultural self-confidence allowed a certain slackness, tolerated conflict as the price of freedom, and sacrificed governmental strength and unity to party squabbling. German lack of confidence and insecurity emphasized discipline in every area and basically supported the continuation of a stable, reliable government authority separate from the parliaments and above the ideological and economic battles of the party arena. But a strong, respectable, mediating authoritarian government could not easily be maintained if the personality at the apex of authority was unreliable and unstable. In the context, Bismarck's extreme expedients in these weeks appear to have been politically necessary and indicate how important he considered the problem of young William to be.

The Puttkamer affair had a comic epilogue. In the meeting of the Prussian State Ministry on June 15 Bismarck gravely and confidentially informed the shocked ministers that two or three days previously, when he had complained to Kaiserin Victoria about the difficulties she had caused him in the dismissal of Puttkamer—for example, that people were now accusing him of having brought it about himself or at least of not resisting it sufficiently, and that he could not free himself from such a suspicion—she had replied, "Do you want him reappointed? The kaiser will do it right away!" He was telling the ministers this "*en faveur de la loi Salique* [the Salic Law, of course, excluded women from the royal succession] and as proof of Her Majesty's fickleness and complete lack of political understanding." The actual scene, however, was undoubtedly quite different: enter the chancellor, with a look of intimate complicity and a knowing smile, who says to the kaiserin, "Does Your Majesty realize the trouble you have caused me? Why, people are saying that *I* was responsible for the fall of Puttkamer," etc. Whereupon Kaiserin Victoria, responding to the bantering tone, asks archly if he wants Puttkamer reappointed, that she can certainly procure the kaiser's signature, thus playing up to his implied suggestion—a previously established pattern—that they were in cahoots, a team that was secretly running things. As for his straight-faced report to the ministers, one imagines that for a statesman in Bismarck's position, beset by all sorts of insoluble problems and overwhelmed with tedious detail, the opportunities for personal amusement were few; he apparently took them where he found them.[39]

34

Death of Kaiser Frederick

KAISER Frederick's health began again to decline almost as soon as he arrived in Potsdam. As early as June 5 he began to complain of headaches and to suffer from a general feeling of weakness and loss of appetite. The same day the *Vossische Zeitung* published a report, no doubt originating with Mackenzie, that declared that there was no doubt the kaiser was suffering from perichondritis, but that there was still doubt as to whether cancer existed or not. On June 9 the *British Medical Journal* announced that the doctors did not know the nature of the kaiser's illness and that the improvement in his condition was continuing. In fact, he was already developing difficulty in swallowing, and on June 10 when he drank some milk it came out through the tube in his neck. The doctors immediately assumed that the esophagus had been perforated, but the autopsy later showed that it must have been deterioration of the epiglottis that had allowed the liquid to flow into the trachea. This difficulty was surmounted by feeding the royal patient through a rubber tube, which further depressed his appetite. At about the same time his temperature began to rise again during the day. In spite of these developments, the *Frankfurter Zeitung* reported on June 11 that the difficulty in swallowing had had no effect on the kaiser's general health, which continued to be satisfactory, and on the twelfth, that the disturbing rumors that had been circulating were exaggerated. Even in its second morning edition on the fourteenth the *Frankfurter* continued to maintain that there was "no special danger at present."[1]

The royal patient himself began to feel apprehensive on June 11, writing in his diary, "What is to become of me?" and mouthing the words, which the kaiserin wrote down, "How am I really? Does it seem to be better? When shall I get well again, what do you think, shall I be sick long?" Then, wringing his hands, "I must get well, I have so much to do!" Count Lerchenfeld reported on the thirteenth that for the last two days Berliners had been aware of the worsening in the kaiser's condition and although genuinely sorry, nevertheless felt a feeling of relief, since his death would put an end to the apparent political crisis. Lerchenfeld did not understand why the kaiserin, knowing of her husband's dubious prospects, should nevertheless have made moves to upset things politically and not have made an attempt to come to terms with the crown prince, upon whom she would soon be dependent. On the other hand, he thought that the German Liberal party had taken good advantage of Kaiser Frederick's short reign to weaken the government as much as possible and create the best possible situation for the next elections. They would be able to counteract the accusation of lack of loyalty to the king much more easily than heretofore.[2]

Bismarck had his last audience with Kaiser Frederick on June 14. The Kaiser had recognized him right away, Bismarck told the ministers, and had held out both hands in a friendly gesture. He was feverish and red in the face but did not seem to have much pain. He had then taken the hand of the kaiserin and placed it in the chancellor's and pressed them together with both of his own. Understanding the gesture—a request that he look out for her—Bismarck had said, "Your Majesty can be sure that I shall never forget that Her Majesty is my queen." Kaiserin Victoria later wrote that she had felt that Bismarck was not moved by this scene, that he seemed rather to be thinking with some relief and joyful anticipation of the demands and possibilities of the coming new regime. Evidently he was now withdrawing that tender sympathy and intensity of personal concern that he had previously turned upon her, his attention and concern being diverted to Crown Prince William, the new center of power. To later observers it might seem admirable for the old man of seventy-three to be so ready to meet new challenges, to be so eager for action. But to Kaiserin Victoria, in her agony, it was a personal abandonment. She felt the change in his attitude, she wrote, "like the thrust of a dagger, and yet I could not hold it against him; for a man of his stamp it was only natural."[3]

The evening of the thirteenth the kaiser's fever had gone up over 104°, and the doctors had decided that the infection must have spread to the lungs. Early in the morning of the fourteenth Berliners began to stream out to Potsdam and to collect along the fence in the park that sealed off the palace of Friedrichskron from Sans Souci. The official bulletin at ten o'clock announced that "the kaiser's condition has taken an important turn for the worse since yesterday evening. His strength is sinking." Both pulse and rate of breathing had markedly increased. At noon the *Frankfurter Zeitung* received a telegram from Berlin conceding that there was no longer any hope. A later telegram reported that almost all the members of the royal family were now in the palace. Notices of the kaiser's death had already been prepared in the ministry secretariat and the Foreign Office.[4]

Kaiser Frederick died at 11:15 A.M. on Friday, June 15, exactly fourteen weeks after his father, on the ninety-ninth day of his reign. Bismarck was informed by telegraph during a session of the Prussian State Ministry. Shortly after noon Kaiserin Victoria telegraphed him, "Everything is now over. Now that he is no more you will certainly always remember his request of yesterday. He dies as a hero, his soul lives with the angels." To her mother she wrote, "His mild just rule was not to be." Now finally she could face the fact. Three days later she poured out her grief to her mother: "The good, the noble, the brave, *patient*, enduring, *pure*—& kind!! Oh such men should *not* die! They have no right I think. They are *wanted* in this sad world—but they also—have *much* to *suffer!!*" Her mother had suggested that she could try to carry on his work, but she saw no hope for that. "I disappear with him, *my task* was with him, *for him*, for his dear People. It is buried in the grave where he will be buried today. My voice will be silent for ever!... We *had* a mission. We felt & we knew it—We were Papa's & your children! We were *faithful* to what we believed & knew to be *right*. We loved Germany. We wished to see her *strong* & *great* not only with the *sword* but in *all* that was righteous in *culture*, in *progress*, & in *Liberty*."[5]

The kaiserin did not want an autopsy and appealed to her son, the new Kaiser William II, who at first granted her wish and ordered that it should be omitted. But Dr. von Bergmann and the other German doctors insisted to the chancellor that German medicine must have the opportunity to vindicate itself against Mackenzie's skulduggeries, and the house rule of the Hohenzollerns called for exact determination of the cause of death of the king. Consequently Kaiser William was persuaded to overrule himself and his mother, and an autopsy was performed, revealing not only that the disease was indeed cancer and that death had been caused by an infection in the lungs, but that nothing at all was left of the larynx— merely an empty hole—and that there was so sign of any ulceration or abscess near the tracheotomy incision. Dr. Mackenzie was asked to write up a report, in which he stated, "It is my opinion that the disease from which the Emperor Frederick III died was cancer. The morbid process probably commenced in the deeper tissues, and the cartilaginous structure of the larynx became affected at a very early date." Mackenzie later wrote in his rather scandalous book, *The Fatal Illness of Frederick the Noble*, that he was consoled by the thought that through his treatment and management of the case "the dangerous methods recommended by Gerhardt and von Bergmann were prevented, and that I thereby not only prolonged the life of the Emperor, but also saved him much suffering." According to Kaiser Frederick's own request, who had wanted to spare Berlin and the country another large-scale occasion for grief so short a time after his father's great funeral, the funeral was to be held privately in Potsdam, where he was to be buried in the Friedenskirche, and it was to be primarily military and confined to the immediate family, representatives of foreign royalty being limited to relatives.[6]

The news of the kaiser's death reached private circles in Berlin by half-past eleven on the fifteenth and began quietly to spread. The first public indication was given by the lowering of the flag to half-mast on the main telegraph office on the Französischenstrasse. At a quarter to twelve on the top of Kaiser Frederick's palace the purple royal standard was displayed at half-mast. Immediately several hundred people assembled, and a man in civilian clothes who emerged from the palace was questioned closely for further details of the kaiser's passing. Shortly after twelve, mourning flags appeared on the princesses' palace and on the opera house. Other public buildings and the old royal *Schloss* soon followed suit. Among the many German imperial flags appeared some that were completely black. Already by a quarter to twelve newspaper extras were being cried on the street, and although they could contain nothing but the barest announcement of the kaiser's death, many people bought them. At a quarter to one the bell of the cathedral began to toll. The stock exchange closed, and the city council adjourned. Crowds streamed toward the Potsdam railroad station to travel out to the palace of Friedrichskron. The evening editions of Berlin papers, on the streets by half-past four, were all edged in black.[7]

In a letter to the grand duke of Baden on June 15, Baron von Roggenbach expressed the general left-Liberal reaction to the death of Kaiser Frederick. It was, he wrote, "the saddest catastrophe that ever happened in history." The evening edition of the *Frankfurter Zeitung* declared in a lead article, "From this crown emanated the radiance of a new era, a time in which the Ideal again came into its own, in which what the great thinkers and poets had promised was to be fulfilled. . . . The good that he did, the greatness that he strove for, it remains a living thing for his family, for the nation, and for the world." Kaiser Frederick, mourned the *Vossische Zeitung*, had been "a Siegfried, who charms the whole world, whose shield shines clear and pure, whose sword banishes gloomy night . . . this knightly prince, in the flower of his manhood snatched away by malignant death." The *Freisinnige Zeitung* wrote that Kaiser Frederick would remain "the image and ensign [*Bild und Banner*] of our future." He had not been able to lead, but had shown the way. "It was a beautiful dream, too beautiful to last. Kaiser Frederick has departed from us like that legendary hero who passed by but left a shining trace." The English *Pall Mall Gazette* quoted the Liberal party leader Gladstone as calling Kaiser Frederick "the Barbarossa of German Liberalism." The left Liberals, out of their sentimental attachment to Kaiser Frederick, seemed to be in danger of doubling the dose of idealism that conveniently fogged over political reality and prevented them from forming a practical, popular program, of placing foremost in their hearts and minds, next to the unattainable future, the equally unattainable past. For them Barbarossa had once more safely been returned to his cave.[8]

In Potsdam, on June 15, at 11:20 A.M. when the purple royal standard in front of the palace of Friedrichskron had been lowered and raised again to half-mast, the public signal that Kaiser Frederick had died, immediately troops came running from their barracks and cavalry galloped up, sealing off the palace and allowing no one to go in or out, including ministers and members of the court. Apparently Kaiser William II wanted to prevent any incriminating papers from being removed, and according to Johanna von Bismarck at least one chest of papers was found in the "shrubbery." He also wanted to catch Mackenzie and his left-Liberal correspondents, and he actually tried to arrest the good doctor, but was talked out of it by Minister von Friedberg. The only progressive correspondent caught in the net was a Mr. Bashford of the London *Daily Telegraph*, who was confined until evening and not given anything to eat, and who subsequently made righteously indignant protests at the British consulate and embassy. Kaiserin Victoria, trying to use the telephone to order her mourning from Berlin, found that she could not get through. The Wilhelmian Era had begun.[9]

35

Afterword

THE Ninety-Nine Days turned out to be something more than merely "a female interregnum." Throughout the whole winter and spring Bismarck had used the slow death of Frederick to try to prepare young Prince William for his imminent reign as German kaiser, and he apparently had been successful. At least momentarily he had turned the prince away from championing a preventive war with Russia and toward trying to win the friendship of the tsar. He had disillusioned the prince in regard to the Stoeckerite, *Kreuzzeitung*, clerical, right-wing Conservative group—his natural political orientation—and had beaten back the attempts of this clique to achieve control over the Junker Conservative party as a whole and to move it out of the cartel and into an association with the Catholic Center. And he had also, in the Battenberg affair and the Puttkamer incident, publicly and dramatically demonstrated the limits of royal authority in relation to ministers, legislatures, and people, and had thereby deliberately diminished the prestige of the crown.

In accomplishing these last two strokes Bismarck had been markedly assisted by the illness of Kaiser Frederick as well as by the imperial couple's political naiveté. In fact, the latter makes one wonder if that might not have been their major contribution to German political development if Frederick had had a long reign: that they would have largely destroyed the exalted mystique that the monarchy had taken on under Kaiser William. But the chancellor was also strongly assisted in his maneuvers by the naiveté and narrow fanaticism of the political parties themselves, both Left and Right. Cassell's *New French Dictionary* defines *querelle d'Allemand* as "a groundless quarrel." Not that it is groundless to the participants, but rather that a reasonably objective outsider cannot discover adequate grounds for it. In fact, reading the heated and vituperative exchanges between democratic Liberals and Junker Conservatives on the floor of the Prussian House of Deputies, the partisans of Kaiser Frederick opposing the partisans of Crown Prince William, one gets the feeling that what the conflicting idealisms on both wings of the House demanded was purity, abstract sanctity, authority—in a word, deity.

Western liberalism, from the time of the Enlightenment, had been aimed partly at demythologizing government, at bringing it down to earth, making it a practical, reasonable, human enterprise. But both the American and French Revolutions had in their basic attitudes been pre-romantic, whereas the German national movement had been rooted in romantic idealism. And the decline and weakening of liberalism, with its rational, science-oriented basis, in the late nineteenth century, as a result of the Long Depression and the social and economic conflicts stemming from rapid industrialization, had promoted a strong new growth of irra-tional idealism of all kinds. And this movement was taking place everywhere in the West, not just in Germany. Anti-Semitism, jingoistic imperialism, racism, revolutionary Marxism, anarchism, and Zionism were the most notable movements that were all now in full swing.[1] Thus the fanatical Christian idealism of the clerically oriented Prussian Junkers was undoubtedly partly rooted in their growing economic and political obsolescence as a ruling class.[2] And the fanatical laissez-faire liberalism of the German Liberals may likewise have been rooted in their growing failure to attract the laboring and peasant masses and convince them of the value of individual independence.[3] The fanatical revolutionary Marx-ism of the Social Democrats completed a three-sided ideological cleavage that had its origins as far back as the experiences of 1848–49.

The strong authoritarian traditions of German society and government also helped to sustain the concept that there should be one ideal solution, cause, program. Nor have the two world wars completely eradicated this idea. Thus it has been possible for a German historian to write fairly recently that "obviously" the problem of reconciling conflicting political interests through political leadership can be solved neither through the "Prussian Ideology (fictitious nonpartisan objectivity [*Überparteilichkeit*], represented by the state bureaucracy), nor the American Ideology (har-mony as the quasi-automatic, natural result of the conflict of interests)."[4] Now, an at least partly objective position above the parties cannot be avoided by any bureaucracy or ruling group if it wants to keep on ruling, so that the Prussian (Junker) claim was not entirely "fictitious." Naturally they served their own interests in the process. Otherwise no ruling elite would ever take on responsibility for the general welfare. It is a matter of anomalies: of an ambiguous gray, not stark black and white. But this definition of the "American Ideology" to an American is stupefying. It is very doubtful that many Americans in the last two hundred years have thought of government in that way. It is, of course, true that our eighteenth-century Founding Fathers tended to think in an overly rational, mechanistic fashion. Thus they were more concerned to prevent tyranny in their new governments than to facilitate consensus, and through their checks and balances produced governmental structures that effectively guard against too rash policies but all too often prevent any responsible initiative. No doubt they assumed with Edmund Burke the "natural," "quasi-automatic" "action and counteraction, which, in the natural and in the political world, from the reciprocal struggle of discordant powers, draws out the harmony of the universe."[5] Yet, with their extensive colonial experience and the extremely intensive political experience of the revolutionary period, they became motivated more by pragmatic concepts of political reality and behavior than by disembodied idealism. It was from a healthy, cynical distrust of human nature that John Adams introduced the principle of separation of powers into the Massachusetts constitution of 1780, from where it moved to the federal Constitution of 1787.[6] James Madison did not expect some ideal harmony to emerge from the clash of factional interests but rather a practical accommodation, a working compromise: "the general combined interest of all the state put together, as it were, upon an average."[7] The contemporary German historian quoted above is actually describing the liberal German ideology rather than the American. Thus Burke's formulation finds its appropriate romantic, idealistic, nineteenth-century organic, developmental restatement in Eugen Richter's declaration at the beginning of the Ninety-Nine Days that only from the conflict of different political, social, and religious tendencies could "the True, Right, and Good work its way out." The Divine Principle. Down-to-earth British empiricism has traditionally provided the basis for American political thought, not the high-flown idealistic systems of Kant, Fichte, Schelling, or Hegel.[8]

But conditions were worse a hundred years ago. Faiths and loyalties were deeper and stronger and more naive in the West. The nineteenth century was posttheistic; people still had the psychological need for an absolute faith. Thus no political consensus was possible in Germany, and the demands from all sides for all or nothing meant that if the attempt at creating a consensus around a compromise program through an appeal to national loyalty was to succeed in raising the emotional commitment of the various parties above the "point of indifference," then German Nationalism would have to take on the appeal of a higher religion. The *Post* had, indeed, already advocated as much in its attack on the orthodox Christian Stoeckerites. But as the *Kreuzzeitung* had naively pointed out, national loyalty—a true national consensus—was not operable on a day-to-day basis in internal affairs, but only under external threat. Germany's international position was necessarily delicate, requiring great restraint and control, as Bismarck had indicated in his February 6 speech. Yet it was not his repeated emphasis then on self-confident magnanimity and restraint that had found the greatest public response, but rather the emotion-laden, somewhat belligerent phrases of *furor teutonicus* and "We Germans fear God and nothing else in the world!" If a domestic consensus could be achieved only through an exalted, unrestrained, potentially aggressive, paranoid nationalism, then Germany, after the chancellor's departure, would herself become an unsettling factor in Europe, inevitably bringing on general war and demonstrating that the experiment of trying to construct a powerful German national state—the dream of the liberals and Bismarck's whole career—was perhaps a mistake.

Lack of consensus and irreconcilably warring ideologies made Bismarck's domination through balance and maneuver not only possible but also necessary. His career was born in the conflicts of 1848, took its first flight in the constitutional conflict in Prussia in 1862, and maintained itself thereafter on the winds of continued domestic and international conflict. He dramatized, stage-managed, and exploited the conflicts brilliantly and with a very special mixture of boldness of tactics, sensitivity of perception, and a basic and typically Victorian cautious apprehension and restraint. He managed conflicts so well that many began to feel that he had arbitrarily created them and that without him they would cease (cf. *Frankfurter Zeitung* on the international tension, above, p. 170). Few realized that when he finally did go, they would come to yearn for his firm control and that the conflicts would be worse. If balancing various elements against each other in an essentially authoritarian but pseudoparliamentary way—appealing to the masses but not attempting to change the social structure—is "Bonapartism," then that is assuredly the correct term for the Bismarck regime. But labeling it does not condemn it. After all, France found two Bonapartist empires (1802–15, and 1852–70) to be necessary for her political development, or three, if one accepts the July Monarchy of Louis Philippe (1830–48) as "Bonapartism without Bonaparte."[9] Or one could extend the number to five if one added the two more recent, twentieth-century careers of Charles De Gaulle. And France in the nineteenth century was not developing as rapidly as Germany, either in population or in rate of industrialization. The stresses and strains were not so great. Most countries that have modernized since have also found some strong man or other to be necessary in the first phase of rapid change. The techniques for organizing the masses in a single "monolithic" political party, however, have advanced considerably in sophistication since the rather modest effort of Bismarck's cartel.[10]

In June 1887, Bill Bismarck, the chancellor's second and cleverest son, wrote to Holstein in regard to Germany's foreign policy, "There remains therefore only a seesaw policy as in the Reichstag: to threaten one with the other." Otto von Bismarck as mediator, as conciliator, as consensus-builder is a rather unfamiliar image. To be sure, his moderation and caution in foreign policy, as in the mild Treaty of Nikolsburg with Austria in 1866, his conciliation of the Prussian Liberals in 1867, and his retreat from the Kulturkampf and conciliation of the Center party in the 1880s, are well recognized, but these moves are mostly ascribed to tactical or ulterior motives. That his whole career consisted in mediating between the absolutist past and the democratic future, the well-known "Bismarck-ian Compromise," is admitted, yet the tendency among liberal historians is to assume that the swing to the Right in 1879 was meant to be final and expressed Bismarck's latent Junker conservatism.[11]

There seems, in fact, to be no reason for such an assumption. He appears to have done his best, in 1887, to prepare a basis in the cartel Reichstag for a moderately liberal regime for Kaiser Frederick. In the above narrative the National Liberals were treated with kid gloves, while the Junker Conservatives were systematically scolded, corralled, and humiliated. To be sure, they were also rewarded materially with the increase in the grain tariff, but the tariff system in general also satisfied some Liberals, and Junker agrarian demands were scaled down substantially in the process. It was also the industrially oriented among the aristocracy, people such as Henckel von Donnersmarck and the other Silesian magnates, who were especially close to the Bismarckian regime. There is nothing at all in the unfolding of the above story that suggests that Bismarck leaned ideologically toward the Conservative side. The image of national unity preached by the *Norddeutsche Allgemeine Zeitung* does not conform to Junker ideals or interests, but, rather, to an accommodation, a middle-of-the-road compromise. He must have known that by pushing Prussia into a larger, dynamic, industrializing, and modernizing German Empire he was inevitably undercutting the bases, both ideological and social-economic, for Junker political supremacy. It is notoriously difficult to identify Bismarck's personal feelings on any topic, but judging by his actions—always the best measure of his intentions—he did not especially care what happened to the Junkers as a class. If they had the wisdom and pliability to follow his lead and to adjust to the new political, social, and economic realities, all well and good. If not, then let God's will be done; he had done his best.

Bismarck, his lieutenants in the government, and his press, while maintaining the amenities regarding loyalty to kaiser and Reich, showed no regard for any principle save state interest—with which, of course, Bismarck identified his own power. Even the monarchy—in spite of public statements about his "feudal loyalty"—was handled coldly, objectively, ruthlessly by him. Bismarck actually, from day to day, showed much more flexibility than the historians who have tried to deal with him. Too often they have tended to be taken in by the public battles and the party verbiage and their own conscious or unconscious partisanship. Also, in his own time and since, it has been more emotionally rewarding to adopt the position of either the democratic Left or the orthodox Right, rather than the much maligned middle: the National Liberal and Free Conservative parties. Nobody loves a compromise, since it has no ideal image, either of the past or of the future, and Bismarck, the compromiser, eventually ended his career forsaken by everyone. To have accepted the existing social classes as he found them, to have recognized the importance of the newly developing industry, and to have tried to reconcile the new power group with the old were only practical politics, as was the attempt to make the truly revolutionary changes he was sponsoring appear to be traditional. In the 1887–88 crisis he found the greatest threat to be the instability of Crown Prince William, and he immediately called in public opinion, the popular, democratic principle, to offset it. Labeling the Bismarck regime "Bonapartist" and then assuming that it supported Conservative interests is self-contradictory. The tendency for such regimes— as the present narrative demonstrates—is to develop an independent, arrogant, self-serving, self-perpetuating, authoritarian stance that identifies the interests of the regime itself with the overriding interests of the state as a whole, the *res publica* (cf. Rottenburg's remark to Rantzau, p. 42).

Recent German scholarship, under the burden of the Hitler period and the continuing presence of authoritarian elements in German life, has tended to emphasize the authoritarian aspects of Bismarck's Reich and has, perhaps naturally, fallen in the process into the same liberal groove of a hundred years ago: suggesting or implying that there was a better alternative, that Bismarck and the preindustrial Junker elite arbitrarily held back a natural modernizing process of emancipation of the masses. But there would seem to be nothing naturally emancipating in industrialization per se.[12] Great Britain and the United States, now as a hundred years ago, appear—mistakenly—to be the models for this analysis.[13] But English liberties go a long way back historically, and the relative ease with which the British democratized their government (not their society) in the nineteenth century was sustained by an incomparable worldwide commercial supremacy. American freedom likewise has been a child not of industrialization (shades of J. P. Morgan!), but of British traditions and very special historical circumstances, notably a whole new continent to exploit. New conditions and new, unfamiliar limitations encountered recently in both countries have already ended their special run of luck and caused severe new strains to appear in the famous Anglo-Saxon consensus.

It is always better to compare German development with that of those people closest to her geographically: with France or with Russia. Such a change in reference leads to very different perspectives. The proper question then becomes not "Why was German liberalism so weak?" but "Why was liberalism so strong in German life? Where did it derive its continuing strength; what were its historical roots?"—questions that cannot be dealt with here. Industrialization has historically not brought liberation to Russia, nor to Japan, China, nor almost anywhere else.[14] It has most characteristically provided old elites with new techniques and instruments of oppression. One may believe fervently that truly democratic governmental and social arrangements are the most practical, flexible, and efficient in the long run for handling modern, complex, highly differentiated societies. But one should not imagine that such arrangements are easily come by— certainly not as an inevitable process according to some formula—or that they are easily maintained once possessed. "Man," says the good old book, "is born to trouble as the sparks fly upward."*

In the critical, revealing crisis period of 1887–88 one finds the left, democratic Liberals rallying zealously to the defense of Kaiser Frederick and especially Kaiserin Victoria. One has to respect the soundness of their instincts, if not the practicality or ideological consistency of their tactics. Reduced by the election of February 1887 to an impotent position in the Reichstag, all they could do was energetically wave their liberal principles in the air. They knew that the imperial couple were devoted to those principles, and there is little doubt that a long reign of Frederick and Victoria—when a more open, flexible, individual-oriented rather than traditional, caste-dominated atmosphere would have prevailed, when Liberalism and a bourgeois, secular-minded progressivism would have been officially authorized—would have made a difference in German development. Leaders of Frederick's own liberal generation, men such as Bennigsen, Miquel, Bamberger, Kardorff, Helldorff, and Generals Loë and Caprivi, all of whom thought in terms of industrialization, modernization, and the necessity of further constitutional development for Germany in the direction of rapprochement between monarchy, aristocracy, and people, would then have had their day. A time of healthy blurring of ideological, economic, and social distinctions, coupled with the acceptance of a greater role for educated public opinion and for party leadership in legislatures and government, might well have ensued.

Not that it would have been easy going; in December 1886 Bismarck had told Robert Lucius, the minister of agriculture, that Crown Prince Frederick William "with his touchiness, his pretensions, unmotivated

---

* Job 5:7.

wishes and suspicions of every kind would do me in in short order." But, judging by later developments, this would have been another reason for providing Liberal ministers to handle the kaiser, letting them act as an absorbent buffer between the old chancellor and the imperial couple. And the presence of actual party leaders in the government would have moved it inevitably in a parliamentary direction. No doubt there would have been exciting battles in parliament and press on one issue or another, "alarums and excursions" of all kinds, in the Bismarckian manner, but in the end the transition to a new, more liberal, more popular, less authoritarian, but more healthy, stable, and responsible regime could conceivably have been made.[15]

Without such royal, traditional authorization and initiative, however, and with an inherently conservative and military-minded ruler such as William II at the top of the authoritarian structure, such a development was now unlikely. In the critical months of 1887–88, while the left Liberals were making symbolic gestures, the National Liberals did not reveal any striking initiative or strength. They rallied to the initiatives of the chancellor or the collective government. But even there they did not do very well in carrying out their own tasks: the National Liberal leadership in the Prussian Landtag—the most important legislative arena in the Bismarckian system—could not understand the Conservative viewpoint adequately in regard to the school-aid bill or manage the Conservatives with sufficient adroitness to hold them in the cartel. The government had to step in itself—the bureaucracy and the crown—to provide the necessary force, discipline, authority. Recent German and American scholarship has been very helpful in pointing out the weight of the authoritarian tradition in German life, in the family and the educational system as well as in politics; the support inherently supplied to authoritarianism by both the Lutheran and Counter-Reformation Catholic churches; the tendency of idealistic philosophy to deify the state and to encourage essentially aristocratic, elitist attitudes among the educated middle classes; and the propagation of the ideals of harmony, of discipline, of submission to authority, which made the acceptance of the idea of the English "loyal opposition" in political life and in the parliaments especially difficult.[16] With all this, however, contemporary liberal German historians have nevertheless insisted on clinging to the old, traditional nineteenth-century liberal stance, a viewpoint expressed in the present narrative by Kaiserin Victoria and the German Liberals: that everything would have progressed naturally in a liberal direction if it had not been for the arrogant intransigence of the preindustrial Junker ruling class aided and abetted by Bismarck.[17]

Such an assumption does not fit the analysis of the deep-rooted nature of authoritarianism in German life; and in the fixation on placing blame on "authoritative circles"—which means ducking it for everyone else—one can see the lingering influence of the authoritarian mind itself even in its opponents. The Junkers could not have maintained their position as well as they did, even with Bismarck's help, if there had been an effective opposition. There was none. No party was eager or even willing to take on the responsibility for governing. Greater freedom to agitate, yes; but agitation and speaking out are not the same as accepting or attempting to seize the responsibility of power. People get the governments they deserve, and if Germany was being governed inadequately, it was essentially because of the lack of schooling in politics of the German rank and file. Also, the basic role played by fear of conflict has not been sufficiently recognized, perhaps because it is still too obvious or too painful to contemplate. It was not merely the result of official authoritarian indoctrination by church and state. Germany did not float free, surrounded by the waves, as did both Great Britain and the United States, but was hemmed in by the French on the one hand and the Poles and Russians on the other. Disunity and political stagnation had been the centuries-long result of that inescapable geographical position. Fear of conquest and thus fear of disunity and conflict were part of the basic warp and woof of German life—and still are.

An even more dispiriting perspective that emerges from the story of the crisis of 1887–88 is the inadequacy of the Junker ruling class itself. As a group they fell all too easily into the hands of Hammerstein and Stoecker. The challenge of the crisis in the dynasty did not arouse a sense of generosity and wider responsibility in them nor a broader perspective. Rather, they reacted in a purely parochial, selfish, partisan way, seeing merely a special opportunity to promote their own ideals and interests and depending on the crown and bureaucracy to assume the responsibility and provide the leadership. The fact that all the other parties were acting similarly does not excuse them, since they were the ruling class. It was Bismarck who forced them to be reasonable and responsible and thus protected their position in spite of themselves. Nor did the bureaucrats show any special initiative. They merely wanted things to run smoothly and knew only their own departments. Nor was there responsibility at the top, with young William. He was cajoled, pressured, intimidated, and tricked into finally adopting a reasonable course, both at home and abroad. But the incident of the tasteless and foolish manning of the palace by the guard on his father's death, in spite of Bismarck's specific admonitions, shows how self-willed, narrowed-minded, and childish he continued to be and how difficult it would be for the elderly, ailing chancellor to control him. With truly responsible statesmanship lacking among the ruling class, the dominant political parties, the bureaucracy, and, at the top of the authoritarian structure, the crown itself, the perspective for the future was bleak. Bismarck's constitution, with its careful balancing of monarchy, aristocracy, and democracy, of Prussian bureaucratic and military power with federalism, was not at fault. With a reasonable monarch, an intelligent chancellor, and a modicum of good will among the parties it would probably have continued to work fairly well. But there would be conflicts, and it was questionable whether the leadership, the parties, the various contending class and interest groups, and the public at large could handle such conflicts calmly and with confidence, or whether they might not become even more hysterical and paranoid, engage in rash and foolish enterprises, and ultimately bring down destruction upon Bismarck's new Germany and upon Europe as well. Even the most skilled gambler cannot maintain a run of luck forever. With William I's longevity, Frederick's cancer, and the personality of William II, Bismarck's luck ran out. And so eventually did Germany's.

List of Sources Cited
in the Notes

ARCHIVES

AA	Politisches Archiv des Auswärtigen Amtes. Bonn.
BAFR	Fürstlich von Bismarcksches Archiv. Friedrichsruh.
BAK	Das Deutsche Bundesarchiv. Coblenz. *Nachlässe* Dietze, Hohenlohe, Rottenburg.
BHSA	Bayerisches Hauptstaatsarchiv. Munich.
FOM	German Foreign Office. University of Michigan microfilm.
FOW	German Foreign Office. National Archives microfilm.
FRK	Freiherr von Franckenstein'sches Archiv. Ullstadt, Kreis Scheinfeld, Bavaria.
GLAK	Generallandesarchiv. Karlsruhe. Reports of Minister to Berlin Adolf Marschall von Bieberstein to Minister-President Turban and Grand Duke Frederick of Baden, 233/34797 (1887), 233/34798 (1888); to *Staatsministerium*, 233/12797; also *Grossherzogliches Familienarchiv*.
GSAB	Geheimes Staatsarchiv der Stiftung des preussischen Kulturbesitzes. Berlin/Dahlem.
GSAM	Geheimes Staatsarchiv. Munich. Reports of Minister to Berlin Count Lerchenfeld to Prince Regent Luitpold and Foreign Minister Crailsheim except as otherwise noted; MA III, 2665 (1887), 2666 (1888).
HHSA	Haus-, Hof-, und Staatsarchiv. Vienna. Reports of Berlin Ambassador Széchényi to Foreign Minister Count Kálnoky, except as otherwise noted; Politisches Archiv 3, Karton 133 (Jan.-May 1888), 134 (June-Dec. 1888).
HSAST	Hauptstaatsarchiv. Stuttgart. Reports of Minister to Berlin Count Zeppelin to Minister-President and Foreign Minister von Mittnacht; E73, *Verz.* 61, 12c.
Pindter	Emil Pindter *Nachlass*. National Archives microfilm; series AHA 2, reel 14.

PRO	Public Record Office. Kew.
RA	Royal Archive. Windsor Castle, Windsor.
SP	Salisbury Papers. Hatfield. Correspondence with Sir Edward Malet, ambassador in Berlin; A/61.
ZSA	Zentral Staatsarchiv. Historische Abteilung 1, Potsdam. *Reichskanzlei*; *Nachlässe* Bamberger, Hammacher. Historische Abteilung 2, Merseburg. Hohenzollern *Hausarchiv*; *Königliche Preussische Staatsministerialprotocolle*, Rep. 90a, B, III, 2b, No. 6 (1887), 7 (1888); *Nachlässe* Busch, Waldersee.

NEWSPAPERS AND SERIALS

DGK	*Deutscher Geschichtskalender*. Editor, Karl Wippermann. Leipzig, 1887–88.
DW	*Deutsches Wochenblatt*. Berlin, 1888.
FZ	*Frankfurter Zeitung und Handelsblatt*. Frankfurt am Main, 1887–88.
Gegenwart	*Die Gegenwart*. Berlin, 1887–88.
Ger	*Germania*. Berlin, 1887–88.
KölZ	*Kölnische Zeitung*. Cologne, 1887–88.
Landtag (1)	*Stenographische Berichte über die Verhandlungen des Königlichen Preussischen Landtages, Haus der Abgeordneten. 16. Legislaturperiode, 3 Session*. Berlin, 1888.
(2)	*Stenographische Berichte über die Verhandlungen des Königlichen Preussischen Landtages, Herrenhaus. 16. Legislaturperiode, 3 Session*. Berlin, 1888.
Nation	*Die Nation, Wochenschrift für Politik, Volkswirthschaft und Literatur*. Editor, Theodor Barth. Berlin, 1887–88.
NAZ	*Norddeutsche Allgemeine Zeitung*. Editor, Emil Pindter. Berlin, 1887–88. The chancellor's more or less official outlet.
NDB	*Neue Deutsche Biographie*. Berlin, 1953–.
NPZ	*Neue Preussische (Kreuz) Zeitung*. Editor in chief, Baron Wilhelm von Hammerstein-Schwartow. Berlin, 1887–88.
NYH	*New York Herald*. Proprietor, James Gordon Bennett, Jr. New York, 1887–88. The *Herald* began its Paris edition in early 1888. Important European reports ran in both editions.
NZ	*National-Zeitung*. Berlin, 1887–88.
Reichstag	*Stenographische Berichte über die Verhandlungen des deutschen Reichstages. 7. Legislaturperiode, 2 Session*. Vol. 101 (1887–88), 102 (1888). Berlin.
Schulthess	*Schulthess' Europäischer Geschichtskalender*. Munich, 1887–88.
Zukunft	*Die Zukunft*. Editor, Maximilian Harden. Berlin, 1892–1922.

BOOKS AND ARTICLES

Ackerknecht   Ackerknecht, Erwin H. *Rudolf Virchow.* Madison, Wis.
                     1953.
Anderson & Barkin   Anderson, Margaret Lavinia, and Kenneth Barkin. "The
                     Myth of the Puttkamer Purge and the Reality of the
                     Kulturkampf: Some Reflections on the Historiography of
                     Imperial Germany." *Journal of Modern History* 54 (1982):
                     647–86.
Arendt   Arendt, Hannah. *The Origins of Totalitarianism.* New York,
                     1958.
Bachem   Bachem, Karl. *Vorgeschichte, Geschichte, und Politik der
                     deutschen Zentrumspartei, 1815–1914.* 9 vols. Cologne, 1927–
                     32.
Bamberger (1)   Bamberger, Ludwig. *Bismarck Posthumus.* Berlin, 1899.
         (2)   ———. *Bismarcks grosses Spiel.* Edited by Ernst Feder.
                     Frankfurt am Main, 1932.
Bedford   Bedford, Sybille. *A Legacy.* London, 1956.
Berdahl   Berdahl, Robert M. "Conservative Politics and Aristo-
                     cratic Landholders in Bismarckian Germany." *Journal of
                     Modern History* 44 (1972): 1–20.
Bismarck (1)   Bismarck, Otto von. *Gedanken und Erinnerungen.* 2 vols.
                     Stuttgart, 1899. *Anhang.* 2 vols. Stuttgart, 1901; vol. 3.
                     Stuttgart, 1921.
         (2)   ———. *Die Gesammelten Werke.* Edited by Hermann von
                     Petersdorff et al. Berlin, 1923–33.
Blackbourn & Eley   Blackbourn, David, and Geoff Eley. *Mythen deutscher Ges-
                     chichtsschreibung: Die gescheiterte bürgerliche Revolution von
                     1848.* Frankfurt am Main, Berlin, and Vienna, 1980.
Böhme   Böhme, Helmut. *Deutschlands Weg zur Grossmacht.* Col-
                     ogne, 1966.
Braudel   Braudel, Fernand. *The Mediterranean and the Mediterranean
                     World in the Age of Philip II.* 2 vols. London, 1972–73.
Bülow   Bülow, Bernhard von. *Denkwürdigkeiten.* 4 vols. Berlin,
                     1930–31.
Burke   Burke, Edmund. *Reflections on the Revolution in France.* Ab-
                     ridged ed. in *Burke and Paine: On Revolution and The Rights
                     of Man,* edited by Robert B. Dishman. New York, 1971.
Busch   Busch, Moritz. *Bismarck: Some Secret Pages of His History.*
                     3 vols. London, 1898.
Bussmann   Bussmann, Walter. *Das Zeitalter Bismarcks; Handbuch der
                     deutschen Geschichte.* Edited by Leo Just. Vol. 3, Pt. 3.
                     Munich, 1952–57.
Cecil   Cecil, Lady Gwendolen. *Life of Robert, Marquess of Salis-
                     bury.* 4 vols. London, 1921–32.

Corti (1)   Corti, Egon Caesar, Count. *Alexander von Battenberg.* Vienna, 1920.

(2)   ————. *Wenn . . . Schicksal einer Kaiserin.* Graz, 1954.

Craig   Craig, Gordon A. *Germany, 1806–1945.* New York, 1978.

DDF   *Documents Diplomatiques Français.* 1 series. Paris, 1929. Reports of Berlin Ambassador Herbette to the French Foreign Ministry.

Dohme   Dohme, Robert. "Erinnerungen an Kaiser Friedrich." *Deutsche Revue* Jahrgang 47 (1922), Band 1: 1–14, 117–31, 246–57, Band 2: 73–84.

Dorpalen   Dorpalen, Andreas. "Emperor Frederick III and the German Liberal Movement." *American Historical Review* 54 (Oct. 1948): 1–31.

Eley (1)   Eley, Geoff. "Capitalism and the Wilhelmine State: Industrial Growth and Political Backwardness in Recent German Historiography, 1890–1918." *Historical Journal* 21 (1978): 737–50.

(2)   ————. *Reshaping the German Right: Radical Nationalism and Political Change after Bismarck.* New Haven, 1980.

Eulenburg   Eulenburg-Hertefeld, Philipp, Fürst zu. *Aus 50 Jahren.* Berlin, 1923.

Eyck   Eyck, Erich. *Bismarck, Leben und Werk.* 3 vols. Erlenbach-Zürich, 1941–44.

Forstreuter   Forstreuter, K. "Zu Bismarcks Journalistik. Bismarck und die *Norddeutsche Allgemeine Zeitung.*" *Jahrbuch für die Geschichte Mittel-und Ost-Deutschlands* 2 (1953), 191–210.

Frank   Frank, Walter. *Hofprediger Adolf Stoecker und die christlich-soziale Bewegung.* Hamburg, 1935.

Freund   Freund, Michael. *Das Drama der 99 Tage.* Cologne, 1966.

Freytag (1)   Freytag, Gustav. *Briefe an die Braut und Gattin.* Berlin, 1912.

(2)   ————. *Briefe an Stosch.* Leipzig, 1900.

(3)   ————. *Der Kronprinz und der deutsche Kaiserkron.* Leipzig, 1889.

Fricke   Fricke, Dieter. "Die Affäre Leckert-Lützow-Tausch und die Regierungskrise von 1897 in Deutschland." *Zeitschrift für Geschichtswissenschaft,* Jahrgang 8 (1960), Heft 7, 1579–1603.

Friedjung   Friedjung, Heinrich. *The Struggle for Supremacy in Germany, 1859–1866.* New York, 1935.

Gagliardi   Gagliardi, Ernst von. *Bismarcks Entlassung.* 2 vols. Tübingen, 1927, 1941.

Gall   Gall, Lothar. *Bismarck: Der weisse Revolutionär.* Berlin, 1980.

Gourevitch   Gourevitch, Peter Alexis. "International Trade, Domes-
                      tic Coalitions, and Liberty: Comparative Responses to
                      the Crisis of 1873–96." *Journal of Interdisciplinary History* 8
                      (1977): 281–313.

GP   *Die Grosse Politik der europäischen Kabinette, 1871–1914.*
                      . . . Edited by J. Lepsius, A. Mendelssohn-Bartholdy,
                      and F. Thimme. 40 vols. Berlin, 1922–27.

Haller   Haller, Johannes. *Aus dem Leben des Fürsten Philipp zu
                      Eulenburg-Hertefeld.* Berlin, 1924.

Hartung   Hartung, Friedrich. *Deutsche Geschichte.* 5th ed. Berlin,
                      1939.

Heffter   Heffter, Heinrich. *Die Opposition der Kreuzzeitungspartei
                      gegen die Bismarcksche Kartellpolitik in den Jahren 1887 bis
                      1890.* Leipzig, 1927.

Herbert   *Staatssekretär Graf Herbert von Bismarck: Aus seiner politischen
                      Privatkorrespondenz.* Edited by Walter Bussmann.
                      Deutsche Geschichtsquellen des 19. und 20. Jahrhun-
                      derts, 44. Göttingen, 1964.

Herzfeld (1)   Herzfeld, Hans. *Johannes von Miquel.* 2 vols. Detmold,
                      1938.

        (2)   ———. "Waldersee und Eulenburg." In *Ausgewählte Auf-
                      sätze* 71–86. Berlin, 1962.

Hess   Hess, Adalbert. *Das Parlament das Bismarck widerstrebte.*
                      Cologne and Opladen, 1964.

Heyderhoff   Heyderhoff, Julius, ed. *Im Ring der Gegner Bismarcks.*
                      Deutsche Geschichtsquellen des 19. und 20. Jahrhun-
                      derts, 35. Leipzig, 1943.

Hillgruber   Hillgruber, Andreas. *Bismarcks Aussenpolitik.* Freiburg,
                      1972.

Hohenlohe   Hohenlohe-Schillingsfürst, Chlodwig Fürst zu. *Denkwür-
                      digkeiten.* 2 vols. Stuttgart, 1906.

Holborn   Holborn, Hajo. *A History of Modern Germany.* 2 vols. New
                      York, 1959–69.

Hollyday   Hollyday, Frederic B. M. *Bismarck's Rival.* Durham, N.C.,
                      1960.

Holstein   *The Holstein Papers.* Edited by Norman Rich and M. H.
                      Fisher. 4 vols. Cambridge, 1955–63.

Hübner   Hübner, Joachim. *Bismarck und Kaiser Friedrich III.* Kiel,
                      1953.

Hunt   Hunt, James C. "Imperial German Protectionism Re-
                      examined." *Central European History* 7 (1974): 311–31.

Huntington   Huntington, Samuel. *Political Order in Changing Societies.*
                      New Haven, 1968.

Johanna   Bismarck, Johanna von. *Johanna von Bismarck: ein
                      Lebensbild in Briefen, 1844–1894.* Stuttgart, 1915.

Johnson   Johnson, John J., Jr. "False Dawn: Bismarck, the Cartel, and the Crown Prince, November 1886 to June 1887." Ph.D. dissertation, University of Illinois at Urbana-Champaign, 1972.

Kampmann   Kampmann, Wanda. "Adolf Stoecker und die Berliner Bewegung." *Geschichte in Wissenschaft und Unterricht* 13 (1962): 558–79.

Kardorff   Kardorff, Siegfried von. *Wilhelm von Kardorff, ein nationaler Parlamentarier im Zeitalter Bismarcks und Wilhelms II, 1828–1907.* Berlin, 1936.

Kaufmann   Kaufmann, Walter, ed. and trans. *Goethe's Faust.* Garden City, 1961.

Kehr   Kehr, Eckart. *Der Primat der Innenpolitik.* Edited by Hans-Ulrich Wehler. Berlin, 1965.

Kennan   Kennan, George F. *The Decline of Bismarck's European Order: Franco-Russian Relations, 1875–1890.* Princeton, 1979.

Krankheit   *Die Krankheit Kaiser Friedrichs III dargestellt nach amtlichen Quellen und den im königlichen Hausministerium niedergelegten Berichten der Aerzte.* Berlin, 1888. Excerpted in *Berliner Politischen Nachrichten,* July 10, 1888; contained in HHSA 79B: 244–46, Sz. to Kál., July 14, 1888.

Krausnick   Krausnick, Helmut. *Holsteins Geheimpolitik in der Ära Bismarck, 1886–1890.* Hamburg, 1942.

Krieger   Krieger, Leonard. *The German Idea of Freedom.* Boston, 1957.

Kumpf-Korfes   Kumpf-Korfes, Sigrid. *Bismarcks "Draht nach Russland."* Berlin, 1968.

Kupisch   Kupisch, Karl. *Adolf Stoecker, Hofprediger und Volkstribun.* Berlin, 1970.

Langer   Langer, William L. *European Alliances and Alignments, 1871–1890.* New York, 1931.

Leuss   Leuss, Hans. *Wilhelm Freiherr von Hammerstein, 1881–1895 Chefredakteur der Kreuzzeitung.* Berlin, 1905.

Levy   Levy, Richard S. *The Downfall of the Anti-Semitic Political Parties in Imperial Germany.* New Haven, 1975.

Lucius   Lucius von Ballhausen, Robert, Freiherr. *Bismarckerinnerungen.* Stuttgart, 1921.

McClelland   McClelland, Charles E. *The German Historians and England: A Study in Nineteenth-Century Views.* Cambridge, 1971.

Mackenzie   Mackenzie, Sir Morrell. *The Fatal Illness of Frederick the Noble.* London, 1888.

Massing   Massing, Paul. *Rehearsal for Destruction.* New York, 1949.

Meisner   Meisner, Heinrich O., ed. "Briefwechsel zwischen … Grafen Waldersee und … Grafen Yorck von Wartenburg, 1885–1894." *Historisch-Politisches Archiv* 1 (1930).

Mittnacht   Mittnacht, Hermann, Freiherr von. *Erinnerungen an Bismarck.* Stuttgart, 1904–5.

Möckl   Möckl, Karl. *Die Prinzregentenzeit.* Munich, 1972.

Nichols   Nichols, J. Alden. *Germany after Bismarck: The Caprivi Era, 1890–1894.* Cambridge, Mass., 1958.

Nipperdey   Nipperdey, Thomas. *Die Organisation der deutschen Parteien.* Düsseldorf, 1961.

Oncken   Oncken, Hermann. *Rudolf von Bennigsen.* 2 vols. Stuttgart, 1910.

Pack   Pack, Wolfgang. *Parlamentarische Ringen um das Sozialistengesetz Bismarcks, 1878–1890.* Beiträge zur Geschichte des Parlamentarismus und der politischen Parteien, 20. Düsseldorf, 1961.

Pflanze (1)   Pflanze, Otto. *Bismarck and the Development of Germany.* Princeton, 1962.

(2)   ———. "Toward a Psychoanalytical Interpretation of Bismarck." *American Historical Review* 77 (1972): 419–44.

(3)   ———, ed. *The Unification of Germany, 1848–1871.* New York, 1968.

Pinkney   Pinkney, David H. "The Myth of the French Revolution of 1830." In *Essays in Honor of Frederick B. Artz.* Edited by David H. Pinkney. Durham, N.C., 1964.

Plumb   Plumb, J. H. *The Origins of Political Stability, England, 1675–1725.* Boston, 1967.

Polizei   *Die Politische Polizei in Preussen. Bericht über die Verhandlungen im Prozess Leckert-Lützow-Tausch am 2., 3., 4. und 7. Dezember 1896 vor dem Landgericht I zu Berlin.* Berlin, 1896.

Ponsonby (1)   Ponsonby, Sir Frederick, ed. *Letters of the Empress Frederick.* London, 1928.

(2)   Ponsonby, Mary. *A Lady-in-Waiting to the Queen.* Edited by Magdalen Ponsonby. New York, 1927.

Poschinger   Poschinger, Margaretha von. *Kaiser Friedrich.* 3 vols. Berlin, 1898.

Pulzer   Pulzer, Peter G. J. *The Rise of Political Anti-Semitism in Germany and Austria.* New York, 1964.

Puttkamer   Puttkamer, Albert von. *Staatsminister von Puttkamer. Ein Stück preussischer Vergangenheit, 1828 bis 1900.* Leipzig, 1929.

Q. Vict.   Queen Victoria. *Letters of Queen Victoria.* Edited by G. E. Buckle. 3d series. London, 1930–32.

Richter   Richter, Werner. *Bismarck.* New York, 1965.

Robinson   Robinson, James Harvey. "The Constitution of the Kingdom of Prussia." *Annals of the American Academy* 5 (1894), supplement, [197–250].

Rodd   Rodd, James, Lord Rennell of. *Social and Diplomatic Memories, 1884–1893.* London, 1922.

Rodes	Rodes, John E. *Germany: A History.* New York, 1964.
Rogge (1)	Rogge, Helmuth. *Friedrich von Holstein Lebensbekenntnis in Briefen an eine Frau.* Berlin, 1932.
(2)	———. *Holstein und Hohenlohe.* Stuttgart, 1957.
Röhl	Röhl, John C. G. "The Disintegration of the *Kartell* and the Politics of Bismarck's Fall from Power." *Historical Journal* 9 (1966): 60–89.
Röhl & Sombart	Röhl, John C. G., and Nicolaus Sombart, eds. *Kaiser Wilhelm II: New Interpretations.* Cambridge, 1982.
Rosenberg	Rosenberg, Hans. *Grosse Depression und Bismarckzeit.* Berlin, 1967.
Rothfels	Rothfels, Hans. *Bismarck und der Staat.* Munich, 1925.
Schnitzler (1)	Schnitzler, Arthur. *My Youth in Vienna.* Translated by Catherine Hutter. New York, 1970.
(2)	Schnitzler, Arthur, and Olga Waissnix. *Liebe die starb vor der Zeit: Briefwechsel.* Vienna, 1970.
Scholtz	Scholtz, Gerhard. *Die Übersprungene Generation 1888.* Heidelberg, 1934.
Schorske	Schorske, Carl E. *Fin-de-Siècle Vienna: Politics and Culture.* New York, 1980.
Seeber	Seeber, Gustav. *Zwischen Bebel und Bismarck: Zur Geschichte des Linksliberalismus in Deutschland, 1871–1893.* Berlin, 1965.
Shanahan	Shanahan, William O. *German Protestants Face the Social Question.* South Bend, Ind. 1954.
Sheehan	Sheehan, James J. *German Liberalism in the Nineteenth Century.* Chicago, 1978.
Spitzemberg	Spitzemberg, Hildegard, Baronin von. *Das Tagebuch der Baronin von Spitzemberg.* Edited by Rudolf Vierhaus. Göttingen, 1960.
Stern (1)	Stern, Fritz. *Gold and Iron: Bismarck, Bleichröder, and the Building of the German Empire.* New York, 1977.
(2)	———. *The Politics of Cultural Despair.* Berkeley, 1961.
Stürmer (1)	Stürmer, Michael. "Bismarck in Perspective." *Central European History* 4 (1971): 291–331.
(2)	———. *Das kaiserliche Deutschland: Politik und Gesellschaft, 1870–1918.* Düsseldorf, 1970.
(3)	———. "Staatsstreichgedanken im Bismarckreich." *Historische Zeitschrift,* 209 (11969): 566ff.
Thimme	Thimme, Friedrich, ed. "Bismarck und Kardorff." *Deutsche Revue* 42 (1917): (1), 46–59, 162–85, 278–88; (2), 24–45, 149–68, 262–79.
Turk	Turk, Eleanor L. "The Press of Imperial Germany: A New Role for a Traditional Resource." *Central European History* 10/4 (1977): 329–37.

Untermeyer   Untermeyer, Louis. *Heinrich Heine: Paradox and Poet.* New
                    York, 1937.
Wahl   Wahl, Adalbert. *Deutsche Geschichte von der Reichsgründung
                    bis zum Ausbruch des Weltkrieges, 1871–1914.* 4 vols. Stuttgart,
                    1926–36.
Waldersee   Waldersee, Alfred, Graf von. *Denkwürdigkeiten.* . . . Edited
                    by H. O. Meissner. 3 vols. Stuttgart, 1923.
Wehler (1)   Wehler, Hans-Ulrich. *Das Deutsche Kaiserreich, 1871–1918.*
                    Göttingen, 1973.
       (2)   ———. *Krisenherde des Kaiserreichs, 1871–1918: Studien Zur
                    deutschen Sozial- und Verfassungsgeschichte.* Göttingen, 1970.
Wentzcke   Wentzcke, Paul, ed. *Deutscher Liberalismus im Zeitalter Bis-
                    marcks.* Vol. 2, *Im Neuen Reich.* Deutsche Geschichtsquellen
                    des 19. Jahrhunderts, 24. Osnabrück, 1967.
White   White, Dan S. *The Splintered Party: National Liberalism in
                    Hessen and the Reich, 1867–1918.* Cambridge, Mass., 1976.
William II   William II, Deutscher Kaiser. *Aus meinem Leben.* Berlin,
                    1927.
Wolf   Wolf, H.-J. *Die Krankheit Friedrichs III. und ihre Wirkung auf
                    die deutsche und englische Öffentlichkeit.* Berlin, 1958.
Wood   Wood, Gordon S. *The Creation of the American Republic,
                    1776–1787.* Chapel Hill, 1969.
Zahn   Zahn-Harnack, Agnes von. *Adolf von Harnack.* Berlin,
                    1936.
Ziekursch   Ziekursch, Johannes. *Politische Geschichte des neuen deutschen
                    Kaiserreiches.* 3 vols. Frankfurt am Main, 1925–30.
Zmarzlick   Zmarzlick, Hans-Günter. "Das Kaiserreich in neuer
                    Sicht?" *Historische Zeitschrift* 222 (1976): 105–26.
Zucker   Zucker, Stanley. *Ludwig Bamberger: German Liberal Politician
                    and Social Critic, 1823–1899.* Pittsburgh, 1975.

Notes

Complete references for each author or publication may be found in the List of Sources Cited in the Notes beginning on. p. 350.

1. "THE CARTEL AND THE CROWN PRINCE"

1. For the unification of Germany, see especially Pflanze (1) and (3). For German history, Rodes, Craig. For Bismarck, Pflanze (1), Gall.

2. On the political impact of the Long Depression, see Rosenberg, Gourevitch.

3. For this development, see Zucker, Sheehan, Seeber.

4. On Crown Prince Frederick William, later Kaiser Frederick III, see, for his personality, Corti (2), Holstein, Freytag (3); for his political orientation, Dorpalen, Bismarck (1), Hübner, Poschinger.

5. Quote, Corti (2), 484–85; Busch, 1: 500.

6. Dorpalen; quote, Holstein, 2: 179; Corti (2), 150–53; cf. Bamberger (2), 32, Lucius, 360, and below, 211.

7. On the crown princess, see Freytag (1), passim.

8. Bismarck (1), 2: 305; *Anhang*, 2: 540; Heyderhoff, 228–29; Holstein, 2: 112–13, 115–19, 203, 211, quote from cr. princess, 2: 204; *Herbert*, 374; cf. Eulenburg, 128–29; Lucius, 324, 338; *Zukunft*, 57: 214.

9. On the German Liberals, see Nipperdey, Sheehan, Seeber; on the position of the parties in the 1862 crisis, see Hess.

10. *Herbert*, 225; Oncken, 2: 524, 531. See also Lucius, 297, 345; *Ger*, Jan. 22, 1887 (2d ed.): 1; Jan. 23 (2d ed.): 2. Cf. Massing, 55.

11. On the seriousness of the military aspect, see Johnson, 22ff.; also Kennan, 120–93; Langer, 379–80; Eyck, 3: 431ff.; Bachem, 4: 152–53.

12. *Reichstag*, 93: 342, 351, 379, 413; *Schulthess*, (1887): 22, 54.

13. *Schulthess*, (1887): 34, 36; *Reichstag*, 93: 379.

14. Heyderhoff, passim.

15. Eyck, 3: 449; *Reichstag*, 93: 402; *Schulthess*, (1887): 45.

16. Mittnacht, 2: 29, 44; Johnson, 53–55. Both Helldorff and Kleist-Retzow urged a conflict with the Reichstag. BAFR, Herbert to Rantzau, D27, Jan. 7, 1887; Herb.'s diary, D48, Jan. 7, 10.

17. Busch, 3: 158–59.

18. Lucius, 307.

19. *Herbert*, 425; original is in English.

20. *Kreuzztg.* (*NPZ*) article quoted in Oncken, 2: 531; Johnson, 56; cf. *NPZ*, May 31, 1888 (173): 1; *Ger*, June 9, 1887 (1st ed.): 2.

21. Heyderhoff, 256; Lucius, 462; Holstein, 2: 69; Thimme, 2: 270; cf. Frank,

153–62. There is a biography of Puttkamer by his son (see Puttkamer); the review of this biography by Eckart Kehr, "Das soziale System der Reaktion in Preussen unter dem Ministerium Puttkamer" (see Kehr), says nothing about Puttkamer but is a superficial and tendentious critique of the Bismarckian Reich as a whole. On Kehr and the Puttkamer "system," see Anderson & Barkin.

22. _Schulthess_, (1887): 62–65, 76–77, 80–83, 85.

23. Bamberger (2), 339; Thimme, 2: 269.

24. The quote is from Eyck, 3: 448. Eyck's account is based mostly on left-Liberal sources. Holstein, 2: 200–201. On the development of the cartel, see especially Johnson, chap. 3. On Frederick, Bismarck, and the National Liberals, Hübner, 165, 167, 173, 180.

25. Holstein, 2: 275; Busch, 3: 163–64.

26. Lucius, 373, 462; cf. Heyderhoff, 256.

2. "CANCER"

1. For the illness of the crown prince, later Kaiser Frederick III, see especially the official report of the German doctors, _Krankheit_, as well as Wolf, Mackenzie, Freund; Heyderhoff, 258. Further bibliography on the case may be found in Wolf and Freund.

2. Corti (2), 403–8, 432–33; Ponsonby (1), 231–32; Heyderhoff, 260; Mackenzie, 21, 188, 191–96; Freund, 47–54; Bismarck (1), 2: 306; Wolf, 3–12, 64–68, 71–75, 85; GSAM, Lerchenfeld to prince regent, May 21, 1887, No. 284/XIX; BAFR, F4, Rantz. to Herb., May 21.

3. Mackenzie, 36–37; Wolf, 71–72, 85; Freund, 78, 99, 109, 122–25, 139; Lucius, 388–90; Freytag (2), 194; HHSA, Karton 132: 24–27, Széchenyi to Kálnoky, private letter, May 25, 1887; cf. Freytag (1), 125, 127; ZSA, Merseburg, _Hausarch._, Rep. 52J, 327^t, cr. pr. to ksrn., May 18, 27; Rep. 51J, 733, Gen. Winterfeld to kaiser, Oct. 24; BAFR, B44, Radolinski to chanc., May 20; GSAM, III: 2665, Lerch. to pr. reg., May 22, 24, 25, 30, June 9, Nos. 286/XX, 290/XXI, 291/XXII, 299/XXIII, 311/XXVI; on Virchow, Ackerknecht, esp. 74–76.

4. Wolf, 75; Freund, 78, 169, 171, 185; Heyderhoff, 276; Lucius, 391; BAFR, D48, Herb.'s diary, May 24, 1887, June 10; B110, Dr. F. Semon to Herb., July 31, Aug. 6, Sept. 8, Nov. 19; ZSA, Merseburg, _Hausarch._, Mackenzie to Radolinski, June 29, Rad. to Stolberg, Aug. 16.

5. Wolf, 22; Lucius, 393–94; Heyderhoff, 261; Freund, 141, 146, 157; ZSA, Merseburg, _Hausarch._, Rep. 51J, 733, Winterfeld to kaiser, Oct. 9, 1887; GLAK, Marschall to Turban, Nov. 14, No. 44; ZSA, Merseburg, _Hausarch._, Rep. 52, FI, 7aa: 280, cr. pr.'s diary, Oct. 7; RA, Z38/80, cr. prcss. to Queen Victoria, Nov. 13.

6. Heyderhoff, 280, quote, 261–62; Eulenburg, 140; Herbert and Dr. Semon citations, n. 4, above; Lucius, 392, 394, quote, 393; _Herbert_, 456, 457; Johanna, 321, 323; Spitzemberg, 235, 238. Cf. Holstein, 3: 213; Bismarck (2), 6c: 361, quote: 14^2: 672; BAFR, F4, Rantz. to Herb., June 17, 1887, Nov. 7, 10; D48, Herb.'s diary, June 11-16, 20; C9, Johanna to Herb., Oct. 21, 23, Nov. 5, 8.

7. Queen Victoria's private physician wrote Mackenzie that the operation was the only hope of saving the crown prince's life and that neither German nor English doctors considered it to be very dangerous. Mackenzie replied that it was

too great a risk. Q. Vict., 1: 360; Freund, 133, 153, 162, 168–69; *Schulthess,* (1887): 195, for cr. pr. quote; Mackenzie, 65; Heyderhoff, 270; Holstein, 2: 355, 357; 3: 227; *Herbert,* 479; BAFR, D4a, Herb. to Bism., Nov. 14; cr. prcss. quotes, Ponsonby (1), 260–61 and ZSA, Merseburg, *Hausarch.,* Rep. 52T, No. 13; Wolf, 87–100; GLAK, Marsch. to Turban, Oct. 15, 17, Nov. 14, Nos. 31, 32, 44, Marsch. to gr. d., Nov. 7, *Grhzg. Fam. arch.,* N451; GSAM, Bavarian member of Bundesrat, Count Klemens von Podewils to pr. reg., Sept. 19, Oct. 12, 15, 16, Nos. 428/LIII, 470/LXII, 472, 475/LXIII; Lerch. to pr. reg., Nov. 9, 11, 12, 13, Nos. 513/LXVII, 516/LXVIII, 517/LXIX, 519/LXX, 522/LXXII; ZSA, Merseburg, *Hausarch.,* Rep. 52, FI, 7aa: 315, cr. pr.'s diary, Nov. 11; BAFR, F4, Rantz. to Herb., Nov. 6, 8; D27, Herb. to Rantz., Nov. 8, 10.

8. BAFR, D27, Herb. to Rantz., Nov. 11, 12, 1887; F4, Rantz. to Herb., Nov. 12, 14; GLAK, *Grhzg. Fam. arch.,* N536, Marsch. to Turban, Nov. 12; HSAST, Zeppelin to Mittnacht, Nov. 13; *Krankheit,* 245; Heyderhoff, 270; Lucius, 402; *Herbert,* 481; Hohenlohe, 2: 422; Holstein, 2: 357; Ponsonby (1), 262–63; Bamberger (2), 369. Cf. report of August Stein (E), *FZ,* Dec. 29 (363:1 mg. ed.): 1; Robinson, 234.

9. RA, Z38/88; Ponsonby (1), 259, 263; Bamberger (2), 369; Hohenlohe, 2: 422; Holstein, 2: 357–58; cf. Corti (2), 494–95. On Winterfeld cf. Rogge (1), 145; Ksrn. Vict. in Corti (2), 494–95.

10. Cf. Ziekursch, 2: 426, 428; Eyck, 3: 507, 543; Wahl, 2: 449–50; Holborn, 3: 299; Richter, 310–11.

11. Holstein, 3: 230; 2: 346–48; Q. Vict., 1: 361; cf. *Zukunft,* 57 (Nov. 10, 1906): 214.

12. Text of *Stellvertretung* order in *NAZ,* Mar. 8, 1888 (116): 3; Lucius, 403–4, 406, 407; cr. pr.'s diary, ZSA, Merseburg, *Hausarch.,* Rep. 52, FI, 7aa: 325–26; BAFR, F4, Rantz. to Herb., Nov. 26, 29, 1887. Cf. *Herbert,* 481–82; *FZ,* Nov. 16 (320:2 mg.): 1; Nov. 18 (322:2 mg.): 1.

13. RA, Z38/95–98; cf. cr. pr.'s diary, ZSA, Merseburg, *Hausarch.,* Rep. 52, FI, 7aa: 326 (Nov. 22), 354 (Dec. 20).

14. Bismarck (2), 6c: 371–73; Corti (2), 432–33; RA, Z38/99; cr. pr.'s diary, ZSA, Merseburg, *Hausarch.,* Rep. 52, FI, 7aa: 326; cf. BAFR, F4, Rantz. to Herb., Dec. 1, 10, 17, 1887.

15. *KölZ,* Nov. 23 (325:2): 1; Nov. 24 (326:3): 1; Nov. 28 (330:1): 1; Dec. 1 (333:1): 2; Dec. 2 (334:2): 1; GLAK, Marsch. to Turban, Nov. 23, No. 49; BAFR, F4, Rantz. to Herb., Nov. 26, 27; D27, Herb. to Rantz., Nov. 26; B100, Rottbg. to Rantz., Nov. 24; Bismarck (2), 6c: 367–69; *DDF,* 6: 651.

16. Corti (2), 434, 436; cf. Ponsonby (1), 270; cr. pr.'s letter dated Dec. 4, sent by Hintzpeter to *Neue Westfälischer Volkszeitung, Westfälischer Zeitung, Der Wächter,* and *Bielefelder Zeitung* on Dec. 8, was published the ninth, and reprinted, along with Hintzpeter's covering letter, in *NAZ,* Dec. 10 (578): 1, and *Ger,* Dec. 11 (283:1): 2; *Zukunft,* 57 (Nov. 10, 1906): 214; Lucius, 396.

3. "THE WALDERSEE-STOECKER MEETING"

1. Salisbury quote, Cecil, 4: 96; Corti (2), 425.

2. *Post* report of the meeting in *Schulthess,* (1887): 190; *NAZ,* Dec. 1 (561): 2; for

a more complete list of those attending, *Deutsch-Evangel. Kirchenztg.* article, reprinted in *Ger*, Dec. 13 (284:1): 2; *FZ*, Dec. 12 (346:evg.): 1.

3. *Schulthess*, (1887): 190; *FZ*, Dec. 2 (336:evg.): 1; Waldersee, 1: 339.

4. The *Post* article is reprinted in *Ger*, Dec. 2 (276:1): 2; *KölZ*, Dec. 1 (333:1): 1; cf. letters to Stoecker and Waldersee from Frhr. v. Mirbach, ZSA, Merseburg, Rep. 92, AII, No. 8, Bl. 7–13; *Börsen-Cour.* article reprinted in *Ger*, Nov. 30 (274:2): 2; *FZ*, Dec. 1 (335:evg.): 1; quotes from *Freis. Ztg.* reprinted in the *FZ* article; Waldersee, 1: 339.

5. For Stoecker's early life, Kupisch; for the Berlin Movement, Levy, 17, 25–27, Kampmann, also Heffter, 19–21.

6. Heffter, 22–29; Johnson, 86–87, 110–11; Frank, 149–64, Stoecker quote, 98; Kampmann, 565–66, 571–72. On anti-Semitism, Massing, Pulzer, Arendt. On Jewish finance, Stern (1).

7. For the attitudes of Frederick William and Victoria, see especially Corti (2), passim; *NPZ*, Nov. 27, 1887 (278, *Beilage*), "Christlich-soziale Partei": 1; Nov. 26 (277), "Predigt zur Eröffnung des Reichstags": 1; Nov. 27 (278), "Advent": 1.

8. *FZ*, Dec. 2, 1887 (336:evg.): 1; *NPZ*, Dec. 4 (284, *Beilage*), "Christlich-soziale Partei": 1. For Böckel, see Levy, 39–65.

9. *NPZ*, Dec. 4, 1887 (284, *Beilage*): 1.

10. For Waldersee, the crown prince, Albedyll, and Winterfeld, cf. Waldersee, 1: 306, 325, 327, 338; Holstein, 2: 356; Dohme, 250; Rogge (1), 145; see above, 29–30. The cr. prcss.'s letter in Ponsonby (1), 270–71.

11. Ponsonby (1), 247; Dohme, 248–49; Hollyday, 234; cf. Heyderhoff, 275–77; ZSA, Merseburg, *Hausarch.*, rep. 52J, *general*. 6, Dec. 20, 26, 1887; Jan. 31, 1888.

12. *NAZ*, Nov. 29, 1887 (558), "Dtld., Hof u. Pers.-Nachr.": 2; Dec. 2 (564), "Dtld., Hof u. Pers.-Nachr.": 1; Dec. 3 (566), "Hof u. Pers.-Nachr.": 1; Dec. 5 (568), "Hof u. Pers.-Nachr.": 2; Dec. 6 (569), "Hof u. Pers.-Nachr.": 2; Bismarck (1), 3: 5–6; Lucius, 410; BAFR, D48, Herb.'s diary, Dec. 1–4.

13. For the *Kreuzztg.* article, see above, 38.

14. *Ger*, Dec. 6, 1887 (279:1): 2–3. The crown prince pasted in his diary a fuller version of the *Posener Ztg.* article, probably the original, identified as from a Halle paper; ZSA, Merseburg, *Hausarch.*, Rep. 52, FI, 7aa: 333.

15. BAFR, B100, ref. to Cremer's subsidy, Oct. 11; Lucius, 409; Bismarck (2), 6c: 199; Frank, 393ff.

4. "THE STOECKER DRIVE BECOMES AN AFFAIR"

1. *NAZ*, Dec. 8, 1887 (574), "Parteibewegg.": 2; *Ger*, Dec. 10 (282:1): 3; *NAZ*, Dec. 11 (579): 1.

2. BAFR, F4, Rantz. to Herb., Dec. 7, 1887; D27, Herb. to Rantz., Dec. 6; B100, Rottbg. to Rantz., Dec. 8, 10; Bismarck (2), 6c: 376.

3. The article appeared in *NAZ*, Dec. 11, 1887 (579): 1.

4. *NPZ*, Dec. 13, 1887 (291): 2. The *Kons. Korr.* article appeared on Oct. 13.

5. *KölZ*, Dec. 12, 1887 (344:2): 1; *NAZ*, Dec. 14 (584), "Pol. Tagesber.": 1; report of Stoecker meeting, *NPZ*, Dec. 14 (292): 6.

6. Waldersee, 1: 343–44.

7. *NPZ*, Dec. 16, 1887 (294): 2; Dec. 17 (295): 2.

8. For the Böckel scene, *Reichstag*, 101: 273–74; *FZ*, Dec. 16, 1887 (350:2 mg.), "Dtr. Rchstg.": 1–2; anti-Sem. mtg., *FZ*, Dec. 17 (351:evg.): 1; *NPZ*, Dec. 17 (295), "Rchstgs. Nachr.": 2; *NAZ*, Dec. 16 (588): 1; Dec. 17 (590): 1–2. Liebermann addressed an anti-Semitic meeting on Dec. 13, where he also discussed various types of anti-Semitism, defending the racial standpoint but in a way conciliatory toward Stoecker: *NPZ*, Dec. 16 (294, 2 *Beilage*), "Antisemiten Versammlg.": 1.

9. *NAZ*, Dec. 20, 1887 (593), "Jour.-Rev.": 2 [erroneously numbered 3]; *FZ*, Dec. 24 (358:1 mg.): 1; the kaiser received the crown prince's chamberlain, Count Radolinski, on the twenty-second and followed this with a long audience with Herbert Bismarck. *NAZ*, Dec. 23 (600): 2.

10. Corti reports that the crown prince's letter to Dr. Hintzpeter appeared in the *Nat. Ztg.* Since Corti worked almost entirely from family archives, this statement suggests that the crown prince's household habitually read the *Nat. Ztg.*; Corti (2), 434.

11. *NPZ*, Dec. 20, 1887 (297), "Pol. Wochen-Übersicht": 1; Dec. 21 (298), "'Hervorragende' Rettgsgedanken. f. die Berl. Bewegg.": 1.

12. *NAZ*, Dec. 22, 1887 (597): 1.

13. *NPZ*, Dec. 23, 1887 (300), "Die Kampfesweise der *NAZ*": 1; Mar. 8 statement quoted in Johnson, 154.

14. For this and the following *Berl. Tgblt.* article, *Ger*, Dec. 23, 1887 (293:2): 1–2. This article was pasted in his diary by the crown prince; ZSA, Merseburg, *Hausarch.*, Rep. 52, FI, 7aa: 355–56.

15. Cf. n. 9, above.

16. Cf. *Ger*, Dec. 1, 1887 (275): 3; Dec. 3 (277:2): 2; Dec. 6 (279:1): 1; Werthern to Hohenl., Jan. 5, 1888, BAK, *Nachl.* Hohenlohe, XBW9.

17. *NAZ*, Dec. 4, 1887 (567): 2; *Nat. Ztg.* article in *NAZ*, Dec. 13 (581): 2; Lucius, 408; *FZ*, Dec. 13 (347:2 mg.): 2; *Magd. Ztg.* quote from *Ger*, Dec. 13 (284:1): 3.

18. *FZ*, Dec. 15, 1887 (349:2 mg.): 2; Dec. 16 (350:1 mg.): 3; (350:2 mg.): 2; (350:evg.): 2; Dec. 17 (351:2 mg.): 3; Dec. 18 (352:2 mg.): 2; Dec. 23 (357:2 mg.): 1; *NAZ*, Dec. 15 (586): 2; Dec. 16 (587): 2; (588): 1; *NPZ*, Dec. 18 (296): 1; Dec. 22 (299), "Aus San Remo": 1; Dec. 23 (300), "Aus San Remo": 1; Dec. 24 (301), "Aus San Remo": 1; Mack. to *Figaro*, *Ger*, Dec. 24 (294:1), "Local-Nachr.": 4; *KölZ*, Dec. 24 (356:2): 1; cf. Waldersee, 1: 344; Lucius, 411; ZSA, Merseburg, *Hausarch.*, Rep. 52J, No. 336a, cr. pr. to Pr. Wm.; gr. d., *NAZ*, Dec. 27 (604): 1; for original text of statement and letter to gr. duke, GLAK, *Grhzg. Fam. arch.*, Bd. 45, Dec. 9, 10.

19. *Schulthess*, (1887): 200, gives the date as Dec. 24, but it is clear from evidence in the contemporary press that it was the twenty-third; the Schulthess text is closest to that run in *Ger*, Dec. 24 (294:2): 2, but lacks a passage printed in both *NAZ*, Dec. 25 (603), "Jour.-Rev.": 2, and *NPZ*, Dec. 25 (302), "Die Versammlg. bei Grf. Waldersee": 1.

20. *Hamb. Korr.* article printed in *Ger*, Dec. 24, 1887 (294:1): 3, and in *NPZ*, Dec. 25 (302), "Die Versammlg. bei Grf. Waldersee": 1; for the *Dts. Tgblt.*, see

KölZ, Dec. 26 (357:3): 1; *Ger*, Dec. 25 (295:2): 1.

21. *FZ*, Dec. 25, 1887 (359:1 mg.): 1.

22. *Ger*, Dec. 24, 1887 (294:2): 2; Dec. 25 (295:1): 3.

23. *NPZ*, Dec. 25, 1887 (302), "Die Versammlg. bei Grf. Waldersee": 1.

24. Reprinted *FZ*, Dec. 28, 1887 (362:2 mg.): 1; *Schulthess*, (1887): 200–201; *NPZ*, Dec. 29 (304), "Die 'Post'": 1. *Schulthess* gives the date as Dec. 28.

25. *NPZ*, Dec. 29, 1887 (304), "Die 'Post'": 1.

26. *Ger*, Dec. 29, 1887 (297:1): 2; *NPZ*, Dec. 31 (306), "Die 'Post'": 1; cf. *FZ*, Dec. 31 (365:2 mg.): 1. A "Promemoria" dated Dec. 26 very similar to the *NPZ* article of Dec. 31 may be found in the Waldersee papers, ZSA, Merseburg, Rep. 92, AII, No. 8, Bl. 18–30; for reports of early negative reactions to the Stoecker meeting, Roggenbach to gr. d. of Baden, Dec. 7, GLAK, *Grhzg. Fam. arch.*, Bd. 56; GSAM, Lerch. to pr. reg., Dec. 7, No. 562/LXXIII.

27. *FZ*, Dec. 25, 1887 (359:1 mg.): 1.

5. "PRINCE WILLIAM AND THE CHANCELLOR"

1. Waldersee, 1: 346.

2. Pr. Wm.'s letter, BAFR, B130, and in Bismarck (1), 3: 7–12; Waldersee, 1: 348; Bismarck (1), 3: 25–26; cf. Herb.'s diary, BAFR, D48, Dec. 31, 1887.

3. On Pr. Wm., Röhl & Sombart; *Zukunft*, 57 (Nov. 3, 1906): 170; Kaufmann, 37; Corti (2), 400.

4. Lucius, 292; this speech of Bismarck's was delivered to the Prussian House of Deputies, Jan. 27, 1863. For Roggenbach's ideas, Waldersee, 1: 322; Heyderhoff, 271, 273. Roggenbach boasted to his friend Stosch that he had given the "same sermon" to William I in the 1850s. Sir G. Strachey to Sir H. Ponsonby, Ponsonby (1), 305.

5. Waldersee, 1: 311; Lucius, 294; Holstein, 2: 360. On Herbert's personality, see also Eulenburg. The crown prince's well-known letter of protest in Bismarck (1), 3: 1–2.

6. Pr. Wm.'s letter, BAFR, B130, and Bismarck (1), 3: 12–14.

7. ZSA, Merseburg, *Hausarch.*, ksrn. to kaiser, Rep. 51T, Lit. P, No. 11; Rad. to cr. pr., Dec. 31, 1887, Rep. 52J *general.* 6; cf. Bism. to kaiser, Bismarck (2), 14^2: 983; HSAST, Zepp. to Mittn., Jan. 3, 1888.

8. BAFR, B130; Bismarck (1), 3: 14–22; cf. Waldersee, 1: 351.

9. *Herbert*, 497; Waldersee, 1: 351–52. On Puttkamer's administration and administrative policies in general, Anderson & Barkin.

10. *Ger*, Jan. 4, 1888 (3:1), "Local-Nachr.": 4; Waldersee 1: 352; Lucius, 413; Holstein, 2: 363; Heyderhoff, 280.

6. "GENERAL WALDERSEE AND PREVENTIVE WAR"

1. Bismarck (1), 3: 12; *Times*, Nov. 9, 1887: 5.

2. See esp. Herzfeld (2); Bismarck (1), 3: 112; Rogge (2), 255; Lucius, 359; Bülow, 4: 609.

3. Herzfeld (2), 73–76; Bachem, 4: 261–62; Waldersee, 1: 308; Bülow, 4: 609–10.

4. Herzfeld (2), 77–78; Waldersee, 1: 306.

5. Waldersee, 1: 334–37; HHSA, Karton 132: 86, Eissenstein to Kál., priv. lttr., Nov. 12 1887; 88–91, Sz. to Kál., priv. lttr., Dec. 12; BAFR, D48, Herb.'s diary, Nov. 1, D27, Herb. to Rantz., Oct. 21, Nov. 11; *FZ*, Nov. 18 (322:1 mg.): 1; Nov. 24 (328:2 mg.): 1; (328:evg.): 1; *Ger*, Nov. 12 (259:1): 1; *KölZ*, Nov. 23 (325:2): 1; text of forged documents, *NAZ*, Jan. 1, 1888 (1): 1–2; (2): 1–2; on Russian securities, see *FZ*, Nov. 27 (361:mg.): 2; *NAZ*, Jan. 12 (19), "Jour.-Rev." (article of *Börsen-Courier*): 2–3; Jan. 18 (29), "Jour.-Rev." (article of *Standard*): 2; for the *Post* article, *FZ*, Nov. 25 (329:2 mg.): 1; Dec. 12 (346:evg.), "Zur Lage": 1; on its authorship, Pindter, 48 (Feb. 12).

6. Waldersee, passim, esp. 1: 337–42, 419–21; *GP*, 6: 3–29, 55–56; cf. Krausnick, esp. 149–66; Hillgruber, 186–88; BAFR, D48, Herb.'s diary, Sept. 22, Dec. 4, 1887; B99, 1, Oct. 4; B100, Oct. 7, 12; D2, Dec. 13; D27, Herb. to Rantz., Nov. 25, Dec. 8, 16; F4, Rantz. to Herb., Dec. 9, 15, 16; F4, copy of Moltke memo., Nov. 30; GLAK, June 30, No. 18; Nov. 20, No. 48; see below, 99; *FZ*, Dec. 12 (346:evg.), "Zur Lage": 1; Dec. 14 (348:2 mg.): 2; Dec. 19 (353:evg.), "Zur Lage": 1.

7. Meisner, 151; Waldersee, 1: 335, 344–45; ZSA, Merseburg, *Hausarch.*, Rep. 52J, *general*. 6, Liebenau to cr. pr., Dec. 20, 1887; *FZ*, Dec. 18 (352:1 mg.), "Tel. Dep.": 3; cf. Pindter, 75, Apr. 4, 1888; 37, Jan. 18; *FZ* quote, Jan. 17 (17:1 mg.), lead article: 1.

8. Speech from throne, *FZ*, Nov. 24, 1887 (328:evg.): 1; Nov. 25 (329:2 mg.): 1; *Times*, Nov. 25: 5; *NAZ*, Nov. 24 (550): 1; Stein tel., *FZ*, Dec. 19 (353:mg.), "Tel. Dep.": 3; BAFR, D27, Herb. to Rantz., Dec. 18; F4, Rantz. to Herb., Dec. 21; *GP*, 6: 56–59.

9. *GP*, 6: 59–63; BAFR, D2, Dec. 29, 1887; D27, Herb. to Rantz., Dec. 20, 21; F4, Rantz. to Herb., Dec. 19, 21; D48, Herb.'s diary, Dec. 18, 20, 25. Herbert wrote his father that Moltke was interested that Bismarck hoped not only to postpone war with Russia but also to avoid it. Such a war would be the most thankless imaginable; BAFR, D4a, Dec. 29.

10. RA, Z40/2; Ponsonby (1), 272.

7. "THE CARTEL AND THE GRAIN TARIFF"

1. Kardorff, 201–2; Oncken, 2: 537; cf. Herzfeld (1), 2: 113; cf. *NPZ*, Dec. 28, 1887 (303): 1.

2. *FZ*, Nov. 11, 1887 (315:1 mg.): 1; *NAZ*, Nov. 11 (528): 1; Nov. 24 (549): 1; (550): 1; Nov. 25 (551): 1; Nov. 26 (553): 2; Dec. 1 (561), "Jour.-Rev.": 2; report on *Handelstag*, *FZ*, Nov. 30 (334:2 mg.): 2. On German peasants and the tariff, see Hunt, 321, 324, 327–28.

3. *FZ*, Oct. 7, 1887 (280:1 mg.): 1; Oct. 10 (283:evg.): 1; Oct. 11 (284:evg.): 1; Oct. 12 (285:1 mg.): 1.

4. *FZ*, Oct. 12, 1887 (285:evg.): 1; Puttkamer blamed not only the liquor tax,

but also the laxity of the National Liberals. ZSA, Potsdam, *Rchskzlei.*, No. 1815, Bl. 139–40.

5. These articles reprinted in *FZ*, Oct. 13, 1887 (286:evg.): 1; (286:2 mg.): 1; Oct. 14 (287:2 mg.): 1; *Ger*, Oct. 14 (235:2): 1–2; Oct. 15 (236:1): 1. Cf. *NAZ*, Oct. 28 (504): 1.

6. *FZ*, Oct. 15, 1887 (288:1 mg.): 1; *NAZ*, Oct. 15 (481): 1; (482): 2; Lucius, 398; *NAZ* quote, Oct. 18 (486), "Pol. Tagesbericht": 1.

7. For these exchanges, *NAZ*, Oct. 23 (495), "Jour.-Rev.": 2; *FZ*, Oct. 26 (299:1 mg.): 1; *Ger*, Oct. 26 (245:2): 1.

8. *NAZ*, Oct. 29, 1887 (505): 1; Barth's article, "Der Anfang vom Ende des Kartells," *Nation*, V/4 (Oct. 22, 1887): 45–46.

9. This exchange reprinted in *Ger*, Oct. 30, 1887 (249:2): 1.

10. *NAZ*, Nov. 1, 1887 (510): 1.

11. *Ger*, Nov. 4, 1887 (252:2), "Der Kampf der Kartellparteien": 1.

12. Cf. *FZ*, Nov. 16, 1887 (320:1 mg.): 1; *NAZ*, Nov. 24 (549), "Jour.-Rev.": 2; *NPZ*, Nov. 27 (278): 2; Jan. 1, 1888 (1), "Mittelparteil. Jahresbilanz": 1.

13. *Reichstag*, 101 (1887–88): 27, 31; *FZ*, Nov. 30, 1887 (334:evg.): 1; Dec. 2 (336:1 mg.): 1; Dec. 6 (340:2 mg.): 2; (340:evg.): 1; Dec. 7 (341:2 mg.): 1; (341:evg.): 1; Dec. 9 (343:1 mg.): 1–2; Dec. 10 (344:evg.): 1; *NPZ*, Nov. 30 (280): 2; *KölZ*, Dec. 7 (339:1): 1; (339:2): 1; *NAZ*, Dec. 3 (565), "Jour.-Rev.": 2; Dec. 7 (571), "Jour.-Rev.": 2; Dec. 9 (575), "Jour.-Rev.,": 2; Dec. 11 (579), "Jour.-Rev.": 2; *Ger*, Dec. 6 (279:2): 1–2. Kleist-Retzow told Rottenburg that pressure must be put on National Liberals and Free Conservatives from Friedrichsruh; BAFR, B100, Nov. 29.

14. *Reichstag*, 101 (1887–88): 173–215, 208–78; *FZ*, Dec. 13, 1887 (347:evg.): 1; Dec. 14 (348:2 mg.): 1–2; (348:evg.): 1; Dec. 17 (351:1 mg.): 1; Dec. 20 (354:evg.): 1; Dec. 21 (355:evg.): 1; *NPZ*, Dec. 15 (293), "Rchstgs.-Nachr.": 2; Dec. 16 (294), "Rchstgs.-Nachr.": 1; Dec. 17 (295), "Rchstgs.-Nachr.": 2; Dec. 18 (296): 1; *KölZ*, Dec. 14 (346:2): 1; Dec. 15 (347:2): 1; *Nat. Lib. Korr.* article, *KölZ*, Dec. 20 (352:2): 1; *NAZ*, Nov. 30 (559), "Jour.-Rev.": 2; Dec. 17 (589), "Jour.-Rev.": 2; *Voss. Ztg.* article, *NAZ*, Dec. 15 (585), "Jour.-Rev.": 2; *Ger*, Dec. 7 (280:2): 1; Dec. 10 (282:1): 1; (282:2): 1; Dec. 20 (290:2), "Ueber die Haltung des Centrums in der Getreidezollfrage": 1; BAK, Rep. 92, 5, 244, Rantz. to Rottbg., Nov. 30; BAFR, B100, Rottbg. to Rantz., Dec. 3, 5, 12.

8. "LEGISLATIVE TERM AND ANTISOCIALIST LAW"

1. *FZ*, Dec. 20, 1887 (354:evg.): 1; *Ger*, Dec. 22 (292:1): 2; *NAZ*, Oct. 18 (485), "Jour.-Rev.": 3; Oct. 19 (488): 1; Oct. 20 (489), "Jour.-Rev.": 2; Dec. 3 (565), "Jour.-Rev.": 2.

2. *Ger*, Oct. 21, 1887 (241:1): 1–2; *FZ*, Oct. 21 (294:evg.): 1; Oct. 22 (295:evg.): 1. On Bamberger, see Zucker.

3. *Kons. Korr.* quote, *NAZ*, Dec. 2, 1887 (564): 1; *Nat. Lib. Korr.* quote, *NAZ*, Dec. 4 (567), "Jour.-Rev.": 1–2; *NAZ*, Oct. 31 (508): 1; Nov. 27 (555): 1; quote, Nov. 4 (515): 1.

4. *FZ*, Oct. 7, 1887 (280:evg.): 1; Dec. 20 (354:evg.): 1; Jan. 8, 1888 (8:1 mg.):

1; *NAZ*, Dec. 2 (563), "Jour.-Rev.": 2; Dec. 3 (565), "Jour.-Rev.": 2; *NPZ*, Dec. 7 (286), "Rchstgs.-Nachr": 1–2.

5. Bism. to Puttk., Rothfels, 380; ZSA, Merseburg, *Stsmin.*, Nov. 3, 1887: 223; Dec. 1: 244; GSAB, *Preussisches Justizministerium.*, Rep. 84a, 8461, Herrfurth to Friedberg, July 27, 1887; Friedberg to Puttk., Aug. 5; Puttk. to Friedbg., Sept. 16; Friedbg. to Puttk., Sept. 23; Puttk. to Bism., w. text, Oct. 6; Boett. et al. responses, Oct. 13-Nov. 1, etc.; GLAK, 233, 12721, Marsch. to Turban, Oct. 18, Nov. 28, 29, 30, Dec. 4, 9, 12; GSAM, MA 76530, min. int. to Crails., Nov. 24; No. 14777, ministry to Lerch., Dec. 1; No. 557, Lerch. to Crails., Dec. 5; Pack, 178–79; *FZ*, Dec. 20 (354:evg.): 1; Dec. 22 (356:evg.): 1; cf. *Ger*, Jan. 11, 1888 (8:2): 1; Jan. 24 (19:1): 2; Johnson, 143ff.; for the Eulenburg incident, Eyck, 3: 308–9.

6. *NPZ*, Dec. 7, 1887 (286), "Zur innerpol. Lage": 1.

7. Ibid.; cf. *Ger*, Dec. 23, 1887 (293:1): 2; *FZ*, Jan. 8, 1888 (8:1 mg.): 1.

8. *FZ*, Oct. 13, 1887 (286:1 mg.): 1; *KölZ*, Dec. 1 (333:1): 1; Dec. 23 (355:1): 1; *NAZ*, Dec. 4 (567): 1.

9. *NAZ*, Oct. 20, 1887 (489), "Jour.-Rev.": 2; *Berl. Tgblt.* article, Oct. 27 (502): 1; Tammany Hall story, *NPZ*, Dec. 6 (285A), "Wahlschwindel u. Aemterschacher in Amerika": 1; Grévy quote, *NPZ*, Dec. 9 (288, *Beilage* 2): 1; Sir H. Ponsonby to Earl of Selborne, Oct. 27, Q. Vict., 1: 357.

10. See esp. *Ger*, Dec. 22, 1887 (292:2), "Ggn. das Soc.ges.": 1.

11. *KölZ*, Dec. 23, 1887 (355:1), "Zur Frage der Ges.gebg. ggn. die Soc.dem.": 1; (355:2): 1; *NPZ*, Dec. 24 (301), "Zur Frage der Verlängrg. u. Verschärfg. des Soz.ges.": 1.

12. As quoted in *FZ*, Dec. 25, 1887 (359:2 mg.): 1.

9. "THE STOECKERITES BREATHE DEFIANCE"

1. *NAZ*, Jan. 3, 1888 (4): 2; Jan. 6 (10): 1; for other articles, *NPZ*, Jan. 4 (3), "Die Versammlg. beim Grfn. Wald. u. die Presse": 1; *Ger*, Jan. 1 (1): 2; Jan. 4 (3:1): 3–4.

2. For the *Magd. Ztg.* and *Rchsbote.*, *Ger*, Jan 4, 1888 (3:1): 3; *NPZ*, Jan. 5 (4), "Die christl.-soz. Partei": 1; Jan. 6 (5, *Beilage* 2): 1–2.

3. *NAZ*, Jan. 5, 1888 (8), "Parteibewegg.": 2; Jan. 9 (14): 1; *KölZ*, Jan. 8 (8:1): 1; *Ger*, Jan. 6 (5:1): 2; Jan. 10 (7:1): 2; cf. Pindter, 32, Jan. 10; ZSA, Merseburg, Rep. 52J, *general.* 6, Liebenau to cr. pr., Jan. 7.

4. *NAZ*, Jan. 14, 1888 (23), "Jour.-Rev.": 2; *Ger*, Jan. 14 (11:2): 1; *NPZ*, Jan. 13 (11, *Beilage*), "Rückblick u. Ausblick": 2; *FZ*, Jan. 13 (13:evg.): 1; Jan. 15 (15:1 mg.): 1.

5. *NPZ*, Jan. 4, 1888 (3), "Die Versammlg. beim Grfn. Wald. u. die Presse": 1–2; Jan. 6 (5): 2; Jan. 8 (7), "Zur Aufklärg.": 1–2; Jan. 11 (9): 2; Jan. 13 (11): 2; Jan. 15 (13), "Die *Nordd. Allg. Ztg.*": 1; *NAZ*, Jan. 13 (22): 1.

6. *NPZ*, Jan. 6, 1888 (5): 1. On Christian Socialist movements in Germany see Pulzer, Shanahan.

7. *NAZ*, Jan. 7, 1888 (12): 1; Jan. 12 (20): 1; Center article in *FZ*, Jan. 11 (11:1 mg.): 1; *NPZ*, Jan. 10 (8): 2.

8. Oncken, 2: 538; *Ger*, Jan. 10, 1888 (7:2): 1; Jan. 13 (10:1): 3; Jan. 15 (12:1):

1; *NPZ*, Jan. 15 (13, *Beilage* 1), "Christl.-soz. Partei": 2; *NAZ*, Jan. 11 (17), "Jour.-Rev.": 2; Jan. 13 (21), "Jour.-Rev.": 2; Jan. 14 (23), "Jour.-Rev.": 2; *FZ*, Jan. 13 (13:1 mg.): 1; Pr. Wm.'s letter, BAFR, B130, and in Bismarck (1), 3: 22–24.

9. *KölZ*, Dec. 21, 1887 (353:1), "Vermischte Nachr.": 2; *FZ*, Dec.21 (355:2 mg.): 1; *Ger*, Dec. 23 (293:1): 1; Waldersee, 1: 349; Holstein, 2: 361; Pindter, 37, 43; BAFR, D27, Herb. to Rantz., Jan. 19, 1888; second Pr. Wm. quote, *Herbert*, 504.

10. Holstein, 2: 361; 3: 244; Pindter, 37; Bism. to staff officers, Holstein, 2: 362; Waldersee, 1: 352.

11. Pindter, 32, 35–36.

12. *NPZ*, Dec. 31, 1887 (306): 2; Jan. 3 (2), "Pol. Rückblick": 1; *Ger*, Jan. 13, 1888 (10:1): 3; Jan. 20 (16:1): 1; Jan. 25 (20:2): 1; *Post* article in *Ger*, Jan. 14 (11:2): 1–2.

13. Waldersee, 1: 352–54; *Herbert*, 498–99; Pindter, 37–38; for Bismarck's earlier dissatisfaction with Puttkamer, Lucius, 279, 322; BAFR, C9, Jan. 20.

14. Quoted in *NAZ*, Jan. 8 (13), "Jour.-Rev.": 2; Jan. 12 (20): 1.

15. These articles reprinted in *Ger*, Jan. 14, 1888 (11:1): 2–3; (11:2): 1–2; *FZ*, Jan. 14 (14:1 mg.): 1; Jan. 15 (15:1 mg.): 1; *Kons. Korr.* in *NPZ*, Jan. 18 (15): 2.

16. *Landtag* (1), 1: 1–3, 48–49, 61–62, 68; *NAZ*, Jan. 14. 1888 (24): 1; *KölZ*, Jan. 14 (14:2): 1; *NPZ*, Jan. 17 (14): 1; BAFR, D27, Herb. to Rantz., Jan. 19; F4, Rantz. to Herb., Jan. 16, 17, 20, 21; D48, Herb.'s diary, Jan. 19, 20, 26; B100, Rottbg. to Rantz., Jan. 20, 22; ZSA, Merseburg, Rep. 52J, *general.* 6, Jan. 21, 22, 25, Feb. 5.

17. Waldersee, 1: 354; *FZ*, Dec. 29, 1887 (363:evg.): 1; Jan. 25, 1888 (25:1 mg.): 1; Jan. 31 (31:2mg.): 3; *Ger*, Jan. 21 (17:2): 1; Jan. 22 (18:1): 2; Jan. 24 (19:1): 1; text of City Mission appeal, *NAZ*, Jan. 31 (51): 9; Stoecker in the Rchstg., *Reichstag*, 102: 796; Meyer in Ldtg., *Landtag* (1), 1: 432–33; *FZ*, Feb. 10 (41:2 mg.): 1; Feb. 14 (45:2 mg.): 2.

10. "THE CHANCELLOR APPEALS TO THE NATION"

1. Waldersee, 1: 354–55; Pindter, 43; *KölZ*, Jan. 31, 1888 (31:3): 1; *Reichstag*, 101: 581; *FZ*, Jan. 29 (29:2 mg.): 2; Jan. 30 (30:evg.): 1.

2. Holstein, 2: 362–63.

3. *Ger*, Dec. 13, 1887 (284:2): 1; Dec. 15 (286:1): 2; *FZ*, Dec. 14 (348:1 mg.): 1; Dec. 15 (349:1 mg.): 1; *NAZ*, Dec. 13 (581): 2; *Volksztg.* article, *NAZ*, Dec. 14 (583), "Jour.-Rev.": 2; the most detailed discussion of the changes introduced by the bill in *NPZ*, Dec. 16 (294): 1.

4. Cf. *Times*, Dec. 17, 1887: 7; quote, Jan. 27, 1888: 5; *NAZ*, Dec. 17 (590): 1; *FZ*, Jan. 27, 1888 (27:evg.): 1.

5. *KölZ*, Jan. 31, 1888 (31:3): 1; *FZ*, Feb. 1 (32:2 mg.): 2; quote, Feb. 7 (38:2 mg.): 3; Spitzemberg, 239–40; Pindter, 46–47; cf. *Ger*, Feb. 7 (30:1): 2; *NAZ*, Feb. 8 (65), "Jour.-Rev.": 2; *NYH*, Feb. 3: 5; Feb. 5: 13; Feb. 6: 4.

6. *FZ*, Feb. 7, 1888 (38:2 mg.): 3; *Magd. Ztg.* article, *NAZ*, Feb. 8 (65), "Jour.-Rev.": 2; *NYH*, Feb. 7: 7; Lucius, 419.

7. *Reichstag*, 102: 723–33; Thimme, 2: 272; Spitzemberg, 240; *Börsen Ztg.* quote, *NAZ*, Feb. 7, 1888 (64): 1.

8. *Reichstag*, 102: 733–35; *KölZ*, Feb. 7 (38:2): 1; *FZ*, Feb. 7 (38: 2mg.): 3; Bismarck's reaction to Rickert's speech, *Hann. Kour.* in *NAZ*, Feb. 9 (67), "Jour.-Rev.": 2; differing reports on action of Soc. Dems., *NAZ*, Feb. 7 (64): 1; Feb. 9 (68): 2; Feb. 22 (89), "Jour.-Rev.": 2; *FZ*, Feb. 7 (38:evg.): 1; *Ger*, Feb. 7 (30:1): 2; (30:2): 11; final passage of Bism.'s speech, Nichols, 5–6.

9. *KölZ*, Feb. 7 (38:1): 2; (38:2): 1; BAFR, D48, Herb.'s diary, Feb. 6; D18, Herb. to Bill, Feb. 6; *Herbert*, 505; *DGK*, (1888) 1: 256; *Weser Ztg.* quoted in *NAZ*, Feb. 10 (70): 1; *NYH*, Feb. 7: 6; Feb. 12: 13; Spitzemberg, 240; Lucius, 419; cf. Lerch. to pr. reg., Feb. 9, GSAM, No. 65/VI; William II, 329.

10. Lucius, 419–20; *NAZ*, Feb. 16, 1888 (80): 2; Feb. 26 (97): 3; *Ger*, Feb. 17 (39:2): 4.

11. Text of Pr. Wm.'s toast in *Schulthess*, (1888): 44; *NAZ*, Feb. 9 (67): 1–2; *NPZ*, Feb. 10 (35): 1; Pindter, 49: *FZ*, Feb. 10 (41:2 mg.): 2; HHSA, 300; Waldersee, 1: 358; cf. ZSA, Merseburg, *Hausarch.*, Rep. 52J, *general*. 6, Pr. Wm. to cr. pr., Feb. 17; GSAM, No. 65/VI, Lerch. to pr. reg., Feb. 9. Herbert had written Bill on Feb. 1 that the previous day Prince William had agreed with his father's statement on the City Mission. "The matter is therefore settled," he wrote, BAFR, D18.

12. Pindter, 46, 48–49.

13. *FZ*, Feb. 7 (38:evg.): 1; *Ger*, Feb. 7 (30:2): 1; Feb. 8 (31:1): 1; Feb. 9 (32:1): 1; Bebel in Rchstg., *Reichstag*, 101: 601; *FZ*, Jan. 31 (31:2 mg.): 1; *Volksztg.* article, *NAZ*, Feb. 17 (81), "Jour.-Rev.": 2.

11. "TRACHEOTOMY"

1. Dr. Bramann's report, BAFR, B44, Mar. 6; *Krankheit*, 245; Lucius, 418, 421; *NAZ*, Feb. 9 (68): 1; Feb. 10 (69): 1; (70): 1; Feb. 15 (78): 1; *KölZ*, Feb. 10 (41:1): 2; (41:2): 1; *NPZ*, Feb. 10 (35A), "Aus San Remo": 1; Feb. 11 (36): 1; Freund, 297–300.

2. Q. Vict., 1: 369, 373, 375–77; Lucius, 412; GLAK, No. 2, Marsch. to Turban, Jan. 6; GSAM, No. 6/II, Lerch. to pr. reg., Jan. 7; RA, Z40/5–8, 9, 11, cr. prcss. to Q. Vict., Jan. 14, 15, 18, 22, 25, 31.

3. *NAZ*, Jan. 15 (25): 2; Jan. 25 (42): 2; Jan. 26 (43): 1; Jan 31 (51): 3; Feb. 1 (53): 2; (54): 1; Feb. 2 (56): 2; *Ger*, Jan. 24 (19:1), "Local-Nachr.": 4; Feb. 1 (26:1): 4; Feb. 4 (28:1): 3; cf. *KölZ*, Feb. 2 (33:2): 1; Mack. to Rad., Lucius, 417; cr. pr. to Berlin pastors, *NPZ*, Jan. 19 (16): 1; Mack.'s Feb. 3 report, *NPZ*, Feb. 7 (32), "Aus San Remo": 1; cr. pr.'s dairy, Corti (2), 440; according to Lerchenfeld, Virchow had reported the presence of cancer cells, GSAM, No. 60/V, to pr. reg., Feb. 7; cf. *NYH*, Jan. 30: 5; Feb. 3: 5.

4. HHSA, 3–4, Sz. to Kál., Feb. 11; *NPZ*, Feb. 11 (36A), "Aus San Remo": 1; Heyderhoff, 284; Lucius, 420; HHSA, Karton 135: 130, Sz. to Kál., priv. lttr., Apr. 7; Hohenlohe, 2: 437; *NYH*, Feb. 10: 6.

5. *NAZ*, Feb. 14, 1888 (76): 1; Feb. 16 (80): 1–2; Feb. 17 (81): 1; cf. article reprinted from *Strassburger Post*, inspired by Dr. Kussmaul, Mar. 3 (108): 1; *Ger*,

Feb. 15 (37:1): 3; (37:2): 1; Feb. 16 (38:1): 3; Feb. 17 (39:2): 2; Feb. 25 (46:2): 4; *FZ*, Feb. 16 (47:2 mg.): 2; *NPZ*, Feb. 24 (47), "Aus San Remo": 1; Feb. 26 (49), "Aus San Remo": 1; Pindter, 50–51, Feb. 17; Lucius, 421–24; Freund, 310–11; RA, Z40/15, 17–19, 22, cr. prcss. to Q. Vict., Feb. 10, 15, 16, 18, 28; Z41/11–18, Mack. to Queen Victoria's physician, Dr. Reid; GSAM, No. 89/VIII, Lerch. to pr. reg., Feb. 19; BAFR, B130, Pr. Wm. to Bism., Feb. 23.

6. *NAZ*, Feb. 16 (80): 2; Feb. 21 (87): 1–2 for *Hann. Kour.* article; *NPZ*, Feb. 18 (42), "Aus San Remo": 1; *Ger*, Feb. 18 (40:1): 3; cf. Feb. 23 (44:1): 2.

7. *FZ*, Feb. 19 (50:1 mg.): 1; *Berl. Pol. Nachr.* article, *Ger*, Feb. 22 (43:1): 2; Lucius, 423; for the constl. provisions, see Robinson, 234 (Art. 56).

8. *KölZ*, Feb. 27 (58:2): 1; *Voss. Ztg.* article in *Ger*, Feb. 29 (49:2): 2; *FZ*, Mar. 1 (61:evg.): 1; Mar. 5 (65:mg.): 1; *NPZ*, Mar. 3 (55), "Aus San Remo": 1; *Ger*, Mar. 4 (53:1): 3.

9. Pindter, 55, Feb. 25; HHSA, Kart. 135: 83–84, Sz. to Kál., priv. lttr., Feb. 27; *Krankheit*, 245; *DDF*, 7: 81, Herbette to Flourens, Mar. 7; Waldersee, 1: 362–63; Heyderhoff, 285; *NAZ*, Feb. 17 (98): 1; Feb. 28 (99): 3; *NPZ*, Feb. 29 (51): 1; Mar. 6 (56A): 1; *Ger*, Mar. 7 (55:2): 1; Mar. 8 (56:1): 1–2; (56:2): 1; *NYH*, Mar. 4: 13; RA, Z41/19, cr. prcss. to Q. Vict., Mar. 3.

10. Holstein, 3: 268–70; Lucius, 421–23; *Ger*, Mar. 8, 1888 (56:2): 1; cf. *FZ*, Mar. 4 (64:2 mg.): 2; Mar. 5 (65:evg.): 2; Mar. 6 (66:1 mg.): 3.

12. "AN ADVISOR FOR PRINCE WILLIAM"

1. Waldersee, 1: 361, 363–65; HHSA, Kart. 135: 87–88, Sz. to Kál., priv. lttr., Feb. 29; cf. GSAM, No. 158/XXIII, Lerch. to pr. reg., Mar. 23. P. Eulenburg enthusiastically agreed with Herbert, May 19, that the prince's intellectual growth was "very striking." BAFR, B40 (3).

2. Holstein, 3: 270; Lucius, 423; BAFR, B130, Pr. Wm. to Bism., Feb. 25; D48, Herb.'s diary, Feb. 26; RA, Z40/24–26, cr. prcss. to Q. Vict., Feb. 28, Mar. 1–2; ZSA, Merseburg, *Hausarch.*, Rep., 51, J21m, kaiser to gr. d. of Baden, Feb. 26; Rep. 52J, *general.* 6, Bism. to cr. pr., kaiser to Rad., Mar. 1; Rep. 52J, 336a, cr. pr. to Pr. Wm., Mar. 2; Pindter, 56, Feb. 27; *NAZ*, Feb. 29 (102): 2; Mar. 1 (104): 1; Mar. 5 (110): 3; *FZ*, Mar. 2 (62:evg.): 2; William II, 342–43.

3. *NAZ*, Jan. 27, 1888 (46): 1; Lucius, 417, 421–22; HHSA, 38, Jan. 28; BAFR, D27, Herb. to Rantz., Jan. 22; D2, Herb. to Bism., Jan. 16; F4, Rantz. to Herb., Jan. 18; *Herbert*, 505 (the misspelling of "irretrievably" is a typo: BAFR, D18, Jan. 29); Hollyday, 234–35; ZSA, Merseburg, *Hausarch.*, Rep. 52J, 323, 336a, cr. pr. to kaiser, Jan. 14, Feb. 4; to Friedbg. Jan. 28; Rep. 52J, *general.* 6, kaiser to cr. pr., Jan. 25; Friedbg. to cr. pr., Jan. 28; Pr. Wm. to cr. pr., Jan. 31, Feb. 23; Bismarck (2), 6c: 387, Bism. to Rad.; HSAST, Zepp. to Mittn., Feb. 5. Herbert wrote Bill that he had had a two-hour talk with Brandenstein "to set him straight." BAFR, D18, Feb. 25.

4. *KölZ*, Mar. 4 (64:1): 2; Mar. 5 (65:2): 1; *Nat. Ztg.* notice in *KölZ*, Mar. 6 (66:2): 1; *FZ*, Mar. 6 (66:1 mg.): 3; *NAZ*, Mar. 6 (112): 2; *NPZ*, Mar. 7 (57): 2.

5. *NAZ*, Feb. 20 (86): 1; Feb. 21 (87): 1; (88): 1; Feb. 22 (89): 1; Mar. 2 (105):

1; (106): 1; Mar. 6 (111): 1; *NPZ*, Feb. 21 (44), "Aus San Remo": 1; Mar. 4 (55A): 1; *Kons. Korr.* article reprinted Feb. 24 (47A), "Aus San Remo": 1; *Ger*, Mar. 3 (52:1): 1–2; *FZ*, Mar. 2 (62:2 mg.): 2; (62:evg.): 1; *KölZ*, Mar. 2 (62:1): 2; Mar. 7 (67:2): 1.

13. "PUTTKAMER ON THE DEFENSIVE"

1. *Hamb. Nachr.* article in *Ger*, Jan. 8, 1888 (6:2): 1; *NPZ*, Jan. 10 (8): 1; BAFR, B99, 1, Rottbg. to Herb., Dec. 24, 1887.

2. Text of bill in *Reichstag, Anlage*, 103: 386–89, No. 71; *NAZ*, Jan. 16 (26): 1; *FZ*, Jan. 17 (17:evg.): 1; Jan. 19 (19:1 mg.): 1.

3. BAFR, B100, Rottbg. to Rantzau, Jan. 18; BAK, Rep. 92, 5, 246, Rantz. to Rottbg., Jan. 19; also BAFR, B101 (copy).

4. *NZ* article reprinted in *Ger*, Jan. 19 (15:1): 1–2; *NPZ*, Jan. 19 (16), "Zum Soz.ges.": 1; *FZ*, Jan. 20 (20:1 mg.): 1; *KölZ*, Jan. 17 (17:2): 1.

5. *NPZ*, Jan. 22, 1888 (19), "Zum Soz.ges.": 1; *FZ*, Jan. 24 (24:1 mg.): 1.

6. *NPZ*, Jan 24 (20): 1.

7. Landtag party strength taken from *Ger*, Dec. 30, 1887 (298:2): 1; the figures assume that two vacancies (Center and Poles) will be filled with members of the same parties as previously; cf. *NAZ*, Jan. 18 (29): 2. On the position of the Junkers and the Conservative party, see Hartung, 132; Böhme, passim; Hess, passim; Berdahl, 7. On the Prussian three-class voting system, Robinson, 238–40 (Arts. 69–74). One of the few factually correct textbook explanations of the system in Rodes, 336–37.

8. *Reichstag*, 101: 527–89; HHSA, 58, Sz. to Kál., Feb. 11; *FZ*, Jan. 23 (23:mg.): 1; Jan. 28 (28:2 mg.): 2; (28:evg.): 1; Jan. 29 (29:1 mg.): 1; Marquardsen, Ibid., (29:2 mg.): 1–2; Jan. 30 (30:evg.): 1; *KölZ*, Jan. 28 (28:2): 1; *Ger*, Jan. 28 (23:1): 1; Jan. 29 (24:2): 1.

9. *NPZ*, Jan. 31 (26): 1; Feb. 1 (27): 2; *FZ*, Jan. 31 (31:2 mg.): 1–2; *Ger*, Feb. 1 (26:1): 1. On the "Puttkamer System" see Anderson & Barkin.

10. *FZ*, Feb. 11 (42:evg.): 1; Feb. 14 (45:2 mg.): 2; (45:evg.): 1; Feb. 15 (46:1 mg.): 1; (46:2 mg.): 1–2; Feb. 18 (49:2 mg.): 1–2; (49:evg.): 1; *Reichstag*, 102: 859–83, 953–91.

11. *Nat. Lib. Korr.* article in *Ger*, Jan. 24 (19:1): 2; see above, 87–88; *NAZ*, Feb. 1 (53): 2; Feb. 16 (80): 1; Feb. 17 (81): 2; *NPZ*, Feb. 7 (32): 1; *Ger*, Feb. 2 (27:2): 1; Feb. 5 (29:1): 2; Feb. 17 (39:2): 1; *KölZ*, Feb. 20 (51:2): 1.

12. *Nat. Ztg.* articles in *Ger*, Feb. 22 (43:1): 1–2; Feb. 24 (45:1): 2–3; *NAZ*, Feb. 26 (97): 1; *Preussische Jahrbücher*, 61: 310–11; *NPZ*, Mar. 1 (52):2.

14. "THE CARTEL UNITES ON THE LEGISLATIVE TERM ISSUE"

1. *Hann. Kour.* article in *Ger*, Jan. 11 (8:2): 1; *Reichstag*, 101: 663–72; *FZ*, Feb. 2 (33:2 mg.): 1–2.

2. *Reichstag* 101: 663–72; *FZ*, Feb. 2 (33:2 mg.): 1–2.; *Reichstag*, 101: 658–63, 681–91; *FZ*, Feb. 4 (35:2 mg.): 1.

3. *NPZ*, Feb. 3 (29): 1; *NAZ*, Feb. 2 (56): 1; *KölZ*, Feb. 2 (33:2): 1; *Kons. Korr.* and *Hann. Kour.* articles, *NAZ*, Feb. 5 (61): 2; Feb. 4 (59): 2; *Nat. Lib. Korr.* article, *KölZ*, Feb. 3 (34:2): 1.

4. *Schulthess*, (1888): 21; *Reichstag*, 102: 738–58, 784–807; *FZ*, Feb. 8 (39:2 mg.): 1; (39:evg.): 1–2.

5. *NAZ*, Feb. 14 (75): 2; *FZ*, Feb. 9 (40:2 mg.): 1–3; (40:evg.): 1; Feb. 12 (43:2 mg.): 1–2; Feb. 15 (46:1 mg.): 1; *NPZ*, Feb. 10 (35): 1; Feb. 15 (39): 2; *Landtag* (1), 1: 331–67, 391–458.

6. *NPZ*, Feb. 4 (30): 2; Feb. 14 (38, *Beilage* 1): 2; *FZ*, Feb. 6 (37:evg.): 1; *Ger*, Feb. 11 (34:2): 1.

7. *Ger*, Feb. 15 (37:2), "Die Verlängrg. der Legpde.": 1.

8. *Ger*, Feb. 4 (28:2): 1.

9. On German parties as pressure groups, see Nipperdey.

10. *Landtag* (1), 2: 881–84; *KölZ*, Mar. 7 (67:1): 1–2; the words from the preamble of the English bill were not quoted by Gneist, but are taken from Plumb, 173–74.

11. *Landtag* (1), 2: 885; *KölZ*, Mar. 7 (67:1): 2; (67:2): 1; *FZ*, Mar. 8 (68:1 mg.): 1; on Gneist's teachings, McClelland, 137–58.

15. "THE GOVERNMENT ASSISTS THE CARTEL"

1. *NAZ*, Jan. 28 (47).

2. *NAZ*, Feb. 4 (60).

3. *NAZ*, Feb. 21 (87).

4. *Landtag* (1), 2: 838–67, *Anlage* 2: 1466–67, No. 74; ZSA, Merseburg, *Stsmin.*, Dec. 27, 1887: 256–57; cf. Mar. 15, 1887: 102–6; *NPZ*, Jan. 17 (14): 1; Feb. 10–12 (35–37), "Die berechtgtn. Fordrgn. der evangel. Landeskirche u. das fin. Angebot des Staats," 1–3: 1; *KölZ*, Mar. 5 (65:1): 1; *Ger*, Mar. 6 (54:1): 1; Mar. 7 (55:2): 1; *Berl. Pol. Nachr.* article, *Ger*, Mar. 8 (56:1): 3; *NAZ*, Mar. 7 (113): 2.

5. Cf. Oncken, 2: 539.

6. Text of law, *Landtag* (1), *Anlage*, 2: 930–41, No. 15; *NAZ*, Jan. 17 (28): 1; *KölZ*, Jan. 24 (24:2): 1; Jan. 25 (25:2): 1; *Ger*, Jan. 25 (20:2): 1; Feb. 8 (31:2): 1; Feb. 9 (32:1): 2; *Landtag* (1), 1: 105–32.

7. *NPZ*, Jan. 26 (22): 1; quote, Feb. 16 (40): 1; *KölZ*, Jan. 28 (28:1): 2; *NAZ*, Feb. 10 (69): 2–3; *FZ*, Feb. 10 (41:evg.): 1.

8. *NPZ*, Feb. 17 (41): 1; Feb. 18 (42): 1; *NAZ*, Feb. 21 (88): 1; Feb. 29 (101): 2; *KölZ*, Feb. 17 (48:2): 1; Feb. 20 (51:1): 1; Feb. 21 (52:2): 1; Feb. 23 (54:2): 1; Feb. 25 (56:2): 1; ZSA, Merseburg, *Stsmin.*, Feb. 22: 42–43.

16. "NEW ATTACKS ON WALDERSEE, THE *KREUZZEITUNG,* AND STOECKER"

1. Waldersee, 1: 359–64; Pindter, 52–54; BAFR, B131, Pr. Wm. to Herb., Feb. 16; *NPZ*, Feb. 15 (39): 1; Feb. 16 (40): 1; Feb. 18 (42): 2.

2. *NPZ*, Feb. 16 (40): 1; *KölZ*, Feb. 17 (48:2): 1.

3. *NPZ*, Feb. 15 (39), "'Natnl.' u. kons.": 1.

4. See report of Hans Unruh to Adolf Marschall von Bieberstein, Dec. 5, 1896, AA, Dtld. 122, Bd. 1, No. 3b; Pindter, 50; *NAZ*, Mar. 6 (112): 2; *NPZ*, Feb. 10 (35): 2; *Ger*, Feb. 10 (33:2): 1–2; Feb. 11 (34:1): 2.

5. *NPZ*, Feb. 12 (37): 2; *Ger*, Feb. 11 (34:2): 1; *Rchsbote*. article, *Ger*, Feb. 11 (34:2): 1.

6. *NPZ*, Feb. 22 (45), "Zur Klarstellg.":1.

7. *Dts. Tgblt.* article, *NAZ*, Feb. 23 (92), "Jour.-Rev.": 2; *NPZ*, Feb. 23 (46A), "Das Dte. Tgblt.": 1.

8. *NPZ*, Feb. 24 (47): 2; Feb. 25 (48): 1; Feb. 28 (50): 2; Waldersee, 1: 363.

9. *NAZ*, Feb. 17 (82): 2; Feb. 18 (84): 2; Feb. 20 (86): 2; *FZ*, Feb. 20 (51:evg.): 1; Feb. 21 (52:1 mg.): 1; *NPZ*, Feb. 18 (42A): 1; Feb. 21 (44): 1.

10. *NPZ*, Feb. 23 (46): 1; *NAZ*, Feb. 23 (92): 1.

11. *FZ*, Feb. 25 (56:evg.): 1; Feb. 28 (59:1 mg.): 1.

12. *NPZ*, Feb. 22 (45): 1.

13. *NPZ*, Mar. 2 (53): 1.

14. *FZ*, Mar. 6 (66:1 mg.): 1.

15. *NPZ*, Mar. 6 (56, *Beilage*): 2.

16. Cf. lead article, "Die 13 Irrthümer des Fürsten Bismarck," based on an article in *Moskovskaya Vedemosti*, *NPZ*, Feb. 29 (51A): 1; Pindter, 57, 59; Hohenlohe, 2: 429; Waldersee, 1: 366, 374. In early February Moltke told Herbert that Waldersee was indispensable, BAFR, D18, Feb. 11; *Herbert*, 349.

17. "PROTESTANT CLERICALS COURT THE CENTER PARTY"

1. *Ger*, Jan. 17 (13:1): 1.

2. *NPZ*, Jan. 20 (17): 1.

3. *Ger*, Jan. 20 (16:2): 1; Jan. 22 (19A): 1; Jan. 27 (23, *Beilage*): 1; Mar. 29 (76, 1 *Beilage*): 1.

4. *Ger*, Feb. 7 (30:2): 1; Feb. 15 (37:1): 2; Mar. 8 (56:1): 4; *DGK*, (1888)1: 287; *Landtag* (1), 2: 891; *NPZ*, Mar. 3 (54A): 2; on Harnack, Zahn, 156–72.

5. *NPZ*, Feb. 18 (42A): 1; Feb. 26 (49A): 2.

6. *NPZ*, Feb. 28 (50): 1; Feb. 29 (51): 2; Mar. 9 (59): 2; *Ger*, Feb. 15 (37:1): 2; Feb. 28 (48:1): 2; Feb. 29 (49:1): 2; ZSA, Merseburg, *Stsmin.*, May 23: 162; Untermeyer, 366–68, w. illus.

7. *Reichstag*, 101: 477–97; 102: 1173–95; 103, *Anlage* 1: 148–50, No. 21; *Ger*, Jan. 26 (21:2): 1; *KölZ*, Mar. 1 (61:2): 1; *NPZ*, Jan. 27 (23): 2; Mar. 3 (54A): 2; Mar. 8 (58A): 1; the certificate-of-competence bill did not reach a third reading.

8. *NPZ*, Jan. 29 (25): 1; (25A): 1; Feb. 1 (27A): 1; Feb. 2 (28): 2; Feb. 3 (29): 2; Feb. 14 (38): 1; Feb. 18 (43, *Beilage*), "Das Zentrum": 2; *Ger*, Jan. 27 (22:2): 1.

9. *NPZ*, Feb. 10 (35): 1–2; *Schulthess*, (1888): 50; *Ger*, Feb. 19 (41:2): 1; Feb. 21 (42:2): 1; quote, Feb. 24 (45:2): 1; *KölZ*, Mar. 3 (63:2): 1; Mar. 5 (65:1): 1; *FZ*, Mar. 2 (62:evg.): 1; *Landtag* (1), 2: 739–43, 778–80, 787–89, 797–98, 824–25; *Anlage* 2: 1464, No. 69.

10. Text of bill, *Landtag* (1), *Anlage* 2: 1464–65, No. 70; *Ger*, Feb. 28 (48:1): 1; Robinson, 226, Art. 24; *FZ*, Mar. 4 (64:1 mg.): 1; *Hann. Kour.* article, *NAZ*, Mar. 1 (103), "Jour.-Rev.": 2; *DGK*, (1888) 1: 296.

11. *Post* article, *NAZ*, Mar. 1 (103): 2; *NPZ*, Feb. 29 (51): 1; *KölZ*, Feb. 28 (59:2): 1; *Ger*, Feb. 29 (49:2): 1; Schorlemer in the House, Feb. 26 (47:2): 2; Mar. 1 (50:2), "An die gläubigen Protestanten v. Ueberzeugg. u. Muth!": 1; *Landtag* (1), 1: 121; *Kons. Korr.* article, *NAZ*, Mar. 1 (103): 2; *Reichsbote* article, ibid.

18. "GREIFFENBERG-KAMMIN AND THE NATIONAL LIBERALS"

1. *NPZ*, Feb. 24 (47): 2; *Ger*, Feb. 24 (45:1): 2; *FZ*, Mar. 5 (65:evg.): 1.

2. *NAZ*, Mar. 7 (113), "Jour.-Rev.": 2; *DGK*, (1888) 1: 178; *Landtag* (1), 2: 872.

3. *NPZ*, Mar. 6 (56): 1; Mar. 7 (57), "Zur Wahl in Kammin-Greiffenberg": 1.

4. *NPZ*, Mar. 7 (57): 1; *NAZ*, Mar. 7 (113): 2; *Ger*. Mar. 6, (54:1): 1; (54:2): 1; Mar. 8 (56:2): 1.

5. *KölZ*, Mar. 5 (65:2): 1; Mar. 7 (67:2): 1; *NPZ*, Mar. 7 (57): 1; *NAZ*, Mar. 6 (112): 1; *Hann. Kour.* article, Mar. 8 (115), "Jour.Rev.": 2–3.

6. F. Hersmann to Hammacher, Apr. 25, 1887, ZSA, Potsdam, *Nachl.* Hammacher, 68, No. 26; *FZ*, Jan. 21 (21:2 mg.): 1; (21:evg.): 1; Mar. 4 (64:2 mg.): 1; Mar. 7 (67:evg.): 1; Mar. 8 (68:2 mg.): 1–2; *NAZ*, Mar. 5 (110): 1; *NPZ*, Mar. 8 (58): 1; *Nat. Lib. Korr.* article, *Ger*, Feb. 18 (40:1): 2; *FZ* on Oechelhäuser, Mar. 7 (67:1 mg.): 1; *Hann. Kour.* article, *NAZ*, Feb. 21 (87): 2. On the National Liberals, Nipperdey, White, Eley (2), chap. 2.

7. *Jen. Ztg.* article, *Ger*, Feb. 22 (43:1): 2; *KölZ*, Mar. 1 (61:1): 2; *Hann. Kour.* article, *NAZ*, Feb. 2 (89), "Jour.-Rev.": 2.

19. "DEATH OF KAISER WILLIAM"

1. *NAZ*, Mar. 5 (111): 3; Mar. 6 (112): 2; Mar. 7 (114): 1; Mar. 8 (116), "Aus Berlin": 2; HHSA, 316, Sz. to Kál., Mar. 6; 344, 346, 352, 354, 356, Mar. 7–8; *NPZ*, Feb. 21 (44): 2; *KölZ*, Feb. 20 (51:3): 2.

2. Oncken, 2: 539; Bamberger (2), 342; Q. Vict., 1: 390; Lucius, 423, 425; *FZ*, Mar. 8 (68:evg.): 1; on Frederick and the imperial idea, Freytag (3), 30; ZSA, Merseburg, *Stsmin.*, Mar. 8: 47–52; Bismarck (2), 6c: 387; GLAK, 233/12797, Bd. 12, *Stsmin.*, Reichsangelegenheiten, Allgemeines, Marsch. to *Stsmin.*, Mar. 8; SP, 203–4, Malet to Q. Vict., Mar. 9; to Salisbury, Mar. 10; GSAM, MA 76067, No. 134, Lerch. to Crails., Mar. 11.

3. *NAZ*, Mar. 7 (114): 2; Mar. 8 (116): 3, 1; Waldersee, 1: 366; *FZ*, Mar. 8 (68:evg.), "Die Krankht. des Ks.": 2.

4. *FZ*, Mar. 9 (69:1 mg.): 3; (69:2 mg.): 1–2; *NAZ*, Mar. 9 (117): 1; *Herbert*, 509.

5. *NAZ*, Mar. 9 (118): 2; *NPZ*, Mar. 10 (60): 2; *Landtag* (1), 2: 937.

6. *Landtag* (1), 2: 939; *Reichstag*, 102: 1385–86; *NAZ*, Mar. 9 (118): 1; Mar. 10 (120): 1; Mar. 11 (121): 2; *FZ*, Mar. 9 (69:evg.): 1; Mar. 10 (70:2 mg.): 1; (70:evg.): 1; cf. Apr. 10 (101:1 mg.): 1; *KölZ*, Mar. 10 (70:1): 1; *NPZ*, Mar. 10 (60): 2, 4; *Ger*, Mar. 11 (59:2): 1; *NZ*, Mar. 10 (163): 2; description of scene in Rchstg., A. Stein, *FZ*, Mar. 10 (70:2 mg.): 1; Herzfeld (1), 2: 115; Pindter, 61, Mar. 10; report of Bundesrat session, GSAM, MA 76067, No. 127/XIV, Lerch. to pr. reg., Mar. 9; No. 135, Lerch. to Crails., Mar. 11; cf. William II, 347.

7. *FZ*, Mar. 9 (69:evg.): 1–2; *NAZ*, Mar. 9 (118): 1–2; *NZ* article, *NAZ*, Mar. 10 (119), "Jour.-Rev": 3. *NYH*, Mar. 10: 3–4; Mar. 11: 12; Mar. 12: 4.

20. "THE NEW REIGN"

1. *NAZ*, Mar. 11 (122), "Pol. Tagesber.": 1; Mar. 12 (123), "Pol. Tagesber.": 1; *NPZ*, Mar. 11 (extra); Mar. 13 (62): 1; *FZ*, Mar. 12 (72:mg.), "Heimreise u. Ankunft K. Frs.": 1; *NZ*, Mar. 12 (166): 1; *NYH*, Mar. 11: 5.
2. *NAZ*, Mar. 11 (121), "Pol. Tagesber.": 1; Mar. 12 (123), "Pol. Tagesber.": 1; *DDF*, 7: 83; *Herbert*, 510; Pindter, 137, Mar. 11, 12; Lucius, 431–33; *KölZ*, Mar. 12 (72:1): 1; *FZ*, Mar. 13 (73:1 mg.): 3; GSAM, Nos. 132/XVI, 136/XVII, Lerch. to pr. reg., Mar. 10.
3. HHSA, No. 19B: 378, Mar. 10; Karton 135: 90–91, priv. lttr., Mar. 10; Ponsonby (1), 293; Corti (2), 276; Lucius, 433; Wentzcke, 2: 437; Spitzemberg, 243; GSAM, No. 143/XIX, Lerch. to pr. reg., Mar. 14; MA 76067, No. 138, Lerch. to Crails., Mar. 12; RA, Z41/30, ksrn. to Q. Vict., Mar. 19; GLAK, No. 13, Marsch. to Turban, Mar. 13.
4. HHSA, No. 19B, Sz. to Kál., Mar. 10; tel. No. 43: 445, Mar. 14; Karton 135: 107–9, priv. lttr., Mar. 24; *NAZ*, Mar. 16 (130), "Hof u. Pers.-Nachr.": 3; Mar. 20 (136), "Hof u. Pers.-Nachr.": 2; *Ger*, Mar. 20 (66:1): 1; (66:2): 2; *NPZ*, Mar. 17 (66): 3; *KölZ*, Mar. 13 (73:1): 1; Mar. 15 (75:1): 1; Waldersee, 1: 376–77; Corti (2), 288.
5. Waldersee, 1: 370–71, 374–75; HHSA, No. 27E: 502–3, Sz. to Kál., Mar. 24.
6. HHSA, Nos. 15a: 321–25, 19B: 381, 26B: 468–70, 27a: 481–82, Sz. to Kál., Mar. 6, 10, 21, 24 respectively; Karton 135: 113–14, priv. lttr., Mar. 24; text of *Stellvertretung* order, *NAZ*, Mar. 24 (144): 1; *DGK*, (1888) 1: 148; *Schulthess*, (1888): 69; ZSA, Merseburg, *Hausarch.*, Rep. 52, E 3, 5, kaiser to Stsmin., Mar. 27; Stsmin. to kaiser, Mar. 28; E 3, 4, Bism. to kaiser, Mar. 29, 30; ZSA, Merseburg, *Stsmin.*, (1888) 69, 75–78; GSAM, No. 158/XXIII, Lerch. to pr. reg., Mar. 23; GLAK, No. 14, Marsch. to Turban, Mar. 27; Lucius, 437–39; cf. *FZ*, Mar. 24 (84:2 mg.): 1; (84:evg.): 1; *KölZ*, Mar. 13 (73:1): 1; *Ger*, Mar. 25 (71:1): 1; (71:2): 1; Mar. 30 (75:1): 1; Bedford, 11–12, 301–2; RA, Z41/29–30, ksrn. to Q. Vict., Mar. 18, 19.
7. ZSA, Merseburg, *Stsmin.*, (1888): 65–66; Stein quote, *FZ*, Mar. 11 (71:2 mg.), "Aus der trauernden Rchshauptstadt.": 1; Mar. 15 (75:evg.): 2; Mar. 16 (76:2 mg.), "Im Dom zu Berl.": 1; Mar. 17 (77:evg.): 1–2; Pindter, 64, Mar. 15; GSAM, No. 150/XXI, Lerch. to pr. reg., Mar. 20; *NAZ*, Mar. 12 (123): 2; Mar. 14 (126): 2; (127): 2; Mar. 20 (137): 2; *KölZ*, Mar. 14 (74:1): 1–2; (74:2): 1; Mar. 17 (77:2): 1; *NPZ*, Mar. 17 (66): 1; Mar. 18 (67): 3; Mar. 29 (76), "Berl. Zuschauer": 2; *Ger*, Mar. 18 (65:1): 1; Mar. 21 (67:1): 2; *NZ*, Mar. 12 (166): 1; Mar. 14 (169, 1 *Beiblatt*): 2; Mar. 16 (173, *Beiblatt*): 2.
8. Waldersee, 1: 375; *NAZ*, Mar. 16 (130): 1–2; *FZ*, Mar. 11 (71:1 mg.): 1.
9. London ref., *FZ*, Mar. 9 (69:1 mg.), "Die Krankht. des Ks.": 3; French press, *KölZ*, Mar. 9 (69:3), "Der Tod des Ks. Wm.": 1; Mar. 10 (70:2): 2; Mar. 12 (72:1): 2; *Kons. Korr.* in *NAZ*, Mar. 11 (121), "Jour.-Rev.": 3; *NPZ*, Mar. 10 (60): 1.

10. *NAZ*, Mar. 16 (131), "K. Wms. letzter Gang": 2–3; Mar. 17 (132), "K. Wms. letzter Gang": 1–2; (133): 1; Mar. 18 (134), "Jour.-Rev.": 2; Mar. 23 (143): 1; *FZ*, Mar. 15 (75:2 mg.): 1; Mar. 16 (76:evg.): 1–2; *NZ*, Mar. 16 (174): 3; *Ger*, Mar. 17 (64:2): 2; *KölZ*, Mar. 16 (76:1): 1–2; (76:2): 1; (76:3): 1; Mar. 17 (77:1): 1; (77:2): 1; *NPZ*, Mar. 17 (66): 1; (66A): 1; Waldersee, 1: 375; Mackenzie, 127–28; *Freis. Ztg.*, *NAZ*, Mar. 18 (134), "Jour.-Rev.": 2; *NYH*, Mar. 17: 5.

11. Pindter, 63–64, Mar. 13, 15, 21; Corti (2), 454; RA, Z41/34, ksrn. to Q. Vict., Mar. 24; test of procls., ZSA, Merseburg, *Hausarch.*, Rep. 52, E 3, No. 4; *NAZ* Mar. 13 (124): 1; Bavarian criticism, GSAM, MA 76067, Nos. 139, 144, Lerch. to Crails., Mar. 13, 14; No. 3721[1], Crails. to pr. reg., Mar. 15; No. 3769[1], Crails. to Lerch., Mar. 16; *FZ*, Mar. 13 (73:2 mg.): 1; *NPZ*, Mar. 12 (extra); Hollyday, 229–31; on Geffcken, *NDB*; *Zukunft*, 57 (Nov. 10, 1906): 213; HHSA, Karton 135: 94–95, Sz. to Kál., priv. lttr., Mar. 13; GLAK, No. 13, Marsch. to Turban, Mar. 13; Bamberger (2), 47; Lucius, 430; Ponsonby (1), 276–79, 291–92; *Ger*, Mar. 16 (63:1): 1; Mar. 17 (64:1): 2; Mar. 20 (66:1): 1; Mar. 21 (67): 1; *DGK*, (1888) 1: 184; *NYH*, Mar. 12: 4; Mar. 13: 5; Mar. 14: 5; Mar. 15: 4; Mar. 19: 4; Mar. 24: 5.

12. ZSA, Merseburg, *Stsmin.*, 54–55, Mar. 9, 1888; HHSA, No. 19C: 386–87, Sz. to Kál., Mar. 10; GLAK, Bd. 12, *Stsmin.*, *Rchsanglhtn./Allg.*, Marsch. to Turban and reply, Mar. 10; GSAM, MA 76067, No. 129, Lerch. to Crails., Mar. 10; Lucius, 429, 437; Waldersee, 1: 371.

13. Freytag (3), 28–29, *KölZ*, Mar. 11 (71:1): 1; Mar. 25 (85:1): 1; Lucius, 432; Corti (2), 456; HHSA, Karton 135: 95–96, Sz. to Kál., priv. lttr., Mar. 14; Nos. 26B: 469–70, 27E: 502, Sz. to Kál., Mar. 21, 24, respectively; Waldersee, 1: 373–74; Spitzemberg, 243; Pindter: 67–68, Mar. 22; *NPZ*, Mar. 14 (63): 2; *FZ*, Apr. 3 (94:mg.): 1.

14. *FZ*, Mar. 12 (72: evg.): 1; *NPZ*, Mar. 13 (62): 1; *KölZ*, Mar. 10 (70:1): 2; Mar. 12 (72:1): 2; *DGK*, (1888) 1: 181; *NZ*, Mar. 12 (165): 1; cf. June 8 (327): 2; *Ger*, Mar. 15 (62:1): 3; Mar. 13 (60:2): 1.

15. *Freis. Ztg.* articles, *DGK*, (1888) 1: 182; *NAZ*, Mar. 13 (124), "Parteibewegg.": 2; *Ger*, Mar. 13 (60:2), "Die Volksempfndg. über die Ereignisse im Kaiserhause": 1.

16. Text of proclamations, *NAZ*, Mar. 13 (124): 1; *FZ*, Mar. 13 (73:2 mg.): 1; Lucius, 433; cf. PRO, FO244, 439, No. 86, Malet to Salisbury, Mar. 15.

17. *Ger*, Mar. 14 (61:1): 2; (61:2): 2; Mar. 15 (62:1): 3; *NZ*, Mar. 13 (167): 2; *FZ*, Mar. 14 (74:1 mg.): 1; *Reichsbote* in *FZ*, Mar. 14 (74:2 mg.): 1; *Weser Ztg.*, *NAZ*, Mar. 14 (127): 1; *DGK*, (1888) 1: 142.

18. *NPZ*, Mar. 14 (63): 1.

19. *Post*, *NAZ*, Mar. 14 (127): 1; *KölZ*, Mar. 13 (73:2): 1; Mar. 14 (74:2): 1; cf. *NZ*, Mar. 13 (167): 2.

21. "POLITICAL RELATIONSHIPS AND MANEUVERS"

1. *NPZ*, Mar. 20 (68A): 1; Mar. 15 (64): 1; cf. *FZ*, Mar. 16 (76:1 mg.): 1; *NZ*, Mar. 14 (169): 1; *Berl. Pol. Nachr.*, *DGK*, (1888) 1: 184.

2. *NZ*, Mar. 16 (174, *Beiblatt*): 1; Mar. 17 (176): 2; Mar. 19 (180): 1; Mar. 28 (198): 1; *NPZ*, Mar. 18 (67): 3; *Ger*, Mar. 18 (65): 1; cf. *FZ*, Mar. 20 (80:2 mg.): 2.

3. *NZ*, Mar. 18 (179), "Nach dem Thronwechsel": 1; *DGK*, (1888) 1: 183; *NAZ*, Mar. 20 (136): 2.

4. *Ger*, Mar. 20 (66:2): 1.

5. HHSA, Nos. 23: 452–53, 29B: 516, Sz. to Kál., Mar. 17, 29 respectively; Lucius, 430; Waldersee, 1: 371, 373–74, 375–77; *NYH*, Mar. 21: 7.

6. Cf. Waldersee, 1: 377, 379; Lucius, 440; Wentzcke, 2: 438 and passim; cf. Freytag (3), 67–73; Hollyday, 133–34.

7. Lucius, 439–40, GSAM, No. 158/XXIII, Lerch. to pr. reg., Mar. 23; No. 176, to Crails., Apr. 1; GLAK, No. 14, Marsch. to Turban, Mar. 27; *NAZ*, Mar. 11 (121): 1; Corti (2), 498, 526–27; *Ger*, Mar. 22 (68:2): 1; *KölZ*, Mar. 15 (75:1): 1; Mar. 20 (8:1): 1; text of kaiser's messages, *NAZ*, Mar. 19 (135): 1; *Landtag* (1), 2: 971; *Reichstag*, 102: 1387–89; ZSA, Merseburg, *Stsmin., (1888)*: 69, 72.

8. Lucius, 462, 425, 433; *DDF*, 7: 83; HHSA, No. 15: 321, Sz. to Kál., Mar. 6; Waldersee, 1: 375; Corti (2), 470, 489, 493, 499–500; *NYH*, Apr. 22: 17; on the ministry, cf. *FZ*, Mar. 28 (88:2 mg.): 1; cf. *NYH*, Apr. 1: 15.

9. ZSA, Merseburg, *Stsmin.*, (1888): 69–73; Lucius, 439.

10. Lucius, 441–43; *NZ*, Mar. 23 (189): 1; *KölZ*, Mar. 27 (87:1): 1.

11. Lucius, 443–44; cf. GLAK, No. 14, Marsch. to Turban, Mar. 27; *NAZ*, Mar. 25 (146): 1.

12. Waldersee, 1: 377–78, 380.

13. ZSA, Potsdam, *Rchskzlei.*, No. 646/8: 178, Wilmowski to Bism., Mar. 21; Lucius, 437–38; Corti (2), 491–92; Waldersee, 1: 379–80; Hohenlohe, 2: 430; GSAM, No. 176, Lerch. to Crails., Apr. 1; GLAK, No. 14, Marsch. to Turban, Mar. 27.

14. Lucius, 437; Hohenlohe, 2: 430; Hollyday, 227–28; on Ernst v. Stockmar, Corti (2), 41, 52–53, 73; Waldersee, 1: 380; *NZ*, Mar. 17 (176): 2; (177): 1; Mar. 20 (182): 1; Mar. 21 (185): 1; *FZ*, Mar. 19 (79:evg): 1; cf. *Pr. Jbb.*, 61 (1888): 408–9.

15. *NYH*, Mar. 14: 5; Mar. 21: 7; *Ger*, Mar. 17 (64:1): 3; Mar. 20 (66:2): 2; Mar. 22 (68:1): 1; (68:2): 1; Mar. 23 (69:1): 2; *NAZ*, Mar. 20 (137): 2; *NZ*, Mar. 21 (185, *Beiblatt*): 1; *KölZ*, Mar. 21 (81:2): 1; *Börsen-Cour.*, in *Ger*, Mar. 21 (67:1): 2; *DGK*, (1888) 1: 183; *FZ*, Mar. 22 (82:2 mg.): 2; Mar. 15 (75:1 mg.): 1; Fred.'s diary quoted by Corti (2), 293.

16. *FZ*, Mar. 22 (82:1 mg.): 1.

17. *KölZ*, Mar. 26 (86:2): 1; Mar. 25 (85:1): 1; Mar. 27 (87:2): 1; *Hamb. Nachr.* quoted by *Voss. Ztg.* in *NPZ*, Mar. 24 (72): 2; *Hann. Kour.* in *NAZ*, Mar. 21 (138), "Jour.-Rev.": 2; *Kons. Korr.* in *KölZ*, Mar. 20 (80:2): 1.

18. *NAZ*, Mar. 24 (145): 1; Mar. 28 (150): 1; Mar. 29 (152): 1; *Daily News* in *KölZ*, Mar. 16 (76:1): 2; *Standard* in *NAZ*, Mar. 15 (128), "Jour.-Rev.": 3; Salisbury letter, Corti (2), 454; *Grashdanin*, in *KölZ*, Mar. 20 (80:2): 1; Mar. 22 (82:1): 1; Mar. 23 (83:1): 1; *Ger*, Mar. 23 (69:1): 2; Mar. 28 (73:1): 1; Oncken, 2: 540; Lucius, 446.

19. *FZ*, Mar. 27 (87:1 mg.): 1; Mar. 28 (88:1 mg.): 1; HHSA, No. 29B: 515–16, Sz. to Kál., Mar. 29; cf. Heyderhoff, 287.

20. *Ger*, Mar. 30 (75.2): 1; Mar. 27 (72:1): 1; (72:2): 1.

21. Holstein, 2: 365–66; *Ger*, Mar. 21 (67:2): 1; *NPZ* Mar. 24 (72): 2.

22. *KölZ*, Mar. 14 (74:2): 1; Mar. 16 (77:2): 1; *Freis. Ztg.* in *FZ*, Mar. 16 (76:evg.): 1; *Ger*, Mar. 16 (63:2): 3; Mar. 25 (71:2): 1; Mar. 28 (73:2): 1; *DGK*,

(1888) 1: 184–85; Hohenlohe, 2: 430; Mackenzie, 138; Pindter, 68–69, 72–73, Mar. 23, 24, 29; *NZ*, Mar. 24 (191): 2; cf. HHSA, Karton 135: 96–97, Sz. to Kál., priv. lttr.

23. *NZ*, Mar. 27 (195): 2; Mar. 31 (202): 2; *Ger*, Mar. 27 (72:2): 1; Apr. 1 (76:1): 1–2; *NAZ* Mar. 31 (155): 2; *KölZ*, Mar. 31 (91:1): 1; *NPZ*, Mar. 31 (78): 2; *FZ*, Apr. 1 (92:2 mg.): 1.

22. "THE BATTENBERG CRISIS"

1. Holstein, 2: 366; Lucius, 445; Freytag (1), 142–43; Waldersee, 1: 381–82; Corti (1), 283–86; Pindter, 72, Mar. 28; *Herbert*, 511.

2. Corti (1), 176–77, 261–63, 277–83; (2), 459; cf. *Herbert*, 377–78, 382, 385.

3. BAFR, D48, Herb.'s diary, Mar. 27, 30, 31, Apr. 1; *Zukunft*, 57 (1906): 99, "Enthüllgn."; Corti (1), 284, 286–89; Pindter, 72, Mar. 28; Holstein, 2: 367; GLAK, No. 16, Marsch. to Turban, Apr. 9; Waldersee, 1: 382; gr. d. of Baden explains necessity of mediation, GLAK, *Grhzg. Fam. arch.*, Bd. 36, to Turban, Apr. 9; cf. *NYH*, Apr. 5: 7.

4. *GP*, 6: 282–87; BAFR, D48, Herb.'s diary, Apr. 3; Holstein, 2: 367; *FZ*, Apr. 8 (99:1 mg.): 3; *KölZ*, Apr. 7 (98:1): 1.

5. *GP*, 6: 282, 287–89; BAFR, D48, Herb.'s diary, Apr. 5; Holstein, 3: 271–72, n. 3; 2: 367; Corti (2), 463; Ponsonby (2), 295; an English request on April 6 to support a new Egyptian loan was answered dilatorily on Bismarck's instructions, PRO, FO244, 439, No. 107. The messages to Vienna and Rome were also read to Bavarian Foreign Minister Crailsheim in Munich and approved by him and the prince regent, GSAM, MA 690, Crails. to Frhr. v. Freyschlag, Apr. 24; Freyschlag to Crails., Apr. 25.

6. Lucius, 485–86; Holstein 2: 143.

7. *KölZ*, Apr. 5 (95:1): 2; (95:2): 1, 2; Pindter, 75–77, Apr. 5–6.

8. Holstein, 2: 368–70; *Zukunft*, 57 (1906(: 99, "Eunthüllgn."; Pindter, 77–78, Apr. 7; Ponsonby (2), 295; Q. Vict., 1: 397; Freund, 365; HHSA, 534, 539–40, 597–600, Sz. to Kál., Apr. 6, 7, 20.

9. Holstein, 2: 368; Ponsonby (2), 294, 301; RA, Z41/38, ksrn. to Q. Vict., Apr. 13, 10.

10. Pindter, 77, Apr. 7; Holstein, 2: 367; *Zukunft*, 57 (1906): 99, "Enthüllgn."; BAFR, D48, Herb.'s diary; ZSA, Potsdam, Bamberger *Nachlass*, no. 188: 4–5; for the effect on the Social Democrats, HHSA, No. 34: 571–72, Sz. to Kál., Apr. 13. Rodd, 136, wrote that Bismarck's causing the Battenberg crisis was "to demonstrate that the throne was not absolute, and . . . to give a premonitory lesson to the heir apparent."

23. "PARTY REACTION"

1. Oncken, 2: 540–41, n. 2; HHSA, No. 34: 569–71, Sz. to Kál., Apr. 13; GSAM, No. 196/XXVIII, Lerch. to pr. reg., Apr. 11; *KölZ*, Apr. 10 (100:1): 2; *FZ*, Apr. 10 (101:2 mg.): 1–2; (101:evg.): 1; *NAZ*, Apr. 12 (172): 2; *NZ*, Apr. 12 (219): 2; Apr. 13 (221): 1; *Ger*, Apr. 13 (85.2): 1; Apr. 17 (88:1): 1.

2. Waldersee, 1: 382–86; cf. ZSA, Potsdam, Bamberger *Nachl.*, No. 166, Bl. 1, E. Richter to Bamb., Apr. 5.

3. Waldersee, 1: 383, 385 n., 387, 390; Holstein, 2: 371.

4. Holstein, 2: 371; BAFR, D48, Herb.'s diary, Apr. 1; HHSA, Karton 135: 122–23, Sz. to Kál., priv. lttr., Apr. 7; *FZ*, Apr. 4 (95:2 mg.): 1–2; Apr. 6 (97:evg.): 2; Pindter, 75, Apr. 3; Corti (2), 460; cf. RA, 1: 56/41, Col. L. Swain to Pr. of Wales, Apr. 13; PRO, FO244, 439, No. 101, Malet to Slsby.; *NAZ*, Apr. 6 (162): 1; *KölZ*, Apr. 3 (93:1): 1; Apr. 6 (96:2): 1; *Zukunft*, 57 (1906): 171; cf. *Ger*, Apr. 6 (79:1): 1.

5. *Schulthess*, (1888): 75; *FZ*, Apr. 7 (98:1 mg.): 3; (98:2 mg.): 1; (98:evg.): 1; Apr. 9 (100:evg.): 1; Apr. 10 (101:evg.): 1; *DGK*, (1888) 1: 164, 166–67.

6. *KölZ*, Apr. 9 (99:2): 1.

7. *KölZ*, Apr. 6 (96:2): 1; Apr. 7 (97:1): 1; Apr. 8 (98:1): 1; Apr. 10 (100:2): 1; *NZ*, Apr. 6 (209): 1; (210): 1; Apr. 7 (211): 1; (212): 1; Apr. 9 (214): 1. Bismarck told Marschall on April 8 that he couldn't "serve Queen Victoria of England." GLAK, No. 16, Marsch. to Turban, Apr. 9.

8. Busch, 3: 172–87; ZSA, Merseburg, Busch *Nachl.*, Rep. 92, No. 41, Bl. 55, 57, Rottbg. to Busch, Apr. 7; Holstein, 2: 270. Herbert wrote his friend Plessen that the kaiser was very much against the marriage, BAFR, D35, Apr. 9.

9. *NPZ*, Apr. 7 (87): 2; Apr. 8 (89): 1; Apr. 10 (91): 1.

10. *NPZ*, Apr. 10 (92): 2; Apr. 11 (94): 1.

11. *Reichsbote* article in *NAZ*, Apr. 11 (170), "Jour.-Rev.": 2; *Dresd. Nachr.* quoted in *Ger*, Apr. 12 (84:1): 1; "Frauenzimmerpol.," *DGK*, (1888) 1: 164, 167; *Schulthess*, (1888): 78; *NAZ*, Apr. 14 (177): 1. In the 1880s the political police were using especially the talents of the notorious Ernst Schumann, or Normann-Schumann and other aliases, for secret operations in the press; see FOW, ACP/296; *Polizei*; Fricke. *FZ*, (Stein), Apr. 11 (102:evg.): 1.

12. *Post* article in *NAZ*, Apr. 7 (164): 2–3; cf. *FZ*, Apr. 1 (92:1 mg.): 1.

13. *NZ*, Mar. 30 (201): 1–2; *NPZ*, Apr. 5 (83): 1.

14. *NAZ*, Apr. 4 (159): 1; Apr. 15 (178): 2.

15. *NPZ*, Apr. 6 (86), "Die Furcht vor dem Reaktionsgespenst": 1.

16. *Ger*, Apr. 6 (79:2): 2; Apr. 7 (80:1): 1.

17. *Ger*, Apr. 7 (80:2): 1; Apr. 8 (81:2): 2; Apr. 10 (82:1): 1; Herzfeld (1), 2: 541–42; Lucius, 448; *Kons. Korr.* report in *NAZ*, Apr. 12 (173): 1; *Dts. Tgblt.* remark in *Ger*, Apr. 13 (85:2): 1; cf. *KölZ*, Apr. 12 (102:2): 1.

18. *Ger*, Apr. 10 (82:1): 1; (82:2): 2; Apr. 11 (83:1): 1; (83:2): 1; Apr. 12 (84:1): 1.

24. "FOREIGN AND PUBLIC REACTION"

1. Ponsonby (1), 295–96; Cecil, 4: 98–99.

2. Ponsonby (1), 296–301; Corti (2), 465; Q. Vict., 1: 397; cf. *KölZ*, Apr. 11 (101:2): 1.

3. *KölZ*, Apr. 7 (97:2): 1; Apr. 9 (99:1): 1; Apr. 10 (100:2): 1; *FZ*, Apr. 11 (102:evg.): 2; *Ger*, Apr. 11 (83:2): 1; *NZ*, Apr. 11 (218): 1; *GP*, 6: 290–92.

4. HHSA, No. 32: 537–38, Sz. to Kál., Apr. 7; Holstein, 3: 272–73.

5. HHSA, No. 32: 538, Sz. to Kál., Apr. 7; No. 34: 566–67, Sz. to Kál., Apr.

13; *FZ*, Apr. 6 (97:evg.): 1; *NZ*, Apr. 6 (210): 1, and following issues; *NYH*, Apr. 6: 7, Apr. 7: 7; Spitzemberg, 247–48; Rogge (2), 311; ZSA, Potsdam, *Rchskzlei.*, No. 2301, passim.

6. Corti (2), 464–65; Corti (1), 290; *NAZ*, Apr. 10 (168): 2; *DGK*, (1888) 1: 161. P. Eulenburg wrote Herbert that there was deep resentment in Munich that all Germany could be endangered by a Prussian princess; BAFR, B40 (3), Apr. 10. Ponsonby (2), 299.

25. "PARTIAL RESOLUTION OF THE CRISIS"

1. Bamberger (2), 343; Hollyday, 242; Pindter, 78, Apr. 7; 83, Apr. 16; Holstein, 2: 368; *FZ*, Apr. 12 (103:evg.): 1; *NZ*, Apr. 11 (217): 2; *KölZ*, Apr. 12 (102:1): 1; (102:2): 1; *NYH*, Apr. 14: 6.

2. GLAK, *Grhzg. Fam. arch.*, Bd. 36, gr. d. of Baden to Turban, Apr. 12; BAFR, B44, ksrn. to Bism., Apr. 12; Lucius, 447; Holstein, 2: 370; cf. Bismarck (2), 14^2: 984; ZSA, Potsdam, *Rchskzlei.*, No. 2301, Bl. 7, 9, 80, 82, 83, 84, Bism. to *Oberpräs.*, Breslau, *Oberbrgmstr.*, Leipzig, Apr. 12, and replies.

3. *NAZ*, Apr. 13 (174): 2; *FZ* Apr. 12 (103:2 mg.): 1; *KölZ*, Apr. 12 (102:3): 1; Apr. 13 (103:2): 1; *NZ*. Apr. 12 (220): 2; Apr. 13 (221): 2; *Ger*, Apr. 12 (84:2): 1; Apr. 14 (86:2): 1; *DW*, Apr. 11 (3): 25–26. Széchényi called the Battenberg campaign in the semiofficial press a "Pyrrhic victory"; HHSA, No. 34: 573, Apr. 13; cf. No. 35: 602–3, Apr. 20; Pindter, 85, Apr. 21; GLAK, *Grhzg. Fam. arch.*, Bd. 36, gr. d. of Baden to Turban, Apr. 12.

4. *DW*, Mar. 28 (1): 1–2.

5. *DW*, Apr. 4 (2): 13–14.

6. *DW*, Apr. 11 (3): 25–26; Apr. 18 (4): 37.

7. Pindter, 80, Apr. 12; *NAZ*, Apr. 12 (173): 1; Forstreuter, 208–9; *NPZ*, Apr. 13 (97): 1; *FZ*, Apr. 13 (104:2 mg.): 1.

8. Cf. *NAZ*, Apr. 14 (176): 1. *Post* statement and comment in *NPZ*, Apr. 14 (100): 2; *FZ*, Apr. 14 (105:2 mg.): 1; kaiser's letter in Bülow, 1: 236; cf. Nichols, 180–81; *FZ*, Apr. 13 (104:evg.): 2; A. Stein's interesting summary of the crisis, *FZ*, Apr. 14 (105:evg.): 1.

9. Spitzemberg, 248–49; on Bismarck's good health in spite of the crisis, GSAM, No. 197/XXIX, Lerch. to pr. reg., Apr. 13.

10. For the Schurz visit, *NZ*, Apr. 30 (255): 2; May 10 (276, 1 *Beiblatt*): 2; June 2 (316, 1 *Beiblatt*): 1; *KölZ*, May 1 (121:2): 2; May 3 (123:2): 1; *Ger*, May 2 (100:1): 1; May 19 (114:2): 2; May 8 (105:1): 2; *NYH*, May 1: 7; May 15: 6; 19: 7; cf. 2: 3; 4: 7; 5: 7; 6: 15; Bamberger (2), 355–56; Pindter, 92; Wentzcke, 2: 441; Bism. quote, article by Dr. Paul Nathan in *Vorwärts*, undated clipping in HSAST, *Nachl.* Haussmann, fasc. 143.

11. Cf. PRO, FO244, 439, No. 111, Malet to Slsby., Apr. 14.

26. "MEDICAL CRISIS IN CHARLOTTENBURG"

1. Lucius, 446; Mackenzie, 141–50, 154–55; Freund, 363–65; Pindter, 80–82, Apr. 12, 15; *Krankheit*, 245–46; HHSA, Karton 135: 131–32, Sz. to Kál., priv. lttr.,

Apr. 13; GSAM, Nos. 180, 197/XXIX; *NZ,* Apr. 7 (212): 1; Apr. 10 (216): 2; Apr. 13 (222): 1; *FZ,* Apr. 16 (107:mg.): 1; *KölZ,* Apr. 14 (104:1): 1; (104:2): 1; Wolf, 151. Bergmann said the kaiser was within fifteen minutes of death, BAFR, D35, Apr. 14.

2. Rad. to chanc., BAFR, B44, Apr. 16; Pindter, 81–82, Apr. 15; GSAM, No. 199/XXX, Lerch. to pr. reg., Apr. 16; HHSA, tel. No. 53: 582, Sz. to Kál., Apr. 16; *NAZ,* Apr. 16 (179): 1; *NZ,* Apr. 16 (227): 1; Apr. 17 (229): 1; *KölZ,* Apr. 17 (107:1): 2.

3. HHSA, tel. No. 56: 588, Sz. to Kál., Apr. 19; tel. No. 62: 636, Apr. 23; tel. No. 63: 641, Apr. 24; GSAM, Nos. 199/XXX, 210/XXXIII, 222/XXXVI, 238/ XXXVIII, 251/XLI, Lerch. to pr. reg., Apr. 16, 20, 26, May 5, 15; Holstein, 2: 372; Lucius, 449; among newspaper reports, esp. *NZ,* Apr. 20 (237, 1 *Beiblatt*): 2; Apr. 24 (246): 1; (247): 1; *FZ,* Apr. 21 (112:2 mg.): 2; Apr. 24 (115:2 mg.): 2; Apr. 27 (118:1 mg.): 3; (118:2 mg.): 1; Apr. 29 (120:2 mg.): 2; May 1 (122:2 mg.): 1; *KölZ,* Apr. 26 (116:2): 1; *Ger,* Apr. 25 (95:2): 1; Apr. 29 (98:2): 1.

4. Spitzemberg, 250; Pindter, 83, Apr. 18; *NAZ,* Apr. 18 (182), "Aus Berlin": 2; *FZ,* Apr. 23 (114:evg.): 1; *KölZ,* Apr. 19 (109:1): 1–2; *Ger,* Apr. 24 (94:1): 1; Apr. 27 (96:1): 1.

5. GSAM, Nos. 205/XXXII, 222/XXXVI, 246/XL, Lerch. to pr. reg., Apr. 18, 26, May 8; statement of male nurse Beerbaum to police, BAFR, B44, Apr. 19; Pindter, 85, Apr. 20, 22; *Ger,* Apr. 5 (78:1): 2; Apr. 6 (79:1): 1; Apr. 7 (80:1): 1; Apr. 10 (82:1): 1; Apr. 20 (91:1): 1; Apr. 21 (92:1): 1; *KölZ,* Apr. 14 (104:2): 1; Apr. 17 (107:2): 1; Apr. 18 (108:1): 1; Apr. 28 (118:2): 1; *DGK,* (1888) 1: 185; *FZ,* Apr. 17 (108:2 mg.): 1; Apr. 19 (110:2 mg.): 2; Apr. 21 (112:evg.): 1; Apr. 23 (114:evg.): 1; Apr. 24 (115:2 mg.): 2; May 1 (122:2 mg.): 1; *NZ,* Apr. 21 (239): 1; (240): 1; Apr. 27 (250, *Beiblatt*): 2; *NPZ,* Apr. 17 (104): 1; Apr. 18 (106): 1; Apr. 20 (109): 1; (110): 1; Apr. 21 (112): 1; Apr. 22 (113): 1.

6. *Volksztg.* article in GSAM, No. 173/XXVI, Lerch. to pr. reg., Mar. 31; Franz Mehring had been editor of the *Berl. Volksztg,* since 1882. Of aristocratic family, Mehring eventually became disillusioned with democratic liberalism. Later in 1888 at the age of forty-three he left the paper and in 1891 formally joined the Social Democrats, becoming their chief literary figure.

7. *KölZ,* Apr. 19 (109:2): 1; Pindter, 84–85, Apr. 19. Twenty-six-year-old Arthur Schnitzler, trained in his father's medical specialty of laryngology, had been sent abroad for further observation and experience and was in Berlin at this time and interviewed Mackenzie with Ernst von Rosenberg, a boyhood friend and Vienna newspaper publisher. The *Kreuzzeitung* included Schnitzler's name in a list of Mackenzie's correspondents (May 17 [151]: 1), which he denied in his autobiography (Schnitzler [1], 245–46). It is very doubtful that the brief interview he describes would have provided sufficient provocation for such a listing, and the striking literary quality of the *Neue Freie Presse* piece raises the suspicion that he may have written it and preferred later to forget about it. Schnitzler (2), 124.

8. Waldersee, 1: 389–90; Holstein, 2: 371; *NPZ,* Apr. 16 (102): 1.

9. Waldersee, 1: 391–93.

10. Waldersee, 1: 391; GSAM, Nos. 205/XXXII, 222/XXXVI, Lerch. to pr. reg., Apr. 18, 26; No. 246/XL, ksrn.'s statement, May 8; Pindter, 86–87, Apr. 23;

NZ, Apr. 22 (242, 1 *Beiblatt*): 2; ZSA, Merseburg, *Stsmin.*, Apr. 21: 113–15; Lucius, 449.

27. "QUEEN VICTORIA ARRIVES"

1. *NZ*, Apr. 15 (226, 1 *Beiblatt*): 1; *Berl. Pol. Nachr.* quote in *NPZ*, Apr. 18 (105): 1; *KölZ*, May 2 (122:1): 2; *Ger*, May 1 (99:1): 2; GLAK, No. 51, Marsch. to gr. d., Apr. 19; HHSA, 594, Sz. to Kál., Apr. 21.

2. Cecil, 4: 101–2.

3. *KölZ*, Apr. 23 (113:1): 2; *NAZ*, Apr. 23 (192): 2; Apr. 24 (193): 1.

4. Q. Vict., 1: 402; Corti (1), 290–91; Hohenlohe, 2: 435; Busch, 3: 187–88.

5. Q. Vict., 1: 404–5; *Zukunft*, 57 (1906): 172; Busch, 3: 187–88, 198.

6. *NZ*, Apr. 25 (248): 3; *Ger*, Apr. 27 (96:1): 1; (96:2): 2; Pindter, 149; Q. Vict., 1: 407–8. That the queen provocatively included Prince and Princess Henry of Battenberg in her entourage was not mentioned in the German press; PRO, FO244, 439, No. 121.

7. *NAZ*, Apr. 27 (198): 1; *GP*, 4: 178; Q. Vict., 1: 409.

8. Ponsonby (2) 303–4; Q. Vict., 1: 408; cf. PRO, FO244, 439, No. 124.

9. HHSA, No. 38A-B: 646–50, Sz. to Kál.; *GP*, 6: 294–98.

10. Busch, 3: 188–89, 198–99, *Die Grenzboten*, 47 (1888), 2. *Vierteljhr.*, 153–64; *FZ*, Apr. 23 (114:evg.): 1.

28. "THE HONORS LIST"

1. Amnesty: *NZ*, Apr. 1 (203:1 *Beiblatt*): 1; Apr. 3 (204): 1; *FZ*, Apr. 1 (92:2 mg.): 1; Apr. 5 (96:1 mg.): 1; (96:evg.): 1; *NPZ*, Apr. 6 (85): 2; text, *NAZ*, Apr. 1 (156): 1; Apr. 5 (160): 2; Lucius, 445; ennoblement: GSAM, No. 213/XXXIV, Lerch. to pr. reg., Apr. 21; *Herbert*, 511, 515; BAFR, B132, 18, Gen. Winterfeld to chanc., Apr. 27; Bismarck (2), 6c: 389; Lucius, 448, 450; *NAZ*, May 8 (215, *Bes. Beilage*): 1–6; *FZ*, May 8 (129:evg.): 1; *Ger*, Apr. 28 (97:2): 2; *NZ*, May 8 (272): 2; (2 *Beiblatt*): 1.

2. Holstein, 2: 373–74; BAFR, B99, 2, Herb. to Rottbg., Apr. 23; *Herbert*, 515–16; Waldersee 1: 393; HHSA, Kart. 135: 144, sz. to Kál., priv. lttr., Apr. 29; *NZ*, Apr. 25 (248, 1 *Beiblatt*): 1; *Ger*, Apr. 27 (96:1): 2; *NAZ*, Apr. 27 (197): 2.

3. *FZ*, Apr. 25 (116:1 mg.): 1; (116:2 mg.): 1; May 6 (127:2 mg.): 2; May 8 (129:2 mg.): 1; (129:evg.): 1; May 19 (140:2 mg.): 1; May 24 (145:1 mg.): 1; (145:2 mg.): 1; Corti (2), 499; BAFR, B44, Kaiser Fr. memo., Apr. 30; D48, Herb.'s diary, Apr. 30; B100a, Rottbg. to Rantz., May 21; ZSA, Merseburg, *Stsmin.*, Apr. 23: 117–19; 24: 120; 29: 122–23; May 6: 132–33; 13: 135–36; Lucius, 453, Holstein, 2: 376–77; Bismarck (2), 6c: 390; Waldersee 1: 402.

4. Lucius, 454; Holstein, 2: 376–77.

29. "THE KAISERIN'S SECRET ADVISOR"

1. *FZ*, May 19 (140:2 mg.): 1; May 6 (127:2 mg.): 2; *NYH*, May 23: 6; Bamberger (2): 342–49.

2. On Bamberger, see esp. Zucker. Bamberger (2), 346–47, 350.

3. Bamberger (2), 352–55.

4. Bamberger (2), 357–61.

5. RA, Z41/43, 46, ksrn. to queen, May 2, 9; Ponsonby (2), 311; GSAM, No. 305/XLVIII, Lerch. to pr. reg., June 17; cf. Bamberger (2), 391–92.

6. For all of the foregoing, Bamberger (2), 361–68.

7. Bamberger (2), 370–73.

30. "BISMARCK, THE CROWN PRINCE, AND RUSSIA"

1. BAFR, D48, Herb.'s diary, Apr. 19, 20, Mar. 26; *DDF*, 7: 81, Herbette to French Foreign Minister Flourens, Mar. 7.

2. Holstein, 2: 374–75; *GP*, 6: 301–7; Bismarck (2), 15: 554–57; BAFR, B130, cr. pr. to Bism., May 10; Waldersee, 1: 395–99. For Bleichröder, see Stern (1).

3. Lucius, 452–53; Holstein, 2: 375–76; Hohenlohe, 2: 436; on Alsace-Lorr., Rogge (2), 314–25.

4. Waldersee, 1: 399, 401; *Herbert*, 517; Pindter, 95, 98–101, 105; Hohenlohe, 2: 437; HHSA, Kart. 135: 153–56, Sz. to Kál., priv. lttr., May 23; GSAM, No. 275, Lerch. to Crails., June 1; *FZ*, May 23 (144:mg.): 1; May 27 (148:2 mg.): 2; *NZ* May 22 (295): 1; May 24 (298): 2; May 27 (306): 2.

5. RA, Z41/57, ksrn. to Q. Vict., June [2]; Rogge (2), 317–18, 323; Hohenlohe, 2: 434–36; *FZ*, May 16 (137:1 mg.): 1; May 22 (143:evg.): 1; May 24 (145:evg.): 1; May 26 (147:evg.): 1; May 30 (151:2 mg.): 1.

6. BAFR, D27, Herb. to Rantz., May 17, May 20; F4, Rantz. to Herb., May 19.

31. "THE GOVERNMENT DISCIPLINES THE CONSERVATIVES"

1. Lucius, 453; HSAST, Zepp. to Mittn., May 21; HHSA, No. 47: 694–95, Sz. to Kál., May 25; *FZ*, May 15 (136:2 mg.): 1; May 22 (143:evg.): 1; Freund, 385; Lucius, 454, 445; BAFR, D27, Herb. to Rantz., May 18.

2. ZSA, Merseburg, *Stsmin.*, Apr. 12: 88–89; *NZ*, Apr. 8 (213): 2; Apr. 10 (215): 1–2; Apr. 13 (221): 2; *DW*, Apr. 11 (3): 26–28; *NPZ*, Apr. 9 (90): 1; *KölZ*, Apr. 11 (101:1): 1; Apr. 23 (113:1): 1; *NAZ*, Apr. 15 (178): 2.

3. *Landtag* (1), 3: 1121ff.; *NZ*, Apr. 15 (226): 2; Apr. 16 (227): 1; Apr. 17 (229): 2; (230): 1; Apr. 20 (237): 1–2; Apr. 21 (239): 2; *KölZ*, Apr. 16 (106:1): 1; Apr. 20 (110:2): 1; *NPZ*, Apr. 17 (104): 1; Apr. 20 (110): 1; *NAZ*, Apr. 17 (181): 1; Apr. 20 (186): 1; *Ger*, Apr. 19 (90:1): 1; Apr. 20 (91:1): 2.

4. *Landtag* (1), 3: 1217–65; *NPZ*, Apr. 22 (113): 2; *KölZ*, Apr. 22 (112:1): 1–2; *NAZ*, Apr. 22 (190): 5; Apr. 27 (198): 1–2; *Ger*, Apr. 22 (93:1): 3; *NZ*, Apr. 22 (242): 2; cf. *FZ*, Apr. 28 (119:1 mg.): 1; *Nation,*: Apr. 28 (5/31),"Proteus": 433–34.

5. *KölZ*, Apr. 23 (113:1): 1; (113:2): 1; Apr. 26 (116:2): 1; *Post* quote in *NZ*, Apr. 23 (244): 1; Apr. 24 (246): 1–2; *Nat. Lib. Korr.* quote in ibid., 2; Apr. 25 (248): 1–2; *NPZ*, Apr. 23 (114): 1; Apr. 25 (117): 1; *NAZ*, Apr. 23 (192): 1; Apr. 26 (196): 1; *DW*, Apr. 25 (5): 50; *Ger*, Apr. 24 (94:1): 1–2; (94:2): 1; Apr. 25 (95:2): 1; *FZ* Apr. 25 (116:evg.): 1.

6. *NZ*, Apr. 26 (250): 1; *NPZ*, Apr. 23 (114): 1; *FZ*, Apr. 27 (118:2 mg.): 1; *KölZ*,

Apr. 27 (117:2): 1; Pindter, 89, Apr. 28.

7. Robinson, Art. 107: 248; ZSA, Merseburg, *Stsmin.*, (1888): 126–27.

8. *NAZ*, Apr. 29 (201): 2; *Ger*, Apr. 28 (97:2): 1; cf. *FZ*, May 2 (123:evg): 1.

9. *NPZ*, Apr. 29 (123): 2.

10. *NPZ*, Apr. 29 (123, 1 *Beilage*): 2.

11. *NZ*, Apr. 29 (254): 1–2.

12. "Official" election figures in *KölZ*, May 3 (123:1): 2; *NZ*, Apr. 30 (255): 1; May 1 (258): 1; May 2 (260), "Abschaffg. der Stichwahlen": 1; May 5 (267): 1; May 6 (270), "Die Stichwahlen": 1; May 8 (273): 1; *NAZ*, May 3 (207): 1–2; May 4 (209): 2; *FZ*, May 1 (122:1 mg.): 1–3; (122:evg.): 1; May 3 (124:2 mg.): 2; *NPZ*, May 3 (129): 1; (130): 2; May 7 (136): 1–2.

13. *FZ*, May 8 (129:1 mg.): 1; May 12 (133:evg.): 1; *Ger*, May 9 (106:1): 1; May 13 (109:1): 1; (109:2): 1; *NAZ*, May 11 (221): 2; May 12 (222): 1; May 14 (224): 1; May 17 (230): 1; May 18 (231): 2; (232): 1; *NZ*, May 16 (285): 1; *NPZ*, May 18 (153): 1.

14. *NPZ*, May 1 (126), "Dunkele Machensftn.": 1.

15. *Gegenwart*, 33/17: 257–61 (Apr. 28); *Kons. Korr.* quote in *NAZ*, May 2 (205): 2–3; May 3 (207): 2; *Post* quote in *Ger*, May 1 (99:2): 1.

16. *NAZ*, May 1 (203): 1.

17. ZSA, Merseburg, *Stsmin.*, (1888): 127–31.

18. *NAZ*, May 4 (210): 1; May 6 (213): 2; *Ger*, May 5 (103:1): 1; *NPZ*, May 7 (136, *Beilage*): 2; BAK, Rep. 92 (Rottbg.), 10:486, d. of Ratibor to Rottbg., May 15; BAFR, B100a, Rottbg. to Rantz., May 16.

19. *NZ*, May 18 (290, 1 *Beiblatt*): 2; June 1 (314): 2; June 4 (319): 3; *NAZ*, May 16 (227): 2; May 20 (235): 2; *NPZ*, May 16 (149): 3; May 18 (153): 2; BAK, Rep. 92 (Rottbg.), 10: 484–85; *Ger*, May 31 (123:2): 2; June 2 (124:2): 1; *FZ*, May 26 (147:1 mg.): 1.

20. *FZ*, May 9 (130:2 mg.): 1; May 12 (133:2 mg.): 1; *NZ*, May 12 (278): 1; *Ger*, May 10 (107:1): 1; *NPZ*, May 11 (142): 1; May 12 (144): 1.

21. *Post* article in *NAZ*, May 13 (223): 2; May 14 (224): 1; *NZ*, May 10 (276): 2; *Ger*, May 13 (109:1): 1; (109:2): 1; *NPZ*, May 13 (145): 1; *Landtag* (1), 3: 1564–65.

22. ZSA, Merseburg, *Stsmin.*, (1888): 143–48, May 15.

23. ZSA, Merseburg, *Stsmin.*, (1888): 151–52, May 16.

24. ZSA, Merseburg, *Stsmin.*, (1888): 148–50, May 16.

25. *NPZ*, May 9 (140): 1; May 15 (148): 2.

26. *FZ*, May 16 (137:1 mg.): 1.

27. *Landtag* (2), 109–33; *NZ*, May 16 (285): 1; *FZ*, May 17 (138:2 mg.): 1–2; Stein article, (138:evg.): 1.

28. ZSA, Merseburg, *Stsmin.*, (1888): 156–58, May 17.

29. *NPZ*, May 6 (135): 1; May 17 (151): 1; May 18 (153): 1–2; *Kons. Korr.* in *NAZ*, May 15 (225): 2.

30. *NPZ*, May 19 (156): 1–2; May 23 (159): 1.

31. *FZ*, May 20 (141:1 mg.): 1.

32. *NPZ*, May 18 (154): 1; May 19 (156): 1; May 20 (157): 1; May 22 (158): 1.

33. *NPZ*, May 24 (162): 1.

34. *Hamb. Korr.*, *NAZ*, May 23 (237): 2; May 15 (225): 2; May 20 (235): 2; *NZ*,

May 19 (292): 1; *Ger,* May 18 (113:2): 1; May 19 (114:1): 1; May 20 (115:2): 1; May 23 (116:2): 1; May 24 (117:1): 1–2; *KölZ,* May 23 (142:2): 1.
35. *NAZ,* May 23 (238): 2; May 24 (240): 2.
36. *FZ,* May 25 (146:1 mg.): 1; cf. (146:evg.): 1.
37. *FZ,* May 25 (146:2 mg.): 1; (146:evg.): 2; May 26 (147:2 mg.): 1–2; (147:evg.): 1; *Landtag* (1), 3: 1599–1646; *NZ,* May 25 (301): 1–2; May 26 (303): 1–2; (305): 1; May 27 (306): 1–2; BAFR, B100a, Rottbg. to Rantz., May 25, 27; *Ger,* May 27 (120:1): 1.

32. "AN OPENING TOWARD THE CENTER"

1. This brief treatment of Bavarian politics is based on Möckl; on Franckenstein, 113–14.
2. Möckl, 94–95, 177–78, 186–88.
3. Möckl, 93, n. 218.
4. Möckl, 65, 70–71, 158–59; *Münch. Allg. Ztg.* quote in *NAZ,* May 15 (225): 2; cf. *Voss. Ztg.* in *Ger,* Feb. 22 (43:1): 1. For Bavarian Center-party disinclinations to be too far separated from the Reich government, cf. FRK, *Fach* 1/20, Baron Max von Soden to Frkstn., Feb. 20, 1887.
5. On Werthern, see Möckl, 60; Pindter, 50, 54, 56; *Ger,* Oct. 27, 1887 (246:2): 1; *NAZ,* Feb. 21 (88): 2; *KölZ,* Feb. 20 (51:1): 1; Holstein, 3: 271, 275–76; Eulenburg quote, BAK, *Nachl.* Eulenburg, Bd. 1, 110; Haller, 32, 35–36; Eulenburg emphasized his view to Herbert, Feb. 16, BAFR, B40 (3); Röhl, 70; Bismarck's negative comments on Eulenburg's reports during this period, FOM, reel 73, Apr. 7, No. 15; Apr. 27, No. 28, frames 378–79; reel 75, Apr. 18, frame 356; BAFR, D27, Herb. to Rantz., June 10; F4, Rantz. to Herb., June 7; D48, Herb.'s diary, Apr. 4, 10; GSAM, Crails. to Lerch., June 5; on Berchem, Möckl, 88, n. 193; Holstein, 2: 186–87.
6. BAK, *Nachl.* Adolf von Dietze, Rottbg. to Dietze, Mar. 24.

33. "THE FALL OF PUTTKAMER"

1. Corti (2), 525–27; Hohenlohe, 2: 440; RA, Z41/49, ksrn. to Q. Vict., May 22; Pindter, 100, 112–13; cf. opinion of gr. d. of Baden in Freytag (1), 143.
2. Pindter, 95; BAFR, F4, Rantz. to Herb., May 25; Corti (2), 476–77, reference to Gagliardi, 2: 474; cf. Pindter, 105, June 2.
3. *Landtag* (1), 3: 1413–27; *NZ,* May 3 (264): 1; May 4 (265): 2; *FZ,* May 3 (124:evg.): 1; May 4 (125:1 mg.): 1; *KölZ,* May 3 (123:2): 1; *NPZ,* May 3 (130): 1; cf. *NAZ,* May 5 (211), "Jour.-Rev.": 2.
4. HHSA, Kart. 135: 145–48, Sz. to Kál., priv. lttr., May 5.
5. *Landtag* (1), 3: 1651–78; *FZ,* May 27 (148:2 mg.): 2; May 28 (149:evg.): 1; June 4 (156:evg.): 1; *NZ,* May 27 (306): 2; text of Jan. 4, 1882, decree, *NAZ,* June 7 (263): 1; cf. PRO, FO244, 439, No. 154, Malet to Slsby., May 28.
6. *FZ,* May 28 (149:evg.): 1; BAFR, D27, Herb. to Rantz., May 26; *KölZ,* May 28 (147:1): 1; *NAZ,* May 29 (247): 2; *Hann. Kour.* in *NAZ,* May 31 (251): 2; *Berl. Pol. Nachr.* article in ZSA, Potsdam, *Rchskzlei.,* No. 673, Bl. 11; *Rchsbote.* in *KölZ,*

May 30 (149:2): 1; GSAM, No. 271, Lerch. to Crails., May 31; *Freis. Ztg.* and *Berl. Pol. Nachr.* in *NAZ*, June 6 (261): 1; Bamberger (2), 376; GLAK, No. 20, Marsch. to Turban, May 31; *Grhzg. Fam. arch.*, Bd. 46, cr. pr. to gr. d. of Baden, May 29.

7. *NZ*, May 31 (312): 2; (313): 1; *Ger*, May 5 (103:1): 1; Lucius, 455, 458; GSAM, No. 271, Lerch. to Crails., May 31; GLAK, No. 20, Marsch. to Turban, May 31.

8. *Freis. Ztg.* in *KölZ*, May 29 (148:2): 2; *Münch. Allg. Ztg.* in *FZ*, May 30 (151:evg.): 1; GLAK, No. 20, Marsch. to Turban, May 31; Bamberger (2), 379–80.

9. GSAM, No. 266/XLIII, Lerch. to pr. reg., May 27: BAFR, F4, Rantz. to Herb., May 23; D27, Herb. to Rantz., May 26; D48, Herb.'s diary, May 29; Pindter, 101–2, May 26; *Ger*, June 5 (126:2): 3; HHSA, Nos. (tel.) 68: 696, May 27; 49: 705–6, May 28; 52: 14, June 4; GLAK, No. 22, Marsch. to Turban, June 4; Bamberger (2), 375; Lucius, 455.

10. Lucius, 456–57; Leuss, 58; BAFR, D48, Herb.'s diary, June 1; GLAK, N536, Marsch. to Turban, coded tel., June 2; No. 22, June 4.

11. Bamberger (2), 374–78; a copy of a 35-page pamphlet entitled *Kgthm. u. pol. Freiheit: e. offenes Wort zu den bevorstehenden Wahlen über Parteiverhältnisse Dtlds.* by Wolfgang Eisenhart was presented to Bismarck on June 2, and is in ZSA, Potsdam, *Rchskzlei.*, 673, Bl. 15. In a letter to Q. Vict. the kaiserin described it as "shameful"; Corti (2), 477.

12. *Berl. Pol. Nachr.* article in *NAZ*, June 1 (253): 1; also included in GLAK, No. 21, Marsch. to Turban, June 1.

13. *NPZ*, June 1 (175): 1; (176): 2; *Voss. Ztg.* in *FZ*, June 2 (154:2 mg.): 1.

14. *KölZ*, June 2 (152:2): 1.

15. *KölZ*, June 4 (154:1): 1; (154:2): 1; cf. *FZ*, June 4 (156:evg.): 1.

16. Heyderhoff, 288; Oncken, 2: 542; Waldersee 1: 403; GSAM, No. 271, Lerch. to Crails., May 31; HHSA, No. 50: 708, Sz. to Kál., May 29; *FZ*, May 30 (151:2 mg.): 1; letter of Wm. II, BAK, Rep. 92 (*Nachl.* Rottbg.), No. 20.

17. GLAK, *Grhzg. Fam. arch.*, Bd. 46, Cr. Pr. Wm. to gr. d. of Baden, May 29; Waldersee, 1: 401–2.

18. *FZ*, May 18 (139:2 mg.): 1; May 19 (140:evg.): 2; May 22 (143: mg.): 3; May 31 (152:2 mg.): 1; *NYH*, June 2: 7; HHSA, No. 51: 2–3, Sz. to Kál., June 2; *NZ*, May 10 (276, 1 *Beiblatt*): 2; June 1 (314, 1 *Beiblatt*): 2; (315): 1–2; BAFR, D27, Herb. to Rantz., May 23; F4, Rantz. to Herb., May 24.

19. GLAK, No. 20, Marsch. to Turban, May 31; GSAM, No. 279, Lerch. to Crails., June 4; Lucius, 457–58.

20. Pindter, 106; *NAZ*, June 5 (260): 1.

21. *KölZ*, June 6 (156:2): 1.

22. Lucius, 458–59; Leuss, 58.

23. Bamberger (2), 382–91; cf. 437–39; cf. *NYH*, June 3: 11; June 5: 6; Corti (1), 296.

24. BAFR, D48, Herb.'s diary; the passage is dated June 6, but all other sources indicate it must have been the seventh; cf. Puttk.'s letter and memo., Leuss, 58; kaiser's letter in Puttkamer, 189, cited in Bamberger (2), 538, n. 110; Lucius, 460–63; Pindter, 111–13, June 16; GSAM, Lerch. to Crails., Nos. 279, 288, 290, June 4, 8; cf. BHSA, BA 570/8, MA 1: 769, Crails to Freyschlag; GLAK, Nos.

23, 24, Marsch. to Turban, June 8, 11; ZSA, Merseburg, *Stsmin.*, (1888): 169–70, June 8; cf. *FZ*, June 12 (164:evg.): 1; *NYH*, June 6: 7; June 10: 11; ksrn.'s account, Corti (2), 525; Bamberger (2), 394–96.

25. *NPZ*, June 4 (180): 2; June 6 (184): 1; June 7 (186): 1; *NZ*, June 6 (323): 1; *Ger*, June 5 (126:1): 1; June 7 (128:1): 1; June 8 (129:1): 2; *Kons. Korr.* article in *KölZ*, June 7 (157:2): 1; *FZ*, June 6 (158:evg.): 1; Rickert's speech, June 4 (156:mg.): 1; *NAZ*, June 8 (266): 1.

26. *NZ*, June 8 (326): 1; *NPZ*, June 8 (188): 1; *KölZ*, June 8 (158:1): 1.

27. *FZ*, June 5 (157:2 mg.): 1 (refers to *Voss. Ztg.*); *NZ*, June 6 (323): 1; Stein article, *FZ*, June 8 (160:1 mg.): 1; (160:evg.): 1.

28. *Post* article in *Ger*, June 6 (127:2): 2; *Dts. Tgblt.*, *Ger*, June 5 (126:2): 1; *Berl. Tgblt.* article in *Ger*, June 7 (128:2): 1; GLAK, No. 23, Marsch. to Turban, June 8.

29. *NAZ*, June 8 (265): 1; cf. *FZ*, June 11 (163:evg.): 1.

30. *Ger*, June 9 (130:2): 1–2; *FZ*, June 9 (161:evg.): 1; *NAZ*, June 8 (265), "Jour-Rev.": 2.

31. Stein, *FZ*, June 6 (158:1 mg.): 1; June 9 (161:evg.): 1; Rickert, June 4 (156:mg.): 1; June 10 (162:1 mg.): 1; *Freis. Ztg.*, in *NZ*, June 9 (329): 1; *Berl. Tgblt.*, HHSA, No. 57: 52–53, Sz. to Kál., June 9; *Ger*, June 10, (131:1): 1–2; *NPZ*, June 11 (192, *Beilage*): 2; June 12 (193): 1.

32. *KölZ*, June 9 (159:2): 1; cf. June 11 (161:1): 1; June 14 (164:2): 1; *NZ*, June 12 (332): 2; *Post* in *Ger*, June 10 (131:2): 1; June 14 (134:2): 2.

33. Waldersee, 1: 403–4; cf. *Hamb. Nachr.* in *Ger*, June 13 (133:2): 1.

34. Cr. pr. to gr. d. of Baden, GLAK, *Grhzg. Fam. arch.*, Bd. 46; Lucius, 461–62.

35. *FZ*, June 10 (162:2 mg.): 1–2; Stein on Zedlitz, June 15 (166:evg.): 2; *NAZ*, June 13 (274): 1; *Ger*, June 13 (133:2): 1; *NZ*, June 12 (332, 1 *Beiblatt*): 1; June 13 (334): 2; *NPZ*, June 12 (194): 1; on Zedlitz, *KölZ*, June 14 (164:1): 1; (164:3): 1; Wahl, 3: 533; HHSA, No. 60: 69, Sz. to Kál., June 14; GLAK, No. 25, Marsch. to Turban, June 14; Lucius, 463, 465; cf. Herzfeld (1), 117–19; Hollyday, 244.

36. Ponsonby (2), 312–14; RA, Z41/61, 62, ksrn. to Q. Vict., June 12, 13; Bamberger (2), 437–39.

37. GLAK, No. 25, Marsch. to Turban; Lucius, 465.

38. GSAM, Nos. 271, 275, 288, 290, Lerch. to Crails., May 31, June 1, 8; HSAST, Zepp. to Mittn., June 1, 9.

39. Lucius, 465.

34. "DEATH OF KAISER FREDERICK"

1. GSAM, No. 293, Lerch. to Crails., June 11; HHSA, No. 55: 28–29, Sz. to Kál., June 7; BAFR, D27, Herb. to Rantz., June 10; *NZ*, June 5 (320): 3; June 8 (327): 2; June 11 (331): 2; June 12 (333): 2; *Voss. Ztg.* article in *FZ*, June 6 (158:2 mg.): 1; June 11 (162: mg.): 3; (162:evg.): 2; June 12 (163:2 mg.): 1; (163:evg.): 2; June 13 (164:2 mg.): 2; June 14 (165:2 mg.): 1; *Brit. Med. J.* in Freund, 389.

2. Kaiser's diary in Freund, 389; Bamberger (2), 428, GSAM, No. 301, Lerch. to Crails., June 13.

3. Lucius, 464–65; Corti (2), 531; Spitzemberg, 253.

4. *NZ*, June 14 (337): 1; *FZ*, June 14 (165:evg.): 2; HHSA, tels. Nos. 70:63,

72:65, Sz. to Kál., June 14; GSAM, No. 302/XLVI, Lerch. to Foreign Ministry, June 14; Mackenzie, 176.

    5. Lucius, 465; HHSA, tel. No. 73, Sz. to Kál., June 15; BAFR, B44, ksrn. to chanc., June 15; RA, Z41/65; Ponsonby (2), 315, 319–21.

    6. GSAM, Nos. 303/XLVII, 305/XLVIII, Lerch. to For. Min., to pr. reg., June 15, 17; HHSA, No. 61: 81, Sz. to Kál., June 16; Pindter, 112–13, June 16; BAFR, D48, Herb.'s diary, June 15; Spitzemberg, 253; Mackenzie, 180, 187; Lucius, 466–67.

    7. *NAZ*, June 15 (278): 1–2; *NPZ*, June 15 (200): 1; *FZ*, June 16 (167:1 mg.): 3.

    8. GLAK, *Grhzg. Fam. arch.*, N 500, Roggenbach to gr. d. of Baden, June 15; *FZ*, June 15 (166:evg.): 1; *Voss. Ztg.* and *Freis. Ztg.* in *FZ*, June 16 (167:2 mg.): 1–2; *Pall Mall Gaz.* in *FZ*, June 17 (168:1 mg.): 3.

    9. GSAM, No. 350/XLVIII, Lerch. to pr. reg., June 17; Spitzemberg, 253; Pindter, 112–13, June 16; Corti (2), 537–39; *NAZ*, June 15 (278): 2; *FZ*, June 16 (167:2 mg.): 1; *Ger*, June 16 (136:2): 1; Malet to Slsby., May 26, identifies Mr. Bashford as correspondent of the *Daily Telegr.*: PRO, FO 244, 439, No. 149.

35. AFTERWORD

    1. Schorske, chap. 3.

    2. See Stern (2).

    3. See esp. Zucker, chap. 6, also Blackbourn & Eley.

    4. Wehler (2), 325, n. 4.

    5. Burke, 152.

    6. On Adams, see Wood, chap. 14.

    7. Madison quote in Wood, 608.

    8. Cf. Krieger's seminal study.

    9. See Pinkney.

    10. See, for example, Huntington.

    11. For example, Böhme, 537–40, 570–72, 579–86; Stürmer (3); (2), 18, 19, 144; (1), 296–97, 306; Wehler (1), 68.

    12. Cf. Wehler (1), 14, 17, 27, 32; and critical of this view, Eley (1) and Blackbourn & Eley. For a critique of Wehler (1), Zmarzlick.

    13. On the problems of using England as a model and the responsibility of American social scientists for encouraging this practice, see Blackbourn & Eley.

    14. Wehler (1) recognizes this fact but does not let it shake his theoretical approach to German development, 228–29.

    15. Lucius, 360; Johnson, 280ff.; for the concept of a "liberal generation" in Germany that might have ruled with Frederick, see Scholtz.

    16. This scholarship is conveniently summarized in Wehler (1), 105–35.

    17. Bamberger (1) takes this view, although he may have known better. For the role of Eckart Kehr in transmitting this old liberal view to the post–World War II generation, see Eley (1) and Anderson & Barkin.

Index

Note on the Author

J. Alden Nichols is professor of history at the University of Illinois at Urbana-Champaign, where he has been teaching since 1961. He is the author of *Germany after Bismarck: The Caprivi Era, 1890–1894* (Harvard University Press).